Israel's Beneficent Dead

Ancestor Cult and Necromancy in Ancient Israelite Religion and Tradition

by

Brian B. Schmidt

Eisenbrauns
Winona Lake, Indiana
1996

Library of Congress Cataloging-in-Publication Data

Schmidt, Brian B.
Israel's beneficent dead : ancestor cult and necromancy in ancient Israelite religion and tradition / by Brian B. Schmidt.
p. cm.
Previously published: Tübingen : J.C.B. Mohr (Paul Siebeck), © 1994.
Revision of the author's thesis (Ph.D.—Oxford, 1992).
Includes bibliographical references and index.
ISBN 1-57506-008-6 (pbk. : alk. paper)
1. Ancestor worship—Biblical teaching. 2. Ancestor worship—Middle East. 3. Dead—Religious aspects—Biblical teaching. 4. Dead—Middle East. 5. Dead—Religious aspects. 6. Bible, O.T.—Criticism, Interpretation, etc. 7. Israel—Religion. 8. Middle Eas—Religion. I. Title.
BS1199.A47S36 1995
291.2′13—dc20 95-45181
CIP

The paper used in this publication meets the minimum requirements of the American National Standard for Information Sciences—Permanence of Paper for Printed Library Materials, ANSI Z39.48-1984.⊗

Dedication

I dedicate this work to the memory of my grandfather, Hiram Ardis Simons, a farm boy-turned-school teacher without whose example and support this book would not have been conceivable, let alone possible. His ten year silence only intensifies my inclination to embrace its results.

To live rationally one must live so that death cannot destroy life.

Tolstoy, *What I Believe*

Preface

Death and life are in the power of the tongue,
those who love ***it*** *will eat its fruits.*

Proverbs 18:21

This book is a significantly revised version of a thesis which I completed in preliminary form in the spring of 1990 and which I defended for the University of Oxford's Doctorate of Philosophy degree in the winter of 1992. I am grateful to the many who saw this project through to its present form. I am particularly indebted to my energetic supervisor, Dr. John Day, for his willingness to dispense of his encyclopedic knowledge and judicious guidance during my dissertation days.

I also wish to offer my thanks to Stephanie Dalley, Ernest Nicholson, Jonas Greenfield, John Barton, and Kevin Cathcart, all of whom plumbed many meanderings during my reading and defending days at Oxford; to John Van Seters, Jack Sasson, and James Vanderkam who provided me with the opportunity to continue my research while teaching in the Research Triangle of North Carolina ever offering their guidance, encouragement, and assistance throughout those formative years; to William Hallo and Wayne Pitard who faithfully offered their research in progress in exchange for my repeated pleadings; and to Gary Beckman, Bertrand Lafont, Piotr Michalowski, and Norman Yoffee for their helpful comments on various portions of this work as it drew ever nearer to publication.

I express my appreciation to Jarl Fossum who suggested J.C.B. Mohr (Paul Siebeck) as a publisher and who kindly supported the submission of my manuscript for consideration; to Bernd Janowski and Hermann Spieckermann for accepting it in the FAT series; and to the University of Michigan for its support in preparing the manuscript for publication. I would like to extend a very special thanks to my editor and research assistant, Harry Weeks, Ph.D. candidate, without whom this book would never have reached its state-of-the-art form. His perseverance, expertise, and technical guidance shall forever remain a model for future projects.

I gratefully acknowledge the many sacrifices made by my wife Kathy and the endurance exemplified by my children Blake and Hayley who have shared the entirety of their short-lived lives with what was for the longest time that invisible third sibling. Finally, I cherish the encouragement and support I received from my family, friends, and colleagues at those crucial moments when doubt got the better of me.

It is only fitting that in closing I anticipate any shortcomings of this book. They are due to the failings and limitations of its author and no other.

Ann Arbor, Spring 1994 Brian B. Schmidt

Preface to the Paperback Edition

With the publication of Eisenbrauns North American paperback edition of *Israel's Beneficent Dead*, I would first like to extend my personal thanks to Jim Eisenbraun, who initially inquired about my interest in such an edition, and second, to Georg Siebeck of J.C.B. Mohr (Paul Siebeck) for accepting the Eisenbrauns proposal.

The publication of this edition has afforded me the opportunity to make corrections to the text. Among others, a number of errors of Hebrew transliteration found their way into the manuscript during the data transfer from the dissertation to the 1994 hardback edition. Most of these errors involved the unanticipated deletion of subscript and superscript diacritics. Philip Johnston deserves credit for bringing to my attention additional instances of such errors. I am once again deeply indebted to Harry Weeks for his diligence and perseverance in providing technical assistance. He single-handedly made the "new and improved" paperback edition a reality.

Ann Arbor, Winter 1996 Brian B. Schmidt

Contents

Abbreviations

AAAS	*Annales archéologiques arabes syriennes*
AAR	American Academy of Religion
AASOR	*Annual of the American Schools of Oriental Research*
ABL	R. F. Harper, *Assyrian and Babylonian Letters* (Chicago 1982–1914)
ACF	*Annuaire du Collège de France*
AEPHER	*Ecole pratique des hautes études, V^e section-sciences religieuses: Annuaire*
AfO	*Archiv für Orientforschung*
AHw	*Akkadisches Handwörterbuch* (ed. Wolfram von Soden, Wiesbaden, 1965-81)
AION	*Annali dell'istituto orientale di Napoli*
AJA	*American Journal of Archaeology*
ANET	*Ancient Near Eastern Texts Relating to the Old Testament* (ed. J. B. Pritchard, Princeton, 1969^3)
AnSt	*Anatolian Studies*
AO	*Tablets in the collection of the Musée du Louvre*
AOAT	Alter Orient und Altes Testament
AOB	*Altorientalische Bibliothek*
AOS	American Oriental Society
ARET	Archivi reali di Ebla: Testi
ARI	*Assyrian Royal Inscriptions*
ARM	Archives royales de Mari
ARMT	*Archives royales de Mari (Textes)*
ArOr	*Archiv orientâlní*
AuOr	*Aula orientalis*
AT	D. Wiseman, *Alalakh Tablets*, (London, 1953)
BA	*Biblical Archaeologist*
BAR	*Biblical Archaeology Review*
BASOR	*Bulletin of the American Schools of Oriental Research*
B.C.E.	Before the Common Era
BDB	F. Brown, S. R. Driver, and C. A. Briggs, *Hebrew and English Lexicon of the Old Testament* (Oxford, 1907)

BHS	*Biblia Hebraica Stuttgartensia* (Hrsg. von K. Elliger und W. Rudolph, Stuttgart, 1983)
BIN	*Babylonian Inscriptions in the collection of J. B. Nies*
BM	*Tablets in the collections of the British Museum*
BN	*Biblische Notizen*
BO	*Bibliotheca orientalis*
BR	*Biblical Research*
BSMS	*Bulletin of Syro-Mesopotamian Studies*
BSOAS	*Bulletin of the School of Oriental and African Studies*
BZ	*Biblische Zeitschrift*
CAD	*The Assyrian Dictionary of the Oriental Institute of the University of Chicago* (I. J. Gelb, et al., Chicago, 1956–)
CBQ	*Catholic Biblical Quarterly*
CBS	R. Labat, *Un calendrier Babylonien des travaux des signes et des mois* (Paris, 1965)
C.E.	The Common Era
ChrH	Chronistic History
CRAIBL	*Comptes rendus des séances de l'académie des inscriptions et belles-Lettres*
CT	*Cuneiform Texts from Babylonian Tablets in the British Museum*
CTA	*Corpus des tablettes en cunéiformes alphabétiques découvertes à Ras Shamra-Ugarit de 1929 à 1939* (Ed. par A. Herdner, Paris, 1963)
DN	Divine Name
dtr	deuteronomistic
DtrH	Deuteronomistic History
EA	*Die El-Amarna Tafeln* (Hrsg. J. A. Knudtzon, Leipzig, 1910–15)
EI	*Eretz Israel*
ET	English translation
G	Basic stem of the verb
GHD	The Genealogy of the Hammurapi Dynasty
GKC	*Gesenius' Hebrew Grammar* (ed. E. Kautzsch, tr. A. E. Cowley, Oxford, 1910^2)
HAR	*Hebrew Annual Review*
H	tablets from Harran
HC	Holiness Code
HSS	*Harvard Semitic Series*
HTR	*Harvard Theological Review*
HUCA	*Hebrew Union College Annual*
IBS	*Irish Biblical Studies*
IEJ	*Israel Exploration Journal*

JANES	*Journal of the Ancient Near Eastern Society of Columbia University*
JAOS	*Journal of the American Oriental Society*
JBL	*Journal of Biblical Literature*
JCS	*Journal of Cuneiform Studies*
JEN	*Joint Expedition with the Iraq Museum at Nuzi*
JEOL	*Jaarbericht Ex Oriente Lux*
JNES	*Journal of Near Eastern Studies*
JNSL	*Journal of Northwest Semitic Languages*
JPS	*The Jewish Publication Society* (A New Translation of the Holy Scriptures According to the Traditional Hebrew Text, Philadelphia, 1985)
JSOT	*Journal for the Study of the Old Testament*
JSS	*Journal of Semitic Studies*
K	tablets from Kouyunjik (Nineveh)
KAI	*Kanaanäische und aramäische Inschriften* (Hrsg. von H. Donner und W. Röllig, Wiesbaden, 1962-64)
KTU	*Die keilalphabetischen Texte aus Ugarit.* Teil 1: Transkription (AOAT 24. Hrsg. von M. Dietrich, O. Loretz, und J. Sanmartín, Neukirchen-Vluyn, 1976)
LAS	*Letters from Assyrian Scholars to the Kings Esarhaddon and Assurbanipal* I,II (AOAT 5/1-2. S. Parpola, Neukirchen-Vluyn, 1970,1983)
LKA	*Literaturische Keilschrifttexte aus Assur*
LTP	*Les textes para-mythologiques* Ras Shamra-Ougarit IV. Èditions Recherche sur les Civilisations. Paris, 1988
LXX	*Septuagint*
MARI	*Mari annales recherches interdisciplinaires*
MSK	Meskéné-Emar
MSL	*Materialien zum sumerischen Lexikon* (ed. B. Landsberger, et al., Rome, 1937–)
MT	Masoretic text
MVÄG	Mitteilungen der Vorderasiatischen/Vorderasiatisch-Ägyptischen Gesellschaft
NAB	*New American Bible*
NABU	*Nouvelles assyriologiques brèves et utilitaires*
NCB	*New Century Bible*
ND	tablets from Nimrud (Calah)
NEB	*New English Bible*
NIV	*New International Version*
OECT	*Oxford Editions of Cuneiform Texts*
OIP	*Oriental Institute Publications*
OLP	*Orientalia Lovaniensia Periodica*

OLZ	*Orientalistische Literaturzeitung*
OrAn	*Oriens antiquus*
P	Priestly Source
PBS	University Museum, University of Pennsylvania, *Publications of the Babylon Section* [=UM] (Philadelphia, 1911–)
PEF	*Palestine Exploration Fund*
PEQ	*Palestine Exploration Quarterly*
PGM	*Papyri Graecae Magicae* (2 vols, ed. H. K. Preisendanz, et al., Leipzig und Berlin, 1928, 1931)
PIBA	*Proceedings of the Irish Biblical Association*
PN	Personal Name
PRU	*Le Palais royal d'Ugarit*
RA	*Revue d'assyriologique et d'archéologie orientale*
RAI	Rencontre assyriologique internationale
RB	*Revue biblique*
RES	*Revue des études sémitique*
RHA	*Revue Hittite et asianique*
RHR	*Revue d'histoire des religions*
RIH	Ras Ibn Hani
RlA	*Reallexikon der Assyriologie*
RN	Royal Name
RS	*Ras Shamra*
RSF	*Rivista di studi fenici*
RSV	*Revised Standard Version*
SEL	*Studi epigrafici e linguistici*
SJT	*Scottish Journal of Theology*
SVT	*Supplements to Vetus Testamentum*
TA	*Tel Aviv*
TAPS	*Transactions of the American Philosophical Society*
TC	*Tablettes Cappadociennes* [=TCL 4]
TCL	Textes cunéiformes, Musée du Louvre
TGUOS	*Transactions of the Glasgow University Oriental Society*
TJT	*Toronto Journal of Theology*
TLZ	*Theologische Literaturzeitung*
TM	*Tell Mardikh (Ebla)*
UF	*Ugarit-Forschungen*
UT	*Ugaritic Textbook* (C. H. Gordon, Rome, 1965; Supplement, 1967)
UVB	*Vorläufiger Bericht über die von dem Deutschen Archäologischen Institut und der Deutschen Orient-Gesellschaft aus Mitteln der*

	Deutschen Forschungsgemeinschaft unternommenen Ausgrabungen in Uruk-Warka
VT	*Vetus Testamentum*
WO	*Die Welt des Orients*
YBC	tablets in Babylonian Collection, Yale University
ZA	*Zeitschrift für Assyriologie*
ZAW	*Zeitschrift für die Alttestamentliche Wissenschaft*
ZDPV	*Zeitschrift des Deutschen Palästina-Vereins*
ZRGG	*Zeitschrift für Religions- und Geistesgeschichte*

Introduction

The following investigation sets out to ascertain whether or not the ancient Israelites believed in the dead's supernatural beneficent powers and, if so, to reconstruct what can be known about the origin, history, and character of that belief. Owing to ancient Israel's lack of speculative discourse on the subject, an examination such as ours must proceed along alternative avenues of inquiry. Therefore, the present study comprises a sustained analysis of the potential ritual expressions of that belief which have been preserved in the textual remains from ancient Syria-Palestine.[1] Two ritual complexes have been repeatedly identified as reflective of the power of the ghost to supernaturally bless the living: those rites affiliated with the cult of the ancestors and those associated with that form of divination known as necromancy.

In the modern study of ancient Israelite religion, the ancestor cult and necromancy have been the topics of considerable inquiry and indications are such that this will continue into the foreseeable future. An increasing number of biblical scholars advocate the view that significant sectors of pre-exilic Israelite society participated in ancestor cult and necromantic rites. These rites, in turn, have often been cited as evidence for an ancient Israelite belief in the dead's supernatural beneficent powers, a belief originating in and deriving its character from the Amorite and Canaanite cultures of the third through second millennia B.C.E.[2]

While it is tempting to argue that recent studies have vindicated the views of late nineteenth and early twentieth century scholars who lacked sufficient textual and artifactual evidence to adequately support their claims, it is more than mere coincidence that the current *opinio communis* approaches the virtual unanimity

---

[1] To be sure, the term Syria-Palestine (or any of its variant forms, e.g., Syro-Palestinian), reflects the dubious conflation of ancient Syrian and Palestinian cultures. Syria-Palestine is adopted herein purely for purposes of evaluating the conflation evident in the history of scholarship. Among others, Rainey 1965a:102–25; Craigie 1981:99–111; 1983:145–67 have rightly criticized the tendency to collapse the ancient cultures of Ugarit and Canaan or Palestine into a single "Canaanite" world.

[2] The *Canaanite and Israelite Religion* session of the Society of Biblical Literature devoted its entire program to the topic at the 1992 annual meeting held in San Francisco and note also the recent treatments by Healey 1989:33–44; Lorenz 1990:21–31; van der Toorn 1990:203–22; Dietrich and Loretz 1990a:57–65, 75–77; de Moor 1990:233–45; Niehr 1991:301–306; Mendenhall 1992:67–81; Hallo 1992:381–401; Ackerman 1992; Levine 1993:468–79.

achieved by the turn-of-the-century scholarship. As a reconstruction of the modern history of interpretation like that of Spronk reveals, much current research derives its impetus from these earlier works.[3] In any case, both the early modern investigations as well as the re-emergent interest in Israelite ancestor cults and necromancy can trace their lineage back to the claims of late nineteenth century social historians. Zealously applying evolutionary and typological models to the history of world religions, these turn-of-the-century intellectuals identified the ancestor cult (in which necromancy was typically included) as the incipient expression of humanity's search for ultimate reality and human destiny. Accordingly, belief in the supernatural and in one's survival after death were given their primal expression in this cult. That is to say, the belief in the dead's superhuman power eventuated into the abstraction "god", while the postmortem persistence of a benevolent ghost provided the stimulus for envisaging a beatific afterlife.[4]

In addition to the dubious nature of this rather outmoded theoretical framework, the history of interpretation has suffered from terminological inaccuracy and methodological isolationism. All too often, the vocabulary reflective of a wide range of mortuary practices has been mistaken as reflective of the ancestor cult or necromancy. Furthermore, recent advances in the anthropology of death invalidate some of the essential underlying assumptions of biblical research on the topic. For example, the available ethnographic record nullifies the long held truisms of a universal response to death and its original expression in the ancestor cult. The diversity of human response to death is everywhere apparent.[5]

In what follows, selected mortuary practices are classified and defined, and where possible, their attendant beliefs identified. Following upon this, the textual data and, to a far lesser extent, the archaeological finds from Syria-Palestine are analyzed in order to test the assumption that the Israelites embraced the belief in the benevolence of the dead and that the origins and character of that belief are to be found in early Canaanite religion.[6] Lastly, the relevant biblical texts are

---

[3] Cf. Spronk 1986:25–83 and the surveys by Margoliouth 1908:444–50; Ribar 1973:4–8. Some of the early advocates include Tylor 1871 in Britain; Halévy 1874 in France; Lippert 1881 in Germany; Oort 1881:350–63 in Holland. For a treatment of earlier nineteenth century scholarship, see Spiess 1877 as noted by Spronk 1986:25–27.

[4] The 1864 work of the French social historian, Numa Denis Fustel de Coulanges, *La cité antique* (= *The Ancient City*, 1873) stands as the starting point for many biblical researches on the ancestor cult both old and new (cf. e.g., Brichto 1973:1–54). For the extent of his influence, cf. Momigliano 1977:325–43; Finley 1977:305–27; Humphreys 1987:459–61. See also the two part foreword to the 1980 edition of *The Ancient City* by Humphreys and Momigliano.

[5] This diverse response in the human record is underscored by Ucko 1969:262–80 and reiterated in the treatments on the anthropology and archaeology of death in Metcalf and Huntington 1991 (first edition 1979); Humphreys and King 1981; Bloch and Parry 1982; Palgi and Abramovitch 1984:385–417; Morris 1987:29–43; 1992:1–30; Bowker 1991.

[6] We can only offer an abbreviated assessment of the archaeological data within the confines of the present context, cf. esp. 4.4.3.

closely examined and their compositional histories reconstructed. Such a strategy provides not only a much needed control for evaluating the comparative data from the worlds of the ancient Near East and beyond, but it also lays an adequate foundation upon which to reconstruct a history of Israelite religion on the matter.

Chapter 1

Mortuary Rites: A Descriptive Glossary

The ancient Israelite ancestor cult and the practice of necromancy have been the objects of an extensive history of interpretation. This chapter is designed to both build upon and to advance that history by defining the terms upon which any substantive examination of the subject must rely. Warrant for such an approach derives in part from the repeated use of terms and models by biblical scholars more at home in the anthropologies of religion and death. In addition to facilitating the evaluation of that history and its use of anthropology, the glossary outlined herein will serve to verify the interpretative decisions made in the textual analyses comprising chapters 2, 3, and 4.

What follows is essentially an 'intellectualist' endeavor. That is to say, we will examine rituals as a means of access to their corresponding beliefs. Due recognition is made of the limitations inherent in the intellectualist study of ancient religion that underlies both the present study and those that have gone before. Critics of intellectualist research have rightly asked: what sectors and ideologies of a given society can a limited data base reasonably represent? Be that as it may, the most formidable obstacle for intellectualist oriented study is the interpretation of ritual as symbol; does a rite have a one-to-one correspondence with a particular belief or are their relationship(s) more complex? The view adopted here is that the intellectualist orientation can stand as a viable avenue of inquiry when applied in conjunction with other approaches. Any rite must be evaluated as part of the larger system of ritual action to which it belongs, for that system uniquely informs the relations between a given ritual and the ideational world. We will, therefore, implement additional approaches such as a structuralist orientation along the lines advocated by Leach as a counter balance to the intellectualist orientation.[1] A direct one-to-one correspondence between ritual and belief is assumed here only in order to answer the question that has formed the starting point for the history

---

[1] Leach 1976. Morris 1992:17–21,201 offers a survey of the state of the art. He discusses ritual, symbol, and the interpretation of mortuary remains as the domain of historical inquiry rather than as an archaeological version of formalist literary theory.

of interpretation, namely, does a given ritual express a belief in the supernatural beneficent power of the dead?

The terms selected for treatment in the glossary represent a variety of *mortuary rites*, some related to, but others that are often confused with, the ancestor cult and necromancy.[2] The corresponding rites selected for analysis fall into one of four ritual complexes: funerary rites, the mortuary cult, the death cult, and 'magical, mortuary rites'. Funerary rites include burial and mourning rites. The mortuary cult includes the regular care or feeding of the common dead or the ancestors as well as the customary commemoration of the dead. The death cult presupposes the veneration and worship of the dead who are usually identified as the ancestors. Magical, mortuary rites involve the manipulation of the dead as sought in necromantic and exorcistic or ghost expulsion rites. Each rite will be defined and illustrated by means of the comparative ethnographic record in order to ascertain whether or not a given ritual possesses the potential for conveying the belief in the dead's supernatural beneficent power.

Funerary rites are typically classified as rites of passage. The rites of passage mark the course of a person through the cycle of life, from one stage to another over time, from one social role, status, or position to another. In the rites of passage, a fundamental, tripartite process can be discerned: separation (from a former status), transition (or liminality), and incorporation (or aggregation, into a new status).[3] *Mourning rites* are performed during the period in which the dead person passes from this life (separation), through death (transition), to the next life (incorporation). With varying degrees of intensity, they take place during the transitional or liminal stage of death which itself may last for an extended period of time (in some cases, for several years). Mourning rites can therefore be subsumed under the more general rubric of funerary rites for funerary rites would also encompass other ritual complexes such as the rites of burial. The period of mourning characteristically ends with the arrival of the dead in the afterworld. In the case of burials, arrival may coincide with interment or an additional time period might be required for the journey to, and arrival in, the afterworld. In the latter case or in cases where burial is not observed, arrival often is signaled by the consumption of the body, whether it be induced naturally (i.e., through decay) or artificially (e.g., by means of cremation or cannibalism).

But what differentiates funerary rites from death cult rites? In spite of advances which have been made in social anthropology since Émile Durkheim's, *The Ele-*

---

[2] The label *mortuary rite* will be employed to designate any practice which falls within the purview of those rites that are recognized as expressive of the human response to death regardless of the presence or absence of the belief in the supernatural beneficent power of the dead. In other words, it might refer to any one of the several terms treated below.

[3] Van Gennep 1960:146–65; cf. Myerhoff, Camino, and Turner 1987:380–86.

mentary Forms of the Religious Life, his definition of the *cult of the dead* remains a standard for historians of religion. He identified the death cult as comprising "repeated standardized practices oriented toward the dead at ritual locations associated with the dead." Durkheim also suggested that death cult practices served "to fulfill the need which the believer feels of strengthening and reaffirming, at regular intervals of time, the bond which unites him to the sacred beings upon which he depends."[4] As it stands, his definition is rather limited in its usefulness, for in several respects it defines the death cult only too vaguely. But before we take up the matter of definition further, a final element in Durkheim's scheme should be mentioned. According to Durkheim, in societies where death cults exist, the belief in the persistence of some aspect of the human personality after death is universally attested.[5] This belief, while perhaps not to be understood as the underlying motivation explaining the existence of all such cults, stands for Durkheim as a common denominator.

Durkheim's distinction between rites and a cult offers some assistance in clarifying the difference between funerary and death cult rites. Rites might comprise practices which appear only in certain and, we would add, temporary circumstances, while a cult comprises a system of practices repeated periodically.[6] More to the point, funerary rites occur between death and the arrival in the afterworld, whereas death cult practices begin with the dead's arrival in the afterworld and continue on a regular basis, perhaps, indefinitely. In any case, funerary rites do not by necessity assume the persistence of man after death.[7] For example, some mourning rites may be intended purely for the benefit of the living. If and when they do presuppose such persistence, if what remains is viewed as existing in the form of a ghost or spirit, it might be construed as potentially hostile until the necessary rites are completed and said spirit is consigned to the next world. Alternatively, the ghost might be considered frail and merely in need of sustenance. In other words, belief in the beneficence of the dead is not an obligatory aspect of the funerary ritual.

The characteristic elements of the death cult are likewise found in the *cult of the ancestors* but with important qualifications attached. Before those are taken

---

[4] Durkheim 1915:63. Nilsson 1950:585–86 adopted Durkheim's definition in his treatment of the cult of the dead in Minoan-Mycenaean religion. Unlike his mentor, Fustel de Coulanges, Durkheim did not view the ancestor cult as the earliest form of religion and against Max Müller, nature religion was not to be given that honor. For Durkheim, totemism was the earliest form of religion. Nevertheless, the ancestral spirit played a central role in his theory as an aspect of the totemic principle.

[5] But cf. Goody 1962:18,379 and for the ancestor cult cf. Fortes 1976:5; Newell 1976:21–29; Singleton 1977:18–25; Hardacre 1987:263.

[6] Durkheim 1915:63 and cf. Thomas 1987:450–59. The observation of Singleton 1977:3 is apropos, "Though all peoples solemnize the burying of their dead, far from all subsequently devote a great deal of their ritual time and energy to remaining on good terms with the departed."

[7] Goody 1962:18.

up however, the most distinctive feature of the ancestor cult over against the death cult must be mentioned, namely the real or perceived kinship ties which bond the living and the dead. The ancestor cult comprises beliefs and practices directed towards dead predecessors. The cult of the dead is directed toward the dead in general while the ancestor cult is a lineage cult.[8]

Regarding the question of the dead's postmortem existence, Fortes has pointed out that certain varieties of the African ancestor cult can exist alongside the sketchiest lore about the mode of existence of the dead. Furthermore, the rites are not necessarily directed towards consigning the ancestors to a spiritual realm of existence in a supernatural world, but towards discorporating them from the social structure. In the African context, the metaphysical implications of western notions of the soul—indestructible essences that animate bodies and succeed them in the timeless realm of God pending resurrection in a corporeal form—are not essential beliefs. Among the Ashanti, an ancestral 'spirit' is not thought of as a kind of nebulous being or personified mystical presence, but primarily as a name attached to a relic such as a stool. The constituent of personality is not imagined to survive in a supernatural realm after death, but is believed to remain behind to look after descendants.[9] Moreover, an ancestor's afterlife is specifically tied to the continued authority he or she can exercise.[10] They might behave either benevolently or malevolently. When the latter is the case, it may be due to the lack of close ties with any one living group which in turn demonstrates that the behavior of the dead does not terminate their status as recipients of ritual.[11]

A second, distinctive feature is the moral influence which the ancestors exercise over their descendants. Ancestors exert positive moral forces and can cause or prevent misfortune, whereas the spirits of the dead in general may exercise powers which achieve amoral or even antisocial ends. That is to say, misfortune at the hands of the ancestors is interpreted as retribution for failure in matters of filial piety. Misfortune at the hands of the dead who lack living relations may be explained as an act of a malicious, arbitrary, or capricious apparition.[12]

---

[8] Ahern 1973:121 has summarized some typical credentials for ancestorhood. She listed "an adult man who is a direct descendant of the lineage-ancestors and who is married, sired male children and handed down property to his sons." There are exceptions of course as in Japan where the responsibilities fell to the female household heads who succeeded deceased mothers-in-law.

[9] Fortes 1965:126–29; cf. Singleton 1977:2–35, esp. pp.18–25 on the semi-personal nature of the ancestral spirit in Africa.

[10] Cf. Fortes 1976:1–16; Newell 1976:17–29.

[11] So Newell 1976:21–29. This serves to qualify the notion that the ancestral spirits were solely benevolent, while the spirits of the dead more generally were malevolent (or vice versa). Thus, with regard to Mesopotamia, the opposing views of Bayliss 1973:115–25 and Skaist 1980:123–28 require qualification in spite of the fact that both invoke anthropological data from Africa.

[12] Cf. Gluckman 1937:117–36; Fortes 1976:9–10 on this distinction between the cult of the dead and the ancestor cult within the African context.

Furthermore, the traditional view that the cult of the ancestors is merely a religious phenomenon fails to take into account the ethnographic data which suggest that it is also an aspect of the living social relations in a given society and closely linked to a society's regulation of inheritance and succession. This equally applies to the *cult of the royal ancestors.* In Africa, for example, the king participates in the cult of his ancestors and may appeal to them on behalf of the nation as any head might do in the limited descent group context. Thus, the royal version parallels the pattern of the lineage cult of the ancestors. However, the national significance of the royal ancestor cult derives more from the political rank of those ancestors being worshipped than from their ancestral status.[13]

The cult of the ancestors might manifest itself in the *cult of the common ancestors*, those non-royal deceased who have real kinship ties with the living. It has been suggested that it may also be made manifest in the cult of the mythic ancestors.[14] It should be pointed out however that the so-called mythic ancestors were never perceived as human procreators begetting and bearing offspring, but were conceived as creators of humanity.[15] Therefore, a more appropriate category for this group might be the mythic heroes and, as such, they would be more suitably located in that complex of rites related to the *hero cult.* The ancient Greek versions of the hero cult provide an excellent example of this ritual complex. Those who might be considered worthy of cultic rites typically possessed some extraordinary quality, though not necessarily a virtuous life. As a member of this class, a given hero might be placed at any one of several points along a continuum as the heroes included a wide array of figures: faded deities, vegetation spirits, epic heroes, the eponymous figures, and heroes who lived in historical times.[16] At the two extremes were those who descended from the world of the gods, like the mythic heroes, and those who became heroes after their death, the legendary or epic heroes.[17]

The mythic heroes were closer to the gods than to the legendary heroes. Nevertheless, the world of the gods and the world of heroes—and of common mortals for that matter—were kept quite distinct. Only a select few like Dionysus and Heracles who were considered *hērōs theos*, might stand as exceptions to this rule.

---

[13] Cf. Fortes 1965:122–42; 1976:1–16.

[14] Cf. Berndt 1970:216–17. For a summary treatment of the mythic ancestors, cf. Long 1987:268–70. Recently, Xella 1982:654–55 has suggested the existence of mythic ancestors within the Israelite context.

[15] Fortes 1976:3–4.

[16] Cf. Farnell 1921:280–342; Burkert 1985:203–15; Garland 1985:1–12,88–93. On the origins of the Greek hero cults, cf. Kerényi 1959:10–22; Coldstream 1976:8–17; Snodgrass 1982:107–19; 1988:19–26; Antonaccio 1987; Whitley 1988:173–82; Garland 1992:31–35.

[17] In the Greek traditions, both can be found in the epic poetry. This probably reflects the mixture of ancient and late traditions, so Burkert 1985:205. Moreover, all such heroes, whether mythic or legendary, fall victim to death, so Kerényi 1959:1–22.

Moreover, kinship ties were typically lacking and an extended period of time usually lapsed before regular rites intended for the hero were instituted.[18] In any case, the Greek hero cult was otherwise not one in which the hero was worshipped or apotheosized like the Olympian gods. Rather, the heroes were at most venerated (see below on the distinction between worship and veneration).[19] It was believed that the heroes, in contrast to the pitiful, ordinary dead, could assist the living by protecting them against enemies and diseases and by opening the wombs of barren women. They were on rare occasion labeled healers or *iatroi.*[20]

Other mortuary rites that are widely attested include the veneration of the dead and the worship of the dead. The *veneration of the dead* assumes the persistence of man after death. Moreover, it presupposes the belief that the dead can influence the high god(s) to act on behalf of the living. The dead obtained this power through their heroic acts or qualities exhibited while living, or thought to be living in the case of the mythic heroes. Not only do the living offer the dead their expressions of gratitude, but the dead receive various forms of inducements from the living. The dead do not appear to have the same degree or quality of divinity as the high god(s), nor can they act independently of the god(s). Therefore, they are not worthy of, and unlike the gods, they do not receive, worship. The same set of criteria applies in the case of the *veneration of the ancestors.*[21]

As a parallel, we offer the Roman Catholic cult or veneration of the saints in which the deceased intercede on behalf of the living. This, the dead can accomplish owing to their acquired access to divine *virtus* or power. The dead gain such an exalted position through the testimony of a virtuous life accompanied by miracles with the latter often considered the divine reward for the former. In this practice, the dead receive veneration or *douleia* but not worship or *latreia* which is reserved only for God.[22]

Goody concluded that the *worship of the dead* implies not only the idea of survival after death, but also the belief that the dead, as superior powers to

---

[18] Coldstream 1976:9; Burkert 1985:204.

[19] Cf. Kerényi 1959:1–6. Characteristically, the sacrifices to the heroes were not the same as those offered to the major gods and the altars were distinct in form and lower in height.

[20] Cf. Farnell 1921:369 for the healing heroes among whom were Asclepius, Amphiaraus, and Achilles. The significance of the term *iatroi* as applied to the biblical Rephaim by the authors of the Septuagint will be taken up in 4.8. On the fate of the common dead in Greece as deserving of pity rather than fear or reverence, cf. Garland 1985; 1992:31–34.

[21] Cf. Jensen 1963:291–92.

[22] The Second Vatican Council made the following pronouncement with regard to the cult of the saints: "Let the faithful be taught, therefore, that the authentic cult of the saints consists not so much in the multiplying of external acts, but rather in the intensity of our active love. By such love, for our greater good and that of the Church, we seek from the saints example in the way of life, fellowship in their communion, and aid in their intercession," cf. Abbot 1966:84; note Hawley 1987 for a more recent assessment of the cult of the saints.

the living, actively participate in the mundane affairs of the living.[23] Goody's definition requires further qualification since, as it stands, it also encompasses the veneration of the dead. The worship of the dead requires that the living serve the dead in a greater capacity. Mere gratitude and care will not suffice. The same goes for inducements. The dead require the highest form of reverence for they can act independently of the high god(s) to affect the world of the living. They are, in effect, equal in power with the god(s). The living must propitiate the dead through the offer of goods, services, words, and other gestures in order to secure their favor. Similarly, our use of *ancestor worship* will be restricted to those acts which reflect the belief that the power possessed by the ancestor is equivalent to that of a deity. However, the ancestral dead are restricted vis-à-vis their extent of influence. While they can directly influence the living like the gods, they do so only within the boundaries of lineal descendancy. In other words, they act only on behalf of the genealogically-related living.

Another related practice reminiscent of the belief in man's persistence after death is the *care for* or *feeding of the dead*. In this case, the dead have not escaped all human frailty and so are perceived as in need of assistance, even sustenance. Care for or feeding of the dead typically carries with it the implicit notion that the dead are weak; they have no power to affect the living in a beneficial way. In the case of the ancestors, the *care for* or *feeding of the ancestors* is motivated by the obligation to continue one's filial duties for immediate lineal predecessors after their death. This keeps the ancestors alive and their presence continually accessible to the living descendants as they partake together of the food offered to the ancestors.[24] Nevertheless, the ancestors are not necessarily viewed as superior beings for they lack power. In order to underscore the fact that such care does not necessitate the belief that the dead supernaturally bestow some benefit upon their devotees, we have excluded the care and feeding of the dead from the category of the death or ancestor cult. For purposes of the present investigation, these ritual complexes along with the commemoration of the dead have been located in what we have designated as the *mortuary cult.*[25]

As in the case of the care for and feeding of the dead, death and ancestor cults should not be equated with the *commemoration of the dead* or *geneonymy*.[26] This form of commemoration is that which perpetuates the memory of the deceased. It does not by necessity assume the persistence of man after death beyond the recall of the dead in the mind of the living. While geneonymy presupposes the

---

23 Goody 1962:18,20–25,379.

24 Cf. Fortes 1976:10–11,14.

25 Hultkrantz 1978:102–03 similarly eliminated the care for and feeding of the dead from the category of the death cult.

26 On geneonymy, cf. Goody 1962:379; Fortes 1965:123–24; 1976:4; Newell 1976:19–20.

mnemonic use of genealogies, it in no way predicates ancestor worship. Beyond its memorializing function, the one remaining function to be highlighted, for purposes of this study, is commemoration's power to legitimate.

The familiar practice of laying flowers at the grave of the deceased or the formal rites enacted at the tomb of the unknown soldier illustrate the secular version of the commemoration of the dead. The recognition of the saints observed in the Church of England in which the dead are remembered for their exemplary lives expresses the same concern but from within a religious context. In both cases, the nonreligious and religious, the living are edified through a process of legitimation in which certain ethical norms exemplified in the former lives of those now dead are revered. But such rites, while perhaps appearing periodically, do not necessitate, as the nonreligious examples demonstrate, a belief that the dead obtain an afterlife beyond the recollection of their years prior to death. Finally, the commemoration of the dead should not be confused with the Roman Catholic practice that goes by the same name. In the case of this rite, the living attempt to produce benefits on behalf of the dead through the worship of the deity (as a response to the doctrine of purgatory). By way of summary, then, those rites expressive of the veneration and worship of the dead or of the ancestors, we have located in the ritual complexes labeled the death or ancestor cult, while those symbolic of the dead's weakness or exemplary acts while living, we have placed in the mortuary cult (which is not to be confused with our use of the term mortuary rite).

We turn now to the magical, mortuary rites. Another practice has arisen in various cultures where the dead, or segments of the dead, are perceived as possessing what some have construed as beneficial powers of significant magnitude. This rite of divination commonly referred to as *necromancy* involves the communication with the dead for the purpose of retrieving information. As Bourguignon has recently defined it, necromancy is "the art or practice of magically conjuring up the souls of the dead . . . to obtain information from them, generally regarding the revelation of unknown causes or the future course of events."[27] While this practice will be treated extensively, this should not be taken to mean that necromancy is to be subsumed under the rubrics of either the death or ancestor cult as has been so often the case in past studies. Precluding such an association is the fact that this

---

[27] Cf. Bourguignon 1987:345. In the end, Bourguignon preferred a more inclusive definition which was not restricted in its usefulness for analyzing traditions of non-Western cultures (p.347). For purposes of the present investigation, however, the definition offered above is appropriate for it has its analogues, if not its basis, in ancient Near Eastern traditions, cf. e.g., 1 Sam. 28:3–25 in 4.5.1. In their treatments of ancient Near Eastern necromancy, Tropper 1989:13–23 and Moore 1990:53–55 have aligned themselves with a definition similar to Bourguignon's broader one. This allows them to associate a variety of practices with necromancy. However, many of their texts do not record procedures for bringing up the ghost, let alone the ghost's supernatural capacity to reveal esoteric knowledge about the future of the living.

practice is not by necessity a regular rite of the established cult, but is only implemented as circumstances warrant (e.g., in times of crisis). Necromancy remains of interest nevertheless, owing to its potential for expressing an ancient Israelite belief in the supernatural beneficent power of the dead. It must be pointed out that, while the ghost imparts no blessing upon its suitor beyond the mere discharge of information, the dead's ability to reveal such esoteric knowledge has been construed in the history of scholarship as a benevolent act of supernatural proportions performed on behalf of the living.[28] Only the medical and magical apotropaic rites aimed at warding off ghosts and/or their affects remain to be treated. However, owing to the exclusively negative orientation of such exorcistic rites—stemming as they do from a horrid fear of the dead—these lie outside the scope of the present investigation.[29]

While several of the above mentioned mortuary rites do not presuppose the persistence of the human after death, others do. Some of those that do might merely portray such an existence as one to be pitied or abhorred. Others require only that the living perform rituals directed at the dead in order to care for the feeble phantom or to expel the malicious ghost. Necromancy and the rites expressive of the veneration or worship of the dead alone comprise quintessential incarnations of the belief in the dead's supernatural power to bless the living. These occupy central place in the following analyses of the textual traditions from ancient Syria-Palestine. By way of conclusion, we offer an illustrated summary of the preceding glossary of terms:

[28] In a forthcoming review in the *Journal of Theological Studies*, Philip Johnston of Wycliffe College, Oxford, inauspiciously follows certain tendencies typical of early modern research. He repeatedly appeals to the phrase, "the interest in the dead," as a heuristic construct encompassing all of the many and varied attitudes that the living possess with regard to the dead. Due to such inexactitude, he wrongly attributes to me the claim that in ancient Israel such an interest in the dead was non-existent prior to neo-Assyrian influence (but cf. the Conclusion). Furthermore, he completely misses the point regarding the rationale for including necromancy in my investigation (cf. this and the preceding page of my work).

[29] Cf. Scurlock 1988:1–102,125–317,363–66 for a treatment of ghost expulsion texts from first millennium Mesopotamia.

Mortuary Rites: A Summary

The Situationally Observed Rites

Funerary

Burial
Mourning

The Regularly Instituted Cults

Mortuary	Death or Ancestor
Care	*Veneration
Feeding	*Worship
Commemoration	

The Magical Mortuary Rites

*Necromancy
(Exorcism)

* The belief in the supernatural beneficent power of the dead is given expression through the performance of this rite or cult.

Chapter 2

The Extra-biblical Textual Evidence from Syria-Palestine: The Late Third to Early Second Millennia B.C.E.

The current interest in the ancient Israelite version of the cult of the ancestors and the practice of necromancy has been stimulated in large part by the recent publication of epigraphic remains from several sites in Syria. Investigators anticipated that these data would shed new light on Israelite mortuary practices and beliefs. This anticipation has been predicated on the geographic proximity of these finds as well as the assumed temporal and cultural affinities which the societies represented in these discoveries share with each other and with early Israel. In the next two chapters, the relevant texts recovered from the ancient Syrian sites of Ebla, Mari, Ugarit, and Emar (along with those from Nuzi) will be examined for indications of death cult rites and necromantic practices. The scant Aramaic, Phoenician, and Palestinian epigraphic remains of the early first millennium will be evaluated in chapter 4.

2.1. The Evidence From Ebla

A scholarly consensus has yet to emerge on matters concerning various problematic aspects of the language and culture of the city-state of Ebla (modern Tell Mardikh).[1] Nevertheless, its cultural and economic ties seem closest with city-states west and north of the Mesopotamian heartland such as Kish, Abu Ṣalabikh, and Mari.[2] However, it now appears that its regional power was significantly less than initially surmised.[3] Moreover, the Ebla archive probably dates from the late third millennium and not earlier and spans the reign of but one ruler,

---

[1] For helpful discussions and bibliography, see Biggs 1982:9–24; 1992:263–70; Viganò and Pardee 1984:6–16; Michalowski 1985:293–302.

[2] Cf. Gelb 1981:52–60; Viganò and Pardee 1984:6–16.

[3] Geller 1987:141–45 concluded that Ebla was under the hegemony of Mari rather than vice versa.

Ibbi-Zikir/Sipish, not five. Lastly, it has yet to be conclusively demonstrated that the archive represents the central royal library.[4]

Evidence indicative of a royal ancestor cult at Ebla has been published by Giovanni Pettinato and Alfonso Archi, as well as by the director of the Italian archaeological mission to Ebla, Paulo Matthiae. The texts published by Pettinato and Archi date from the Early Bronze IV period. They supposedly record offerings made to the deified, dead royal ancestors. Matthiae's architectural data date from the Middle Bronze. These monumental remains preserve royal tombs presumably located near the temple of the chthonic god Rasap where rites of the royal ancestor cult were performed. According to these authors, the Eblaite royal ancestor cult presupposed not only contact with the dead, but also their regular worship as tutelary deities endowed with the power to supernaturally bless the living.[5]

2.1.1. The Eblaite King List

Archi has published the central text documenting an Eblaite royal ancestor cult, his so-called king list (*TM* 75.G.2628), which he interprets as recording offerings to ten deceased and deified kings, each represented by their statues, as well as to several major deities. The kings are listed in retrograde order and are referred to collectively as the en-en, the deified, deceased "kings" or "rulers" (cf. obv. III.6 below). In Archi's estimation, each king is identified by the construction dingir + royal name (hereafter RN), "divine So-and-so."[6] His edition of the text is reproduced below:

---

4 Cf. Michalowski 1985:293–302.

5 The apparent underlying assumption in the work of these authors is that the origins of tutelary deities can be traced back to an earlier stage at which they were ghosts of the dead. This approximates the late nineteenth century evolutionistic model constructed by Fustel de Coulanges.

6 Archi 1986:213–17; 1988a:103–12; cf. Biga and Pomponio 1987:60–61. Fronzaroli 1988:1–33; 1989:1–2; 1993:163–85 has published a reconstructed ritual series comprised of *TM* 75.G.3205+3218 (= ARET 3.178) an edited fragment *TM* 75.G.3132 (= ARET 3.112) and previously unedited fragments *TM* 75.G.4828+4843+4883+4889. According to the author, this composite text preserves a funerary liturgy in which the new king honors (*ig-da-ra-ab*) the royal ancestors. His interpretation relies to a large extent on details contained in Archi's view of the king list and Pardee's view of the so-called Ugaritic king list (on which, see below and 3.1.6.). Although Fronzaroli's text does make reference to é *ma-dím*, "the mausoleum," to si-dù, "lamentation" (or *dì-mu-mu*, cf. 2.1.2.), and to the calendrical nature of the rites, there is nothing in the text that establishes the deceased's supernatural powers. The associated rites are intended for the dynastic personal god identified in the construction dingir + RN as we will argue below. The ritual context of a royal coronation provides the underlying social setting.

Part 1

Obv.	I.	1.	[10 udu]
			[dingir]
		3.	[*ìr-k*]*ab*-[*d*]*a-mu*
			[dingi]r
		5.	[*í*]*k-rí*-[*i*]*š*-<*ḫa*> LAM
			dingir
		7.	*a-dub-a-mu*
	II.	1.	dingir
			kum-da-mu
		3.	dingir
			i-šar-ma-lik
		5.	dingir
			en-àr-da-mu
		7.	dingir
			ba-da-mu
		9.	dingir
	III.	1.	*i-bí-da-mu*
			dingir
		3.	*a-gur-li-im*
			dingir
		5.	*a-bur-li-im*
			en-en

Part 2

		7.	2 udu
			^{d}*ì-da-kul*
	IV.	1.	*wa*
			^{d}BE-*mí*
		3.	2 udu
			^{d}*ra-sa-ap*
		5.	*wa*
			^{d}a-dam-ma
		7.	2 udu
			^{d}*a-gú*
Rev.	I.	1.	*wa*
			^{d}*gu-la-du*
		3.	1 udu
			[^{d}x-*r*]*a-ru*$_{12}$
		5.	[*da*]-*rí*-[*í*]*b*^{ki}
			[1 ud]u
		7.	^{d}GÁ×SIG$_7$-*ra*
	II.	1.	lú *da-da*(-)EN
			[*á*]*š-da*
		3.	1 x̣ x̣
			(lacuna)
	III.		(lacuna)

Part 3

Rev.	III.	x+1.	(broken)	[(An offering of sheep)
			dingir-dingir-dingir	for] the deities
			uru-uru	[of] the cities,
		3.	al$_6$-dab$_5$	[who(se images?)] reside
	IV.	1.	*in*	in
			da-rí-íb^{ki}	Darib
		3.	(broken)	
	V.		(broken)	

Several considerations argue against Archi's interpretation while still others favor an alternative rendition. If, for the sake of argument, one assumes a mortuary context for the ritual, it is curious that the text records nothing as to its regularly repeated observance as one would expect in the case of a royal ancestor cult rite.[7] Moreover, the deceased kings who do receive offerings at contemporary Pre-Sargonic Lagash in the en-en-né-ne account lists and at Old Babylonian Mari in the *kispum* offerings are *not* preceded by the dingir or *ilu* sign; they are not deified.[8] That statues of dead, royal ancestors are nowhere mentioned in the en-en-né-ne or *kispum* texts should caution against Archi's unsubstantiated assumption that at Ebla, such statues were used as the place of deposit for offerings.

Neither dead kings nor their statues were included in the Lagash níg-giš-tag-ga account lists as recipients of offerings alongside the major deities, temples, and cultic paraphernalia. They were only present in the form of their votive statues. We would have expected the royal Lagash ancestors to be included in these texts had they been deified, in which case they should have received offerings of a similar capacity as those uniformly distributed to the gods, temples, and cultic paraphernalia.[9] If we grant for the sake of argument that in *TM* 75.G.2628, the names listed do represent the dead, deified, Eblaite ancestors, then in view of what might be inferred from the Lagash evidence, we would have expected the en-en at Ebla to receive an amount approximating that offered to the gods in section 2, but the ancestors are allocated far less (i.e., half if the ten sheep were distributed equally).

Archi's comparison with what he identifies as related rituals in the Ugaritic text *KTU* 1.161 and in the Old Babylonian text *BM* 80328 (the Genealogy of the Hammurapi Dynasty, hereafter GHD) actually favors the association of the Eblaite ritual with funerary rites not the ancestor cult (for the funerary nature of these texts, cf. 3.1.7.1. and 3.1.9.). Lastly, if en at Ebla designates an official of lower authority than a king (with all that the latter term implies with regard to independence and sovereignty), we would have a rite unique only to Ebla, for then non-royal dead would be depicted as having obtained divine status and as having

---

[7] Fronzaroli's text mentioned in the previous footnote was published after Archi's king list. While it does record the regularity of the associated mortuary rites, it does not indicate that the dead possessed supernatural beneficent powers.

[8] On the en-en-né-ne texts at Lagash, cf. Kobayashi 1984:43–65. For the Mari *kispum* offerings, cf. 2.2. Kobayashi suggested that the rulers and their wives mentioned in the Lagash texts were the living offerers and that the statues mentioned were votive or prayer statues *contra* Talon 1974:167–68. Talon conjectured that these statues represented the dead participants in funeral feasts. For treatments of the Pre-Sargonic Lagash materials, cf. Deimel 1920:32–51; Rosengarten 1960(esp. chapter 7); Bauer 1969:107–14; Kobayashi 1984:43–65; 1985:10–30; Cohen 1993:37–64,470–81.

[9] Cf. Kobayashi 1984:56–57 and his tables II and III.

been the objects of ancestor cult rites.[10] However, this is nowhere attested in Syria or Mesopotamia. Rather, the deceased king was the sole recipient of both the status of divinity and the performance of cultic rites, and then only for a relatively limited span of time in Mesopotamian history.[11]

In the final analysis, we must even reject Archi's assumed mortuary context for the ritual. With good reason, Archi vacillates over the function of the dingir sign as a divine determinative preceding each of the ten names. When it precedes the name of any one of these individuals, it is written in its own case whereas when it accompanies one of the known deities later in the text, it is not written in its own case, e.g., ^{d}ì-da-kul. He recognizes that a straightforward reading of the phrase dingir + RN would render "the god of Such-and-such a king."[12] We invoke the Sumerian texts from Pre-Sargonic Lagash once again in order to illustrate what was conceptually possible for the phrase dingir + RN. These texts record the fact that individual kings of the Ur-Nanshe dynasty took as their personal god a particular deity named Shulutula. Belief in personal gods of various kinds was widespread and the dingir sign alone could be employed to designate a personal god.[13] It was common practice to refer to the personal god without recourse to a specific god name and to make offerings to that god.[14] Among royalty, it was customary for the personal god of a dynastic king to be inherited by his successor son.[15] This explains the references to the personal dynastic god as the "god of the

10 As suggested by Michalowski 1985:294–95,297; 1988b:267–77, the term en might have been only a bureaucrat heading one of the many major organizations in the city, "the one in charge." His argument assumes that the archive does not represent the central royal library.

11 So Hallo 1980:190; 1988:54–66; 1992:387ff. who dates the origin of this phenomenon to midway through the reign of Naram-Sin of Akkad but who incorrectly extends it beyond the accession of Hammurapi of Babylon into late second millennium Syria (i.e., Ugarit, cf. 3.1.). On the ideology of divine kingship in early Mesopotamia, see also Michalowski 1988a:19–23.

12 Cf. e.g., the phrases dingir *En-àr-Da-mu* and dingir *Isar-Ma-lik* which appear in both the so-called king list and in *TM* 75.G.570, but in the latter case he translates "the god [of] Enàr-Damu . . . the god [of] Isar-Malik," in Archi 1985:281; 1986:215 against 1988:106–07 n.9; Biga and Pomponio 1987:60–61.

13 Cf. Vorländer 1975:9; Kobayashi 1989:22–42. Kobayashi (p.22 and n.4) has reiterated the fact that the more common designation for the personal god is dingir-an-ni, "his god," and that in the following Lagash dynasties, the personal god of Enentarzi was Mesandu and that of Uruinimgina, Ninshubur.

14 On the personal god, cf. Vorländer 1975:5–120; Jacobsen 1976:147–64; Albertz 1978:96–158; Klein 1982:295–306; Groneberg 1986:93–108. Some of the epithets of the personal god include "my god," "god of my fathers," "my creator," "my shepherd," "my father," etc., cf. Vorländer 1975:8–25 for an inventory of epithets. In royal circles, the personal god could be identified as a well known member of the pantheon (e.g., Shamash, Sin, Adad, Nergal) and one who represented the human protégé in the divine assembly, so Vorländer 1975:8–117,149–64; Jacobsen 1976:157; Klein 1982:296; van der Toorn 1985:44. On other occasions, certain of the high gods such as Shamash could be approached by an individual to intercede on his/her behalf before the personal god, cf. the edition of *LKA* 139:24–27 in van der Toorn 1985:Appendix #3.g.

15 Jacobsen 1976:159; Klein 1982:295; van der Toorn 1985:4,24.

fathers."[16] Lastly, it was also a known practice among royalty to erect statues of their personal gods and to place them in temples or chapels.[17] Shulutula received offerings in the Lagash cult and was identified by the same construction attested in the Eblaite king list, dingir + RN, ^{d}šulutula dingir en-te-me-na, "Shulutula, god of Entemena."

These considerations make Archi's appeal for support to the so-called Ugaritic king list, *KTU* 1.113, unconvincing. Not only does this text represent a chronological (and cultural?) distance of more than a millennium, but more importantly, the nature of the attendant ritual is equally problematic (cf. 3.1.6.). In fact, Liverani viewed *KTU* 1.113 as a ritual list of the personal god(s) of the former Ugaritic kings. He acknowledged that the names mentioned in *KTU* 1.113 represent the deceased kings of Ugarit and that each is preceded by the lexeme *'il*, but it was the deity designated by the generic *'il* who functioned as the object of a legitimating ritual and not the dead kings. For Liverani, the *'il* + RN element was to be rendered "the god of Such-and-such a king."[18] The use of the phrase dingir + RN at Lagash—and perhaps in the Eblaite king list—lends support to Liverani's interpretation of *KTU* 1.113.[19] In any case, one cannot assume, as so often the case, that dead kings at Ugarit were designated gods on the basis of the Emar and Nuzi texts, for the relevant details are equally debatable. The *ilānu* or *ilū*, "gods," in parallelism with the *eṭemmū*, "ghosts of the dead," and the *mētū*, "dead," at Nuzi and Emar do not refer to the same group, i.e., the deified dead. They more likely refer to two distinct groups of numina both worthy and demanding of the household head's cultic observance.[20]

---

16 Cf. Vorländer 1975:12–14,155–58; Jacobsen 1976:159 and the qualifications of Klein 1982: 296–97. In the light of the fact that the personal gods might comprise members of the pantheon, the pluralized form of this epithet "gods of the fathers" could function as an appropriate heading for a god list or a text recording offerings for the gods as in the Ugaritic text *KTU* 1.118:1, on which cf. 3.1.3.

17 Gudea of Lagash placed a statue of his own god, Ningishzida, in a chapel attached to the temple which he had built for the city goddess, Baba. His reasons for doing so were to strengthen the power of his throne, to enable him to judge rightly, and to lengthen the days of his life, in other words, to legitimate his dynasty, cf. Jacobsen 1976:156.

18 For this view of 1.113, cf. Liverani 1974:340–41 and 3.1.6. Pardee 1988:173 n.25 argued that this makes little sense owing to the lack of mention of specific god names. But he did not acknowledge the fact that the personal gods often occur without their specific names, cf. the sixteen epithets listed in Vorländer 1975:8–25.

19 Even if one were to assume that *KTU* 1.113 was a mortuary ritual, in the light of the documented enactment of funerary rites on behalf of one of the (non-deified!) deceased kings at Ugarit (cf. *KTU* 1.161 in 3.1.9.) and the absence otherwise of ancestor cult rites there (cf. 3.1.), it is going well beyond the limits of the evidence to posit that the underlying ritual in this text is something more than funerary in nature.

20 The same goes for their occurrence together in the Neo-Assyrian version of the Legend of Etana. For our treatment of the Nuzi and Emar evidence, cf. 3.2.; for our assessment of the remaining data cited in support of the deified status of the dead, cf. 4.5.1.

The preceding factors point to a different cultic context for *TM* 75.G.2628 from that outlined by Archi. Common knowledge and scribal practice could readily explain the absence of the god's name in this accounting list. *TM* 75.G.2628 more likely preserves echoes of a ritual in which the current dynast legitimated rule by aligning his administration with that of his predecessors. It is not too difficult to imagine the names actually being recited in the course of the associated ritual observance. The names were proclaimed in retrograde order down to that of the immediate predecessor of the living king. As each of the ten offerings were made to the dynastic god, the name of each former king of the dynasty was recited as the protégé of that god, "the god of Such-and-such a king (#10), the god of Such-and-such a king (#9) etc. . . . " While the significance of such a ritual would approximate a commemorative act on behalf of the dead Eblaite dynastic kings, it is not expressive of an Eblaite belief in the royal dead's puissant beneficence.

2.1.2. Offerings and Lamentations for the Dead Kings

In a treatise designed to outline the fundamental elements of the official cult at Ebla, Pettinato listed several offering texts which supposedly testified to the existence of a royal ancestor cult. According to him, two texts in particular stand out. They mention "(slaughtered) sheep" offerings (udu [íb-tag]) made for "the lamentations [of] the kings" (si-dù-si-dù en-en) during the eleventh month.[21] The associated rites were performed in the royal palace garden or ^{giš}kiri$_6$ which supposedly contained a royal hypogeum or ki-sur, where the deceased kings were interred.[22]

Pettinato based his interpretation of si-dù-si-dù as "lamentations" on the equation of Sumerian si-dù and Eblaite *dì-mu-mu* attested in bilingual lexical lists from Ebla.[23] For *dì-mu-mu*, he offered the Akkadian cognate *dimmatu*, "lament,"

[21] Pettinato 1979b:31–32 = 1979c:115–16. These administrative lists include *TM* 75.G.1764:I. 26–III.4; r.III.5–12, cf. Pettinato 1979a:104; 1979b:47 = 1979c:130–31; *TM* 75.G.2238:IV.21–25; XII.21–26; cf. Pettinato 1979a:158; 1979b:79,84 = 1979c:163, 168. A third text is mentioned in Pettinato 1979a:42; 1980:XLVIII [Catalogue no. 714 *sic* > 713].

[22] Pettinato 1979b:31–32 = 1979c:115–16. The garden is mentioned in *TM* 75.G.1764:III.10 and the so-called hypogeum in *TM* 75.G.2238:XII.22; *TM* 75.G.1274:IV.7; cf. Pettinato 1980:68. His view has been adopted by Xella 1983:288; 1985:75; Healey 1984:251; Spronk 1986:140–41; del Olmo Lete 1986b:62–64.

[23] *TM* 75.G.2001; cf. Pettinato 1979a:131; 1982:33. The relevant lines cited in Pettinato 1979b:31 and n.159 = 1979c:115 and n.159 are v.XII.4–5; see also Pettinato 1982:320. Pettinato 1979a:94; 1982:33,320 mentions another bilingual lexical list *TM* 75.G.1678:v.XII.14–15 [Catalogue no. 1116] which equates si-dù-si-dù and *dì-mu-mu*.

from *damāmu*, "to mourn (for the dead)."[24] In support of Pettinato's proposal, del Olmo Lete has noted that the offerings for the lamentations of the kings are immediately preceded by offerings to a-mu-a-mu, "the (dead) fathers," and to the so-called chthonic god Rasap (= Resheph), and are followed by additional offerings to Rasap.[25]

Like Archi's proposal, Pettinato's presents several problems. First is the fact that there is no evidence in the texts for the regular observance of this ritual lamentation. The second involves the significance of the terms si-dù and en at Ebla. That Sumerian si-dù and its lexical equivalent, Eblaite *dì-mu-mu*, refer to lamentation is debatable. The root *d-m-m* in West Semitic can also signify "to be silent."[26] Besides, as we noted above, en at Ebla might refer to officials of a standing lower than that of the king. Finally, the ambiguity inherent in the syntactic value of the genitival en-en in si-dù-si-dù en-en makes Pettinato's proposal difficult to accept outright.

If si-dù does signify lamentation, then the question arises, does the "of" in the "lamentations of the en-en" signify lamentations on behalf of the deceased en-en, i.e., "lamentations for the (dead) en-en" as Pettinato claims, or were the en-en those who performed the lamentations, i.e., "lamentations by the (living) officials"? Mourning over the death of a dignitary by foreign officials comprised one component in the international diplomatic protocol of Mesopotamia. Customary elements of international mourning included the arrival of the news of death *via* a messenger, the immediate reaction of grief by the recipient which involved, among other gestures, the shedding of tears, fasting, and lamentation, and the dispatch of an envoy laden with funerary gifts and grave goods to be presented at the funeral.[27] Perhaps si-dù-si-dù describes living en-en waiting in silence for a divine revelation, "the silent deliberations of the (living) officials." In Mesopotamia and Syria-Palestine, ritual lamentation is also associated with invigoration or fertility rites and the rituals related to the hidden god.[28] The en-en might be Eblaite or foreign officials who make offerings and cultic lamentations to the god(s).

---

[24] See *CAD* 3(1959):59–60,143; *AHw* 1(1965):155,170; cf. *d-m-m* in Hebrew, Ugaritic (*KTU* 1.16:I.26), and Arabic (*damā*). Pettinato is followed by Archi 1988:106 n.10; Fronzaroli 1988:13.

[25] Del Olmo Lete 1986b:69 n.38. *TM* 75.G.2238:IV.21–25; XII.21–26. The term, a-mu-a-mu, occurs in XI.30; the term, Rasap, in IV.8–9,15–16; XII.7–8,13–14,19–20; v.I.2′-3′. On a-mu-a-mu, cf. Pettinato 1979b:17,20 = 1979c:101,104; Xella 1983:288; 1985:75.

[26] On this significance of *d-m-m*, cf. Baumann 1978:260–65 and note his bibliography.

[27] Cf. Artzi 1980:161–70 and the recently published letters from Tell Asmar in Whiting 1987:48–51,59–63.

[28] Cf. Podella 1989.

As to Pettinato's remaining arguments, gardens in Syria-Palestine and Mesopotamia functioned in a variety of ways, burial plots being only one.[29] Pettinato's view of ki-sur as "hypogeum" is severely weakened since, as he admits, this is entirely dependent upon his view of si-dù-si-dù en-en.[30] Lastly, the contextual support cited by del Olmo Lete is problematic. The defunct status of a-mu-a-mu is unlikely (cf. 2.1.4.) and Rasap is probably depicted in his role as the god of plague or pestilence rather than as patron god of a supposed Eblaite royal ancestor cult (cf. 2.1.5.).

In conclusion, the en-en of Pettinato's texts might be living officials, local and foreign, who performed the expected mourning rituals on behalf of some politically distinguished, but presently unidentifiable, departed soul. The attested observance of mourning as international protocol and the lack of evidence in support of Eblaite ancestor worship or veneration favors this interpretation. Among many other observances, these occasions, perhaps, included the offering of mutton (udu) in order to feed the weakened dead or to insure the arrival of the deceased in the netherworld. What most characterized these rites however, was the cultic lamentation performed by the en-en.

2.1.3. The Eblaite Version of the *marzēaḥ*

According to the late Mitchell Dahood, Ebla records the earliest attestation of the West Asiatic institution known as the *marzēaḥ*. In one administrative text, three women receive variegated dresses on ud *mar-za-u*$_9$ itu *i-ši*, "the day of the *marzēaḥ* in the month of Ishu(?)."[31] In another more recently published, three garments are allocated for *Du-da-sa* ugula *mar-za-u*$_9$, "Dudasa, superintendent of the *marzēaḥ*."[32]

Although not directly applicable, the consensus is that membership in this confraternity in first millennium Syria-Palestine may have required the observance of death cult practices at feasts held on behalf of former members (more on this to follow).[33] However, based on the proposal that Hebrew *bêt marzēaḥ*

[29] For the various cultic functions of gardens in the ancient Near East, see Andrae 1952:485–94; Ebeling 1959:147–50; Oppenheim 1965:328–33; Jacobs-Hornig 1978:34–39; Wiseman 1983:137–44.

[30] Pettinato 1979b:31 = 1979c:115; 1980:68. On this dubious basis, he also equated ki-sur with ki-a-nag, the place of burial and funerary rites. On the ki-a-nag, cf. now Kobayashi 1985:10–30.

[31] *TM* 75.G.1372:I.1–v.I.3, in Pettinato 1980:XLV-XLVI,309 [Edition no. 46]; cf. Pope 1981:179 n.65; Fabry 1984:12; Dahood 1987:99; Archi 1988:103 n.2.

[32] *TM* 75.G.1443:XI.1–3, cf. Pettinato 1981:88 and Archi 1985:31.

[33] For bibliography and summary of views on the *marzēaḥ* institution, cf. 3.1.5.; 4.3.1.; 4.6.1.

is synonymous with *bêṯ mišteh*, "house of drinking," in Jer. 16:5–8,[34] Dahood suggested that a parallel semantic relation occurs much earlier and involves Eblaite *mar-za-u₉*. When one compares the above text with another at Ebla in which two garments are offered to the god Rasap ud *maš-da-ù* dumu-nita-*šu*, "on the day of the drinking feast of his son," for Dahood, the parallel becomes apparent.[35] If one assumes for the sake of argument that the Eblaite terms *mar-za-u₉* and *maš-da-ù* can be equated with their Hebrew counterparts *marzēaḥ* and *mišteh* respectively, then Dahood's proposal demands careful evaluation.

Nevertheless, the available evidence indicates that the death cult relations of the *marzēaḥ* were nonexistent prior to the first millennium (cf. 3.1.5. for Ugarit). Moreover, our two texts make no explicit mention of such relations and the *bêṯ marzēaḥ* and *bêṯ mišteh* in Jer. 16:5–8 are not synonymous institutions (cf. 4.6.1.). Therefore, we are, for the present, compelled to reject any possible connections of Eblaite *mar-za-u₉* and, for that matter, *maš-da-ù* with the death or ancestor cult.

2.1.4. Eblaite Ancestral Gods and the Cult of the Dead

The names of three deities which show up in the offering lists as recipients of sheep offerings have been cited as testimony to a cult of royal ancestors and sundry other persons of prominence. According to Xella, the deities a-mu-a-mu, ^{d}a-mu, and ^{d}en are "the fathers," "the divine father," and "the divine king(s)" respectively. Xella concluded that the a-mu-a-mu referred not to royal personages per se, but to other individuals who had obtained a rank of such importance so as to warrant their receiving offerings in the official cult subsequent to death. The ^{d}a-mu was the divinized ancestor of the king and the ^{d}en were the defunct former kings (viewed collectively). ^{d}a-mu was the forerunner of Ugaritic *'il'ib*, the so-called "divinized ancestor" (but, cf. 3.1.3.), while ^{d}en anticipated the Ugaritic *mlkm* and *rp'um*, the "dead, deified kings and heroes" (cf. 3.1.7. and 3.1.8.).[36]

Several obstacles impede our acceptance of Xella's proposals. First, the context of *TM* 75.G.2238, the text cited by Xella, offers no support for the dead or deified status of the a-mu-a-mu.[37] Second, no dingir sign precedes the a-mu-a-mu and,

---

[34] Cf. e.g., Bright 1965:110–11; Porten 1968:180–81; Pope 1977b:216,221; now Lewis 1989:138–39.

[35] Dahood 1987:99. For the text, *TM* 75.G.1264:IV.15–17 [Edition no. 2], see Pettinato 1980: 22,29.

[36] Xella 1983:288; 1985:75; cf. Ribichini 1985:66–67. Archi 1979–80:168 identified Eblaite ^{d}en-en as "the ancestors," but cited no textual reference in support. Furthermore, he did not take up this datum in his survey of the subject in 1988.

[37] Cf. Pettinato 1979b:17,85 = 1979c:101,168; Archi 1988:108.

as mentioned already, this is the primary criterion by which one ascertains the (dead) deified status of an associated individual, that is according to the Eblaite ancestor cult interpretation. The a-mu-a-mu more likely represent living persons who function as the offerers, not the recipients, in *TM* 75.G.2238.[38]

Lines XI.29–XII.4 read as follows: 2 udu a-mu-a-mu GABA ^{d}AMA-ra *mi-na-ì* su-du$_{8}$, "two sheep [of (= from)] the fathers [for] receipt [by] AMA-ra, Minai has delivered."[39] The role of recipient is taken up by the deity AMA-ra rather than the a-mu-a-mu. Pettinato, followed by Archi, had viewed ^{d}AMA-ra in XII.2 as a month name, but one would expect a preceding itu as even Pettinato acknowledged.[40] Sollberger suggested that ^{d}AMA-ra at Ebla is a god name.[41] This deity is also attested in the Abu Ṣalabikh god lists.[42]

We turn now to Xella's two remaining forms ^{d}a-mu and ^{d}en. The dingir sign preceding a-mu and en in the offering lists functions not as the divine determinative, but as the noun denoting deity "the god of So-and-so."[43] Thus, ^{d}a-mu should be read as dingir a-mu, "the god [of] the father," and ^{d}en as dingir en, "the god [of] the en."[44] The gods intended in these references are perhaps the personal gods. They show up repeatedly but are never explicitly identified with a known deity, which, as we noted above, was common practice.[45]

---

[38] Even if a-mu-a-mu can be equated with the deceased, they are neither deified nor recipients of ancestor cult rites as typically understood. Our approach also applies in the case of *TM* 75.G.2403:I.16–II.5, cited in Archi 1988:107, where a-mu again lacks the preceding dingir sign: 2 udu ^{d}*ra-as-ap in* sa.za$_{x}^{ki}$ *ir-ak-da-mu* nidba *in* u$_{4}$ *gi-ba-lu* nidba a-mu-*sú*, "2 sheep [for] Rasap in the palace, Irak-Damu has offered at the time of the g. [of] the offering [of (= from?)] his father." Elsewhere Irak-Damu is designated dumu-nita en, "the son of an en." Archi 1988:108 and n.13 identified the en as Ibrium.

[39] For a-mu-a-mu, see *TM* 75.G.2238:XI.30. Pettinato suggested for GABA (XII.1), "middle (of the month of ^{d}AMA-ra)," but Archi 1985:282 offered "receipt," cf. also *CAD* 7(1960):183, Akkadian *irtu*, "chest, back."

[40] Cf. Pettinato 1979b:84 = 1979c:168; Archi 1988:108. They translated the text as follows "2 sheep [for] the fathers . . . (month) AMA-ra, Minai has taken in possession." On the month name (^{d})AMA-ra with accompanying itu at Ebla, cf. *TM* 75.G.427 *passim*; Pettinato 1981:151–52.

[41] Sollberger 1986:9.

[42] Cf. Alberti 1985:9 (line 125).

[43] Archi 1988:107–10; cf. 2.1.1. esp. n.18; Pettinato 1979b:20 = 1979c:104 and cf. Viganò and Pardee 1984:11. Archi 1988:108 recognized the inconsistencies in rendering the dingir sign, for it shows up in several instances with en and amu but in its own case.

[44] For dingir a-mu, see *TM* 75.G.2075:II.27; IV.11; *TM* 75.G.2238:IX.20; *TM* 75.G.11010+:III.6; VIII.17′,21′ in Pettinato 1979b:20,64–65,82,94,99 = 1979c:104,148–49,166, 178,183; add now *TM* 75.G.2717:III.16–19; *TM* 75.G.2635:II.18–21; *TM* 75.G.10103:II.11–14; IV.6–10; *TM* 75.G.2403: 22–26; ARET 2 15:III.11–IV.5 in Archi 1988:107. For dingir en, see *TM* 75.G.2238:V.21–22; 11010+:V.16; VII.33; Pettinato 1979b:20,80,96,98 = 1979c:104,164,180,182; add now *TM* 75.G.2403:27–31; *TM* 75.G.2398:III.22–26; *TM* 75.G.1246:III.1–7; *TM* 75(*sic*).G.2647:4′-8′; *TM* 75.G.2520:IX.4–10; ARET 4 5:III.10–13; IV.14–17 in Archi 1988:109,111–12.

[45] Employing the same questionable logic which led him, in the final analysis, to view dingir + RN, "the god [of] RN," as a dead, deified king who received offerings in the royal ancestor cult, Archi

Archi also included dingir a-mu *ma-lik-tum*, "the god [of] the queen's father," and dingir dingir *ma-lik-tum-ma-lik-tum*, "the 'ghosts' [of] the dead queens," in his version of the Eblaite royal ancestor cult.[46] Moreover, similar practices on behalf of royal family members have been supposedly gleaned from the Mari archives (but cf. 2.2.) and the roughly contemporary en-en-né-ne economic archives at Pre-Sargonic Lagash record offerings to the former rulers, their mothers, wives, and daughters as well. It should be recalled, however, that neither were the names of those deceased persons of royalty who received offerings at Lagash preceded by the dingir sign, nor were their names included among the offering lists for major deities, temples, and other implements in the níg-giš-tag-ga texts.[47] The Eblaite scribes had another group of recipients in mind in these instances, namely the personal dynastic god of the queen's father and the personal gods of the queens.

2.1.5. Eblaite Rasap and the Cult of the Dead

Matthiae theorized that the monumental remains from the Middle Bronze western palace area of the Amorite period preserve evidence of an Eblaite royal ancestor cult. He argued that the close proximity of a royal necropolis and the Rasap temple at Ebla pointed to the existence of this cult.[48] His characterization of the temple as dedicated to Rasap was, in part, influenced not only by the proximity of what he identified as the royal graves, but also by the equation of Rasap and Nergal, the Sumerian god of the netherworld, in a bilingual syncretistic god list from Ebla.[49] However, burials prima facie do not prove the existence of an ancestor cult and the

1988:107–12 unfortunately concluded that these two phrases likewise pointed to such a cult. "The god [of} the father" was, for Archi, the dead, deified Ibrium, former king of Ebla, and "the god [of] the en" was "the god [of the person of] the king," by which we understand him to mean, the dead, deified king, for he offered little else by way of elucidation.

46 Archi's texts include: 1 udu dingir a-mu *ma-lik-tum Ḫir-du-du* nidba, "1 sheep [for] the god [of] the father [of] the queen, Ḫirdudu has offered," *TM* 75.G.11010+:VIII.20–24; cf. Archi 1988:108 and udu dingir-dingir *ma-lik-tum-ma-lik-tum Ìr-'a-ak-Da-mu* nidba, "4 sheep [for] the gods [of] the queens, Irak-Damu has offered," *TM* 75.G.10167:I.26–II.2 in Archi 1988:111.

47 So Kobayashi 1984:43–65, esp. pp.49–50,56–57; cf. 1985:10–30, esp. pp.10–13.

48 Matthiae 1979:566; 1981:61; 1984:30; 1990:349–54.

49 Matthiae 1984:30; cf. *TM* 75.G.2000:v.X.15′; Pettinato 1981:136–45 (esp. p.143); 1982:17, 290. Cf. also *TM* 75.G.1875:v.V.9′-10′ in Pettinato 1982:XXXI,72. Matthiae also cited the discovery of a sculpted ritual basin in the temple complex as evidence for connecting the temple and Rasap. On the basin are depicted a banquet scene and two series of soldiers which Matthiae viewed as reflective of Rasap's role as god of war. If the depiction on the basin is to be connected to Rasap, it only underscores the curious silence concerning Rasap's role at Ebla as patron of the royal ancestor cult, for one would have expected that role or at least his more general chthonic role and not simply his role as warrior god to be associated with evidence found in an area supposedly designed for royal ancestor cult rites.

supposed royal character of the tombs is not at all certain.[50] Even Matthiae was forced to acknowledge that the stratigraphic limitations at Ebla were unlike the data from Avaris which he cited as support.[51] Lastly, the problems in identifying burial remains and deposits as artifacts of royalty are legion.[52]

With the exception of his equation with Nergal in the bilingual god list, Rasap's supposed underworld role remains otherwise unattested at Ebla.[53] In fact, the underworld role of Rasap or Resheph is not documented before the late second millennium. At Ugarit, he fills only the minor role of gatekeeper. *KTU* 1.78:3–4 reads *špš ṯǵrh ršp*, "Shapash, her gatekeeper is Resheph."[54] In any case, Rasap and Nergal might have been equated at Ebla and Ugarit based on their similar roles as gods of plague and pestilence or metalworking.[55] Even if Rasap attained the role of a chthonic god at Ebla, it is another matter altogether to attribute to him the position of patron deity over a royal ancestor cult in the absence of any explicit supporting evidence for such a role.

2.1.6. Summary

We thus conclude our evaluation of the relevant Eblaite texts. The belief in the supernatural beneficent power of the dead is nowhere attested in the texts or material remains of Ebla. Even if we were to grant for the sake of argument that Eblaite en designated the king, unequivocal evidence is presently lacking for the regular care for or feeding of, let alone the veneration or worship of, the royal ancestors. Ebla likewise testifies to neither a general death cult nor to a domestic ancestor cult. The same applies with the practice of necromancy.[56] The available

[50] Cf. Matthiae 1979:563–69; 1981:55–65; 1984:18–32.

[51] Matthiae 1984:30. For Avaris, cf. Bietak 1979:249–61.

[52] Cf. the evaluation of Woolley's royal graves at Ur by Moorey 1977:24–40; 1984:1–18.

[53] On the Eblaite literary evidence concerning Eblaite Rasap, see Dahood and Pettinato 1977:230–32; Pettinato 1979b:25–26 = 1979c:109–10; Müller 1980:7; Dahood 1987:97; Sollberger 1986:9,11.

[54] *Contra* Cooper 1987a:1–7; Fulco 1987:343, Resheph is not netherworld king at Ugarit. He is never explicitly located in the Ugaritic netherworld. In fact, his association with Shapash might refer to those gates offering passage only to and from heaven's interior on the analogy of the Babylonian model proposed by Heimpel 1986:127–51; cf. 3.1.7.3.

[55] In the light of *KTU* 1.78, Resheph's equation with Nergal in the Ugaritic pantheon lists *KTU* 1.118:26 and *RS* 20.24:26, cannot secure Resheph's status as underworldking. Besides, these lists contain mere approximations (cf. line 15: *kṯr* // Ea), even innovations (cf. line 12: *kṯrt* // *sasurātum*), so Healey 1985:115–25. Dalley 1987:61–66, followed by Handy 1992:678–79, has proposed that Resheph is the West Asiatic name given to Nergal as patron deity of metalworking (cf. esp. pp.62,65). On the unlikelihood of a deity Malik's involvement in the cult of the dead at Ebla, see Heider 1985:98–100 against Müller 1980:11–14; cf. Sollberger 1986:10.

[56] While various types of incantations are attested at Ebla, necromancy per se is not, cf. Krebernik 1984.

Eblaite archives and archaeological record simply do not substantiate the existence of such practices. What the Ebla archives do suggest is that whatever political office the term en designated at Ebla, whether an important bureaucratic official or a king, great emphasis was placed on the honor due the personal god of such an individual (cf. dingir + RN, dingir + en) and those of their forefathers (cf. dingir + a-mu) for they, alongside the other major gods of the pantheon, received offerings in the cult. These rites took place on the occasion of the new king's coronation (if the rites reflected in Fronzaroli's text are taken into account). Other texts suggest the possibility that on the occasion of the funeral of a politically important person and in conjunction with the norms of international protocol, the Ebla court received foreign "ens" or dignitaries who made offerings and lamentations alongside local ens on behalf of a recently deceased person of political prominence.

2.2. The Evidence from Mari

The texts from ancient Mari (modern Tell Ḫarīrī) provide extensive documentation for regular offerings on behalf of the dead royalty and other persons of prominence in early second millennium Syria. The *kispum* offering along with its associated ritual comprise the primary data for Mari mortuary rites.[57] Also relevant in this regard is the *pagrā'um* offering owing to its presumed connection with the underworld god Dagan and the *kispum* offering. It remains to be seen whether or not these data preserve rites associated with a royal ancestor cult at Mari and the attendant belief in the dead's supernatural capacity to perform benevolent acts on behalf of the living.

---

57 For the *kispum* at Mari, see Birot *ARMT* 9(1960):283–87; Burke *ARMT* 11(1963):139–40; Birot *ARMT* 12(1964):23–24; Ribar 1973:88–135; Talon 1978:53–75; Sasson 1979:125–28; Birot 1980:139–50; Sasson 1982:339; Bonneterre 1983:26–31; Bottéro 1983:173–74; Wilcke 1983:50–53; Dalley 1984:122–25; Sasson 1985:447; Tsukimoto 1985:57–78; Finet 1985:89–90; Charpin and Durand 1986:163–70; Wilcke 1986:11–16; Finet 1987:242–44; Malamat 1989:96–103. *Kispum* occurs in at least eighty-six texts from Mari, some published, others only listed by museum number. Tsukimoto 1985:57 n.224, n.225, and n.226 lists sixty-five [for *ARMT* 9:114:iii:29; v:33, read 121:iii; v; add 225:6; omit 11:225 and add 279]. See also *ARMT* 1:65; 3:40; 7:9; *RA* 64(1970):35 [Text 28]; *Mari* 12803; cf. *ARI*(1):25 [Text 39:6 Terqa], but see 2.2.2. Add Materne 1983:197 n.12 [Text x:135:iv]; *ARMT* 23 (1984):60; *ARMT* 23(1984):248; Charpin 1984b:88–89 [Texts 30–36]; Charpin 1985a:259–60 [texts 10146, *A*.1403, 11125]; Wilcke 1986:11–16; Sasson 1987:586 [Text *M*.10004]. In a new collation, Durand 1985c:159 n.55 read *kispum* in *ARMT* 19:253:4 (see below).

2.2.1. The *kispum* Ritual

In a letter which Kibri-Dagan, governor of Terqa, sent to his king, Zimri-Lim at Mari, the wishes of the god Dagan at Terqa are communicated to Zimri-Lim through the medium of a *muḫḫûm* priest, "the god sent me: Hurry and write to the king so that he might consecrate the *kispū* to the *eṭemmum* (or ghost) of Yaḫdun-Lim."[58] Leaving aside both the puzzling questions of this Yaḫdun-Lim's identity[59] and the exact nature of the *kispū* offerings mentioned,[60] this datum decisively corroborates the mortuary character of the well-attested "*kispum* for the kings" at Mari, the *kispum ša šarrāni*. The recently published ritual text, *Mari* 12803, from the reign of Shamshi-Addu, removes all doubt as to the mortuary nature of the *kispum* offerings. In *Mari* 12803, not only do the statues or *lamassātum* of the dead kings,[61] Sargon and Naram-Sin, receive *kispum* offerings in the course of what might comprise a regularly observed ritual calendar,[62] but other dead persons of prominence do as well.[63] Still another text lists *kispum* offered during the tenth

---

58 *ARMT* 3:40:13–18: *ilum*^{lum} *iš-pu-ra-an-[ni] ḫu-mu-uṭ a-na šar[rim] šu-pu-ur-ma ki-ìs-pí a-na i-ṭe*$_4$*-em-[mi-im] ša Ia-aḫ-du-un-L[i-im] li-ik-ru-bu.* Similarly, Wilcke 1986:11–16 has recently published a text in which a female prophet(?), Dagan-naḫmis, receives a dream prompting the offering of *kispum* (cf. further 2.2.6.).

59 That is, whether he is a former king of Mari or the prematurely deceased son of Zimri-Lim. For Yaḫdun-Lim as Zimri-Lim's prematurely deceased son, cf. Dossin 1938:111 and 1939:106 on *a-na ki-ma-ḫi-im ša Ia-aḫ-du-un-Li-im mār šarrim.* On additional references to a tomb of one Yaḫdun-Lim, cf. *ARMT* 16/1(1979):216; Dalley 1984:137 n.16; Durand 1985b:404; now Charpin and Durand 1989:18–19 who, in the light of *ARMT* 3:40, located the tomb at Terqa. It appears that the references to a former king named Yaḫdun-Lim do not point to Zimri-Lim's father as Ḫatni-Addu filled this role and Yaḫdun-Lim and Ḫatni-Addu were two different people, so Charpin and Durand 1985:337, but cf. Sasson 1984a:116 n.1.

60 That is, whether they are funerary offerings or royal ancestor cult offerings and whether they simply point to the care for, the feeding of, or the commemoration of the dead. Cf. Tsukimoto 1980:129–38 for examples of the *kispum* offering as a funerary gift outside of Mari.

61 Birot 1980:143, 146–47 concluded that the *lamassātum* of Sargon and Naram-Sin *Mari* 12803:i:5–7, are their statues residing *ina bīt* ^{giš}*kussi*^{ḫá}, "in the hall of thrones." On the *lamassu* as statues at Mari, cf. now Durand *ARMT* 21(1983):379,385 [Texts 222,223,226,228,238,307 and see 22:204]. The *lamassu* also appear in the form of a vase in *ARMT* 7:265:7′; 13:16:6,10; 42:6; an ornament in 7:123:3. Bayliss 1973:124; Talon 1978:64 have speculated on the use of statues in the *kispum* ritual. Hallo 1988:54–66 proposed that the cult of the divine king prevalent from the Sargonic to Old Babylonian periods employed statues of the dead, deified king.

62 *Contra* Malamat 1989:98. Unlike the *kispum ša šarrāni*, the *kispum* in *Mari* 12803 was not offered on the first and sixteenth of the month, but at ITU ŠE.KIN.TAR U$_4$ 1–KÁM BA.ZAL-*ma*, "the going out of the first day of the month of Addar," (col. i:1). Additional *kispum*, perhaps, took place at other set times (on other days of the same month?, cf. col. i:9,27–28 and Tsukimoto 1985:74–76). Some took place on U$_4$-*um bi-ib-li-im*, "the day of *biblum*," (col. ii!1–3) and others on U$_4$-*um gi-im-ki-im*, "the day of *gimkum*," (col. ii:7). Cf. Birot 1980:139–50, esp. p.145 and n.2 for the proposal that the text reflects a liturgical calendar and see Charpin and Durand 1986:165.

63 We follow the reading of Charpin and Durand 1986:165 n.115: *ki-is-pu-um a-na* LUGAL-*ki-in* ⌈x⌉ *na-ra-am*-30 ^{lú}*Ḫa-na*^{meš} *ia-ra-di ù a-na šu-ut nu-um-ḫe-e ù* DID<L>I-Ḫ[I-A] *ki-is-pu-um an-nu-*

month (i.e., annually?) for either the common dead or for the "fathers" or royal ancestors, *ana kispim ša abbê*. Whether the common dead or the royal ancestors should be the preferred interpretation of *abbê* is impossible to decide as the term is problematic.[64]

A more recently published dispensary list has been cited as evidence for *kispum* offered to the dead, deified queen mother of Zimri-Lim, Addu-duri, *ana kispim ša* ᵈ*Addu-dūri*.[65] The dingir sign preceding the name Addu-duri is simply the determinative accompanying a theophoric element in a personal name, i.e., ᵈIM. Besides, we would not expect the deceased human recipient in this one instance of the Mari *kispum* to be deified. None of the other eighty or so references to the *kispum* at Mari designate the deceased kings as deified (and we would certainly expect the deification of dead kings if others of importance such as a queen mother were deified). It should be noted, in this regard, that the editor of *Mari* 12803 has pointed out that the names of the long deceased kings, Sargon and Naram-Sin, mentioned in *Mari* 12803 are not preceded by the dingir sign.[66]

It is often asserted that the *kispum* entailed a communal meal with both living and deceased participants. Although the *kispum* is occasionally listed in consignments for the royal meal or *naptan šarrim*, it probably had nothing to do with normal meals. To be sure, the king's presence was required at the regular *kispum* ritual where food, such as honey, KUM bread, sour bread, or cake, and drink, such as *šipkum* or *alappānum* beer, fine meal, and sesame, as well as oil, were typically

---

ú-[um] ik-ka-sà-[ap], "The *kispum* (offered) to Sargon, Naram-Sin, to the Ḫanean *yaradu*, and to those of Numḫa, and to various others, this *kispum* has been offered," (lines 16–23). Cf. also Birot 1980:141–47 and Tsukimoto 1985:73–78. The Ḫanean *yaradu* have been viewed as settled Ḫaneans, so Tsukimoto 1985:76–77 (< *warādum*, "to settle down,"); or, more explicitly, as deceased Ḫaneans, so Malamat 1989:99–100 (< Hebrew *yārōḏ*, "to descend,"); cf. Birot 1980:144. The term might refer to Ḫanean "descendants," although here deceased ones, but cf. Charpin and Durand 1986:166 n.121. On another group of the politically important deceased who receive offerings, the *malikū*, cf. 2.2.1.1.

64 Text #36:2–3 in Charpin 1984b:89, 118 *a-na ki-is-pí-im* [*š*]*a ab-bé-e*. Note *Mari* 12803:i:2–3, *ki-is-pu-um i-na li-ib-bi* URU Á.DAM[ki], "the *kispum* (offered) in the town and its environs." Birot 1980:139–40, 144 suggested for *abbê, abbû* = *nammaštû* = Á.DAM, "population, settlement," cf. *AHw* 1(1965):5; 2(1972):728; *CAD* 1(1964):48; 11(1980):233–34. In Text #36, Charpin 1984b:89,118; Charpin and Durand 1986:165 n.113; Durand 1987b:70 and n.102 read *abbê*, "fathers," a plural of *abu*, i.e., deceased royal ancestors or tribal chieftains(?). Cohen 1993:259–61,454–62 details the problems with relating *abbê* to "father(s)" and proposes instead offerings to the *ab/pum* or mound covering a passage to the netherworld, or with Beaulieu 1988:36, perhaps a canebrake or marsh where the dead were buried.

65 For the text, cf. Materne 1983:197 n.12 (lines 9–10) *a-na ki-is-pí-im ša* ᵈ*addu-du-ri*. If Addu-duri was the widow of Ḫatni-Addu, so Batto 1974:64–72, and if Ḫatni-Addu was Zimri-Lim's father, so Charpin and Durand 1985:33, then she might have been Zimri-Lim's mother. The syntactic parallel *a-na ki-is-pí-im ša* LUGAL[meš] in the same text (lines 13–14) favors ᵈ*Addu-dūri* as the recipient, not the offerer.

66 Birot 1980:146–47.

offered to the defunct predecessors.[67] However, the relatively small quantity of food suggests that it was sufficient only to satisfy the requirements of the cultic functionaries or, by analogy, the needs of the dead, but not both the living and the dead.[68]

Likewise, the identification of the *kispum* as a "funerary offering" is grossly inaccurate. To be sure, the practice of placing gifts at the grave is attested at Mari, e.g., offerings *ana kimāḫim ša* PN, but *kispum* is never described as such.[69] By a wide margin, the texts depict it as a regular food offering presented to the dead. We know of only three instances, all of which come from ancient sites other than Mari, where the *kispum* was placed in the grave at burial.[70] At Mari, the standard practice entailed *kispum* offerings at regular intervals; the *kispum* for the *šarrānu* was offered on the first and sixteenth of the month, while the offerings for the *malikū* (see 2.2.1.1.) were made only on the first of the month. In both cases, these offerings would have been made long after the funerary rites had ceased. Nevertheless, special occasions or circumstances might warrant the unscheduled enactment or even the postponement of the regular *kispum* ritual.[71]

As to the exact religious or ideological significance of the royal *kispum* rites at Mari, we are left with very few clues. We do gain some assistance from *Mari* 12803. The underlying ritual series apparently functioned as a means for Shamshi-Addu to link up his dynasty with the ancient dynasty of Akkad from which he derived his claim to power.[72] The ritual served to legitimate existing dynastic political structures by reaffirming their link with the past. Beyond this, however, it is difficult to reconstruct such religious beliefs or concerns as those having to

---

[67] Cf. *ARMT* 9:226 for a list of some of these foodstuffs and now Lafont 1984:252 [Text 248] where meat consignments are atypically listed among the *kispum*. Cf. also Wilcke 1986:11–16 for other kinds of bread and beer. On the presence of the king at Mari during the regular *kispum* rituals (the *kispum ša šarrāni*), see Talon 1978:64; Sasson 1979:125; 1985:447, but note that in the rather distinct ritual of *Mari* 12803, the *kispum* was to be performed before the arrival of the king (cf. col.i:1). *ARMT* 10:50:14 may allude to king Zimri-Lim's neglect of his duties on behalf of the dead, so Sasson 1983:289.

[68] Ribar 1973:91–92 pointed out that the fifty *qa kispum* corresponds to the low end of the scale for the royal table or the *naptan šarrim*, that three *qa* represent the daily ration for an individual, and whereas the royal table consignments widely vary, those of the *kispum* do not (cf. *ARMT* 9:212, 98,71,193). On the *naptan šarrim*, cf. also Glaeseman 1978; Sasson 1982:326–41. At best, only a small number of the living could have attended such a communal meal. The reference to *kispum* as a "meal" NÍG.DU in *Mari* 12803 has in view its exclusive function vis-à-vis the dead (col.i:4) and for our view of the GHD in which those invited to "eat and drink and bless" the king are exclusively the living, cf. 3.1.7.1.

[69] E.g., *ARMT* 7:58:3; Dossin 1938:111; 1939:106; cf. *CAD* 8(1971):370; Tsukimoto 1980:132–35; Parayne 1982:25 n.98. Add the newly published texts *ARMT* 21:347; Charpin 1984b:109–10 [Text 50]; Limet 1986:6,169,176–77 [Texts 17, 539, 565, and 571] and cf. the texts on p.30 n.1.

[70] Cf. Tsukimoto 1980:129–38; 1985:140–45.

[71] Cf. Birot *ARMT* 12(1964):23; Talon 1978:64; Sasson 1979:125–28; Tsukimoto 1985:58–60.

[72] So Birot 1980:147–48 followed by Tsukimoto 1985:229–32; Malamat 1989:98 n.98.

do with the care for, feeding, veneration, worship, or the commemoration of the deceased kings and prominent persons of Mari. These issues will be discussed in greater detail in the final section 2.2.6., where we summarize our evaluation of the Mari evidence.[73]

2.2.1.1. The Royal *kispum* and the Offerings for the *mālikū*

Two aspects of the royal *kispum* ritual call for further elaboration, the occurrence of the *kispum ša šarrāni* alongside offerings *ana malikī(/im)*, "for the *malikū*,"[74] and the *kispum* rites enacted *ina rapiqātim*, "in the garden." The *malikū* (or *mālikū*) at Mari have been understood to represent demons,[75] infernal ghosts,[76] counselors,[77] non-royal departed men of distinction,[78] princes[79] or other non-reigning members of the royal line.[80] While the *malkū* may denote either demons or infernal ghosts in Old Babylonian oil omens and Standard Babylonian literary texts,[81] nowhere at Mari do the *malikū* appear as such.[82] Besides, it is highly unlikely that the name of a class of wholly evil chthonic beings would have gained the level of popularity needed to be incorporated into the royal cult as

---

73 The GHD is frequently cited in support of (1) the legitimating function of the Mari *kispum*, particularly *Mari* 12803, and (2) the festive banquet which supposedly accompanied the Mari *kispum*, but cf. 3.1.7.1. where the former is significantly nuanced and the latter is rejected in favor of an alternative reconstruction of the ritual underlying the GHD.

74 Tsukimoto 1985:65 and n.254 mentions twenty-two texts and lists three instances where offerings *ana malikī* occur alone, *ARMT* 7:8; 12:282,342. The regular lack of mimation points to a plural form. For more recently published texts, cf. Finet 1985:87–90; Durand 1988a:490,501–03; see below.

75 Cf. von Soden *AHw* 2(1972):595.

76 Cf. Nougayrol 1968:60; now Finet 1985:90.

77 Bottéro *ARMT* 7(1957):190; Wiseman 1965:125.

78 So Wiseman 1965:125 followed by Tsukimoto 1985:68–69.

79 Cf. e.g., Burke *ARMT* 11(1963):139.

80 So Charpin and Durand 1986:165,168–69. Durand 1985c:159 n.55 also proposed the designation "chiefs of the tribe."

81 For the omen texts, see Pettinato 1966 [Texts 1,2]. The *malkū* occur alongside the ghosts, or *eṭemmū*, and the demons, or *kūbū*, cf. Aro 1961:604, and at the end of a series of bad apodoses, so Heider 1985:153–55. They appear in the Shamash Hymn along with the gods, or *ilu*^{meš}, (line 7) and the demons, or ^{d}*kūbū*, and the Anunnaki, or ^{d}*anunnakū* (line 31); see Lambert 1960:126–27 (but read ^{d}*kūbū*, not ^{d}*kūsū*, in line 31 with Römer 1973:313). In the text in Ebeling 1931:56–58 (K.7856:19–21), the *malkū* are listed as recipients of offerings alongside the Anunnaki and *ilānu*^{meš} *a-ši-bu-ut erṣetim*^{tim}, "the gods who inhabit the earth."

82 Sasson 1979:126–27; 1985:448 has suggested that the offerings for the *nīš ilim*, "oath on (the life of) a god," like the offerings to the *malikū*, are closely related to the *kispum*. If so, the hypothetical malevolence of the Mari *malikū* is further confuted. The relation of the deity Malik (in personal names only) and the *malikū* at Mari remains enigmatic, see Müller 1984:965; Heider 1985:102–13; Olyan and Smith 1987:273.

beneficiaries of offerings alongside the *šarrānu* and to become an element in Mari personal names.[83] More satisfactory are the interpretations of *malikū* which depict them as defunct counselors or princes, but definitely not former kings (or rulers of equal standing) owing to the fact that the *malikū* receive smaller offerings on a less frequent basis than the deceased *šarrānu*.[84]

Preference for either the counselor or prince interpretation of Mari *malikum* has been predicated on the number of roots one recognizes for Semitic *m-l-k* and the likelihood of that root's appearance at Mari. Although there may be some question as to whether or not one or more distinct roots of *malākum* exist, philologists generally acknowledge a multiplicity of roots.[85] In fact, the West Semitic root *malākum*, "to have authority," from which derives *malikum*, "king, ruler," is distinct from the East Semitic *malākum*, "to counsel," from which derives *malikum*, "counselor." The West Semitic *malākum* shows up at Ugarit.[86] The form *namlakātum* = *mamlakātum*, "kingdom," found at Mari likewise favors the presence, there, of a root *malākum*, "to have authority."[87] In any case, counselors at Mari are otherwise designated *wedûtum*.[88] These considerations slightly favor the prince interpretation over the counselor.

However, the attested epithet *mār šarrim*, "son of the king," at Mari would render less likely the meaning "prince" for *malikum*, that is if the specific office is meant. Nevertheless, it would not altogether eliminate the regal aspect of the *malikū*, for their frequent mention alongside the deceased *šarrānu* as recipients of offerings in the royal cult strongly favors some status of royalty.[89] The *malikū* at Mari might represent rulers of vassal kingdoms under Mari's hegemony. Although

83 For lists of Mari (Amorite) personal and divine names with the *malikum* element, see Gelb 1980:321–23; Heider 1985:416–17; Beyer 1985:101.

84 So Talon 1978:65–66; Sasson 1979:126; Tsukimoto 1985:65,255–60. Only twice in twenty-two instances alongside the *kispum ša šarrāni* does *maliku(m)* appear with mimation in *ARMT* 9:121:V:43 and 12:85:10. The singular could stand as a collective, so Tsukimoto 1985:67, or an individual, e.g., the god Malik, so Heider 1985:111. The collective is more likely, for the plural is the regular form (note that Heider 1985:108 n.200 must restore *-im* in *ARMT* 9:123:12).

85 Cf. the major dictionaries, *AHw* 2(1972):592–94; *CAD* 10(1977):154–58.

86 In an Ugaritic Akkadian text, the following phrase appears: *ù* ^{lú}*ḫa-za-nu* URU^{ki} *ù* ^{lú}UGULA A.SÀ^{meš} *la-a i-ma-li-ik* UGU-*šu*, "neither the mayor of the city nor the overseer of the fields will have authority over him." The verb *imallik* is the present form of *malākum*, "to have authority," cf. *PRU* 3(1955):135; Sivan 1984:179–80; Huehnergard 1987:147.

87 Cf. *AHw* 2(1972):728.

88 Cf. Charpin and Durand 1986:168 n.130; *ARMT* 1:14:7; 73:8; 104:9; *ARMT* 4:80:5; *ARMT* 5:73:8,13; *ARMT* 7:190:9; 227:8′,12′.

89 *ARMT* 8:46:5′; Dossin 1939:106; cf. now Charpin and Durand 1986:168 n.130. The GHD and the Ugaritic text *KTU* 1.161 demonstrate that in addition to deceased kings, others of political prominence might be the objects of ritual observance. However, these texts do not reflect rites associated with a royal ancestor cult. As noted previously, they preserve funerary rites or, perhaps, commemorative rites on behalf of dead heroes and kings as part of a larger series of coronation rites, cf. 3.1.7.1.; 3.1.9.

the nominal form of the West Semitic root *m-l-k*, "to have authority," is usually translated by the English "king," its non-absoluteness has been recently reiterated.[90] Furthermore, the kings or rulers of local city-states of Syria-Palestine, the *malikū*, were frequently subjects of the East Semitic city-state rulers of Mesopotamia, the *šarrānu* (note for example the roughly contemporary Assyrian interregnum at Mari). Such a hierarchical relationship between living *šarrānu* and *malikū* is perhaps reflected in the El-Amarna archives.[91] This same political hierarchy might be presupposed in the Mari lists wherein the dead *šarrānu* receive both larger and more frequent offerings than the *malikū*. In other words, these former rulers of local city-states have become the deceased recipients of offerings alongside the former kings of Mari, the *šarrānu*. The lower political status of the *malikū* at Mari adequately explains why in the royal cult, the *malikū* received smaller offerings and on a less frequent basis than the *šarrānu*.[92] The fact that they receive differing quantities of offerings favors the notion that a genuine sociopolitical distinction underlies the former roles of the dead *malikū* and *šarrānu* at Mari.

In closing, I draw attention to a recently published letter written to Zimri-Lim, king of Mari, by Ishme-Dagan, king of Ekallātum and son of Shamshi-Addu. Finet interpreted the enigmatic text as follows. A lone *malikum* appears as the object of an unidentifiable ritual. Ishme-Dagan explains that although he had initiated the prescribed "*malikum*" ritual, he was unable to complete the ceremony in the absence of an expert in the rite of the *malikum*.[93] Therefore, he had written to Zimri-Lim to request that their emissaries negotiate the immediate dispatch of one so skilled.[94] Durand has conjectured that *malikum* signifies a divinatory

---

90 Cf. Handy 1988:57–59 who has stressed that English "ruler" is more in keeping with the relative political power attached to the term.

91 See Weber in Knudtzon 1915:1225–26 on ^{lú}*malik šarri*, "vassal ruler of the king," in *EA* 131:23 (p.557). In Moran 1987:349 = 1992:212, the editors prefer counselors, but if two separate roots exist for *m-l-k*, the West Semitic "to have authority" and the East Semitic "to counsel," we might expect the West Semitic at Amarna. Note also that in *EA* 131:21, *malik*^{meš} *šarri* is a gloss to $^{\text{lú.meš}}$*rabiṣi*, the highest Egyptian official in Syria-Palestine, so Rainey 1970:76. What is clear is that the *malikum* at Amarna held a subordinate political position to the *šarrum*.

92 Malamat 1989:102 judged that the *malikū* were the more remote rulers or sheikhs of seminomadic times "so remote that their actual names could not be recalled," while the *šarrānu* were the 'civilized' kings of the more recent past, but the texts nowhere list the names of the *šarrānu* either. On the significance of the exclusive collectivity attached to both groups, cf. our remarks in the concluding summary 2.2.6.

93 Finet 1985:89 [Text A.674:5–10]: *ma-li-kam ka-ar-ba-k*[*u*] [*ù ma-*]*li-ku-um it-ta-ab-ši ù mu-di pa-ar-ṣí-im ša ma-li-ki-im an-ni-ki-a-am ú-ul i-*[*b*]*a-aš-ši*, "I have vowed a *malikum* and (the time for) the *malikum* has arrived, but there is no expert in the *malikum* rite here." Durand 1988a:490 and n.40 rendered *malikam karbāku*, "I am obtaining a *malikum* sign for that which I requested in my prayers."

94 Malamat 1989:102 assumes that this text uniquely documents at Mari the desire to make contact with the ancestral ghosts of the kings. He qualifies this, however, by pointing out that, while the text

sign of judgment much like the *erištum* mark of omen texts.[95] In his opinion, the judgment might manifest itself by the appearance of an apparition, the *malikum*. He cited two newly published texts in support. The one, perhaps, makes mention of the arrival of the apparition as "the 'judgment' of Addu."[96] The other mentions a woman by the name of Yataraya who "gives a (good) counsel," that is a *malikum*.[97] This *malikum* might refer to a ritual aimed at obtaining the "counsel" of the gods with no reference to the ghost of a dead king in view. In any event, this proposal is dependent upon the questionable presence of East Semitic *malākum*, "to counsel," at Mari.

2.2.1.2. The *kispum* Offered in the Royal Garden

One Mari text records the apportioning of *naptan šarrim*, "the king's meal," *ina rapiqātim*, "in the (tilled?) garden."[98] A second text notes that the king's meal is apportioned as *niqî Ištar ina kirê šarrim*, "a sacrifice to Ishtar in the king's garden."[99] Still another records the enactment of a second type of offering apportioned from the king's meal, the *kispum* offered *ina rapiqātim*, "in the (tilled?) garden."[100] Based on these shared ritual loci and Landsberger's proposal that *rapāqum* means "to turn the earth (with a spade)," Burke offered for the derivative *rapiqātum*, "flower bed of a tilled garden," and concluded that this was a royal burial place where *kispum* rites took place.[101] As gardens typically served as burial places in antiquity, the *kispum* ritual, perhaps, took place in the palace gardens where the royalty was buried.[102]

---

comes from Mari, it actually records an attempt on the part of the king of Assyria, Ishme-Dagan, to perform the *malikum* rite as communicated to Zimri-Lim, king of Mari.

95 Durand 1988a:489–91, 501–03. On *erištum*, cf. *CAD* 4(1958):299–300. Durand understands *malikum* to be related to East Semitic *malākum*, "to counsel," cf. *CAD* 10(1977):169a.

96 Text A.490 in Durand 1988a:501–03 *ma-li-kum ša* ^{d}IM.

97 Text M.7141 in Durand 1988a:490 ^{f}*Ia-ta-ra-ia i-nu-ma ma-li-ka-am id-di-nu*.

98 *ARMT* 12:466:r.12–13.

99 *ARMT* 12:267:5.

100 *ARMT* 11:266:15:13–15. On the relation of the *kispum* and the *naptan šarrim*, cf. *ARMT* 9:173; 11:266; Glaeseman 1978:9,12,157–58. Tsukimoto 1985:61–62 concluded that *rapiqātum* is a place name, but the term never shows up with the ^{ki} determinative. The toponym is *Rapiqum*^{ki}, cf. *ARMT* 16/1(1979):28; 23:94:2; 24:22:19; cf. the name *Rapiqa* in 22:2:15:II′:10′.

101 Cf. Landsberger 1937:185–87; Burke *ARMT* 11(1963):136 n.15 and p.139 n.17 and cf. Aramaic *r-p-q*, "to dig up," e.g., Jastrow 1903:1491–92.

102 Cf. 2.1.2. Two Sumerian texts testify to the burial of prominent persons in gardens. The earliest is a royal inscription of Urukagina, last of the Pre-Sargonic rulers of Lagash gi.^{d}en.ki.ka.ka adda$_{x}$ ù.túmu., "when a dead person is taken to the garden of Enki," cf. Lambert 1956:172–73 [lines 15–16]; Talon 1978:63. The second is an Ur III court document concerned with a plot of family real estate kiri$_{6}$.a ki.maḫ gala.maḫ uru.ka ì.me.a bí.in.[e]š.a., "he discovered that the tomb of the grand

Al-Khalesi argued that located just south of court 131 of Zimri-Lim's palace was Unit 5 or the Gallery of Paintings, which he identified as a *bīt kispī*, "funerary complex." It included what he identified as royal burials (rms. 117–19, 124–26) and dining halls (rms. 121–23, 219–21) complete with kitchens and storerooms (rms. 222–26, 255–56).[103] Durand suggested that the *kispum* ritual took place in a different location, rm. 65, which he tentatively identified as "the hall of thrones" or *bīt* <giš>*kussi*ḫá mentioned in *Mari* 12803:i:7,10. Rm. 65 was west of Al-Khalesi's Unit 5 and southwest of court 131.[104] Margueron identified court 106 just west of court 131 as the most likely location for the garden or gišKIRI6 LUGAL where the king's meal or *naptan šarrim* was served. He equated court 106 with the Court of the Palms or *k[i-sa-lum š]a* gišGIŠIMMAR of *Mari* 12803:iii:21–22. Owing to the fact that the *kispum* was offered in the (tilled?) garden and associated with the *naptan šarrim*, then court 106 might have served as the location for the *kispum* ceremonies.

Although a royal burial plot may have been uncovered within the Old Babylonian palace complex at Mari,[105] it is more likely that gardens connected with *kispum* rites functioned to memorialize the kings, their bodies lying in rest elsewhere. Terqa, the home of the dynasty, has been proposed as the royal cemetery, for it is from this city that the letter to Zimri-Lim at Mari is sent requesting his written response to Kibri-Dagan of Terqa. It should be recalled that the latter sought to consecrate the *kispū* to the *eṭemmum* (ghost) of Yaḫdun-Lim who probably laid at rest in a tomb located in Terqa (cf. 2.2.1.).[106]

2.2.2. The *bīt kispī* and the *bīt Dagan*

According to a text found at Terqa, *ARI* 39, Shamshi-Addu built in that town É KI.SI.GA *bīt qūltišu bīt* d*Dagan*, "the É KI.SI.GA, his house of silence, the house of

---

chorister of the city was in the garden," cf. Falkenstein 1956–57:165 [Text 101:13–14]; Talon 1978:63. Kennedy 1987:231–34 has described the garden in later Roman death cults as a place of burial and where food and flowers were grown for the funerary banquet and in support of the endowment.

103 Al-Khalesi 1977:68–72; 1978:4. For the floor plan of the Mari palace complex, cf. Durand 1987b:50–51. Against Al-Khalesi, cf. Talon 1979:331–33; Margueron 1982(I):340 n.479 [his Secteur F = Al-Khalesi Unit 5 = Durand F]; 1983b:185–86; Tsukimoto 1985:60. On Al-Khalesi's use of the questionable reading *bīt kispī*, cf. 2.2.2.

104 Durand 1987b:54–57,108–09; cf. Birot 1980:143–45; Margueron 1982:360, 363 and n.589.

105 Parrot 1975:96, but cf. Tunča 1984:48–49; Moorey 1984:15. Durand 1987b:61 n.74 cites Margueron who identifies Parrot's grave as a cistern and on p.109 n.211, Durand cites Margueron's recovery of a large grave in the small eastern palace where the *kispum* might have been performed.

106 *ARMT* 3:40; cf. Moorey 1984:15; Charpin and Durand 1989:18–19. It is not impossible that Kibri-Dagan intended to send the appropriate diplomatic official to Mari to offer the *kispum* in order to observe expected international protocol, for which see Artzi 1980:161–70.

Dagan."[107] The É KI.SI.GA has been equated with *bīt kispī*, "house of offerings to the dead," which in turn has been identified with the house of Dagan.[108] If correct, then we have evidence which not only identifies the location (of the gardens?) where the *kispum* ritual was performed, but which also connects the god Dagan with the royal ancestor cult at Mari.[109] But the expected spelling of the Sumerian equivalent to *bīt kispī* is É KI.SÌ.GA, not É KI.SI.GA. Elsewhere, the latter has the meaning "place of silence" and, therefore, may stand in apposition to *bīt qūltišu*. Such a grammatical construction—Sumerian temple name + Akkadian gloss + house of DN—is attested in another inscription of Shamshi-Addu.[110] In other words, a "house of offerings to the dead" is nowhere in view, rather a house of silence is identified as Dagan's temple in *ARI* 39.

Even if we suppose for the sake of argument that *bīt kispī* is the correct reading, its relation to the house of silence, or *bīt qūltišu*, and the house of Dagan, or *bīt* ᵈ*Dagan*, remains enigmatic.[111] In the absence of decisive contextual evidence, the apposition could signify a number of relationships among the three structures. In the final analysis, this text can establish neither the cultic location of the *kispum* ritual nor the patronage of Dagan in the royal ancestor cult.

2.2.3. Dagan, Lord of *pagrū*

At Mari, support for the ancestor cult also rests on an inference derived from Dagan's epithet *bēl pagrê*, "Lord of *pagrū*." This epithet, supposedly, indicates not only Dagan's connection with the royal ancestor cult, but that of the *pagrum* offering as well.[112] The epithet *bēl pagrê* has been rendered: lord of corpse

[107] *ARI* (I):39:6, p.25. For *bīt qūltišu* as "house of silence" cf. *AHw* 2(1971):927; *CAD* 13(1983):302; Grayson 1987:59–60.

[108] So Grayson 1972:24–25; Menzel 1981(I):52; Dalley 1984:122–23. Menzel conjectured that the *bīt Dagan* at Ashur is to be equated with a *bīt kimaḫḫi* documented there. While the latter is in all likelihood to be associated with rites in the Ashur temple and É KI.SÌ.GA can designate a grave or *kimāḫum* (cf. Tsukimoto 1985:30 n.135, 235), Menzel's equation of the *bīt Dagan* and the *bīt kimaḫḫi* at Ashur depends upon the equation of the *bīt Dagan* at Terqa (Shamshi-Addu) with the conjectural *bīt kispī* proposed by Al-Khalesi (on which, see below).

[109] So e.g., Healey 1977b:50.

[110] Cf. Tsukimoto 1980:137 n.29, 1985:70–73; Charpin 1985c:86, 1986:217 and n.2. The other Shamshi-Addu text is *AOB* 1(1926):8:6–8, pp.22–23: É AM.KUR.KUR.RA *bīt ri-im ma-ta-a-tim bīt* ᵈ*Enlil*. The Enlil temple or É AM.KUR.KUR.RA is equated with the house of the wild bulls of the lands.

[111] We note the conjecture of Lambert 1987:403–04 that Sumerian KI.SÌ.GA (not KI.SI.GA!) might have originally meant "silent place" where offerings were made to the dead ancestors and later developed a meaning to cover the offerings made at this quiet place. These offerings were designated *kispum* in Akkadian.

[112] *ARMT* 10:63:15. On this view of *bēl pagrê*, see Roberts 1972:19; Talon 1978:71; Wyatt 1980:377; Dalley 1984:125.

offerings, lord of corpses (= a netherworld god), lord of funerary offerings, or lord of human sacrifices.[113] Akkadian *pagrum* and the related ritual attested at Mari, the *pagrā'um*, have been attributed the following meanings: bloody sacrifice, corpse or cadaver, sacrifice of (for) the dead, sacrifice of the stele, or slaughtered animal.[114]

Pagrum without further qualification can denote the corpse of a fallen soldier or a slain animal, but the debate arises over its use in sacrificial contexts.[115] Not a single instance from its handful of occurrences at Mari can establish *pagrā'um* as a sacrifice associated with mortuary matters.[116] Neither the connection with Dagan *via* the epithet *bēl pagrê* nor the mention of the *pagrum* given to Dagan, *pagram ana* ᵈ*Dagan inaddin*,[117] are sufficient in themselves to substantiate the mortuary nature of *pagrā'um*. The royal ancestor cult or death cult associations of Dagan and *pagrum/pagrā'um* are otherwise entirely lacking at Mari. Nowhere in the Mari archives is mentioned Dagan's supposed role as patron deity of the royal ancestor cult.[118] Furthermore, recently published Mari texts make the interpretation of *pagrum* as human sacrifice untenable and demonstrate that *pagrā'um* refers to animal sacrifices, specifically carcasses of dead animals (i.e., not live sacrifice).[119] In fact, the *pagrā'um* offering could consist of a sacrificial bullock distributed among those present.[120] In another instance, Dagan, having become angered over the issue of *pagrum*, was appeased with an offering of slaughtered mutton.[121] In sum, none of the Mari texts mentioning the *pagrum/pagrā'um* offering point to any association with mortuary rites, let alone the royal cult, or the royal ancestor cult in particular. In those few cases where we gain some assistance from the

---

[113] Cf. Dalley 1984:125 for the various positions; note Lambert 1985a:533.

[114] Cf. Birot *ARMT* 14(1974):217–18; *AHw* 3(1981):1581. On the formation of *pagrā'um* from *pagrum* as a relational adjective formed on the analogy of a place name, cf. Birot *ARMT* 14(1974):217; Wilcke 1986:13 n.10 and its explanation as a *nisbe* formation in Malamat 1989:97 n.91.

[115] Cf. the examples cited in *AHw* 2(1972):809 *pagru* (2) "Leiche, Kadaver."

[116] Cf. Dossin 1948:132:51 com.133 [= Ellermeier 1968:26:51]; *ARMT* 2:87:7–22; 2:90:22; 10:51:16,18; 10:63:15; 14:12:4′; 18:38:5; 19:303:3; 21:62:1,42; 70:6; 76:2; 147:5; 23:561:16.

[117] For this text, see Dossin 1948:132 lines 51–52 [= Ellermeier 1968:26 lines 51–52]. Ebach 1971:367–68 translated *pagrum* here as "Totenopfer," while Dalley 1984:125 offered "(human) corpse." A neutral stance is taken by Sasson 1979:131. Cf. also Healey 1977b:50; Talon 1978:70; de Tarragon 1980:69 and n.49.

[118] Cf. 2.2.2.; 2.2.4.; the recent survey by Lambert 1985a:525–39, esp. 532, 538, but note p.533 where he rendered the epithet *bēl pagrê* as "lord of funerary offerings."

[119] When associated with *niqû*, *pagrā'ū* refer to offerings of animal blood, so Durand *ARMT* 21(1983):71–72,160 n.20.

[120] Cf. *ARMT* 21:62:43; 147:5 as well as the comments by Durand *ARMT* 21(1983):160 n.20.

[121] Cf. *ARMT* 18:38:5; Durand *ARMT* 21(1983):71–72,160 n.20. Villard *ARMT* 23(1984):533 note *e* discussed the most recently published text, 561:16, in which the *pagrā'um* ritual is either accompanied by offerings of silver or is purchased with silver.

contexts, the evidence indicates that the *pagrum/pagrā'um* was offered by non-royal personages.[122]

2.2.4. The Parallel *kispum* and *pagrā'um* Rituals

One datum remains that has been cited in support of the connection between the *pagrā'um* offering and the royal ancestor cult, and again Dagan's assumed role in that cult forms the basis of the proposal. In 2.2.1., we quoted from a letter, *ARMT* 3:40, sent by Kibri-Dagan, governor of Terqa, to the king of Mari. In this letter, Dagan at Terqa, through the medium of a *muḫḫûm* priest, exhorted Zimri-Lim to offer *kispū* to the ghost of his departed (father or son?) Yaḫdun-Lim.[123] So it appears that Dagan takes on a direct role in matters *kispum*.

In another severely damaged text, *ARMT* 2:90, Dagan again instructs the king to perform certain rites, and again he does so through the medium of a *muḫḫûm* priest, that is, if we are justified in restoring that term in the text.[124] The king then orders the *niqû pagrā'ī* or offerings of animal blood. Owing to the fact that it is Dagan who instructs the king through the medium of a *muḫḫûm* priest in both texts and that *ARMT* 3:40 is related to mortuary matters, *ARMT* 2:90 has been given a comparable mortuary interpretation by Malamat and others.[125]

Needless to say, one cannot assume that whenever the god Dagan, a *muḫḫûm* priest, and a sacrifice are mentioned together as they are in the above two letters, a mortuary rite is at hand. Elsewhere, the *pagrā'um* offering is never explicitly related to mortuary matters as we have seen in 2.2.3. Moreover, in its eighty plus instances, the *kispum* offering is never directly related to the *pagrā'um* offering. It should be recalled that the *pagrā'um* offering remains otherwise unconnected with the royal cult, that is with perhaps the exception of the text in question, *ARMT* 2:90. But the extensive lacunae make any interpretation of this text tentative at best.

Finally, *ARMT* 3:40 is not a sufficient basis upon which to argue for Dagan's patronage of the royal ancestor cult at Mari. While his demands recorded in this

---

122 Cf. Wilcke 1986:13 n.10.

123 *ARMT* 3:40:7b–18. For lines 7b–9, see the following footnote and for lines 13–18, see 2.2.1.

124 *ARMT* 2:90. According to Malamat 1966:220, *muḫḫûm* can be reconstructed in line 16. The several lacunae in lines 13–17a have been restored on the basis of *ARMT* 3:40:7b–9: [*u*$_4$-*um tup-pì an*] *ni-e-em* [*a-na ṣe-er*] *be-lí-ia* [*ú-ša-bi-lam* ^{lú}*muḫḫûm š*]*a* ^{d}*Da-gan*, "On the same day I sent this letter to my lord, the *muḫḫûm* priest of Dagan. . . . "

125 The phrase *niqû pagrā'ī* occurs in *ARMT* 2:90:18(?),22. Jean *ARMT* 2(1950):65; Finet *ARMT* 15(1954):238; Ebach 1971:365–68 understood this phrase to designate "sacrifices for the dead." Talon 1978:69–70 tentatively equated the *niqû pagrā'ī* with the offerings *ana malikī*, but assumed the shared identity of Malik and Dagan at Mari in the absence of supporting data.

one instance relate to a royal mortuary practice, such scant evidence cannot make Dagan the patron deity of any cult. Besides, as one among several major gods of the Mari pantheon, his influence and authority, no doubt, spanned a wide range of religious concerns.[126] In fact, only in this one instance in eighty is Dagan mentioned alongside *kispum*. This strongly favors his relative non-involvement with mortuary matters at Mari.

2.2.5. The Cult of the Dead, Deified *Itūr-Mer*

The deity Itur-Mer occupied one of the two most important positions among the gods of Mari.[127] The other was taken up by Dagan. As the god of the region of which Mari was the largest and most important town, perhaps he was regarded as patron deity of the Mari kingdom. In two recently published texts, Itur-Mer gives Shamshi-Addu "the land of Mari and the bank of the Euphrates (and its domains)."[128] This passage verifies the regional extent of Itur-Mer's influence. It also elucidates an epithet of Itur-Mer found elsewhere at Mari, *šar Mari*^{ki}, "the ruler of Mari." This title should be rendered "the ruler of the *kingdom of* Mari."[129]

These factors favor Itur-Mer rather than Dagan as the unidentified deity given the title, *šar mātim*, "ruler of the land," in Mari god lists.[130] Besides, Dagan is actually listed separately from *šar mātim* in one list of gods at Mari.[131] Temples, a city gate or precinct ká ^{d}*Itūr-Mer*, *šangum* priests, *muḫḫûm* prophets, a *qilāsātum* feast, and a festival of musicians all devoted to Itur-Mer underscore his importance at Mari.[132] Nakata has suggested that Itur-Mer was originally a mortal hero or

---

126 As Dalley 1979:290 has pointed out, we have no unequivocal evidence for a Dagan shrine at Mari. Despite Dagan's epithet, *bēl Terqa*, in *ARMT* 10:62, his exclusive patronage of Terqa, the home of the Mari dynasty, remains in doubt as Dagan shows up separately from *bēl Terqa* in a god list at Mari, cf. Lambert 1970:247–50.

127 For helpful treatments on Itur-Mer, see Nakata 1974:323–33; Dalley 1979:289–90; Sasson 1979:133; Lambert 1985a:533–35,538–39.

128 Cf. Charpin 1984a:42–44,69,71 [Text 1:4–6]; Lambert 1985a:538–39; Charpin and Durand 1986:145–46; Grayson 1987:56–57: ^{d}*i-túr-m*[*e-er*] *be-li ma-at ma-ri*[^{ki}] *ù a-aḫ* ^{id}*pu*[*rantim*] (*ù nam-la-ka-ti-šu*), and for the added *ù nam-la-ka-ti-šu*, "and its domains," cf. the related text in Charpin 1985b:91; Grayson 1987:57.

129 *ARMT* 10:63:16; cf. 10:66:18; 10:72:11–12. Note that the phrase is not *šar* ^{uru}*Mari*^{ki}, "ruler of the city of Mari," but "ruler of Mari." His dominion over the entire Mari kingdom would explain why his more restricted relationship to the town is rarely attested, so Lambert 1985a:539.

130 Cf. Dalley 1979:289–90; Lambert 1985a:529 n.4.

131 Cf. Lambert 1970:249–250; Lambert 1985a:531.

132 *ARMT* 10:10:6; 13:26:10; 10:51:4; 21:333:43′, 22:167:8′; and 7:263:i:6–7, 22:276:i:36–42; 9:176:5 respectively. On other temples possibly dedicated to Itur-Mer, cf. Dalley 1979:289–90 and Durand 1987a:611–12. On the *šangum* priest and the royal cult, Beyer 1985:176–83. On the

former king of Mari who was deified after his death.[133] That Itur-Mer was once a human figure is supported by the fact that while unique among divine names, the personal name form **iprVs*-DN is well attested in Akkadian onomastics. Furthermore, Nakata argues that the *Itūr* element in personal names is quite common at Mari and should not be taken as an epithet of the god Mer.[134] However, it is more likely that Itur-Mer once represented an old storm god of northern Mesopotamia and Syria as Lambert has suggested.[135]

In any case, Nakata's proposal that Itur-Mer became the patron deity of a mortuary cult at Mari might find support in a recently published text where Itur-Mer is entitled *bēl pūdim*, "lord of *pūdum*" (line 2), and where it is noted that the fourteen "sons of *pūdum*" assemble to pay homage to him (lines 31–33). The individuals comprising the accompanying list of names (lines 3–30) have been identified as priests or possibly merchants.[136] Elsewhere, the "sons of *pūdum*" are depicted as attendants of a feast held in the Gallery of Paintings (or court 131, the court adjacent to Al-Khalesi's conjectured funerary complex or *bīt kispī*, cf. 2.2.2.). Prior to their attendance at that feast, they banqueted in the temple of the netherworld god Nergal which might suggest not only their chthonic connections, but also Itur-Mer's.[137] Another Mari text might likewise relate Itur-Mer and the royal, mortuary cult. It records Zimri-Lim's repeated trips to the *bīt kimti*. It was Itur-Mer's *šangum* priest who, having dreamt of Zimri-Lim's pilgrimages, deemed them misspent owing to the permanence of his kingship.[138] Moran tentatively identified the *bīt kimti* as a "mortuary chapel" as suggested by its use

---

enigmatic *qilāsātum* feast, see Bottéro *ARMT* 7(1957):343; Burke *ARMT* 11(1963):132–33; cf. now von Soden 1985:277; 1987:102. On the festival of musicians, see *ARMT* 9:176:5; cf. 7:267:5′.

133 Cf. Nakata 1975:15–24; Dalley 1979:289–90. If Nakata is correct, owing to his continued rule over the "land of" Mari long after Itur-Mer's supposed death, the epithet *šar mātim* should not be restricted in its reference to his actual reign while a living ruler, *contra* Dalley 1979:290.

134 Following Nakata 1975:15–24. He cited *ARMT* 3:40:13–18 as his Mari evidence for Itur-Mer's identity as a deified human, but, as we have shown, this text proves nothing of the sort. He also cited the deification of the *eṭemmum* of departed persons of prominence in Mesopotamia; but, as we have demonstrated, this phenomenon is not attested at Mari; cf. also 4.5.1. against the deification of the dead in Mesopotamia.

135 Cf. Lambert 1985a:533–35.

136 *ARMT* 23:436; cf. pp.385–87. Lines 31–33 read: ŠUNIGIN 14 DUMU^{meš} *pu-di-im ša a-na pu-lu-uḫ-ti* ^{d}*i-túr-me-er ka-aṣ-[ru]*. Sasson 1985:447 proposed that Itur-Mer presides as patron deity over what stands as the best candidate for the Mari version of the *marzēaḥ*. Our findings vis-à-vis the non-mortuary relations of the *marzēaḥ* prior to the first millennium eliminate this datum as support for Itur-Mer's patronage over a mortuary or ancestor cult at Mari (cf. 3.1.5.).

137 So Durand 1987b:52 and n.38 [Text *M* 15249:6]; *ARMT* 23:494:6. *ARMT* 7:263:10′-11′ perhaps records a group entitled the *pu-da-at šarrim*, but cf. *CAD* 2(1965):305 where the *pu-da-at* are viewed as a type of sacrifice.

138 *ARMT* 10:51:8–15: *i-na šu-ut-ti-ia* ^{d}NIN-*bi-ri iz-zi-iz-za-am-ma ki-a-am iq-bé-em um-ma ši-i-ma di-ru-[t]um na-a[m-l]a-[k-t]a-[šu] ù pa-lu-um du-ur-šu a-na* É *ki-im-tim a-na mi-ni-im i-te*$_{9}$-*né-el-li*, "In my dream Belet-biri stepped up to me and spoke as follows. Thus she (spoke): . . . is

in a much later tomb inscription of Sennacherib. In the final analysis, however, Moran rejected the reading *bīt kimti* for the Mari text.[139]

2.2.6. Summary

This completes our analysis of the Mari evidence. The numerous dispensary lists, the royal letters, the commemorative royal inscription from Terqa, and *Mari* 12803 document regular offerings made to the dead kings (*kispum ša šarrāni* and *kispum ša abbê*[?]), to the deceased vassal rulers (offerings *ana malikī*), to others of political prominence (the *Mari* 12803 *kispum*), and, perhaps, even to the general populace (*kispum ša abbê*[?] and cf. *kispum ina libbi* URU Á.DAM^{ki}).[140] However, our findings with regard to the *pagrum* and *pagrā'um* offerings render highly unlikely any ancestor or mortuary cult associations for these offerings or for the god Dagan at Mari. Finally, regardless of his purported euhemeristic origins, Itur-Mer's role in mortuary rites at Mari appears plausible although the associated rites do not necessarily signify the belief in the deceased's supernatural beneficence (on which, see further below).

Three factors have been identified as supposedly supportive of the *kispum* ritual as essentially an Amorite innovation indigenous to north Syria. First, texts which mention the *kispum* offering date from the Old Babylonian period and later, but not earlier.[141] Second, various Amorite elements dominated the geopolitical map during this period—this applies to both so-called 'peripheral' sites as Mari as well as to the Mesopotamian 'heartland'. Third, it has been suggested that the Amorite ethos emphasized genealogical, tribal, and ancestral relationships while the Sumero-Babylonian element did not.[142] One might then assume that the *kispum* had been introduced into the Mesopotamian heartland from north Syria coincident with the ascendancy of the Amorite dynasties there. It was subsequently adopted

---

his kingship, and the rule is his permanent possession. Why does he keep going up to the 'family house?'."

139 Moran 1969:42–43, but cf. p.56. He appointed Dagan as patron deity of this cult, but as we have argued above, and as the mention of the priest of Itur-Mer suggests, Itur-Mer stands as a better candidate. The relevant line in the Sennacherib text can be found in *OIP* 2:151:13. Moran's initial reading was: *e-kal ta-ap-šu-uḫ-ti šu-bat da-ra-at bīt ki-im-ti šu-ur-šu-du ša* ^{d}*Si-in-aḫ-ḫé-er-ri-ba*, "Palace of rest, eternal residence, irremovable family dwelling of Sennacherib," (lines 1–4a) and cf. *CAD* 8(1971):377; *AHw* 1(1965)479.

140 Cf. now Malamat 1989:96–107 for a recent summary of the Mari evidence.

141 The same can be generally said of the Sumerian equivalent, KI.SÌ.GA. For the relevant texts, cf. Tsukimoto 1985:26–38.

142 So Hallo 1983:7–18, esp. pp.9–12.

by the various peoples inhabiting Syria-Palestine of the first millennium such as the Arameans and Israelites.[143]

However, rites on behalf of the royal ancestors are well attested in "Pre-Amorite," and for that matter "Pre-Akkadian," Mesopotamia. As noted in 2.1.1., the Sumerian culture at urban centers like Pre-Sargonic Lagash engaged in such rites. The Lagash mortuary cult might have influenced the cults of other centers as well.[144] Admittedly, the Lagash rituals may be unlike those attested at Mari in some respects, but they share several elements in common. Although the term KI.SÌ.GA (= *kispum*) as yet does not show up at Pre-Sargonic Lagash, a variety of analogous offerings comprising food, drink, and animals as well as clothing were made to the ancestors of the Lagash royal family on a regular basis. Furthermore, these rites often took place at the ki-a-nag or mortuary shrine, at least this was the case for the deceased ensis or lugals and their wives.[145] As noted previously, a similar shrine has been proposed for Mari, either the Court of the Palms or the hall of thrones (cf. 2.2.1.2.).

In fact, the rites on behalf of the Mari royal ancestors have more similarities with those at Lagash than they do with the cult of the dead, deified kings of the dynasty of Akkad.[146] Neither in the Lagash nor in Mari rites for the royal ancestors are the deceased royalty deified. None of the recipients of ritual are preceded by the dingir (*ilu*) sign. However, the royal ancestor cult established for the worship of the deceased Sargonic kings coincides with their posthumous deification.[147] At both Lagash and Mari, the dead royalty are referred to only as collectives in the lists, at Mari as *šarrānu* and *malikū* and at Lagash as en-en-né-ne. They are not listed individually by name as is the case with the deified Sargonic

143 Cf. e.g., Xella 1988:219–25. Greenfield 1973:46–52; 1987:70–71 argued that the *kispum* ritual evolved during the period of Amorite domination in order to allow for conforming to West Semitic usages and was eventually adopted by the Israelites *via* the Arameans. Dietrich and Loretz 1980b:381–82 assumed that *pagrum/pgr* was the West Semitic synonym for *kispum* and that the Ugaritic text *KTU* 1.161 was a later (Amorite) reflex of *Mari* 12803. Pope 1981:176 concluded that the *marzēaḥ* was the West Semitic equivalent to the *kispum*.

144 Like that at Ur III Nippur, cf. Cohen 1993:34–67,118. On p.458, Cohen notes that the earliest reference to the ab-è festival is found at Pre-Sargonic Lagash. A related festival, the *Ab/pum*, which he understands to refer to a mortuary cult, is found later at several other sites throughout Mesopotamia, cf. esp. pp.354–65.

145 Cf. Kobayashi 1984:43–65 and 1985:10–30. Bertrand Lafont has cited *BIN* IX 440 ki-a-nag ma-al-ku-um lugal-lugal-e-ne as a Sumerian parallel to *kispum ša šarrāni* and offerings *ana malikī* (private communication).

146 On which, cf. Hirsch 1963:5,13,16,24,30 and Hallo 1988:54–66. If the earliest documentation for this cult comes from the Ur III period and not Sargonic times, could not the cult in honor of the dynastic kings of Akkad have been the ideological creation of the kings of the Ur III dynasty projected into contexts about earlier times as a means to establish an historical precedent for their own deification?

147 So Hallo 1988:54–66. The same has been proposed for the kings of the Ur III dynasty, cf. Klein 1981:35.

kings. Neither ritual complex concerned itself with the worship or veneration of the *divine* monarchs as is the case with the cult in honor of the Sargonic kings.

Presently, we lack any reference to the *kispum* offering or to rites for the royal ancestors from the reigns of the Amorite rulers who preceded Zimri-Lim at Mari, Yaggit-Lim and Yaḫdun-Lim.[148] Not before the reign of Zimri-Lim's foreign predecessor, Shamshi-Addu I, king of Ekallātum, is the *kispum* attested at Mari.[149] In fact, we now have a handful of Mari *kispum* references from the so-called Assyrian period.[150] But only with the beginning of the subsequent reign of Zimri-Lim, do the occurrences significantly increase.[151] In contrast however, similar rites for the royal ancestors were already being performed in Mesopotamia as attested in the texts from the earlier Sumerian and Akkadian dynasties.[152] In any case, references to the *kispum* offering itself show up in the texts of the contemporary Old Babylonian Amorite dynasty of Hammurapi in Babylon which eventually took control of Mari.[153]

In sum, contrary to the consensus, the Mari rites exhibit no innovations which might be considered uniquely Amorite. They simply approximate the mortuary rites attested in the older Sumerian texts from Lagash. This renders the *kispum* offering more an adaptation of an existing Sumerian practice than an actual Amorite or, for that matter, Akkadian innovation. Furthermore, its diffusion might have migrated from east to west, where it seems to have enjoyed only sporadic popularity among the privileged classes. Assuming that an annual festival for the dead underlies the observance held during the month of a-bè or *Ab/pum* at various sites in Mesopotamia, then it would be safe to conclude the Mari *kispum ša abbê* rite might have non-Amorite origins. It might have its precursor in the a-bè festival

---

148 Durand 1985c:159 n.55 has reconstructed an isolated reference to *kispum* in a *šakkanakku* period text, *ARMT* 19:253:4 based on a new collation [*k*]*i-is-pum*. The original editor, Limet, read only [x x]*pum*. Durand suggested that 19:214, also a *šakkanakku* text, records offerings to the prominent dead although *kispum* per se is not mentioned. Two other *kispum* texts, *RA* 64(1970):35 [Text 28] and Wilcke 1986:11–16 have been dated to the reign of Sumu-Yamam by Wilcke, p.12 n.2. He based his dating on the name of a palace official, Ḫamatil, who shows up in both texts. But a Ḫamatil is attested in the reigns of Yaḫdun-Lim, Sumu-Yamam, and in the Assyrian period. Therefore, it is not possible to isolate these two texts in any one of these periods on this basis alone.

149 Cf. *ARMT* 7:9; 12:3,85,96; *Mari* 12803.

150 In addition to the texts cited above, cf. the seven texts in Charpin 1984b:88–89,103–06 [Texts 30–36]; the three texts in Charpin 1985a:260 [Texts 10146, A.1403, 11125].

151 Most *kispum* texts date to the reign of Zimri-Lim, so Talon 1978:60; Sasson 1979:125–28; 1985:447.

152 Cf. Tsukimoto 1985:29–38, esp. p.35 for possible references to KI.SÌ.GA as a mortuary offering in earlier periods.

153 It was Hammurapi who conquered Mari after Zimri-Lim came to power and we have references to *kispum* from Babylon dated to his reign, cf. Tsukimoto 1985:39–41. The reasons for our exclusion of the GHD as an Old Babylonian reference to the *kispum* are outlined in 3.1.7.1.

which first appears at Pre-Sargonic Lagash.[154] In other words, rites for the royal ancestors were already a well-established institution in Mesopotamia prior to both the appearance of Amorite groups in the historical record and the introduction of *kispum* offerings at Mari. That the *kispum* rites for the royal ancestors at Mari are not uniquely Amorite or Syrian is further substantiated by our findings vis-à-vis the Syro-Palestinian textual evidence from the mid second millennium onwards. In spite of an abundance of textual witnesses for the periods of Syrian history following the Amorite domination of Mari, we have no indication that regular rites for the royal ancestors continued uninterrupted as an Amorite or Syrian tradition. No such cult is evidenced at Ugarit (cf. 3.1.) or Emar (cf. 3.2.2.), although funerary and commemorative rites (but not necessarily any corresponding cults) are documented in the texts from these sites.[155]

If we can assume that the dead *šarrānu* of the Mari *kispum* texts were former Mari kings and that they were perceived as genealogically related to the current dynasty—admittedly, neither point is certain—then we can offer some speculation on the function of the *kispum* based on other texts from Mari. *Mari* 12803 functioned to legitimate politically existing institutions or dynasties by linking them to the past and the offerings *ana malikī* extended that legitimating power regionally. The *malikū*'s commemoration in regular mortuary ceremonies in the Mari cult alongside former Mari kings served to reinforce Mari's existing political relations with the regional vassaldoms. Moreover, the offerings *ana malikī* might comprise part of those mortuary rites practiced within the sphere of international diplomacy by foreign dignitaries such as we find in the mourning over the death of a king or, as in the present case, a vassal ruler.[156] But was the belief in the supernatural beneficent power of the dead embraced at Mari? It is unlikely that these rites presupposed worship or veneration of the royal ancestors. Both the Mari and comparative evidence suggests otherwise.[157] The non-deification of Mari kings is especially underscored in the *kispum* and sheep offerings made to (the statues of?) Sargon and Naram-Sin in *Mari* 12803. Neither of these names is preceded by the dingir (*ilu*) sign although it is specifically these two kings who were deified in the earlier Akkad and Ur III periods.[158]

---

154 Cf. Cohen 1993:118,248,458,462.

155 Durand 1989:85–88 has speculated that a non-royal ancestor cult is attested at Emar, but cf. 3.2.2.

156 Cf. Artzi 1980:161–70.

157 Most recently Cohen 1993:463 assumed that in addition to memorial rites observed in the month of *Abu*, benign and malevolent ghosts from the netherworld joined the living in a death cult feast. He anachronistically invoked the first millennium *Maqlû* rites to support his claim, a claim which presupposes an undefined time span and geographic distribution.

158 Cf. Birot 1980:146–47. Moreover, that the *kispum* was presented first to Shamash and only then offered to Sargon and Naram-Sin in *Mari* 12803 further reflects the lower station of the dead kings over against the gods.

The thesis that the dead kings and vassal rulers at Mari were not venerated or worshipped finds additional support in their characteristic depiction as a collective group. Recent studies of Chinese and Japanese ancestor cults offer a plausible explanation for the collective grouping of the dead kings at Mari and vassal rulers. Like their East Asian counterparts, the unidentified Mari royal ancestors might have merged into an impersonal collectivity by virtue of their genealogical distance. That is to say, they were perceived as only remotely influential with regard to the continuity of the current Mari dynasty. From this we would infer that as a class, the *šarrānu* were not recognized as the immediate ancestors of the existing Amorite dynasty.[159] The dead kings at Mari, therefore, would have exercised no power to influence the living.[160] In addition to its legitimating function then, the Mari *kispum* might have expressed merely the concern to care for and/or to feed the dead.[161]

Lastly, in the absence of any textual witness for an extended cosmography of the world of the dead at Mari, we cannot be certain that these rites presupposed an extended lore regarding the dead's mode of existence. The lone mention of the term *eṭemmum*—that being of the Yaḫdun-Lim of *ARMT* 3:40—does not obviate this fact. Such would be the case even if it were viewed as related to the regularly observed royal ancestor cult, a point we shall grant for the sake of argument.[162] As we mentioned in chapter 1, we know of comparative examples where the dead are personified in the ancestor cult but where the intent is not to consign them to or equip them for some spiritual existence in a supernatural realm as might be the case with other types of mortuary practices. Rather the intent is to discorporate them from the social structure.[163]

---

159 Perhaps they comprised the former non-Amorite dynasties at Mari and/or dynasties of Mesopotamia e.g., the ancient dynasty of Akkad as suggested by the mention of Sargon and Naram-Sin in *Mari* 12803. If this in fact were the case, then the mention of these two names would be exceptional and indicative of their commemoration and not just their care.

160 Cf. Fortes 1976:8–11; Newell 1976:20–23; Hardacre 1987:264. In the Japanese ancestor cults, the dead individual goes through a second symbolic death and after some time has lapsed requiring daily ritual attention, the deceased is placed among the remote communal ancestors who no longer require regular care, but are commemorated nevertheless, in periodic community rites.

161 However, if we could be certain that the Yaḫdun-Lim of *ARMT* 3:40 was Zimri-Lim's father, then we might have an instance in which reference is made to an individual ancestor of immediate continuity and therefore one, perhaps, possessing power to affect the living. Even so, veneration would be the highest form of religious observance we might expect given our evaluation of the Mari evidence overall. Of course, the text might merely allude to the need to feed the neglected ghost, otherwise it or the gods might retaliate.

162 As pointed out previously (cf. 2.2.1.), these *kispū* may designate those intended to be placed at the grave at the time of burial for the ghost of Yaḫdun-Lim. On the funerary *kispum* offerings, cf. Tsukimoto 1980:129–38. In other words, this text might reflect only the concern to care for the *weak* ghost of Yaḫdun-Lim (father or son of Zimri-Lim?) as it completes the necessary rites of passage.

163 Fortes 1965:125–29; cf. Singleton 1977:18–25 who emphasizes the anthropocentric semi-personal spirituality, the atheistic religiousness, and evanescent eschatology of the African ancestor

While it appears that in addition to deceased royalty other groups of politically prominent dead could receive *kispum* offerings, the evidence does not support the notion that at Mari a belief in the supernatural beneficent power of the dead was embraced by the royal court. The primary focus of these rites was their legitimating function. They might have served to commemorate the dead as well. Moreover, Mari attests to neither a domestic ancestor or death cult, nor, for that matter, to the practice of necromancy. Finally, although Wilcke conjectured that the *kispum ša šarrāni* mentioned in conjunction with the dream of one Dagan-naḫmis points to a necromantic rite, in fact, the text is much too abbreviated to say anything about the purpose and nature of the associated rite.[164]

---

cult as opposed to the theism, afterlife, and substantial spirituality intrinsic to the epistemological framework which so often informs the analysis of ancestor cults in other societies by Westerners.

164 Wilcke 1986:13. For supposed evidence for a private ancestor cult in the Old Babylonian heartland, see now *CBS* 473 in Wilcke 1983:49–54; Kraus 1987:96–97 which comprises a prayer to the moon god Sin on behalf of a commoner's deceased relatives of four generations. Of course, the offered bread and water may simply reflect the care for the weakened dead. It dates to the thirty-third year of Ammiditana. For additional, relevant texts from Old Babylonian Mesopotamia, cf. Malamat 1989:97.

Chapter 3

The Extra-biblical Textual Evidence from Syria-Palestine: The Mid to Late Second Millennium B.C.E.

The oft-cited texts from Ugarit or modern Ras Shamra and the newly published texts from Emar or modern Tell Meskéné preserve the principal witnesses to mortuary rites in Syria(-Palestine) of the latter half of the second millennium B.C.E. The contemporary epigraphic data from Nuzi or modern Yorgan Tepe in northern Iraq have recently resurfaced in treatments on the Emar texts owing to a number of relevant elements which they share. In the ensuing pages, we will offer an analysis of the texts from each of the sites that might bear on the belief in the supernatural beneficent power of the dead.

3.1. The Evidence from Ugarit

Like the transition from Ebla to Mari, the transition from Mari to Ugarit is not without reason. Besides their geographical and chronological proximity, we know that these two city-states had extensive cultural contact.[1] Moreover, their religious traditions held several elements in common as illustrated by the many Syro-(Palestinian) deities which they shared.[2] The Ugaritic texts have been examined repeatedly for second millennium Syro-(Palestinian) evidence supporting the Canaanite origin of Israelite death and ancestor cult practices.[3]

---

[1] Sasson 1984a:110–20; 1984b:246–51 treats the frequent mention of Ugarit at Mari and their repeated diplomatic exchanges. Mari appears in an Ugaritic text as a known religious cult center, cf. *KTU* 1.100:78.

[2] On the pantheons at Mari and Ugarit, cf. Lambert 1985a:525–39; Healey 1985:115–25 respectively. We doubt Lambert's equation of Ea and El based on El's supposed subterranean abode. Besides, Ea is equated with Kothar at Ugarit, cf. Nougayrol 1968:45; Healey 1985:118. Nevertheless, the deities Shamash/Shapash, Dagan, Ishtar/Ashtartu, Adad/Baal and, perhaps, Il/El and Malik/Malku found in personal names, play significant roles in the religions of both city-states.

[3] This aligns with the interpretation of the material data by Schaeffer 1939:49–56; Sukenik 1940:59–65; Angi 1971:1–93; but cf. 4.4.3.

The renewed interest in the Ugaritic evidence owes much of its impetus to the more recent publication of *KTU* 1.161, a text replete with mortuary rites. The publication of this text immediately led to the re-evaluation of previously available texts. To the Ugaritic texts we now turn.

3.1.1. A *kispum*-like Offertory Text

KTU 1.142 records offerings inscribed on a clay liver model: 2

dbḥt. byy.bn	Sacrifices of *Byy*, son
ṭry[4] *.l ‘ṯtr*[ ]	of *Ṭry*, for *‘ṯtr*[ ]
d. b qbr	who is in the grave.

Death cult advocates view the plural construct *dbḥt* as food offerings to the deceased *‘ṯtr* and invoke the *kispum* offerings as a parallel. According to this view, the mentioned offerings were brought to the grave subsequent to burial on a regular basis and are therefore indicative of death or ancestor cult practices.[5] Like the liver models found at Old Babylonian Mari, the twenty plus known liver models from Ugarit were produced and collected in order to facilitate recognition, diagnosis, and prescription in the art of divination. The model itself, which graphically records the description of the observed feature based on the analysis of a specific liver, functions as the protasis, while the inscription on the model records the apodosis or the concomitant instruction. Like its Mari analogues, 1.142 reflects a particular historical occasion on which a haruspicinal rite was enacted.[6]

This leads to the conclusion that the sacrifices *dbḥt* in 1.142 are not *kispum*-like offerings made on a regular basis. Nevertheless, the instruction to offer sacrifice may have coincided with the burial of *‘ṯtr*[ ], in which case *dbḥt* would show some affinity to the *kispum* offerings included with the burial (cf. 2.2.1.). However, such offerings do not qualify as death cult practices, but reflect instead an occasionally

---

[4] Cf. Pardee 1989:42–43 who reads *ṭry* against *šry* of *KTU*.

[5] Cf. Nougayrol 1968:31–33; Dietrich and Loretz 1969:172–73,176; 1990a:12–13; Healey 1975:237 n.35; Xella 1979:838 n.2; 1981a:186–87. Spronk 1986:145, followed by Lewis 1989:45 n.198, identified only "funerary offerings" in this text. Heltzer 1973:95–96 saw behind *‘ṯtr* the goddess Ashtarte as a buried deity which has its analogue in the Persian period inscription from Pyrgi at least as typically interpreted, cf. e.g., Soggin 1975:112–19; Roschinski 1988:602–05; 4.1.

[6] Cf. Nougayrol 1968:32; Courtois 1969:91–119; Dietrich and Loretz 1969:165–79; Gurney 1981:147–52; Biggs 1983:519–21; now Meyer 1990:214–80, esp. p.269.

attested funerary rite. It might reflect a concern to appease a malevolent ghost,[7] or to feed a weak, neglected one whose cause had been taken up by the gods.[8] In the final analysis, the belief in the supernatural beneficence of the dead is nowhere made explicit or necessarily presumed as underlying the ritual reflected in *KTU* 1.142.

3.1.2. The Dagan Stelae

Two inscribed stelae were discovered in the rubble from a wall of a stone building identified as a temple in the eastern acropolis of Ugarit.[9] The fact that the accompanying inscriptions, *KTU* 6.13 and 6.14, mention the god Dagan suggested to the Ras Shamra expedition that he was patron of the adjacent temple.[10]

Albright surmised that the two stelae were used in the cult of the dead at Ugarit[11] and Roberts concluded that the inscriptions designated Dagan as the recipient of sacrifices for the dead. In defense of the mortuary associations of the stelae and their inscriptions, Roberts cited the underworld role of Dagan at Ugarit based on cuneiform texts from various sites in Mesopotamia and Syria, and particularly those from Mari.[12] Our translation follows:

[6.13]	*skn.d š'lyt*	The stele upon which Tharelli offered
	ṯryl.l dgn.pgr	to Dagan, a *pgr*:
	[*š*] *w 'alp l 'akl*	[a sheep] and a bullock for a meal.

[7] Cf. Avishur 1981:13–25; de Moor 1980b:429–32; 1981–82:106–19; de Moor and Spronk 1984:237–50 for a supposed ghost expelling incantation text from nearby Ras Ibn Hani, *RIH* 78/20, but cf. Caquot 1984:163–74; Caquot, de Tarragon, and Cunchillos 1989:53–60 who view this text as a demon (non-ghost!) expelling incantation.

[8] In ancient Greece, reprisals for neglect of the ancestors might come from the gods rather than the inert dead, so Garland 1985:118–20.

[9] Concerning their discovery, see Schaeffer 1935:155–57 and pl.xxxvi. The stele containing text *KTU* 6.13 is housed in Paris and 6.14 in Aleppo.

[10] For the original transcriptions and translations, cf. Dussaud 1935:177–80, pl.31. For recent discussions and bibliography, cf. de Tarragon 1980:67–70; Xella 1981a:297–99; Segert 1982:241; Tsukimoto 1985:71; Spronk 1986:149–51; Healey 1986:29–31; Lewis 1989:72–79; Bordreuil and Pardee in Yon 1991:302–03,334.

[11] Cf. e.g., Albright 1957:246–47. In this treatment, Albright followed Neiman 1948:55–60. Cf. also Ebach 1971:365–68; Greenfield 1973:48.

[12] Roberts 1972:19.

[6.14]	*pgr. d š'ly*	A *pgr* which *'zn* offered
	'zn.l dgn.b'lh	to Dagan, his lord:
	[š w 'a]lp.b mḫrm/t	[a sheep and a b]ullock *bmḫrm/t.*[13]

Roberts' view of Dagan's underworld role and his resultant conclusion that the stelae are associated with a death or ancestor cult are unwarranted. The various lines of evidence adduced in favor of Dagan's underworld role in Syrian religion have each been addressed in 2.2. and none were found to be convincing for Mari.[14] If these stelae and their inscriptions played a death or ancestor cult role, such a role must be established on other grounds.

Albright initially interpreted *pgr* as "mortuary offering," but later as "funerary stele."[15] Other proposals include "altar," "stele," "sacrifice," "corpse" or "(human) cadaver."[16] The supposed parallelism between *skn.d š'lyt* in 6.13 and *pgr.d š'ly* in 6.14 has been cited as support for viewing *pgr*, like *skn*, as "altar" or "stele."[17] But the reverse argument has been employed by others in order to interpret *skn* as "alimentary offering" in light of *pgr*, "sacrifice."[18] In any case, the fact that in *KTU* 1.17:I:26, *skn* is the object of the verbal action conveyed by *nṣb*, "to set up" or "to erect," renders "alimentary offering" for *skn* in 6.13 obsolete (cf. 3.1.4.). Besides, contrary to general opinion, the two inscriptions evince dissimilar structures: 6.14 is elliptical in nature, for *skn* in 6.13 has no genuine parallel.[19]

The function of the term *skn* might best be understood in the light of the Syrian cult of bétyles now documented at Ebla, Mari, Emar, and Mumbaqat.[20] In this cult, the *sikkānu(m)*, or 'sacred stone', was considered the abode of the deity, and at times, even the deity itself. If Ugaritic *skn* is to be identified with *sikkānu*, then *skn* in our texts represents a sacred stone in which, so it was believed, the deity

13 The enigmatic *bmḫrm/t* has been rendered "inviolable offering" Albright 1969:106 n.30; "in that order" so Ebach 1971:366; "sanctuary" with Ribar 1973:37 n.23 (following Mendenhall's suggestion based on Old South Arabic); "total destruction" so Healey 1977b:46, "total dedication" Healey 1986:30; "for total dedication" or "in the sacred precinct" with Healey 1988:106–07; "at the burnt offering altar" so Dietrich and Loretz 1981:297–98; "in the morning" so Spronk 1986:150; "for the designated offering" with Lewis 1989:75 and n.23; or "a plough-ox(?)" so Bordreuil and Pardee in Yon 1991:303.

14 Cf. 2.2.2.–2.2.4. *contra* Roberts 1972:19 followed now by Lewis 1989:72–79.

15 Albright 1969:106 n.30 (originally published in 1942); 1957:246; cf. Ebach 1971:368.

16 For surveys of previous proposals, see Ribar 1973:18–19; Healey 1977b:43–51; de Tarragon 1980:67–70; Xella 1981a:298–99.

17 Neiman 1948:57.

18 Dussaud 1935:178.

19 Cf. Ebach 1971:367; de Tarragon 1980:68; Segert 1982:241. The last views the stelae as "quasi-parallel."

20 For Mari, cf. Durand 1985a:79–84; for Emar, cf. Arnaud 1980a:117; 1980b:254 and n.45; 1981:34; 1986:338–46; Fleming 1992:75–79. For these and Mumbaqat, cf. Dietrich, Loretz, and Meyer 1989:133–39 and Charpin 1992:6–7. For Ebla, cf. Durand 1988b:5–6.

dwelt.[21] Obviously in 6.13 and 6.14, the deity in question would be Dagan. This new documentation also clarifies the meaning of *skn* in the mythological texts at Ugarit. In *KTU* 1.17:I:26,44 and II:16, the phrase *skn 'il'ib* occurs. If, as we shall demonstrate below, *'il'ib* refers, not to some deified ancestral ghost, but to the "gods of the fathers," then *skn 'il'ib* probably refers to the "bétyles of the gods of the fathers."[22] Of particular interest to us is the frequent mention of Dagan in connection with the cult of bétyles at both Mari and Emar.

A "bétyle of Dagan," *sikkānum ša* ^{d}*Dagan*, has been recently documented at Old Babylonian Mari.[23] At Late Bronze Emar, the bétyles were used in cultic ceremonies and often dedicated to Dagan. His temple is also mentioned in some contexts.[24] Furthermore, in the Emarite cult of bétyles, a ritual is attested in which an animal was slaughtered and the bétyles rubbed with its oil and blood. The remaining portions were then eaten by those in attendance. Again, the deity involved is Dagan. He also shows up in some mysterious role during a related night vigil which in turn might suggest that his bétyle was included among those used.[25]

In the light of the data from Mari and Emar, we view the two occurrences of (*l*)*dgn* in 6.13 and 6.14 as references to the two bétyles or *skn*(*m*) of Dagan upon which our two texts are inscribed. Thus, as at Emar, the ritual inferred from 6.13 and 6.14 might have entailed the rubbing of fat and blood of a sacrificial animal designated *pgr* on a bétyle of Dagan at Ugarit. This in turn was followed by a communal meal, as suggested by the term *l'akl* in 6.13:3.[26]

As for *pgr* in 6.13 and 6.14, various lines of evidence converge to establish the general range of meaning for Ugaritic *pgr* in offering contexts. The fact that *pgr* occurs with the causative of the verb *'ly* in 6.13 and 6.14 suggests its offertory function. This view of *pgr* finds support in the offertory contexts of the cognate *pagrum* and its derivative, *pagrā'um*, attested at Mari. In 1.39:12,17, the phrase, *špš pgr*, is followed by terms designating offerings, one grain, (*w*) *ṯrmnm*, and

---

21 Following Durand 1985a:82 n.10.

22 The *'il'ib* would then comprise those gods worshipped by Danil's forefathers and identified in the god and offering lists as the members of the pantheon (cf. 3.1.3.). The god lists included *KTU* 1.47:4; 1.118:3 (alphabetic) = *RS* 20.24:3 (cuneiform); and the ritual texts: 1.148:2,10,26; 1.109:21.

23 Durand 1985a:81–83 [Text *A* 652:(3′–4′),11′].

24 Arnaud 1986:338–46,350–66,369–70 [Texts 370:41,43; 373; 375].

25 So Arnaud 1980a:117; 1981:34. Cf. now 1986:352,359 [Text 373:57b–58a]: *sikanāti* Ì^{meš} ÚŠ^{meš} [*ipaš*]*āšu*, "The betyles are rubbed with fat and blood"; [lines 196–97]: *ina pānī nubatti* ^{d}KUR *ina berat* ^{na_4}*sikanāti êtīq*, "in the night vigil, Dagan passes among the betyles." Perhaps, Ugaritic *bmḥrt* in 6.14:3 should be rendered "by the morning light," that is, before daybreak in view of *ina pānī nubatti*.

26 Cf. Healey 1988:107 for the alternative view of these stelae as records of sacrifices originally set up in a sanctuary.

one animal, *gdlt.*[27] The term *gdlt* may specify one kind of offering from the class *pgr*, while (the conjunction *w* and) *ṯrmnm* may point to an independent class of offerings, probably meal offerings.[28]

Other supporting evidence for the offertory nature of *pgr* comes from the parallel structure of two other texts, *KTU* 4.182 and 4.316. It would seem that *pgr* designates the name of a month in the Ugaritic cultic calendar *yrḫ pgrm.* In 4.182:35–40, the following sequence of months occurs: *nql, mgmr*, and *pgrm*, while in 4.316:1–5 (cf. *UT* 1160:1–5), the sequence is *nql, mgmr*, and *dbḥm.* If the former sequence is a partial representation of the consecutive order of months in the Ugaritic calendar, then the month officially designated *pgrm* was also depicted as a month characterized by the making of sacrifices or *dbḥm.*[29] Its use, both as the name of a month and, as we shall see forthwith, as an epithet of a major deity like Shapash, substantiates the relative importance of *pgr* in the Ugaritic cult.

The form *špš pgr* occurs in 1.39:12,17 and 1.102:12. In 1.102, a list of divinities, *pgr* functions as a divine epithet, "Shapash of *pagrū*," and finds a general analogue at Mari in *bēl pagrê*, "(Dagan) lord of the slain animal sacrifices."[30] In the immediate context of line 12, each of the deities listed is accompanied by an epithet (lines 11–13): *'nt ḫbly špš pgr 'iltm ḫnqtm.* In 1.39:17–18, *špš pgr*, like *'nt ḫbly* and *'iltm ḫnqtm*, is listed with its designated offering, or *gdlt*, immediately following.

The offertory nature of *pgr*, its designation as an official month of the cultic calendar, and its employment as an epithet indicate that the term *pgr* in 6.13 and 6.14 probably designates a class of offerings and that these offerings were of special import. But in none of this evidence does *pgr* have connections with ancestor or death cult rites, let alone human sacrifice.[31] This is consistent with our findings with regard to Mari *pagrum/pagrā'um.*[32] Therefore, the assumption that *pgr* is associated with mortuary matters on the basis of its dedication to two gods,

---

27 Cf. de Tarragon 1980:33,67; Xella 1981a:365.

28 Cf. *ṯrm* alongside *lḥm* in 1.16:VI:11–12; 1.18:IV:19,29–30.

29 Cf. de Tarragon 1980:26–28. For additional references to this month name, cf. 4.172:2; 4.193:2,7; 4.266:2; 4.366:2.

30 Xella 1981a:297–99 views *dgn pgr* in 6.13:2 as the god name followed by an epithet, but, as Segert 1982:241 notes, *pgr* in 6.14:1 is what is offered to Dagan. This applies in 6.13:2 as well. Besides, Mari ^{d}*Dagan bēl pagrê* is not an identical parallel to the hypothetical Ugaritic *dgn pgr*.

31 In what might constitute a severely damaged Ugaritic version of the *Šumma izbu* recently published by Arnaud 1982:217 [Text *RS* 1979.26], the editor read [*pa*]*grum* (line 6′), which he interpreted as a human corpse and as the recipient of mourning rites *bakû* (cf. line 12′). But neither sacrifice nor the ancestor cult suggest themselves.

32 Cf. 2.2.2.–2.2.4. Dagan's death cult role is not necessarily reflected in his equation with Enlil, *contra* Montalbano 1951:395 and most recently Wyatt 1980:377. It should be recalled that Enlil played many roles unrelated to the netherworld. For the relevant texts *CT* 24:6:22 = 22:120, see Lambert 1967:131. Dagan is associated with the underworld in a ritual commentary, cf. Lambert 1968b:109–10, but it is late, syncretistic, and Babylonian.

Dagan and Shapash, both deities with supposed underworld roles in the underlying rituals reflected in these texts, is unwarranted. Besides, Shapash, like Dagan, may have received a *pgr* offering for reasons other than her chthonic associations. In any case, not only Ugaritic *pgr*, but also Dagan, lack any death or ancestor cult associations.[33]

Finally, the archaeological data necessitate consideration. Archaeological matters actually complicate the picture regarding the relation of the two stelae to the Middle Bronze building adjacent to their find spot. Both were found outside the building in question, supposedly a Middle Bronze temple. This edifice was identified as Dagan's temple solely on the basis of the texts inscribed on the two stelae, but there is little evidence otherwise for a Dagan temple at Ugarit (cf. 1.104:13). In fact, in one Ugaritic text, Tuttul is identified as Dagan's cult center (1.100:15). Besides, others have identified the patron deity of said building as El. Moreover, the stele housed in Paris has a projection designed to fit a socketed base, but no such base is recorded in the report findings pertaining to the building and its environs.[34] Lastly, the persons named in 6.13 and 6.14 are identifiable members of the Late Bronze royal house (*ṯryl* 2.34:2 and *'zn* 4.93:II:8) and the use of the alphabetic script points to a Late Bronze period dating for the stelae. Thus, it is very likely that the stelae had been completely removed from their original context and transported to the area adjacent to the wall of the Middle Bronze building. Not only does this favor the view that the stelae had no connection with the earlier temple, but it also points to the possibility that the stelae were relocated and buried at this location. The burial of such monuments is a well known practice.[35]

3.1.3. The Deity *'Il'ib*

Another datum frequently cited as indicative of the existence of death or ancestor cult practices at Ugarit is the term *'il'ib*, often rendered "the divine ancestor/father."[36] According to this view, in 1.17:I:26 and II:16, a 'sacred stone' is erected in honor of the divine ancestor: *nṣb skn 'il'ib*, while in 1.109:19, libations and offerings are purportedly made on his behalf through the aperture leading to

[33] Cf. similarly Healey 1988:106.

[34] Cf. Schaeffer 1935:155–56.

[35] For recent reviews, cf. Healey 1986:29–31; 1988:107. On the ritual burial of statues of gods, cf. Nielsen 1954:103–22. Sasson 1966:136 n.57 suggested that during the month *yrḫ pgrm* (cf. its Alalakh parallel *a-ra-aḫ pa-ag-ri*), the gods, that is their statues, were buried either for cultic or practical reasons as they may have been in a deteriorated state.

[36] So Goetze 1938:278 n.80; Albright 1968:141–42,204–05; 1969:106 and n.31. Gray 1966:174 conjectured that this 'ancestral' deity was a dead ancestor, a connection that is not always so straight forward in treatments of *'il'ib*.

his tomb: *b'urbt 'il'ib*.[37] Now *'il'ib* shows up frequently in cultic texts and is attested in the pantheon lists as well.[38] Moreover, the term occurs in two or three mythological passages in the Aqhat texts 1.17:I:26,44(?) as *'il'ibh*, and 1.17:II:16 as *'il'iby*. Morphologically speaking, interpreters have viewed these occurrences of *'il'ib* in one of two ways. Either the form comprises one word or is to be divided into two elements, *'il* and *'ib*. As one word, *'il'ib* has been derived from the Arabic lexeme *la'aba* and translated "divinized sacred stone."[39]

Others have related it to major deities such as Akkadian Ilaba, Eblaite ^{d}a-mu, or Hittite Zawalli, all of which supposedly represented deified ancestors at one stage or another.[40] Be that as it may, a major deity is unlikely in those mythological contexts where *'il'ib* appears, for the accompanying possessive suffixes *-h* and *-y* favor a personal god, a deified ancestor, or some other sacred object of worship.[41] This fact has resulted in independent proposals for the mythic *'il'ib* and cultic *'il'ib*.[42]

Assuming *'il'ib* is comprised of two elements, a connection with the concept of deity is unanimously recognized for *'il*. The term is attributed either an adjectival force, i.e., "divine" or a nominal one. With the exception of its mythological references, a nominal form *'il* might render either the deity El or the more general "god(s)." While some have viewed *'il* as the divine determinative based on this supposed function of *'il* in the so-called Ugaritic king list 1.113 (on which, cf. 3.1.6.), this use is unlikely in the case of *'il'ib* since none of the other gods listed in the cultic texts are so designated.

The second element, *'ib*, has proven to be more problematic. It has been equated with *'ab*, "father," with the added possibility of an adjectival force, i.e., "paternal." The vocalic change *'i* > *'a* has been explained variously.[43] For *'ib*,

37 Gray 1978:102; Xella 1981a:53–54; Spronk 1986:145, 148–49 connect *'urbt* with the tomb opening through which regular offerings were made to the dead. But in 1.4:V:23, *'urbt* parallels *ḥln*, a palace lattice or window, cf. 1.4:VII:18. Besides, such tomb openings may have served as a means of ventilation or fumigation, cf. 4.4.3. The new datum *RIH* 78/20:3: *kqṭr 'urbtm*, "like incense from an aperture," supports this latter function for *'urbt*.

38 Cf. 1.41:35; 1.56:3,5; 1.87:38; 1.91:5; 1.109:12,15,19,35; 1.138:2; 1.139:1; 1.148:10,23; *RIH* 77/2B:3,6 (= *RIH* 77/26:3,6?). The alphabetic pantheon lists include 1.47:2; 1.118:1; probably 1.74:1.

39 Van Selms 1954:100–01; Astour 1966:279 n.25; but cf. Gray 1965:109 n.2; Caquot 1969:260.

40 For Ilaba, cf. Roberts 1972:35,125; Lambert 1981:299–301; for ^{d}a-mu, cf. Xella 1983:288; 1985:75; for Zawalli, cf. Xella 1981b:85–93.

41 So Lambert 1981:301.

42 Following Lambert 1981:301. This approach also is assumed by de Moor 1980a:184–87 esp. n.66.

43 Albright 1968:141–43 "influence of the labial consonant;" Hoffner 1967:385–401 "diphthong contraction;" Müller 1975–76:70 "conscious differentiation;" Healey 1977a:256 n.6 "sandhi;" de Moor 1980a:184 n.66 "vowel harmony." Note the variants *'iḫ* (2.41:18) and *'aḫ*, "brother" (1.6:II:12), cf. Segert 1984:178 and ^{d}*ib*.ú and ^{d}*ab*.ú; and cf. Nougayrol 1968:218 [Text *RS* 22.344 + 23.24:132].

Albright proposed "ghost, shade which returns to the earth."[44] Hoffner offered "sacrificial pit." Thus, *'il'ib*, "god of the pit," would be a member of the *'ilm 'arṣ*, "the gods of the earth" (i.e., of the netherworld).[45] According to this view, *'il'ib* would also be a deity related to necromancy and the cult of the dead.

However, behind Hoffner's proposal stands a complicated etymological and phonological argument.[46] Furthermore, it is severely weakened by the fact that Ugarit offers no supporting evidence for the use of pits or a god of the pit in necromancy. Lastly, both of the above proposals ignore the equations preserved in the parallel Akkadian and Hurrian god lists from Ugarit: Ugaritic *'il'ib* (1.118:1) = Akkadian DINGIR *abi* (*RS* 20.24:1) "the god of the father(s)" = Hurrian *en atn* (1.42), "the god, the father." These confirm the antiquity of "father" and "god" as elements in *'il'ib*.

It would appear that the best solution to this dilemma is the recognition of two homonymous forms of *'il'ib*. We would then have a major deity in the pantheon and offering lists but a divinized ancestor in the mythological texts. In the case of the former, the most likely candidate appears to be Ilaba although another proposal has been offered, "El, the father," or the personification of El's fatherhood over all living things. This rendering has been suggested on the basis of reading *'il'ib 'arṣ wšmm* in 1.148:23–25, but this is doubtful.[47] While the ancestral ghosts supposedly provide the least problematic approach for the mythological references to *'il'ib*, it is at this juncture that interpreters part company. For example, Lambert tends to interpret the *'il'ib* of the mythological texts in the light of his proposed deity, Ilaba, of the pantheon and offering lists. The Old Akkadian god Ilaba, in its later form *'il'ib*, served everyone as a private family god.[48] On the other hand, Healey concludes that the ancestral ghost of the mythic contexts also fits the lists. According to Healey, the Akkadian pantheon list upon which Lambert based his proposal has a false etymology of a confused and obscure term.[49]

We offer an alternative solution to this veritable impasse. As generally recognized, *'il'ib* normally stands at the head of the various lists of gods. A notable exception is 1.47. Here, *'il'ib* occurs in line 2 and is preceded by *'il ṣpn* in line 1,

---

44 Albright 1968:141–43, cf. Arabic *'āba*, "to return," and see further 4.3.2. for the possible connection of this Arabic root and Heb. *'ôḇ*, "One-who-returns."

45 Hoffner 1967:385–401; 1974:130–34; following Vieyra 1961:47–55; cf. Sumerian ab(làl), Assyrian *apu* B, Hittite *api*, "pit."

46 Cf. 4.3.2.

47 The other proposals seem less likely. See 2.1.4. against ^{d}a-mu. De Moor 1980a:184–86, in his proposal "El, the father" overlooked the *š* offering separating *'il'ib* and *'arṣ wšmm* in 1.148:23–25 and reconstructed the conjectural reading DINGIR.AD ^{d}KI [*ù* AN] in *RS* 26.142:13′-14′, a fragmentary Ugaritic Akkadian pantheon list, on which cf. Nougayrol 1968:321.

48 Cf. Lambert 1981:301. De Tarragon 1980:151–57, esp. p.156, embraced a similar view.

49 Healey 1985:119; cf. 1979:355 where he noted that its occurrence at the head of the pantheon might be explained by seeing here the divine ancestor *par excellence*.

which has been interpreted either as the deified mountain Zaphon or the god of Zaphon.[50] The problem with both of these proposals is that mount Zaphon or *ṣpn* and Baal, the god of Zaphon, *b'l ṣpn* are mentioned later in the list (cf. 1.47:5,15; and cf. 1.118:4,14; and *RS* 20.24:4,14).[51] A better solution is to view *'il ṣpn* as a title or heading of the entire list or minimally, of the first ten lines, i.e., "the gods of Zaphon."[52]

Several god lists at Ugarit, whether written in Ugaritic, Akkadian, or Hurrian, contain summarizing headings. For example, the Akkadian list *RS* 19.85 begins with the heading *ilānu* ^{meš} *Ugarit*, "the gods of Ugarit," followed by the names of individual gods, e.g., ^{d}IM, ^{d}*padrai*, etc.[53] Moreover, several such texts contain multiple headings with as many as three consecutive headings in one list. An Akkadian cultic pantheon list from Ugarit, *RS* 26.142, shares several affinities with one of the lists mentioned previously, 1.118.[54] It also shares another with both 1.47 and the Hurrian list 1.116 discussed below. Like the lists 1.47 and 1.116, *RS* 26.142 contains an introductory section containing multiple headings. Each heading refers to a distinct group of gods. *RS* 26.142 begins as follows (lines 1′–4′):

[. . . . .]	
[*il*]*ānu* $^{\text{[meš gi]š}}$*sikkūru*	The gods of the bolts,
ilānu ^{meš} *da-ad-me-ma*	The gods of Dadmema(?)
ilānu ^{meš} *la-ab-a-na*	The gods of Labana(?)

As in the other lists, a lengthy inventory of the major gods follows e.g., ^{d}IM . . . etc. (lines 7′–24′). Each is entered separately as the recipient of cultic offerings (lines 5′–6′ list sacred implements). We would argue that *'il'ib* has a similar summarizing function both in the lists and in the Aqhat texts. In this case, both *'il* and *'ib* would comprise plural forms "the gods of the(/his/my) fathers," with

50 Mullen 1980:268–69 viewed *'il ṣpn* as "divine Zaphon," Baal's mountain, with the *'il* element functioning as a divine determinative. De Tarragon 1980:156 conjectured an anonymous deity of Zaphon similar to *'il'ib*, while Baal is favored by others.

51 Against the view of de Tarragon 1980:156, Healey 1985:117 noted that, unlike *'il'ib*, *'il ṣpn* is never the recipient of worship either here or in its three remaining occurrences 1.3:III:29; IV:19; 1.101:2. Moreover, its restoration in a lacuna in the offering list to gods, 1.148:1, is unjustified. However, like de Tarragon, Healey wrongly assumed that *'il'ib* was an individual deity worshipped in the cult (see below).

52 Following Healey 1985:117–18.

53 Cf. *PRU* 6 (1970):no. 132 = *RS* 19.85.

54 For *RS* 26.142 and a discussion of the various elements shared by these two lists, cf. Nougayrol 1968:320–22, esp. p.320.

the *'ib* of the Aqhat texts standing for the fathers collectively.[55] Further data from the god lists found at Ugarit are in agreement with this interpretation. To begin with, it is compatible with Akkadian DINGIR *abi*. The latter form, *abi*, might be defective for the plural *abbī*.[56] Moreover, DINGIR might be plural in spite of the absence of a plural indicator, whether the determinative meš or the reduplication of DINGIR, for this is not uncommon for forms intended to be read as such at Ugarit.[57]

The enigmatic Hurrian evidence is also of interest. Not only is the plural Hurrian *en atnbn* = *enna attannibina*, "the gods of the father," quite common,[58] a similar Hurrian form might occur at Ugarit in a section comprising lines 10–29 of the offering text 1.116. As recognized by the original editor, the form in question, like its immediate predecessor, functions as a title or heading for what follows. Both introduce the major gods who receive offerings in the cult. Like the Ugaritic alphabetic lists, the individual entries that follow begin with the names of major gods, in this case, El:[59]

wbbt.ašḫlm	In the temple, sacrifice:
enšt.šlnnštm	both to the *šalanna* gods,
enšt.atn[ ]*m*	and to the gods [of?] the fathers;
eld.tšbd....	to El, to Teshub, (etc ...)

Laroche reconstructed the dative plural *št* = *šta* in *atn*[*št*]*m* = *attanna*[*šta*]*ma* making the form apposite to *enšt* = *ennašta*, "the gods-fathers."[60] He assumed that this was the plural of *en atnd* = *en(n)i attannida*.[61] Nevertheless, Laroche recognized the fact that the form *en atnbn* = *enna atannibina*, "the god of the father," is far more common. In the case of *enšt atn*[ ]*m* in 1.116:12, is it possible to read *atn*[*ẑ*]*m* with the plural genitive and translate *enšt atnẑm* = *ennašta attannaše-ma*, "to the gods [of] the fathers?" If so, this form would not represent the plural syntactic equivalent of *en atnd*.[62]

---

55 In their analyses of the references in the mythic texts, both Lambert 1981:299 and de Moor 1980a:184 n.66 recognized the possibility of plural forms for both *'il* and *'ib* when followed by the suffixed pronouns *-h* and *-y*.

56 So Lambert 1981:299.

57 Cf. Huehnergard 1987:147,300,720. With Healey 1985:119, the alternative remains that the Akkadian has a false etymology of a confused and obscure term.

58 So Laroche 1968:523; 1976–77:63–64.

59 Cf. Laroche 1968:499–504,523; 1976–77:63–64; Xella 1981a:317–21.

60 Xella 1981a:317 followed the reading of *KTU* : *inṯt atn*⌈*ṯt*⌉)[ ]*m*. Admittedly, as the editors recognized, the two characters in question remain highly problematic.

61 Cf. Laroche 1968:503,523; for *en atnd*, see *RS* 24.254:2.

62 Laroche 1968:523. For the morphological justification of our proposal, see Laroche 1968:530–32. He also noted the ambiguity inherent in the determinative suffix or article *-n* in Ugaritic Hurrian which can represent either the singular or plural, and the intermingling of the genitive and dative

Turning now to the cultic texts, we find that *'il'ib* on occasion can head any one of several sub-lists of gods contained within a cultic god list. In some lists, *'il'ib* receives more numerous and qualitatively superior offerings (e.g., gold and silver) than the known individual gods. In 1.148:9b–10, *'il'ib* is lavished with various offerings (*'alpm, 'ṣrm, gdlt, šlmm*), but each of the following individual gods, including even El, is allocated only a single offering, either a *š* or an *'alp*. In 1.91:2–5, 1.109, and *RIH* 77/2B, *'il'ib* heads a list of deities who receive offerings from the king. In 1.91:5, *'il'ib* is followed in line 6 by *'il bldn*. Both terms are headings. *'il bldn* is perhaps to be read as "the gods in Ldn."[63] These two headings precede the mention of individual gods beginning with Pidray (line 7). In 109:12,15,19, the offerings made to *'il'ib* again far outnumber those designated for the individual gods. In *RIH* 77/2B:3, *'il'ib* is offered gold and silver, then a series of other offerings (line 6) before El is ever mentioned (line 7).

In other instances, while the known individual gods receive offerings, *'il'ib*, like the other headings, receives nothing. In line 23 of 1.148, the term *'il'ib* immediately follows *'il ḫyr* which Xella interprets as "the gods of the month of *Ḫyr*" and, like the *'il ḫyr*, *'il'ib* receives no offerings. However, each of the following individual deities receives a *š* offering.[64] The fact that *'il'ib* is treated in a fashion similar to that of the known headings for god lists and cultic lists, but differently from the known individual gods in those lists, favors the notion that *'il'ib* is an abridgment or heading and not a single deity. We interpret the form as "the gods of the fathers," the gods worshipped throughout several generations of the royal dynastic line.

This interpretation works in the Aqhat references as well. Thus, *nṣb skn 'il'ibh/y*, "one who sets up the bétyles of the gods of his/my fathers," would no longer comprise a reference to the divinized ancestor(s), but to those well-known gods of the pantheon worshipped by one's predecessors.[65] Our proposal for *'il'ib* gains further support from the *ilānu abbī* or DINGIR.MEŠ AD.MEŠ of the cuneiform sources, "the gods [of] the fathers." These were not the divinized ancestors, but well known members of the pantheon and, in particular, the personal or family

---

plural endings on nouns *ž* = *še* or *ša*. Tsumura 1993:40-41 assumes *'il'ib*'s central death cult role at Ugarit, translates the form as "god-father," gives undeserved weight to the ambiguous Hurrian phrase *en atnd*, but all the while acknowledges that *'il'ib*'s absence from what he deems as the crucial death cult text 1.161 (cf. 3.1.9.).

[63] Cf. de Tarragon 1980:168 and Xella 1981a:341.

[64] *Contra* Xella 1981b:93 who wrongly attributed to *'il'ib* the following *š* offering which instead goes with *arṣ w šmm* of the next line. In 1.109:19, the phrase *w b 'urbt. 'il'ib* has a similar introductory function in a sub-list and the same sequence, sacrifice + recipient, follows; *.š b'l*, etc.

[65] An alternative would be to view the *'il'ib* of the god lists and cultic lists, "the gods of the fathers," as a corresponding morphological plural of an otherwise independent singular *'il'ib*, "god of the father(s)" (= DINGIR *abi*?), attested in the Aqhat texts, cf. also 1.41:35 = 1.87:38.

gods.[66] Thus, Akkadian DINGIR *abi* (*RS* 20.24:1), "the god of the father(s)," and Hurrian *en atn* (1.42), "the god, the father," are, if not rough equivalents, then innovative theological approximations of *'il'ib*.[67] A comparison of other entries shared by these god lists reveals numerous such innovations on the part of the scribes.[68]

3.1.4. The Duties of the Faithful Son

Several scholars have seen evidence for a (royal) ancestor cult in the Aqhat text, 1.17:I:26b–33. According to this line of argument, the ideal son is one who *nṣb skn 'il'ibh*, "sets up the stele of his divine ancestors," as an act of filial piety (line 26 and cf. line 44 and II:16).[69] Should the context of 1.17:I:26 point to ancestor cult connections for *'il'ib* , then our previous conclusions regarding *'il'ib* must be reconsidered. Our interpretation of this line and its immediate context are reflected in the following translation and defended below:[70]

nṣb.skn.'il'ibh.	One who sets up the stelae of his fathers' gods,
bqdš ztr.'mh.	in the sanctuary, the *ztr* of his clan(?);
l'arṣ.mšṣ'u.qṭrh	from the earth, one who sends up his smoke,
l'pr.ḏmr.'aṯrh.	from the dust, one who protects his chapel;
ṭbq.lḥt n'iṣh	one who puts the lid on his revilers' abuse,
grš.d.'šy.lnh	one who expels those who act against him;
'aḫd.ydh.bškrn.	one who holds his hand when he is drunk,
m'msh [k]šb' yn.	one who carries him when he is sated with wine;
sp'u.ksmh.bt.b'l	one who serves his wheat/corn in Baal's temple,

[66] Cf. Vorländer 1975:12–14 (Mesopotamia), pp.155–58 (Syria-Palestine); Groneberg 1986:101–07; Charpin 1990:59–78; add DINGIR^{me}-*ni ša abīya* in a text from El-Qitar published by Snell 1983–84:159–70. *'l'b* of *'bd'l'b* in Diringer 1934:233–35 is probably an epithet "servant of the fathers' gods." *'lh 'bh*, "the god of his father," in *KAI* 214:29 and *'lhy byt 'by*, "the gods of the house of my father," in *KAI* 217:3 stand for groups of major gods, cf. *KAI* 214:2,8; 215:22. The term *'il'ib* is attested in a badly damaged Old Canaanite Lachish inscription, cf. Ussishkin 1983:155–57; Cross 1984:71–76.

[67] Cf. now DINGIR *a-ba* at Emar in Fleming 1992:300 [Text 380:17].

[68] E.g., *b'l ṣpn* (*KTU* 1.118:4) // ^{d}*adad bēl ḫuršân ḫa-zi* (*RS* 20.24:4); *kṯ[r]t* (1.118:12) // ^{d}*sa-sú-ra-tum* (*RS* 20.24:12); cf. Healey 1985:123 for still others.

[69] Goetze 1938:278; cf. Albright 1944:35; Gaster 1950:275; Koch 1967:211–21; Greenfield 1973:48; Pope 1977a:164; 1981:160 n.4; Healey 1979:353–56; de Moor 1985:407–09; Avishur 1985:49–60; Spronk 1986:146–47. Cf. also 1.17:I:44–46; II:1–2,16–17; see the commentary in del Olmo Lete 1981:368–69. Van Selms 1954:101 saw this as evidence of death cult rites for the common man.

[70] Cf. also the recent collation, translation, and analysis of Margalit 1989:146,247–81.

[w]mnth.bt.'il.	his grain offering in El's temple;
ṭḫ.ggh.bym [ṯ'i]ṭ	one who plasters his roof on a miry day,
rḥṣ.npṣh.bym.rṯ	one who washes his clothes on a filthy day.

The crucial terms for the ancestor cult interpretation are *'il'ibh*, *ztr*, *'mh*, and *qṭrh*. The term *ztr* is a *hapax legomenon* and has had numerous explanations. Recent defenders of the ancestor cult interpretation offer "thyme" or "marjoram," the latter being supposedly attested elsewhere in mortuary rites.[71]

While the third term is generally viewed as the preposition *'m* with the suffixed pronoun, advocates of an ancestor cult reading offer "his clan," that is, those members long gone, which for them poses a fitting parallel to *'il'ibh*, "his divine ancestor(s)."[72] Most interpreters agree on the meaning of *qṭrh*. It has to do with smoke or incense like its Semitic cognates, although the less likely alternatives "vapor" or "spirit (in the sense of a ghost)" have been suggested.[73]

While de Moor's reading of "marjoram" for *ztr* is possible, his argument stands or falls with his reading of *z'tr* in 1.43:3 and the supposed death cult context of that text. Both the reading *z'tr* and the death cult interpretation of 1.43:1–4 are debatable. His reading of *z'tr* is based on the photograph in Herdner against the more recent *KTU* edition which reads an erasure (cf. line 3 below):[74]

de Moor	KTU
k t'rb.'ṯtrt.ḫr.gb	*k t'rb.'ṯtrt.ḫr.gb*
bt mlk.'šr.'šr.b.bt 'ilm	*bt mlk.'šr.'šr.⌜b⌝.* (Eras.) *bt.'il⌜m⌝*
kbkbm.z(')tr mt	*kbkbm.*(Eras.) *trmt.*
lbš[.]wktn.'ušpǵt ḫrṣ	*lbš[.]w ktn.'ušpǵt*

---

[71] For "thyme," cf. Pope 1977a:164; 1981:160 n.4; for "marjoram," cf. de Moor 1985:407–09; both derived from Akkadian *zatēru*, Arabic *za'tar*. A Hittite loanword from *sittar*, "votive (sun) disk," has been proposed, cf. now Avishur 1985:51, but according to Margalit 1989:270 and n.17, Hittite loanwords in Ugaritic literary texts are rare. Huehnergard 1987:69,122 discusses the possibly related form *[z]u-ut-ta-ru* at Ugarit.

[72] Cf. e.g., Goetze 1938:278; Gaster 1950:272; Dietrich, Loretz, and Sanmartín 1974:451; Healey 1977a:256; 1979:355; Spronk 1986:147.

[73] For Semitic *qṭr*, "smoke" or "incense," cf. now the survey of Nielsen 1986:52–59. Albright 1944:35 proposed "spirit;" Driver 1956:143 "vapor;" de Moor 1985:409 and Spronk 1986:149 "smoke," but assumed that a departed spirit was in view. The objections of Lewis 1989:60–62 to "smoke" or "incense" overlook the separative local use of the preposition *l-* "from" in Ugaritic, for which cf. *KTU* 1.5:VI:11–12 *'il . . . yrd l ks'i*, " . . . El . . . came down from (his) throne," a reference to El's throne descent in mourning over Baal's death.

[74] Cf. de Moor 1985:408 and n.6 followed by Spronk 1986:146 and n.4. For significantly different interpretations of 1.43 from that of de Moor and Spronk, cf. de Tarragon 1980:98–107; Xella 1981b:86–90; Caquot, de Tarragon, and Cunchillos 1989:161–63.

De Moor translates these lines as follows: "When Athtartu of Hurri enters the pit, the house of the king serves a banquet in the house of the star gods. Marjoram of death, a garment and a chemise, neck-piece of gold. . . . " The term *gb* in 1.43:1 may denote any convex shaped object, e.g., a room, a grotto, a mound, a (human) back, an eyebrow, a cistern, but for Ugaritic, "pit" is tenuous at best.[75] The syntax of lines 2–3 is difficult owing to the problematic word division and traces of the erased letter. Furthermore, de Moor's "star gods," *'ilm kbkbm*, if indeed these two terms are to be syntactically related in this fashion, designate heavenly beings, not netherworld deities.[76] Lastly, *g̱trm* of lines 9–17, which has been viewed by some as one of the dual, deified ancestors, Gathar-wa-Yaqar, for which supporting evidence is lacking, does not secure the ancestral cult interpretation of lines 1–3. The term probably has to do with strength like Akkadian *gašru*, thus *g̱trm*, "the strong ones."[77]

Returning to 1.17:I, the term *'mh* has been understood as qualifying *ztr* in the following manner, "the *ztr* of (= offered to) his clan" that is, those members long gone or his divine ancestors as elaborated by the parallel *'il'ibh*. But apart from this alleged instance, *'m* in Ugaritic seldom if ever has this meaning. In more than one hundred and fifty occurrences it represents the preposition "with."[78] Even if clan is meant, a death cult interpretation remains uncertain. The phrase could refer to "the *ztr* (offered by) his clan." At best, we can only identify an unnamed sanctuary and, perhaps, some domestic rites involving marjoram.

To be sure, incense was used in Mesopotamian mortuary rites, but in the text at hand, *qṭr* may simply reflect a funerary rite in which incense was placed at the tomb for aromatic purposes.[79] Others have taken *qṭr* as alluding to the ghost of the departed, but this has little to commend it for parallels are nowhere cited in support.[80] In any case, we are not obliged to see a death cult ceremony in 1.17:I:27, for if it is the departure of the ghost to the otherworld that is in view,

---

[75] For a summary of other interpretations of *gb*, cf. de Tarragon 1980:100–01.

[76] As recognized even by his student Spronk 1986:157.

[77] *Contra* Spronk 1986:158; cf. pp.181–82. The form *g̱tr* in 1.108:2, which is crucial to his argument, is problematic owing to the damaged context: [–]*g̱tr.w yqr*. In any case, the two forms may represent epithets, not names of deceased ancestors, cf. Blau and Greenfield 1970:12–13; now Cooper 1987a:4; note the further listing of epithets in 1.108:6ff.

[78] So Pope 1977a:163–64 followed by Pardee 1980:288.

[79] Cf. e.g., the text cited in Bayliss 1973:123–24.

[80] So Caquot, Sznycer, and Herdner 1974:422 n.*q*; de Moor 1985:409; Spronk 1986:149. Healey 1979:356 concluded that while man's life departs like smoke *km.qṭr* (cf. 1.18:IV:25–26,37; add *kqṭr 'urbtm* in *RIH* 78/20:3), there is no evidence of *qṭr* itself meaning "ghost." In any event, Healey's conjecture is necessitated only by adhering to a strict synonymous parallelism for lines 28–29.

its arrival there may have merely concluded the funerary and mourning rites.[81] In light of the succeeding clause, *qṭr* might instead refer to the smoke rising from the household fires.[82]

Two other terms deserve treatment. Protecting the "place" or *'aṯr*, from dust hardly refers to a cultic location where death cult practices were enacted. The rendering of *'aṯr* as "mortuary chapel" is dubious. The Akkadian *ašīrtu* cited in support simply denotes a cultic room in a private house. The term *ksm(-h)* in line 31 is not to be equated with Akkadian *kispum.*[83] Rather, in view of its use in the sacrificial contexts of 1.41:19; 1.87:20; 1.39:9; 4.269:4,20,30; 4.345:2,4,9; and the parallel *[w]mnt(-h)*, "grain offering," in line 32, *ksm* probably designates a grain served, or *sp'u*, but not eaten, by the offerer.[84]

In sum, mortuary connections are simply lacking in 1.17:I. Like the other duties of the faithful son mentioned, those in lines 26b–28a,31b were observed while the father was alive, yet inebriated or, perhaps, afflicted as probably the cases with the duties of roof mending and garment washing suggest (lines 29–30,32–34). The rites involving marjoram(?) *ẓtr* and incense *qṭr* refer to those expected of the ideal son. Like those expected of the ideal king, they were intended for the family gods rather than for the dead.[85]

3.1.5. The Ugaritic Version of the *marzēaḥ*

Opinion is widely divided over the supposed death and ancestor cult associations of the Ugaritic version of the *marzēaḥ*. Some recognize the *marzēaḥ* solely as a death cult institution while others fail to see any connection between the two. Also there are those who maintain that the death cult depicts only one aspect of the *marzēaḥ* institution.[86] The number of proposed cognate etymologies serves to underscore this disparity of opinion: *rzḥ*, "to cry out," *rzḥ*, "to unite oneself,"

[81] Cf. Thomas 1987:450–59, esp. pp.451–52 for cases where the ghost's arrival in the afterworld concludes the funerary rites. Funerary and mourning rites are among those comprising the heir's duties at Nuzi, so Greenfield 1982:311, and probably at Emar, cf. 3.2.–3.3.

[82] Following Gaster 1950:275–76 and n.2.

[83] *Contra* Albright 1944:35 n.38; Ginsberg 1969:150.

[84] On the reading *[w]mnth*, cf. Cassuto 1975:200. On *ksm/kśm* as a type of grain, cf. Gordon 1965:422. Gordon noted that *ksm* is distinguished from wheat and barley in 4.269 and 4.345 (= *UT* 1099 and 2091). De Tarragon 1980:44–45 favors "cups" with *ksm* a plural of *ks*.

[85] Cf. the deeds of Idrimi in Oller 1977:16 (lines 88–91) for an example of the tasks expected of the ideal king in service to the gods.

[86] Pope 1972:190–94; 1977b:214–21; 1981:174–79; Porten 1968:179–86 viewed the death and ancestor cult connections of the Ugaritic *marzēaḥ* as its most important feature. Eissfeldt 1969:187–95; L'Heureux 1979:206–12,218–21; Fabry 1984:11–16 argued that it has nothing to do with mortuary matters. Others such as Greenfield 1973:48–49; 1974:451–55; de Tarragon 1980:144–47; Loretz

rzḥ, "to make a noise, to be loud," *rzḥ*, "to fall down from weakness and remain prostrate without power to rise." Not only do these proposals possess slight explanatory power, they are all but nullified by the equally plausible explanation of the origin of the term as a non-Semitic loanword (of unknown meaning).[87]

As we pointed out earlier, Ebla might record the earliest attestation of the term in *mar-za-u₉*, but for the present the Eblaite evidence offers no help vis-à-vis the mortuary connections of the West Asiatic *marzēaḥ* (cf. 2.1.3.). The same can be said for the proposal that the *marzēaḥ* institution was known at Mari and Amarna.[88] At Ugarit, the term occurs in numerous economic and legal texts but in only one mythological context, 1.114:15.[89] Based on the presumed equation of Ugaritic *mrzḥ* and *mrz'*, it has been restored elsewhere at Ugarit and thereby associated with the *rp'um*, the supposed dead ancestors (cf. ⌜*m*⌝(?)*rz'y* in 1.21:II:1,5, a Rephaim text).[90]

Research concerning the *marzēaḥ* has changed little since the cogent summary outlined by Greenfield over a decade and a half ago.[91] The Ugaritic *marzēaḥ* had both institutional and cultic functions. As a matter of practice, it comprised an assembly which celebrated a festival dedicated to a specific deity, e.g., Anat (4.642:1–7) or Shatrana (*RS* 15.70:4,7,11,16; without divine determinative)![92] Nevertheless, the conclusion that the Ugaritic *marzēaḥ*, like the much later Greek *thiasos*, was characterized by wanton drinking is troublesome. The evidence for this generalization is based on a single passage, one which is found in a mythological context, 1.114: *'il yṯb bmrzḥh yšt* [.*y*]*n*. *'d šb'*, "El continues to sit at his *marzēaḥ*, he drinks wine to satiety" (lines 15b–16a). Eissfeldt, for example, assumed a rigid correspondence between the "divine" and "earthly" versions of

1982:87–93; Barstad 1984:127–42; Barnett 1985:2*-3*; Spronk 1986:196–202; King 1988a:137–39; 1988b:34–37 considered the death and ancestor cult relations as only one of its aspects.

[87] Eissfeldt 1966:165–76 held that *rzḥ*, "to cry out," reflected the Israelite *marzēaḥ*, while *rzḥ*, "to unite oneself," represented the practices of the *marzēaḥ* of the Syrian religious world. Pope 1972:193–94 suggested the third etymology, while Greenfield 1974:452; Avigad and Greenfield 1982:125 n.32 concluded that an unknown foreign loanword is in view. Meyer 1979:603–04 offered what appears to be a variation on *rzḥ*, "to cry out," with his "to make a noise, to be loud."

[88] For the Mari evidence, cf. 2.2.5. Against the lone El-Amarna datum *ma-ar-ṣa-ú* with *CAD* 10/1(1977):290 or *ma-ar-ṣú-ú* with *AHw* 2(1972):617 in *EA* 120:21, cf. Moran 1987:330–31 n.11 = 1992:199 n.11. Against the proposal of Barnett 1985:1*-6*, followed by Gubel 1989:47–53,127–133, that the West Asiatic *marzēaḥ* is depicted in a banquet scene on a relief from Ashurbanipal's palace at Nineveh, cf. 4.3.1.

[89] Cf. *LTP* 1:15 in Pardee 1988:13–74, esp. pp.54–60.

[90] The form has been less convincingly restored in other mythological passages as well, cf. 1.1:IV:4 ⌜*m*⌝[*rzḥ* . . .]; Gibson 1978:39; Spronk 1986:170,176 for 1.21:II:9 [. . . *mrz'*]*y*; 1.22:II:2 [. . . *mrz'y*].

[91] Greenfield 1974:451–53; cf. now Barstad 1984:135–38; Fabry 1984:12–13; Pardee 1988:54–59.

[92] For *RS* 15.70, see Nougayrol 1955:130 and pl.17.

the *marzēaḥ* at Ugarit.[93] However, in the absence of confirming evidence from the administrative texts, reconstruction of historical elements from Ugaritic myth is problematic.[94] Besides, a lone reference to wanton drinking cannot prove that such was characteristic of an institution or practice otherwise well attested at Ugarit. Besides, untamed imbibing might simply function to adorn the landscape of the social setting depicted at this point in the myth's plot development.

A member of the *marzēaḥ* was designated "a man of the *marzēaḥ*," alphabetic *mt mrzḥ* (3.9:13) and syllabic LÚ^meš^ *marziḫi* (*RS* 14.16:3, etc.), or "a son of the *marzēaḥ*," alphabetic *bn mrzḥ* (4.399:8).[95] The head of the organization was given the title *rb*. As an institution, the *marzēaḥ* had its own special meeting place, É LÚ^meš^ *mar-ze/za-i*, "the house of the men of the *marzēaḥ*" (*RS* 15.70:4,7 and 15.88:4).[96] Another text depicts the actual establishment of a *marzēaḥ* institution, *mrzḥ d qny šmmn b.bt w*, "the *marzēaḥ* which Shamuman established in his house" (3.9:1–4). Shamuman functioned as the head or *rb* of the *marzēaḥ* (3.9:12).[97] Its members comprised the higher economic strata of society. This is confirmed by the mention of a large sum of money in a broken text (*RS* 14.16).[98] These funds were either the high penalties imposed on its members for breach of contract (3.9:11) or the dues required for membership (3.9:17). In addition to a house, the *marzēaḥ* owned such valuable property as fields and vineyards, cf. *šd kr*[*m*] (4.642:3) and *eqel karāni* (*RS* 18.01:5).[99] Ownership of *marzēaḥ* property was confirmed and transferred by the king as indicated by the mention of "Niqmepa, son of Niqmaddu, king of Ugarit" (*RS* 15.88:2–3) and his successor "Ammishtamru, son of Niqmepa, king of Ugarit" (*RS* 15.70:2–3,19–20) who were apparently involved in such proceedings.

But what evidence exists that would suggest any mortuary associations of the Ugaritic *marzēaḥ*? The Ugaritic evidence cited in past discussions consists of two texts, 1.114 and 1.21. Otherwise, the mortuary connections of the West Asiatic *marzēaḥ* date from much later periods and originate at other locations.[100] While most interpreters view 1.114 simply as a divine drinking bout, Pope has attempted

---

93 Eissfeldt 1969:193; cf. similarly Pope 1972:178.

94 Following Sasson 1981a:81–98.

95 The equivalent alphabetic and cuneiform expressions argue against reading *mt* in *mt mrzḥ* as "the dead of the *marzēaḥ*" with Halpern 1979–80:135. For *bn mrzḥ*, cf. Palmyrene *bny mrzḥ'*.

96 For *RS* 15.88, see Nougayrol 1955:88 and pl.20.

97 For treatments of 3.9, see Miller 1971:37–49; Fenton 1977:71–76; Halpern 1979–80:121–40; Friedman 1979–80:187–206; Dietrich and Loretz 1982:71–76; Spronk 1986:197–98. Cf. also *rb mrzḥ'* of the Nabatean and Palmyrene texts and the critique of Friedman 1979–80:197–98 against a proposed verbal form.

98 For *RS* 14.16, see Virolleaud 1951:163–79.

99 For *RS* 18.01, see Nougayrol 1956:230 and pl.77.

100 Cf. our treatment of the first millennium evidence in 4.1.; Greenfield 1974:451–55, esp. 452 n.14; Barstad 1984:135–39, esp. n.81.

to reconstruct a death cult ritual in this text.[101] His citation of a late isolated rabbinic use of Aramaic *ṣûḏniṯā'*, as indicative of a meal served to mourners and as cognate to *ṣd* in line 1, must be evaluated over against the widely recognized use of Ugaritic *ṣd* as the verb "to give a banquet" without any inherent connection with mortuary rites.[102] This is a foundational datum for Pope's interpretation.

Second, his interpretation of *yrḫ gbh*, "mixed his tripe," in lines 4–5 as a reference to the drinking of juices from a deceased relative's body must be rejected in the light of the regular use of *yrḫ* to designate the moon god Yariḫ (or simply "month"). In no other instance in the Ugaritic corpus does this form possess a meaning connected with moisture or liquids as Pope presupposes.[103] Pope cited *klb* in lines 5 and 12 as further evidence for a death cult context. The widely attested role of dogs in death cult rituals of divergent cultures prompted this hypothesis.[104] But, not only did Pope fail to identify the dog's exact function in our text, others have seen *klb* in lines 5 and 12 as references to the canine-like behavior of the inebriated moon god.[105] In any case, Virolleaud did not restore *klb* in line 5 in the *editio princeps*, but rather left the space blank. Moreover, his reading of *rlb* in line 12 was confirmed by the editors of *KTU* and *LTP* although both tentatively read ⌜*klb*⌝ in line 5.[106]

The actual form attested in the Rephaim texts (1.21:II:1, cf. also lines 5 and 9) is *mrz'* which, beginning with Eissfeldt, has been viewed as a variant of Ugaritic *mrzḥ*. This conclusion is based on the supposed analogous orthographic variants in Ugaritic Akkadian: *mar-zi-i* (*RS* 18.01:7,10) and *mar-zi-ḫi* (*RS* 14.16:3).[107] However, it is not at all certain that the phoneme *ḥ* which lies behind *mar-zi-ḫi* (*RS* 14.16:3) ultimately lies behind *mar-zi-i* and *mar-za-i* (*RS* 15.88:4,6), both of which presume the presence of the phoneme '. The equation has been based

---

101 Cf. Pope 1972:170–203; note 1979–80:141–43; 1981:177–78. For recent treatments of this text with extensive bibliographies, see L'Heureux 1979:159–69; Margalit 1979–80:65–120; Cathcart and Watson 1980:35–58; Spronk 1986:198–201; Pardee 1988:13–74.

102 With Loewenstamm 1980:372,410–22 against Pope 1972:175. Others view the form as derived from a verb "to give chase, roam" attested in Ugaritic, Arabic, and Akkadian, cf. e.g., Cathcart and Watson 1980:41,44.

103 Pope 1972:179.

104 Pope 1972:183–89. Pope's additional arguments are still less convincing. The forms *yqṯqṯ* in line 5 and *ylmn* in line 8 may denote noises made to drive away the ghosts, so Pope 1972:181, but this hinges on his prior arguments as does his view of El's drunken stupor as an experience of death intended to join the worlds of the living and the dead, cf. Pope 1972:178,202.

105 Cf. Loewenstamm 1969:72,74; L'Heureux 1979:160,166; Margalit 1979–80:69,81–82; Cathcart and Watson 1980:37; note *KTU*'s reading *km klb* in line 5. Spronk 1986:198–99 took an approach which both eliminates Pope's view and avoids the function of *klb* as a simile.

106 Cf. Virolleaud 1968:545,549–50 against Loewenstamm 1969:71–77.

107 So Eissfeldt 1969:195. Similarly, L'Heureux 1979:142 n.43 added that the ' is the voiced equivalent to the unvoiced *ḥ* evincing a supposed partial assimilation to the voiced *z*.

a priori on the equation of the similar alphabetic forms. This not only betrays a circularity of reasoning, but creates other obstacles as well.

First, the intervocalic voicing of *ḥ* to *ʿ* would be exceptional for Ugaritic Akkadian.[108] The resultant vocalization based on *mar-za-i* would be *marzaḫi*, a *maqtal* form, but this is not what we would expect in view of the remaining Ugaritic forms and Hebrew *marzēaḥ*. We would expect *marziḫi*, a *maqtil* form.[109] In other words, with regard to the occurrences of the Ugaritic form of *marzēaḥ*, the syllabic writing system at Ugarit is as ambiguous as the alphabetic.[110] Even if the underlying assumption that the *rp'um* represented chthonic beings were the correct one, and this is by no means certain (cf. 3.1.7.), their relation to the *marzēaḥ*, actually *mrzʿ*, in 1.21:II:1,5,9 remains ambiguous. The damaged state of the passages in question and the absence of the requisite data proving such a presumed correlation prohibits us from saying more.[111] Furthermore, even if we were to assume that *marzēaḥ* is mentioned in these passages, we have the added issue of the host who invited the *rp'um* to the *marzēaḥ*. If it is El, as suggested by lines 8–9: *wyʿn ʾil* [*mrzʿ*]*y*, "And El replied . . . my *marzēaḥ*," then we might have a divine banquet attended by the mythic heroes or *rp'um*.[112] Finally, even if one concluded, based on this lone datum, that the *marzēaḥ* played a part in Ugaritic death or ancestor cults, one clearly cannot extrapolate from this that such a role was an important one, for the numerous legal and administrative texts indicate otherwise. They lack any such mortuary associations, but rather focus on the economic and social interests of its members.

These concerns rather than the hypothetical mortuary connections of the *marzēaḥ* or, for that matter, the drinking habits of its members, lie behind each of its references at Ugarit. El's banquet in 1.114 is no exception, for, while drinking is a major part of the plot, only the wider social setting remotely resembles what can be confidently reconstructed from the administrative and legal texts, namely a festive occasion celebrated by the highest echelons of society. In conclusion, the association of the Ugaritic *marzēaḥ* with mortuary matters has yet to be established.[113]

---

108 Cf. Huehnergard 1987:278.

109 Huehnergard 1987:271–2.

110 So Pardee 1988:176 n.48. Cf. also Huehnergard 1987:178,239–40,244,272,278. Note the supposed West Asiatic loan *mrz*(ʾ)-*nn* in the Hurrian text *RS* 24.278:12 in Laroche 1968:515.

111 L'Heureux 1979:206–12; Fabry 1984:13 dismissed the death cult associations of the *marzēaḥ* at Ugarit and rejected the underworld connections of the *rp'um*.

112 Cf. similarly L'Heureux 1979:142. Pope 1972:192 preferred Danil but he viewed him as mourning the death of his son Aqhat and as inviting the shades of the dead, the *rp'um*, to his *marzēaḥ*.

113 Lewis 1989:80–88 came to the same conclusion independently.

3.1.6. The Ugaritic King List

Frequently, *KTU* 1.113 has been cited as evidence for the existence of a royal ancestor cult at Ugarit. Two particulars of the text have occasioned this interpretation: the repeated element *'il* which precedes what have been identified as the names of former Ugaritic rulers on the reverse of the text and what appears to be some sort of cultic ceremony recorded on the obverse, the exact nature of which has eluded interpreters. Interpreters refer to this text as the Ugaritic king list. My own collation of the text reads as follows:[114]

Obverse	Reverse (L)	Reverse (R)
[ ]⸢x *w*⸣*rm tph*	[ ]	[ ]
[ ]*l'umm l n'm*	[ ]	[ ] ⸢*ṯ*⸣*t*⸢*m*⸣[
[ ]⸢*w*⸣ *rm ṯlbm*	[ ]	[ ]*q*⸢*m*x⸣'
[ ]*pr l n'm*	[ ]	[ ]*mp*⸢*p*⸣
[ ]⸢x⸣ *mt w rm tph*	[ ]	*'il 'ibr*⸢*n/'a*⸣
[ ]*ḥb l n'm*	[ ]	*'il y'ḏrd*
[ ]*ymǵy*	[ ]	*'il nqmp'*
[ ]⸢*r*⸣*m ṯlbm*	[ ]⸢*p*⸣[ ]	*'il 'ibrn*
[ ]⸢'⸣*m*	[ ]⸢*d*⸣[ ]	[ ] ⸢'⸣*mrp'i*
[ ]*ḥ* ⸢*n*⸣ '⸢*m*⸣	[ ]*mp*[ ]	[ ] *nqm*⸢*p*'⸣
[ ]⸢x⸣[ ]	[ ]*t*⸢x*r*⸣	*'il* ⸢*'i*⸣[
	(Edge)	
	[ ]	*'il nqm*[
	[ ]	*'il 'ibrn*
	[ ]	*'il nqmd*
	[ ]⸢x⸣	*'il yqr*

This list, particularly its obverse, has been described as having some affinities with the genres of ritual, incantation, prayer, and hymn.[115] However, Pardee has

---

[114] Virolleaud 1968:561–62 published the obverse, but the reverse was published later in the *KTU* edition of 1976. Wilson 1977:121–22 discussed the reverse without aid of the *KTU* edition while Kitchen 1977:131–42 first commented on it extensively. Cf. now de Tarragon 1980:124–25; Xella 1981a:288–91; del Olmo Lete 1986a:83–95; Pardee 1988:165–78 (= *LTP* 5); Lewis 1989:47–52. Preliminary remarks can be found in Virolleaud 1962:94–95; Schaeffer 1963:214–15; Rainey 1965a:107. Variant readings from previous editions might be partially explained by progressive deterioration of the text.

[115] Kitchen 1977:140.

pointed out that 1.113 lacks the terminology of the Ugaritic rituals.[116] Moreover, the genre of prayer is inadequate, for 1.113 has far less repetition than the Ugaritic prayers as represented by *KTU* 1.119.[117] If by hymn, certain biblical psalms are meant, we lack Ugaritic parallels. While the repetition of formulae might be vaguely reflected in a psalm such as 136, this is too late to provide a working model for 1.113.

Although 1.113 reveals a curious absence of ritual terminology, it is wrought with mythological vocabulary e.g., *tp*, *ṯlb*, *mǵy*, and *rm*.[118] This fact along with the supposed poetic form of 1.113 and its presumed mortuary correlations has led Ribichini and Xella to the conclusion that *KTU* 1.113 and 1.161 shared the same cultic function.[119] But, if, as we shall argue below, 1.113 has an altogether different function and 1.161 represents a coronation text with an accompanying funerary liturgy (and not the Ugaritic version of the regularly observed *kispum* ritual, cf. 3.1.9.), then their supposed similarities dissipate.

Pardee has classified 1.113 as a "para-mythological" text, that is, one which employs mythological elements for practical ends. He identified its setting as a festival in which the dead, deified Ugaritic kings were invoked by the accompaniment of music. Pardee, following the consensus, concludes that it has a supposed parallel in the Old Babylonian GHD wherein the dead kings are invoked (but cf. 3.1.7.1.). Furthermore, the obverse shows similarities to *KTU* 1.100, an incantation text, in its tendency for word repetition and etched horizontal lines separating the poetic stanzas.[120] 1.100 exhibits a repeated summons addressed to twelve different deities. While 1.113 contains no explicit mention of known deities, the twelvefold summons in 1.100 might provide a working model for understanding the enigmatic *nʿm* in lines 2,4,6, and 10 of the obverse of 1.113. This term has been identified by several scholars as the title of a living king summoned to a ceremony.[121] It is likewise used as a title for the heroes Keret and Aqhat of the mythological texts, both of whom might have functioned as kings in their respective legends. However, it is a gross inaccuracy to state that the term *nʿm* is not applied to deities.[122] It is so used in 1.23:1,23,60,67 in reference to Shahar and Shalim, the *ʾilm nʿmm*, and in 1.24:25 in reference to the moon god Yariḫ, *nʿmn*

[116] Pardee 1988:170,172.

[117] For 1.119, see Watson 1984:360–62 and the bibliography cited there.

[118] The term *tp*, "tambourine," occurs in the mythological context of 1.16:I:41 and with *ṯlb*, "flute," in 1.108:4. *mǵy* and *rm* show up in poetic and mythological contexts. The *hapax legomenon lʾumm* might be the poetic form for "peoples," so Pardee 1988:170.

[119] Ribichini and Xella 1979:150 n.29.

[120] Pardee 1988:170,172,175–78.

[121] So Kitchen 1977:140; Xella 1981a:289,291. Spronk 1986:155 suggested Radmanu of 1.3:I:2, but his readings of 1.17:VI:30–32 and 1.3:I:2 are questionable, cf. *KTU* and Pardee 1980:274 respectively.

[122] So Kitchen 1977:140 followed by Lewis 1989:51.

'ilm.[123] This fact coupled with the invocation of gods depicted in the literary parallel 1.100 argue in favor of identifying *n'm* in 1.113 as a title of a god rather than as a title of a king. This is given added support by the use of the tambourine or *tp*, and flute or *ṯlb*, in a benediction to the god *Rp'u* in *KTU* 1.108:4.[124] Interpreters who assume that an ancestor cult context stands behind the ceremony reflected in 1.113 have proposed several deities for *n'm*: Baal, *Rp'u*, Malik, and Mot.[125] However, in the absence of decisive contextual support, the exact identity of the god who is given the title *n'm* remains for the present enigmatic.

In spite of the widely accepted position that 1.113 records rites directed to the dead, deified kings of Ugarit, there is, in actuality, no textual basis for this view, that is apart from a predisposition to interpret *'il* + RN as a reference to a deified king. As we noted in 2.1.1., Liverani offered a more adequate interpretation of the phrase. The repeated element *'il* + RN referred not to rituals aimed at deified, defunct Ugaritic kings (for which evidence is lacking), but to those dedicated to the personal god of the former kings who might have been a major god of the pantheon.[126]

His proposal gains support from 1.100 and 1.108. The address to the numerous deities in 1.100 and the use of the same musical instruments in 1.108 in the benediction to the god *Rp'u* point to 1.113 as a text associated with a ritual directed to a deity. Like 1.100, 1.113 more likely reflects a ceremony in which a god or gods are invoked or whose names are simply orally recited. Alternatively, as in the case of the Eblaite king list, 1.113 perhaps comprises a list of dead kings each successively associated with the dynastic personal god known by all and so designated by the generic term *'il*. The list was recited in the cult and accompanied by ritual offerings for the purpose of legitimating the current dynasty.

---

123 Cf. del Olmo Lete 1981:429 and p.453 respectively.

124 The mention of these instruments in two different texts is not sufficient evidence alone to identify *rp'u* as the god of 1.113.

125 Cf. Pardee 1988:170–71 for a survey of proposals.

126 Liverani 1974:340–41. The conjecture that the full list of kings contained some thirty names or more is problematic. This conjecture is based on the presence of the vertical line runing down the lefthand side of the right column of the reverse of the tablet. This line has been interpreted as an indicator of the list's continuance to the end of the tablet. My own examination of the tablet in the summer of 1994, however, revealed that the vertical line spans three, or at most, six lines. The reverse of the text begins with four lines (12′–15′) that lack the vertical line. Beginning at line 16′, the vertical runs alongside the next three (16′–18′). From here, it disappears due either to the damage of the text or to its original absence in this portion. In any case, it does not reappear at line 22′ where the surface of the text is well preserved. When considered alongside the observation—again based on personal examination of the tablet—that the left column of the reverse preserves only three fully legible signs (see the transcription), it is possible that the vertical line was accidental and not a marker of separate columns. The reverse might contain several lines that span the entire width of the tablet in one, not two, columns. The kings' names would then be elements within longer lines beginning on the far left of the reverse and ending on the far right.

Recall that our interpretation of *'il* + RN finds its precedent in the Sumerian royal inscriptions where the personal god of the king was identified by means of dingir + RN, *'il* + RN's corresponding formula which is also attested in the Eblaite king list. As we pointed out in 2.1.1., the personal god of king Entemena of Lagash was identified as ^{d}šulutula dingir en-te-me-[na], "Shulutula, god of Entemena."[127]

While the exact identity of the god in 1.113 remains obscure to the modern reader, undoubtedly common knowledge sufficed to identify the name of the deity of the royal dynasty designated *'il* + RN.[128] Common knowledge might also explain the significance of a possible related rubric as well. As we argued in 3.1.3., the dynastic personal god along with other gods worshipped by the royal family might have been given the collective designation in Ugaritic, *'il'ib*, "the gods of the fathers." In fact, the identity of some of these gods is probably to be found in the names of those deities listed under the rubric *'il'ib* in the cultic texts.[129] Thus, we conclude that, like the Eblaite king list, 1.113 comprises a list of the former kings, each of whom is associated with the dynastic personal god. In the light of the text's obvious concern with dynastic continuity, this god in all likelihood was to receive cultic ritual for the purpose of political legitimation.[130]

It goes without saying that we reject the related proposals that 1.113 exhibits similarities with either 1 Samuel 28, an account of necromancy, the *marzēaḥ*, or the *kispum*. First, there is no indication that the invocation had as its goal the appearance of the dead as in 1 Samuel 28. Second, the Ugaritic *marzēaḥ* knows no practice involving music or singing, not to mention that its mortuary connections are nowhere apparent. Finally, music has yet to appear in the *kispum* ritual and 1.113 makes no mention of *kispum*-like offerings.[131] Even if we could establish its mortuary associations, 1.113, like 1.161, might reflect a ceremony intended for a single occasion and one lacking any concern for the dead's supernatural beneficent powers.

---

127 Cf. Vorländer 1975:9; cf. pp.151–52 for possible examples from Syria-Palestine of the second to first millennia B.C.E.

128 Pardee 1988:173 n.25 rejected Liverani's view and cited the GHD in favor of the ancestor cult connections of 1.113, but the chronological proximity of the GHD is not close, it was used on the lone occasion of Ammiṣaduqa's coronation, none of the listed individuals are divinized, and so its assumed ancestor cult affiliations are equally problematic, cf. further our treatment in 3.1.7.1.

129 In the light of the mention of musical instruments in 1.113, *n'm* might refer to an anonymous singer who performs for the god as *n'm* does in 1.3:I:19 or *n'm* might depict an individual granted an affirmative omen having enticed the god for a verdict with music, cf. Levenson 1985:66.

130 What we have proposed remains preferable in spite of the fact that the exact nature of the ritual reflected in the Ugaritic king list remains uncertain in every detail. We should also note that Schaeffer 1963:215 suggested that two distinct scripts from two independent hands are present on the obverse and reverse and so the texts of the two sides might not be related. If this is the case, a major datum for the ancestor cult adherents is even more ambiguous than generally acknowledged.

131 Pardee 1988:176–78. Xella 1981a:291; Pardee 1988:177 suggested offerings in line 4 [ ]*pr* either *pr*, "bull," or *ḫpr*, "rations."

As a final note, we should make mention of del Olmo Lete's thesis that Ugaritic theophoric names such as *ydb'il, y'arš'il, 'mtr*, etc., of 1.106 and 1.102 represent the dead, deified dynastic ancestors who, along with the major deities mentioned, receive cultic offerings, (e.g., *gdlt*, cf. 1.106:3–5). These three names also occur alongside the name *yrgbb'l* in 1.102:16–20. According to del Olmo Lete, *yrgbb'l* is a title of king Niqmaddu based on 1.6:VI:57–58, *nqmd mlk 'ugrt 'adn yrgb b'l ṯrmn*, "Niqmaddu, king of Ugarit, Lord, Baal terrified, Ṯrmn."[132]

Nevertheless, del Olmo Lete's proposal is heavily dependent upon those works in which the diffusion of ancestor and death cults at Ugarit is a given. His citation of such texts as 1.113 and 1.161 (cf. 3.1.9.) and such entities as the *rp'um* (cf. 3.1.7.) as support for his proposal must be set aside.[133] Finally, the types of theophoric names that he treats are typically attributed to living persons. In fact, according to Stamm, these names are those of living officials of high rank who brought offerings to the cult. Stamm pointed out that the recipients of offerings in 1.106:1–2, which are known deities for the most part, are preceded by the *l*-preposition, e.g., *l ršp ḥgb 'ṣrm* and *l 'inš 'ilm šrp*, whereas the offerers, including the above three names, as in lines 3–5, precede the mention of their gift, e.g., PN + *gdlt*.[134]

3.1.7. The Ugaritic *rp'um*

In the six decades since the discovery of the Ras Shamra texts, the *rp'um* have been categorized as gods, shades of the dead, and/or living persons.[135] The first two categories, although widely accepted, create significant interpretative difficulties. The third relates little else beyond the fact that such entities existed in the mythological traditions, although not necessarily in the historical traditions. Be that as it may, the growing consensus is that the *rp'um* are synonymous with or

[132] Del Olmo Lete 1986b:55–71; 1986a:83–95. Del Olmo Lete 1986a:84 classified the above three names as *'inš 'ilm*, "divine persons" (cf. 1.106:2), and located them in 1.39:20–21, a sacrificial agenda supposedly related to the royal funerary liturgy where the phrase *'inš 'ilm* occurs again. Of course, in the absence of decisive evidence for the mortuary connections of 1.39, the *inš 'ilm* might simply refer to those in service to the gods, "the men of the gods," like kings, priests, or prophets.

[133] In particular, he drew upon the works of de Tarragon 1980:167; Xella 1981a:83–84.

[134] Cf. Stamm 1979:753–58; note Herdner 1978:29. In any case, *yrgbb'l* in 1.6:VI:58 has been identified as a place name found in Tuthmosis III's toponymic list. On *yrgbb'l* as a possible place name in 1.6:VI:58, see Herdner 1978:4–5.

[135] Cf. the surveys of L'Heureux 1979:116–25; Cooper 1981:460–67; Caquot 1981:351–56.

include the dead, deified kings and that, as founders of the dynasty, they exercised their supernatural, beneficent powers in the royal ancestor cult.[136]

According to the editors of *KTU*, the root *r-p-'* occurs in approximately thirty-six instances where the reading is undisputed.[137] It is reconstructed in another sixteen contexts often based on the repetition of similar lines, sometimes without change, but in other instances with predictable variation.[138] Nonetheless, some readings formerly endorsed must now be discarded.[139] The form also appears in a handful of personal names, perhaps as a theophoric element.[140]

3.1.7.1. The Related *Ditānu* Name

The *Ditānu* name, or *dtn*, parallels the *rp'i 'arṣ* on three occasions in the Ugaritic texts (1.15:III:3–4,14–15; 1.161:2–3,9–10). Owing to the controversial nature of the evidence concerning the *rp'um* that dates from periods both prior to and contemporary with Ugarit, we shall offer a brief analysis of the related form, *dtn*. The working assumption is that the *dtn* name might provide a traditio-historical model by which to provisionally reconstruct the development of the *rp'um* concept. Although the limitations of such an approach are obvious, it nevertheless demonstrates that the significance of both the *dtn* and *rp'u* names can be understood quite independently of any ancestor cult associations.[141]

From Ur the following Old Babylonian compound form is attested ME-^{d}*di-ta-an*. The divine determinative suggests that the name had become associated with

136 Cf. e.g., the numerous treatments of *KTU* 1.161 listed in 3.1.9. and the remarks by Healey 1986:27–32.

137 In the Shapash hymn: 1.6:VI:46. In the Keret legend: 1.15:III:3,14. In the Aqhat legend: 1.17:I:18,35; 1.17:II:28; 1.17:V:4–5,14,33–34; 1.17:VI:52; 1.19:I:20,36–37,38–39,47; 1.19:IV:36. In the Rephaim texts: 1.20:II:6; 1.21:II:3,9,11; 1.22:I:8,21,23; 1.22:II:19; in the following texts: 1.82:32; 1.108:1,19,21,24; 1.114:28 (verb, but ambiguous); 1.161:2,4,5,8,9,24; *RIH* 77/8A(+13+21B):14′.

138 In the Keret legend: 1.15:III:3. In the Aqhat legend: 1.17:I:1,37,42; 1.19:IV:17,18. In the Rephaim texts: 1.20:I:1; 1.20:II:1,7; 1.22:II:3,5,8,10,20,25; and in 1.108:22.

139 In the Keret legend, 1.14:I:7, *rp'at* is now read as ⸢x⸣*rwt*. In 1.82:28, [. . . *rp*]*'im* is now read as [. . .]*hm*. The form *yrp* comes at the very end of 1.21:II:5, but the beginning of line 6 is missing (i.e., no *aleph* sign exists).

140 Gröndahl 1967:180 and cf. p.84: *Rap-a-na*, *A-bir*$_x$*-pi-i*, *Abdi-rap-i*, *Am-mu-ra-pi*, ^{f}*Bitta-ra-ap-i*, *'abrp'u*, *'ilrp'u*, *'bdrp'u*, *'mrp'i/'mpr*, *rp'an*, *rp'iy*, *rp'iyn*, *yrp'u*, *yrp'i*.

141 Lipiński 1978:91–110 has collected much of the pertinent data on the *dtn* name in earlier periods e.g., *Tidinu*, *Titinu*, *Tidnim*, *Tidanum*, *Didanum*, *Datnim*, and *Datnam*. His conclusion that it was simply a tribal name derived ultimately from the animal name for antelope and never a personal name is problematic, cf. e.g., *Ditānu*'s use as a personal name in the obelisk of Man-ishtusu in Gelb 1957:294 and at Ebla. Lipiński's work also assumes a unified tradition history for all occurrences of the name.

sacred powers, but the exact significance remains obscure.[142] In any case, the religio-political notoriety of the *Ditānu* name was such that it was incorporated into the official cult, for in the Old Babylonian GHD, *Ditānu* occurs in line 6 as a name possessing heroic dimensions and one that was recited in the royal cult. The various groups listed in the GHD, both those individuals in lines 1–28, of which *Ditānu* is one, and those in lines 29–38, have been commonly viewed as the ghosts of the dead who were summoned and who receive offerings and rites or *pāqidum ù sāḫirum*. In other words, according to this interpretation, the GHD comprises a *kispum* ritual.[143] Lines 39–43 reflect a ritual setting in which the ghosts of the dead were invited to a communal meal in the hope that they might bestow their supernatural blessings upon the new king.

However, apart from the possible commemoration of the royal ancestors reflected in lines 1–28 (see below), mortuary practices, and in particular those indicative of a belief in the dead's supernatural power, are otherwise lacking. Nowhere are those terms that are typically associated with the mortuary cult like *kispum* or *eṭemmum* mentioned. None of the individuals mentioned in the GHD are deified. The divine determinative is nowhere present. Moreover, the GHD was tied to a single historical occasion, the coronation of Ammiṣaduqa, king of Babylon (cf. lines 41–43), and so it was not observed as part of a regularly occurring cultic calendar. Even if one were to assume for the sake of argument that the GHD preserved a mortuary rite like a funerary liturgy (as some have suggested for the Ugaritic text *KTU* 1.161, cf. 3.1.9.), it is unlikely that such involved the attendance of the living *and* the dead at a communal meal as part of a *kispum* festival meal.[144] In any event, one can hardly justify assigning to a mortuary setting, the term *pāqidum* and the couplet "eat this" or *aklā* and "drink this" or *šitiā* (lines 39–40) in the absence of explicit internal evidence for such associations of the underlying ritual.[145]

It is the GHD's explicit coronational ritual setting that informs the present interpretation of the text. Typical coronational elements attested in Ur III to Neo-

---

142 Is it "the sacred powers of *Ditānu*" or "the sacred powers of the (personal) god of *Ditānu*" that are in view? For the text, cf. Figulla and Martin 1953:nos. 497:11; 581:11.

143 Cf. Finkelstein 1966:95–118; Malamat 1968:163–73 esp. n.29; Lambert 1968a:1–2; Röllig 1969:265–77; Wilson 1977:44–45,107–114; Tsukimoto 1985:68–69; Charpin and Durand 1986:159–70. On the supposed connection of *pāqidum*, "care," and *sāḫirum*, "invoke(?)" (< *zakārum*), in line 38 with the *kispum* ritual, cf. Finkelstein 1966:113–16; Lambert 1968a:1–2; Charpin and Durand 1986:163–70. See Tsukimoto 1985:68–69 n.272 for *sāḫirum*, "venerate" (< *saḫārum*).

144 Cf. 2.2.1.; Tsukimoto 1985:61.

145 The *pāqidum* < *paqādum*, can refer to one who cares for the elderly, cf. Greenfield 1982:309–16. Eating and drinking clearly signify a festive occasion, but in the absence of characteristic terminology of the ancestor cult, the nature of that feast must be established on independent grounds. The significance of the term *sāḫirum* is problematic so it cannot be cited in support of any particular interpretation.

Babylonian texts include: divine election, assembly of nobles and dignitaries, preparatory purification, the king's presentation, investiture with insignia, giving of a throne name, acclamation of the king with blessing, the enthronement, homage, swearing of oaths, affirmation by the king, celebration, and sacrifice.[146] A re-examination of the GHD, with its coronational setting providing the crucial interpretative framework, suggests the following series of ritual enactments: the assembly of the living nobles and dignitaries (lines 29–35), the celebration (lines 39–40), and the acclamation of the king with the blessing of the people and, perhaps, the gods (but not the dead; lines 41–43). Moreover, the merrymaking reported in lines 39–40 (cf. "eat this," "drink this") points to the coronational celebration accompanied by sacrifices to the deity. These ritual elements find some analogues from a Middle Assyrian coronation ritual published in 1937 by K. F. Müller. That text contains such coronational elements as the presentation before the deity (Ashur; col.i:30–32), offerings and sacrifice to the deity (Ashur; col.i:37–41), the investiture with scepter and (*kulūlu*) crown (col.ii:15–28), acclamation with blessing (col.ii:30–38,42–49), enthronement (col.iii:1), assembly of nobles and dignitaries (col.iii:2–3), payment of homage (col.iii:4–14), and swearing of oaths before the divine witness, the solar deity (represented as Ṣalmu;[147] col.ii:7–8).

Lines 1–19 of the GHD comprise a genealogical list consisting of eponymous ancestors followed by the kings of the first dynasty of Babylon in lines 20–28. In view of the absence of unequivocal death or ancestor cult rites in the GHD, the names in lines 1–28 are interpreted here as having been recited as part of a commemorative rite. As noted in our introduction, such geneonymy or commemoration is not to be equated with ancestor veneration or worship although both ritual complexes presuppose the mnemonic use and perpetuation of pedigrees and genealogies. Simply put, recognition of demonstrable ancestry does not predicate ancestor worship.[148] In other words, the names do not represent those shades who were invited to participate in a *kispum* festival complete with food and drink. The public recitation of the names of venerable figures of the past is followed in lines 29–43 by a summons for the living in attendance to participate in a communal meal. This is the significance of the imperatives *aklā*, "eat this," and *šitiā*, "drink this," in lines 39–40. Finally, a petition for the living to lavish blessings upon the new king Ammiṣaduqa immediately follows in lines 41–43 (cf. the imperative *kurbā*, "bless," in line 43).

---

146 Cf. also 3.1.9. for our treatment of *KTU* 1.161. Other major texts preserving coronational elements include: Ur-Nammu, the investiture of Kingu and Marduk in Enuma Elish, the Middle Assyrian coronation ritual discussed below, and the Nabopolassar epic, cf. Müller 1937; Ben-Barak 1980:55–67; Wilkinson 1986; add Tell Asmar 1931–T299 in Whiting 1987:48–51.

147 Following Dalley 1986:85–101.

148 So Fortes 1965:123–24; 1976:4; Newell 1976:19–20.

Each in their "turn" (BAL = *palû*), those groups listed in lines 29ff. commemorated the dynastic dead on the special occasion of the coronation of Ammiṣaduqa.[149] The term ERÍN = *ṣābum* in lines 29–30, we render as "soldiers," rather than the "people," for the general population is referred to by way of the merism comprising the whole of lines 29–38. In those lines, both the powerful and the powerless of society are specified as invitees. In addition to the active military (lines 29–31) and the nobility (lines 34–35), the invitees include other military contingents (line 32) as well as disabled veterans or *ù* AGA.UŠ *ša ina dannat bēlišu imqutū*, "those who have suffered injury for their lord"(line 33).[150] Still another group was also invited, the indigent of society or those who had "no one to care for them or to be solicitous[?] to them" or *ša pāqidam ù sāḫiram lā išû* (lines 36–38).

The invitation of those able to defend and rule along with those maimed and powerless reveals Ammiṣaduqa's concern to secure his place among the ruling class and the military as well as to achieve popular appeal. By including for commemoration the names of the former kings and the names of eponymous, warrior heroes of former ages like *Ditānu*, Ammiṣaduqa solidified his allegiance with his contemporaries who could identify themselves, whether they be the political elite or the military in his employ, with the names recited in the ritual. This suggests that the coronational aspect of the ritual underlying the GHD is far more extensive and detailed and that mortuary rites are lacking, the lone exception being the commemorative rite reflected in lines 1–28. In order to illustrate each of the distinct elements in these two interpretations, the text as edited by Finkelstein and a comparative chart are included below (text, p.76; chart, p.77).

My version of the coronation interpretation of the GHD underscores the importance attributed to great warriors of the past such as *Ditānu*. That an ancient warrior elite is given such a primary role in the underlying ritual, stands as a heretofore neglected criterion in the selection of names included in the GHD.[151] If *Didānu* is a variant of *Ditānu*, then in the Assyrian King List-A:i:4,10 (hereafter AKL-A) the name is also portrayed as an ancient nomad of heroic stature as well as a king. The name is identified as one of the "seventeen kings who lived in

---

149 Röllig 1969:273 viewed the Amorites, Ḫaneans, and Gutians as contemporary contiguous political groups. Charpin and Durand 1986:169 postulated a surviving warrior contingent related to those deceased apparitions supposedly invited to the feast. On pp.166–67, they viewed BAL = *palû*, "turn," in lines 29–32 as indicative of the successive groups who come, each at their turn, to receive a portion of the offerings. We take all those mentioned in lines 29–43 to be alive.

150 The presence of the verbal form *im-qú-tu* from *maqātum* does not necessarily signify "to fall" in the fatal sense. It can signify "to suffer downfall (said of a diviner)," "suffer injury/defeat" or perhaps simply "to fight," cf. *CAD* 10(1977):240–51 esp. pp.242–43 [##1b,1d1′,4].

151 The GHD does not identify the individuals listed before Sumu-abim, the first king of Babylon, as kings, cf. lines 1–19.

The Genealogy of the Hammurapi Dynasty:
Text and Translation

Obverse

1. ^{I}*A-ra-am-ma-da-ra*
2. ^{I}*Tu-ub-ti-ya-mu-ta*
3. ^{I}*Ya-am-qú-uz-zu-ḫa-lam-ma*
4. ^{I}*Ḫe-a-na*
5. ^{I}*Nam-zu-ú*
6. ^{I}*Di-ta-nu*
7. ^{I}*Zu-um-ma-bu*
8. ^{I}*Nam-ḫu-ú*
9. ^{I}*Am-na-nu*
10. ^{I}*Ya-aḫ-ru-rum*
11. ^{I}*Ip-ti-ya-mu-ta*
12. ^{I}*Bu-ḫa-zu-um*
13. ^{I}*Su-ma-li-ka*
14. ^{I}*Aš-ma-du*
15. ^{I}*A-bi-ya-mu-ta*
16. ^{I}*A-bi-di-ta-an*
17. ^{I}*Ma-am*(?)-x-[-x-x(?)]
18. ^{I}*Šu*-x-*ni*(?)-x[-x(?)]
19. ^{I}*Da-a*⸢*d*(?)⸣-x[-x-x(?)]
20. ^{I}*Su-m*[*u-a-bu-um*]

Reverse

21. ^{I}*Su-mu-la-*[*ìl*]
22. ^{I}*Za-bi-um*
23. ^{I}*A-píl-*^{d}*Sīn*
24. $^{I\,d}$*Sīn-mu-ba-lí-*[*iṭ*]
25. ^{I}*Ḫa-am-mu-ra-p*[*í*]
26. ^{I}*Sa-am-su-i-lu-n*[*a*]
27. ^{I}*A-bi-e-šu-*[*uḫ*]
28. ^{I}*Am-mi-di-ta-*[*na*]

29.	BAL ERÍN MAR.[TU]	Turn of the Amorite soldiers,
30.	BAL ERÍN *Ḫe-a-*[*na*]	Turn of the Ḫanean soldiers,
31.	BAL *Gu-ti-um*	Turn of the Gutians,
32.	BAL *ša i-na tup-pí an-ni-i*	Turn of (those) not recorded
	la ša-aṭ-ru	on this tablet
33.	*ù* AGA.UŠ *ša i-na*	and any soldier who
	da-an-na-at	*suffered injury*
	be-li-šu im-qú-tu	while on perilous campaigns
		for his lord,
34.	DUMU.MEŠ LUGAL	princes,
35.	DUMU.MÍ.MEŠ LUGAL	princesses,
36.	*a-wi-lu-tum ka-li-ši-in*	all 'persons'
37.	*iš-tu* ^{d}UTU.È.A	from East
	a-du(!) ^{d}UTU.ŠÚ.A	to West
38.	⸢*ša*⸣ *pa-qí-dam*	who have no one to care for them
	ù sa-ḫi-ra-am la i-šu-ú	or to be solicitous(?) to them,
39.	*al-ka-nim-ma an-ni-a-am*	come, eat this,
	a-⸢*ak*⸣*-la*	
40.	*an-ni-a-am* ⸢*ši-ti*⸣*-a*	drink this,
41.	*a-na Am-mi-ṣa-du-qá*	(and) bless Ammiṣaduqa
	DUMU *Am-mi-di-ta-na*	the son of Ammiditana,
42.	LUGAL KÁ.DINGIR.RA^{ki}	the king of Babylon
43.	*ku-ur-ba*	

The Genealogy of the Hammurapi Dynasty: A Rite of the Ancestor Cult or Coronation?

As An Ancestor Cult Ritual		As A Coronation Ceremony
	Lines 1–28	
Invocation of royal dead to attend (*kispum*) ancestor cult feast		*List of Heroic & Royal Ancestral Names* (to be commemorated by recitation)
	Lines 29–38	
Appearance of the dead		*Assembly and Procession* Call for the invitees to assemble in order to commemorate the dead
	Lines 29–31	
Appearance of ghosts of dead royalty listed in lines 1–28		Active military participate
	Lines 32–33	
Appearance of ghosts of unknown soldiers		Disabled military participate
	Lines 34–35	
Appearance of ghosts of dead nobility		Nobility participate
	Lines 36–38	
Appearance of slighted ghosts of the dead		The indigent participate
	Lines 39–40	
Call for royal dead to consume and imbibe		*Celebration & Sacrifice* by the living
	Lines 41–43	
Blessing of new king by the ghosts of the royal dead		*Acclamation of King with Blessings* by the living

tents."[152] In other words, the eponymous bearer of that name was viewed as a glorious military leader who was only subsequently identified in the tradition as a king or lugal.[153]

The remaining data related to the *Ditānu* name consist of several Amorite and Ugaritic personal names.[154] Although the exact significance of the name in these contexts remains obscure, its occurrence in personal names provides additional testimony for its notoriety. Whether or not it functions as a theophoric element in names like *su-mu-di-ta-na* that might comprise genitive compound names remains debatable. The evidence which we have surveyed indicates that divine properties of the name are lacking or, at best, are rare and enigmatic (cf. e.g., ME-^{d}*di-ta-an*).[155]

The legitimating function of the ritual underlying the GHD and the political importance of the *Ditānu* name provide crucial information for interpreting the roles assigned to the *qbṣ dt/dn*, the *rp'i 'arṣ*, and the *mlk(m)* at Ugarit as well as the function of the so-called royal funerary liturgy, *KTU* 1.161 (cf. 3.1.7.2.–3.1.9.). The name *dtn* is found in the compound *bn dtn* in 4.69:II:9, VI:29 and 4.422:52, in the para-mythological text 1.124:11,14, as *bpḫr qbṣ dtn // btk rp'i 'arṣ* in 1.15:III:2–3,14–15, as *ddn* in a damaged offering text *RIH* 78/11:1–2, and in 1.161. In the thirteenth century administrative list 4.69, the *bn dtn* represent one social class among many who receive the highest level of state payment for services rendered in the capacity of *mrynm*, "warriors," (cf. I:1 and II:9) and *khnm*, "priests," (cf. VI:22,29).[156] That the *bn dtn* are depicted as owners of great herds in 4.422 confirms their important social status.

---

[152] Cf. Kraus 1965:123–40, esp.126; Wilson 1977:86–114.

[153] An Old Babylonian votive text from Nippur(?) describes a foreigner who came to Babylonia to make offerings at its sanctuaries *[am-m]i-iš-ta-mar* [x *d*]*i-da-ni-um* [*ra-b*]*i-an* MAR.DÚ, "Ammishtamar, [the ruler of] the Didanum, [lead]er of the Amorites," cf. Fossey 1911:248–49; Stol 1976:87; Heltzer 1981:5 and n.33; Frayne 1990:810. The only known royal name for this period is Ammishtamru I of Ugarit, cf. Kitchen 1977:139 and Heltzer 1981:5–6 *contra* Frayne 1990:810. If correct, this text connects the Ugaritic dynasty, the *Ditānu* name, the Amorites, and, as we shall argue below, the *rp'u(m)* (= *rabûm*, "to be great," > *rabi'anu*, "leader, chief").

[154] Cf. Gelb 1980:295 and the syllabic cuneiform names in the Ras Shamra recension of ḪAR-*ra* = *ḫubullu* XX-XXII in Landsberger 1974:48(col.IV:20–22),50(lines 26–28): *am-mi-di-da-na*, *am-mi-di-da-na-ḫé-gal*, BÀD-*am-mi-di-da-na*^{ki}, ^{d}UTU-*di-da-na* and BÀD^{d}UTU-*di-da-na*^{ki}; in *RIH* 77/3(+24):6,11, recently published by Arnaud and Kennedy 1979:321: ^{d}*am-mi-di-t*[*a-na*] and ^{d}UTU-*di-d*[*a-na*].

[155] On the occurrence of divine names or theophoric elements in genitive compound names in Amorite, cf. Huffmon 1965:118–25.

[156] On the *mrynm* = *maryannu*, cf. Rainey 1965b:19–20; Reviv 1972:219–22 who conclude that the chariot was not the crucial factor making the *maryannu* an elite soldier class. Nevertheless, groups like the *bn dtn* who fulfilled the roles of *mrynm* and *khnm* no doubt comprised influential political forces at Ugarit.

In *KTU* 1.124, an individual named *dtn* and another entitled *'adn 'ilm rbm* (lines 1–2) engage in dialogue over the fate of a sick child.[157] The latter is generally identified as El or Baal "Lord of the Great Gods,"[158] but this creates the potential problem of El or Baal consulting a lesser class of being. Scholars have reversed the roles of *dtn* and the *'adn* in lines 1–4 in order to compensate for this apparent difficulty, but claims that this supposedly violates the clear syntax of the passage have also been voiced. On the one hand, Pardee, who published a recent collation of the text, identified *'adn* not as El or Baal, but as *yqr*, one of the kings mentioned in 1.113 (line 26′) and the deceased founder of the Ugaritic dynasty. Thus, *'ilm rbm* would not refer to the major gods of the pantheon, but to the divinized, deceased kings or "the many 'gods'."[159] On the other hand, Tropper has rendered *'adn 'ilm rbm* as "the (chief) incantation priest of the royal ancestors." He cited as support the *ba*^{ca}*lat-'ôḇ* of 1 Sam. 28:7 and understood 1.124 to reflect a royal necromantic ritual.[160]

Both proposals are based on the assumption that a royal ancestor cult can be documented at Ugarit, that necromancy was intimately connected with that cult, and that *'il* in 1.113 reflects a deified and dead Ugaritic king. We have argued that the *'il* element in 1.113 designates the personal dynastic god who was inherited by each successive king (cf. 3.1.6.). Therefore, the identities of *'adn* and *'ilm rbm* and the role of the *'adn* and *dtn* are open to alternative interpretations. With the dismissal of their status as deified, dead kings, the comparison of the *'ilm rbm* with the *ilānu rabûtu*, the determiners of fates in Enuma Elish, is greatly strengthened.[161] This in turn favors the view that *'adn* is El or Baal. However, neither of these gods would consult the *dtn* whom we have come to know through our analysis thus far, for *dtn* lacks the requisite prophylactic powers to warrant the petition of a major deity. Therefore, we see *dtn* consulting the *'adn* in lines 1–3, not vice versa.[162] In sum, 1.124 preserves a tradition in which *dtn* was viewed as an important mythic figure who played a subservient role to El or Baal in the

157 For helpful bibliographies and new editions of 1.124, cf. Dietrich and Loretz 1988:329–31; 1990a:205–40, esp. pp.205–07; Pardee 1988:179–180; Tropper 1989:151–56.

158 However, Dietrich and Loretz 1980a:395–96, followed by Spronk 1986:193–94, proposed Baal. Pope 1977a:179 was also reluctant to identify *'adn* as El.

159 Cf. Pardee 1983:127–40; 1988:179–92. Spronk 1986:194; Dietrich and Loretz 1988:330 have adopted Pardee's view of *'ilm rbm*. Cf. Pardee 1988:167 n.8,171 for a revision of the chronology of the Ugaritic kings as outlined by Kitchen 1977:131–42.

160 Tropper 1989:151–56; 1989:154 has adopted Pardee's view of *'ilm rbm*.

161 Notwithstanding their distinct roles, *contra* Pardee 1983:132–33; 1988:184–86. On the equation of the *'ilm rbm* and the *ilānu rabûtu*, cf. Mullen 1980:186 n.122. Tropper 1989:154 n.161 equated the *'ilm rbm* and the *ilū rabûtu* who represent the Anunnaki, but his proposal falters due to the assumption that an ancestor cult connection can be established for the *dtn* name and 1.124.

162 Astour 1975:281; Lipiński 1978:94; Caquot 1981:355; Pardee 1983:131; 1988:183 read line 4 as follows: *w y'ny nn dtn*, "Ditan answered him (= the Lord of the great/many gods)," and understood the line as expressive of *dtn*'s supernatural role in giving instructions to heal the sick

search for a remedy for the sick child (cf. *mṯpt* in lines 3,12). This concurs with the lack of reference otherwise to the name *dtn* as a supernaturally empowered, beneficent ghost in Ugaritic myth and ritual.[163]

We turn now to the legend of king Keret where the phrase *bpḫr qbṣ dtn* is found parallel to *btk rp'i 'arṣ* in 1.15:III:3–4,14–15. Keret has been promised the blessing of future progeny by El after having lost both his wife and his "scion," *špḥ*, // "heir," *yrṯ*, (1.14:I:24–25). He is then praised with the following words:

m'id rm krt	Be greatly exalted, Keret,
btk rp'i 'arṣ	among the *Rp'i 'Arṣ*,
bpḫr qbṣ dtn	in the assembly of
	the Gathered Ones of *Ditānu*[164]

These lines reveal a striking similarity to lines 2–3,9–10 of 1.161 (cf. 3.1.9.) and their significance likewise has been variously understood. They have been viewed as (1) depicting Keret's blessed afterlife with an esteemed place among the long-departed ancestors,[165] or (2) as expressive of Keret's power to overcome childlessness which is the same power that the ghosts of the dead were believed to possess in overcoming death. Thus, it can be said that he became one of them.[166] Parker has proposed that these lines refer to the ancestors as precedents for the blessing which Keret can expect in the next life.[167] Our findings thus far with regard to the existence of an ancestor cult at Ugarit would suggest that an alternative

---

child. Notwithstanding his remarks in 1983:128; 1988:180 ["the reading {'*dtn*'} is probable"], a glance at the photograph and handcopy in Pardee 1988:180–81 demonstrates that the supposed *dtn* reading is all but obliterated. My own examination of the tablet in the summer of 1994 revealed the total obliteration of letters with the possible exception of a single wedge that might represent the t, but the wedge might be only one that is part of a more complex sign. In any case, the reading *w y'ny nn dtn* in line 4 and in lines 13–14a might be translated with the *'adn* instructing *dtn*, with *dtn* in the vocative case, "then he (*'adn*) answered him, 'O' Ditanu, (You shall reply . . .)."

163 For the possible mention of *ddn* in connection with royal offerings, cf. the ritual text *RIH* 78/11:1–2. The reading and interpretation remain enigmatic for it is severely damaged: *d*]*bḥ m*[*l*]*kt*]*ddn š šrp*, "sacrifice [to/of?] the queen [by or to?] Ddn(?), a sheep wholly burnt . . . ," cf. Bordreuil and Caquot 1980:354–55; Xella 1981a:357–58.

164 The term *qbṣ* is the (plural) construct passive participle. *Contra* Lipiński 1978:97, the term is used in biblical Hebrew to denote the living far more often than the dead.

165 Levine and de Tarragon 1984:655.

166 Spronk 1986:189.

167 Parker 1989:87–98. In support, he cites several biblical passages in which a marriage blessing occurs and where the ancestors are referred to as models or precedents. Ruth 4:11b–12 is the closest in form because it too comprises a *royal* marriage blessing. In response, the much later biblical passages cannot take precedence over the internal evidence at Ugarit (see below), and as Parker also recognizes, the variability in form of what he identifies as the marriage blessing precludes forcing the elements of any one representative such as the Keret passage into a formalized generic pattern. His reinterpretation of *b-pḫr*, "in the assembly . . . ," and *btk*, "among . . . " as "in comparison with," is

approach to the interpretation of these lines be given serious consideration.[168] The previous lines record that subsequent to a dream theophany in which El promises Keret offspring, Keret was able to procure a son by leading a military campaign against the realm of Udm (cf. 1.14:III–1.15:I). Under threat of siege, its king, Pabil, offered Keret a new wife, Hurraya, who then gave birth to numerous offspring.

In the GHD and in *KTU* 1.161 (cf. 3.1.9.), the new king is the son of the recently deceased. It is my contention that, in both texts, the former king, his dynastic predecessors, and the heroic warriors of antiquity including the legendary *Ditānu* are all commemorated by the new king and others present. In 1.161:13–16 the new king also performs the additional rites of (burial and) mourning in honor of his recently deceased father. In other words, these texts are expressive of a king's concern to secure a son who would not only succeed him, but more importantly, see to it that the royal funeral as well as the royal commemorative rites were properly performed on his behalf and to maintain his memory after death.[169] The memory of the recently deceased king is upheld in 1.161 where the living *qbṣ ddn* and *rp'i 'arṣ* assemble to commemorate his name. It is this same royal aspiration that is explicitly expressed in Keret's hope to be exalted among the living *qbṣ dtn* and *rp'i 'arṣ*.

---

therefore rather strained (cf. p.90). Finally, he follows the consensus interpretation of the *rp'i 'arṣ* as dead rulers at Ugarit. The same criticisms can be leveled against Ford 1992:76.

[168] Cf. also the arguments of Van Seters 1983:201–02 against the view that the Keret legend preserves elements of an Ugaritic ancestor cult. Our interpretation only superficially resembles the proposal of de Moor 1976:324 wherein Keret's success in obtaining numerous offspring is recognized by a solemn meeting of the (living) chiefs of the tribe of *Ditānu*. Ford 1992:73-101 has most recently upheld the post-mortem status of the Ugaritic *rp'um*. His treatment however falters on several grounds. He overlooks the strongest arguments in favor of a living element, i.e., the mention of the *bn rp'yn* and *bn dt/dn* in the administrative texts. He over emphasizes the role of sacral kingship in the Keret legend and the large number of children Keret is supposedly awarded. While sacral kingship certainly has a major role in the legend, I have argued that in the immediate context of the mention of the *rp'i 'arṣ*, it is the military prowess that is underscored. As to the number of children Keret is awarded, the text repeatedly refers to the singular scion or heir Keret seeks. Elsewhere only two sons are mentioned in the text. The only exception is the exaltation of Keret in 1.15:II:23–24 where the poetic couplet alludes to seven, yea eight sons, but given the factors just mentioned this should be understood as hyperbole for emphasis on the certitude of the event. In any case, Ford's reliance on Brichto's conclusion that what one wished for in the next life was numerous children, must be reassessed. The citation from Gilgamesh XII (Ford 1992:75) nowhere mentions the care of the dead. The various concerns are those that the father enjoys while living. What one hoped for in the next life was a single heir who, out of filial piety, would care for the weakened dead. Finally, Keret's concern to obtain a son was the natural reaction of a military hero against whom the odds are mounting with every new campaign. The writer might have intended the reference to Keret's campaign against Udm as a closing admonition to the military hero in his twilight years whose resolve was in need of strengthening. The rewards of victory would ever increase in value.

[169] Sasson 1981a:96–98 suggests that we should expect to find the aspirations of the Ugaritic royalty expressed in the life of a paradigmatic hero like Keret.

This completes our survey of *Ditānu*. By Old Babylonian times, socio-religious importance was imputed to the name. In an isolated compound name, ME-^{d}*Di-ta-an,* it is closely associated with sacred powers although the exact nature of those connections remains obscure. While the GHD testifies to its incorporation into the royal cult as the name of an ancient hero worthy of commemoration, the name is not preceded by the divine determinative. In other words, *Ditānu* is not deified. Ugarit evinces a remarkable degree of continuity with these earlier traditions. *Dtn* maintained its prominence as a mythic hero tradition and the name was eventually awarded a prominent place in the cult. This was partially the result of its continued identity as the patron name of a politically influential living warrior nobility, the *bn dtn* and/or *qbṣ dtn*. Although the name was neither deified nor portrayed as a ghost with supernatural beneficent powers worthy of veneration or worship, it did serve as the recipient of commemorative rites. In sum, the *Ditānu* name was neither employed at Ugarit in a distinct Amorite royal version of the ancestor cult as the object of worship or veneration nor as the empowered ghost in necromantic ritual as some have suggested in the case of *KTU* 1.124.

3.1.7.2. The *rp'um* as Gods

Virolleaud understood the *rp'um* to be minor deities in the service of Baal. There were only seven or eight *rp'um* and *rp'u b'l*, "Baal the healer" or "Baal has healed," in 1.22:I:8, was their leader.[170] This understanding of *rp'u b'l* is not at all certain and a more fitting interpretation of this phrase is offered below (cf. 3.1.7.3.). Furthermore, Virolleaud wrongly concluded that the *rp'um* anointed Baal on the occasion of his enthronement. He based this on a mistaken translation of 1.22:II:14–18.[171] Needless to say, he has few, if any, followers today. The *rp'um* have been classified as gods also on the basis of the parallel *'ilnym* in the Shapash hymn 1.6:VI:46–47 (cf. also the damaged 1.21:II:3–4).[172] But in view of the more commonly occurring *'ilm*, "gods," in Ugaritic, the exact meaning of *'ilnym* has eluded scholars. Some have sought to clarify the term by citing the similar form *'lnm* in Phoenician and Punic wherein the affixed *n* is viewed as designating the numeric plural (> "gods").[173]

170 Virolleaud 1940:77–83.

171 Cf. L'Heureux 1979:116–19,171–74.

172 The additional references cited by Mullen 1980:261–62 all occur in lacunae.

173 Cf. Segert 1976:112 for the Punic and Phoenician forms. In *KAI* 117, a first century C.E. Latin-Punic bilingual inscription from El Amruni (Libya), line 1 of the Neo-Punic reads *l'l[n]' r'p'm '* . . . , "for the gods of the Rephaim . . . ," not *l'l[nm] 'r'p'm*, "for the deified Rephaim . . . ," according to Vattioni 1980–81:293–99 followed by Garbini 1986:13–14; cf. 4.1. (*'ln*, if that is in fact the correct

Nonetheless, the Phoenician-Punic evidence is much too late to be considered decisive. Besides, *'lnm* never occurs with the corresponding *-y-* infix. The Ugaritic term *'ilnym* is probably comprised of the divine term *'il* with a doubly hypocoristic expansion: *-ānu* plus *-iy-*, a *niṣbeh* formation "the godly ones(?)."[174] The most that can be safely asserted is that while *'ilnym* is probably related somehow to the concept of deity (< *'il*), its exact nuance remains perplexing.[175] The precariousness of equating the *rp'um* with the *'ilnym* is further illustrated by the argument in favor of chiastic structure in 1.6:VI:46–48 with *'ilnym* and *'ilm* parallel on the one hand, and *rp'im* and *mtm* on the other, rather than *rp'im* and *'ilnym* followed by *'ilm* and *mtm*, the order given in the text (cf. 3.1.7.3. for the relevant lines).[176] If the *mtm* were to be understood as "humanity" or "the warriors" as suggested by the context of the Baal myth, then the *rp'um* would not be related to the gods, but with living mortals or more specifically, heroic warriors (see below).

Others have cited as evidence for the divine status of the *rp'um*, the personal names from Ugarit in which *r-p-'* supposedly functions as a theophoric element designating the name of a deity, e.g., *abdi-rapi*, "the servant of Rapi'u."[177] The significance of the root in these cases is uncertain. It may function as an appellative (G ptc.) e.g., *abdi-rapi*, "the Servant heals."[178] Forms like *'ilrp'u*, "El heals," at Ugarit and ^{d}IM-*ra-pi*, "Addu/Baal heals," at Mari demonstrate that the *-rapi* element is not theophorous.[179] Finally, it should be pointed out that neither the *rp'um* nor, for that matter, the singular *rp'u* (assuming that the latter is a divine name or epithet of a deity) show up in the god lists or sacrificial lists at Ugarit. We would expect, at least on occasion, such major or minor deities which were originally ancestors to be represented in these and related lists. This is apparently the case with the corresponding *mlkm* and *mlk*, at least as viewed by the consensus of scholarship, but more on these will follow (cf. 3.1.8.).

---

reading, is generally recognized as a variant of *'ln*). The Latin reads *D*[*is*] *M*[*anibus*] *SAC*[*rum*]. In any case, this text is too late to directly impact our investigation.

174 L'Heureux 1974:268 n.14. Virolleaud 1940:83 took the term to be an adjective from *'lwn*, "oak tree," or a gentilic connected with Eylon mentioned in Josh. 19:43.

175 Previously, help was thought to be at hand in the couplet *'ilnym* and *'ilm* in 1.3:IV:34–35, but the reading *'ilm* is doubtful, *contra* Horwitz 1979:38. *KTU* reads ⌜x⌝*lm* not *'ilm* in 1.3:IV:34 (= *CTA* 3.IV:78).

176 Cf. Spronk 1986:162–63. Assuming that the *mtm* designated "the dead," he concluded, and we believe, wrongly, that the *rp'um* were to be related to both the gods and the dead.

177 Jirku 1965:82–83.

178 Cf. L'Heureux 1979:215–16. This is particularly the case if the root has the alternative meaning "to be strong," so Brown 1985:170–73, rather than the assumed "to heal, make whole." Cf. 3.1.7.5.

179 Huffmon 1965:264.

3.1.7.3. The Dead *rp'um* and the Goddess Shapash

In spite of its current popularity, the view that the *rp'um* comprise the shades of the dead also has its difficulties. Prior to the publication of 1.161, this view was based on the Hebrew and Phoenician data, the connection of the *rp'um* and the supposed mortuary related *marzēaḥ*,[180] and the equation of the *rp'um* with the *mtm*, the latter being interpreted as "the dead ones" in the Shapash hymn 1.6:VI:46,48. It is generally assumed that the sun goddess functions in the Shapash hymn as *psychopomp*, transporter of the dead to and from their netherly abode.[181]

In any case, the Hebrew and Phoenician evidence is much later and should not take precedent over the internal evidence from Ugarit in interpreting a much earlier, and perhaps distinct, tradition as we have there (see below). Moreover, we rejected above any inherent mortuary associations of the Ugaritic *marzēaḥ* as well as the supposed connection of the *rp'um* and the *marzēaḥ* (cf. 3.1.5.). Finally, Shapash's netherworld connections, and thereby those of the *rp'um*, cannot be substantiated on the basis of the Shapash hymn or, for that matter, the Baal-Mot texts 1.6:I-VI more generally. In 1.6:I:7–8, Shapash is depicted as having *yrd b'arṣ*, "descended to the *'arṣ*," where she met the goddess Anat. It was here that Anat recovers what remained of Baal after Mot ruthlessly smote him. According to 1.5:VI:29–30, this region was located at the *dbr*, "outback," or *šd šḥl mmt*, "steppe by the shore/stream of the realm of death."[182] In 1.6:I:16–18, Shapash lifts Baal's corpse on to Anat's shoulder whereupon Anat carries him to mount Zaphon for burial.

It appears that the outback or steppe was not the netherworld, for had Baal been killed by Mot in the netherworld, Anat's retrieval and burial of Baal would have been superfluous.[183] Rather, this region was located at *ǵṣr 'arṣ*, "the edge of (inhabitable) earth," or *ksm mhl'iyt*, "the edge of the water regions," according to 1.4:VIII:4; 1.5:VI:4–5; 1.16:III:3–4.[184] Like the steppe in Mesopotamian

---

180 Cf. esp. Pope 1972:170–203.

181 So Caquot 1959:90–101.

182 Cf. de Moor 1971:183,186 and Clifford 1972:83–84 for these renderings of *dbr* and *šd šḥl mmt*. For *dbr*, cf. Hebrew *dōḇer*, "steppe, outback." For *šd*, cf. Hebrew *śāḏeh*. For *šḥl*, cf. Arabic *sāḥil*, "shore," or Syriac *šāḥlā*, "stream," (both assume a contiguous body of water). The term *mmt* is a local formation.

183 So Gibson 1978:74 n.4; L'Heureux 1979:195–96; M. Smith 1985:311–14. Margalit 1980b: 155–57 recognized this incongruity in the scene, but upheld Shapash's role as *psychopomp* and rearranged the order of the texts.

184 We equate El's mountain *hr 'il* (1.4:II:36 and cf. *ǵr ll* = *p'n 'il* via *pḫr m'd* in 1.2:I:20,30) and the mountain at whose base was located the netherworld entrance *ǵr trǵzz* // *ǵr ṯrmg* // *tlm* (1.4:VIII:2–4). Thus, the stream/shore by the realm of death makes up part of the *nhrm*, "two rivers," and *thmtm*, "two seas," where El's mount was located (1.4:IV:21–22; 1.6:I:33–34; 1.17:VI:47–48). These waters

cosmography, it was situated at the edge of both earth and underworld.[185] To be sure, in 1.6:I:17–18, Baal did descend to the netherworld from atop mount Zaphon through *ḫrt 'ilm 'arṣ*, "the hole of the chthonic gods," but only subsequent to receiving the proper funerary rites as administered by Anat.[186] But the point to be underscored is that Shapash is not portrayed in these lines as having descended to the netherworld.

Our conclusion finds its analogy in a thesis similarly concerned with the netherworldly relations of the Babylonian sun god Shamash. Heimpel has argued that Shamash remained at all times in the heaven and never passed into the netherworld. In contexts where it was previously assumed that Shamash was located in the infernal world, it is more in keeping with the data as a whole to view Shamash as located in heaven's interior whence he concerns himself with the matters of the dead and whence his radiance penetrates the netherworld.[187] This reconstruction provides the fitting background for understanding the recently published description of Shamash in a Neo-Babylonian necromantic ritual, "O Shamash, the judge, you bring those up from above down below, those from below up to above."[188] In another related text, it is probably Shamash who is petitioned to bring up a ghost from the netherworld.[189] In other words, neither text necessarily assumes Shamash's presence in the netherworld, only the exercise of his power and influence to bring up the dead from there.

The Ugaritic goddess Shapash is mentioned thrice more in *KTU* 1.6, but in none of these instances is she located in the netherworld: 1.6:II:24–25; III:24–IV:1; and VI:22–29.[190] In the last, she delivers El's verdict from mount Zaphon in favor of Baal over Mot. It is this passage, in particular, that provides the linchpin for

---

separate earth and netherworld and represent the West Asiatic approximation of the *apsû*, cf. Lambert 1985b:451; 1985a:537.

185 For the Mesopotamian conception, cf. Bottéro 1980:31–32; 1982:376; 1983:190,192.

186 In 1.19:III:6,20–21,41, *ḫrt 'ilm 'arṣ*, "the hole of the chthonic gods," is that place wherein Danil would place Aqhat once he found his remains and performed the customary mourning rites.

187 Heimpel 1986:127–51. On the significance of the sun deity's light reaching to the netherworld and retrieving the dead, cf. 3.1.9.2.

188 Cf. Finkel 1983–84:11 [Text *K* 2779:13b-14a]: ^{d}UTU DI.KU$_5$ *ša e-la-a-ti ana šap-la-a-ti ša šap-la-a-ti ana e-la-a-ti túb-bal*. *Contra* Finkel, the verb *abālu* can be rendered "to bring" rather than "to carry" when it takes the ventive, cf. *CAD* 1(1964):14 and Scurlock 1988:328. This text adapts namburbi-type phraseology to induce a ghost rather than the namburbi's typical function to avert the evil resulting from contact with a maligning ghost, cf. Finkel 1983–84:7.

189 Against Scurlock 1988:322–23 and with Finkel 1983–84:9. The text reads: GIDIM *e-ṭú*^{l}*-ti li-š[e-l]a-an-ni*, "May he bring up a ghost from the darkness for me," [Text *BM* 36703:ii:3]. The verbal form is the Š causative of *elû* with *lū*-precative prefix. In the handful of Mesopotamian necromantic texts published by Finkel, various gods participate in the rites and Shamash plays a central role. Shamash is repeatedly invoked and is offered gifts on altars dedicated to his cult.. Moreover, the previous text portrays his role as raiser of the dead. For the role of the sun god as raiser of the dead in necromancy, cf. also the depiction of Helios in Betz 1992:72–73 [*PGM* IV.1928–2005].

190 *Contra* Caquot 1959:90–101, esp. 93–98.

interpreting the Shapash hymn within the context of 1.6:I-VI. By delivering her verdict in the final struggle between Baal and Mot, Shapash displays her role as judge of the gods. When this is viewed in the light of 1.6 more generally, her role as judge of humankind also comes to the fore. Repeatedly in 1.6, Mot threatens to devour mankind (II:17b–19a and V:24–25), but by her judgment against Mot, Shapash ultimately thwarts his evil scheme thereby saving all of humanity along with Baal. These two aspects of the sun deity's role as judge conform with what we know of Shamash's function in Mesopotamia.[191] In fact, Shapash's epithet, *nrt 'ilm*, "Illuminator of the gods," found repeatedly in 1.6 (I:8–9,13; II:24; IV:8,17) has its parallel in an epithet of Shamash, *nūr ilāni*. This epithet is generally taken as a reference to Shapash's wise judgment.[192]

Assuming that the closing hymn should possess a significant degree of continuity with the larger myth, we should point out that the preceding contexts nowhere present humanity as dead. Rather, humankind is only threatened with an annihilation that is never actualized.[193] Moreover, having found no unequivocal evidence in the myth or elsewhere in the Ugaritic texts that Shapash journeyed to the netherworld, there is no reason to view *mtm* in 1.6:VI as "the dead (ones)" as is so often the case.[194] As previously noted, Shapash fixes the fate of those dwelling in the divine realm and those in the earthly realm by limiting the power of Mot. Her judgments are universal, effectual for both gods and men. This fact offers the most likely context for understanding the elements of the concluding hymn. The term *mtm* refers to "humanity" or, perhaps, "warriors," hence the corresponding merism, *'ilm* or "gods" and *mtm* or "men."[195] This in turn supports the view that these lines in the Shapash hymn comprise a chiastic structure in which the *rp'um* are to be associated with the *mtm*, "men" or "warriors," and the *'ilnym* with the *'ilm* or "gods."

---

[191] See e.g., Frymer-Kensky 1987:162–63.

[192] Cf. e.g., Healey 1980a:239.

[193] Cf. Healey 1977a:94,184,196, but in line with his view of the *rp'um* as shades of the royal dead, Healey considered the hymn to be a later addition to the myth and concluded that these lines portray a democratization of the dead *rp'um* at Ugarit.

[194] Cf. now Dietrich and Loretz 1990b:57–65. The view of M. Smith 1984:377–80; Dijkstra 1985:147–52 that Kothar-wa-Ḫasis in 1.6:VI:49b–53 is spell-caster and knower (of ghosts) wrongly assumes a netherly background for the hymn. In lines 49b–50, Kothar-wa-Ḫasis functions as Shapash's weapons' maker. In 1.2:IV:7–16, he fashions clubs for Baal in the course of his battle with Yamm. Philo of Byblos records the tradition that Chousor was one of two brothers who discovered iron, how to work it, and thereby invented the hook, lure, line, and raft, cf. Eusebius *Preparatio Evangelica* 1.10.11 and the translation of Attridge and Oden 1981:45–79.

[195] The form *mtm* occurs in parallel to *ǵzrm* in 1.22:I:6. It is usually rendered "the dead" as in 1.6:VI:48, but in light of the parallel terms in both contexts, it more likely represents "men, heroes, warriors," cf. del Olmo Lete 1981:585 and 1.3:I:13 *mt šmm*, "men of the heavens." The Akkadian cognate *mutu* can denote a warrior, cf. *CAD* 10(1977):316.

The remaining interpretative problem in the hymn is the form *tḥtk* in lines 45b–47.[196] Some interpreters view it as the preposition *tḥt* with the suffix and understand the passage to convey the notion that Shapash is located in the netherworld along with the *rp'um* and *'ilnym*, "Shapash the *rp'um* are under you // Shapash the *'ilnym* are under you."[197] Others have suggested a prefixed verbal form of *ḥtk*, "Shapash, you rule the *rp'um* // Shapash, you rule the *'ilnym.*"[198] While the latter rendition can be made to conform with our understanding of the passage, it too is generally taken to refer to Shapash as judge of the dead *rp'um* and *'ilnym*. Based on our previous arguments, either proposal would suffice but with the qualification that a figurative meaning is meant, namely that Shapash has authority over these groups not that she is necessarily located in the netherworld (or that they are located there).

In 1.22:I:8–9, *mhr b'l*, "the warriors of Baal," and *mhr 'nt*, "the warriors of Anat," are depicted alongside *rp'u b'l*, "the *rp'u* of Baal."[199] They are also associated with the *ǵzrm*, "heroes," of line 7. Finally, in 1.20:II:3–4, the *rp'um* are depicted as harnessing their horses and mounting chariots. These passages strongly suggest that not only did major deities gather about them others of lesser status such as (mythic) warriors, but that included among these warriors were the *rp'um*. The *rp'um* along with others probably assisted Baal in his two engagements with Mot's company outside the netherworld, both at the steppe separating earth and netherworld and on mount Zaphon, the location of the final battle. Likewise, Shapash's retinue might have accompanied her to the steppe and to mount Zaphon where she confronted, or, in the case of the former, might have confronted, Mot and his cohorts. This could adequately explain the mention of the *rp'um* in the closing lines of the Baal-Mot myth without having to assume that the *rp'um*, or for that matter, the *mtm*, are netherworld shades.

The couplet *'rb špš // ṣb'i'a špš* in *'rb špš lymǵ krt // ṣb'i'a špš b'lny* in 1.15:V:18–19 (cf. 1.19:IV:47–49) is often cited in support of the netherworld journey of Shapash, and by implication, the defunct nature of those who comprise

---

[196] For a convenient survey of opinions, cf. Lewis 1989:36 n.155.

[197] It can no longer be assumed that the term *rp'im* represents a noun in the oblique case as the *aleph* may be syllable closing, i.e., *rapi'ūma*, cf. the works of Verreet 1983:223–58; 1984:307–21; 1985:324–30.

[198] For *ḥtk* with a juridical force, see Cross 1968:44–45 n.24 against Healey 1980b:408–09. The proposed derivation of del Olmo Lete 1983:171 *nḥt*, "to descend," against Margalit 1980b:197–99 Akkadian *taḫu* III, "juxtapose," assumes a netherworld descent.

[199] De Moor 1976:323–45 assumed that in 1.20–1.22, the *rp'um* were shades of the dead. The texts are sufficiently damaged so as to render such a conclusion tentative at best. His student Spronk 1986:165–77 maintained this view on the basis of 1.6:VI:45–49! For a view of 1.20–1.22 different from that of de Moor or Spronk, cf. del Olmo Lete 1981:404–24 and the bibliography cited there. de Moor 1976:325–29; Healey 1977a:177–80 viewed *rp'u b'l* as an epithet of Baal "Baal Rapi'u," but the immediate context, in particular, the parallel *mhr b'l* and *mhr 'nt*, militates against this.

her entourage.[200] To be sure, when seen in the light of 1.16:I:36–37 and II:24–26, the couplet unfolds as an announcement of the death of Keret "the setting of Shapash, Keret will meet, the host of Shapash, our lord." But this in no way necessitates Shapash's netherworld descent. Following Heimpel's Babylonian model, the western door of heaven is the destination of such a journey. From there the sun goddess and her host enter heaven's interior while the newly departed journey along those pathways leading to the netherworld such as the *ḫrt 'ilm 'arṣ*, "the hole of the chthonic gods."[201]

In sum, the *rp'um* of the mythological texts are nowhere portrayed as the shades of the dead.[202] This is crucial to understanding the mention of the *rp'um* in 1.161 (cf. 3.1.9.). While the exact significance of *'ilnym* remains elusive, the identification of the *rp'um* as heroic warriors is secure. With this background in mind, the relevant lines of the Shapash hymn take on the following significance:[203]

špš rp'im tḥtk	A	Shapash, the *rp'u*-warriors are under you,
špš tḥtk 'ilnym	B	Shapash, the *'ilnym* divinities are under you;
'dk 'ilm	B′	Your witnesses are the gods,
hn mtm 'dk	A′	Behold, humans are your witnesses.

3.1.7.4. The Living *rp'um*

Several writers have argued for the presence of living historical *rp'um* at Ugarit. Gray concluded that the *rp'um* in 1.20–1.22 were human agents or cult functionaries who accompanied the king on his visits to the threshing floors or *grnt* and plantations or *mṭ't* in order to promote fertility (cf. 1.20:II:6–7).[204] According to Ryan, the *rp'um* constituted living chariot warriors similar to the *mrynm* or

200 Cf. now Dietrich and Loretz 1990c:75–77.

201 Following Heimpel 1986:148–50; cf. similarly del Olmo Lete 1981:308.

202 The form *rp'i yqr* in *RIH* 77/8a+13+21B:14′ (= *RIH* 77/21:14) does not support the chthonic nature of the *rp'um*, cf. Levine and de Tarragon 1984:656 against Bordreuil and Caquot 1979:301–03; Bordreuil 1981:46; de Moor 1981–82:119 and n.55. In view of the text's fragmentary nature, *yqr* may simply be an epithet like the parallel *n'm* in line 15′, rather than the name of the deceased founder of the Ugaritic dynasty, and the parallel *šd qdš* of line 13′ may be "the field of the temple," not "the holy *šēdu* ghost."

203 The above reconstruction allows for the possibility that Resheph was Shapash's underworld gatekeeper, cf. *špš ṯǵrh ršp*, "Shapash, her gatekeeper is Resheph," in *KTU* 1.78:34 and in 2.1.5., in spite of Shapash's absence in the Eblaite evidence cited there. Of course, Resheph might be keeper of those gates to heaven's interior that lead to the netherworld as we argued previously.

204 Gray 1949:127–39; 1952:39–41.

maryannu.[205] Aistleitner viewed those *rpu'm* in 1.15:III as human princes.[206] For Healey, the *rp'um* originally constituted an early Amorite tribe related to *Ditānu*, remnants of which may have persisted at Ugarit (where they also later came to designate the dead in general).[207] Along similar lines, Heltzer understood the *rp'um* of 1.15:III to encompass a Sutean sub-tribe known as the Rabba'um attested at Mari (although he recognized their status as shades in other texts).[208]

The basic weakness inherent in each of these proposals is the underlying assumption that the data from the mythological texts provides a reliable source for reconstructing historical elements, for none of these authors cite references to the *rp'um* in the non-literary texts from Ugarit.[209] The only proposal known to this writer which employs data from the non-literary texts is that of S. H. Margulies (*sic*?) as noted by Sperling. He suggests that the *bn rp'iyn* (*sic rp'iym*) in 4.232:8 were a guild under the patronage of the divine *rp'um*. As intriguing as this datum is, Sperling unfortunately neither cites his Margulies source nor offers a statement on Margulies' view of the identity or social function of the *bn rp'iyn*. Beyond the fact that they received payment from the royal treasury and that their name derives from a root *r-p-'*, Sperling offers little else.[210]

The data from 4.232 when considered alongside the general framework of Heltzer's thesis might provide the kind of historical confirmation needed to identify a living element among the Ugaritic *rp'um*. Heltzer concluded that the *rp'um*, or more precisely, the *rp'i 'arṣ*, were the Rabbeans, a West Asiatic tribe attested at Mari. This points to the plausible identity of the *bn rp'iyn* as a Rabbean tribe, rather than a guild. As provocative as Heltzer's specific thesis is, it presents serious problems on several counts. First, we lack independent confirmation,

205 Ryan 1954:110–12; similarly Margulis 1970:292–304; Sperling 1971:79; L'Heureux 1974: 265–74; 1979:201–23; Loewenstamm 1976:403–07; Healey 1989:33–44 for a review of scholarship on the identity of the *rp'um*/Rephaim since Ryan. On the relation of the *maryannu* and the chariot, cf. Rainey 1965b:19–20; Reviv 1972:218–28, esp. pp.119–22.

206 Aistleitner 1967:295. Cf. also Sauer 1966:1590–91; Mendenhall 1973:160.

207 Healey 1977a:195.

208 Heltzer 1978:5–20; cf. Heltzer 1981; Margalit 1981:151–58. Ginsberg 1946:23,41 labeled the *rp'u(m)* in 1.15:III as "humans," but offered no further elaboration. Ford 1992:73 cites as the reasoning for the identification of the *rp'um* as living beings, the inappropriateness which the presence of the dead would have presented in the situation described in the Keret legend, a wedding ceremony. This is somewhat of a straw man since signficantly more convincing arguments have been put forward by scholars in support of the living *rp'um* at Ugarit (see below).

209 Cf. the apposite remarks by Sasson 1981a:81–98 regarding the limitations of this general approach. He underscored the need for confirming data from the non-literary texts. Rainey 1974:188; Pardee 1981–82:266–67; Pope 1983:67–69 set forth similar arguments against the living *rp'um*.

210 Cf. Sperling 1971:79. The affixed *-iy-* and *-n* on *rp'* could conceivably comprise a doubly hypocoristic expansion, the former being the common *niṣbeh* formation, thus, "the ones of *rp'u*" (= *rp'um*!). For examples of similarly constructed names in Ugaritic, cf. Gordon 1965:63; Segert 1984:43.

whether from the non-literary texts or otherwise, that the Rabbean tribes were known at Ugarit. Furthermore, his etymological argument falters in that a more suitable etymology for Rabbean is to be found in *r-b-y* or *r-b-b*, and not in *r-b-' = r-p-'* as the spelling *Rabbayu* in *ARMT* 1:6:9 demonstrates.[211] Furthermore, Heltzer assumes an early date for the mythological texts (and/or their traditions) in order to locate the Rabbeans at Ugarit in the first centuries of the second millennium, but the dating of these texts remains enigmatic.[212] He also presumes that the Suteans, of which the Rabbeans supposedly comprise a subgroup, are mentioned in the Ugaritic texts, so that one would expect them to show up there as well. However, the supposed Sutean references in the Ugaritic texts involving the term *št* are minuscule and consequently, interpretations of *št* abound.[213]

3.1.7.5. The *rp'um*: Mythic Heroes and Earthly Warriors

In what follows, we offer an alternative paradigm for the characterization of the Ugaritic *rp'um*. The fact that the independent *Ditānu/dtn* and *rpu'm* traditions meet in 1.15:III and later again in 1.161 and that they both possess heroic warrior dimensions justifies the proposal that the former might provide an apt comparison for reconstructing a tradition history of the *rp'um*. Other considerations support this as well. The economic texts from Ugarit inform us that the *bn dtn* were employed by Ugarit as elite warriors or *mrynm* (4.69:I:1, II:9). Likewise, Ugarit employed the *bn rp'iyn* alongside the *mrynm* (4.232:8,33). All of these groups received payment from the royal treasury for services rendered.

Prior to the accession of Ammurapi, Ugarit's last king, Hittite hegemony in the region had all but eclipsed. Ugarit found itself in need of strengthening its defenses as well as its resolve. This need was only heightened as news of the invading sea peoples reached Ugarit. These factors might explain the establishment of such warrior contingents as the *bn dtn* and *bn rp'iyn*, soldiers or mercenaries alongside the *mrynm*. In the light of these factors and the warrior-like character of their mythic counterparts, the *rp'um*, we tentatively propose that the *bn rp'iyn* and the

---

[211] Cf. e.g., Albright 1968:94 n.140; Lipiński 1978:96 n.30.

[212] Cf. e.g., Sasson 1981a:86–87 and n.12, n.13.

[213] Cf. Margalit 1976:181–88; 1981:131–58, who proposed the references to the Suteans. He lists other renderings in 1976:181–83 as does del Olmo Lete 1981:633–34 (*št* I-V). The phrase *mhr št* appears only once with certainty in 1.18:IV:27. Whether or not the phrase refers to a "warrior of Sutū" (= a Sutean), awaits confirmation, but cf. now Margalit 1989:337–39.

bn dtn comprised contingents of living warriors in the service of the royal court at Ugarit.[214]

On the analogy of the *Ditānu* traditions surveyed in 3.1.7.1., we would tentatively suggest that, like *dtn* in 1.124, *rp'u* of 1.108 came to designate a legendary hero. This figure in turn served as the eponym for the band of living warriors, the *bn rp'iyn*. As a result of military engagements, dead from among these detachments inevitably increased. Having organized themselves in response to Ugarit's call, many warriors from the *bn rp'iyn* (and *bn dtn*) fell in battle. These realities eventually led to the *rp'um* concept taking on a specifically postmortem dimension as expressed exclusively in the epithet *rp'im qdmym*, "the ancient Rephaim," in 1.161.[215] So what was originally an historical reality and a mythical heroic concept, with a significant increase in war dead at a crucial moment in Ugarit's history, became affiliated with the underworld. This transformation also finds an analogue in the role which the *Ditānu* name plays in the GHD. Although the circumstances and contributing factors are irrecoverable, *Ditānu* in the GHD clearly represents a deceased legendary hero. However, in no case were these various names at Ugarit or in the GHD endowed with supernatural benefic powers. *Ditānu* was merely commemorated and the *rp'im qdmym* at Ugarit were likewise commemorated or, as weak shades, called to attention in the netherworld to prepare for the arrival of the recently deceased king down below (cf. 3.1.9.).

1.15:III points to additional motivations for the specific inclusion of the *rp'i 'arṣ* and *qbṣ ddn* in the ritual underlying 1.161. The son's loyalty to his father compelled the new king to perform the expected commemorative rites by means of which his father's name would be eulogized within the ranks of the living warrior-nobility, the *rp'i 'arṣ* and *qbṣ dtn*.[216] If the aspirations of the Ugaritic kings were indeed expressed in the life of a paradigmatic hero like Keret, then as death approached, the realization of that royal hope was the charge of the successor-son. This is clearly the focus of the ritual reflected in 1.161 which originates in the royal cult. It demonstrates a clear dependency upon the tradition reflected in 1.15:III of the Keret legend. 1.161 records mourning rites in honor of Niqmaddu III, the former king. The *rp'i 'arṣ* and the *qbṣ ddn* play central roles in these rites, for not only is Niqmaddu's death ritually mourned by his son, but Ammurapi eulogizes his father's name in the presence of the living *rp'i 'arṣ* and the *qbṣ ddn* (see below).

---

[214] Cf. also *bn ddn* as read in Yon 1991:140–41 for *KTU* 4.760:5. Unlike the case with the term *dtn*, a god related to *rp'*, namely *rp'u*, might be attested in the para-mythological texts at Ugarit. For the existence of the deity *rp'u*, cf. 1.108:1; 3.1.9.; de Moor 1976:328–29.

[215] Cf. also L'Heureux 1979:189,204.

[216] Concerning this type of educational and political role which such literary traditions as the Keret legend fulfilled in Ugaritic society, cf. Sasson 1981a:96–98.

The repeated occurrence of *rp'um* in military and heroic contexts and the inadequacy of alternative hypotheses reopens the question of the significance of Ugaritic *r-p-'*. As noted by several writers, the Ugaritic *rp'um* are nowhere described as "healers" or "healed ones," "gathered ones" or "fertilizers,"[217] nor is the figure *rp'u* to be identified as El or Baal, both of whom have been considered healer deities, nor as Mot, Molek, or Resheph.[218] Perhaps, it has an associated semantic and etymological cognate in Akkadian *rabā'um*, "to be large, great," and its derivative, *rabium* (< *rabûm*), "leader, chief."[219] Thus, the *rp'um* would be "the Great Ones" or "the Mighty Ones."[220] Aistleitner had proposed Akkadian *rubûm, ruba'um*, "prince," as cognate to Ugaritic *r-p-'*.[221] However, this might unnecessarily impute an inherent regality to the *rp'um*. Our survey indicated that the *rp'um* were portrayed as a military contingent lacking any inherent royal associations. Royalty only became attached to the name and tradition secondarily. The non-royal nature of the *rp'um* stands in spite of the depiction of the ruler Danil as a *mt rp'i* for he was renowned for his accomplishments as a warrior hero or *ǵzr*. Besides, his supposed royal status has been called into question.[222] The same applies in the case of king Keret. This mythic prototype of regality yearned to

[217] Cf. Burns 1970:172; Loewenstamm 1976:406 "there is not in any text a clear reference to an act of healing [*rᵊpû'â*], be it healing the sick, reviving the dead, or restoring fertility to man or earth;" 1980:320 n.1 "the Ugaritic root *r-p-'* is nowhere attested in the unequivocal sense of 'to heal';" cf. esp. Brown 1985:115–30,146–47 against these alternatives.

[218] L'Heureux 1979:169–72,212–15 suggested El; de Moor 1969:176, followed recently by Spronk 1986:180–81, proposed Baal; Parker 1972:104 noted the possibility of Mot (but rejected it); Pope 1977a:169–72,181–82 advanced Molek; Cooper 1987a:1–7 offered Resheph. Parker 1972:97–104 has ably defended *rp'u*'s independent status. Caquot and Sznycer 1980:19 viewed *rp'u* as the personification of the *rp'um*.

[219] Cf. *AHw* 3(1980):936,938; Stol 1976:73–89. Others offered "to heal," thus, the *rp'um* are the "healers," so Gröndahl 1967:180 and especially de Moor 1976:324–26; or the "healed ones," so L'Heureux 1979:215–18; Good 1980:40; still others "to fertilize," thus, "the fertilizers," so Gray 1949:127–39; 1952:40; 1965:146 and n.5; Jacob 1960:58–59; Tromp 1969:176–80; Pope 1977a:167; Lipiński 1978:95; and finally others "to gather," so Ginsberg 1946:41; Driver 1956:155. Ugaritic *r-p-'* eliminates the alternative Hebrew root *r-b-h/y*, "to sink down," most recently advocated by White 1980:858. For a recent criticism of these views, see Margalit 1989:253 and n.6.

[220] Cf. also Loewenstamm 1976:406. This would result in two Northwest Semitic roots, *r-p-'* I, "to heal," found, for example, in Hebrew, and *r-p-'* II, "to be great, numerous." This has been independently endorsed by Brown 1985:115–48,160–73.

[221] Aistleitner 1967:295; cf. Sauer 1966:1590–91. Mendenhall 1973:160 who posited "an archaic north Syrian root *r-p-'* meaning 'lord'." The same might be assumed for *r-p-'*, "to be large, great," and would explain the consistent presence of the *p* in later West Semitic languages.

[222] Cf. Dressler 1976:152–53 for a critique of Danil's status as king. The meaning of *mt hrnmy* which, like *ǵzr*, frequently parallels *mt rp'i*, has eluded scholars. The suffixed *-y* has been viewed as a gentilic ending resulting in numerous proposals: Hermel (Egyptian *hrnm* near Kadesh on the Orontes), Albright 1953:26–27; Hinnom (as entrance to the netherworld), Pope 1977a:166; a location on the eastern shore of the Kinnereth Sea, Barton 1941:213–25; or between the Kinnereth and Hermon, Margalit 1981:149–50. Cf. Astour 1975:283–84; Margalit 1989:251–60 for summaries of these and other views.

beget a son who would in turn perform those funeral rites fit for a great warrior. At his death, he fancied being memorialized within the ranks of the living warrior contingents, the *rp'i 'arṣ* and *qbṣ dtn*. Keret could expect this honor, for we know that, on at least one legendary occasion, he led his great army in victorious battle against a foreign ruler, Pabil of Udm.

That an Ugaritic king might obtain an intimate association with the militarily significant *Ditānu* and *rp'um* names finds support in the mention of two titles given to one Ammishtamar in the Old Babylonian votive text mentioned in 3.1.7.1. This individual has been identified as Ammishtamru I of Ugarit who is proclaimed the ruler of the *Didānum* and leader, or [*rabi*(')]*ānum*, of the Amorites. The connection between the Ugaritic king, the *Ditānu* warriors, and the *rp'um* is explicit, that is, if the term *rabi*[']*ānu* or "leader" from *rabûm* is to be related to Ugaritic *r-p-'*. If so, this datum directly joins the living *rp'um* traditions and the Amorites, thereby suggesting an additional element they both share in turn with the *Ditānu* traditions.[223]

3.1.8. The Ugaritic *mlk*(*m*)

The Ugaritic *mlkm,* along with the *malikū* from Mari and the later Canaanite-Israelite *mᵊlāḵîm* have been taken to represent dead kings who were venerated or worshipped in the royal ancestor cult.[224] In other words, the *mlkm* are to be equated with or compared to the *rp'um*. One must now also consider the *imlikū* attested at Emar, the divine warriors and guardians of the entrances to Nergal's infernal city.[225] Arguments in support of a chthonic aspect of the Ugaritic form *mlkm*, the supposed pluralization of the singular *mlk*, are often derived directly or indirectly from the supposed chthonic character of *mlk*. The form *mlk* has been interpreted as the chthonic deity Malik or as a reference to the deceased Ugaritic king. The plural form *mlkm* shows up in two alphabetic god lists at Ugarit, *KTU* 1.47:11 and 1.118:32, while a parallel god list *RS* 20.24:32 records the corresponding Akkadian term ᵈ*ma-lik*ᵐᵉš. The plural form *mlkm* is also attested in the recently published omen text *RIH* 78/14:4′ and in a so-called Rephaim text 1.22:I:16–17. Besides the five occurrences of the singular form *mlk* in 1.161:11–12,15,25–26, the form *mlk 'ṯtrh* is attested in 1.100:41, the form *mlk b'ṯtrt* in 1.107:17, and the phrase *rp'u mlk 'lm . . . 'il yṯb b'ṯtrt 'il ṯpṭ b hd r'y* in 1.108:1–3a. The related

---

223 Admittedly, the text is rather damaged, therefore, any conclusion drawn on the basis of these titles is tentative at best.

224 See most recently Heider 1985:102–147,383–408.

225 So Arnaud 1985:235.

singular Akkadian form ^{d}*ma-lik* shows up in *RS* 20.121:81 (for additional citations, see below).

We will first survey the supposed chthonic associations of the singular form *mlk*. The mention of *mlk* in the serpent incantations, 1.100:41 and 1.107:17, has been cited as proof for the existence of an Ugaritic deity Malik (for the phraseology, see above).[226] While this is most likely the case, the posited netherly character of this deity at Ugarit is doubtful.[227] The basis for the netherly character of Malik lies in the supposed equation of *mlk* with one or more of the better known Ugaritic gods allied to the netherworld, e.g., Baal, Resheph, Mot, or *Rp'u* (Rapi'u).[228] We shall treat each of these proposals shortly. Others cite, in this regard, the chthonic affiliations advanced on behalf of the locale, Ashtaroth, or *'ṯtrt*, in 1.100:41 and 1.107:17 as well as the parallel Edrei or *hd r'y* in 1.108:3. The correlation with Baal is based on the assumption that *Rp'u* is the chthonic aspect of Baal and so *Rp'u* is to be equated with *mlk*.[229] The circularity in argument is self-evident. According to this line of argument, the identification of Baal and *Rp'u* is revealed in the phrase *rp'u b'l* in 1.22:I:8, but, as we have already noted, the parallel phrases *mhr b'l* and *mhr 'nt* strongly suggest that the initial element *rp'u* in *rp'u b'l* comprises a group of warriors, "the Mighty Ones of Baal," (cf. 3.1.7.3.). In any case, we would expect the presence of the conjunction *-w-* joining a compound divine name such as that proposed for *rp'u b'l*, cf. e.g., *Kṯr-w-Ḫss*, "Kothar-wa-Ḫasis."[230]

However, assuming that *Rp'u* is a deity, it is not to be equated with Malik, for where *mlk* appears in close connection with other gods at Ugarit, it clearly functions as an epithet. For example, El, who likewise is not to be identified with *Rp'u*, is given the epithet *mlk* (cf. 1.6:I:35–36). Having detached Baal from *rp'u*, we can safely note that Baal is likewise given the *mlk* epithet, but in this instance as part of his eternal kingship or *mlk 'lmk* (1.2:IV:10). Now *mlk* in 1.100:41 and 1.107:17 is not an epithet, but if it were to be viewed as such, one could not simply equate it with *Rp'u*'s epithet in 1.108:1, *mlk 'lm*, for the two constructions, *mlk* + geographical name and *mlk 'lm*, are not the same.[231] In any case, the *mlk* of

[226] The evidence for this deity at Ebla, Abu Ṣalabikh, and Mari remains controversial. In all three cases, the evidence derives solely from personal names, cf. Nakata 1974:377–87; Heider 1985:96–98;102–13; Lambert 1985a:533; Beyer 1985:101 who added the additional personal names from the indices of *ARMT* 21 and 22. Olyan and Smith 1987:273, in their review of Heider, suggested that the *malik* element may be an epithet even when divinized. Occurrences of Milku or ^{d}*Milku* are attested at Emar, cf. Arnaud 1986:460,466 [Texts 472:62′,473:15′]. Whether this recipient of offerings represents a deity or epithet remains unclear.

[227] For a different position, cf. Day 1989:46–55.

[228] For a survey of some of these positions, cf. the independent assessment of Day 1989:31–46.

[229] Cf. Spronk 1986:187–88,232–33.

[230] The Phoenician god *b'l mrp'* is not immediately relevant to the Ugaritic material owing to its late date.

[231] Olyan and Smith 1987:273–75 view *mlk* in 1.100 and 1.107 as an epithet.

mlk (b)'ṯtrt(h) in 1.100 and 1.107 designates the deity, "Malik in Ashtaroth," for the remaining personal names in 1.100 are those of gods, each followed by their address (see further below).

Malik's equation with Resheph relies on the prior identification of Resheph in the supposed epithet *rp'u mlk 'lm.*[232] In Egyptian texts, Resheph is given the titles *ḳḥ3 ḏ.t* and *nb nḥḥ*, "lord of eternity," indicating that he was perceived to be "eternal king of the netherworld."[233] As these titles comprise rough equations of Ugaritic *mlk 'lm*, it has been argued that *rp'u* in *rp'u mlk 'lm* must be an epithet for Resheph. But as we have already pointed out, Resheph at Ugarit is nowhere described as the ruler of the netherworld. On the contrary, he is portrayed only in the role of the sun goddess' gatekeeper which, as we intimated previously, might locate him in heaven's interior rather than in the netherworld.[234] Be that as it may, *rp'u* should not be considered an epithet in the phrase *rp'u mlk 'lm.*[235] The phrase *mlk 'lm* is used at Ugarit in reference to the king of Egypt.[236] It finds its identical parallel in Hebrew where it also functions as a divine epithet *meleḵ 'ôlām* (Jer. 10:10 used of Yahweh). In view of this and Akkadian *šarru dārû*, "king of eternity," as well as the Egyptian epithets cited above, *mlk 'lm* alone constitutes an epithet, while *rp'u* specifies a name of deity.

The correlation of Malik or *mlk* and Mot is based on the idea that Mot was esteemed, in some sense, as king of the netherworld.[237] Mot's royal seat *ṯbt*, throne *ks'a*, kingship *mlk*, and scepter of rule *ḫṭ mṯpṭ* are mentioned in 1.6:VI:28–29, while in 1.4:VIII:12–14 and 1.5:II:15–16, we hear again of his throne *ks'u ṯbt* as well as his royal inheritance *nḥlt*. Nevertheless, Mot is nowhere given the title king or ruler of the netherworld at Ugarit. Furthermore, as we shall demonstrate below, the chthonic associations of *mlk* at Ugarit are otherwise entirely lacking, so while the concept of rulership may be common to both, this in no way inextricably seats the latter on the netherworld throne. This stands in spite of the possible identity of *mlk* with the ^{d}*ma-lik* of *RS* 20.121:81.

^{d}*ma-lik* in the Old Babylonian, double columned, Weidner list is equated with Nergal who has been identified as the Mesopotamian king of the netherworld

232 Heider 1985:137–39 in dependence upon Cooper 1987a:1–7.

233 Cf. Cooper 1987a:1–7.

234 Cf. 2.1.5. n.76 and 3.1.7.3. The form *ršp* in the alphabetic god list, *KTU* 1.118:26, has as its Mesopotamian equivalent, ^{d}*nergal* in line 26 of the Akkadian god list *RS* 20.24. We would categorize Resheph's equation with Nergal, the sometime Mesopotamian king of the underworld, as an attempt on the part of the Ugaritic scribe merely to approximate the respective domains of the two gods. See Healey 1985:122–23 for additional examples of such approximations. In any case, they may be equated owing to their shared roles as gods of pestilence or war and metal working, see 2.1.5. and Dalley 1987:61–66.

235 So Cooper 1987a:1–7.

236 *PRU* 5(1965):no.8.9.

237 Lehmann 1953:361–71; Mulder 1965:57–64,70; Cooper 1981:446 citing a suggestion by Pope.

(^{d}U.GUR).[238] But what is attested in Mesopotamia for one period is by no means indicative of what transpired in Syria during another. Besides, although one would have expected perhaps Mot, it is Resheph and not Malik or *mlk*, who is in some vague sense equated with Nergal at Ugarit (cf. 1.118:26 = *RS* 20.24:26). Neither *mlk* or ^{d}*ma-lik* of the god lists have clear chthonic connections.

In the expression *mlk (b)'ṯtrt(h)* of 1.100:41 and 1.107:17, the form *'ṯtrt* has been interpreted as a divine name.[239] However, a toponymic interpretation appears more likely, for as we pointed out previously, the incantation 1.100 comprises a list of several deities along with their habitats.[240] While it might represent the Ashtaroth situated in the Transjordanian Bashan region of the Hebrew Bible, the notion of a netherworld location for mythical Bashan must be rejected.[241] Day has made a reasonable case for identifying Bashan as the mountain of the gods (possibly Hermon) in Ps. 68:16,23(ET 15,22) . He also concluded that, while it attains mythological coloring, Bashan is nowhere attributed a netherly locale (although the netherworld entrance was probably located at the mountain's base, but this is quite different). Lastly, Bashan's link with Ugaritic *bṯn*, "serpent," cited as exemplary of biblical Bashan's chthonic symbolism, is unconvincing, for the Hebrew cognate is *peṯen*, "snake," not *bāšān*.[242]

There are several other texts in which scholars have identified the god Malik, or *mlk*. De Moor advanced the suggestion that *mlk* shows up in 1.108:12 as well as in 1.41:48 in the phrase *ḥl mlk*, "the host of *mlk*."[243] The severely damaged context of 1.108:10ff. precludes any certainty for this reading in 1.108.[244] In any case, the term *ḥl* has been generally taken to be derivative of *ḥll*, "to desacralize, profane."[245] This would favor reading *mlk* as king or ruler not as the deity Malik. The same uncertainty attends *zbl mlk 'llmy* in 1.22:I:10 which Pope rendered "Prince *Mlk*

---

238 The same equation is made in a late Assyrian god list from Ashur. For both texts, cf. Lambert 1971:474; 1985a:533 n.16.

239 Levine and de Tarragon 1988:497 cited another recently published text *RS* 1986.2235:17 where *mlk 'ṯtrth* appears.

240 On these texts, see now Levine and de Tarragon 1988:481–518, esp. pp.497–98. On the place names, cf. Astour 1968:19–21; Pardee 1978:73–108; Xella 1981a:224–50.

241 The Bashan location was proposed by Margulis 1970:293–94 (now) Margalit 1981:152–56. Pope 1977a:170–71,174, followed by Heider 1985:396, proposed the chthonic association of Bashan. We note that interpreters often discuss this datum in support of the chthonic nature of the Ugaritic *rp'um* and the Rephaim of the non-poetic Hebrew texts, cf. the reference to "King Og of Bashan—one of the last of the Rephaim—who resided in Ashtaroth and Edrei" (Josh. 12:4) and 4.8.

242 Day 1985:113–19.

243 De Moor 1972(II):17 followed by Spronk 1986:187.

244 Cf. Pardee 1988:76; note the *KTU* readings for 1.41:48, [.*ḥl*]*mlk* and for 1.87:52, [. *w ḥl.mlk*].

245 Cf. Xella 1981a:63,74. The term *mlk* shows up in 1.91:2,7,11, but Xella 1981a:335–45 argued that 1.91 is an economic text and not a liturgical or religious one. It deals with consignments of wine used in royal sacrificial ceremonies.

the Wise"[246] and *rp'u mlk 'lm* in 1.108:1 which Heider has interpreted as "Rapiu, *Mlk* the Wise," Rapiu, in this case, being a title of the god Malik, or *mlk*.[247] The epithet "wise" is the key interpretative issue in these two instances.

The epithet "wise" is based on Arabic *'alima*, but this etymology for the Ugaritic *'lm* is not at all certain.[248] In view of *zbl mlk šmm* in 1.13:26–27, *mlk* in *zbl mlk 'llmy* in 1.22:I:10 may be no more than a noun or adjective forming part of a title.[249] In the end, whether one takes *mlk* in 1.108:1 to be a deity or an epithet depends largely upon one's interpretation of *rp'u* in *rp'u mlk 'lm* in 1.108:1. Is it an epithet of a well known deity or an independent deity in its own right? We argued above that the term *rp'u* constituted an independent deity and *mlk 'lm*, a title. Having said that, while a deity *mlk* is attested in 1.100 and 1.107, any preconceived notions about its chthonic qualities must await future substantiation. In sum, arguments derived directly or indirectly from the character of the singular Ugaritic form *mlk* in favor of a chthonic element in the *mlkm*, the supposed pluralization of the singular *mlk*, must be rejected.

To the *mlkm* we now turn. The plural *mlkm* have been interpreted as dead kings and/or minor chthonic deities and, at times, even equated with the dead *rp'um*.[250] The *mlk* of 1.161:11–12,25–26 signifies two deceased Ugaritic kings, probably Ammishtamru II and Niqmaddu III.[251] That they are deceased is confirmed by the rites observed on Niqmaddu's behalf and by the fact that these *mlk(m)* are located in the netherworld (cf. 3.1.9.1. and 1.161:25 *tḥt. 'mṯtmr. mlk*, "go down to Amishtamru, the king").

Another text has been cited as support for the chthonic nature of the *mlkm*. In 1.22:I:16–17, the phrase *q'l mlkm* has been translated "the hall of kings" or "the heights where the kings" sit.[252] Healey concluded that these were deceased kings.[253] This would apparently fit the context of a netherly gathering of the *mtm*, "the dead," *ǵzrm*, "the (dead) heroes," *rp'u b'l*, "the Rephaim of Baal," as

---

246 Pope 1977a:167. Spronk 1986:171,174–75 offers "the highness, the king, the unrelated" and follows de Moor 1976:342 in viewing *'llmy* as a compound, but at this point, their argument becomes unnecessarily complex. For a more likely explanation based on *'l(l)m*, "time long past, remote antiquity," cf. Caquot 1976b:299; and Astour 1980:234 and n.83 "the highness, the king of yore."

247 Heider 1985:127. We translate *rp'u mlk 'lm* as "*Rp'u*, the king of yore."

248 So Rosenthal 1970:10; cf. Cooper 1987a:4 n.43.

249 So Olyan and Smith 1987:273–74.

250 For recent surveys of the various views, cf. Heider 1985:113–41; Spronk 1986:187–88.

251 De Moor 1976:343 identified the *mlkm* as Amishtamru I and Niqmaddu II, but mortuary rites observed on a single historical occasion as in the case of 1.161 suggest more immediate deceased royal ancestors. In the GHD, Ammiṣaduqa performs commemorative rites for his deceased father Ammiditana, cf. 3.1.7.1.

252 For "hall," see de Moor 1972(II):12–13. For "heights," see Caquot, Sznycer, and Herdner 1974:177 n.*b*; cf. *gbl // q'l* in 1.3:VI:7–8. See also Ribichini and Xella 1979:153 and n.42.

253 Healey 1978a:91; cf. now Spronk 1986:176.

well as the "hosts of filth" or *ḥyl ḫḫ* in lines 6–10, and "those who pass over" or *'brm* in line 15, but as we have argued previously, the first three entities are not to be identified as chthonic beings (cf. 3.1.7.3.). The same applies to the latter two, for their underworld affiliations are dependent upon those postulated for the former.[254] The *'brm* (and cf. the Hebrew equivalent *'ōḇᵊrîm*, Ezek. 39:11) have been interpreted as "the ancestors passed away," or "those who came over" the river of death.[255] But owing to the ambiguity of the context, others are able to offer "traveler(s)" without any chthonic attachments implied.[256] Lastly, the significance of *q'l* is uncertain. The form *mlkm* has been taken as an adjectival genitive and *q'l* as "fig cake," thus, "royal fig cake."[257] Still others have offered for the phrase "blossoms fit for kings."[258]

The *mlkm* which show up in the two alphabetic pantheon lists, 1.47:11 and 1.118:32, have been viewed as singular forms with enclitic *-m* and as added confirmation that a deity *mlk* was known at Ugarit.[259] But others have argued that ^{d}*ma-lik*^{meš} in *RS* 20.24:32, the parallel Akkadian pantheon list to 1.118:32, unequivocally secures *mlkm*'s plural status.[260] This however must be qualified for Huehnergard has recently pointed out that the determinative ^{meš} often appears on singular forms in peripheral Akkadian and may not, per se, be taken as an unambiguous marker of the plural.[261] Thus, ^{d}*ma-lik*^{meš} in *RS* 20.24:32 might represent a singular form (cf. ^{d}*ma-lik* in *RS* 20.121:81) and the *-m* on *mlkm* in 1.118:32 might be enclitic, but when viewed together and in conjunction with the *malikū* from Mari, we give slight preference to the plural for these Ugaritic forms. In any event, this is a dubious datum upon which to establish a royal ancestor cult at Ugarit.

It has been suggested that the inventory of deities and numina that stands behind 1.118 and 1.47 derived from the cult. This in turn would add support to

---

254 Spronk 1986:171, following de Moor 1969:174 n.54, renders *ḥyl ḫḫ* as "the host of filth." Del Olmo Lete 1981:423 favors the reading *ḥyly* following *CTA* against *KTU* and on p.551 lists alternative meanings for Ugaritic *ḫḫ*.

255 Cf. Pope 1977a:173, following Raṭosh 1970–71:549–68; Spronk 1986:175.

256 So L'Heureux 1979:153 and cf. del Olmo Lete 1981:423.

257 Pope 1977a:168,176.

258 E.g., L'Heureux 1979:153,157.

259 Cf. the discussion in Healey 1975:235–38. Gordon 1965:434 equated *mlkm* with Milkom. Dhorme 1956:60 rendered *mlk* in 1.91:2 and 1.41:50 as the deity, but cf. Xella 1979:833–38; 1981a:335–45.

260 Nougayrol 1968:60,339 followed by Healey 1975:235; 1985:120; Heider 1985:117. Astour 1966:280–81 viewed *mlkm* as divinized *mlk* sacrifices as suggested by the inclusion of cult objects, such as *'uṯḫt*, "censor" and *knr*, "lyre," and sacrifices, such as the *šlm*, "peace offering." But *šlm* might be the deity *Šlm* who appears at the end of offering lists, cf. 1.39:8 and 1.41:17, so de Tarragon 1980:159, or better yet, "completed," so Xella 1981a:327 or, perhaps, "divinized health," so Caquot 1979:1404.

261 Huehnergard 1987:147,300,720.

the ancestor cult interpretation of *mlk* and *mlkm*.[262] Healey stated that it replicates the "canonical" list of Ugaritic gods and was apparently influenced by the ritual of 1.148, a text which contains a similar god list. 1.148 begins with the heading *dbḥ ṣpn*, "sacrifices of Zaphon," and 1.47 with the heading *'il ṣpn*, "the gods of Zaphon." Furthermore, 1.118 lists several divinized cultic objects.[263] But this is very slight evidence indeed upon which to assign 1.118 and 1.47 a cultic function. We know that god lists had non-cultic functions e.g., as scholarly endeavors for the purpose of collecting information or propagating a particular theological doctrine.[264] In cases where a god list had a cultic function, such is easily detectable. For example, in the case of the Mari pantheon list published in 1950 by Dossin, the numbers of sheep assigned to the deities are clearly recorded.[265] But no such inventory taking is evident in 1.118 or in the Ugaritic lists with the exception of 1.148.[266] In fact, 1.148 actually supports our argument. Where god lists were used in the cult, the practice of registering the deities along with their respective offerings was observed in the scribal tradition. In any case, even if one were to concede that 1.118 was intended for the cult, in the absence of any dating formulae, we would have no way of knowing if it was used on a repeated basis.

The term, *mlkm*, now appears in *RIH* 78/14:4′: *yrḫ.kslm.mlkm.tbṣrn*, "in the month of Kislev, you/they shall watch the *mlkm*" or "the *mlkm* shall be observed." According to the editors, this is the first such omen text attested at Ugarit. It apparently originates in the royal court (cf. *mlkn*, "our king," in line 7′).[267] Healey initially identified the *mlkm* here as the demonic aspect of the *mlkm*, but subsequently recognized the more likely possibility that they are foreign, hostile, living rulers, for other such apodoses are couched in the natural, not the supernatural, sphere.[268]

In conclusion, 1.161 provides the only data from which we can extrapolate an unequivocal netherly connection for the Ugaritic *mlk* or *mlkm*. In this text, *mlk* represents a deceased king. As to *mlk*'s character or function, 1.161 intimates only that such a one resided in the netherworld and was summoned to gather down

---

262 Nougayrol 1968:43; de Tarragon 1980:151 regarded 1.118 as a model for cultic practice.

263 Healey 1985:122–23.

264 Cf. Lambert 1971:473–79, esp. p.478.

265 Dossin 1950:41–50 and cf. the lists discussed by Lambert 1971:478; 1985a:528–32.

266 Healey 1985:116–17; 1988:104–05 discussed repeated markings on 1.118 and *RS* 20.24 and concluded that these were some type of check mark. On the analogy of another Mari pantheon list first published by Talon 1980:12–17, and cf. Lambert 1985a:528–32, these marks are more likely aids to copying rather than indicators of the number of offerings received by each entry in the Ugaritic lists.

267 Bordreuil and Caquot 1980:352–53.

268 Healey 1985:124 n.25; 1988:108. The brevity of the omen precludes any decision on the matter. Recall that in the Mari text recently published by Finet 1985:89, cf. Durand 1988a:489–91,501–03, a *malikum* likewise plays a possible role in divination and in the royal cult, but cf. 2.2.1.1.

below in order to receive and escort the royal throne on its journey toward the recently deceased king's abode (cf. 3.1.9.). As such, a dead *mlk* exhibited no supernatural beneficent powers. If the *mlk*(*m*) of 1.161 are to be equated with the *mlkm* in 1.118:32, then one might conclude that the latter's parallel in *RS* 20.24:32, ^{d}*ma-lik*^{meš}, points to the deification of the Ugaritic *mlk*(*m*). But this is unlikely, for nowhere in the Ugaritic texts otherwise are dead kings deified (cf. 3.1.6. and 3.1.9.) and that includes 1.161 and 1.113. In fact, 1.161 gives no indication that the *mlk*(*m*) possessed supernatural beneficent powers. Therefore, it is best to view the ^{d}*ma-lik*^{meš} of the Akkadian god list only as a vague approximation of its Ugaritic analogue *mlkm*.[269] Nevertheless, a link between the Ugaritic *mlkm* and the *malikū*, "vassal rulers," in the *kispum* texts from Mari, irrespective of their function and supposed postmortem powers, might find confirmation in the equation of ^{d}*ma-lik*^{meš} and *mlkm* at Ugarit.[270]

In closing, we should mention that what we have concluded leaves open the question of child sacrifice or *molk-* sacrifices at Ugarit. Egyptian reliefs of the New Kingdom might depict the inhabitants of Syro-Palestinian cities under attack as sacrificing their children (for a later parallel, cf. the tradition in 2 Kgs. 3:27).[271] Despite the efforts of such scholars as Herdner to identify such a practice at Ugarit, the only textual witness worthy of serious consideration remains controvertible.[272] The same applies in the case of the material evidence.[273] We now turn to examine *mlk* and *KTU* 1.161 in greater detail.

3.1.9. *KTU* 1.161: Funerary Liturgy or Coronation Litany?

Just over a decade and a half have passed since the initial publication of *RS* 34.126 (= *KTU* 1.161) by M. André Caquot.[274] In the search for the identity of the Ugaritic *rp'um* and the Rephaim of the Hebrew Bible, *KTU* 1.161 has quickly won center stage. The deciding role which 1.161 has played in the reconstruction

---

[269] Following Healey 1985:122–23; Huehnergard 1987:10.

[270] Cf. Handy 1988:57–59 for the more general meaning "ruler" for Ugaritic *mlk*.

[271] Cf. Spalinger 1977–78:47–60. Ackerman 1992:121 and n.53 notes Stager's suggestion that the children were alive and were being transferred from a lower level to a higher one in the city.

[272] Cf. *KTU* 1.119:31 [*b*]*kr b'l.nš*[*q*]*dš*, "A firstborn, Baal, we shall sacrifice;" Herdner 1972:693–703; 1978:7,36; Astour 1980:235 n.6; but see Xella 1978:127–36; Day 1989:18 n.11 who read [*d*]*kr* instead of [*b*]*kr*, "male;" note Ackerman 1992:122–23.

[273] Cf. Schaeffer 1962:77–83; but see Bieńkowski 1982:80–89, esp. p.81, who found no evidence of ritual cremation evincing violent death or a human sacrificial context, or for that matter, cremation in general, at Ugarit.

[274] The tablet was discovered at Ras Shamra in 1973. The first transcription of the text was published two years later by Caquot 1976a:426–29. For a discussion of the subsequent collations and photographs, cf. Pitard 1987:75–77; Bordreuil and Pardee 1991:151–63.

of Canaanite-Israelite beliefs about ghosts and demons is amply illustrated by the impressive number of articles and essays published on the text over the past fifteen years.[275]

A virtual consensus has formed with regard to the interpretation of 1.161 and consequently the identity and role of the *rp'um* at Ugarit. The ritual elements are generally understood to reflect a funerary liturgy which initiated the royal ancestor cult. The *rp'um* are the (semi-)divine dead kings and heroes who were summoned from the netherworld so that they might exercise their supernatural power to bless the living. For most scholars, this interpretation of 1.161 also provides the context for understanding those references to the *rp'um* elsewhere in Ugaritic myth, legend, and ritual. Moreover, on the basis of this view of *KTU* 1.161, interpreters have advanced similar reconstructions for the biblical Rephaim. At least those Rephaim of the non-narrative portions of the Hebrew Bible are viewed as having been ancient dead, divinized kings who, being polemically stripped of their supernatural beneficent powers, were thereafter transformed into the weakened, democratized dead and relegated to Sheol.

3.1.9.1. The Compositional Setting

On the whole, early studies tended to confuse rather than clarify the compositional setting of *KTU* 1.161. This was due in part to the readings published in the early editions of the text. Illustrative of this fact is the reading of the heading in line 1. Lipiński proposed *spr dbḥ qlm*, "booklet of the sacrifice of a child." This reflects his understanding of 1.161 as a ritual related to child sacrifice and the cult of the dead.[276] In his most detailed treatment of the Rephaim, Caquot read *spr dbḥ 'ilm* and concluded that this text was a poem intended to accompany sacrifice

---

275 Cf. the bibliography in Pitard 1987:75 n.2 and add to the twenty-one or so treatments listed there, the following: Caquot 1976b:296–97; Gaster 1976:97–106; Healey 1977a:i-v (postscript); 1978a:89–91; 1980a:240; 1989:33–44; Margalit 1980b:192,197–99; 1980a:251 and n.34; de Tarragon 1980:57–59,73–74,106; Dijkstra, de Moor, and Spronk 1981:374–78; Michalowski 1983:245; de Moor 1981–82:116–17; Pope 1981:159–79; Sapin 1983:178–79; Talmon 1983:235–49; Verreet 1983:234–36,240–41,247,256–58; 1984:307–22; 1985:324–30; Barnett 1986:112–20; Dalley 1986:89; del Olmo Lete 1986a:92–93; Spronk 1986:189–93; Taylor 1984:13; 1985:315–18; 1988a:151–77; Pardee 1987:211–17; 1988:176–78 and n.49, n.54; Lewis 1989:5–46; Caquot, de Tarragon and Cunchillos 1989:103–10; Tropper 1989:144–50; Bordreuil and Pardee 1991:151–63; Ford 1992:73–101; Tsumura 1993:40–55.

276 Lipiński 1978:98. He understood *mlk* in lines 12,26 as "*molk*-sacrifice," a sevenfold sacrifice (cf. *ṯ'y* in lines 27–30). The reading of *qlm*, upon which his general interpretation depended, must be rejected in favor of *ẓlm* (see below).

to the gods.[277] Most commentators recognize the reading of *KTU* as confirmed by Pitard: *spr dbḥ ẓlm*. However, even with this reading secure, interpretations of line 1 abound (cf. 3.1.9.2.).

As noted above, the reverse is true of the interpretation of 1.161 as a whole. Dietrich and Loretz thought the text reflected a *marzēaḥ* feast and assumed that the latter was part of the cult of the dead.[278] More frequently, 1.161 has been compared with the royal Mesopotamian *kispum* ritual and the GHD in particular.[279] In 1978, Pitard, having outlined what he believed to be the essential components of the *kispum* ritual—an incantation and an invocation of the dead, food offerings, and libations as well as the optional element of haruspicies—proceeded to interpret 1.161 along similar lines.[280] Others have identified additional elements in common with the *kispum* ritual.[281] Dietrich and Loretz identified several elements that *Mari* 12803 shared with 1.161. Both texts list offerings made to the images of the deified kings at the foot of their thrones (cf. *lamassātu* in *Mari* 12803:i:5 and *ẓlm* in 1.161:1) and the sun deity functioned in some aspect of its role as chthonic god in both. Based on these commonalities, the authors equated *dbḥ ẓlm* (< *ẓll*) of 1.161 "sacrifices to the shades" with the *kispum* of *Mari* 12803:I:2, "offering(s) to the ancestors."[282]

A typical ancestor cult setting for 1.161 includes announcing the celebration in honor of the "shades" (line 1), the summons of the illustrious dead to ascend in order to supernaturally bless the living (lines 2–12), the new king's mourning for his deceased father (lines 13–17), the solar deity's descent and retrieval of the illustrious dead (lines 18–26), sacrifices in honor of the illustrious dead (lines 27–30), and the blessing of the new king, the queen, and the city of Ugarit by those illustrious dead (lines 31–34).

---

277 Caquot 1981:354. He included within the category of gods the *rp'um* whom he interpreted as the deceased royal ancestors based on his view of 1.113.

278 Dietrich and Loretz 1983:23. L'Heureux 1979:192; Margalit 1980b:199 and n.1 also mentioned this possibility but rejected it. Against the death cult relations of the Ugaritic *marzēaḥ*, cf. 3.1.5. We should mention that 1.161 offers no indication that it was a feast per se.

279 De Moor 1976:333 n.72 was the first to suggest a comparison of 1.161 and the GHD. His proposal has been followed by most subsequent writers.

280 Pitard 1978:67,69,72. 1.161:2–12 comprise the invocation, lines 13–17, the food offerings, lines (18–19) 20–26, the libations, and lines 27–30, seven extispicies to determine the decision of the dead (lines 31–34 indicate that the rite was efficacious). On p.72, he concluded "in some, if not all, cases, haruspicies were carried out in Mesopotamian *kispum* rituals . . . " and, in n.30, he cited Nougayrol 1967:222–23 in support, but the latter cited only one text, *BM* 78564. Tropper 1989:129,144–50 has proposed a similar understanding of the text in which 1.161 comprises a necromantic incantation for the purpose of obtaining the active involvement of the ancestors in the present, but see below.

281 Pope 1977a:178 read *qlm* in 1.161:1 and connected it with the *bīt qūltišu* (= *bīt kispī*?) of the Shamshi-Addu inscription discussed in 2.2.2.

282 Dietrich and Loretz 1980b:381–82; cf. 1983:21

Nonetheless, a regularly observed ritual does not stand behind the text of 1.161. The benediction (lines 31–34) indicates that it was composed for the specific historical occasion of a new king's coronation, that of Ammurapi.[283] In this respect, 1.161 has its closest parallel in the GHD, but the GHD likewise lacks any indication of its regular use. It too is tied to the singular occasion of a royal coronation (cf. 3.1.7.1.). Therefore, 1.161 cannot be classified as a regularly occurring *kispum* ritual. At most, funerary or mourning rites are mentioned alongside various coronation rites (see further below).[284]

As noted previously in our treatment of the GHD (3.1.7.1.), a number of divergent Mesopotamian texts attest to as many as eleven distinct, but variable, elements of the coronation ceremony; divine election, assembly of the nobles and dignitaries, preparatory purification, the king's presentation before the deity, investiture with insignia, giving of a throne name, acclamation of the king (or blessing of the gods and people), enthronement, paying of homage and swearing of loyalty oaths, affirmation by the king, and celebration. Sacrifice was occasionally offered as well.[285] As noted previously the Middle Assyrian coronation ritual published by Müller contains seven of these elements: the presentation before the deity (Ashur; col.i:30–32), offerings and sacrifice to the deity (col.i:37–41), the investiture with scepter and (*kulūlu*) crown (col.ii:15–28), acclamation with blessing (col.ii:30–38,42–49), enthronement (col.iii:1), assembly of nobles and dignitaries (col.iii:2–3), payment of homage (col.iii:4–14) and swearing of oaths before the divine witnesses (including in this case, the solar deity represented as Ṣalmu; col.ii:7–8).[286]

---

[283] Levine and de Tarragon 1984:654,659 speculated that 1.161 was a *canonical* liturgy used whenever succession took place and assumed that the ritual, while funerary in nature, initiated the cult of the dead. Pitard 1978:69 proposed that separate texts circulated which recorded the full list of ancestors found in 1.161 and the GHD, since all the ancestors were invoked during the *kispum* ritual, cf. also L'Heureux 1979:192. While these are plausible proposals, *Mari* 12803 lists only Sargon and Naram-Sin by name and *ARMT* 3:40 mentions only one Yaḫdun-Lim, cf. 2.2.1 and the *kispum ša šarrāni* at Mari may refer to only a select group of ancient kings. In any case, funerary rites do not necessarily presuppose the existence of death cult rites.

[284] As we pointed out in 2.1., a cultic occasion like that reflected in 1.161 with its attendant coronational and funerary rites might find its reflex in ancient Near Eastern international diplomacy wherein attendance at the coronation and funerary rites legitimating the continuance of a dynasty was considered protocol, on which cf. Artzi 1980:161–70. The underlying ritual setting of 1.161 might have initiated regular commemorative rites like those that regularly occasioned the offerings for the *malikū* at Mari (see further below).

[285] Cf. Wilkinson 1986:242–71 who also adds as a possible element the anointing with oil which while not explicit in Mesopotamia was observed in the adjacent regions. His work significantly expands that of Ben-Barak 1980:56–67 who identified only three elements in the Mesopotamian coronation ceremony: the convocation, the installation, and the acclamation.

[286] Cf. Müller 1937. Dalley 1986:93,97–98 suggested that *ṣalmu* refers to the solar deity as depicted in the form of the divine emblem, the winged disk. If correct, this would provide still another parallel for 1.161 (cf. line 1 *ẓlm* = *ṣalmu* and 3.1.9.2.).

Several of these find analogues in 1.161. The assembly of nobles and dignitaries, the presentation before the deity, the acclamation of the king, and sacrifices to the gods are each possibly attested in 1.161.[287] The assembled nobles and dignitaries comprise lines 2–5,9–10 (see below). The acclamation of the king is to be found in the closing lines, lines 31–34, the presentation before the deity is reflected in line 18, and (seven) sacrifices to the deity are recorded in lines 27–30 and anticipated in line 1 by the phrase, *spr dbḥ ẓlm*, (cf. 3.1.9.2.). In the light of the eleven or so possible elements attested, the relative brevity of 1.161 can be explained along the lines offered by Ben-Barak for the abridged version of Nabopolassar's coronation. As is likely in the case of our text, war was either underway or imminent so the concern for the confirmation and blessing of the gods took precedence resulting in an abbreviated account. Admittedly, this may not necessarily reflect what transpired in typical coronational procedures.[288]

The assembly of nobles and dignitaries is ubiquitous in coronational procedures attested from Ur III times onwards.[289] In the Middle Assyrian coronation text, mentioned previously, nobles or *rabānu* and princes or *ša rēš šarrāni* gather to kiss the feet of the new king, offer him gifts, and give their blessing before the people.[290] In a recently published epic which contains a coronational ceremony for Nabopolassar, king of Babylon, the ^{lú}*rubû* ^{meš} *ša māti*, "nobles of the land," and ^{lú}*rabûtu* $^{\text{meš kur}}$*Akkadi* ^{ki}, "the dignitaries of Akkad," assemble and kneel before the king, greet and pray for him, and bless him in the sight of the people.[291] Another recently published Old Babylonian text from Tell Asmar mentions *siprū mātim*, "the ambassadors of the whole land," and *ammurum kalušu*, "all the Amorites," who gather for the funeral of Abda-El, an Amorite chieftain, in order to honor him and his successor during the coronation.[292]

In 1.161, the summons of the *rp'i 'arṣ* and the *qbṣ ddn* reflects the characteristic assembly of the coronation ritual. Just as in the funeral of Abda-El wherein the Amorites are assembled to pay their respects to the dead and to offer their blessing upon the new king, so it is in the case of 1.161 wherein the Amorite-related *Ditānu* and the *rp'um* elite are assembled.[293] The details of the text support the notion

287 Both Bordreuil and Pardee 1982:128 and Levine and de Tarragon 1984:654 recognized the presence of the acclamation of the king in 1.161, but failed to acknowledge the pervasiveness of coronational elements preserved throughout the text.

288 Ben-Barak 1980:67.

289 Cf. e.g., de Vaux 1961:102–07; Wilkinson 1986:242–71 and esp. p.266 where the assembly is documented for texts dating from the Ur III period through to the Neo-Babylonian period.

290 Cf. Müller 1937:4–19; Ben-Barak 1980:61–62; Wilkinson 1986:306–316.

291 *BM* 34793 in Grayson 1975:78–86 cf. Ben-Barak 1980:56–60; Wilkinson 1986:317–20.

292 Tell Asmar 1931–T299:1–55 in Whiting 1987:48–51; cf. pp.59–63,115 for similar texts.

293 If the etymological proposal of Aistleitner wherein Ugaritic *r-p-'* is equated with Akkadian *rubûm*, *rubā'um*, "prince," were correct, then we would have a virtual semantic equivalent between *rp'i 'arṣ* of 1.161 and the ^{lú}*rubû* ^{meš} *ša māti* of the Nabopolassar coronation ceremony, but cf. 3.1.7.5.

that an assembly of living persons of prominence is in view. In the ritual descent of Niqmaddu's throne (lines 20–26), nowhere are the *rp'i 'arṣ* or the *qbṣ ddn* explicitly located in the 'land below'. In view of this as well as our arguments in 3.1.7., L'Heureux's observation concerning the need for the Ugaritians to qualify the term *rp'um* is apposite, "it would hardly be necessary to specify that these *rp'im* are *qdmym* if the word *rp'm* originally and of itself referred to the dead."[294]

However, L'Heureux wrongly included in the *rp'im qdmym* all of the names in lines 4–8 (see our translation that follows). We would incorporate within this group only the individuals listed in lines 6–7, Sdn-w-Rdn and Ṯr 'llmn, for the text locates only these two as identifiable members of the *rp'im qdmym* in the netherworld in lines 22b–24a. But how do we interpret the fact that the two names, Ulkn and Trmn of lines 4–5 with the accompanying epithet *rp'u*, are nowhere located in the netherworld? The existence of a living element from among the *rp'um* and the absence of a deceased element in the other texts from Ugarit supports the living status of Ulkn and Trmn. They represent assembled warriors, nobles, and/or dignitaries in 1.161. Thus, the presumed similarities which 1.161 and, for that matter, the GHD share with the regularly observed *kispum* ritual are only apparent. In any case, *Mari* 12803 lacks any mention of the living king and nobility, appears as part of the liturgical calendar, explicitly records *kispum* offerings beginning on the second day of Addar (line 1) and repeated perhaps thereafter at the appointed times, and has no explicit ties to a coronation ceremony.[295] Had *Mari* 12803 been tied to a particular occasion such as a royal funeral and coronation, and not to a regularly observed cult, then on the analogy of 1.161 and the GHD, one would have expected the mention of the deceased father, Ilakabkabu, and his successor son, Shamshi-Addu, in 12803.

The question remains then, in what capacity are the dead summoned or called in lines 6–8,11–12 and again in lines 22b–25. Tropper, like interpreters before him, identified all those entities in lines 2–12,22b–25, as apparitions invoked in order to bestow their supernatural blessings upon the new king.[296] If 1.161's affinities with coronation procedures accurately reflect the religio-political concerns of the underlying ritual, then the blessings of lines 31–34 are those of the deity and the living people. In other words, the dead were not summoned from the netherworld to return to the world above. In lines 20–25, the throne is portrayed as descending to the netherworld (cf. 3.1.9.2. on lines 20–26) and is received down below by Sdn-w-Rdn, Ṯr 'llmn, that is, the dead *rp'im qdmym*, and Amishtamru, the dead king or *mlk*. The writer of 1.161 not only presupposes their location in the netherworld in his initial summons in lines 6–8,11–12, he never lets them

---

[294] L'Heureux 1979:204; cf. p.189 and 1.161:8,24.

[295] Cf. Birot 1980:145; Tsukimoto 1985:73–78.

[296] Tropper 1989:144–50.

leave that region as lines 20–26 demonstrate. The call or summons merely alerted the dead to prepare to receive the soon-to-descend throne.[297] For the benefit of the living in attendance, the call or summons also served a legitimating function fulfilled through the recitation of these names within the constraints of an artificial genealogical framework (i.e., geneonymy). The other entities generally understood to return to the world above from below, namely, the *rp'i 'arṣ*, the *qbṣ ddn*, Ulkn, and Trmn (lines 2–5,9–10), are never explicitly depicted as located in the netherworld.[298] They comprise instead those living who attended the ceremony. In sum, 1.161 is not an otherwise unattested funerary liturgy with accompanying 'necrophany'. We have identified the following coronational and funerary (*) elements in 1.161:

I. Heading: A Coronation Ceremony with Sacrifices [and oath swearing] before *Ẓalmu* (line 1)

II. First Call for the assembly of the living warrior-nobility (lines 2–5)

*III. Summons of the deceased warrior heroes of old [to prepare to receive the soon-to-descend throne of Niqmaddu] (lines 6–8)

IV. Second Call for the assembly of the living warrior-nobility (lines 9–10)

*V. Summons of the recently deceased kings [to prepare to receive the soon-to-descend throne of Niqmaddu] (lines 11–12)

*VI. Mourning by the new king for his predecessor-father [with the shedding of tears to invigorate Niqmaddu during his journey to the netherworld] (lines 13–17)

VII. Presentation of the new king before the solar deity, Shapash (lines 18–19)

*VIII. Ritual netherly descent of the deceased predecessor's throne (lines 20–26)

IX. Sacrifices to the solar deity, Shapash (lines 27–30)

X. Acclamation of the new king with blessing (lines 31–34)

---

297 Note that Niqmaddu is not one of those to whom the throne descends, cf. line 26. Perhaps too the dead were to transport it to its proper place in anticipation of Niqmaddu's eventual arrival following the liminal stage of death (cf. 1.2.).

298 This may explain their different titles and epithets from those located below.

KTU 1.161

1.	*spr. dbḥ. ẓlm*	The account of the sacred celebration before Ẓalmu:
2.	*qr'itm. rp'i. 'a*[*rṣ*]	"Have you called the Rephaim of the Land?
3.	*qb'itm. qbṣ. d*[*dn*]	Have you summoned the Gathered of Didanu?
4.	*qr'a. 'ulkn. rp*[*'a*	He called Ulkn, the Rapha,
5.	*qr'a. trmn. rp*[*'a*	He called Trmn, the Rapha;
6.	*qr'a. sdn. w. rd*[*n*]	He called Sdn-w-Rdn,
7.	*qr'a. ṯr. 'llmn*[	He called Ṯr 'llmn,
8.	*qr'u. rp'im. qdmym.*	They called the Ancient Rephaim;
9.	*qr'itm. rp'i. 'arṣ*	Have you called the Rephaim of the Land?
10.	*qb'itm. qbṣ. dd*[*n*]	Have you summoned the Gathered of Didanu?
11.	*qr'a. 'mṯtmr. m*[*l*]*k*	He called Amishtamru, the (defunct) king,
12.	*qr'a. 'u. nqm*[*d*] *mlk*	He called, yea, Niqmaddu the (defunct) king;
13.	*ks'i. nqmd tbky* [.]	At the throne of Niqmaddu, you must weep,
14.	*wydm'. hdm. p'nh*	as he who sheds tears at his footstool;
15.	*lpnh. ybky.ṯlḥn.*	Before him, he must weep at the table,
	mlk] (16) *w. ybl'. 'udm'th*	so that the (defunct) king might swallow his tears;
17.	*'dmt. w. 'dmt.*	Gnashing of teeth and more gnashing of teeth.
	'dmt (18) *'išḫn. špš.*	With gnashing of teeth, I bow down, O Shapash.

	w. ’išḫn (19) *nyr. rbt.*	I bow down, O Great Light,
	‘ln. špš. tṣḥ	Lift me up O Shapash, please shine!
20.	*’aṯr* [*.b*]*‘lk. l. ksh.*	After your Lord, O throne,
	’aṯr (21) *b‘lk.*	After your Lord to earth descend,
	’arṣ. rd.	
	’arṣ. (22) *rd.*	To earth descend
	w. špl. ‘pr.	and be low in the dust;
	tḥt (23) *sdn. w. rdn.*	Go down to Sdn-w-Rdn,
	tḥt. ṯr (24) *‘llmn.*	Go down to Ṯr ‘llmn;
	tḥt. rp’im. qdmym	Go down to the Ancient Rephaim;
25.	*tḥt. ‘mṯtmr. mlk*	Go down to Amishtamru, the king,
26.	*tḥm ’u. nq*[*md*]. *mlk*	May you remain warm, yea, Niqmaddu, O king;
27.	*‘šty. w. ṯ*[*‘y.*	One and an offering.
	ṯn. w.] *ṯ‘*[*y*]	Two and an offering.
28.	*ṯlṯ.*[*w*]. *ṯ‘y*	Three and an offering.
	[*’arb‘*] *.w. ṯ‘*[*y*]	Four and an offering.
29.	*ḫmš. w. ṯ‘y.*	Five and an offering.
	ṯṯ[*w.*] *ṯ‘y*	Six and an offering.
30.	*šb‘. w. ṯ‘y.*	Seven and an offering.
	tqdm. ‘ṣr	The sacred assembly is convened!
31.	*šlm. šlm. ‘mr*[*p’i*]	Peace! Peace to Ammurapi!
32.	*w. šlm. bnh.*	and peace to his sons!
	šlm. [*ṯ*]*ry*[*l*	Peace to Ṯaryelli!
33.	*šlm. bth.*	and peace to her house!
	šlm. ’u[*g*]*rt*	Peace to Ugarit!
34.	*šlm. ṯġrh*	and peace to its gates!”

3.1.9.2. Notes to *KTU* 1.161

Line 1: The form *spr* has been interpreted as “the written record,” “account,” or “instruction” of the sacrifice or celebration of *ẓlm*. The mention of *dbḥ* in line 1 and the language of lines 13–17,27–30 support the text’s underlying ritual nature. 1.161 should be viewed as a descriptive, not a prescriptive, ritual. Although the words of the king are quoted in the lament and petition sections, explicit ritual instructions are otherwise lacking.

Line 1: *dbḥ* is in the genitive case. While the term commonly refers to sacrifice, it can denote the broader ceremonial occasion involving a processional. In 1.148:1, *dbḥ* appears as the title of such a sacred celebration "for Zaphon" *dbḥ ṣpn* that is, for the gods of the pantheon.[299] In 1.142:1, *dbḥt* is found in a mortuary context where offerings are placed at the grave on one particular occasion following burial; but, contrary to consensus, this is not directly analogous to the function of *dbḥ* in 1.161 (cf. 3.1.2.).

Line 1: *ẓlm* was initially rejected by Caquot in favor of the reading *qlm*.[300] He subsequently suggested *'ilm* in spite of the availability of *KTU*'s reading *ẓlm*.[301] The collations of Bordreuil and Pardee, and Pitard have confirmed the reading *ẓlm*. Pope suggested a connection with "darkness," or, less likely, with "statue." He favored *ẓlm*, "darkness," over *qlm* since funeral feasts were nocturnal affairs.[302] Healey offered "shadows, or possibly protectors, which would also fit."[303] Pitard proposed "shadow, shade (but not 'shade-of-the-dead')," and "shadows," perhaps, "protectors" (cf. Hebrew *ṣēl* < *ṣālal*).[304] Xella initially mentioned two possibilities for *ẓlm*, "statue" or "man," but preferred the latter, noting Akkadian *ṣalālu*, "to be at rest, repose," as a third alternative. In his full length treatment of 1.161, he opted for "statue."[305] Margalit suggested "shady ones."[306] Bordreuil and Pardee offered "funerary sacrifice (literally 'for a man')," that is to say, for a dead man.[307] Dietrich and Loretz offered "shades" but then "statue of the dead."[308] Levine and de Tarragon proposed "patrons," that is, protectors.[309] Having abandoned his earlier reading *qlm*, de Moor, along with Dijkstra and Spronk, suggested a plural form of *ẓl*, "shade," (Hebrew *ṣēl*) and compared 1.4:II:27 and Qoh. 7:12.[310]

---

299 Cf. Virolleaud 1968:582; de Tarragon 1980:56,98–99,103,109–10. These authors assumed a meaning "banquet," but there is no hint of a funerary meal in the text. The latter appears to have realized this in Levine and de Tarragon 1984:651 "sacred celebration." In any case, this is not a *marzēaḥ* feast associated with the cult of the dead, *contra* Dietrich and Loretz 1983:23.

300 Caquot 1976a:427 followed by de Moor 1976:333; Healey 1978b:83; L'Heureux 1979:189; cf. Pope 1977a:178; Pitard 1978:65,67.

301 Caquot 1981:354.

302 Pope 1977a:178 followed by Lewis 1989:10–12. We note in response, not all such ceremonies were enacted at night, no indicators in the text suggest a nocturnal affair, and *ẓlm*, "darkness," is otherwise unattested at Ugarit (see below).

303 Healey 1978b:85.

304 Pitard 1978:68; 1987:78.

305 Cf. Xella 1979:838; 1981a:283–84.

306 Margalit 1980b:199.

307 Bordreuil and Pardee 1982:122,126.

308 Cf. Dietrich and Loretz 1980b:382; 1983:18.

309 Levine and de Tarragon 1984:651–52.

310 Dijkstra, de Moor, and Spronk 1981:375.

He cited Bottéro's suggestion that Akkadian *ṣillu* described the ghost of the dead in the Old Babylonian LÚ professions list *mušēlû ṣilli*, "the one who brings up the 'shade'," (cf. *mušēlû eṭemmi* in the same lexical series).[311] The combined ideas of protection, specifically that of a king as in the case at hand, and shade, that is, "a dead one," could produce the semi-technical term "royal netherworld protector(s)."

The isolated instance of *ṣillu* as "ghost of the dead" is dubious and the lack of parallels for *ṣillu* as protector in relation to the netherworld militates against this interpretation.[312] Moreover, while Ugaritic *ẓl* (< *ẓll*), "shade, protection(?)," occurs twice (*ẓl*(-)*mt*, "shadow of death," 1.4:VII:55; and cf. 1.8:II:8) or three times (*bẓl ḫmt*, "in the shade of a tree," cf. 1.14:III:55), and the related *mẓll*, "house, shelter," four times (1.4:I:12,17; IV:52,56), in none of these occurrences is a shade of the dead implied.[313] Besides, one would expect the second *l* of the root *ẓll* to show up in such a plural form, whether "shades" or "protectors."

A stronger case can be made for the interpretation of *ẓlm* as "statue," and in this instance that of a dead Ugaritic king, Amishtamru (as well as perhaps that of Niqmaddu, cf. lines 11–12?). Bayliss theorized that in the royal *kispum* rituals, dead kings were represented by their statues as were the gods.[314] Although not directly relevant, Hittite royal dead were represented in rituals by their statues before which offerings were made.[315] Tsukimoto cited the Middle Bronze text *PBS*[= UM] 2/2 in which the *kispum* ritual is combined with what he identifies as the rite of the king's statue or *ṣalam šarri*.[316] Recall that *Mari* 12803:I:5–7 records *kispum* and sheep offerings to the *lamassu* statues of kings Sargon and Naram-Sin. It also highlights the roles of the royal throne (I:7; IV:4′ and cf. 1.161:13) and of the sun deity (I:12–15 and cf. 1.161:18–19) in such mortuary rituals.

Among the texts from level 7 at Alalakh is a record of items made of silver intended to be placed in the grave of a dead king. The term ^{d}alam = *ṣalmu* occurs in

---

311 De Moor 1981–82:117 and n.50; Bottéro 1980:28 and n.28, cf. p.40 and n.200.

312 The form *mušēlû* might refer to an act of removal or taking away, cf. the causative of *elû* in *CAD* 4(1958):134 [#11d]. So *mušēlû eṭemmi* might be an exorcist or "one who removes the ghost" and not a necromancer. For the texts, cf. Finkel 1983–84:1; Tropper 1989:58–62, esp. pp.59–60; our treatment in 4.5.1.

313 As noted by Pitard 1978:68, but cf. Michel 1984:5–20, esp. p.13. De Moor 1980b:430, followed by Spronk 1986:189 and n.3, reads two words *'ap ẓl* in *RIH* 78/20:15, but the *editio princeps* of Bordreuil and Caquot 1980:346–50 reads one: *npẓl*, cf. also Caquot 1984:163–76.

314 Bayliss 1973:124. Kobayashi 1984:43–65 has argued that, at Pre-Sargonic Lagash, statues of the ancestors were not used in ritual. For the custom of erecting statues of the royal predecessors more generally, cf. the surveys of *CAD* 16(1962):80–82 and Cassin 1982:365–66 and for later Hittite and Aramean practices, see Hawkins 1980:213–25; cf. 4.1.2.-1.4.

315 Cf. Otten 1951:58 who cited three short texts dealing with these statues.

316 Tsukimoto 1985:88–89. The text is *PBS*[= UM] 2/2:108:7. For the view that *ṣalam šarri* is a variant form of the god Ṣalmu (= Shamash), cf. Dalley 1986:85–101.

AT 366:12,20 which Na'aman understood as a statue of a god.[317] However, alam = *ṣalmu* might represent a dead king's statue in the later inscription from Alalakh containing Idrimi's autobiography.[318] In fact, that autobiography is written on the statue of king Idrimi and his statue is the one referred to as ^{d}alam in line 99 of the text inscribed on the statue. His statue was possibly the object of some commemorative rites and as such served as a means of political legitimation. Having been toppled from its throne by invaders, Idrimi's statue was then buried to avoid further desecration.[319]

In the light of ^{d}alam in Idrimi's autobiography, the function of his statue, and in spite of the significant time lapse, ^{d}alam in *AT* 366 might signify a dead king's statue to which silver items were offered *anna ša* ^{d}alam, "for the approval of the royal divine statue," (lines 12,20).[320] This statue was placed in the dead king's grave at burial *šarri ana kupuri imdud / iddinu* (lines 6,15). Thus, Alalakh ^{d}alam = *ṣalmu* would refer to the statue of a deceased king to which offerings were made prior to its deposit in the royal grave. Similarly Birot, commenting on *Mari* 12803, noted that *lamassu*, when so used, functioned as a synonym of *ṣalmu*, the Akkadian cognate of *ẓlm*.[321] For most interpreters, such a construction as (*spr*) *dbḥ ẓlm*, "sacrifices for the statues (of the dead kings)," presupposes the royal ancestor cult as the underlying cultic setting. Nevertheless, 1.161's affinities with coronation procedures and the absence of royal ancestor cult rites or funerary rites involving grave offerings favor another ritual occasion.

Dalley has recently argued that in Mesopotamia from the mid second millennium onwards the term *ṣalmu* designated the god Ṣalmu, another name for the sun god, Shamash. Ṣalmu appears in oath swearing contexts as reflected in the

317 Na'aman 1981:47–48.

318 For the text of Idrimi's autobiography and the supposed royal ancestor cult associations of this statue, cf. Oller 1977:17,140–41; Sasson 1981b:323–24; Mayer-Opificius 1981:287–89; Spycket 1981:329–34; Moorey and Fleming 1984:77. On p.145, Oller discussed the significance of alam = *ṣalmu* in the autobiography. It should be noted that the form occurs in lines 92 and 103 of the same text without the divine determinative.

319 Cf. Oller 1977:1; Sasson 1981b:324.

320 Perhaps, the form *anna* is to be related to (the accusative of?) *annu*, "approval, positive divine answer (through extispicy)," cf. *CAD* 1/2(1968):134–36 and esp. p.125a and not the interjection "indeed," p.125b with Na'aman 1981:47.

321 The first consonant of this term alternates between *ẓ* and *ṣ* in early South Arabian, cf. Biella 1982:226,425; Beeston 1962:no.9.6 for their frequent interchange. At Ugarit, *ẓ* and *ṣ* interchange, cf. *yẓhq* (1.12:12) / *ṣhq*, *ẓ'i* (1.12:14) / *yṣ'*, and *ymẓ'a* (1.12:37) / *mṣ'* and Freilich and Pardee 1984:25–26. [ ]*ṣlm pn*⸢*y/h*⸣[ ] in 2.31:61 remains mute if the *-m* is the pl. ending on a term with a damaged initial letter. In *RIH* 78/20:8 *bẓlm* occurs which we translate as "(at the) statue" // *bqdš*, "(at the) sanctuary." For bibliography, see Dijkstra 1985:150 n.22; add Saracino 1984:69–83; Caquot 1984:163–76.

Middle Assyrian coronation ritual treated above.[322] The term presupposed the iconographic presence of the divine emblem, the winged disk, upon which loyalty oaths were sworn to the royal dynasty. Dalley also saw in Alalakh ^{d}alam = *ṣalmu* a reference to the deity Ṣalmu = Shamash. It was this deity who issued the items of silver in *AT* 366.[323] Given the fact that the solar deity Shapash plays the central divine role in 1.161 (lines 18–19), perhaps, the term *ẓlm* in 1.161:1 should be read as Ṣalmu, the iconographic emblem of the solar deity. That Ṣalmu in line 1 might refer to a distinct designation for the sun goddess in 1.161 in addition to the mention of her specific name, Shapash, in lines 18–19, finds its analogy in the occurrence of Ṣalmu or Ṣalmu-šarri alongside Shamash in texts like the Middle Assyrian coronation.[324] The name Ṣalmu in 1.161 would thus presuppose the presence of the winged disk. The disk might have served as the focal point of the coronation ritual and as the emblem upon which oaths of loyalty to the ruling Ugaritic dynasty were sworn.[325]

Lines 2–12: *qr'itm, qb'itm, qr'a, qr'u*. Interpreters have analyzed these forms as G active perfects (with the alternative of rendering the latter two as imperatives) either of instruction, prescription, or address. A jussive force has also been proposed.[326] The active perfect avoids the need for an otherwise questionable *-m* enclitic with Ugaritic verbal forms as suggested for *qr'it-m // qb'it-m*,[327] although it creates an alternation between singular and plural forms and assumes that 1.161 contains ritual instructions.

Based on *qr'i* in 1.100:2, which Levine and de Tarragon analyzed as a G 3fsg perfect with *i* theme vowel as indicated by the aleph *i* sign (*qari'at*), these authors interpreted *qr'itm // qb'itm* in 1.161 as 2mpl perfects.[328] However, several writers analyzed *qr'it* in 1.100:2 as a fs participle *qari'tu*, the most recent being Verreet. Besides, Ugaritic *qara'a* (*qr'a*, 1.161) and *qara'at* (*qr'at*, 1.116:1–2) conform with the vocalization of the perfect in other Semitic languages, so the existence of a *qatila* perfect in Ugaritic is doubtful.[329] This confirms what Verreet has demonstrated more generally, namely that the aleph *i* in final position in

---

[322] Cf. 3.1.9.1.; Dalley 1986:85–101, esp. pp.93,97–98. On p.97, Dalley concluded that Ṣalmu also shows up in royal burial rites as the ^{d}alam at Alalakh as *AT* 366:12,20 suggests, but this is controvertible in light of the use of ^{d}alam on the Idrimi statue to represent the royal statue.

[323] Dalley 1986:89 and n.22 following Na'aman 1981:47–48.

[324] For references to Shamash (col.i:45, ii:7, iii:18,33) and Ṣalmu (col.ii:7–8, iii:37) in the Middle Assyrian coronation ritual, cf. Müller 1937:10–11,16–17; for examples from god lists and legal contracts, cf. Dalley 1986:88–91.

[325] Cf. Dalley 1986:94–96.

[326] Dietrich and Loretz 1983:19 and n.16.

[327] So Pitard 1978:68, but cf. Good 1980:41; Levine and de Tarragon 1984:652.

[328] Levine and de Tarragon 1984:652; similarly de Moor 1976:341–42 and n.108 *qari'tumu*.

[329] Verreet 1983:240–41 and cf. p.241 n.145, for other writers who reject the *qatila* perfect (Rainey, Gordon, Dietrich, Loretz and Sanmartín, and Tsevat); add Pardee 1979:406.

third aleph verbs and nouns can function as a syllable closing, vowelless aleph irrespective of the preceding (or following) vowels designated in the script.[330] Verreet's work is also important for our treatment of other forms in 1.161 (e.g., *rp'im*, line 8 and *ks'i*, line 13, see below).

Good suggested that the verbal forms in lines 2–3 and 9–10 are 2pl internal passives. This avoids having to interpret the final *-m* as enclitic and it does away with the presence of ritual instructions alternating with the singular forms in the following lines. He also proposed that *rp'i* in line 2 could remain in the accusative case since with passive verbs, the accusative case with bound forms might designate the vocative as in classical Arabic.[331] Bordreuil and Pardee have rendered all of the verbs of lines 2–12 as internal passives with vocatives, the lone exception being *qr'u* in line 8.[332] The following *rp'im* which they understood to be in the oblique case, *rapi'īma*, requires an active verb. This form does not represent the vocative in the accusative case with a 2pl verb since, in their view, the verbal form *qr'u* is 3pl; nor is it the subject of a passive verb since this would demand the nominative case. In any event, Taylor analyzed *qr'u* as a 2mpl internal passive "you are summoned" and *rp'im* as the plural oblique in the accusative with the vocative force "O heroes of old."[333] But Verreet's recent work has exposed the uncertain evidence cited in support of an internal passive in Ugaritic.[334]

Dietrich and Loretz applied Verreet's findings to 1.161 in an attempt to remove the difficulties with regard to the person, number, and voice of the verbs and the case of the related nouns. They rendered the verbs of lines 2–3, 9–10 as jussives and the forms in lines 4–8, 11–12 as imperatives: *qr'u* in line 8 (2mpl) and *qr'a* in lines 4–7, 11–12 (2fpl).[335] According to these authors, both men and women took active parts in the ceremonies as is possibly the case in *KTU* 1.40.[336] They also suggested new grammatical analyses for *ks'i* and *'ibky* in line 13 and *rp'im* in line 24 in view of Verreet's theory concerning the vowelless aleph. The

---

330 Verreet 1983:256–57. It can also represent *'i*, cf. p.258. On the Ugaritic aleph, add Segert 1984:22–23, but cf. Marcus 1987:489–90. Verreet 1983:242,247,257 views the verbs in lines 2–12 as perfects and vocalizes the forms as follows: *qara'tumu*, *qaba'tumu*, and *qara'a*. He does not treat *qr'u* of line 8.

331 Good 1980:41.

332 Bordreuil and Pardee 1982:126 who follow Singer 1948:1–10 on the vocative significance of the oblique case.

333 Cf. Taylor 1986:315–18.

334 Cf. Verreet 1983:234–36; 1985:324–30. Forms like *y'uḫd* previously read as passives of one kind or another, Verreet reads as *ya'ḫudu*, an active imperfect, just like *y'iḫd* = *ya'ḫudu*. In both cases, whether *'u* or *'i*, the aleph is vowelless and closes the syllable.

335 Dietrich and Loretz 1983:18–19. On this understanding of the verbs, see similarly Pope 1977a:177.

336 On *KTU* 1.40, see Xella 1981a:253–67, esp. pp.260–62; de Moor and Sanders 1991:283–300.

form *ks'i* was rendered *kussi'a*, the accusative singular, *'ibky* as *'abkiyu* 1cs (but read now *tbky* in line 13), and *rp'im* as *rapi'ūma*, the nominative plural.[337]

Xella translated the forms in lines 2–12 as perfects. The change from plural to singular coincides with the change from general reference to specific *rp'um* and with the change of subject. This avoids the necessity of postulating designated male and female roles for 1.161, the supporting evidence for which is clearly exceptional (i.e., *KTU* 1.40). Del Olmo Lete prefers the rhetoric/imperative alternation frequent in the hymnic form, "Have you invoked . . . " *(qr'itm)*/ "Invoke . . . !" (*qr'a*; cf. 1.4:III:30–36).[338] The present rendition is essentially a combination of Verreet, Xella and del Olmo Lete which offers the benefit of circumventing the instructional imperative.

Both *q-r-'* and *q-b-'* in 1.161 has been generally understood to convey the invocation of the dead who ascend to the world above and who possess the supernatural power to bless the living. In 1 Sam. 28:15, *qāra'* + *l^{ə}-* has this significance where king Saul explains the reason for having invoked the dead prophet Samuel and this passage has undoubtedly influenced interpretations of *q-r-'* and *q-b-'* in *KTU* 1.161. But the one "called" in 1 Samuel 28 is clearly depicted as a ghost and the ritual setting is unequivocally necromancy. The situation is altogether different in 1.161. Those usually considered the dead heroes, the *rp'i 'arṣ*, are living attendees, and those others identified as dead, the *mlkm* and *rp'im qdmym* (lines 6–8,11–12), remain below as weak shades lacking the powers of the dead depicted in 1 Samuel 28 or in the Mesopotamian necromantic incantations of the first millennium B.C.E. (for which, cf. 4.5.1.).

Where the dead function as the objects of the verb *q-r-'* in 1.161 (lines 6–8,11–12)—unlike the occurrence of *qāra'* + *l^{ə}-* in 1 Sam. 28:15—Ugaritic *q-r-'* lacks the *l-* preposition and is governed by accusative objects instead.[339] Owing to the remaining problematic contexts where *q-r-'* occurs in Ugaritic, its cognates in biblical Hebrew and early Aramaic offer worthy comparisons.[340] When *qāra'* + accusative personal object appears in biblical Hebrew, as in 1.161, it can denote the notification of the object located in one cosmological sphere to perform a task

337 Dietrich and Loretz 1983:19.

338 Del Olmo Lete 1986a:92–93.

339 The distinction between the summoning of the living in lines 2–5,9–10 and the commissioning of the dead in lines 6–8,11–12 might be indicated stylistically by the absence of parallel *q-b-'* verbal forms in lines 6–8,11–12.

340 The verb *q-r-'* without *l-* repeatedly appears in the Rephaim texts, 1.21:A and 1.22:A with *rp'im* or *rp'um* as possible accusative object (recall that the aleph might be vowelless and syllable closing in such cases), but the problems inherent in using the fragmentary and multi-authored Rephaim texts for reconstructions of the religious significance of the Ugaritic *rp'um* are legion, cf. Pitard's recent edition, 1992a:33–77. On Ugaritic *q-b-'*, see Gaster 1976:103 n.B; Dahood 1977:527–28 and Taylor 1984:13. The Akkadian equivalent of Ugaritic *q-b-'* is now attested at Ugarit *qabû* (< *qabā'u*) in *RS* 1980.389:2,4, cf. Arnaud 1982:218.

assigned by a superior personal subject in another, in other words a commissioning. This is its significance in Isa. 13:3 and 46:11 where the deity commissions those on earth to perform tasks. The commission does not necessitate that the object or hearer cross over into the cosmological sphere of the summoner. Rather, those commissioned perform tasks within their own world. Likewise in *KAI* 214:13, king Panamu(wa) recalls how Hadad had commissioned him, (*yqrny*, prefixed verbal form of *q-r-'* + accusative personal object) to build a statue of the god and his own "place" (*mqm*, a palace or tomb?). This semantic function of *q-r-'* conforms with the commissioning of the weak dead down below in 1.161 to prepare for, to receive, and to escort to his netherly dwelling, the imminently arriving and recently deceased king following his throne (lines 6–8,11–12).

Lines 2–3, 9–10: *rp'i 'arṣ // qbṣ ddn*. In 3.1.7., we proposed that the Ugaritic texts portrayed the *rp'i 'arṣ // qbṣ dt/dn* as mythic warrior heroes lacking any link with the netherworld. A living element within the *rp'um* was also identified in the dispensary lists which date from the last days of Ugarit, the *bn rp'iyn*. In the present text, 1.161, the coronation of Ammurapi, also from the latter days of Ugarit, such living warriors are identified as the *rp'i 'arṣ*. Their status as living warriors is given added support by the affinities which 1.161 shares with Syrian and Mesopotamian coronation rites. In such ceremonies, living nobles and dignitaries are called to assemble for the new king's coronation (cf. 3.1.9.1.). Their assembly apparently gave the new king civil and sacral legitimation.

Line 13: *ks'i*. Interpreters have assumed that the *aleph* represents the case of the noun and were thereby forced to argue that the throne was personified and so it was given a vocative plural force (but cf. *ksh* in line 20).[341] However, the plural of *ks'i* would be *ks'at*. Irrespective of the accompanying vowel, the Ugaritic *aleph* sign with third *aleph* nouns in syllable closing position is vowelless according to Verreet.[342] Thus, *kussi'a* should be rendered in the accusative case as the object of the verb *tbky*.

Line 13: *tbky*. This reading is preferred by Pitard although it remains in doubt.[343] The verbal form is the G 2ms imperfect *tabkiyu*, "you shall weep," and refers to Ammurapi. If the alternative reading *'ibky* were preferred, it would not necessitate analyzing it as the rarely attested imperative with prosthetic *aleph* for the *aleph* sign when prefixed to verbal forms might signify the vowelless *aleph* prefix, thus *'abkiyu*, "I will weep."[344]

---

341 Cf. e.g., Bordreuil and Pardee 1982:123,126; Levine and de Tarragon 1984:652; Taylor 1985:315–18; 1988a:151–77; Lewis 1989:19–20.

342 Verreet 1983:256–57.

343 Pitard 1987:78–81, but cf. Pardee 1987:212–13.

344 Verreet 1984:309 but cf. Rainey 1987:396.

Line 15: *ṯlḥn mlk*. The term *mlk* was formerly read as *ml'a* and cited as evidence for the mention of food offerings. It is not in genitival relationship with *ṯlḥn*. Based on the stichometry of lines 15–16, *mlk* is best understood as a case of enjambment, a phenomenon proposed by previous commentators at several other points in the text. It would then be included in line 16 with the following *w*.[345] The *w* is either a *mater lectionis* for the vowel of the nominative case i.e., *mlkw* = *malku* or it might represent a following emphatic conjunction.

Line 16: *'udm'th*. The mention of tears has not attracted the attention of scholars other than to suggest a common mourning rite. But the magical power of tears has played a central role in funerary rituals in other societies. For example, in the funerary feasts of the Torajas, the Galelarese, and the Javanese of Indonesia, tears were thought to possess the power to revive the dead as well as express grief and mourning. In Scandinavian mythology, Baldr, the beautiful son of Odin, having been killed could leave the netherworld of Hel and return to live among the gods only if all things in creation shed tears for him.[346] In our text, tears, in addition to their expression of sorrow, might have possessed the power to temporarily invigorate (or quench the thirst of) the ghost of Ammurapi's father during his otherwise debilitating journey to netherworld.[347]

Lines 17–20. The lamentations of the king in lines 17–19a are followed in lines 19b–20 by the royal petition to the goddess Shapash for personal restoration. As they stand, lines 17, 18–19a, 19b, and 20 exhibit extreme imbalance and confusion.[348] In past treatments, this has been partly rectified by positing enjambment

---

345 Stichometric analysis provides a descriptive approach for approximating the length of lines, for line length has served as the basis for establishing the parameters of Ugaritic prosody. The first column below displays our stichometric analysis. The column's first number indicates the number of words per line, the second, the number of syllables, the third, the number of *morae*, the fourth, the number of letters, and the fifth, the number of vocables. The second column displays a syntactic-semantic analysis indicating the possible relationships between parallel words or phrases. Column three contains a vocalized text arranged in poetic lines:

cols. 1		2		3
(3/10/12/12/24)	c	b	a″	*lipanêhu yabkiyu ṯulḥana*
(3/10/11/13/24)	d	b″	a‴	*malku yibla'u 'udma'atihu*

Left unchanged, lines 15 and 16 display a major imbalance in lineation: (4/12/13/15/29) and (3/9/10/11/21).

346 Cf. Gaster 1950:15–16; Moon 1987:360–61. Hvidberg 1962:55–56 offered a similar interpretation of Anat's weeping for the dead Baal in 1.6:I:9–10 and cf. 1.19:II:61–74, but this went hand-in-hand with his interpretation of the Baal-Mot myth as a seasonal fertility cult drama, so the tears were viewed as reviving the vegetation.

347 Gaster 1976:101–02 offered the explanation that the tears simply served to quench the thirst of Niqmaddu.

348 (3/13/16/13/29), (3/9–11/11/12/22), (5/13/15/15/32), and (4/11/12/14/27) respectively.

for these lines. Not previously proposed however, was the enjambment of the third occurrence of *'dmt* in line 17. It is, in fact, separated from the two preceding occurrences by the absence of the conjunctive *w*. Thus, we suggest that the final *'dmt* functions as the adverbial accusative of *'išḫn* in line 18.

Line 17: *'dmt*. Pope has offered the Arabic cognate *'ad̲ama*, "to seize with the teeth, bite, chew violently," as an expression of violent grief.[349] This is particularly appropriate to the context.

Line 18: *'išḫn*. This form has been most frequently analyzed as an imperative with prosthetic *aleph*. In the light of Verreet's findings, a prefixed verbal form of *šwḫ/šḫḫ*, "to bow down, sink down," with suffixed *n* would be likely.[350] The subject then would be the living king who laments the death of his father.

Line 19: *'ln*. This form is generally rendered as a preposition or adverb *'l* with the pronominal suffix *n*. We read the form as *'alîni*, the internal causative imperative of *'ly* with 1cs suffix "lift me up!."[351] As such, it serves as the complement to the king's sinking down, for now the king petitions Shapash to restore and exalt him. How Shapash accomplishes the king's restoration is described at the end of line 19.

Line 19: *tṣḥ*. Commentators typically understand this portion of line 19 as an introductory formula preceding a speech of Shapash in lines 20ff. and the form *tṣḥ* has been derived from a root *ṣw/yḥ*, "to shout, cry out." But words of incantation or the like are not normally put in the mouth of a god.[352] Besides, a portrayal of the sun goddess as calling out (*tṣḥ*) seems out of place. Caquot offered *ṣḥḥ*, "to gleam, be dazzling."[353] A similar alternative might be *nṣḥ*, "to shine," as found in Syriac. In other words, Ammurapi petitions the sun goddess to offer her invigorating power to one stricken with grief. But line 19b might also comprise the king's presentation before the deity, with the appearance of the sun goddess' light, which the king sought, signaling her sanction of his claim to the throne. That a shrine of Shapash might provide the backdrop for the coronation ceremony with its attendant mourning rites contained in 1.161 is supported by the sun goddess' great popularity in the Ugaritic cult (cf. e.g., 1.41. etc.), and also by the fact that she had a cultic place built in her honor, a *bt špš* (cf. 6.24:2). Whether this comprised a sanctuary within the royal complex or an independent structure is difficult to determine. Although *Mari* 12803 does not comprise a close generic parallel to 1.161, it does mention a sanctuary of the sun god and it has

---

349 Pope 1977a:180.

350 For this etymology, cf. Pitard 1978:71. Others proposed *ṣḥn*, "to be hot," with the sun goddess as subject, following Caquot 1976a:427.

351 Cf. Segert 1984:68–69 for the internal causative in Ugaritic.

352 So Pitard 1978:71.

353 Caquot 1976a:428.

been suggested that that rituals might have been enacted in an area within the royal palace dedicated to Shamash.[354]

Lines 20–26: *'aṯr . . . 'arṣ rd.* A number of commentators have taken these lines to refer to Shapash's netherworld descent, but both our negative findings with regard to the presumed netherworld descent of the sun deity at Ugarit and the specific criticisms against this interpretation of 1.161:20–26 suggest otherwise (cf. 3.1.7.2.).[355] The interpretation which has the throne descending to the netherworld "after its Lord," Niqmaddu, has been recently defended and sufficient comparative evidence has been cited which depicts the importance and presence of the royal throne in the netherworld.[356] The question remains as to how this descent was thought to be accomplished. During the ritual the throne was placed in the royal tomb alongside the king. In a recently published Neo-Assyrian text describing a royal funeral, the regalia of the dead king was first presented before the sun god Shamash and then placed in the royal tomb.[357]

The throne is depicted as descending not to Niqmaddu, but to others already resident in the netherworld (lines 22b–25). With the dead heroes and kings below commissioned (lines 6–8,11–12), the appropriate funerary rites of mourning (and gift giving) completed (lines 13–17), and the sun goddess' sanction of the new king announced (lines 18–19), Niqmaddu's throne was placed with his body in the tomb which was then shut and sealed. The throne was then ritually commanded to descend to the netherworld where the dead heroes and kings were waiting to receive it and then transport it to Niqmaddu's netherly abode. Thus, the throne preceded Niqmaddu to the netherworld in anticipation of his arrival there which would take place only after the extended process of decay. Thus, assuming that *aṯr*

---

354 Durand 1987b:108 n.209 and lines I:12–15. Birot 1980:143,146 concluded that a temple of Shamash was in view.

355 Taylor 1988a:151–77 has summarized the criticisms against this position; (1) Shapash would have to speak to herself but the second person suffix on *b'lk* in line 21 proves otherwise and (2) no one in the context could be considered "the Lord" of Shapash who would have the authority to order her to descend.

356 Cf. Taylor 1988a:151–77. The critique of Lewis 1989:40–44 not only sets aside this view prematurely, but cannot stand in the light of our findings regarding the lack of reference in the Ugaritic texts to the sun goddess' location in the netherworld, cf. 3.1.7.3. Tsumura's arguments against Taylor are likewise unwarranted. If thrones are depicted in the netherworld as are food and water, then if the latter are also described as having descended below, it is plausible that thrones did the same. This finds confirmation in the inclusion of royal regalia and furniture in the tomb of a king, cf. Foxvog 1980:67-75 and McGinnis 1987:1-11. Isa. 14:9 is mute in this regard, the descent or "pre-existence" of thrones in the netherworld is not view; either scenario might have served as backdrop here. The assumption that the funerary meal was shared by the living and the dead who ascended to be present is unwarranted and Tsumura cites no texts in support (he interprets 1.161 in this fashion, but the circularity in argument is self-evident).

357 Cf. *K*.7856 in McGinnis 1987:1–11, esp. pp.2,4 and for a recently published text from the Pre-Sargonic period listing grave goods including such furniture as a bed, cf. Foxvog 1980:67–75.

is the preposition, it would convey a directional force, not the temporal sequence of descent. The scribe's intention in recording *tḥm 'u. nqmd. mlk*, "May you remain warm, yea, Niqmaddu, O king," in line 26 (see below) must be taken seriously. It comprises a reference to the sun goddess' special care for the dead king during the transition, or rite of passage, from the world of the living to the world of the dead.

Line 20: *ksh*. Some interpreters read *ksh* as "cup." This was motivated in part by the desire to conform the details of 1.161 with those commonly attributed to the regular *kispum* ritual. Once food offerings had been identified in the reference to *ṯlḥn ml'a*, "the full table," of line 15, one could expect to find the corresponding libations as in this line. The majority of commentators nevertheless read here a scribal error for *ks'i*, "throne," and in view of the recent collations, the reading *ml'a* in line 15 is no longer valid as we noted above.[358]

Lines 22–25: *tḥt*. Most view this as the preposition "beneath, under." Alternative nouns have also been proposed.[359] Margalit offered a verb based on Akkadian *taḫu* meaning "juxtapose."[360] Del Olmo Lete advanced the root *nḥt*, "to descend." Throughout the text, the author demonstrates a propensity for using and repeating verbs: *q-r-'// q-b-'* (lines 1–2,9–10), *q-r-'* (lines 3–8,11–12), *b-k-y* (lines 13,15), *'išḫn* (line 18 twice), *y-r-d* (lines 21–22) and, we would add, the verbal root *n-ḥ-t* in lines 22b–25.[361] Only one preposition, *'aṯr*, is repeated and then only twice in line 20 (but others like Pitard read *aṯr* as a noun "place," cognate with Akkadian *ašru*). We tentatively analyze the form *tḥt* as a G volitive, *tiḥḥata*, "go down," parallel to the preceding imperatives.[362] The root *n-ḥ-t* occurs elsewhere in Ugaritic in 1.23:47 *nḥtm* (ptc.) and 1.2:IV:18 *ynḥt* (D stem) and the assimilation of the *nun* in the G stem would be expected.[363]

Line 26: *tḥm*. Interpreters typically emend this form to *tḥt* owing to the latter's four previous occurrences. However, the root *ḥmm*, "to be warm, heated," and the likelihood that Niqmaddu had yet to arrive in the netherworld as he was

[358] Cf. most recently, Taylor 1988a:155 n.9; Lewis 1989:24–35 for summaries and bibliography. Tsumura 1993:49-50 rejects the vocative use of *lksh*. While de Moor's insistence in favor of the vocative, as noted by Tsumura, is unwarranted, Tsumura's rejection of the vocative here is likewise unjustified, since as he acknowledges it does in fact appear in the type of parallelism in question. Other considerations must be brought to bear on the question. In any case, the stylistic parallelism between *lksh* and *arṣ rd* in no way necessitates their semantic synonymity (*contra* Tsumura 1993:52). Again, other considerations must be given precedence.

[359] Cf. Healey 1978b:85,87 "throne" and Cecchini 1981:27–32 "subterranean region."

[360] Margalit 1980b:197–99.

[361] del Olmo Lete 1983:171.

[362] On the volitive, cf. Rainey 1987:397–99 who concluded that the Ugaritic volitive is more intensive than the jussive.

[363] Cf. *tēḥat* in Prov. 17:10, 3fs or 2ms < *nāḥēṯ*. In biblical Hebrew, *n-ḥ-t* in the Qal assimilates the initial *nun*.

only recently or was about to be buried recommend the alternative of positing a request by Ammurapi that Shapash give warmth to his father Niqmaddu during his journey toward that chilly destination.[364] The presence here of yet another verb is consistent with the author's propensity as pointed out above.

Line 27: *ṯ'y*. This form is commonly translated "to make sacrifice" and finds immediate support in the mention of *dbḥ* in line 1. The term is well attested at Ugarit.[365]

Line 30: *tqdm 'ṣr*. The latter has been unanimously rendered "bird" by commentators, but the assumed mention of birds might in fact oppose this interpretation, for we know that in Mesopotamia the sacrifice of birds to chthonic beings (here Shapash) was prohibited.[366] Hebrew offers an interesting alternative in *'āṣar*, "to retain," cf. *'ᵃṣārāh*, "sacred assembly."[367] The form here is the G passive participle *'aṣīru* used collectively (lit. "those retained"). In view of the cultic context and the Hebrew analogue, we translate *'ṣr* as "the sacred assembly," a reference to the completed gathering and the near completion and climax of the ceremonies.[368] The verb *tqdm* we read as the D passive preterite *tuqaddamu*, thus, "the sacred assembly is convened."[369]

In our view, 1.161 preserves a coronation ritual that incorporates mourning rites on behalf of Niqmaddu, Ammurapi's father and former king of Ugarit and the public recitation of Niqmaddu's name on that cultic occasion points to a commemorative rite in his honor. The depiction of Ammurapi as the living recipient of blessing, along with several elements characteristic of a coronation, suggest its use on that special occasion. The coronation rites were intended to secure the oath of loyalty from the royal and military establishments as well as perhaps the general population. A royal ancestor cult rite is nowhere in view. The weakened dead below are merely alerted to receive and then to deliver Niqmaddu's throne to its netherly abode and perhaps to escort him there upon his arrival below.

---

364 This was anticipated alongside the invigoration/sustenance offered through the swallowing of tears. Gaster 1976:102 and n.54 noted the Tyrolean custom of kindling a fire for the purpose of warming the ghosts of the dead, but he posited this for *'išḫn* in lines 18–19 of our text.

365 Cf. de Tarragon 1980:58–59.

366 For an example of this, cf. the text in Thureau-Dangin 1921:65,79,85 [*AO* 6451:42]; note Oppenheim 1977:191; *CAD* 7(1960):213. The prohibitions against bird and ox sacrifices to Belet-ṣeri and Eresh-kigal are unqualified (line 42), while those against sheep offerings to Shakkan (in the temple of Shamash) and against offerings of beef to Kharru (in the temple of Sin) are restricted to a specific sacred locale (lines 40–41).

367 Cf. *EA* 138:80,130: *ḫaṣāru* and Sivan 1984:207; Moran 1987:366 n.18 = 1992:224 n.18. Ugaritic *ǵṣr* is related to Arabic *ǵḏr*, "to cut, separate," and not Hebrew *'-ṣ-r*, cf. Margalit 1980b:256.

368 For feminine nouns lacking the feminine marker at Ugarit, cf. Segert 1984:49 (par.52.2).

369 On the Ugaritic preterite, cf. Rainey 1987:397–99.

3.1.10. Summary

The belief in the supernatural beneficent power of the dead as expressed in ancestor worship or veneration and necromancy is not documented in the texts from Ugarit. Several of the frequently cited data fall entirely outside the realm of mortuary rites while others that do fall within their purview cannot be categorized as rites of the death or ancestor cult or as necromantic rites. Examples of non-mortuary elements at Ugarit include: the compound term *'il'ib* which designates "the gods of the fathers" and functions as a collective in the legends and as a heading in the pantheon lists; the *marzēaḥ*, an organization generally engaged in property transactions and a sponsor of festive occasions wherein overindulgence might on occasion get out of hand; the term *pgr*, a designation for a sacrificial animal dedicated to a god; and a mythic figure *dtn* who, in one text, petitioned the gods for a remedy on behalf of a sick child. Furthermore, the ritual underlying 1.113 neither entailed the worship of the dead kings of Ugarit nor their divinity. Rather, it presupposed the worship of the dynastic god inherited by each king upon his ascension to the throne. The public recitation of the god's name alongside that of each defunct member of the dynasty served to "genealogically" legitimate the existing political infrastructure. Finally, our findings vis-à-vis the absence of the explicit deification of kings at Ugarit has not only significantly impacted our understanding of the nature of royal ideology at Ugarit, but it has also eliminated a crucial datum supporting the notion that the dead were worshipped or venerated there.

Moving ever so cautiously from ritual texts to narrative legends, our findings would suggest that the question posed to the fatally stricken king Keret, "do gods die?" (*'u'ilm tmtn*, cf. *KTU* 1.16:I:10ff.) is not reflective of Ugaritic royal ideology. Rather, it is the query of a naive and confused, but desperate, child whose father lies stricken on his death bed. To be sure, the ambiguity is heightened by the description of Keret as a son of El or *bn 'il*. Keret had thus far experienced only "non-death" or a perpetual lifespan (*bl mt*) like the gods as the expanded description of *bl mt* in the Aqhat legend depicts it. There Anat offers the hero a "non-death" wherein he could count the years with Baal, the months like the sons of El (*bn 'il*) in festive perpetuity (1.17:VI:25–33).[370]

Nevertheless, some clues to royal ideology may be found in Keret's response. His reaction to his son's query was twofold. He requested that his son shed no tears and that he instead retrieve Keret's daughter before death arrived. No ideological

[370] Whether Anat's is an empty or genuine offer remains a point of some debate. Spronk 1986:151–61 dubiously suggests that the offer to Aqhat was a prestigious status in the netherworld wherein he would return to the land of the living in the annual New Year's festival. It was not an offer of eternal life, but cf. Pope 1987:452–63.

rationalization is offered in the face of king Keret's death so as to sustain his divine status postmortem.[371] No appeal to an afterlife like the gods is made because no such ideological element was readily accessible. Ugaritic kings were not deified after death. Deification was therefore mere *Hofstil* at Ugarit, for death emptied it of its power.[372] A direct answer to his son might have gone like this, "yes, in spite of courtly decorum, gods, if they be kings, do die the death of all men and they thereby loose whatever divine status they had obtained while alive." As so eloquently put by Aqhat when offered "non-death" by the goddess Anat, the best a mortal could hope for was a decent burial and the perpetuation of one's memory, so, "pick up your bow and make a name for yourself that will not be forgotten while you still can."

This perspective is also consistent with the commemorative rites we identified elsewhere in the Keret legend. The legend reveals that a king aspired to be memorialized at death as one worthy of exaltation by the living warrior elite known as the *rp'i 'arṣ* and *qbṣ dtn*. As 1.161 demonstrates, this ambition could be expressed through the public recitation of a king's name at his funeral. Other mortuary rites identified in our analysis of 1.161 include the funerary rites of ritualized mourning enacted on behalf of a deceased king, the ritual transfer of the throne to the recently deceased king's netherworld abode by the weakened ghosts of former kings, or the *rp'im qdmym*, and the temporary offer of sustenance (tears?) to the recently deceased king while on his netherly journey.[373]

3.2. The Evidence from Nuzi and Emar

In addition to the textual traditions from Ebla, Mari, and Ugarit, the written remains from Emar demand consideration. Already in their brief published history, scholars have repeatedly cited the Emar texts as evidence for the ancient Syrian belief in the supernatural beneficent power of the dead and the Nuzi evidence has been frequently invoked as confirmation of such an interpretation.

---

371 Here, we assume for the sake of argument that deification is an accurate portrayal of his title *bn 'il*.

372 Recall that posthumous deification should be distinguished from divine royal status attained while living, *contra* Spronk 1986:154 n.2, but cf. Healey 1984:249.

373 Recall that *KTU* 1.142 (3.1.1.7.) might point to offerings made at the grave as a means of appeasing a potentially angry ghost or of feeding the weak whose cause had been taken up by the gods. For arguments against post-funerary offerings at Ugarit based on a detailed analysis of the archaeological remains, cf. Pitard 1990:1–18; 1991:1–13; 1992b:1–21; see 4.4.3.

3.2.1. The Evidence from Nuzi

Mourning and burial rites are well attested at Nuzi.[374] That death and ancestor cult rites were observed at Nuzi has also been suggested. The Nuzi terms *kipsu*, *kispātu*, and *kipsātu* have each been offered as derivatives of *kispum* with metathesis cited as the explanation for the first and last forms.[375] Moreover, commentators have identified the *ilānu* at Nuzi as dead (deified) ancestors, for they show up alongside the *eṭemmu* on three occasions and appear as the recipients of *kipsātu*, the supposed Nuzi equivalent to *kispum*, in *AO* 15546.[376]

Tsukimoto rejected the connection of *kipsu* and *kispātu* with *kispum* and opted for *kipsātu* as the Nuzi rendition of *kispum*. He identified *kipsu* in *HSS* 13:383:4,7 with the form *kibsu* from Nimrud, a reference to the customary payment to the temple treasury.[377] Furthermore, he cast doubt on the view of *kispātu* in *AASOR* 16:66:31 as the name of "the month of the funeral offerings of *iškiški*" *arḫu kispātum ša iškiški*. Tsukimoto concluded that one would expect the syntactic construction *araḫ kispāti* or *araḫ ša kispāti*.[378] As analogues, he cited *araḫ pagri* and *araḫ ša balāṭi isinni akīti*.[379] Moreover, the designation, *kispātum ša iškiški*, is nowhere attested and the form *iškiški* is a *hapax legomenon*. Thus, Tsukimoto preferred the metathesized *kipsātu* as the most likely candidate for *kispum* at Nuzi. The decisive datum for Tsukimoto was the mention of *kipsātu* as offerings to the DINGIR^{meš} or *ilānu* in *AO* 15546. The Nuzi connection of the *ilānu*, which he viewed as the ancient ancestors, with the *eṭemmū*, which he viewed as the recent ancestors, confirmed his hypothesis that *kipsātu* was the Nuzi rendition of *kispum*.[380] In other words, one could expect the mention of *kispum* in this context.

---

[374] For mourning only: *bakû*, cf. *JEN* 1:8:11–12; 4:404:16; 4:410:12; 6:595:12; *HSS* 19:18:23–24; 19:56:15–16; 19:101. For burial only: *qebēru*, cf. *RA* 23(1926):91 [Text 5:21]; *RA* 23(1926):127 [Text 51:9]. For mourning and burial: *bakû ù qebēru*, cf. *JEN* 1:59:19–23, *HSS* 9:22:11–15, 19:11:20–25, 19:28:21–24, 19:38:23–26, 19:39:10–11, *RA* 23(1926):144 [Text 9:14–16], *JAOS* 47(1927):40–41 [Text 3:19–23], *Sumer* 32(1976):117, 133 [Text 2:24–25 = *IM* 6818]. See also the comments by San Nicolò 1933:285–86 and Greenfield 1982:311.

[375] The form *kipsu* is found in *HSS* 13:383:4,7; *kispātu* is attested in *AASOR* 16(1936):44–45 [Text 66:31]; *kipsātu* is recorded in *HSS* 14:152:7; *RA* 56(1962):59–60 [Text *AO* 15546:4–5]. For their possible connection with *kispum*, cf. Pfeiffer and Speiser 1936:115; Cassin 1962:60; *CAD* 8(1971):426; Mayer 1978:147; Tsukimoto 1985:98–106; Cohen 1993:367 n.2.

[376] Cf. Tsukimoto 1985:104–05; Rouillard and Tropper 1987a:354–56. The *ilānu* and *eṭemmu* occur side by side in *JEN* 5:478:6; *HSS* 19:27:11; YBC 5142:30–31.

[377] Tsukimoto 1985:95 *contra* Mayer 1978:147. For the Nimrud text *ND* 2319:8, cf. Parker 1954:41; *CAD* 8(1971):339.

[378] Tsukimoto 1985:106 acknowledged the fact that the phrase probably referred to the name of the month, but rejected its connection with funerary offerings.

[379] Cf. *CAD* 1/II(1968):261.

[380] Tsukimoto 1985:104–05 and cf. n. 386 where he suggests that the *eṭemmū* became *ilānu* once they lost their identifiable character.

That *kispum*-like offerings were made to the "gods" and "ghosts" has found added support in YBC 5142:30–31 where, upon the death of the testator, the heir was expected to continue to "serve" the "gods" and "ghosts" as formerly done by the now defunct father *ilāni ù eṭemmīya ipallaḫšu.*[381] Some scholars have assumed that this text also points to both the "gods" and the "ghosts" as figurines, for they appear to be objects passed on to the respective heir(ess).[382] Moreover, like the *eṭem kimti*, "the family ghost," the *ilānu* dwell in family houses *ilānīya āšib bītīya*, "my gods who inhabit my house," thus suggesting that they are dead ancestors.[383] In recent discussions these considerations have served to confirm (1) the equation of the *ilānu* and *eṭemmu*, (2) their identity as deified ancestral ghosts, (3) their function and ability to supernaturally bless the living, and (4) their representation in the form of figurines.[384]

Although provocative, this reconstruction remains highly conjectural. The fact that *kipsātu* occurs in two offering contexts, both of which lack any corroborative evidence for a mortuary context, hardly inspires confidence that what is involved is the *kispum* offering. Furthermore, the lone depiction of the *ilānu* and the *eṭemmū* as recipients of service or *palāḫu* insures neither the status of the *ilānu* as dead, deified ancestors nor the veneration or worship of the hypothetical *ilānu-eṭemmū*.

The term *ilānu* at Nuzi characteristically represents either the gods of the pantheon and/or the personal family or clan gods.[385] Moreover, we noted earlier that service to the gods was a duty expected of both the ideal son and the king. So, what may be outlined here are the duties to both the personal gods and to the ghosts, not to the remote and immediate ancestors who are referred to as, simply, the deified ancestors (cf. further 4.5.1.). This, in turn, would favor an alternative explanation for the nature of the *ilānu* who inhabited family dwellings. They are not ancestral ghosts, but personal gods who dwell in such sacred buildings as a family's private chapel.

The portrayal of both the *ilānu* and the *eṭemmū* as figurines is likewise questionable, at least in the case of the latter. In view of their laconic character, the relevant texts may simply record the heir's loss of the right of access to the "gods"

---

381 For this text, cf. Lacheman and Owen 1981:386–87,413; Paradise 1987:203–13; Rouillard and Tropper 1987a:355–56.

382 Two other texts which mention both the "gods" and the "ghosts" record the denial of rights to the disinherited son. *JEN* 5:478:6–8: *i-na* DINGIR^{meš} *ù a-na e-ṭe*$_4$*-em-mi* (erasure) A.ŠÀ^{meš} *ù* É$^{\text{há.meš}}$ *la i-la-aq-qa*$_4$ which Rouillard and Tropper 1987a:355 translate "he shall not receive the gods or the ghosts or the fields or the houses," and *HSS* 19:27:11: *ú-ul* D[INGIR^{meš}]*-ia* ⌈*ú*⌉-[*ul*] ⌈*e*⌉*-ṭe*$_4$*-em-mi-ia*, "not my gods or my ghosts," (the remaining context is damaged).

383 On their potential role as personal protective gods, cf. *RA* 23(1926):90 [Text 5:20]; Deller 1981:62; for their supposed equation with the *eṭem kimti*, cf. Rouillard and Tropper 1987a:356.

384 Cf. e.g., van der Toorn 1990:203–22.

385 For their designation as high gods, cf. Cassin 1958:18; Mayer 1978:145. For their designation as personal gods at Nuzi, cf. Vorländer 1975:63–66.

and "ghosts." That is to say, the disinherited heir could neither pray to the personal gods for protection at their shrines on family property nor have access to the family property where he could continue to "serve" the family dead at their graves. Paradise rendered the crucial text, *JEN* 5:478:6–8, as follows, "he shall not have rights to the gods and (ancestral) ghosts. Fields and houses he shall not receive," rather than, "he shall not receive the gods or the ghosts or the fields or the houses," following Rouillard and Tropper (see above).[386] It is therefore conjectural at best to assert that like the *ilānu*, depicted elsewhere at Nuzi,—which we take to be personal gods and not deified dead ancestors—the *eṭemmū* too were figurines. Lastly, and most importantly for our purposes, the mentioned service to the *eṭemmū* might entail simply the care for and feeding of or the commemoration of the dead ancestors. Owing to the fact that the exact nature of the service remains for the present inscrutable, one certainly cannot assume that it was motivated by a belief in the supernatural beneficent power of the dead.

In sum, the background central to understanding the inclusion of the *eṭemmū* in the inheritance texts from Nuzi is the location of their graves where service was to be rendered on sacred portions of family property. In other words, the fact that the disinherited heir would lose access to the "gods" and "ghosts" serves to underscore the point that he/she would not receive the family property. The underlying premise is this: access to and the presence of the personal gods in sacred buildings on family land symbolized the divine legitimation of ownership while the location of tombs housing the family ghosts on that same land established the genealogical rights to ownership.

3.2.2. The Evidence from Emar

The French archaeological expeditions to modern Meskéné, ancient Emar, have resulted in the recovery of several hundred cuneiform texts dating to the Late Bronze Age. Those published in the volumes of the *Recherches au pays d'Aštata Emar* constitute a wide range of literary genres and verify Emar's importance within the contemporary Hittite empire. These texts also furnish extensive textual evidence for the religious practices and beliefs of its Syrian inhabitants.[387] For example, various mortuary rites were apparently observed at Emar. A *kissu* feast of Ninkur refers to the *nugagtu* and although the function of this office is otherwise

[386] Paradise 1972:311 n.218. He had earlier added *la i-qe-er-re-eb* in the erasure against the rendition of Rouillard and Tropper 1987a:355. On this text, cf. also *CAD* 4(1958):397.

[387] Cf. Arnaud 1985:231–36.

irrecoverable, it probably refers to a "lamentation priestess."[388] Furthermore, an Emar version of the LÚ I lexical series lists *uruḫḫu*, "priest performing funerary rites." Whether or not this reflects an actual social reality at Emar remains to be seen.[389] An Emarite version of the *marzēaḥ* is perhaps also attested, *marzāḫu*. However, not only does the context lack any explicit mortuary associations, but the reading of the relevant line is controvertible.[390] It has been tentatively suggested that the offerings *ina bāb kimāḫi*, "at the gate of the grave," and offerings *ana abî*, "to the fathers(?)," at Emar refer to a regular monthly cycle of rites for the dead.[391] In the final analysis, the significance of these rites and their corresponding beliefs remains for the present obscure.

The genre of testament provides the most convincing evidence for the observance of death and ancestor cult practices at Emar. In several texts, the testator expresses the wish either to call (upon?) (*nabû* A) or, perhaps, lament (*nabû* B) his *ilānu*, "gods," and his *mētū*, "dead."[392] In one text, two sons inherit their dead father's estate. The sons are bequeathed several duties, one being to "honor" (*kunnû*) the "gods" or *ilānu* and the "dead" or *mētū* of their father.[393] In two other texts, the testator describes his daughter as both son and daughter, the identification of which enabled the daughter to claim the right of inheritance in the absence of sons.[394] As was the case with the two sons mentioned above, the daughter is endowed with certain tasks previously minded by her father. Among others listed

---

388 Arnaud 1980a:118; 1985:233; 1986:327 [Text 369:48],387 [Text 388:3]. In 388:6,57, a deity ^{d}*Šuwala* is mentioned as the object of ritual sacrifice and singing for whom the editor gives the alternative, but highly speculative, translation "Cheol!"

389 Cf. Civil 1987:5.

390 For one possible reading, cf. Fleming 1992:269 [Text 446:91′–92′]: $^{lú.meš}$*mar-za-ḫu ša mi-Ki* (case?). For an emended reading, cf. Arnaud 1986:422 [Text 446:91′–92′]: lú.meš ninda$^{!}$ *za-ri sa*$_{x}$-*mi-di*$^{!}$. However both Fleming and Arnaud read ^{iti}*mar-za-ḫa-nu* as the month name for this section of the ritual calendar [Text 446:85′].

391 Fleming 1992:299–300. Against his alternative proposal that Emarite *abû* is related to the Hurrian pit or *api* where contact with the dead took place, cf. 4.5.1. For the text, cf. Arnaud 1986:431–32 [Text 452:32′–33′,35′,39′–40′,50′,52′]. On p.296, Fleming also tentatively rendered the phrase *u*$_{4}$-*mi ḫu-us-si* [Text 452:1] as "the day of remembrance" on the basis of a gloss from the root *z-k-r* on Akkadian *ḫasāsu* in *EA* 228:18.

392 DINGIR^{meš}-*ia ù me-te-ia lu-ú tù-na-ab-bi*, "She shall call upon/recite the names of my gods and my dead." The verb is *nabû* A, "to name, call," or *nabû* B, "to lament," cf. *CAD* 11(1980):32–39; *AHw* 2(1971):699–700. Similar phraseology appears in at least three other texts, cf. Sigrist 1982:242; Huehnergard 1983:11–12; Arnaud 1987:233 [Text 13:6–7],238 [Text 16:25–27]. Cf. Durand 1989:85–86 for a convenient list of references; note the text in Arnaud 1986:197–98 [Text 185:2′-3′].

393 Sigrist 1982:243–45 [Text 1:25–27] ^{m}*i-túr*-DA *ù ip-ḫur*-^{d}*da-gan* DINGIR^{meš} *ù mi-ti ša a-bi-ka a-bi-šu-nu u*$_{2}$-*ka-an-nu*, "Itur-Da and Iphur-Dagan shall honor the gods and the dead of Abika, their father," and cf. Arnaud 1987:237–39 [Text 16:25–27]. Sigrist assumed that honoring one's deceased father entailed instituting regular offerings (pp.244–45). The verb is *kunnû*, "to honor (a deity or dead person)," cf. *CAD* 8(1971):540–42.

394 Huehnergard 1983:28; 1985:430.

is the duty of "naming, calling (upon?)" (*nabû* A), or, perhaps, "lamenting" (*nabû* B), the *ilānu*, "gods," and the *mētū*, "dead."[395]

While Arnaud specified the rendering, "to invoke," for the verb *kunnû* which, as it stands, is rather ambiguous,[396] Durand understood both this term and *nabû*, "to call," in a more technical sense, "to pronounce the name," and presupposed an ancestor cult background. He cited the Mari and Ugaritic materials in support.[397] Accordingly, the dead were deified and were to be summoned to appear in order that they might bless the living.[398] However, the related act of "speaking the name" as observed on behalf of the ancestors in Mesopotamia (*šuma zakāru*) might point to a commemorative act and not to ancestor veneration or worship. A straightforward reading of the Assyrian text often cited in support demonstrates that it expresses merely the concern to memorialize the recently dead along with the olden dead: *šumka itti eṭemmē azkur*, "I have recited your name along with the ghosts of the dead (*eṭemmū*)," *šumka itti kispī azkur*, "I have recited your name while (offering) the *kispū*."[399] This is clearly the significance of the acts in the biblical traditions which accompany the related *hazkîr šēm*, "reciting the (dead's) name," (2 Sam. 18:18) and *hāqîm šēm-hammēṯ*, "perpetuating the dead's name," (Ruth 4:10).

Now if lamenting of the "gods" and the "dead" were in view in these texts, that is to say that *nabû* B rather than *nabû* A was the underlying root, then at least in the case of the *mētū*, we might have additional data for the observation of funerary or, more specifically, mourning rites at Emar.[400] More to the point, if mourning rites were reflected in the use of the term *nabû* (i.e., "lamenting" *nabû* B), then the case for the chthonic nature of the *ilānu* would be strengthened. Nevertheless, the "gods" might be chthonic gods other than the dead who require ritual lamentation. Even assuming this scenario, the dead's supernatural beneficent powers are nowhere in view. In any case, the frequent use of *ilānu* to designate the

---

[395] Huehnergard 1983:11–19 [Text 1:8], 26–29 [Text 2:11] and cf. Ben-Barak 1988:87–97.

[396] Arnaud 1987:237 n.39.

[397] Durand 1989:87–88.

[398] So also van der Toorn 1990:203–22.

[399] For the text, cf. *CAD* 4(1958):400a; see Ribar 1973:31 who likewise views commemoration as the ritual present here.

[400] For *mētū* we would have expected *mītūtū*. Huehnergard 1983:28 tentatively took the form *me-te-ia* to be the irregular plural of *mītūtīya*, cf. also his qualified translations on pp.15,19. Durand 1989:87 made a distinction between the *mītū* "the clan dead" (cf. e.g., Sigrist 1982:243–45 and Arnaud 1987:237–39 line 26 DINGIR^{meš} *ù mi-ti ša a-bi-ka a-bi-šu-nu ú-ka-an-nu*) while the *mītūtū* designated "the dead in general" (cf. e.g., the texts in Huehnergard 1983:11–19,26–29). Arnaud 1986:197 understood the form to represent "lesser divinities."

major gods and personal gods suggests that at Emar the same applies in the use of the term even when found coupled with forms of *mētū* (cf. further 4.5.1.).[401]

In fact, there are several points that favor *nabû* A, "to call," over *nabû* B, "to lament." First, the other two verbs that occur at Emar with the couplet "gods and the dead" as their object, *palāḫu* and *kunnû*, do appear independently in conjunction with the cult of the gods and in no case is lamentation in view. Second, the appearance of previously unattested verbal forms in the D pattern like *nabû* A is well attested at Emar.[402] Third, as Fleming points out, the related variant phraseology with gods and goddesses or personal protective deities serving as objects of *nabû* shows that the underlying ritual is not restricted to lamenting the dead.[403] Fourth, that same variant might suggest that the dead played only a minor role within the context of inheritance or that as members of a larger class of numina, they are mentioned only as representative of that class. The mentioned gods are thus the same as those referred to elsewhere at Emar as DINGIR-*li* É.GAL, "the gods of the main house," and DINGIR-*li ša* $^{lú.meš}$*aḫ-ḫi*, "the gods of the brothers." These gods were the family and clan gods who were housed (i.e., their images) in private chapels at Emar.[404]

In sum, the customary duties of honoring the gods and the dead (*kunnû*) would include the invocation of the gods on the one hand and on the other the concern to care for or to feed the dead and their commemoration. Both of these religious concerns could fall within the range of rites and beliefs reflected in the semantic range of the verb *nabû* A. But if the gods in these texts are the personal family gods as would be most fitting in a testamentary context, then the mere public recitation of their names along with those of the dead might be in view. Such rites would reflect a domestic version of that which was suggested for the so-called king lists from Ebla and Ugarit (cf. 2.2.1. and 3.1.6.). The ritual in those instances comprised a legitimation rite which identified the dynastic god with the dead as well as the living dynasts through the recollection of the dynastic genealogy. The

---

401 Snell 1983–84:159–70 assumed that the phrase DINGIR.ME-*ni ša a-bi-ia a-na še-bu-te al-ta-kà-a-an*, "I have put the gods of my father as witnesses," in a text from El-Qitar (lines 23–24) refers to the ancestors as *ilānu* as at Nuzi and Emar. Despite the text's similar concern to regulate inheritance, it is the gods of the pantheon and/or personal gods who commonly function as witnesses to legal agreements, not the dead ghosts. Moreover, the gods here are not described as one of the objects of inheritance.

402 Huehnergard 1989:173–74.

403 Fleming 1993:178. The Akkadian reads: DINGER^{meš}*ia* ^{d}*iš$_8$-tár* ^{meš}*-ia lu-ú ta-nab-bi*.

404 *Contra* van der Toorn 1993:1–27 who cites as support the dubious Ugaritic and biblical evidence as well as the ambiguous Hurrian and Hittite data for deification of the dead, but who nevertheless admits that DINGIR and GIDIM occur together only in Akkadian texts written in Anatolia and cf. Pitard 1993:14. In any case, his interpretation of the rite of the *ḫukku*-bread as a *kispu* ritual following Durand does not consider the possibility that what might have transpired was a celebration of the sale of property by the family or clan gods (see further below).

formulaic phrase "the god of So-and-so" was repeated with the substitution of each deceased successor's name while the relevant offerings were performed. In any case, whether these mortuary rites underlying the references to the gods and the dead took place on a regular basis or during the funerary period at Emar is impossible to decide.

In addition to the references in which the *ilānu* are mentioned alongside the *mētū*, Durand has cited other textual data in support of a domestic ancestor cult at Emar. He concluded that in several texts where Arnaud had read the term *kuburu*, "heavy (silver)," in fact, what was involved was a mortuary rite observed at the site of the family *qubūru*, "grave." For Durand, this in turn presupposed a mortuary context for the rites and offerings involving the *ḫukku*-bread in which the *ḫukku*-bread or offering was broken or carried out and the table was anointed. In one instance, the immediate context also mentions the performance of an offering designated by the verb *kasāpu*, the cognate of *kispu*.[405] Thus, the *ḫukku*-bread was a *kispu* offering. According to Durand, these rites were occasioned by the sale, transfer, and potential alienation, of family property. The brothers participated in these rites adjacent to the family grave(s) or *qubūru*. This signified the cessation of their rites to honor (*kunnû*) the dead.[406] In at least one text, the duty of honoring the gods and the dead follows a reference to the family grave.[407] But even if one should assume that Durand's proposal stands, these references neither portray the rites as regularly observed nor do they point to the active participation of the dead, let alone whether or not the belief in the ghost's supernatural beneficent power underlies their observance. The rites involving the dead may simply constitute rites intended to preserve the memory of the ancestral dead, to care for the dead, and to confirm, as a final act before transferring the family property, the living's ownership of the land by perpetuating the names of their ancestors who had previously possessed that property.

In any event, Scurlock has challenged Durand's connection of *kuburu* with *qubūru*. First, the mention of the family tomb in other such documents occurs as part of the description of the house and not in the closing formulae as would be the case in the Emar texts. Second, it is unlikely that family tombs attached to larger estates would be sold for one shekel as demanded by Durand's interpretation when the estates sold for a price ranging from a fourth of a mina to three hundred shekels. Third, the land for sale is described as "unbuilt ground" which would not adequately explain the inclusion of the family cemetery or *qubūru* in that sale of property. Fourth, the *kuburu* formula most closely approximates the *atru* formula

405 Cf. Arnaud 1986:31–32 [Text 20:18–20; 109:17–19; 110:23–25].

406 Durand 1989:85–88.

407 Cf. Durand 1989:85–86; for the text, see Sigrist 1982:243–45 [Text 1:10–11,25–27]; Arnaud 1987:237–39 [Text 16:10–11,25–27].

found in Babylonian contracts and is therefore more likely an additional payment which each of the brothers received as part of the sale. The sale therefore entailed a purchase price, a communal meal involving *ḫukku*-bread, and an additional payment or *kuburu*-payment to each of the brothers.[408]

In closing, we mention the Emarite deity Milku or ^{d}*milku*,[409] and the ^{d}*imliku* found in offering lists. Arnaud views the last as the divine warriors and guardians of the entrances to Nergal's infernal city.[410] Whether or not they represent dead "rulers" like the *malikū* at Mari and the *mlkm* at Ugarit remains to be ascertained. Based on the equation of ^{d}*malik* and Nergal in the Old Babylonian Weidner god list (*OECT* 1:9:2:8), one might be tempted to equate ^{d}*milku* with Nergal at Emar. This would explain the apparent depiction of the ^{d}*imliku* as protégés of Nergal; they are simply the pluralization of ^{d}*milku*. But it should be noted that ^{d}*milku* is listed separately from Nergal as the recipient of offerings in at least one ritual text from Emar.[411]

3.2.3. Summary

The Nuzi and Emar texts preserve a variety of non-royal mortuary practices. Funerary rites such as burial and lamentation are well attested. The repeated mention of the "gods" or *ilānu* in parallel to the "ghosts" or *eṭemmū* at Nuzi and the "gods" or *ilānu* alongside the "dead" or *mētū* in inheritance texts from Emar has been cited in support of the equation of the gods and the dead, their identity as deified ancestors, and their supernatural power to bless the living. At Nuzi both entities are either served (*palāḫu*) by the heir(ess), or he/she is denied ownership of them. At Emar, the names of both are recited (or perhaps lamented) and honored. However, the absence of the deification of the dead in Syro-Palestinian traditions and the fact that these numina appear together in non-poetic contexts favor their complementarity over their equivalency. Two distinct domestic ritual complexes, the care and the recitation of the major or personal gods (*ilānu*) and the feeding and commemoration of the family dead (*eṭemmu* or *mētū*) were responsibilities passed down the family line. As we suggested previously, access to and the presence of the personal gods in sacred buildings on family land symbolized the divine legitimation of ownership while the location of tombs housing the family ghosts on that same land established the genealogical rights to ownership. In the final analysis, neither Nuzi nor Emar attest to ancestor worship or veneration, or, to

---

408 Scurlock 1993:15–16.

409 Cf. Arnaud 1986:460,466 [Texts 472:62′; 473:15′].

410 Cf. Arnaud 1985:235; 1986:354,373 [Texts 373:124′; 378:41].

411 Cf. Arnaud 1986:466 [Text 473:14′: ^{d}NÈ-IRI$_{11}$GAL; line 15′: ^{d}*mil-ku*].

necromantic practices expressive of the corresponding belief in the supernatural beneficence of the dead.

Our findings in chapters two and three strongly suggest that an indigenous belief in the supernatural beneficent power of the dead remains unattested for the Syrian cultures represented at Ebla, Mari, Ugarit, and Emar of the third to second millennia. Our findings with regard to these Syrian sites provide the necessary background for what ensues: a detailed analysis of the relevant biblical traditions which will be further supplemented by an examination of the first millennium extra-biblical texts recovered from Syria and Palestine.

Chapter 4

The Textual Evidence from the Hebrew Bible

Having set forth in the preceding chapters what can be confirmed with regard to the belief in the benevolent power of the dead in Syria(-Palestine) of the pre-first millennium, an examination of the relevant evidence preserved in the Hebrew Bible is now in order. Marked swings in the pendulum have characterized the history of interpretation apropos of Israelite ancestor cults and necromancy. The pendulum appears to be decidedly on the move again in the direction of *apex pro*, for the number of those scholars who advocate that such practices and their corresponding beliefs were embraced by Israelite society is clearly on the rise.[1]

Before examining the relevant texts of the Hebrew Bible, however, the pertinent Syro-Palestinian epigraphic evidence from the early to mid first millennium B.C.E. deserves mention. In past treatments, biblical scholars have cited occasional references to supposed ancestor cult practices in the contemporary Aramaic, Phoenician, and Palestinian inscriptions. This has lent support to the notion that such practices were indigenous to the cultures of Syria and Palestine and that Israel had embraced these practices early on under the influence of these local populations.

4.1. The Extra-biblical Textual Evidence from Syria-Palestine: The Early to Mid First Millennium B.C.E.

First to be considered is the relevant Aramaic evidence. The primary datum cited as indicative of an Aramaic royal ancestor cult is the Hadad inscription or *KAI* 214. Despite the several lacunae in the immediate context, the phrase in line 21 *wyzkr 'šm pnmw*, "and (he) invokes the name of Panammū(wa)," has been viewed

[1] E.g., Heider 1985:383–400; Lang 1988b:144–56; 1988a:12–23; Smith and Bloch-Smith 1988:277–84; Lewis 1989; Tropper 1989 have each expressed a general alignment with this view. For a survey of modern research and the current revival of earlier theories affirming the existence of such cults in ancient Israel, cf. Spronk 1986:25–54.

as the invocation of the dead ancestor, Panammū(wa) I, the eighth century king of Sam'al. However, the reading of line 21 is debatable. Not only is the first term restored from an extensive lacuna i.e., [*wyzk*]*r*, but the meaning of *'šm* has been variously understood.[2] While the following collation is given in the edition of Donner and Röllig: [. . .]*r 'šm pnmw*, the verb [*wyzk*]*r* is frequently reconstructed on the basis of line 16: *wyzkr 'šm hdd*.[3]

However, lines 16 and 21 are not directly parallel, for the object of one is a known deity and of the other, a royal personage. Moreover, in view of the difficulties of the text, a reconstruction of line 21 on the basis of line 16 would presuppose the conjuration of an Aramean royal ancestor in the absence of collaborative support. Such a proposal needs a more substantial Aramean base than what line 21 alone can offer.[4] This has led interpreters to cite in support the practice of "reciting the name" as observed on behalf of the ancestors both in Mesopotamia (*šuma zakāru*) and in Israel (*hazkîr šēm*). But as pointed out previously (3.2.2.), this rite probably points to a commemorative act and not to an act necessarily expressive of ancestor veneration or worship. As mentioned previously, such is the significance of the expressed concern to "remember the (dead's) name," or *hazkîr šēm*, in 2 Sam. 18:18 and to "perpetuate the name of the dead," or *hāqîm šēm-hammēṯ*, in Ruth 4:10. In any case, ethnographic data make clear that commemorative rites or geneonymy can function to legitimate political structures just as effectively as the royal ancestor cult.

While it is frequently assumed that the reference in line 21 is to the dead king Panammū(wa), it might be the living Panammū(wa) who is in view. This is intimated in the opening lines of the related Panammū(wa) inscription or *KAI* 215 wherein mention is made of political unrest during Panammū(wa)'s reign. The historical background to *KAI* 214 might have involved a political coup about to take place in which case it was anticipated that one of Panammū(wa)'s sons would eventually take the throne. The concern expressed by the living Panammū(wa) in *KAI* 214 would then be his well-being as king *emeritus* "may he [= his reigning

---

[2] Müller 1893:52–53; 1894:572–73; Conder 1896:64 took *'šm* in both lines 16 and 21 to refer to either "guilt" or to a "sin offering": "remember the guilt before/sin offering of Hadad" (line 16) and (note the lacuna!) "[. . .] a sin offering of Panamu."

[3] Donner and Röllig 1971–73:39 followed by Gibson 1975:66.

[4] Cf. the mention of *akalšu*, "his bread," and *mêšu*, "his water," in the ninth-century bilingual Tell Fakhariyah inscription as offerings made to the gods, Adad and Shala, in the curse formulae of lines 16–18 (Aramaic = Assyrian lines 26–30). Greenfield and Schaffer 1985:51–53 cite this text as evidence for an Aramaic version of the royal *kispum* rite, but the context offers no support for such an interpretation, and Adad and Shala might have been given such offerings for reasons unconnected with mortuary concerns. This curse might reflect the belief that food offered first to a god was capable of conferring divine blessing upon the one who consumed it thereafter, for which cf. Oppenheim 1977:189. In any case, we lack data for the patronage of Adad and Shala in mortuary matters.

son] (continue to) remember the name of Panammū(wa)" that is, may he let him continue to live and may he honor him.

We turn now to a second datum cited in *KAI* 214 as indicative of a royal ancestor cult practice, the repeated phrase *t'kl nbš pnmw 'mk/ hdd wtšty nbš pnmw 'mk/hdd*, "May the *nbš* of Panammū(wa) eat with you/Hadad and may the *nbš* of Panammū(wa) drink with you/Hadad," (lines 17,21b–22a). These lines have been understood to refer to food and libation offerings for the ghost of Panammū(wa).[5] But not only is the reading *t'kl* in its two occurrences conjectural (cf. line 17: [*t'*]*kl*; line 21: *t*[*'*]*kl*), the attendant translation of the larger phrase is not at all certain.[6] Nevertheless, if we assume for the sake of argument that *t'kl* and *wtšty* are the correct readings and that they refer to "eating" and "drinking" we might render the passage as follows: "may the *nbš* of Panammū(wa) eat *at the same time as* you/Hadad and may the *nbš* of Panammū(wa) drink *at the same time as* you/Hadad."[7] In fact, if *KAI* 214 records the last will and testament of *Qrl*, the father of Panammū(wa), as suggested by Müller[8] then we might have a reference to the living Panammū(wa) and to the royal banquet following his coronation.[9] Given such a scenario, the above mentioned lines would express his anticipated feasting with Hadad who would have been present at the coronation in the form of his statue.[10] The passage would then preserve the hope that at his coronation celebration, the living Panammū(wa) might commune with Hadad, his dynastic god.

Alternatively, if the political unrest mentioned earlier stands in the background, then this expression would comprise Panammū(wa)'s hope to remain alive after his ouster "May the *nbš* of Panammū(wa) (continue to) eat with you/Hadad and

---

[5] Cf. e.g., Gaster 1950:275; de Moor 1972(II):31; Greenfield 1973:47; 1987:68,70–71; Donner and Röllig 1971–73:220–21. Others have seen in these lines rudimentary indications of beatific afterlife, cf. e.g., Halévy 1894:35–37; Astour 1980:228; Healey 1984:251; Spronk 1986:208; Smith and Bloch-Smith 1988:283.

[6] Müller 1893:53,62, following the edition of von Luschan and Sachau 1893:49, completely omitted *t'kl* in both instances and interpreted *wtšty nbš pnmw 'mk/ hdd* as "and may you bind up the spirit of Panamuwa with you/Hadad," a petition for Hadad's protection of *Qrl*'s heir. He took *šty* to mean "to intertwine," cf. Hebrew *šty* II.

[7] Caquot 1976b:303 and n.3 rendered the form *'m*, "with," in the above phrases temporally rather than locally "May the spirit of Panamuwa eat/drink at the same time as you (= Hadad)." This eliminates the supposed belief that the king's departed spirit was feasting *with* his god.

[8] Following Müller 1893:54,62; 1894:573.

[9] In private communication, Greenfield noted the possible coronational background of the text, cf. the phrase "When my son (*bny* = Panamuwa) grasps the scepter and sits upon my seat . . . " (lines 15,20). We take *bny* as the singular noun with 1cs suffix (final *mater î*?).

[10] Cf. Wilkinson 1986:262–63. Among others, the hymn to Ur-Namma B describes a banquet held by the king for the gods immediately after his election. The use of *nbš* in *KAI* 214 would be similar to the use of Hebrew *npš* in connection with one's inclination toward his god, cf. Ps. 63:10(ET 9), or the emotional states of joy and bliss, cf. Ps. 86:4.

may the *nbš* of Panammū(wa) (continue to) drink with you/Hadad." In the final analysis, the contribution of these lines from *KAI* 214 to the reconstruction of Aramaic religion is, to say the least, problematic. In fact, Teixidor concluded with regard to *KAI* 214, "the Cilician region of which Panamu was king was never a land of Semites and consequently the Aramaic inscription may express convictions which are not Semitic."[11]

The remaining Aramaic evidence attests to both mourning rites and the erection of memorials in honor of the deceased. It also lays stress on the inviolability of the tomb.[12] An Aramaic version of the *marzēaḥ* is as yet lacking for the pre-mid first millennium and the later evidence remains for the most part, if not entirely, silent on the matter of its ancestor cult connections.[13]

The contemporary Phoenician evidence likewise lacks any indication of death and ancestor cult practices.[14] The lone exception might be Puech's recently proposed rendering of *KAI* 30:2b–3. His reading results in the mention of offerings for a deceased man or hero *wh'š 'š ḥ[dl] [h]š[l]mm lqbr z' k'l hgbr z'*, "and the man who puts a stop to the peace offerings at this tomb for this man/hero . . . " (lines 2b–3).[15] The author recognized the highly conjectural nature of his reconstruction and offered the viable alternative *ḥll*, "desecrate," for *ḥdl* in line 2b and *hdbr* for *hgbr* in line 3.[16] This would remove any mention of repeated offerings to the

11 Teixidor 1987:371. Although the epithet *'lh 'bh* in lines 29–30 of *KAI* 214 has been identified as the "divine father" or deified ancestor, it is generally identified as an epithet of Rakib-El who was known to be the patron god of the dynasty. Cf. also 3.1.3. Rakib-El is described elsewhere with similar idiom, *b'l.bt.* (*KAI* 214:16) or *b'l.byt.* (*KAI* 215:22), "the Lord of the house)(or of the family)," and as one of "the gods of the house of my father," *'lhy.byt.'by* (*KAI* 217:3).

12 Cf. e.g., The Panamuwa inscription (*KAI* 215, eighth century B.C.E.), the Sinzeribni inscription (*KAI* 225, seventh century B.C.E.), and the Si'gabbar inscription (*KAI* 226, seventh century B.C.E.). It is impossible to determine whether or not the memorial set up in honor of the deceased in these cases involved regular rites beyond the funeral. In any case, veneration and worship are not mentioned or depicted. These are silent on the matter of the benefic power of the dead.

13 A lone Elephantine ostracon in Porten 1968:184–86 mentions the *marzēaḥ* but makes no mention of its mortuary associations, and cf. Bryan 1973:168–69. Sayce 1909:154–55 read only *mr* ||| in line 3, but following Lidzbarski 1915:119–21 most read *marzēaḥ*. The Nabatean inscriptions are silent on its mortuary associations, cf. Negev 1961:134–37; 1963:113–17; Naveh 1967:187–89; Zayadine 1986:465–74; Negev 1987:287–90. One text mentions Obodas as patron of the *marzēaḥ*, see Dalman 1912:92–94 [Text 73:2]; Lidzbarski 1915:278; Ingholt 1967(I/1):48 [Text 5]. Whether or not this is a dead, deified Nabatean king, Obodas I, or a personal god by the same name, remains a point of debate, cf. Bryan 1973:226; L'Heureux 1979:209; Fabry 1984:13–14 against Lewis 1989:90. For the Palmyrene inscriptions, cf. Bryan 1973:170–97,213–25 against the proposals vis-à-vis the supposed mortuary associations, so Porten 1968:183 and/or its beatific motifs, so du Mesnil de Buisson 1962:456,467–69.

14 Cooper 1987b:316 concluded "there is insufficient evidence to permit the reconstruction of a Phoenician cult of the dead . . . ," but he qualified his statement by identifying the Phoenician *marzēaḥ* as the ritual banquet of the cult of the dead.

15 Puech 1979:19–26.

16 Puech 1979:24.

dead. Even if such were in view, they might have been offered either as funerary offerings or as expressions of the care or commemoration of the dead.

The Phoenician version of the *marzēaḥ* is only sparsely attested.[17] The mention of Shamash as patron of the *marzēaḥ* in a dedicatory inscription on a fourth century B.C.E. bronze *phialē* may simply reflect the sun deity's function as judge in commercial legal matters.[18] Mortuary associations are otherwise lacking.[19] The Phoenician *rp'm* are mentioned in three texts.[20] The relevant contexts are of little help beyond the establishment of the chthonic nature of the mid first millennium *rp'm*.[21] The question remains whether they were considered simply as the weak shades of the dead in general, or dead kings, or, in line with our proposal vis-à-vis the Ugaritic *rp'um*, mythic warriors with whom the distinguished living members of society sought to be associated postmortem.

The last viewpoint might find confirmation elsewhere in the Phoenician evidence. In line 2 of *KAI* 30, the text newly collated by Puech, if the reading *hgbr* is correct, it might refer to the special status of a deceased individual, as a "hero." At Ugarit, we found that the cognate *ǵzr* repeatedly showed up parallel to *mt rp'i* where both forms functioned as titles of the legendary hero Danil. In view of our findings concerning the Ugaritic *rp'um* (cf. 3.1.7.), we would venture the proposal that as death drew nigh, members of the higher echelons of Phoenician society sought to insure their having obtained the esteemed status of hero at death by per-

---

[17] Cf. the fourth century B.C.E. inscription in Avigad and Greenfield 1982:118–28; Guzzo Amadasi 1987:121–27; the fourth-third century B.C.E. tariff discovered at Marseilles, France, *KAI* 69, and cf. Bryan 1973:158–63 for bibliography; the first century B.C.E. inscription on a commemorative stele of the Sidonian colony at Piraeus, the port of Athens, *KAI* 60, and cf. Bryan 1973:163–67; Gibson 1982:148–51 for bibliography.

[18] Against the view that in this text libations are offered by the *marzēaḥ* of Shamash to the dead (reading *'nsk* with prosthetic aleph from *nsk* "to pour") so Catastini 1985:111–18, cf. Guzzo Amadasi 1987:121–22 who returned to the reading of the editors, Avigad and Greenfield 1982:126–28, *'nḥn*. Peckham 1987:83 assumed the ancestor cult background of all three texts and cited the biblical evidence in support, but cf. 4.3.1.; 4.6.1.

[19] Ashurbanipal's palace relief has been cited as indicative of the *marzēaḥ*'s spread to Mesopotamia from Phoenicia, so Barnett 1985:1*-6*. That the *rp'm* are depicted in this relief has been unconvincingly argued by Gubel 1989:47–50. In view of the lack of mortuary connections of the pre-Hellenistic *marzēaḥ*, cf. 4.3.1. and 4.6.1., such elements are better explained otherwise. Besides, this would be the first explicit association of the *marzēaḥ* with a victory celebration and with the involvement of the enemy dead (the severed head of the Elamite king is illustrated in the reliefs). We would expect the involvement of dead benefic ancestors, not the dead of the enemy.

[20] *KAI* 13 and 14, the Tabnit and Eshmunazar inscriptions. Both date from the sixth century B.C.E. and were found at Sidon. Cf. also *KAI* 117, the Latin-Punic bilingual inscription of the first century C.E. from El-Amruni, Libya.

[21] Cf. *KAI* 13:7b–8 *'l y[k]n l[k] zr' bḥym tḥt šmš wmškb 't rp'm*, "may you have no seed under the sun nor a place of rest with the *rp'm*"; *KAI* 14:8b–9a *'l ykn lm mškb 't rp'm w'l yqbr bqbr w'l ykn lm bn wzr' tḥtnm*, "may they have no place of rest with the *rp'm* and may they not be buried in a grave and may they have no son or seed to succeed them."

petuating their memory as *rp'm* among the living.[22] It is a well documented fact that the Phoenician royalty did seek to perpetuate their names among the living.[23] The repeated use of funerary stelae to commemorate the dead also illustrates this aspiration.[24] The royalty also sought longevity, for the kings of Byblos of the tenth to fifth centuries B.C.E. prayed for lengthy reigns and long life.[25]

The concurrent Palestinian inscriptional evidence might preserve a scattered allusion or two to the malevolent actions of ghosts, but no mention is made of ancestor cult or necromantic rites or of an associated belief in the beneficence of the dead. The Uriyahu graffito dating to the early eighth century B.C.E. and incised in Tomb 2 at Khirbet el-Qom (inscription 3) might refer to the deity's protection of the dead, but this is not necessarily indicative of a belief in a beatific afterlife.[26] The protection invoked is that, perhaps, sought during the liminal stage marking the deceased's journey to the netherworld when maligning apparitions might attack the deceased while most vulnerable. These malevolent demons are nowhere identified as ghosts. In any case, if supernatural powers are invoked

---

22 In any case, the divine status of the Phoenician *rp'm* cannot be established on the basis of the first century C.E. text *KAI* 117:1 *l'l[nm] 'r'p'm*, "for the deified *rp'm* . . . ," with most commentators who assume the equation of *'lnm* and *'lnm*, cf. e.g., Sperling 1971:79. Vattioni 1980–81:297–98 has revived the alternate reading *l'l[n]' r'p'm*, "for the gods of the *rp'm* of. . . . " Likewise the Persian period inscription from Pyrgi, *KAI* 277, cannot be cited as proof of the dead's status as divine. In lines 8–9, the burial of a god, or *qbr 'lm*, is mentioned, but the god here is generally viewed by scholars as a representation of any one of several known deities, whether Ashtarte/Aphrodite, Melqart, or Adonis/Tammuz and not as a deceased mortal, cf. e.g., Soggin 1975:112–19; now Roschinski 1988:602–05 against Knoppers 1992:105–20.

23 Cf. the curse of Yehawmilk, a Byblian king, against anyone who would remove the written form of his name after his demise in *KAI* 10:11b–15.

24 Cf. the use of *mṣbt* in Phoenician texts at Umm el-'Amed in Magnanini 1973:85–86 [Text 6],88 [Text 12]; at Kition in Guzzo Amadasi and Karageorghis 1977:48–53 [Texts B1–4],56–58 [Texts B5–6],88–100 [Texts 40–45]; in the western Mediterranean [Texts *KAI* 53 (Athens), 60 (Piraeus), 78 (Carthage), 100 (Dougga), 149 (Maktar), 163 (?), 165 (near Guelma) 202 (Äfis)]; cf. Tomback 1978:194 [Texts 2a,2c,4a].

25 *KAI* 4–7,10; cf. 25:5–7; 26A:III:2–6; C:III:19–20.

26 *Contra* Spronk 1986:307–11 following Mittmann 1981:143–44. Spronk's proposal depends upon unlikely textual readings, radical emendation justified on the basis of three supposed scribal errors, and his curious omission of lines 5–6. For a different rendering of the text, cf. Hadley 1987:51. Puech 1992:127–28 sees the inscription as possessing apotropaic powers. This function of the inscription is confirmed by its having been etched above an engraved right hand hanging in the position of an amulet: (1) *'ryhw.hqšr.ktbh* (2) *brk.'ryhw. lyhwh* (3) *wmṣryh.l'šrth.hwš'lh* (4) *l'nyhw* (5)*wl'šrth* (6) [. . . . .]*h*, "Uriyahu conjured his inscription. Blessed be Uriyahu before Yahweh, from his adversaries by his Asherah save him. By Oniyahu and by his Asherah." He also interprets some graffiti incised in tomb 1 of the same site as possessing magical and apotropaic powers, for the inscribed letters *'alep*, *'alep*, *bet*, and *mem* might represent the initials of the four signs of the zodiac: "lion(-scorpion)," "lion," "virgo," and "libra."

against these demons they are those of the deity and not those of the dead.[27] The preceding survey strengthens our earlier verdict that the presumed Syro-Palestinian origin for the Israelite belief in the benevolence of the dead remains unattested in the textual evidence.

4.2. The 'Canaanite' Origins of Israel's Belief in the Beneficent Dead

While certain of the biblical traditions transmit a syncretistic "Canaanite" origin for practices such as selected mourning rites (Deut. 14:1), necromancy (Deut. 18:11), and what many have identified as ancestor cult rites (e.g., Deut. 26:14), a strong case can be made for the highly rhetorical character of at least part of that origins tradition. As our foregoing treatment reveals, the Syro-Palestinian and, in particular, the Ugaritic texts do not document the observance of ancestor cult rites or necromancy by the regional populations of the late second to mid first millennia.[28] Furthermore, though selected biblical texts convey an ancient Canaanite origin as underlying the Israelite mourning rites of self-mutilation, biblical traditions elsewhere attest to the "orthodox" observance of these rites in early Yahwistic circles (cf. Deut. 14:1 in 4.4.1.).

That the biblical writers might resort to such a rhetorical strategy is verified by the prospect that other practices and beliefs found in biblical traditions such as those associated with the cult of Asherah and child sacrifice are artificially attributed to similar syncretistic Canaanite origins. The Asherah origins tradition comprises a deliberate rhetorical polemic with a distinct deuteronomistic (hereafter dtr) orientation. It is more likely the case that Asherah was the consort of El early on, but as later Yahwism appropriated the El traditions, so the inclusion of Yahweh to El resulted in Asherah becoming Yahweh's consort.[29] As dtr Yahwism

[27] Puech 1992:127–29 also views the late seventh century Ketef Hinnom amulets that contain a benediction closely related to that preserved in Num. 6:24–26 as having been placed in the tomb for the dead in order to continue the protective and apotropaic roles which they had fulfilled for the living.

[28] The question of whether or not they accurately reflect geographically, chronologically, and culturally distanced Canaanite religious practices and beliefs as depicted in the biblical traditions further obfuscates matters.

[29] Cf. Olyan 1988:1–22,38–61 followed by M. Smith 1990:80–114. M. Smith 1990:7–12 lists the following points in favor of the "Israelite inclusion of Yahweh into the older figure of El": (1) the divine element in the name Israel is an El name not a Yahwistic one, (2) Deut. 32:8–9 depicts Yahweh as one of the sons of El who received Israel as his nation, (3) there are no biblical polemics against El, (4) the El name developed into a generic designation for god as a result of Yahweh's inclusion into El, (5) Exod. 6:2–3 reflects a tradition in which only the name of El Shaddai not Yahweh was made known to the patriarchs, (6) the inscriptional onomastica identifies Yahweh with El, (7) the characteristics and epithets of El become those of Yahweh in Israel, and (8) Yahweh and El exhibit a similar compassionate disposition toward humanity.

came to dominate major sections of the biblical traditions, the Asherah traditions were then eradicated or suppressed. Thus, the resultant portrayal of Asherah's Canaanite and non-Israelite origin serves as a diversion for what once might have constituted the forefathers' worship of a goddess. Other traditions such as those concerning the Judahite kings Hezekiah, Manasseh, and Josiah were likewise radically altered in conformity with dtr Yahwism. Hezekiah and Josiah were not reforming traditionalists as the dtr traditions would have it. Rather they were, in all probability, religious innovators and Manasseh, rather than an apostate innovator, was a reforming traditionalist (and a non-Yahwistic innovator, more on this below).[30]

Thus, the biblical writers' proposed Canaanite origin of Israelite self-mutilation and necromancy is sufficient to raise suspicion as to the historical veracity of such traditions. In fact, like the terms Hittite and Amorite *as employed by the biblical writers*, the term Canaanite does not correspond to any specific political or ethnic entity known from the extra-biblical texts of the second and first millennia B.C.E. For the biblical writers, the terms Hittite, Amorite, and Canaanite functioned instead as ideological symbols for the indigenous non-Israelite inhabitants of Palestine. They in turn came to epitomize the foreign occupations which persistently threatened 'biblical' Israel's claim to the land and its blessings.[31]

Such constraining precedents enhance the likelihood that a similar anti-Canaanite rhetorical polemic informs the prohibitions against mortuary practices like self-mutilation and necromancy. We offer, by way of illustration, a summary analysis of the first Isaiah passages that refer to the practice of necromancy, Isa. 8:19; 19:3; and 29:4 (for further details cf. 4.3.2.-5.). With good reason, an increasing number of scholars recognize the exilic or post-exilic redaction of first Isaiah (as part of a more comprehensive redaction of the whole of Isaiah) regardless of the nature and extent of that redaction.[32] Some of the decisive criteria favoring the exilic to post-exilic redaction of chapters 1–35 include: (1) the role of Babylon in 13:1–14:23, (2) the overthrow of Babylonia by the Medes in 13:17; 21:2, (3) the lack of condemnation of Persia and Media in the oracles against the nations (chapters 13–23), (4) the destruction of Jerusalem, (5) the Babylonian

---

[30] Cf. Ahlström 1982:68–80. For other examples of dtr rhetorical distortion e.g., the reform cult of Jeroboam (1 Kgs. 12:25–33) and the portrayal of an alleged Canaanite-Israelite deity Molek (1 Kgs. 11:7; 2 Kgs. 23:10; Jer. 32:35), cf. Olyan 1988:11–13.

[31] Following Van Seters 1972:64–81; 1975:46–51; see now Lemche 1991a followed by Thompson 1992:167–69.

[32] For a survey of approaches, cf. now Seitz 1991 and note esp. pp.29,189–91. For helpful critiques of the nature, scope, extent, and social setting of a systematic and comprehensive dtr redaction of the pre-exilic and exilic prophets, cf. Brekelmans 1989:167–76; Porter 1989:69–78.

exile, (6) the restoration, (7) the use of Torah as wise instruction, and (8) the centrality of retributive justice.[33]

In addition to the fact that chapter 1 and chapters 65 and 66 share numerous thematic and linguistic elements suggesting the same post-exilic redactional hand, both reflect what has been typically identified as a dtr orientation.[34] Isa. 1:29–31, and possibly 1:19–20, preserve a characteristic dtr polemic against cultic apostasy and 3:10–11 reflects the typical dtr distinction between the righteous and the wicked and their reward and punishment.[35] Furthermore, both Isa. 2:8 and 17:8 contain the dtr expression *maʿaśēh yāḏayw*, "the work of one's hands." 17:8 mentions *wᵊhāʾašērîm wᵊhāḥammānîm*, "the Asherahs and the incense altars," which is also indicative of dtr redaction.[36] Here, the dtr tradition has portrayed Asherah religion as syncretistic and Canaanite in origin (as mentioned above) and has inserted this polemic into the earlier traditions of first Isaiah.

These factors serve as precedent for the hypothesis that an exilic or post-exilic redaction with a dtr orientation stands behind those traditions in first Isaiah having to do with necromancy as well as those having to do with ancestor worship and veneration should they be found to exist. An examination of the evidence pertaining to necromancy reveals that it remains unattested in the pre-exilic prophetic traditions of Hosea, Amos, and Micah, in the Elijah-Elisha traditions, and in the exilic prophetic traditions. The terms *ʾôḇ* and *yiddᵊʿōnî* (or their variant forms) found in Isa. 8:19; 19:3; and 29:4 appear otherwise only in the dtr traditions at Deut. 18:11; 1 Sam. 28:3–25; 2 Kgs. 21:6; and 23:24.

The non-Isaianic origin of *ʾôḇ* and *yiddᵊʿōnî* is further highlighted by the fact that in the post-exilic text Isa. 65:4 (cf. 4.6.4.) the biblical writer polemicizes against a form of necromancy associated with an incubation rite performed in gardens, but neither *ʾôḇ* nor *yiddᵊʿōnî* are mentioned. If the hand responsible for chapters 65 to 66 is the same hand responsible for the post-exilic redaction of chapters 2–66 as well as for the composition of chapter 1,[37] and if these two terms were original to first Isaiah, then we would have expected the redactional hand

---

33 Following Sweeney 1988:1–25,123–33.

34 The themes shared by chapter 1 and chapters 65–66 include cultic apostasy, judgment as a means for restoration, and the separation of the righteous from the wicked. The shared vocabulary includes: *gan*, "garden," 1:29; 65:3; 66:17; *bāḥar*, "choose," 1:29; 65:12; 66:3–4; *lōʾ ḥāp̄aṣ*, "no delight," 1:11; 65:12; 66:3–4; *bōš*, "shame," 1:29; 65:13; 66:5; *ʾēlîm*, "trees," 1:30; 65:22; "burning" 1:31; 66:15–16,17; and "unquenched fire" 1:31; 66:24; cf. Sweeney 1988:21–24; Gosse 1992:52–66; for dtr influence, cf. Sweeney 1988:196 and n.12.

35 Cf. Sweeney 1988:129–33,183; Gosse 1992:64–65 against Brekelmans 1989:167–76 who neglected to consider the above arguments for an exilic or post-exilic redaction of first Isaiah and the dtr character of 1:29–31.

36 On the dtr character of 2:8 and 17:8, cf. Weinfeld 1972a:324.

37 Cf. Sweeney 1988:21–24.

acquainted with first Isaiah and responsible for 65:4 to have made mention of the *'ôḇ* and *yiddᵊʻōnî*.

A comparison of the Isaiah passages with those necromancy texts original to the Deuteronomistic History (hereafter DtrH), 2 Kgs. 21:6 and 23:24,[38] demonstrates that the former assume that necromancy was a Judahite practice in king Ahaz's day, while the 2 Kings passages depict its introduction not before the days of Manasseh. Had traditions concerning Ahaz's observance of necromancy existed, surely these would have been integrated into the evaluation of Manasseh's predecessors. Such traditions would have established an earlier precedent for imputing the sin of necromancy to the Judahite monarchy. Were these traditions accessible, one would have expected the DtrH to mention Ahaz's embrace of necromancy, its proscription by Isaiah, and its inclusion in Hezekiah's reform, but these are nowhere to be found.

That Manasseh's reign provides the *terminus a quo* for Israel's appropriation of necromancy gains further impetus in the likelihood that necromancy was a foreign practice 'appropriated' by the Israelites from their Mesopotamian overlords not before Manasseh's reign. The following points support this proposal. Our analysis has shown that outside the biblical traditions, necromancy remains unattested in Syria or Palestine in the pre-Hellenistic periods.[39] In pre-first millennium Mesopotamia, necromancy is attested only rarely, if at all. However, references to Mesopotamian necromancy and necromantic incantation texts significantly increase during the mid to late first millennium B.C.E. (cf. 4.5.1.).[40] This corresponds with the growth in popularity of various forms of divination with which the late Assyrian kings became preoccupied.[41] Furthermore, the late Assyrian preoccupation with divination coincided with Mesopotamian—Assyrian, then Babylonian—sovereignty over the region of Syria-Palestine beginning in the eighth century B.C.E. Necromancy was one of those forms of divination which the

---

38 For the late redactional character of Deut. 18:11 and 1 Sam. 28:3–25 and their dtr orientation, cf. 4.4.2.; 4.5.1.

39 Moore 1990:53–55 so generalizes the definition of necromancy as to include the *marzēaḥ* and the expulsion of ghosts, but neither are applicable. The first lacks mortuary concerns in the pre-Hellenistic periods and the latter is not reflective of the dead's beneficent powers, but of its malevolence. As pointed out earlier, Tropper 1989 also defines necromancy broadly, but at times fails to document the associated belief in the dead's supernatural benefic power. Not only are his Egyptian and Hittite texts questionable examples (pp.27–46,110–22), but his Ugaritic texts (pp.123–60) are as well in view of our findings in 3.1. On the Egyptian data, cf. 4.3.3.

40 Cf. the texts in Parpola 1970:107; 1983:120; von Weiher 1983:100–03; Finkel 1983–84:1–17; Scurlock 1988:5–8,103–12,318–42; Tropper 1989:76–103.

41 Cf. Spieckermann 1982:227–306,307–72; Pečírková 1985:155–68; 1987:162–75; Starr 1990: XIII–LXVII.

late Assyrian kings endorsed.[42] Various lines of evidence indicative of Assyrian and Babylonian religious influence on the local Canaanite-Israelite religion of this period suggest that with the Assyrian imposition of vassalship on Manasseh's Judah, Mesopotamian political, religious, and economic influences intensified (cf. 4.5.2.).[43] These observations all point to a mid first millennium Mesopotamian background for the references to necromancy in Isaianic passages like Isa. 8:19; 19:3; and 29:4.

The proposal that the Isaiah passages, 8:19; 19:3; and 29:4, comprise *redactional* additions (cf. further 4.3.–5.) has four points in its favor: (1) the evidence for the late redaction of the whole of first Isaiah, (2) the discrepancy between the Isaiah and DtrH accounts regarding Judah's initial appropriation of necromancy (was it in Ahaz's or in Manasseh's reign?), (3) the intensification of Mesopotamian religious influence, first Assyrian, then Babylonian, on Judahite religion beginning with Manasseh's reign, and (4) the resultant impetus that influence provided for necromancy's introduction into Israelite (specifically Judahite) religion and tradition. The dtr character of the redactional processes scattered throughout Isaiah 1–35 and the dtr phraseology that 8:19; 19:3; and 29:4 share with Deut. 18:11 and 1 Sam. 28:3–25 point to a distinctly dtr orientation for 8:19; 19:3; and 29:4.[44] Their insertion not only enhanced the dtr tradition's authority by identifying itself with the prophet Isaiah and by thrusting necromancy's condemnation well into Judah's past, but it also intensified necromancy's abhorrence by attaching its observance to the apostate king Ahaz—the first Judahite king to also endorse human sacrifice (cf. 2 Kgs. 16:3 and Isa. 28:15,18?)—and to the general Judahite population (cf. further 4.5.2.).[45]

These considerations suggest that the Canaanite origins tradition for Israelite necromancy is the product of a rhetorical strategy intended to enhance the authority of dtr ideology. The polemical rhetoric involved four distinct, but at times, overlapping tactics: (1) projecting necromancy back into Israel's traditions about earlier times, (2) ascribing to it a Canaanite origin, (3) associating it with the cults

---

[42] Cf. the letter to king Esarhaddon dated 672 B.C.E. in Parpola 1970:107; 1983:120 [Text 132]. A translation of the text is provided in 4.5.1. See also Finkel 1983–84:1,3; Tsukimoto 1985:159; Tropper 1989:76–83.

[43] The question of whether Israel's acquaintance with Mesopotamian necromancy found expression in the biblical traditions as a vestige of a historically verifiable, Israelite, religious syncretism of pre-exilic times or merely as a literary topos employed by a later ideological strategist (or both!) is addressed more fully in 4.5.3.

[44] The consultation of the dead (*dāraš 'el-hammēṯîm*) occurs only in Deut. 18:11 and in Isa. 8:19; 19:3 (cf. *dāraš 'el-hā'iṭṭîm*, "consult the ghosts,") and the consultation of the netherworld gods (*'ᵉlōhîm 'ōlîm/dāraš 'el-*[*hā*]*'ᵉlōhîm*) appears only in 1 Sam. 28:13 and in Isa. 8:19; 19:3 (cf. *dāraš 'el-hā'ᵉlîlîm*, "consult the false gods").

[45] Cf. Day 1989:58–64 for the covenant of death in Isa. 28:15,18 as an allusion to the cult of Molek observed during Ahaz's reign, but see our interpretation of Isa. 28:7–22 in 4.3.4.

of the 'apostate' Judahite kings, Ahaz and Manasseh, and (4) identifying as its most ardent critics such culture heroes as Moses, the founder of the nation, the great prophet Isaiah, and Josiah, the righteous Davidic king. So, the antiquity of the rites, their foreign origin, and their condemnation by venerable religious figures of the past establish the desired precedent for defining the social location of practices associated with the dead within the narrative worlds of the dtr and later traditions. It is with this interpretive context in mind, that we turn to examine those biblical texts that scholars have identified as reflective of Israel's ancient belief in the benevolent dead as embodied in the ancestor cult and in necromancy.

4.3. The Pre-exilic Prophetic Literature

In this section, several prophetic passages will be examined, the oracles or contexts of which many commentators have dated to the pre-exilic era. Nevertheless, the secondary nature of some of these texts remains a matter of continued debate. Therefore, we must establish the compositional histories of the relevant passages in our attempt to reconstruct a hypothetical history of Israelite religion vis-à-vis ancestor cults and necromancy. At least three considerations justify our examination of necromancy and ancestor cults together. First, beliefs associated with necromancy closely approximate those connected with the ancestor cult. Both of these ritual complexes express a belief in the supernatural benevolent power of the dead, at least as it has been defined in our introduction. Second, the history of interpretation has assumed a close association between Israelite necromancy and ancestor cults.[46] Third, owing to the nature of both the comparative and biblical data associated with necromancy, that tradition, once reconstructed, can offer a potential working model for the reconstruction of the history of ancestor cult practices in ancient Israel. Having so argued, we do not intend to suggest that these two practices have the same ritual or social settings. Necromancy is not inherently related to inheritance or legitimation like the ancestor cult at least as traditionally understood.

---

[46] Cf. e.g., most recently Rouillard and Tropper 1987b:235–54; Lewis 1989.

4.3.1. Amos 6:7

Clearly, the earliest text cited in discussions on Israelite ancestor cult practices is Amos 6:7.[47] Greenfield labeled the *marzēaḥ* mentioned in v.7, a funerary cult, for in 6:9–10, the death of Samaria's wealthy class and their burial by close relatives is anticipated.[48] Pope, who ventured little distinction between the rites associated with the funerary feast and those connected with what he labeled the cult of the dead, explicitly stated that the *marzēaḥ* in Amos 6:7 exhibits features characteristic of the latter and he has upheld this position to the present.[49] Before offering an evaluation of these and other related proposals, our analysis of the pericope and an English translation of 6:4–7 will be offered. Within the doom oracle spanning 6:1–7, 6:1–2 comprises a woe cry, 6:3–6 encompasses an accusation section, and 6:7 contains a concluding pronouncement of judgment:[50]

	(4)
haššōḵᵊḇîm ʻal-miṭṭôṯ šēn	"Those who lie on beds of ivory,
ûsᵊrûḥîm ʻal-ʻarśôṯām	who loll on their couches,
wᵊʼōḵᵊlîm kārîm miṣṣōʼn	who feast on lambs from the flock
wāʻᵃgālîm mittôḵ marbēq	And on calves from the stall.
	(5)
happōrᵊṭîm ʻal-pî hannāḇel	Those who hum snatches of song to the tune of the lyre[51]—

[47] Nevertheless, Vermeylen 1977–78(II):563–64 viewed 6:7 as a later dtr redaction. He argued that vv.6b–7 appear to interrupt an otherwise complete oracle beginning in v.3 and ending with v.11. Furthermore, the vocabulary does not favor the authenticity of the verse: *mirzaḥ* (!) occurs only one other time and then in a later passage (Jer. 16:5); *sᵊrûḥîm* contains a *mater lectionis* whereas in v.4 it is written defectively; and the verb *gālāh* is found principally in reference to the deportation of the people at the dtr level of the book (5:5; 7:11,17). On the dtr redaction of Amos, cf. Schmidt 1965:168–93; now Coote 1981.

[48] Greenfield 1974:453; cf. 1973:48–49. King 1988a:139 has employed a similar line of argument, although in 1988b:37 he was more cautious, cf. also Polley 1989:88–91; Andersen and Freedman 1990:566–68.

[49] Pope 1977b:216 "The mention of ivory beds, feasting, music and song, wine bibbing, and perfume oil in Amos 6:4–7 . . . are all features of the funeral feast in the *marzēaḥ*(-house), or drinking house." In 1987:459, Pope cited the inebriation reflected in *marzēaḥ sᵊrûḥîm*, "sprawler's banquet," within the context of the following observation "From ancient times to the present celebrations of death have been commonly accompanied by drinking of alcoholic beverages to excess." Cf. also Coote 1981:35–39; Loretz 1982:87–93.

[50] Cf. the *JPS* translation. The meaning of v.3 is uncertain.

[51] For *nēḇel* as "lyre," not "harp," cf. Freedman 1985:48–51. On this and the following clause, cf. Wolff 1977:276.

kᵊḏawîḏ ḥāšᵊḇû lāhem kᵊlê šîr	Like David, invent for themselves instruments of music.
	(6)
haššōṯîm bᵊmizrᵊqê yayin *wᵊrē'šîṯ šᵊmānîm yimšāḥû*	Those who drink from the wine bowls And anoint themselves with the choicest oils—
wᵊlō' neḥlû 'al-šēḇer yôsēp̱	But they are not concerned about the ruin of Joseph.
	(7)
lāḵēn 'attāh yiglû bᵊrō'š gōlîm *wᵊsār mirzaḥ sᵊrûḥîm*	Assuredly, right soon they shall head the column of exiles; and the *marzēaḥ* of lolling[52] shall come to an end."

Amos's repeated accusations of social injustice has led commentators to view this oracle as motivated by the social elite's exploitation of the peasant population in their quest for wealth and populance. Clear, as well, is Amos's condemnation of their lack of vigilance.[53] Nevertheless, Barstad has recently argued that a polemic against foreign deities was the foremost concern of 6:1–7 and not the opulent feasting of the upper classes and that Amos is therefore to be viewed as a monotheist like Hosea. For external support, he cited the comparative evidence associating the *marzēaḥ* with patron gods. For Barstad, the sacral nature of the *marzēaḥ* provides an implicit backdrop to Amos's polemic in 6:7. For internal support, he listed several passages illustrative of Amos's polemic against the worship of foreign gods, two of which demand detailed evaluation, 5:26 and 8:14.[54]

Commentators since the time of Wellhausen have viewed Amos 5:26 as a later addition.[55] Some have maintained the dtr redactional nature of v.26 on the basis of the idealization of the wilderness wandering evident in 5:25–27.[56] Others have done so on the basis of the mention of two lately attested Mesopotamian astral

---

[52] Others translate *sᵊrûḥîm* as "revelry." Either rendering eliminates the assumption that *mirzaḥ* should be translated "revelry" as the following adjective would be redundant.

[53] Cf. e.g., most recently King 1988a:137–62; 1988b:34–44.

[54] Barstad 1984 also treated 2:6–8; 4:1; 6:13. On the latter two, cf. Polley 1989:89–94. The phrase *'ᵉlōhêhem* in 2:8 is translated "their god" by most commentators, not "their gods," and so Amos is attacking what he viewed as an unacceptable Yahwistic practice.

[55] So Schmidt 1965:188–91; Willi-Plein 1971:37–39. Cf. Harper 1905:140 for thirteen different interpretations of this passage.

[56] Cf. Kraus 1966:112–14; Wolff 1977:264–66.

deities Kewan, or *kêwān*, and Sakkuth, or *sakkûṯ*, in v.26 (and cf. the phrase *kôḵaḇ ʾᵉlōhêḵem*, "of your astral deity/ies," in v.26b).[57] These points argue against or, at least, neutralize the position of Barstad. Amos 8:14 is likewise problematic. The phrase *bᵊʾašmaṯ šōmᵊrôn* is often emended to read "Ashima (*ʾăšîmāʾ*) of Samaria" but according to 2 Kgs. 17:30, this Syrian(?) goddess was not introduced into the northern kingdom until after the Assyrian conquest of Samaria. Others have rendered this phrase "the guilt of Samaria" as the term *ʾašmaṯ* could be construed as derivative of *ʾašmāh*. But, this term occurs only in late texts and has likewise resulted in the attribution of 8:14 to a later hand. In any case, the mention of patron foreign deities is nowhere to be found in 6:1–7.[58] This is merely an inference made by Barstad on the basis of the occasional association of local *marzēaḥ*s with patron deities in the comparative material.

As to the mortuary associations of *mirzaḥ*, the construct form of *marzēaḥ*, nothing in 6:1–7 points to such a connection. While the allusion to the burial of relatives in vv.9–10 could be taken as suggestive of the *marzēaḥ*'s mortuary associations, within the context of a pronouncement of judgment it most likely refers to their death as the expected outcome of divine judgment and therefore stands as an independent element with no direct relation to the *marzēaḥ*. As most interpreters acknowledge, the mortuary associations of *marzēaḥ* in Amos 6:7 must be established on the basis of what we can know of the *marzēaḥ* from the comparative data. The Eblaite, Ugaritic, Aramaic, and Phoenician texts, examined previously, lacked mortuary elements of the *marzēaḥ*.[59] The only exception to the comparative material is a lone possible reference in the later Nabatean inscriptions. In other words, such associations were by no means intrinsic to the pre-Hellenistic *marzēaḥ*.[60]

Thus, chronologically, geographically, and culturally, the comparative evidence favors the non-mortuary nature of the *marzēaḥ* and confirms our conclusion that the *marzēaḥ* in Amos 6:1–7 does not refer to the dead or to foreign gods. Rather, this text condemns the preoccupation of the wealthy class with a luxurious life-

---

57 Against McKay 1973:68,123 n.4 who argued that the presence of Assyrian deities does not necessarily date the passage after 722/1, see Lemche 1985:310 n.15. In any case, Borger 1988:70–81 has shown that while plausible, the Assyrian deities interpretation must for the present remain conjectural.

58 Cf. the *opinio communis* outlined in Soggin 1987:96–101,140–41 and the discussion in Polley 1989:91–94, where the interpretation of the guilt of Samaria and the god of Dan in 8:14 is reiterated which in turn results in both phrases referring to unacceptable Yahwistic practices. For a survey of views, cf. Holloway 1992:426.

59 Moreover, ancestor cult relations are entirely lacking in what has been questionably interpreted as the *marzēaḥ* depicted in the banquet scene from the roughly contemporary palace relief of Ashurbanipal, cf. Barnett 1985:1*–6*, followed by Gubel 1989:47–53.

60 Moreover, the mortuary associations of the *marzēaḥ* at Palmyra might have developed under the influence of the Greek *thiasos*.

style to the neglect of the needy. The issue as Amos saw it was Israel's unethical behavior, not her illegitimate, syncretistic(?), religious practices.

In the final analysis, however, the possibility that in an isolated instance the *marzēaḥ* might have been associated with mortuary matters in pre-Hellenistic times cannot be easily dismissed. Nevertheless, such could be explained as simply due to the practice of social fraternities in antiquity to acknowledge the death of one of their illustrious members by a solemn funeral. This, by no means, establishes an intrinsic connection between this institution and mortuary rites or more specifically ancestor practices. This point will be developed in greater detail in our treatment of Jer. 16:5, the later and, we should underscore, lone remaining biblical reference to the *marzēaḥ* (cf. 4.6.1).

4.3.2. Isaiah 8:19–23(ET 8:19–9:1)

Isaiah 8:19–23(ET 8:19–9:1) constitutes part of the closing section of an original independent unit spanning 6:1 to 8:18 or 9:6(ET 7); the so-called Isaianic *Denkschrift*. This unit is generally recognized as pre-exilic in date as it comprises the memoir of the prophet Isaiah on the occasion of the Syro-Ephraimite crisis. Thus, 8:19–23(ET 8:19–9:1) potentially provides us with the earliest biblical tradition concerning the Israelite practice of necromancy. Having said as much, the terms *hā'ōḇôṯ* and *hayyiddᵊ'ōnîm* in v.19 continue to exercise interpreters as to their intended referents: do they represent the ghosts of the dead, their images, or the practitioners who inquire of those ghosts/images? Both the compositional history of Isa. 8:19–22 as well as the specific mortuary associations of the *'ôḇ* and *yiddᵊ'ōnî* play principal roles in determining the answers to these and other related questions.

As to the mortuary associations of *'ôḇ* and *yiddᵊ'ōnî*, the *'ôḇ* in 1 Sam. 28:3,7,8, and 9 clearly denotes a ghost of the dead as it refers there to Samuel's shade, and by way of its repeated association with *yiddᵊ'ōnî* elsewhere, we can tentatively propose the same semantic field for the latter.[61] That ghosts of the dead are in view is further verified by the occurrence of the above two terms alongside *mēṯîm*, "the dead," in 8:19. Deut. 18:11 confirms this, as *šō'ēl 'ôḇ wᵊyiddᵊ'ōnî*, "the inquirer of the *'ôḇ* and the *yiddᵊ'ōnî*," is followed by the appositional expression, *dōrēš 'el-hammēṯîm*, "one who consults the dead" or "the necromancer."[62] Lastly, both terms are paralleled by the term *'iṭṭîm*, "shades," in Isa. 19:3, the Akkadian

---

[61] Cf. 4.5.1. for a detailed treatment of 1 Sam. 28:3–25.

[62] This in turn supports the summarizing function of *meṯîm* in Isa. 8:19.

cognate of which is *eṭemmu*, "ghost of the dead."[63] We will return shortly to the question of the exact referent(s) intended by these terms.

As far as the compositional history of these verses is concerned, the preceding section 8:16–18 is generally recognized as forming the conclusion to the Isaianic memoir or *Denkschrift* beginning at 6:1. However, many commentators have concluded that 8:19–23(ET 8:19–9:1) comprise a later, perhaps two-layered, expansion on that memorial and dates from the time of the exile or later.[64] As such, it applies Isaiah's prophecies to the Babylonian capture of Jerusalem and ascribes that disaster to the people's illicit practices.[65] As set forth in 4.2., several lines of argument point to the likelihood of exilic or post-exilic redactional elements in first Isaiah and the dtr character of at least some of those elements. The evidence also suggested the redactional nature of Isa. 8:19; 19:3; 29:4 and the dtr orientation of these passages.[66] It was pointed out there that neither the terms *'ôḇ* and *yiddᵊʻōnî* nor their plural forms are attested in any other pre-exilic or, for that matter, exilic prophetic tradition. However, both terms are found in distinct dtr narrative and legal texts (Deut. 18:11; 2 Kgs. 21:6; 23:24) or later narrative and legal texts possessing elements common to the dtr tradition (1 Sam. 28:3–25).[67] We offer our translation of 8:19–22 below:

(19)

wᵊḵî yō'mᵊrû 'ᵃlêḵem	And when they say to you,
dirᵊšû 'el-hā'ōḇôṯ	'Consult Those-who-return
wᵊ 'el-hayyiddᵊʻōnîm	and the Knowers who chirp
hamᵊṣapṣᵊpîm	
wᵊhammahgîm hᵃlô'-ʻam	and mutter! Does not a people
'el-'ᵉlōhāyw yiḏrōš bᵊʻaḏ	consult their (chthonic) gods,
haḥayyîm 'el-hammēṯîm	the dead on behalf of the living?'

63 *Contra* Burns 1979:8 who understood the term as "sorcerers." For a detailed treatment of Isa. 19:3, cf. 4.3.3.

64 Cf. Budde 1928; Steck 1972:188–206; Wildberger 1972:343–44,356; Müller 1975–76:65–76; Barth 1977:152–56; Clements 1981:3–8,70–71,101–03; Kaiser 1983:114–17,200–02; Kilian 1986:47.

65 According to several commentators, 8:19–22 comprises a twofold addition to that memorial, vv.19–20 followed by vv.21–22. Although Vermeylen 1977–78(I):24,228–32; 1977–78(II):694 accepted the exilic date, he argued for the unity of vv.19,21–22 and viewed vv.20,23a(ET 9:1a) as a later expansion from the same period. This is supported by the intimate connection of the motifs of consulting the dead and the gods on the one hand and distress and darkness on the other, for which cf. 1 Sam. 28:3–25; Prov. 1:24–28; Micah 3:4–8.

66 *Contra* Brekelmans 1989:173–74, linguistic arguments for dtr redaction elsewhere in Isa. 1–35 do exist, cf. e.g., Isa. 1:19–20,29–31; 2:8; 3:10–11; 17:8; and our discussion in 4.2.

67 Cf. also 1 Chr. 10:13; 2 Chr. 33:6; Lev. 19:31; 20:6,27; 4.5.1.–3.

(20)

lᵊṯôrāh wᵊliṯʻûḏāh	(Look) to the law and to the testimony
'im-lō' yō'mᵊrû kaddāḇār hazzeh	if they do not speak according to this word
'ᵃšer 'ên-lô šāḥar	in which there is no sorcery.[68]

(21)

wᵊʻāḇar bāh niqšeh wᵊrāʻēḇ	They will "pass on"[69] through it (=Sheol) oppressed and hungry,
wᵊhāyāh ḵî-yirʻaḇ wᵊhiṯqaṣṣap̱	and when they hunger, they will be enraged,
wᵊqillēl bᵊmalkô ûḇē'lōhāyw	and will curse their king and their gods[70]
ûp̱ānāh lᵊmāʻᵊlāh	and turn upwards or look

(22)

wᵊ'el-'ereṣ yabbîṭ	down at (lower) earth,[71]
wᵊhinnēh ṣārāh waḥᵃšēḵāh	Surely (there will be) distress and darkness
mᵊʻûp̱ ṣûqāh wa'ᵃp̱ēlāh	with no daybreak; Straitness
mᵊnuddāḥ	and gloom with no dawn.[72]

The verbal form *yō'mᵊrû* in v.19 lacks an appropriate antecedent in vv.16–18.[73] This confirms the redactional nature of vv.19–20a as does *lᵊṯôrāh wᵊliṯʻûḏāh*

[68] For our rendering of v.20, see Hayes and Irvine 1987:166–67. However, we take the phrase *'ên-lô*, to denote (the lack of) possession, cf. *BDB* p.513 para.5b. We connect *šāḥar* with its cognate form in the exilic context of Isa. 47:10b–12 (cf. v.11 and the related *sōḥārayiḵ* in v.15 and Akkadian *sāḫiru* "charm, sorcerer"). This text is likewise concerned with the condemnation of such practices.

[69] The verb *ʻāḇar* might refer to the "passing over" from life to death in Ezek. 39:11–16 but any supposed connections with Ugaritic *ʻbrm* in *KTU* 1.22.I:15 are doubtful *contra* Pope 1977a:173–75; Spronk 1986:229–31. In 8:21, the netherworld imagery underscores the distress of the wicked.

[70] Heider 1985:330–31 read "they will curse by Molek and by their gods," and explained the *-w* in *mlkw* as the result of dittography with the initial *w* in *ûḇē'lōhāyw*).

[71] Wildberger 1972:355–58; Kaiser 1983:202 concluded that this is not metaphoric as it refers to the conjuring up of the dead.

[72] Heider 1985:328–32 made reference to an unpublished paper by J. Glen Taylor who pointed out the netherworld imagery of no dawn (v.20), inhabitants famished and cursing (v.21), palpable darkness (v.22) and suggested that the antecedent of *bāh* in v.21 is Sheol.

[73] Cf. Gray 1912:157–60; Wildberger 1972:343.

in v.20, a (secondary) allusion to v.16, *ṣôr tᵊʿûḏāh ḥᵃṯôm tôrāh*. The inverted word order evident in v.20 suggests that *tôrāh* in v.20a reflects the post-exilic understanding of the term to designate a specific body of teaching or the written divine law as in several late additions to Deuteronomy (cf. e.g., 1:5; 28:61; 31:9,26) and not the more general "wise instruction" of first Isaiah as recorded in v.16. The post-exilic redactor employed the *written* law in his polemic against alternative modes of revelation and so contrasted the prophetic word with that revelation sought through necromancy. The threat of enacting the death penalty for practicing necromancy in dtr related references in the Holiness Code (hereafter HC, cf. Lev. 20:6,27) suggests that such a "heterodox" technique for ascertaining the future posed a serious challenge to deuteronomistic "orthodoxy."[74]

The negative interrogative particle *hᵃlôʾ* opening v.19b clearly governs both objects of the verb *yiḏrōš*, *ʾᵉlōhāyw*, "its (= a people's) gods," and *hammēṯîm*, "the dead." As it is unlikely that Isaiah would have urged a people to consult their dead on behalf of the living, the enticement to necromancy must be continued (in the form of two questions) to the very end of v.19.[75] To be sure, the close proximity of *ʾᵉlōhāyw* and *hammēṯîm* within the context of an enticement to necromancy has elicited the close attention of commentators.[76] It is often asserted that the gods here and in 1 Sam. 28:13 are to be equated with the dead, the emphasis being on the deceased's preternatural or deified state.[77] Against this, it is proposed in our treatment of 1 Sam. 28:3–25, that the oft-cited cuneiform evidence wherein the term, *ilu*, "god," when found parallel to *eṭemmu*, "ghost of the dead," or *mētu*, "the dead," does not identify the dead as gods. In fact, various gods, or *ilānu*, are petitioned in necromantic rites of the mid to late first millennium for their assistance in retrieving a ghost. This suggests that *ʾᵉlōhîm*, "gods," in 8:19 and 1 Sam. 28:13 are references to those gods and netherworld deities summoned to assist in the necromantic ritual (cf. 4.5.1. for a detailed defense of our position).

Given the presence of necromantic practices in this dtr redactional text, it remains for us to ascertain some specifics concerning the terms *ʾōḇôṯ* and *yid-dᵊʿōnîm*. To begin with, not only are their referents debated, but the etymology of *ʾōḇôṯ* remains disputed.[78] While the etymology of *yiddᵊʿōnîm* presents no difficulty, the significance of *y-d-ʿ*, "knowing," remains problematic and is likewise

74 Cf. Wildberger 1972:343; Clements 1981:101–02.

75 Some commentators have concluded that the enticement to necromancy ended with v.19a and v.19b was to be viewed as the beginning of the prophetic response with two questions "should not a people consult its God (or should they consult) the dead on behalf of the living?," cf. the *RSV*; most recently Watts 1985:125–28; Oswalt 1986:230,237.

76 The LXX read the accusative singular of *theos* and 1QIs[a] read the singular *ʾlwhw*.

77 Cf. e.g., Lewis 1989:131.

78 For recent surveys and bibliographies, cf. Hoffner 1974:130–34; Wildberger 1972:349–50; Lust 1974:133–42; Ebach and Rüterswörden 1977:57–70; 1980:205–20; add Burns 1979:1–14; Heider

bound up with the question of its intended referents: are these "knowers," i.e., the dead who have special knowledge about the future, the "familiar ghosts," i.e., the ancestral dead, or are these the practitioners who have the special knowledge enabling them to communicate with the dead? We will defer our response here to our treatment of the *'ōḇôṯ*.

For *'ōḇôṯ*, at least three interpretations have been put forward e.g., "the revenants,"[79] "(the ghosts which issue from) the pit,"[80] and "the fathers" or "ancestors."[81] The second option has received substantial criticism and is generally rejected. In Hebrew, the plural form of *'ôḇ*, *'ôḇôṯ*, is more frequent, but plural "pits" do not seem to be indicated in the presumed non-biblical parallels. Second, there remains some question as to the problematic phonemic relation of the *p* and *b* in Sumerian ab, Akkadian *apu*, Hittite *api*, all supposedly signifying "pit," and Hebrew *'ôḇ*. Third, no explicit connection with "holes" is evident in the Israelite form of necromancy (at least not as depicted in 1 Sam. 28:3–25).[82]

As to etymology, preference is given here to the connection with Arabic *'āba*, "to return." To date, no damaging criticisms of this proposal have been offered. Thus, we translate *'ôḇ* as "the One-who-returns."[83] On the other hand, the association with Hebrew *'āḇ*, "father," presents several difficulties. If one assumed this etymology, the woman of Endor in 1 Sam. 28:7 who rouses the ghost of Samuel would have to be labeled *'ēšeṯ ba'ᵃlaṯ-'ôḇ*, "the controller of a father." However, unless one could demonstrate that the writer intended familial relations between the woman of Endor and Samuel, or for that matter Saul and Samuel, it is unlikely that Hebrew *'ôḇ* intended any such associations.[84] This proposal

---

1985:249–50 (and under the relevant texts); Spronk 1986:251–57; Rouillard and Tropper 1987b:235–54.

[79] Albright 1969:202 n.32, followed by Lewis 1989:56,113 n.36, has recently resurrected "revenants" (cf. Arabic *'āba* "to return"). For earlier commentators who upheld this view, cf. van Hoonacker 1897–98:157.

[80] So Hoffner 1967:385–401 based on Vieyra 1961:47–55 and Gadd 1948:88–89.

[81] Spronk 1986:253–54; Rouillard and Tropper 1987b:238, following Dietrich, Loretz, and Sanmartín 1974:450–51; Lust 1974:136–37; Müller 1975–76:70, have upheld "fathers" (cf. Hebrew *'āḇ*). Another suggestion is "bag, bottle" based on the *hapax legomenon 'ôḇ* in Job 32:19 with the proposed etymology "to be hollow," cf. van Hoonacker 1897–98:157. H. P. Smith 1899:240 suggested "human skull" based on the same etymology.

[82] For additional criticisms, cf. Lust 1974:134; Dietrich, Loretz, and Sanmartín 1974:451; Müller 1975–76:68–70; Margalit 1976:146; Healey 1977a:254–56; Cohen 1978:73–74 n.144; Burns 1979:10.

[83] Lust 1974:135 rejected this position, for the French "revenant," or, as Lust further defines the term, "ghosts of the deceased who can be called up through a spiritist," would not have been an acceptable concept in the first millennium B.C.E. But 1 Samuel 28 provides as close a parallel as one could hope to find! Nevertheless, we recognize the fact that the Arabic is unattested in earlier phases of Semitic, so Hoffner 1974:131.

[84] Cf. the similar criticism of Ebach and Rüterswörden 1980:207. Spronk 1986:254 attempted to circumvent this objection by arguing that in 1 Samuel 28, *'ôḇ* had become a general designation

also requires a protracted and unconvincing argument involving the Canaanite shift *ā* to *ō* as well as a highly speculative theological motivation for the vowel change, i.e., to dissociate the highly regarded fathers from the condemned practice of necromancy.[85] Lastly, circularity is evident as well in the argument that an ancestor cult is implicitly assumed as the intended rival in such a contrast.

At least four possibilities have been proposed for the identity of the referents of *'ōḇôṯ* and *yiddᵊ'ōnîm*: (1) the pit (at least in the case of *'ōḇôṯ*), (2) images of the dead, (3) those who conjure up the dead, and (4) the ghosts of the dead. The first can be eliminated owing to its dependence upon the etymological argument derived from Sumerian ab, Akkadian *apu*, and Hittite *api* which we have rejected for the reasons already outlined. That an image might on occasion be in view has been recently reiterated.[86] The key to this interpretation lies in the significance of *'ôḇ* and *yiddᵊ'ōnî* as objects of such verbal actions as "make" (Qal of *'āśāh:* 2 Kgs. 21:6, 2 Chr. 33:6), "burn" (Piel of *bā'ar*: 2 Kgs. 23:24), "destroy" (Hiphil of *kāraṯ*: 1 Sam. 28:9), and "drive out" (Hiphil of *sûr*: 1 Sam. 28:3). According to the image interpretation, these actions as described, favor material objects over "ghosts of the dead." Therefore, some type of image would appropriately fit the contexts.

Lust, one of the advocates of this position, recognized the fact that the above verbs can be applied to persons as well, but in the end he rejected this possibility for "when considered together however they [the verbs] rather refer to a material object." Lust did note, however, the use of *'āśāh* in Gen. 12:5, where slaves are said to have been "acquired." Such a notion might likewise apply to the hiring of a professional class.[87] Lust also failed to mention that *'āśāh* is used in conjunction with another professional class, the "priests," or *kōhᵃnîm*, and designates their having been "appointed" (cf. e.g., 1 Kgs. 12:31; 13:33; 2 Kgs. 17:32; 2 Chr. 2:17(ET 16)). In any case, it is certainly conceivable that the writers who advocated the laws of burning or expulsion had in mind persons who engaged in such illegitimate practices. Lev. 20:27 makes clear that such persons were to be stoned to death should the *'ôḇ* or the *yiddᵊ'ōnî* be found "in them," or *bāhem*. Surely this is not a reference to an image, pit, or professional.

---

for all spirits of the dead, but he neither offered support nor did he explain how the ancestors were distinguished from the dead in general. In any case, his view that an ancestral spirit of the woman of Endor might have acted as an intermediary between her and other spirits, contradicts Saul's request in v.8. Saul specifically asks her to divine (Qal of *qāsam*) and bring up (Hiphil of *'ālāh*) the *'ôḇ* which Saul should name. This was not one of her ancestors. Spronk's comparison with Ugaritic *'il'ib* and Aramaic *'b'* as read by his mentor de Moor in *KAI* 214:16 must also be rejected, cf. 3.1.3.

[85] So Lust 1974:136, following Lods 1906(I):248.

[86] Heider 1985:250 n.506; Spronk 1986:253; Rouillard and Tropper 1987b:236, following Wohlstein 1967:350–51; Wildberger 1972:349–50; Lust 1974:137–38.

[87] Lust 1974:137 and n.6.

In spite of Lust's rejection of the "ghosts of the dead" interpretation, these verbs can adequately accommodate the ghosts of the dead as their objects. Ghosts, or, figuratively speaking, those rites and cults associated with them, might be appointed or instituted (*'āśāh*), exterminated or purged (Piel of *bā'ar* and cf. the formula *bi'artā hārā' miqqirbekā* "you shall purge the evil from your midst," e.g. Deut. 21:21), cut off, i.e., forbidden (Hiphil of *kārat*, cf. 1 Sam. 20:15), and rejected or put aside (Hiphil of *sûr*, cf. e.g. Josh. 11:15; Ps. 66:20). Moreover, where it was previously assumed that necromancers were in view, the evidence favors ghosts as the fitting referents.[88] Besides, as we noted above, Lev. 20:27 surely eliminates the practitioner as well as the image interpretations as the *'ôb* and the *yiddᵊ'ōnî* are depicted there as possessing persons or as residing "in them," or *bāhem*.

In fact, Isa. 8:19–23 provides an exemplary test case for our proposal. The raised ghosts are described as "chirping" (*hamᵊṣapṣᵊpîm*) and "twittering" (*hammahgîm*). In line with a few LXX translations, commentators have taken such sounds to indicate the methods employed by mediums and wizards to deceive their clients *via* ventriloquism, but this interpretation lacks support from the immediate contexts of the passages in question. The *'ôb* in Isa. 29:4 is likewise depicted as "chirping" (*tᵊṣapṣep*), but in this case, the ghost is clearly located in the netherworld, or *'āpār* ("dust"), so the necromancer or image interpretations are again eliminated. As pointed out above, the portrayal of the dead as birds is sufficiently documented for the ancient Near East which points to their ability to take flight from the netherworld. This is the possible conceptual and ritualistic backdrop for 29:4 .[89]

In only two instances is a practitioner explicitly mentioned and, in both, rather than designating that necromancer by the unqualified use of the terms *'ôb* and *yiddᵊ'ōnî*, an extended phraseology is employed. In Deut. 18:11, the necromancer is described as *šō'ēl 'ôb wᵊyiddᵊ'ōnî* (Qal ptc. of *šā'al*), "one who asks of 'the One-who-returns and the Knower' " or *dōrēš 'el-hammētîm* (Qal ptc. of *dāraš*), "one who consults the dead." In 1 Sam. 28:7, the woman of Endor is named *'ēšet baᵃlat-'ôb* "the controller of the One-who-returns." Therefore, where the *'ôb* and *yiddᵊ'ōnî* function as the objects of such verbal actions as "inquire" (*dāraš* + *'el*: Isa. 8:19; 19:3; 1 Chr. 10:13), "ask" (*šā'al*: Deut. 18:11; + *bᵊ*- 1 Chr. 10:13), "divine" (*qāsam* + *bᵊ*-: 1 Sam. 28:8), "turn to" (*pānāh* + *'el*: Lev. 19:31; 20:6), and "seek unto" (Piel of *bāqaš* + *'el*: Lev. 19:31), they are best viewed as the ghosts of the dead.

---

88 This is also the opinion of the translators of the *JPS*.

89 Cf. Spronk 1986:100 and the bibliography in n.2. This might stand behind the comparison of the voice of the living with that of the *'ôb* from the (lower) earth (*mē'ereṣ*) in 29:4. It is as if the living are as good as dead.

By way of summary, nowhere do the unqualified terms *'ōḇôṯ* and *yiddᵊʿōnîm* require the practitioner interpretation. In fact, several contexts make the ghost interpretation preferable (esp. Lev. 20:27; Isa. 29:4), while others would readily avail themselves of the same. This eliminates the notion that the *yiddᵊʿōnî* designates one who has the special knowledge needed to communicate with the dead. Moreover, in none of the uses of *yiddᵊʿōnî* are familial ties apparent. In fact, 1 Samuel 28 speaks directly against this (see above). So "familiar ghost" is less likely a meaning than simply "knowers," i.e., ghosts who have superior knowledge of the affairs of the living. Finally, when the background of crisis and despair and the resort to unconventional modes of revelation are seen in the light of the dtr redacted text, Deut. 18:11, (cf. 4.4.2. and the parallel Lev. 19:31 and 20:6,27), dtr Isa. 19:3 (cf. 4.3.3.), and the exilic text, Isa. 47:10b–12, where the same or similar divining practices are condemned, an exilic or post-exilic date becomes all the more compelling.[90]

In conclusion, Isa. 8:19–22 is an example of necromancy, that is to say, the calling up of the deceased for purposes of ascertaining the unknown or predicting the future. Unlike prescriptions for expelling a ghost owing to some malevolent influence it might exert, in necromancy the active presence of the ghost is desired. Although it is often assumed that necromancy shares such a *modus operandi* with death or ancestor cults, no clear examples of such a common goal has been documented in Syro-Palestinian texts. Besides, in the survey offered in chapter 1, we outlined the distinctive characteristics of the corresponding ritual complexes and underlying beliefs associated with necromancy on the one hand and the death or ancestor cult on the other.

4.3.3. Isaiah 19:3

Like Isa. 8:19, 19:3 makes mention of *hā'ōḇôṯ*, "the Ones-who-return," and *hayyiddᵊʿōnîm*, "the Knowers," but in this instance, they are depicted as reflective of necromantic practices indigenous to Egypt. Commentators frequently attribute this connection to the author's ignorance of Egyptian magic and religion. Others conclude that this is in keeping with his characteristic Yahwistic bias which finds support in the dependence of the verse upon expressions found elsewhere in the book, 8:19 and 29:4 being prime examples.[91]

As both vv.1–4 as well as the entire oracle against Egypt, vv.1–15, play a crucial role in determining the contribution of v.3 to our investigation, their

---

[90] Cf. Wildberger 1972:344; Clements 1981:101–103.

[91] Cf. e.g., Kaiser 1980:101.

compositional histories require detailed analysis. 19:1–15 falls into three parts: vv.1–4 portray the collapse of the religious and civil order, vv.5–10 depict the failure of the Nile floods, Egypt's economic base, and vv.11–15 describe the helplessness of her political leaders in the face of disaster. The oracle against Egypt is located within the larger, originally independent, collection of oracles against foreign nations (chapters 13–23). Like many such oracles in the prophetic books, vv.1–15 date to a period following the time of the proclamation of the prophet as it presupposes later historical circumstances. In fact, 19:1–15 reveals a heavy dependence upon other passages in the book, and particularly the other oracles against the nations.[92] The repudiation of Egypt and its political strength differs considerably from that found in undoubtedly Isaianic passages such as 20:1–6; 30:1–5; and 31:1–3.[93] Furthermore, the author's style, replete as it is with wooden repetitiveness, is inferior to the elegance and conciseness of the Isaianic hand.[94] When these arguments in support of a post-Isaianic composition are set over against the depiction of Egypt's instability (v.2) as well as her political independence and subsequent domination by a foreign ruler (v.4, cf. Ezek. 30:12), one must look for a period, or periods, in which the themes of conquest and instability come to the fore. Accordingly, the exilic to post-exilic time span best suits the compositional setting of vv.1–15.[95] This finds added support in the arguments outlined in 4.2. for the exilic or post-exilic redaction of Isaiah chapters 1 to 35 as a unit.

As mentioned above, the *'ōḇôṯ* and *yiddᵊʿōnîm* in 19:3 have been viewed as symptomatic of the author's ignorance of Egyptian beliefs or characteristic of his Yahwistic bias.[96] It is clear that ghosts of the dead were considered benevolent numina in Egyptian magical traditions.[97] However, matters complicate when it comes to the Letters to the Dead so often cited in support of an Egyptian version

---

[92] Vermeylen 1977–78(I):320–21 listed as additional elements for the late composition of the oracle: the struggling fratricide (v.2, cf. 3:5), the spirit of Egypt (v.3, cf. 30:1; 31:3), the recourse to necromancy and enchanters (v.3, cf. 3:2–3; 8:19), the incapacity of the planners (v.4, cf. 3:4), the princes of Zoan (vv.11,13, cf. 30:4), the folly of the sages (v.11, cf. 29:14), the plan of Yahweh (v.12, cf. 14:24–27), the staggering drunkard (vv.13–14, cf. 28:7–8; 29:9), the vomit (v.14, cf. 28:8), the spirit poured out by Yahweh (v.14, cf. 29:10; 31:3), and the head and the tail, the palm branch and the reed (v.15, cf. 9:13(ET 14)).

[93] Clements 1981:166–67.

[94] "Egypt" is awkwardly repeated seven times in four verses.

[95] Van der Toorn 1988:209 completely ignored the arguments against an eighth century date. With Kaiser 1980:99, the late date eliminates the Egyptian campaigns of Esarhaddon and Ashurbanipal. He proposed 404–343 B.C.E., the period between the revolt of Amyrtaios and the final reconquest by Artaxerxes III Ochos. Vermeylen 1977–78(I):321 proposed the Egyptian campaign of Nebuchadrezzar (605 B.C.E.) based on the fact that the author was unaware of the post-exilic additions to the book.

[96] Cf. e.g., Kaiser 1980:101; van der Toorn 1988:209.

[97] Cf. Demarée 1983; the extensive review by Schulman 1986:302–48; Baines 1991:150–61.

of necromancy.[98] While contact with the dead is certainly in view in the letters, the prominent aspect of the dead depicted in these letters is their (manipulated) hostility or confrontational posture.[99] Moreover, the letters are not necromantic rites according to the definition offered in chapter 1 and as illustrated by 1 Sam. 28:3–25. The dead in the letters are neither explicitly summoned to the immediate presence of the living nor do they dispense special knowledge concerning the fate of the living.[100] They are requested instead to cease haunting the living, to initiate a haunt, to take legal proceedings against a malevolent ghost, or to dispense knowledge about the underworld.[101] Demarée assumed that the *3ḫ íḳr*, "able ancestor," intervened beneficently in the birth of a healthy child in one such letter, the Chicago jar stand, but the context makes clear that the ghost was to banish the afflicting numina which might attack the mother-to-be.[102] In other words, while advantageous side effects might accrue to a letter's sender, the action performed by the dead is explicitly hostile or it is couched in legal terminology and downplayed as merely confrontational. As acknowledged even by Demarée, the *íḳr* or "able" ghost in the Louvre bowl might be hostile as indicated by the use of a tick differentiating between the determinatives *mwt* and *mwtt.í*.[103] In the final

98 Cf. e.g., Tropper 1989:27–46.

99 Cf. Ritner 1987:159–75; Wente 1990:210–19.

100 *Contra* Tropper 1989:27–46. The same applies in the case of spells in the Book of the Dead where the ghost is depicted as revealing the fate of those in the underworld including its own, not the fate of the living, cf. Allen 1974:141,214 (Book of the Dead spells 148 [21st dynasty] and 190). In the Demotic stories of Setna Khaemuas in Lichtheim 1980:125-51, a concern with events transpiring in the netherworld is evident. Owing to the fact that these are literary texts not rituals, in cases where the dead are portrayed as visiting the world of the living, an exceptional phenomenon might be in view (and not a commonly known necromantic ritual). If one should assume that some ritual complex related to necromancy lies behind this element in the stories, it might well be one adopted of late from the Greek ritual world. In any case, the appearances of the dead in these stories do not entail predicting the future fate of the living. Another literary text is often cited in this regard, the Teaching of King Amenemhat I in Simpson, Faulkner, and Wente 1973:193-97. However, this is a case of a wise admonition placed in the mouth of a dead king speaking from the underworld. The practice of necromancy is nowhere described or presumed. Thus, to glean elements from these literary texts in order to reconstruct a hypothetical early necromantic tradition in Egypt is methodologically troublesome. It would entail extensive generalizations involving a variety of textual data representative of several periods of Egyptian culture. The late Egyptian Ghost Story or Story of Khonsaemhab in Simpson, Faulkner, and Wente 1973:137–41 concerns favors for the dead not vice versa. In addition to the examples of contact with the dead cited by Borghouts in Finkel 1983–84:15 and n.64, cf. Borghouts 1976:11–12 (no.12),24 (no.33),29–30 (no.41).

101 Cf. Wente 1990:210–19; Baines 1991:150–61.

102 Demarée 1983:213–18; cf. Gardiner 1930:19–22.

103 Demarée 1983:215 n.105. These observations are not mutually exclusive of the proposal that the *3ḫ íḳr* was venerated (?) in the mortuary cult as intermediary between the gods and the able ancestor's descendants, on which cf. Demarée 1983; Schulman 1986:302–348, esp. pp.316,346. The aspect stressed in the letters is the hostile power of the *3ḫ íḳr* regardless of its potential beneficence attested elsewhere in *non*-necromantic contexts.

analysis, while contact with the ghost was practiced in ancient Egypt, necromancy like that reflected in 1 Samuel 28 remains unattested.

In any case, the dtr propensity for rhetorical polemic makes it extremely difficult to ascertain whether or not the redactional hand responsible for 19:3 was concerned with the accuracy of his portrayal of necromancy as an Egyptian practice. Given the arguments in 4.1. and 4.3.2. for the extensive dtr influence on first Isaiah, the dtr character of *'ōḇôṯ* and *yidd^{ə}'ōnîm*, and the absence of necromancy in Egyptian sources, 19:3 is best understood as exemplary of a rhetorical strategy similar to that in the legal traditions wherein the supposed Canaanite origins of necromancy serve to legitimate its condemnation. In other words, what the various biblical traditions share in common vis-à-vis necromancy is their attribution of *foreign* origins to the practice. As we shall argue in 4.5.1.–2., underlying the biblical rhetoric of its foreign origins is the historical reality of Mesopotamian necromancy from the mid to late first millennium. In fact, 19:3 preserves a clue to the Mesopotamian origin of Israelite necromancy in its exceptional use of the Hebrew *hapax legomenon*, *'iṭṭîm*, "the ghosts of the dead." This term is in all likelihood the cognate of Akkadian *eṭemmu*. The term *eṭemmu* is the common term for "ghost of the dead" and is the numen repeatedly referred to in the first millennium necromancy incantations from Mesopotamia. Our translation of Isa. 19:3 reads as follows:

win^{ə}ḇaqqāh rûaḥ-miṣrayim b^{ə}qirbô	Egypt will be drained of spirit,
wa'^{a}ṣāṯô '^{a}ḇallēa'	and I will confound its plans;
w^{ə}ḏār^{ə}šû 'el-hā'^{e}lîlîm	So they will consult the false
w^{ə}'el-hā'iṭṭîm	gods and the shades,
w^{ə}'el-hā'ōḇôṯ	the Ones-who-return
w^{ə}'el-hayyidd^{ə}'ōnîm	and the Knowers.

Like *hā'ōḇôṯ* and *hayyidd^{ə}'ōnîm*, the terms, *hā'^{e}lîlîm* and *hā'iṭṭîm*, function as the objects of the verbal form *w^{ə}ḏār^{ə}šû*, "they will consult. . . ." While the analysis of *'^{e}lîlîm* remains problematic, Preuss suggests that it "was created as a disparaging pun on, and as a diminutive of, *'ēl*" (cf. *k^{ə}sîl*, "fool," where the suffixed *-îl* may likewise function as a diminutive ending).[104] The similar use of this term in late and dtr passages such as 2:8,18,20; 10:10,11 (cf. also 1 Kgs. 18:33–35 and Isa. 36:18–20); and 31:7 lends further support to the post-Isaianic redaction of 19:3.[105]

---

104 Preuss 1977:285. According to the author, its relation to the adjective *'^{e}lîl*, "weak, worthless," must be recognized as well.

105 Cf. Vermeylen 1977–78(I):138–39,321.

As pointed out above, *'iṭṭîm* is cognate with Akkadian *eṭemmu*, "ghost of the dead."[106] Others have compared Arabic *'aṭṭa*, "emit or utter a sound or noise,"[107] or Ugaritic *'uṭm*. The former, while possible, is less likely than the Akkadian and the exact meaning of the latter remains to be verified owing to its lone occurrence in Ugaritic.[108] The presence of an Akkadian loan gains further support from the close resemblance shared by the couplet *ilānu*, "gods,"// *eṭemmū*, "ghosts of the dead," found in cuneiform sources and the couplet *'ᵉlîlîm*, "false gods,"//*'iṭṭîm*, "ghosts of the dead," preserved in 19:3 (in spite of the latter couplet's polemical thrust). In both instances, two distinct classes of numina are in view, the major, personal, or netherworld gods on the one hand and the ghosts of the dead on the other. This in turn might suggest that *hā'ōḇôṯ* and *hayyiddᵊ'ōnîm* in 19:3b comprise specific subcategories within the class of beings designated *'iṭṭîm*.[109]

4.3.4. Isaiah 28:7–22

Early in this century, commentators like Daiches suggested that the antagonists of 28:7–22 practiced necromancy and that in 28:10,13, Isaiah was mimicking the phrases spoken during their "séances."[110] Recently van der Toorn has attempted to advance Daiches' proposal by explicating the sense of continuity it gives to the whole of 28:7–22.[111] This line of interpretation offers a very attractive solution to the crux of v.10 (and v.13). According to van der Toorn, 28:7–8 contain Isaiah's description of the rites performed by certain cultic prophets while in attendance at a

---

[106] Cf. Jirku 1912:11–12; Kaufman 1974:50,143 n.23; Cohen 1978:42. The doubling of *ṭ* has been explained as a marker of the plural.

[107] Cf. e.g., Gray 1912:324; Perles 1914:109; Lane 1863–93(I):66.

[108] *KTU* 1.5:I:5; cf. Ginsberg 1936:186. Some commentators suggest the Arabic as cognate, see del Olmo Lete 1981:213,524 for a survey of opinions.

[109] For the proposal that the gods, when found parallel to the dead, do not refer to the deified status of the dead, but either refer to the netherworld gods summoned in necromantic rites, cf. 4.5.1. or to the major or personal gods cf. 3.2.1.–2. and Finkel 1983–84:1–17. Note that for *'ᵉlîlîm*, the LXX reads *tous theous*, "the gods," although in 19:1 the LXX reads *ta cheiropoieta*, "made by human hands," for MT *'ᵉlîlê miṣrayim*. *Contra* Lewis 1989:133–34, this does warrant the conjecture that the LXX had as its *Vorlage* Hebrew *'ᵉlōhîm* in 19:3, for gods and their images could be viewed simply as aspects of the same referents, cf. e.g., Isa. 42:17 and Exod. 20:23.

[110] Daiches 1921:6; cf. e.g., Wade 1911:180; König 1926:254.

[111] Van der Toorn 1988:199–217. He argued for the essential unity of vv.7–22. Vv.7–13 is traditionally viewed as earlier than vv.14–22 based on the view that the religious offices of priest (*kōhēn*) and prophet (*naḇî'*) of v.7 are not to be equated with the *'anšê lāṣôn* of v.14 who rule (*māšal*) the people of Jerusalem. He speculates that the latter need not be viewed only as political leaders, for the cultic prophets influenced political life through their religious utterances, cf. pp.200–01.

marzēaḥ feast.[112] At this feast, the participants sought inebriation in order to enter into a visionary trance and thereby provide a medium or mouthpiece for the dead. 28:10 records Isaiah's mimicry of the birdlike twitterings and groans produced by the necromancers turned ventriloquists (and cf. LXX *engastrimuthous* in Isa. 19:3). These sounds were viewed as the dead's oracular message uttered by the living while in a drunken stupor, or *šᵊmû'āh*, (v.9 and cf. the similar use of Akkadian *egirrû* and Greek *klēdon*).

Thus, *laʿᵃgê śāp̱āh*, "strange lips," and *lāšôn 'aḥereṯ*, "foreign tongue," of v.11 as well as *'anšê lāṣôn*, "self-confident chatterboxes" or "men of nonsensical talk," of v.14 are to be understood as references to the necromancers and their esoteric language. The author further hypothesized that the prophets were required to interpret these unintelligible sounds in order to decipher the message communicated by the dead. For van der Toorn, the crucial datum suggestive of the divinatory or, more specifically, necromantic associations of this passage is the parallel mention of *māweṯ*, "death," and *šᵊ'ôl*, "netherworld," in v.15 (cf. also v.18). These are to be understood as personified beings, the deities, "Death" and "Netherworld," who offer their protection to those who perform the necessary divinatory rites and so the relevant lines are to be taken literally. Our rendition of Isa. 28:15 follows:[113]

kî 'ᵃmartem kārat̲nû b̲ᵉrîṯ	We have concluded a covenant
'eṯ-māweṯ	with death,
wᵊ'im-šᵊ'ôl	and with the netherworld
'āśînû ḥōzeh	we have made a pact;
šîṭ šôṭēp̱	when the overpowering scourge[114]
kî-yaʿᵃḇōr	comes along,
lō' yᵊḇô'ēnû	it shall not reach us,
kî śamnû k̲āzāḇ maḥsēnû	for we have made lying our refuge,
ûḇaššeqer nistārᵊnû	and in deceit we take shelter.

Halpern has independently proposed a similar interpretation of Isaiah 28. The priests and prophets are participants in the ancestor cult and believe that they can manipulate the deity while in a state of alcohol-induced ecstasy. According to this line of interpretation, v.10 contains Isaiah's mockery of the priests' and prophets' verbal 'babyisms' for the vomit and ordure they produced while hallucinating

---

[112] Van der Toorn 1988:213 cited the Ugaritic text *KTU* 1.114 as illustrative of the common role inebriation obtained in the *marzēaḥ* banquet, but cf. 3.1.5.

[113] Van der Toorn 1988:202–04. He also speculated that *kāzāḇ*, "Lie," and *šeqer*, "Deceit," refer to the gods Chemosh and Milcom/Moloch.

[114] For the reading *šōṭ* with qere and 1QIs^a, cf. Day 1989:59 n.101. The following verb *yaʿᵃḇōr* is the qere reading, cf. v.18, the kethibh being *'āḇar*.

under the influence. As support, the author suggested that *ṣaw* and *qaw* in v.10 comprise a wordplay on the terms *qîʾ*, "vomit," and *ṣōʾāh*, "excrement," of v.8 thereby enhancing the accusation that the priests and prophets had indulged in coprophilia.[115] Like van der Toorn, Halpern viewed Death and Sheol in vv.15 and 18 as underworld deities worshipped by the priests and prophets. In the light of this netherly context of v.18, Halpern concluded that *hammaṣṣāʿ* of v.20a is best viewed as a technical term for "funerary bench" with its accompanying "shroud," or *hammassēḵāh*, in v.20b.[116] But for Halpern, it was not vv.15 and 18 that supplied the crucial data in support of a divinatory backdrop for this passage. Rather, v.7 functioned for the author in this capacity. Here the priests and prophets are depicted as seeking oracles or visions, as indicated by the form, *bārōʾeh*, "in seeing."[117]

In response, it should be noted that rites related to the ancestor cult or necromancy are nowhere explicitly mentioned in Isa. 28:7–22. While a form of divination may be in view in v.7 and ecstatic utterances of an inebriated priest, perhaps, in v.10—both of these proposals are controvertible—neither necessitates the presence of rites involving the dead. Besides, others have interpreted v.7 without any reference to professional prophetic practices such as visions and divination. For example, Driver argued that the *RSV* translation, "they err in vision, they stumble in judgment," offers a poor parallelism with the "strong drink," or *šēḵār*, and "wine," or *yayin*, of v.7. He read *rōʾeh* as *rōweh*, "intoxication," following Theodotion's *methē* and the Peshitta's *rwāyûtâ*, "intoxication," and translated *šāḡû bārōʾeh* (= *bārōweh*), as "given up to tippling," and added that *rāʾāh* = *rāwāh*, "to drink one's fill," occurs in a number of other passages as well.[118]

In any case, the supposed mention of the gods of Death and Sheol in vv.15 and 18 cannot be employed as decisive proof or supporting evidence in favor of this interpretation. Against the reliance of van der Toorn, and for that matter, Halpern, on 28:15,18 as indicative of necromantic practices, it should be pointed out that most interpreters construe these lines as figurative for taking the necessary precautions to avert impending disaster. Many have seen in these terms allusions to political agreements either with Assyria (to spare the tipplers when Assyria invades) or with Egypt (against the Assyrians). Assyria is most likely.[119] Even

---

[115] Halpern 1986:113–14.

[116] Halpern 1986:109–21.

[117] Halpern 1986:114. Like van der Toorn, Halpern 1986:118 cited the Ugaritic text *KTU* 1.114 as illustrative of the association of drunkenness, excretion, and death in the *marzēaḥ* feast, but cf. 3.1.5.

[118] Driver 1968a:52. Cf. the translation of the *NEB*, "lose their way through tippling," (margin); Isa. 22:9; 53:10; Jer. 31:14; 46:10; Ps. 36:9(ET 8); 40:13(ET 12); 50:23; 60:5(ET 3); 91:16; Job 10:15; 20:17; 31:7; 33:21.

[119] See the recent surveys in van der Toorn 1988:202 and Day 1989:60–62. Day's criticism of the covenant with Egypt is most convincing. Nevertheless, the covenant with death is best taken

the position that chthonic deities are in view does not necessitate that one embrace the necromantic interpretation. Day has recently argued that Death and Sheol refer to the Molek cult and child sacrifice.[120] In other words, a necromantic or death cult orientation of a literal rendering appears probable only if one concludes that the prior arguments for necromantic or death and ancestor cult practices in Isaiah 28 are convincing.[121]

Nevertheless, if we were to assume for the sake of argument that necromancy or rites related to the ancestral cult constitute the illicit practices for which this prophetic oracle was intended, then Halpern's suggestion that the priests and prophets functioned as imitators of the dead might hint at a Mesopotamian backdrop for the causal clause ending v.8, "for (*kî*) all the tables are full of vomit, no place is without filthiness."[122] That is to say, just as it is with the Mesopotamian dead who, having been abandoned by the living, must eat their dung,[123] so it shall be for the priests and prophets who drink to excess in hopes of imitating the dead or of receiving a message from Yahweh. When they die, they will find their netherly diet to consist of vomit and excrement. According to this view, the author's allusion to this their ultimate fate underscores his exhortation to reject their methods and message.

This brings us to the compositional history of 28:7–22. If behind the phrase *bᵊrîṯ 'eṯ-māweṯ*, "the covenant with death," in 28:15,18, there stands an implied contrast with Yahweh's covenant which brings life and if the dtr traditions were responsible for at least the proliferation of covenant ideology expressing Yahweh's relationship with Israel, then we have additional evidence for the dtr redaction of this chapter and chapters 1–35 more generally.[124] Again, supposing those commentators are correct who advocate the presence of necromancy in Isaiah 28, based on our findings vis-à-vis the exclusively dtr association of those texts

---

to refer to the fatal outcome of Israel's political jockeying having not put her faith in Yahweh, cf. Nicholson 1986:115. Death and Sheol are personifications of the party with whom the agreement was made (whom we take to be Assyria), so Burns 1973:338, but cf. his less convincing treatment in 1989:29–30.

120 Day 1989:58–64.

121 Cf. Day 1989:61–62 for additional criticisms of the necromantic interpretation: (1) Isa. 28:15,18 do not speak of the dead in the plural which is what would be expected if necromancy was in view and (2) consultation is not the same as a covenant. Cf. also the critique of Tropper 1989:326–30.

122 We would understand the perfect form *mālᵊ'û* as descriptive of a future event as if it were already past (i.e., the so-called prophetic perfect).

123 Cf. Xella 1980:151–60 who applied the significance of this Mesopotamian topos to 2 Kgs. 18:27 and Isa. 36:12.

124 Recall that the covenant lawsuit, or *rîḇ*, in Isaiah 1 might indicate the presence in chapters 1–35 of the covenant idea as an expression of Yahweh's relationship with Israel, cf. e.g., Kaiser 1983:12. The "father-son" metaphor common in ancient treaty parlance supports this view as well, for which cf. Fensham 1971:121–35.

which make mention of this divinatory art, we would have additional support for the dtr redactional nature of this passage and Mesopotamian influence would best explain its presence here. This in turn would support the view that the covenant with Death/the pact with the Netherworld was made with Assyria in order to avert disaster. But it was too late, for Assyria would soon break covenant and destroy Israel (cf. v.18). The descriptive language of impending invasion presupposes some familiarity with Mesopotamian religion (more on this below, cf. 4.5.2.).

4.3.5. Isaiah 29:4

Isa. 29:1–8 comprises a description of Jerusalem's salvation.[125] Like the previous Isaianic passages, the date and authorship of this passage remain disputed. Clements, for example, concluded that 29:1–4 were Isaianic and were, therefore, composed just prior to 701 B.C.E. when the possibility of an Assyrian siege of Jerusalem grew imminent, while 29:5–8 were added later by a Josianic redactor. His division is based on the observation that 29:5–8 reflect a dramatic change in perspective, for the foes are no longer the agents of Yahweh, but have become his enemies. Thus, these verses attempt to interpret Sennacherib's failure to take Jerusalem in 701 as a victory for Yahweh and to establish the inviolability of Zion (v.7).[126]

Kaiser, on the other hand, rejected an Isaianic nucleus to 29:1–8. To begin with, the warning lacks a typically Isaianic reproach with reasons derived from the present rather than the future. Secondly, the allusion to David in v.1a is ambiguous. Moreover, according to this line of interpretation, it contains a non-historical conception of deliverance. With regard to v.4 specifically, Kaiser argued that the insertion of the phrase, "and it shall be," in v.4b (Hebrew *hāyāh*) is indicative of a redactional hand and the same shows up in vv.2b (2x),5a,5b,7a, and 8a.[127] Lastly, Kaiser concluded that in 29:1–4, the prophet predicts Jerusalem's destruction. This reflects the hand of an exilic writer. These observations support our contention that where the term *'ôḇ* (cf. v.4) and/or the term *yiddᵊʻōnî* appear in the Isaiah traditions, we have likely evidence for the presence of dtr ideology. In other words, 29:4, like 8:19 and 19:3, is redactional in nature and, we would argue, based on the additional arguments set forth above, dtr in orientation (cf. 4.2. and 4.3.2.–3.) The writer argues that such calamity will befall the city that

---

125 So Kaiser 1980:264. It begins with a woe oracle, vv.1–3(4), and ends with a description of salvation beginning with v.5b(–8). The form *tippāqēḏî* in v.6a should be understood in a positive sense following the editor of *BHS*.

126 Clements 1981:234–35.

127 Kaiser 1980:264–65.

her voice will be reduced to the sound of a ghost chirping in the netherworld. The overtures to death suggest the Babylonian destruction of Jerusalem. The following illustrates our interpretation of Isa. 29:4:

wᵊšāp̱alt mē'ereṣ tᵊḏabbērî	"Brought low,[128] you shall speak from (lower) earth,
ûmē'āp̱ār tiššaḥ 'imrāṯēḵ	from the dust your speech shall issue.[129]
wᵊhāyāh kᵊ'ôḇ mē'ereṣ qôlēḵ	your voice shall be like One-who-returns from (lower) earth,
ûmē'āp̱ār 'imrāṯēḵ tᵊṣap̱ṣēp̱	from the dust your speech shall chirp."

The *JPS* translation views the simile, *kᵊ'ôḇ*, in v.4c as referring to the ghost's voice "your speech shall be like a ghost's from the ground," whereas the *RSV* interprets the comparison as one in which Jerusalem's voice comes up from the netherworld just as a ghost was believed to do (not merely its voice). To be sure, either rendition provides a fitting analogy for the deadly fate of the city. The former assumes that voices of the dead could be heard rising from the ground, the latter suggests that the ghost itself could return to the land of the living. Both notions are attested in the Hebrew Bible. The former is implied in the final clause of our passage (29:4d) where the *'ôḇ* is heard "chirping" (*tᵊṣap̱ṣēp̱*; cf. 8:19) from the "dust" or netherworld (*'āp̱ār*). The latter is assumed in 1 Sam. 28:8 where Saul requests that the woman of Endor bring up (Hiphil of *'ālāh*) the *'ôḇ* which he should name.

This passage is of particular interest owing to the Assyrian backdrop of vv.1–8. Given our arguments for the late Mesopotamian origin of Israelite necromancy (cf. 4.2 and 4.5.2.), we understand the use of the first person in the woe oracle of vv.1–5a (or at the least vv.2–5a) to convey the Assyrian king's proclamation to Judah. As such, it displays a convincing degree of familiarity with Mesopotamian divination and has, as its precedent, the proclamation of the Assyrian king spoken by the Rabshakeh in 2 Kgs. 18:28–35. Moreover, both doom accounts make mention of Assyrian afterlife beliefs, that is if the eating of dung and drinking of urine in 2 Kgs. 18:27 refers to one's anticipated existence in the netherworld.[130]

The efficacy of necromancy assumed in 29:4 stands in stark contrast to the polemical posture of 8:19 where such efficacy is categorically denied. But 29:4 agrees with the perspective found in 1 Sam. 28:3–25, where the efficacy of necro-

---

128 For similar phraseology, cf. Akkadian *šapliš ina erṣetim*, "below in the earth (= netherworld)."

129 Various proposals accompany *tiššaḥ*: < *šḥḥ*, "to be low," so Irwin 1977:51, < Arabic *saḥḥa*, "poured out" thus "issue," so Driver 1968b:51, and < *śyḥ*, "to utter," so Dahood as noted by Irwin 1977:51; cf. Job 7:11.

130 Cf. Xella 1980:151–60.

mancy is likewise assumed. In any case, the metaphoric use of necromancy for the abject weakness and mortal fate of Jerusalem's inhabitants in Isaiah 29 hardly stands if such notions concerning the beliefs about the world of the dead were entirely dismissed by the author. Thus, the dtr redacted denunciation of necromancy in 29:4 is best understood as a response to the Mesopotamian belief embraced by some sectors of Judahite society of the redactor's own day, that the conjuration of and communication with the dead truly enabled one to obtain knowledge about the living's future. The dtr redactor sought to demonstrate that the preferred source of revelation is Yahwistic prophecy. As in 1 Sam. 28:6, the post-Isaianic dtr redactor of Isa. 29:10 portrays the cessation of Yahwistic prophecy as coincident with the adoption of necromancy. This backdrop not only provides the conceptual basis for the simile in v.4., but further underscores 29:4's intriguing contradiction with 8:19 where an altogether different rhetorical strategy is employed. It should be recalled that in 8:19, necromancy's power is entirely rejected as a stratagem for advancing Yahweh as the only true source of revelation.

4.3.6. Summary

Our examination of the Isaianic traditions concerned with necromancy reveals that a rhetorical strategy designed to disparage competing ideologies was executed by a post-Isaianic redactor with a dtr orientation. As a reaction to Mesopotamian religious influence upon the Israelite/Judahite culture of the redactor's own day, that polemic was inserted into Isaianic traditions about such former times as those set in the days of king Ahaz of Judah (8:19). The redactor attributed necromantic rites not only to 'wayward' Judah (8:19), but also to foreign empires such as those of Egypt (19:3) and Assyria (29:4?). Judahite necromancy was thereby depicted, within the literary landscape of the Isaianic traditions, as an originally alien form of divination. The resulting impression is twofold. According to dtr ideology, late Judah had fallen under the pervasive influence of several foreign cultures in the chief matter of her belief in the genuine source of supernatural power. Would Judah place her loyalty with Yahweh or with the foreign gods and the empowered dead whom those gods controlled? Secondly, the dtr ideology's Isaianic redaction depicted the dtr Yahwistic condemnation of necromancy as an ancient (not late), traditional (not innovative), and, therefore, definitive (nonsectarian) mandate.

Our investigation also revealed that like necromancy, the ancestor cult was of no apparent concern to the pre-exilic prophets. This became evident in our assessment of Amos 6:7 and in the resultant image of the pre-exilic Israelite *marzēaḥ*. Furthermore, the lack of mention of ancestor cult rites in first Isaiah and in other prophetic traditions concerned with pre-exilic times corroborates the argument that this deafening silence points to the historical absence of ancestor worship or veneration in pre-exilic Israel and Judah. The Syro-Palestinian evidence which we examined in chapters 2 and 3 and in 4.1. renders doubtful the notion that such silence can be explained by resorting to the argument that while ancestor cult rites did exist among the local Canaanites and Israelites, these rites presented no ideological threat to the then extant forms of Yahwism. The Canaanite origins of necromancy are nowhere explicitly mentioned in the Isaiah passages. The extra-biblical data suggest that such a cult was nonexistent in the contemporary religious traditions of Syria-Palestine and so it can no longer be assumed that the ancestor cult or its attendant belief in the supernatural beneficent power of the dead was long indigenous to the region. Of course, our investigation leaves open the question of the existence of other mortuary rites and cults that were not expressive of this belief.

In fact, our findings concerning necromancy also offer an argument by analogy as they suggest that the period spanning the last days of the southern kingdom through to the exile and beyond provides a more likely context than any time previous for the potential foreign introduction of the belief in the supernatural beneficent dead into Syria-Palestine. Unlike the case of necromancy, however, the dtr tradition never polemicizes against the ancestor cult in its redaction of first Isaiah. In chapter 1, we suggested that ancestor worship and veneration presuppose the same belief as necromancy in the supernatural beneficent power of the dead. Therefore, we would have certainly expected to find a dtr, ideological polemic against ancestor worship and veneration had these beliefs in fact existed and had their corresponding rites been enacted in the days prior to or contemporary with the dtr tradition.

Looking ahead, critics have also identified a number of passages in the legal and narrative traditions of the Hebrew Bible that purportedly document Israel's embrace of the Canaanite ancestor cult during the days of the early monarchy. The attendant assumption is that the belief in the supernatural power of the benefic dead was part of the nation's early heritage. To these texts we now turn.

4.4. The Deuteronomic Legal Texts

In this section, passages from the book of Deuteronomy will be examined for evidence of ancestor cult practices and necromancy. The three relevant texts fall within the confines of the legal section spanning chapters 12 to 26. Each of these texts has been scrutinized in past treatments on the Israelite ancestor cult:

14:1, a command outlawing selected mourning rites, 18:11, a prohibition against necromancy, and 26:14, a passage traditionally viewed as a proscription against offerings made to the dead.

4.4.1. Deuteronomy 14:1

Self-laceration and tonsure—the cutting of one's own flesh and the removal of one's own head or facial hair—are portrayed in the Hebrew Bible as two of the more bizarre responses to death. Their unique status is confirmed by their having been singled out from among the numerous mourning rites mentioned as the only ones to be deemed ritually impure.[131] As the pretext for their proscription, their supposed Canaanite origins are often cited by scholars and the ritual setting typically envisioned is either the Canaanite cult of the dead or the Baal fertility cult. In this regard, modern scholarship has simply adopted the dtr perspective. The rites of self-laceration and tonsure are outlawed only in a handful of legal texts. Deut. 14:1 is the *locus classicus* for their biblical ban:[132]

bānîm 'attem lᵊyhwh	You are the sons of Yahweh
'ᵉlōhêḵem lō' ṯiṯgōḏᵊḏû	your God; you shall not cut your-
wᵊlō'-ṯāśîmû qorḥāh bên	selves or make any baldness on your
'ênêḵem lāmēṯ	foreheads on account of the dead.

[131] This is a more inclusive definition of tonsure than the mere shaving of the crown of the head as practiced in much later monastic orders. The ban on the rites of tonsure (*pāra'*) in Lev. 10:6; 21:10; and Ezek. 44:20a is restricted to the high priest. It is coupled with the ban on rending the high priestly vestments and presupposes the taboo on gashing as 21:18 (*ḥārum*) suggests. The polluting power of non-sacrificial blood might also explain the lack of explicit mention of gashing in the texts.

[132] Their ritual significance is also highlighted by means of their depiction as rites of supplication and purification and as acts of public humiliation when performed by one upon another. For self-laceration as an act of supplication, cf. 1 Kgs. 18:28 and Hos. 7:14 and see below. In Deut. 21:12, a foreign woman, captured in war, who is chosen as a marriage partner is permitted to "shave her head," or *gillᵊḥāh 'eṯ-rô'šāh*, pare her nails, put off her captive's clothes, remain in the house, and mourn for one month before consummating the marriage. Although the immediate context mentions mourning (cf. *bāḵāh* in v.13b) and the broader context might suggest an act of humiliation, shaving here constitutes a rite of purification. This is its significance in Num. 6:9(18?) for the Nazirite defiled by contact with a corpse and in Lev. 14:8,9 for the recently healed leper. In Deut. 21:12, the woman, who has experienced "social death" and has been contaminated through contact with corpses including, perhaps, those of her father and mother, is permitted to mourn over her loss (cf. v.13). Isa. 7:20 preserves an example of tonsure alongside shaving of other body areas as acts of humiliation. In 2 Sam. 10:4, Ḥanun, the Ammonite king, seized David's ambassadors, cut off half their robes, and their beards (*wayᵊgallaḥ*) as an act of humiliation. Zech. 13:6 mentions wounds inflicted upon a prophet for prophesying falsely (cf. vv.3,6b) *contra* Roberts 1970:76–77.

In two texts of the HC, Lev. 19:27 and 21:5, the shaving of the head and beard as well as the gashing of the flesh are likewise proscribed. These passages portray tonsure and self-laceration as mourning rites, not as rites of initiation, supplication, or humiliation. The immediate context makes explicit the mortuary associations of these rites. The phrase "on account of the dead," *lānep̱eš*, in 19:28 clearly indicates that a mortuary rite is in view. Leviticus 19 also includes a prohibition against necromancy (19:31) and the terms *'ôḇôṯ* and *yiddᵊʿōnî* refer to ghosts, "the Ones-who-return" and "the Knowers," rather than to the hypothetical names of ritual practitioners such as "mediums" and "wizards."[133] Matters are much the same in the case of 21:5. 21:1–6 concerns priestly defilement resulting from the performance of rites on behalf of the dead. In fact, 21:1 comprises the overarching legislative principle for the prohibitions spanning vv.1 to 6, "And Yahweh said to Moses, 'Speak to the priests, the sons of Aaron, and say to them that none of them shall defile himself for the dead (*lᵊnep̱eš*) among his people'." But as v.2 indicates, the case of a deceased immediate blood relative might be an exception.[134]

Earlier biblical scholars such as George Adam Smith associated mourning rites, including self-laceration and tonsure, with the Canaanite cult of the dead which in turn was cited as justification for their being banned. Such an interpretation still has many followers today. Smith also concluded that Deut. 14:2, the reason for Israel's abstention from self-laceration and tonsure, implicitly alluded to the divinity of the dead mentioned in v.1, "for you are a people consecrated to Yahweh your God" (rather than to the godly dead). Moreover, for Smith the phrase "sons of Yahweh your God" in 14:1 and the broader context of laws against foreign gods (13:2–19(ET 1–18)) implied the worship of the ancestral dead in 14:1.[135] Scholarship went so far as to suggest that these two rites expressed humanity's fear of the dead in the most intensified way, self-mutilation being a desperate attempt to disguise oneself from ghosts on the haunt or to soften the envy of the dead. According to earlier scholars, this fear also provided the impetus for the Canaanite cult of the dead. It served to appease the ghosts.

A second, and somewhat related, tendency of commentators has been to construe the prohibition against self-laceration and tonsure as a reaction to Canaanite practices specifically related to fertility. According to this view, a passage like 1 Kgs. 18:28, where the prophets of Baal cut themselves to entice Baal's response,

133 Cf. 4.3.2.; Lev. 20:27 where the *'ôḇ* is said to reside in an individual; Isa. 29:4 where the *'ôḇ* is depicted as chirping or speaking from beneath dust or the earth (= netherworld).

134 On the use of *nep̱eš* in these passages to designate the dead, cf. *lānep̱eš* in 19:28; Lev. 21:1 and cf. 22:4; on *nap̱šōṯ mēṯ* in 21:11, cf. Seligson 1951.

135 G. A. Smith 1918:185; cf. Wensinck 1917:96–97; Morgenstern 1966:105–06. These mourning rites would then be employed as acts of supplication, on which see below.

suggests that these customs were characteristic of fertility rites observed in the Baal cult and so they serve as the object of Deut. 14:1. In more recent treatments, texts from Ugarit have been cited in support of the 1 Kgs. 18:28-type background to the prohibition in Deut. 14:1.[136]

An Akkadian text preserved at Ugarit which the original editor entitled "the Just Sufferer" (*RS* 25.460) lists mourning rites observed on behalf of a man near death. One of those mourning rites is the laceration of the body. Line 11 reads: "My brothers are bathed with their blood like ecstatics."[137] In the Ugaritic Baal cycle, El and Anat mourn the death of Baal (*KTU* 1.5.VI:17b–20a, 1.6:I:1–3a) and among the mourning rites performed by these gods are self-laceration and tonsure.[138] The reference in the Aqhat legend to professional mourners, "slashers of the flesh," or *pẓǵm ǵr*, is less certain however (*KTU* 1.19:IV:11,22).[139] These acts have been commonly viewed as referring to mourning rites performed in the Ugaritic cult on behalf of Baal like those mentioned in 1 Kgs. 18:28 and, as I have pointed out above, it is supposedly this Canaanite connection that provides the rationale for their being forbidden in Deut. 14:1.[140] Underlying the "Canaanite explanation" is the history of religions' assumption that the traditio-historical method can offer access to the phenomenal world of pre-exilic Israel *via* the biblical texts. It is only fitting that the analysis of those biblical texts follows a similar history of traditions' trajectory in order to test the validity of such an approach on its own merits. Each rite will be treated separately beginning with the pre-exilic prophetic traditions; first tonsure, then self-laceration.

In response to Yahweh's impending judgment of the north, the author of Amos 8:10 foresees Israel's mourning, lamentation, her donning of sackcloth, and the tonsure of the head or "baldness," *qorḥāh*. In Micah 1:16, Yahweh offers tonsure as a legitimate means for the inhabitants of Samaria and Jerusalem to express their grief over the imminent exile of their children. The verbal forms employed are the Qal (fs) imperatives of *qāraḥ*, "to make bald," and *gāzaz*, "to shear." Similarly, the hand responsible for Isa. 3:24 envisions "baldness," or *qorḥāh*, as one form of grieving among others to which the Jerusalemites will resort when judgment strikes. In Isa. 22:12, Yahweh explicitly commands *qorḥāh* along with

---

136 Cf. e.g., Craigie 1976:230; Mayes 1979:238–39; Spronk 1986:244–47; Lewis 1989:100–01.

137 Cf. Nougayrol 1968:267,269 [Text #162:11′]: *aḫu-ú-a ki-ma maḫ-ḫe-e* [*d*]*a-mi-šu-nu ra-am-ku*.

138 *KTU* 1.5:VI:17b–20a: *ǵr b'abn ydy psltm by'r yhdy lḥm wdqn yṯlṯ qn ḏr'h*, "He scratched his skin with a stone, incisions with a flint, he cut his cheeks and beard, he raked his upper arm," cf. also 1.6:I:1–3a. See de Moor 1971:190–201; Spronk 1986:245–47; Dietrich and Loretz 1986:101–10; Lewis 1989:100–01 for treatments of these passages.

139 *Contra* Fenton 1969:69–70. For recent evaluations, cf. del Olmo Lete 1981:397, 607,610; Margalit 1989:440–41.

140 Cf. e.g., Gray 1965:65 and de Moor 1971:200–01.

weeping, mourning, and girding with sackcloth in anticipation of Jerusalem's fall. A line from a roughly contemporary oracle of doom against Moab, Isa. 15:2, lists *qorḥāh* as a mourning rite known among the Moabites alongside weeping, wailing, beard shaving (*gᵊrûʿāh*), and sackcloth. In sum, the pre-exilic prophetic traditions condone tonsure in spite of the recognized observance of this rite among the local populations. The same scenario obtains in the exilic prophetic traditions.

Jer. 7:29 depicts Yahweh as entreating Judah to mourn its impending doom by "shearing their locks" and, as in Micah 1:16, the Qal (fs) imperative of *gāzaz* is used.[141] As was the case with the pre-exilic traditions, tonsure continued as a legitimate practice in Judah and in the communities of the exile. This is confirmed elsewhere in Jeremiah (16:6; 41:5) and in Ezekiel (7:18) in spite of the fact that it was also a rite, as one among several to be performed in response to Yahweh's judgment, attributed by these writers to several of the local populations: Philistia (Gaza and Ashkelon; Jer. 47:5), Moab (48:37 and Isa. 15:2), or Phoenicia (Tyre; Ezek. 27:31).

Outside the prophetic traditions, the legitimacy of tonsure continued to be endorsed in later biblical traditions. In Job 1:20, part of the post-exilic framework of the book, Job's "shearing of the head" is depicted as an appropriate act of mourning.[142] Lastly, mention should be made of Ezra 9:3. Having heard that the returnees were intermarrying with the locals, the grief-stricken Ezra tears hair from his head and beard.[143] While this constitutes an act of grief, it is not on behalf of the dead (although the threat of social extinction presents itself).

Along with the practice of tonsure, the gashing of the flesh (*lᵊhiṯgōḏēḏ*) is viewed as an acceptable expression of mourning in the book of Jeremiah (cf. 16:6; 41:5).[144] In a much later text, Job 2:8, a form of the rare *hiṯgārēḏ*, "to scratch oneself," appears. It is generally understood as Job's attempt to scrape off his boils. But the verse might point to an act of mourning in view of the mention of his covering himself with ashes. The verb *lᵊhiṯgārēḏ*, "to scratch oneself," might be read as *lᵊhiṯgōḏēḏ*, "to cut oneself," the verbal form repeatedly associated with self-laceration, that is if a *dalet* was mistook for a *resh*, a well-attested scribal error.

A rather unique instance of self-laceration occurs in the pre-exilic passage, Hos. 7:14. As opposed to the commonly held opinion, 7:14 does not explicitly

---

141 The phraseology employed is *gozzî nizrēḵ*, "shear your locks."

142 The phraseology employed is *wayyāḡoz ʾēṯ-rōʾšô*, "and he sheared his head."

143 The phraseology employed is *wāʾemrᵊṭāh miśśᵊʿar rōʾšî ûz(ᵊ)qānî*, "I tore hair out of my head and beard."

144 Jer. 5:7 in the MT reads a form of *hiṯgōḏēḏ*, but many Hebrew manuscripts read a form of *hiṯgōrēr*, "to lodge with," and the LXX reads *katéluov*, "to lodge with."

depict the mentioned rites as rites of supplication to the Canaanite god, Baal.[145] The issue is Israel's insincerity in performing the rites, not the rites themselves:

A They do not cry to me *from their hearts*
    B when they wail upon their beds;
    B′ for grain and new wine they gash[146] themselves,
A′ but they are *faithless* to me.

In support of a Baalistic reading, advocates cite 7:16a where they emend MT *lōʾ ʿāl*, "not upwards," to *labbaʿal*, "to (the) Baal," (and cf. *BHS*). But in support of the MT, the LXX reads here *apestráphēsan eís oúdèn*, "turn aside to nothing." Although Hos. 2:10(ET 8) attributes Israel's grain and new wine as given over to Baal, in 7:14 the author makes the claim that these were originally Yahweh's gift to Israel. The implication is that Israel knowingly rejected this origin. But beyond this point, the two texts unfold quite differently. 7:14 goes on to underscore Israel's ritual hypocrisy, while 2:10(ET 8) depicts her syncretistic apostasy. In other words, a Baalistic backdrop is lacking in 7:14. Moreover, nothing is said in 2:10(ET 8) of the ritual gashing as in 7:14. In the final analysis, neither wailing nor gashing are proscribed, rather Israel's faithless attitude is the object of Hosea's dirge. The rites are depicted as legitimate acts of supplication *to Yahweh* as expressed in the verse's ABB′A′ pattern (see above). This clearly influences how one might prefer to read 1 Kgs. 18:28, but more on that below.

The foregoing traditio-historical analysis demonstrates that self-laceration and tonsure were legitimate forms of mourning and supplication down to Ezekiel's time and, perhaps, beyond (if Job 1:20 and 2:8 and Ezra 9:3 are relevant). Nevertheless, some have argued that the frequent attestation of these rites can be explained as the result of the prohibition in Deut. 14:1 not being known or enforced.[147] But this hardly offers an adequate solution to *Yahweh's* repeated adjuration to observe tonsure as an expression of mourning and to self-laceration as an act of supplication to Yahweh. Contrary to the proscription in Deut. 14:1 and, for that matter, Lev. 19:27–28 and 21:5, both tonsure and self-laceration are portrayed as acceptable ritual expressions in the pre-exilic and exilic prophetic traditions.

In the light of the prophetic testimony, one might date Deut. 14:1 later than Jeremiah.[148] Given such a scenario, the two passages from the HC, Lev. 19:27–28;

---

[145] So e.g., Mays 1969:111–12; Andersen and Freedman 1980:473–75.

[146] Several Hebrew mss read *yit̲gôd̲ād̲û* (< "to gash oneself"), for MT *yit̲gôrārû* (< "to lodge with"), and the LXX reads *katetémnonto*. In 1 Kgs. 18:28 *kai katetémnonto* = Hebrew *wayyit̲gōd̲ ᵊd̲û*. This favors the mention of laceration in Hos. 7:14. On v.14a, see Andersen and Freedman 1980:474–75.

[147] Cf. e.g., Wright, Shires, and Parker 1953:2.42.

[148] Bertholet 1899:44; Horst 1961:61–62.

21:5, should likewise be viewed as later than Jeremiah. As a case in point, Jer. 41:5 mentions laceration and the shaving of the head as eighty men from Shechem, Shiloh, and Samaria approach the house of God to make offerings with "their beards shaved," *mᵊg̱ullᵊḥê zāqān*, their garments torn, "and their bodies gashed," *ûmiṯgōḏᵊḏîm*. With the Babylonian invasion having just taken place, perhaps these men sought to purify themselves after having been defiled while mourning over the loss of, and coming into contact with, slain loved ones (cf. Numbers 19 and 31). In fact, the narrative goes on to describe how these faithful northerners tragically met their own doom at the hands of one Ishmael, the chief officer of Gedeliah, the governor whom Ishmael had murdered the day before! They ended up themselves as defiling corpses according to the author of Jeremiah 41. For our author, perhaps the death of these northerners symbolized their polluting power.

In view of Jer. 41:5, George Adam Smith concluded with regard to the tradition-history of Deut. 14:1, "unknown to Jeremiah, Ezekiel, and to those Shechem Jews who, in obedience to the central law of D, brought their offerings to the temple, this law [Deut. 14:1] cannot have formed part of the original code of D; but it is an exilic or post-exilic addition."[149] In other words, after the capture of Jerusalem, Israelites from the former northern kingdom who remained loyal to the Josianic reform (as evidenced by their pilgrimage there) would hardly have observed mourning rites banned by the very law code which they were attempting to obey.[150] In fact, the prohibition against laceration and tonsure is not found among the laws forming the basis for the Josianic reform in 2 Kings 23 which are viewed by many as embodying the so-called *Urdeuteronomium*.[151] Thus, Deut. 14:1 is most likely a later addition to Deuteronomy and Job 1:20 and 2:8, and perhaps Ezra 9:3, would push the ban on self-mutilation back into the post-exilic period. Deut. 14:1 would then comprise an expansion on a law against self-laceration and tonsure preserved in the HC. The earliest stage of the legislation was directed at the priests (Lev. 21:1,5) which in turn was expanded to incorporate the people (Lev. 19:27–28). In both, these rites are enacted "on account of the dead" (*l-* + *nep̱eš*). The priestly law, in all likelihood, preceded the law for the people, for to suppose the reverse, that the law for the people preceded the priestly regulation, would create unnecessary redundancy.[152] Like Lev. 19:27–28, Deut. 14:1 records a later expansion on the law as embodied in Lev. 21:1,5.

---

[149] G. A. Smith 1918:184–85.

[150] On Jer. 41:5, cf. Nicholson 1975:139–40 and n.5.

[151] For a list comparing the laws in Deuteronomy attested in 2 Kgs. 23, cf. Nicholson 1967:3–4; now Preuss 1982:1–12, esp. p.4.

[152] Bertholet 1899:44 viewed Deut. 14:1 as dependent upon Lev. 19:27–28. Noth 1965:143 saw 19:27b as a secondary addition. For a different view on the relation of these Leviticus passages and Deut. 14:1, cf. Cholewiński 1976:295–96,299–300.

As for the Canaanite theory, we stated previously that 1 Kgs. 18:28 supposedly epitomizes the biblical tradition's polemic against ritualistic gashing by the association of this act with the Baal cult. However, the context nowhere explicitly condemns the specific act of self-laceration committed by the Baal prophets. If this rite were indeed a "magical" mourning rite for Baal, one would have expected an author who throughout the episode polemicizes against the Baal cult to do the same in the case of self-laceration (cf. vv.21,27,29).[153] When this lack of condemnation is seen in the light of Hos. 7:14 where gashing is performed in the Yahweh cult, and in light of texts like Jer. 16:6; 41:5; and Ezek. 7:18 which depict self-laceration as an acceptable act in the Israelite society portrayed therein, it suggests that for the dtr hand responsible for 1 Kgs. 18:28, self-laceration was a legitimate act of supplication in both the Baal and Yahweh cults. In other words, it did not fall within the purview of the author of 1 Kings' larger rhetorical polemic. This would explain why it was allowed to stand uncondemned in 1 Kings 18. The phrase *kᵊmišpāṭām*, "according to their custom," in v.28a would then simply denote the distinct manner in which the prophets of Baal performed this rite over against how an Israelite might have observed the same.[154]

If we suppose that self-laceration was an act of supplication observed in the respective cults of Yahweh and Baal of the first millennium and that the biblical authors assumed its acceptable status, then the arguments for Deut. 14:1 as a prohibition against laceration on the basis of some supposed Canaanite origin are clearly wrongheaded. Moreover, a magical fertility rite involving self-laceration and tonsure among the Canaanites remains otherwise unattested. But most telling of all is the fact that the act in 1 Kgs. 18:28 is one of supplication to a deity, while that in Deut. 14:1 is one of mourning on behalf of a dead human.[155] Furthermore, contrary to general opinion, the texts from Ugarit do not substantiate a Canaanite fertility background for 1 Kgs. 18:28 or Deut. 14:1. In fact, "The Just Sufferer" text explicitly portrays laceration as an expression of mourning on behalf of a human about to die. There is no indication in the text that a magical fertility rite for Baal is involved. Baal never shows up in the text. It is the Mesopotamian god Marduk who is repeatedly mentioned. More importantly, the provenance of the text is not Ugarit or its environs, but rather some more easterly location, probably

---

153 The verb *wayyiṯnabbᵊʾû* in v.29, "they (= the prophets of Baal) raved on," (cf. *RSV* and *JPS*) is used with a pejorative force in 1 Sam. 18:10; 2 Kgs. 9:11; Jer. 29:26.

154 Cf. also Jones 1984(II):320.

155 1 Kgs. 18:28 does not mention tonsure. Ironically, none of the advocates for a Canaanite background have suggested that *lāmēṯ* in Deut. 14:1 might refer "to the Dead One," i.e., Baal (or Mot?), as has been suggested for *lᵊmēṯ* in 26:14. Such an interpretation would presuppose the presence of two acts of supplication in 14:1, as in the case of 26:14; but this interpretation lacks contextual support.

between Aleppo and Mari.[156] Thus, to label this text, or the practices mentioned therein, as representative of a first millennium Canaanite religious rite hardly evokes confidence. More to the point, the reference to laceration *via* the simile "like ecstatics" in the text cannot substantiate the Baalistic associations of such mourning rites. The ecstatics alluded to more likely lacerated themselves as an act of supplication to Marduk. We know that such rites commonly associated with mourning also functioned as rites of supplication in Mesopotamian cultures.[157]

The mourning of El and Anat is more difficult to assess. As mentioned above, it is often assumed that El and Anat perform these acts as seasonal rites of fertility. In this instance, these rites represent a type of imitative magic to revitalize Baal. It is also assumed by interpreters that these rites were observed in the Ugaritic cult as well. This reconstruction in turn supposedly explains the rites performed by the Baal prophets in 1 Kgs. 18:28.[158] Besides the fact that the context is severely laconic, the myth offers no explicit support for the efficacy of the mourning rites in the revitalization of Baal. In any case, the seasonal-fertility interpretation of the Baal-Mot myth remains problematic.[159] Furthermore, we presently lack any clear references to mourning rites or their magical power in the Ugaritic cult. "The Just Sufferer" text is not original to Ugarit, so the ecstatic who performed such acts alluded to there should not be associated with the Ugaritic cult.[160] In the final analysis, the mourning of El and Anat more likely embodies mortuary rites performed on behalf of the recently deceased.[161] That is to say, neither magical rites of revitalization nor acts of supplication are in view. Hos. 7:14's depiction of self-laceration as a fertility rite performed in the Yahweh cult and the preceding analysis of the Ugaritic texts confirm the dubious character of 1 Kgs. 18:28 as an explication of Deut. 14:1. The a priori assumption that Deut. 14:1 prohibits a magical fertility rite for Baal is unwarranted. The relevant texts simply do not substantiate this interpretation. If a fertility rite were the object of Deut. 14:1's proscription, it would more likely be associated with the non-dtr Yahwistic cult reflected in Hos. 7:14, but the setting underlying Deut. 14:1 and the significance of the form *l-m-t* speaks against this.

---

156 Following Nougayrol 1968:265–67; Roberts 1970:77.

157 For instances of mourning rites used as acts of supplication in the ancient Near East, see the lengthy note in Gruber 1980(II):471 n.3; cf. Dan. 9:3.

158 Cf. e.g., Gray 1965:252.

159 Cf. the criticisms of Grabbe 1976:57–63 on the myth and ritual school's seasonal-fertility interpretation of the Baal-Mot myth and those of J. Z. Smith 1987:521–27 who identifies this and its pattern of mythic and ritual associations as the "naturist" version of the myth and ritual of the dying and rising god.

160 The late first millennium evidence cited by de Moor 1971:200–01 as well as his reliance on precise calendrical dating is likewise unconvincing.

161 De Moor 1969:226 acknowledged this possibility.

Likewise, a death or ancestor cult rite is not apparent in Deut. 14:1. What is of concern is the observance of two mourning customs. There is no mention of, or allusion to, those mortuary rites which extend beyond the dead's arrival in the netherworld. Furthermore, nothing in the text indicates that the dead were viewed as possessing supernatural beneficial powers. In conclusion, the Canaanite background cannot adequately account for the performance or proscription of these two rites of self-mutilation. On its own, a Canaanite polemic cannot explain why self-laceration and tonsure were singled out from among the many rites of mourning that ancient Israelites and "Canaanites" both observed.

If, as the preceding traditio-historical analysis might suggest, the prohibition against self-laceration and tonsure is reflective of an exilic or post-exilic setting, then one should search for other stimuli underlying the introduction of this proscription. One alternative is to examine the comparative evidence reflective of those contemporary cultures with which the biblical authors who wrote those proscriptions were familiar. Laceration and tonsure are attested as mourning rites among several ancient Near Eastern peoples.[162] Alster noted that Inanna's Descent to the Netherworld (Sumerian and Akkadian versions), Gilgamesh, Enkidu, and the Netherworld (Sumerian and Akkadian versions) and the Epic of Gilgamesh (Akkadian) contain mythological reflections of mourning rituals involving self-laceration and tonsure.[163] Rowley cited additional references in the classical Greek literature.[164] The texts found at Ugarit suggest that this was the case for second-millennium Syria, although we have as yet no evidence for their observance as mourning rites among first millennium inhabitants of Syria-Palestine. Recall that 1 Kgs. 18:28 depicted laceration as an act of supplication, not mourning.[165] Podella has examined iconographic representations of mourning on first millennium terra cotta figurines from Philistia. Laceration or tonsure as mourning or supplication rites are lacking, although he did cite a first millennium figurine from Rhodes that depicts a self-laceration rite.[166]

The focus narrows with the observation that the DtrH preserves a tradition in which Mesopotamian religious customs were introduced into Israel at least as early as the days of Sargon II if not in the days of Tiglathpileser III. Although the nature of such traditions is difficult to assess, investigators have offered evidence for a genuine historical process of religious influence on the basis of such texts as 2 Kgs.

---

162 For general surveys, cf. Driver 1902:156; Gaster 1981:590–604.

163 Alster 1983:1–16.

164 Rowley 1963:54 n.2.

165 To assume that the existence of these rites in early Canaanite culture presupposes their continuance in the Canaanite context is unwarranted in the absence of confirming data.

166 Podella 1986:263–69.

17:24–41.[167] Whether Mesopotamian religion was imposed upon or voluntarily accepted or gradually assimilated by Judah is not of concern to the present line of argument. What is of ultimate importance is the likelihood that at least the writing elite of ancient Israel possessed some knowledge of Mesopotamian religion.

It would appear that other royal Assyrian funerary customs were known to the biblical writers. The funerary custom of "making a fire" for a dead king, *śārap śᵊrēpāh*, is mentioned in the exilic text, Jer. 34:5 (Zedekiah) and in the post-exilic texts, 2 Chr. 16:14 (Asa) and 21:19 (Jehoram). This practice is probably modeled on the royal Assyrian practice of burning a (funerary) fire (cf. Akkadian *šuruptu šarpat*).[168] Zwickel has recently argued that the funerary fires of Israelite kings like Asa and Zedekiah (but not Jehoram) were borrowed, but modified, apotropaic rituals of the Assyrian royal court. They were probably introduced during the time of Esarhaddon, the Assyrian monarch contemporary with the Judahite king, Manasseh.[169] If this practice constitutes an Assyrian rite that had been appropriated by the biblical writers, it is significant to note that they did not deem "making a fire" an object worthy of an explicit polemic.

Be that as it may, such a familiarity with contemporary Mesopotamian funerary and mourning ritual might explain the post-dtr and priestly condemnation of self-laceration and tonsure as acts of mourning. The annals of Sargon II record Merodach-Baladan II's reaction to the news that the Elamites would not deliver him from the hands of Sargon: "he threw himself to the ground, he rent his [garmen]t, he took up the razor, and he uttered a lament."[170] Another depiction of tonsure as an expression of mourning is preserved in the inscription dedicated to Adad-guppi, the mother of the Babylonian king Nabonidus. In the closing section of the inscription, a third person account narrates Nabonidus's instruction to his armies on the occasion of his mother's funeral "the troops of the entire land cut their hair. . . ."[171] The Greek historian, Xenophon, observed during an engagement of Assyrian and Persian forces led by Cyrus that as the Persian forces breached the fortress walls, "the Assyrian women . . . tore their cheeks" for fear of their impending death and that of their children.[172] He also recorded the same act

---

167 Miller and Hayes 1986:339,345–46,370–72, but for several important qualifications, cf. 4.5.2.; Holloway 1992.

168 Cf. Parpola 1983:7–8 [Letter #4],190–92 [Letter #195],270–72 [Letter #280].

169 Zwickel 1989:267–77.

170 Lie 1929:54–55; Gruber 1980(II):471–72: *qaq-qa-riš ip-pal-si-iḫ* [*na-aḫ*(?) *lap-*]*tuš iš-ru-ṭa nag-la-ba iš-ši-ma ú-šá-aṣ-ri-ḫa bi-ki-tu*.

171 Cf. Gadd 1958:56–65 (H_2 A:III:30′-31′): *ṣabū māti ka-la-ma pi-i*[*r* (?)*tu-šu-nu*] *ú-ga-al-li-bu-ma*; *ANET* 1969:562; This reference, however, might be to tonsure as a purification rite at the close of the mourning period, for the troops perform this act only after a seven day wait and accompany it with cleansing rites.

172 *Cyropaedia* iii.3.67: *hai gunaikes tōn 'assurion . . . druptomenai* (*pareian*).

performed by Armenian women who were sure their king would be put to death after he had answered Cyrus wrongly.[173]

When the references in these texts are coupled with the literary arguments in favor of a late compositional date for the biblical prohibition against these rites, then the era of Mesopotamian hegemony in Palestine offers a more appropriate setting for the eventual ban on what were formerly two legitimate rites of mourning. Either they were banned for as yet some unknown reasons with the Mesopotamian world providing merely the imaging "wood" for the author's polemical "fire," or they were outlawed in response to their potential confusion with similar contemporary Mesopotamian customs. Dan. 9:3 is suggestive in that while this text records the use of fasting and the donning of sackcloth and ashes as acts of supplication for the Israelite *in Mesopotamia* of the post-exilic period, laceration and tonsure go unmentioned.

In sum, the pre-exilic and exilic prophetic traditions viewed these rites as legitimate expressions of grief and supplication. Their proscription in Israel's legal traditions arose in a subsequent period. Given the late provenance of these prohibitions, the ideological reaction might have been aimed at selected religious practices of the contemporary Mesopotamian world. The impression one gains from such an historiographic approach is that the biblical writers' rhetorical strategy involved three maneuvers: (1) the projection of these rites into the distant past, (2) their association with Canaanite culture, and (3) their condemnation placed in the mouth of the nation's first great prophet, Moses. Clearly, such a strategy would have enhanced the legitimacy of that ideology underlying their proscription.

In the final analysis, however, like the proposed Canaanite polemic, the Mesopotamian polemic also falls short vis-à-vis its explanatory power. Although it potentially provided a hypothetical social context contemporary with the author that served as the impetus for the proscription of the rites of mutilation, it alone does not explain adequately the fact that while some mortuary practices held in common with Mesopotamia were outlawed, others such as the funerary rite of making a fire were not. There must be more to the ban against self-laceration and tonsure from among the many funerary rites that Israel shared with her neighbors.

Interpreters have on occasion invoked the anthropological model outlined by Mary Douglas in her treatment of pollution laws in order to explain the biblical prohibition against the observance of self-laceration and tonsure. Douglas proposed that a complex and comprehensive Israelite system of classification and social organization lies behind the biblical pollution laws. The rationale behind these laws was the standard of normality or wholeness. Following Douglas, Carmichael

---

173 *Cyropaedia* iii.1.13: *hai dè gunaikes anaboēsasai edruptonto, ōs iochomenou tou patros kai apolōlotōn sphōn ēdē*, "and the women cried aloud and tore their cheeks as if it were all over with their father and they had already lost."

viewed these rites as constituting an entanglement of life and death. They, therefore, posed a threat to the ordered state of Israelite society.[174] Likewise, Wenham suggested that the resultant disfiguration was to be excluded from an Israelite social system which had as its standard, normality. This finds an analogy in the laws for the sanctity of the priesthood in Lev. 18:18–21, and those concerning skin diseases in Leviticus 13–14.[175]

Underlying these proposals stands an ordered Israelite society having had developed its own coherent set of symbols, a society breaking with its chaotic past and, if not Canaanite in origin, then at least heavily indebted to such influence. In spite of her rejection of Canaanite influence as a sufficiently comprehensive framework against which to interpret all of Israel's pollution laws, Douglas projects a similar "confrontation of cultures" scenario onto a presumed historical landscape that lies behind the biblical texts. She characterizes the Israel striving to withstand the hostile intrusion of anomaly as "a people surrounded by powerful, rapacious enemies."[176] But when did the society exist which could develop the larger classification program of a coherent symbolic system? Could such a society ever exist? Do the texts necessarily presuppose an historical reality in which a homogeneous Israelite society is faced with its chaotic Canaanite environment or should we have in view competing ideologies and sets of symbols as expressed in a well-defined corpus of literature in which life was ordered and interpreted for a future utopian Israelite society? The liabilities of an historicist application of the anthropological method are truly laid bare when one notes that it is not being applied to a society that can actually be observed, but to a society only partially known to us through its very incomplete literary traditions.

Be that as it may, when detached from such historicist underpinnings, anthropological theory and ethnographic data can help to elucidate both the enactment and proscription of these rites. What then gave rise to their observance?[177] Perhaps the answer lies in their function as socially constructive expressions and producers of both hostility and suffering arising out of the anger and sorrow due to death. Moreover, in instances where other members of society, who themselves experience no direct loss, participate in these acts, the performance of these rites can also serve to reaffirm social solidarity. Self-mutilation as mourning also facilitates the identity of the living with the dead in the most socially explicit manner—in terms of one's physical appearance. At least in the case of self-laceration, the resultant scarification also stands as a *permanent* public reminder of the constant threat of

---

174 Carmichael 1976:1–7, but cf. his earlier work, 1974:78–80.

175 Wenham 1979:272.

176 Douglas 1975:304–05.

177 For much of what follows, I am indebted to the works of Metcalf and Huntington 1991; Bowker 1991.

death's imminent encroachment upon the world of the living. It also serves as a lasting impression of the inevitability of death.[178]

As for their proscription, Douglas proposed that pollution beliefs are a central means of defining norms and the strength of those beliefs indicates the strength of concern with the definition of behavior. Such beliefs are designed to protect the "most vulnerable domains, where ambiguity would most weaken the fragile structure" of a given society, real or imagined.[179] The restrictions placed on rites of mourning are best seen in this light, for mourning rites are liminal rites of the life cycle marking the transitional phase from life to death. They represent an anomaly blurring the boundaries between life and death and, in some sense, a convergence of the living's identity with that of the dead. Given these factors, one would expect to find in the Hebrew Bible a comprehensive list of forbidden mourning rites, but curiously, only self-laceration and tonsure are singled out as the objects of such restriction. There must be still more to their being reclassified in the pejorative manner that they are.

As intimated above, no other rite of mourning attested in the Hebrew Bible—including the (ritual) descent to the netherworld—can approximate the symbolic power of self-laceration and tonsure to identify the living with the dead. These rites offer an *unparalleled* identification of the living with the dead and an *unprecedented* reminder of death's intrusion upon the world of the living. Moreover, the irreversibility of the markings embodies death's inevitability and its ever-present threat.[180] Thus, the intimacy and permanence of death's association with life were expressed too vividly in these rites to forgo their censorship in the tightly constructed and ordered world portrayed in the priestly and dtr legislations. Their inclusion in the various prescriptive lists functioned to insulate the social system idealized in the narratives from such socially destructive knowledge.

In conclusion, neither a death nor an ancestor cult underlies the rites recorded in Deut. 14:1. What is of concern is the observation of two mourning rites of self-mutilation, laceration and tonsure. In fact, there is no mention of, or allusion to, those mortuary rites which extend beyond the burial of the dead. Nevertheless, our analysis of these rites provides a starting point for evaluating the biblical authors' treatments of other mortuary rites such as necromancy and, perhaps, the ancestor cult. These considerations we will take up again in the conclusion to our study.

---

178 Tonsure also conveys a degree of permanence in that the resultant alterations last well beyond the normal mourning period.

179 Douglas 1975:58.

180 Cf. now Feldman 1977:79–108.

4.4.2. Deuteronomy 18:11

With Deut. 18:11, we return to the topic of necromancy. The practitioner *šōʾēl ʾôḇ wᵊyiddᵊʿōnî*, "he who inquires of the One-who-returns and the Knower," is one among a seven or eight item list of forbidden mantic offices spanning vv.10–11.[181] This passage along with its immediate context, 18:9–14, comprises a portion of the so-called *Ämtergesetze*, or laws of the officials, spanning 16:18–18:22. Since at least the time of Wellhausen, critics have argued for the redactional nature of the *Ämtergesetze*.[182] More recently, Lohfink identified the whole of 16:18–18:22 as a dtr sketch of a constitution for the restoration of the nation composed during the exilic period.[183] The basis for his proposal is the strong affinity between the *Ämtergesetze* and characteristic dtr language. For example, the repeated forms *yrš* (16:20; 17:14; 18:12,14), *twʿbh* (17:4; 18:9,12 [2x]), and *hʿbyr bʾš* (18:10) are typical of dtr phraseology.[184] Furthermore, "torah" (*tôrāh*; 17:9,11,18,19) is found otherwise only in later dtr redactional layers of Deuteronomy.[185]

Lohfink also pointed out that the law in 18:1–8 allows every rural Levite to offer sacrifice at the central sanctuary (presumably Jerusalem), although 2 Kgs. 23:9, part of the Josianic reform, did not grant this right.[186] Thus, according to

---

[181] Based on the arguments presented in 4.3.2. for the identity of the *ʾôḇ* and the *yiddᵊʿōnî* as ghosts, the phrase, *šōʾēl ʾôḇ wᵊyiddᵊʿōnî* stands in apposition to "the necromancer" *dōrēš ʾel-hammēṯîm*, "He who consults the dead ones." Likewise, the phrase, *dirᵊšû ʾel-hāʾōḇôṯ wᵊʾel-hayyiddᵊʿōnîm*, in Isa. 8:19 is semantically paralleled by *yiḏrōš . . . ʾel-hammēṯîm*. Note also that the LXX omits the copula throughout Deut. 18:10–11 and recall that asyndeton is rare while apposition is common in biblical Hebrew, so Emerton 1962:129–38; Joüon 1991:477–81,649–53.

[182] Wellhausen 1899:357; cf. Dillmann 1886:328; Merendino 1969:405; Preuss 1982:136–38; Rüterswörden 1987.

[183] Lohfink 1971:143–55; cf. 1981:87–100; 1982:953–85; 1988:425–30; Braulik 1988:63–92. Dion 1978:42–44; 1985:200–21 narrowed the boundaries of Lohfink's exilic constitution to 17:14–18:22.

[184] Lohfink 1981:92; 1982:953–85. For *yrš*, cf. the dtr texts 1 Kgs. 14:24; 21:26; 2 Kgs. 16:3; 17:8; 21:2. It shows up only in the parenetic framework, introduction and conclusion (never in the pre-dtr laws): 6:1,18; 7:1,17–24; 8:1,7,20; 9:1–6; 10:11; 11:5,8–12,22–25,29,31; 12:1,2,10,29 (2x); 15:4; 19:1,14; 21:1; 23:21(ET 20); 25:19; 26:1; 27:2,3,4,12; 28:21,63; 29:1–7(ET 2–8); 30:16,18. These are viewed as dtr additions. For *twʿbh*, cf. the dtr texts 1 Kgs. 14:24; 2 Kgs. 16:3; 21:2 and the dtr text Deut. 12:31. For *hʿbyr bʾš*, cf. the dtr texts 2 Kgs. 16:3; 17:17; 21:6 and the dtr text Deut. 12:31 (*śrp bʾš*).

[185] 1:5; 4:8,44; 27:3,8,26(2x); 29:20,30,40; 31:9,11,24,26; 33:4,10. Lohfink 1971:152–53 viewed 17:9–11 as an older text dealing with inquiry directed to God that was applied to Torah. This reapplication in turn has resulted in internal tensions within the pericope.

[186] The generally accepted position that 2 Kgs. 23:4–20 deliberately presents Josiah as in conformity with the demands of the law of Moses is presupposed here, cf. also Mayes 1983:131. While any comparison of these two passages runs into the difficulty of explaining the relationship between the priests and Levites, Emerton 1962:129–38 has argued with regard to the phrase, *kōhᵃnîm hal(ᵊ)wiyyim* kōl-šēḇeṭ lēwî*, "the priests, the Levites, the whole tribe of Levi," in Deut. 18:1, that asyndeton is rare while apposition is very common; cf. Joüon 1991:477–81,649–53.

Lohfink, Deut. 18:6–8 must be later as it could not be part of the law book which instigated, at least in part, the Josianic reform.[187] Owing to the fact that the priests are mentioned again in 17:18 as caring for the Torah—a far reaching claim for the once rural, but now unified Levites—this text too is to be considered post-Josianic and therefore dtr.[188]

As with the *Ämtergesetze* in general, the law of the prophet which comprises vv.9–14 (the negative section) and vv.15–22 (the positive section), has likewise been assigned a complex redactional history.[189] Of special interest is the fact that some critics assign 18:11, where *'ôḇ* and *yiddᵊʻōnî* occur, to the earliest compositional stratum. But the early compositional date for 18:11 is founded upon the (often unstated) premise that the verse preserves an old law reflected in Isa. 8:19; 19:3; 29:4; and 1 Sam. 28:3, 7–9.[190] García López reconstructed four stages in the compositional history of Deut. 18:9–22: (1) a primitive text, vv.10aα, 10b, 11, 12a; (2) a proto-deuteronomic redaction, vv.9a, 14, 15a, 21, 22aβ; (3) a redaction completed by the Dtr historian, vv.9b, 10aβ, 12b; and (4) a redaction related to DtrH and the concerns of Jeremiah, vv.15b–20, 22aα, 22b.[191] The weakness inherent in such a reconstruction is not the recognition that a dtr hand is present in 18:9–14 and vv.15–22. Rather, it is the presumption that vv.10–12a are old. Moreover, when this presumption of antiquity for vv.10–12a is coupled with the theory of multiple dtr redactions, critics are unnecessarily forced to postulate as many as four layers of redaction for vv.9–14.

In any case, the argument for the early attestation of *'ôḇôṯ* and *yiddᵊʻōnîm* in v.11 rests on shaky ground. In addition to their occurrence in what we identified earlier as dtr redactional passages, Isa. 8:19; 19:3; and 29:4,[192] the *'ôḇôṯ* and *yiddᵊʻōnîm* occur otherwise only in the dtr texts 2 Kgs. 21:6 and 23:24, in three texts from the HC, Lev. 19:31; 21:6,27, and in still later texts of the Chronicler, 1 Chr.

---

[187] Hoffmann 1980:208–226 is more skeptical about the existence of a law book per se forming the basis of Josiah's reform. Accordingly, the account of the law book's discovery is fictitious. 2 Kgs. 23:4–20 depends upon some vague historical traditions about a reform in Josiah's time and is a collection in one place of all references to the reform.

[188] Lohfink 1971:149. Mayes 1979:278–79; Preuss 1982:137–38,180 distinguish between the rural Levites of Deuteronomy 18 and the priests of the high places in 2 Kings 23.

[189] See the summary of views in García López 1984:290–95; add Mayes 1979:279–83; Preuss 1982:138–39; Rüterswörden 1987:85–87.

[190] Cf. e.g., G. A. Smith 1918:231.

[191] García López 1984:290–308. The author left the status of v.13 undecided. Seitz 1971:235–43 assumed the antiquity of v.11 in his reconstruction: (1) a pre-deuteronomic text–vv.10–12a; (2) a deuteronomic collection–vv.9, 12b, 14–15; (3) a deuteronomic elaboration—vv.16–18; and (4) a dtr elaboration—vv.19–22. He viewed v.13 as simply late. Cf. also the redactional levels identified by Mayes 1979:279–80: (1) the oldest stage—vv.10–12a; (2) a deuteronomic legislation–vv.9, 12b; (3) a post-dtr addition to the law–vv.15–18 (v.14 is a connecting link); and (4) a still later addition—vv.19–22. Verse 13 is an isolated later addition.

[192] Cf. 4.3.2.–5.; Barth 1977:152–56,184–90,285–90.

10:13 and 2 Chr. 33:6 (= 2 Kgs. 21:6). Furthermore, they are entirely absent in the remaining prophetic traditions both pre-exilic and exilic. Neither Amos nor Hosea, nor the Elijah-Elisha traditions for that matter speak out against the *'ôḇôṯ* and *yiddᵊ'ōnîm*. Likewise, 1 Sam. 28:3–25 (vv.3,7–9) evinces extensive evidence for its dtr or post-dtr character (cf. 4.5.1.). In fact, even the existence of a supposed pre-Deuteronomic level for the texts of DtrH has been recently challenged.[193]

The language of Deut. 18:9–14 further supports the notion that a dtr hand is at work, for it has clear links with dtr and other late texts. This is the case for v.9b: *hgwym hhm*, "those nations,"[194] for v.9bα: *(t)lmd l'śwt*, "learn to imitate,"[195] and for 9bβ: *ktw'bt hgwym*, "detestable ways of the nations."[196] Moreover, v.9b cannot be separated from v.9a as the latter, beginning as it does with a *kî* clause, demands an apodosis for the protasis and it can no longer be presumed that vv.10–12a formed the original apodosis of a hypothetically older v.9a, for as we shall argue shortly, the antiquity of these verses is in doubt. Likewise, the stereotypical opening to the law in 18:9a, *ky + bw' + 'rṣ*, is also found in 7:1; 8:7; 17:14; and 23:21(ET 20), all of which have been identified as forming part of the parenesis of the book.[197] Based on the fact that the form *yrš* shows up in each of these texts and that this form never shows up in the pre-dtr laws of Deuteronomy, Lohfink assigned all of these parenetic verses to a dtr hand.[198] He also argued for the dtr origins of the terms *ntn* and *'rṣ* in 18:9a.[199]

The dtr character of 18:9–12 gains additional support from the detailed analysis of García López in spite of his propensity to atomize the pericope based on the assumed antiquity of vv.10–12a and to assign half and quarter verses to as many as four redactional strata. He astutely noted the linguistic affinities between 18:9–12 and the dtr text 2 Kgs. 16:3 (as indicated below by the underscored text):[200]

	2 Kgs. 16:3		Deut. 18:9–12
v.3ba	*wgm 't-bnw h'byr b'š*	v.10a	*l'-ymṣ' bk m'byr bnw wbtw b'š*
v.3bB	*kt'bwt hgwym*	v.9b	*l'-tlmd l'śwt kt'bt hgwym hhm*
v.3bc	*'šr hwryš yhwh 'tm mpny bny yśr'l*	v.12b	*ky . . . yhwh 'lhyk mwryš 'wtm mpnyk*

[193] For the dtr or post-dtr redaction of 1 Sam. 28:3–25, cf. Schunck 1963:84–85, 94–96; Hoffmann 1980:293–300; Van Seters 1983:261–300; Foresti 1984:86–90,130–36. Against a pre-Deuteronomic level for DtrH, cf. McKenzie 1991.

[194] Deut. 28:65; 29:17(ET 18); Zech. 14:3; the dtr addition, Deut. 17:14.

[195] Cf. Deut. 4:1,5,14; 6:1; 20:18. 17:19 also uses *l-m-d*.

[196] Deut. 20:18; 1 Kgs. 14:24; 2 Kgs. 16:3; 21:2; Ezek. 16:4; Ezra 9:1; 2 Chr. 28:3; 33:2.

[197] Cf. also the related 12:29; 19:1; and 21:1.

[198] Lohfink 1981:92; 1982:953–85; 1988:427–28.

[199] Lohfink 1981:92–96.

[200] García López 1984:296–97.

He also pointed out that the formula *h'byr bn*(–) (*wbt*[–]) *b'š* in v.10a shows up only in late texts.[201] In fact, the entire list of forbidden practices in Deut. 18:10b–12a are, with the lone exception of *ḥbr ḥbr* (owing to its rare occurrence), most frequently attested in passages of the DtrH: 1 Sam. 28:3,7,9; 1 Kgs. 14:24; 20:23; 2 Kgs. 9:22; 16:3; 17:17; 21:2,6; and 23:24. Lohfink also listed the extensive parallels between Deut. 18:10b–11 and dtr 2 Kgs. 21:6 (the brackets indicate additions, not parallels):[202]

2 Kgs. 21:6	Deut. 18:10b–11
wᵊheʿᵉḇîr-'eṯ bᵊnô bā'ēš	*maʿᵃḇîr bᵊnô-ûḇittô bā'ēš*
	[*qōsēm qᵊsāmîm*]
wᵊʿônēn	*mᵉʿônēn*
wᵊniḥēš	*ûm*(ᵊ)*naḥēš*
	[*ûm*(ᵊ)*ḵaššēp̱ wᵊḥōḇēr ḥāḇer*]
wᵊʿāśāh 'ôḇ wᵊyiddᵊʿōnî(*m*)	*wᵊšō'ēl 'ôḇ wᵊyiddᵊʿōnî*
	[*wᵊḏōrēš 'el-hammēṯîm*]

In view of its dtr character, it appears that Deut. 18:10–12 is an expansion on 2 Kgs. 21:6, but more on this below. Once 18:11 is assigned to a dtr hand, the same must be attributed to v.12a, for at the least this first half of v.12 presupposes v.11. Moreover, the suffix on *'wt-m* in v.12b presupposes *hgwym hhm* in v.9b and is therefore dependent upon at least that half verse. In addition, the forms *yrš* as well as *mpny*, both of which have been labeled as dtr by Lohfink, show up in v.12b (and recall the comparison of v.12b with the dtr text 2 Kgs. 16:3).[203] Deut. 18:14 likewise contains a reference to *yrš*, while the phrase *mqrb-*(*m*)*'hy-* in vv.15 and 18 has close affinities with 17:15, a passage in the law of the king, 17:14–20. The whole of the law of the king is generally recognized as dtr owing to its language, presumed setting, and the analogies it shares with 1 Sam. 8:5–20; 10:17–25, and 1 Samuel 12.[204] Finally, as regards vv.16–22, commentators generally acknowledge the dtr origin of these closing verses.[205] By way of summary then, the extensive dtr language present throughout Deut. 18:9–22, and, as has been and

---

201 García López 1984:297 n.49; cf. Lev. 18:21; 2 Kgs. 16:3; 17:17; 21:6; 23:10; (Jer. 23:35; Ezek. 16:21; 20:26) 20:31; (23:27); 2 Chr. 33:6.

202 Lohfink 1988:428. He also included 1 Sam. 28:7–9 which we take to be part of a dtr or post-dtr addition to the DtrH spanning 28:3–25, cf. 4.5.1.

203 Lohfink 1982:661,674–75.

204 Cf. e.g., *yrš* and *ky* + *bw'* + *'rṣ* in 17:14; Lohfink 1971:149–51, 1988:427–28; Preuss 1982:137. Mayes 1979:271, although he acknowledged the presence of dtr additions to 17:14–20 (vv.16,18–19,20b), viewed the dtr texts in 1 Samuel as dependent upon Deuteronomy 17.

205 Cf. Preuss 1982:138. Mayes 1979:279–80,282–83; García López 1984:300–04 recognized the dtr origins of most of vv.16–22.

will be argued throughout, the inclusion of what is otherwise a late concern to condemn necromancy in v.11 points to the work of a dtr hand. This reconstruction gains additional support from a detailed examination of the other mantic practices mentioned in Deut. 18:10–11.

The rite of human sacrifice as reflected in the phrase *ma'ᵃḇîr bᵊnô-ûḇittô bā'ēš*, "the one who makes his son or his daughter pass through the fire," was part of the Yahwistic cult in pre-exilic (and exilic?) times, but the dtr circle or those later traditions susceptible to dtr influence attached this practice to a cult devoted to a "Canaanite" deity named Molek and then condemned it. As for its original legitimacy in the Yahwistic cult, Isa. 30:33 clearly connects Yahweh and the Tophet and if no such connection was intended in this allusion to Assyria's destruction, then one would have expected some disclaimer to that effect. In any case, the sacrifice of the first born to Yahweh and the Molek sacrifice were probably closely related, if not one and the same cult.[206] Although the former required that first born sons be sacrificed to Yahweh while the latter listed children generally, and of both sexes, as sacrifices to Molek, the fact that daughters could substitute for sons as first born heirs, as Num. 27:1–8 and the texts from Emar and Nuzi demonstrate,[207] favors their commonality. In other words, the two traditions reflect the same or similar cult but from complementary perspectives, one from the more particular and the other from the more general. Therefore, texts that refer to the sacrifice of the first born to Yahweh such as Gen. 22:1–14; Exod. 13:2,12–13,15; 22:28–29(ET 29–30); 34:19–20; Micah 6:6–7; and Ezek. 20:25–26,31 are to be related to the Molek cult. Moreover, Molek's connections with Baal (cf. Jer. 2:23; 3:24; 19:5; 32:35) are more likely part of the inventive dtr rhetorical polemic to "Canaanize" what was once a non-dtr but Yahwistic practice.[208]

Whether or not Molek and Yahweh are to be equated, in the end, begs the question (but cf. 4.6.3.). Passages like Jer. 7:31; 19:5; 32:35; Ezek. 23:38–39; Lev. 20:3; Zeph. 1:5 indicate that the Molek cult was considered by some sectors of Israelite society as part of the Yahweh cult. Furthermore, the location of the Molek cult in the Hinnom Valley might only attest to its controversial role in the Yahweh cult. It may have been observed in the temple precinct in Ahaz's (and Hezekiah's?) and Manasseh's day, but moved to the Valley in the initial stages of

---

206 The evolutionary scheme proposed by Ackerman 1992:138–39 presupposes an early date for the processes underlying the relevant Pentateuchal texts. Against her equation of Baal Hamon and El (p.137), cf. Day 1989:37–40. For an independent argument in favor of their partial connection, cf. most recently Levenson 1993:18–24.

207 Cf. Ben-Barak 1988:87–97.

208 In fact, the unqualified form of the law of the first born in Exod. 22:28–29(ET 29–30) might have its echo in Ezek. 20:26 as neither presuppose the option of redeeming the first born found in the parallel and, we would suggest, later legislative texts, Exod. 13:2,12–13,15 (P) and 34:19–20 (P, not J).

Josiah's reign and again thereafter as Jer. 7:31–32; 19:5; and 32:35 suggest.[209] It should be noted that the two references in 2 Kgs. 16:3 and 21:6—not to mention its observance in the north mentioned in 17:17—do not locate the Molek cult at Tophet and Josiah's defilement of Tophet in 2 Kings 23:10 does not explicitly attribute its observance there to either Ahaz or Manasseh. In other words, the Molek cult as portrayed in dtr and related traditions was probably not restricted to Tophet. In fact, texts like 2 Kgs. 21:3–6 and 23:11–12 assume the worship of several deities such as Baal, Asherah, the host of heaven, and the solar deity as taking place in the Jerusalem temple precinct. Furthermore, in 2 Kgs. 23:10, the author might only be highlighting the Tophet as the major cultic location dedicated to what he conceived as the Molek cult. In other words, it was not the only Molek shrine.

Granting for the sake of argument that Molek was Yahweh's chthonic aspect or an independent netherworld deity of the Yahwistic cult in late pre-exilic Judah, we would hardly expect the dtr or related traditions to openly acknowledge that reality. 2 Kgs. 21:3–6 depicts the worship of several deities in the Jerusalem temple precinct as "syncretistic" and "Canaanite" in origin. Such a perspective is clearly the invention of a dtr rhetorical polemic in the case of Asherah, for she was the consort of Yahweh in earlier non-dtr forms of Yahwism. The association of the god Molek with human sacrifice in particular might also be the purposeful invention of the dtr and related traditions. Convincing extra-biblical evidence for Molek's (= Malik's) chthonic associations, let alone his patronage of the cult of child sacrifice, has yet to be recovered from Syria-Palestine (cf. 3.1.8.). In other words, the dtr traditions attempted to artificially distance human sacrifice from Yahweh and the Yahwistic cult, whereas the non-dtr traditions did not. The dtr traditions made Molek the patron deity of the cult, but extra-biblical evidence for Molek's status as patron of human sacrifice is lacking.[210] In fact, the texts from Ugarit cast doubt even on his more general chthonic associations.[211]

A similar rhetorical strategy was implemented in the case of the second mantic practitioner listed in Deut. 18:10, *qōsēm qᵊsāmîm*, "the augur." Both Isa. 3:2 and Micah 3:6–7,11 establish the legitimacy of this practice in pre-exilic Yahwistic religion, but it too is later condemned in dtr circles (1 Sam. 15:23; 28:8; 2 Kgs. 17:17) and dependent texts.[212] A possible reference to augury in the redacted text, Isa. 2:6, not only supports the dtr concern to condemn such a practice, but it also offers a possible clue to its perceived origin. That Isa. 2:5–9 is a dtr addition

[209] The DtrH does not depict Hezekiah as purging the Molek cult, cf. 2 Kgs. 18:1–4!

[210] Cf. also Olyan 1988:11–13; M. Smith 1990:132–38.

[211] A god list from Ugarit equates Resheph, not Malik (= Molek?), with Nergal; cf. 3.1.8.

[212] Jer. 14:14; 27:9; 29:8; Ezek. 12:24; 13:6,7,9,23; 21:29,34(ET 21,29); 22:28; Isa. 44:25; Zech. 10:2.

is supported by the dtr expression which shows up in v.8 *ma'ᵃśēh yāḏāyw*, "the work of x's hands."[213] Likewise, the verb *hištaḥᵃwāh* in v.8 might evince dtr influence.[214] These and other data confirm the view that vv.5–9 comprise a later dtr addition to 2:6–21(22).[215] For example, critics insert *qôsᵊmîm*, "augurs," before *miqqeḏem* in v.6 following the targum and appeal to haplography in the MT, "Surely you have rejected your people, O' house of Jacob, because they are full of augurs from the East, and of soothsayers like the Philistines and *they strike hands with foreigners*."[216] If correct, the formerly legitimate augur is in this late text described as a foreign import from Mesopotamia and condemned (or, less likely in view of the passages to follow, the author intends only to condemn a foreign version of augury irrespective of its specific origins).

The condemnation of the augur is taken up again in the story of Balaam in Numbers 22–24 which is likewise a late composition.[217] In 22:7, the elders of Moab and Midian carry *qᵊsāmîm bᵊyāḏām*, that is, "fees for augury in their hand" for Balaam's hire.[218] Balaam is generally recognized as a foreign seer.[219] It is most curious that this foreign version of augury is not initially condemned by the narrator.[220] However, in the story of Balaam's ass, 22:22–35, a secondary addition, the writer polemicizes against Balaam and, indirectly, his foreign augury.[221] In Josh. 13:22, a late P addition, the prophet Balaam is labeled the augur, or *haqqôsēm*.[222] Not only does this text confirm the later foreign associations of augury, it also alludes to the *raison d'être* for its eventual condemnation. In spite

---

213 Cf. Deut. 4:28; 27:15; 2 Kgs. 22:17; Weinfeld 1972a:324; 4.1.

214 Cf. Weinfeld 1972a:321.

215 Cf. Wildberger 1972:95–96; Barth 1977:222–23; Kaiser 1983:6,56–66 and esp. his survey of opinion on pp.63–66 and n.33. Sweeney 1988:176 viewed vv.6b–9a as original to the oracle, but was forced to exclude v.9b from consideration in order to claim that this pericope of accusation would lack a judgment statement and therefore could not have stood independently on its own.

216 Although v.6c is problematic, it clearly refers to Israel's illicit relations with the nations.

217 So Rouillard 1985 whose work is not treated by Moore 1990. Note that the episode of Agag is mentioned in 24:7, a story attributed to Saul's day in what is recognized as a late text, 1 Samuel 15. Moreover, vv.17–18 speak of the wars of David against Edom and Moab. Rouillard proposed four redactional stages for the Balaam story; (N1) 22:2–21,36–23:26 [650–40 B.C.E.], (N2) 22:22–35 [after Josiah's reform], (N3) 23:27–24:6 [exilic], and (N4) 24:7–24 [soon after the exile]. Having compared the Balaam story and Second Isaiah, Van Seters 1986:245–47 dated Rouillard's N1, N3, and N4 to the exilic period, while N2 constituted a secondary addition.

218 Following the *RSV*.

219 Some commentators take 22:5 as indicative of Balaam's Syrian origins where he is identified as the son of Beor at Pethor, by the River in the land of Amaw. 23:7 places Balaam in Aram. Budd 1984:254 (n.5b) noted both the Syrian and northern Mesopotamian locations of Amaw proposed by scholars, but preferred to identify Balaam as a Mesopotamian seer (cf. p.272).

220 This verse is found in Rouillard's N1 stratum and is Josianic in date according to the author.

221 Rouillard's N2.

222 Cf. Josh. 13:21–22; Numbers 31. On the whole of Josh. 13–19 as a late P addition, cf. Van Seters 1983:331–37.

of its earlier legitimacy, augury's foreign influence was cited as the rationale for its proscription.[223]

Both the "soothsayer," or *mᵊʿônēn*, and the "sorcerer," or *mᵊkaššēp*, of Deut. 18:10 require a detailed treatment. At first glance, Micah 5:11(ET 12) and Isa. 2:6 appear to substantiate the ban on these two practices during pre-exilic times (recall that Isa. 2:6 also mentions the augur). However, the dtr status of Micah 5:9–13(ET 6–14) has been repeatedly defended.[224] The presence of the Hiphil of the verb *k-r-t* suggests dtr influence (vv.9,10,11,12(ET 10,11,12,13)).[225] Moreover, as pointed out above, the phrase *maʿᵃśēh yādêka*, "the work of x's hands," in v.12b(ET 13b) is a characteristic dtr expression[226] as is the verbal form *hištaḥᵃwāh*, "bow down," in the same half verse.[227] Furthermore, the root *n-ṭ-š* in v.13 is typical of dtr-Jer.[228] As outlined above, Isa. 2:6 likewise exhibits evidence of a dtr hand. The soothsayer shows up otherwise only in dtr passages of the DtrH (2 Kgs. 21:6), in late prophetic passages (Jer. 27:9; Isa. 57:3), in the HC (Lev. 19:26), and in the Chronicler (2 Chr. 33:6 = 2 Kgs. 21:6).

Likewise, the sorcerer is attested in a dtr text of the DtrH (2 Kgs. 9:22), in late prophetic texts (Jer. 27:9; Isa. 47:9,12; Nahum 3:4; Mal. 3:5; Dan. 2:2) and in the Chronicler (2 Chr. 33:6 = 2 Kgs. 21:6).[229] In exilic and post-exilic prophetic traditions, this office is connected with Mesopotamian influences, particularly Babylonian (Isa. 47:9,12) and Assyrian (Nahum 3:4).[230] In sum, soothsayers and sorcerers are depicted as late comers to Yahwistic religion, as foreign, namely, Mesopotamian imports and are therefore condemned.

The next practitioner, the "diviner," or *mᵊnaḥēš*, is never mentioned in pre-exilic or exilic prophetic texts. It occurs in dtr texts of the DtrH (1 Kgs. 20:33; 2 Kgs. 17:17; 21:6), in the HC (Lev. 19:26), and in the Chronicler (2 Chr. 33:6 = 2 Kgs. 21:6). Like the practice of augury, it is also found in the late story of Balaam, Numbers 22–24.[231] Balaam is described as one well versed in the foreign arts of

---

223 In the notice that Balaam was killed by the Israelites, the priestly perspective aligned itself with the dtr tradition.

224 Willi-Plein 1971:96–97. Jeremias 1971:330–54, esp. pp.343–46; Mays 1976:25–27,124–25 date the passage to the exile. For dtr language throughout chapters 4–5, see Wolff 1982:132–35 and note the reference to Babylon as the place of exile in 4:10. For a survey of opinion, cf. Renaud 1977:262–71 whose conclusion that 5:9b–13(ET 10b–14) is pre-exilic owing to its close relation to Isa. 2:6–8 does not adequately take into account the compositional history of the latter passage.

225 Cf. Lohfink 1981:97.

226 Cf. Deut. 4:28; 27:15; 2 Kgs. 22:17; Weinfeld 1972a:324.

227 Cf. Weinfeld 1972a:321.

228 Jer. 12:14; cf. Deut. 29:27(ET 28); 1 Kgs. 14:15; Amos 9:15, all with reference to the exile; see Wolff 1982:132–33.

229 For the references in the Yahwist, Exod. 7:11 and 22:18(ET 19), see below.

230 Cf. also Mal. 3:5; Dan. 2:2.

231 Rouillard's N1 and N3.

divining (23:23, cf. also 24:1) and augury (23:23, cf. also 22:7). Again, as noted above, it is indeed surprising that there is no condemnation of Balaam as diviner and augur except in the secondary addition of Num. 22:22–35.[232] In 23:23, part of the earliest section of the story, there is no denunciation.[233]

Finally, the "charmer," or *ḥōḇēr ḥāḇēr*, is likewise never mentioned in pre-exilic prophetic texts, but like the sorcerer, the charmer is later depicted in Isa. 47:9,12 as having Babylonian connections (cf. vv.1,5 and Dan. 2:2). Having concluded that Hebrew *ḥ-b-r* was cognate with Akkadian *ubbūru*, "bind magically," Held has recently suggested that Isa. 47:9,12 comprises a satire on Neo-Babylonian magic.[234]

In sum, none of the first six mantic practices listed in Deut. 18:10–11 were condemned in pre-exilic prophetic traditions. Neither Hosea nor Amos nor, for that matter, the Elijah-Elisha school stood in opposition to them. Two of the practices, human sacrifice and augury, were compatible with earlier Yahwistic religion and only later condemned in dtr circles. The remaining four, soothsaying, sorcery, divining, and charming, were not attested in pre-exilic texts. This might indicate that the biblical writers came to be first acquainted with these in the exile or thereafter. In any case, when they do show up in later dtr texts or texts influenced by dtr ideology, they are depicted as illicit practices.

The prophetic traditions connect the forbidden status of these practices to their foreign attachments. In three, sorcery, divining, and charming, Mesopotamian associations are explicit. Nevertheless, the "foreign origins" tradition as a basis for proscription was clearly improvised in the case of augury, for it was depicted elsewhere in biblical traditions as compatible with earlier pre-exilic Yahwistic religion. As we pointed out previously, such purposeful distortion is characteristic of the dtr ideology. The same rhetorical strategy is evident in the dtr polemics against Manasseh, the alleged bull cult of Jeroboam, the cult of Asherah, and, perhaps, the cult of human sacrifice. Admittedly, in the case of sorcery, divining, and charming—all possible late comers to Israelite tradition—the stated Assyrian and Babylonian influences might reflect genuine instances of foreign "syncretism" of what was a (polytheistic) Yahwistic cult or their similarity with extant Israelite forms gave rise to the ban on their observance. Whether these attachments are

---

232 Rouillard's N2.

233 Rouillard's N1.

234 Held 1982:76–85 (English summary p.254*; *Maqlu* I:4–5); cf. M. Smith 1984:379 and n.11. It also shows up in Ps. 58:6(ET 5). The connection with Ugaritic *ḥbr* in *KTU* 1.6:VI:49 and *RIH* 78/20:10 by Avishur 1981:16,22–23, followed by M. Smith 1985:377–80 and Dijkstra 1985:147–52, is questionable, cf. Bordreuil and Caquot 1980:348,350; de Moor 1980b:429,431; Caquot 1984:163–76 who connect Ugaritic *ḥbr* with Hebrew *ḥāḇēr*, "companion."

real or contrived as in the case of augury, the foreign origins played a central role in the dtr polemic against these practices.[235]

Another observation that was alluded to earlier lends support to the exilic or post-exilic compositional setting for at least vv. 10–11 of Deuteronomy 18. Of the various lists of illicit practices which include the *'ôḇôṯ* and *yiddᵊʻōnîm*, Deut. 18:10–11 is clearly the most expansive with its list of seven or eight mantic practices.[236] A comparison of the related lists in 2 Kgs. 21:6 and 2 Chr. 33:6 indicates that the inventory tended to expand over time. The addition in 2 Chr. 33:6 to the five item list in 2 Kgs. 21:6 involves an office attested only in late prophetic texts, namely, the sorcerer (cf. dtr Micah 5:11(ET 12); Jer. 27:9; and Isa. 47:9,12). In Deut. 18:10–11, the sorcerer and three other offices, the augur, charmer, and consulter of the dead, were added to what probably comprised an earlier inventory of outlawed mantic offices. These items are otherwise condemned only in late texts (Isa. 47:9,12 and dtr 2:6 and 8:19). Thus, Deut. 18:10–11 might comprise a late stage in an ever expanding inventory of illicit mantic offices.

Admittedly, foreign, but non-Mesopotamian, origins are attributed to some of the above practices. In 1 Kgs. 20:33, the Syrians are depicted as diviners, while in 2 Kgs. 9:22 sorcery appears in Phoenician dress. Moreover, the augur and the soothsayer are found among the Philistines in 1 Sam. 6:2 and Isa. 2:6 in spite of the fact that the augur was compatible with pre-exilic Yahwistic religion. The diviner and sorcerer are depicted in Egyptian dress in Gen. 30:27; 44:5,15; and Exod. 7:11 (cf. also Exod. 22:18(ET 19)). Nevertheless, the preponderance of references assume Mesopotamian influence. In other words, easterly magical traditions were negatively influential in the formation of the biblical traditions' idealized world and the passages depicting foreign, but non-Mesopotamian, connections might point to a subsequent rhetorical expansion on that dtr perspective. In these instances, the geographic boundaries were widened so as to include other foreign, but local, non-Israelite peoples with but one exception, Egypt. In 4.3.2.–4., we identified a similar process as having taken place in the (post-)dtr redaction of Isaiah wherein necromancy was rhetorically ascribed Egyptian attachments. The compositional histories of the texts identifying foreign but non-Mesopotamian origins offer additional support for the late association of these mantic practices with the local populations: (1) 1 Kgs. 20:33 and 2 Kgs. 9:22 probably constitute later additions to DtrH,[237] (2) Isa. 2:6 is a dtr addition, (3) 1 Samuel 1–7 might be

235 We should also point out that the biblical traditions nowhere explicitly identify Balaam as a necromancer. This strengthens our proposal that this form of divination was peculiar to mid first millennium Mesopotamia and was understood as such by the biblical writers; cf. 4.5.1.

236 Cf. the following passages for lists of three or more: Lev. 20:2–6; 1 Sam. 28:3,7–9; 2 Kgs. 17:17; 21:6; Isa. 8:19; Jer. 27:9; 2 Chr. 33:6.

237 So Jones 1984(II):337–39,450–54.

the product of an exilic dtr hand,[238] (4) Exod. 7:11 and 22:18(ET 19) might be part of a P or dtr redaction, and (5) the Genesis texts might be modeled on passages in the DtrH.[239] In other words, contrary to the impression one might gain by reading only Deut. 18:10–11, none of the practices therein possess a distinctively "Canaanite," historical origin.

In conclusion, Deut. 18:10b–12a comprises a late expansion on a dtr inventory proscribing various mantic practices. Its "Canaanizing" of the various practices listed is clearly a rhetorical strategy designed to polemicize against contemporary cults competing with dtr-Yahwism. It reflects the same working rationale as that which gave rise to the ban on mourning rites of self-mutilation: to define norms and eradicate anomaly by implementing a rigid classification scheme. This was part and parcel with the larger enterprise of constructing a new self-identity in the aftermath of the Babylonian invasions and maintaining control over the supernatural.

A similar classification strategy was used in antiquity to classify and control the worlds of demons. Zoological, polymorphic, meteorological, astrological, anatomical, topological, and behavioral criteria were used in classifying the demonic. A dominate strategy in first millennium Mesopotamian demonology entailed a combinatory logic resulting in a polymorphic scheme whereby zoological and anthropomorphic elements were combined to create a demon. A given quality represented by an animal was abstracted creating an awe-inspiring exemplary member of that animal group. This in turn was combined with various human attributes in order to make that force or power an imaginary one. This served to distinguish that animal-human member from the individual ordinary member. Finally, those demons who were defeated in cosmic battle by the anthropomorphic gods of the pantheon in Assyro-Babylonian theology could become beneficent protective spirits.[240]

The dtr traditions, however, opted for a somewhat different ideological strategy. The location of the various mantic practices in Deuteronomy 18 in the land of Canaan more closely approximates the kind of demonological topology attested

---

238 So Van Seters 1983:346–53.

239 For exilic references to divining in the Yahwistic History, Gen. 30:27; 44:5,15, cf. e.g., Van Seters 1992:277–333.

240 Cf. Wiggerman 1992:143–64. However, Green 1984:80–105 (and cf. Wiggerman 1992:143–64) added that the difference between demons and monsters or protective spirits depended more upon their function in a given period than on any essential character trait attached to them, cf. also Schiffman and Schwartz 1992:35. Wiggerman 1992:164 notes that monsters were a class distinct from the gods, demons, and ghosts of the dead, or *eṭemmū*. They appear only sporadically with the divine determinative or the horns of divinity in art, they do not appear in diagnostic omens and no incantations exist against them. He sees a similar distinction at the level of function between demons and monsters or protective spirits. Monsters assisted the gods and although they unpredictably might wreak violent death and destruction, they were never the cause of diseases like the demons.

for example in Egypt of the Late Period. In Egypt, all things associated with the liminal world of the frontier or periphery were demonized.[241] As mentioned above, the dtr rhetorical strategy entailed secondarily altering the distant foreign attachments of the practices listed so as to include in Deut. 18:10b–12a the local non-Israelite populations. These peoples, the "Canaanites," in turn came to symbolize pre-exilic antagonisms in the land. But in line with the biblical *Tendenz* to avoid the explicit mention of demons by name, our author implemented a rhetorical strategy in which those competing supernatural forces typically organized in other traditions by the classification of their personification as demons have been organized instead according to the corresponding ritual practitioner.[242]

It should be noted that in Mesopotamia some monsters—and we would add demons—might have derived their form from the cultic or ritual setting where priests and ritual professionals dressed in animal-human hybrid form.[243] Perhaps in Deut. 18:10b–12a, the dtr hand implemented a rhetoric of reversal in which the ritual professionals are substituted for their demonic protagonists which, as we pointed out, would be consistent with the dtr suppression of the demonic world. The fact that the ghosts of the dead are explicitly mentioned in 18:11 might suggest that the concurrent classification systems of demons and monsters—assuming that such existed in ancient Israelite society—did not originally include the ghosts of the dead. This in turn supports our contention that the transformation of the Israelite dead from frail shades into supernaturally powerful beneficent ghosts was a relatively late development and that the list in Deuteronomy 18 is a late conflation.

The dtr or post-dtr redaction of necromancy in Deut. 18:11, a passage portraying the formative period of Israel's origins, not only served to rhetorically 'demonize' the indigenous populations of Canaan, but it also established the antiquity of the dtr polemic. Moreover, by placing the dtr condemnation in the mouth of Moses, the founder of the nation, the authority of dtr Yahwism was indisputably validated.

4.4.3. Deuteronomy 26:14

Deut. 26:12–15 continues the law on the tithe where 14:22–29 left off. In recent treatments, this passage has become a *crux interpretum* in the debate over whether or not pre-exilic Israel embraced a death or ancestor cult and the concomitant belief

241 For Late Period Egypt, cf. e.g., Meeks 1971:25–26.

242 Note the repeated use of the participle forms to denote the corresponding professions: *maʿᵃḇîr bᵊnô-ûḇittô bāʾēš, qōsēm qᵊsāmîm, mᵊʿônēn, mᵊnaḥēš, mᵊḵaššēp̱, ḥōḇēr ḥāḇer, šōʾēl ʾôḇ wᵊyiddᵊʿōnî,* and *dōrēš ʾel-hammēṯîm.*

243 Cf. Wiggerman 1992:148–49.

in the supernatural beneficent power of the dead. Death cult advocates have cited it as the clearest example,[244] while their opponents have listed it as the only text worthy of mention although they dismiss it in the final analysis.[245] But before the arguments on either side can be adequately evaluated, the compositional history of the text must be examined. The verse reads according to our interpretation as follows:

lōʾ-ʾāḵaltî ḇᵊʾōnî mimmennû	I have not eaten any of it (the tithe) in my mourning,
wᵊlōʾ-ḇiʿartî mimmennû bᵊṭāmēʾ	nor have I removed any of it in a state of uncleanness,[246]
wᵊlōʾ-nāṯattî mimmennû lᵊmēṯ	nor have I given any of it on account of a dead person.

Critics have repeatedly underscored the dtr character of the preceding section, vv.1–11, particularly the credo in vv.5–10, as well as the succeeding section, vv.16–19.[247] While the same has been posited for vv.12–15, others have recognized the presence of older material that has been adapted by a dtr redactor to a new context. Mayes, for example, proposed that old material had been reworked by a later hand in both vv.12 and 14a.[248] That later material is present is indicated by the phrase *lipnê yhwh ʾᵉlōhêḵā*, "before Yahweh your God," in v.13. This presupposes, scholars have argued, centralization and depends upon the law in 14:22–29 and points to a post-Deuteronomic hand. Furthermore, the phrase *šāmaʿtî bᵊqôl yhwh ʾᵉlōhāy*, "(I) obeyed the voice of," in v.14 is dtr[249] as are the notions of God's dwelling in heaven and looking down on earth in v.15.[250] However, the internal tensions evident in vv.12–15 point to the possibility that not all was the product of the dtr circle. Verse 12 states that the tithe was to be given to

[244] Brichto 1973:29 saw Deut. 26:14 as reflective of an Israelite ancestor cult for which provision was normally made except in the case of the tithe. Ribar 1973:75–76, followed by Lewis 1989:103–04, sought to leave open, but clearly preferred, the periodic nature of the offering as part of a death cult. Spronk 1986:39,49,241,248 viewed this verse as evidence for the ongoing care of the dead, but not their veneration.

[245] Cf. e.g., Heidel 1963:204–06.

[246] Perles 1914:109–10 equated *bᵊṭāmēʾ* of v.14b with Akkadian *eṭemmu* and translated "I have not made burnings for a spirit of the dead."

[247] For 26:1–11 and esp. the so-called credo in vv.5–9, cf. Rost 1965:11–25; Childs 1967:30–39; Seitz 1971:243–48; Mayes 1979:46,332–35; Preuss 1982:144–46. On the lateness of the phrase "my father was a wandering Aramean," or *ʾᵃrammî ʾōḇēḏ ʾāḇî*, in v.5, see Van Seters 1975:33–34 against Mayes 1979:334. For 26:16–19, cf. Mayes 1979:46,337–40; Preuss 1982:147–48.

[248] Mayes 1979:46,244–45,332–37; 1983:36 and n.30,39.

[249] Cf. 27:10; 28:1,2,15,45,62; 30:3,8,10.

[250] Cf. 1 Kgs. 8:30 and 2 Chr. 30:27; Jer. 25:30 and Zech. 2:13, all late passages. See also Weinfeld 1972a:326; Preuss 1982:144.

the Levite, sojourner, fatherless, and widow, but v.14 assumes three ways in which this might not have been fulfilled. The stress on ritual purity in v.14 suggests that the tithe was given to Yahweh rather than to the poor as recorded in v.12. Thus, according to Mayes, the tithe in v.12 comprised older material reapplied in a new context.[251] Such tensions in the text led Mayes to postulate that in v.14a, a dtr redactor has incorporated an ancient confession of cultic purity.[252]

However, the tensions observed by Mayes are not as pronounced as he assumes. While v.14 records three ways in which an Israelite might not fulfill his obligation to the Levite, sojourner, fatherless, or the widow, the difficulty need not be viewed at the level of a supposed redactional seam. Rather, it may well be that a deliberate contrast was made by the narrator. What the narrator underscores by means of the required pledge in v.14 as elsewhere is that no depletion of the tithe was excusable, even for what might be considered otherwise worthy religious causes. Such an interpretation is in keeping with the thrust of v.12 where the stress lies on the giving of the tithe in full measure, "when you have *completed* (*kî t̲ᵊk̲alleh*) tithing all the tithe of your yield . . . ," and v.13, "I have *completely* removed the holy portion. . . . " The same concern can be seen in vv.13b and 14b where *complete* obedience to the *miṣwôt̲* is underscored. It will be argued below that such causes, as are alluded to in Deut. 26:14, are all associated with the act of mourning. The negative pledges comprising vv.14a,14b,14c are aimed at three corresponding situations related to mourning that gainsayers might cite as solemn exceptions to the law of the tithe.

Verse 14a mandates that while one was "in mourning," or *bᵊʾōnî*, no portion of the tithe was to be eaten in place of one's regular food supply (on *bᵊʾōnî*, see below). Verse 14a might anticipate a common tendency to substitute the tithe set aside for the needy for one's regular staple in the event that one's staple had been contaminated by direct or indirect contact with the dead. It should be recalled that unclean food was to be eaten only after a long wait, a seven day period of purification. It was first to be washed and sprinkled on the seventh day (cf. Num. 31:23).[253]

Furthermore, v.14b might reflect an incident wherein the tithe had been stored in open earthenware, but was handled and thus contaminated by an unclean person owing to his/her previous contact with a corpse. According to stipulations like that recorded in Num. 19:15, the earthenware was to be broken and its contents thrown out. However, the hand responsible for v.14b demands that the importance of the tithe as a means to sustain the destitute take precedent over such purity legislation. Finally, verse 14c decrees that one could not give any portion of the tithe to others

---

251 On the tithe, cf. Gen. 14:20; 28:22; Lev. 27:30–31; 1 Sam. 8:15,17; Amos 4:4.
252 Mayes 1979:335–36.
253 Cf. Wright 1985:213–23; 1987:169–72,196–99.

in mourning regardless of how solemn such an act might have been viewed. Given the possible backdrop of mourning underlying the two previous clauses, this is how we view the implied significance of the force of the preposition *lᵊ-* in the phrase *lō'-nāṯattî . . . lᵊmēṯ*. We translate the *lᵊ-* as "on account of" (see further below). Simply put, the needs of the starving outweigh those of the mourner.

So if vv.12–15, and in particular v.14, do not evince the redactional tensions proposed by Mayes, then the entire pericope, like the remainder of the chapter, might derive from a dtr hand. Nielsen has in fact argued for the dtr character of the whole of chapter 26. According to the author, since 27:4–8 was an original element of Deuteronomy rooted in northern traditions now reshaped, then this would imply that chapter 26 is dtr as it intrudes upon what originally incorporated Deut. 12–25 and 27:4–8. As Nielsen pointed out, even those critics who had assigned chapter 26 to the *Urdeuteronomium* nevertheless recognized its supplementary character.[254] In the final analysis, the likely presence of a dtr hand throughout chapter 26 will necessitate that we weigh heavily those concerns characteristic of dtr ideology as well as its stimulus in our treatment of the underlying mortuary practices of 26:14.

We turn now to the significance of Deut. 26:14 for the subject of the Israelite ancestor cult. The form *lᵊmēṯ* in v.14c has given rise to three interpretations of the clause *wᵊlō'-nāṯattî mimmennû lᵊmēṯ*, "nor have I given any of it on account of/to a dead person." It refers either to (1) food given by friends to their grieving neighbors as an act of consolation "on account of a dead person," or to (2) food offered "to the dead," whether temporarily or periodically in order (a) to sustain them and/or (b) to gain their favor, or to (3) food given "to the Dead One," that is, a chthonic deity, either Baal or Mot.[255] Options two and three are variants on the death cult interpretation (the lone exception being the *temporary* offering up of food to the dead). Owing to the lack of support from the context of chapter 26, we reject the third as highly conjectural. The common use of *(lᵊ)mēṯ* to refer to the dead also speaks against this option. However, the situation is quite different in the case of the second. Its advocates have resorted to the material remains from Syria-Palestine to buttress the death cult interpretation of the passage. Ribar, a recent advocate of the death cult hypothesis, leaned heavily upon the Middle Bronze/Late Bronze material remains from Megiddo and Ugarit. With regard to the Ugaritic finds, he followed the lead of Schaeffer, the original director of the French expedition to Ras Shamra, who concluded that the archaeological

---

254 Nielsen 1977–78:77–89, esp. p.83.

255 For the first two proposals, cf. the surveys of Driver 1902:291–92; G. A. Smith 1918:297. For the third (Baal), cf. Cazelles 1948:54–71; 1966:106, followed by Wijngaards 1973:253–55; (Mot) Gray 1965:65, followed by Craigie 1976:323; Mayes 1979:336–37.

evidence from the site pointed to a death cult.[256] Ribar in turn applied Schaeffer's reconstruction of the Ugaritic finds to the remains at Megiddo in order to bolster a similar death cult interpretation of the remains there as originally advocated by Schumacher, Megiddo's excavation director.[257] For Ribar, the holes in the ceilings of tombs as well as the presence of associated clay pipes, storage jars, and pits pointed to repeated offerings to the dead. It is this type of observance which is reflected textually in Deut. 26:14c.[258]

Schaeffer had argued for a death cult at Ugarit on the basis of the ceiling holes using the following logic: (1) the dead were in need of sustenance; (2) therefore, libations were regularly administered in response to this belief, (3) for a similar practice with matching devices for pouring libations is clearly attested among the Mycenaeans and (4) Mycenaeans were among the inhabitants of Ugarit. Schaeffer's material evidence consisted of various devices for pouring libations: (1) a pit located beside a tomb with an accompanying (2) gutter leading to the tomb, (3) windows in funerary vaults assuring the dead's access to the libations, (4) large jars built into the walls of tombs equipped with cups for pouring, (5) cup-marks sunk in stone at the entrance to a tomb and a gutter leading to a pit lying beneath the floor at the tomb's center, (6) stone slabs covering the various pits with holes bored through the center to allow the dead's ready access to the libations, and (7) large jars with the bottom removed located near some of the tombs used in the performance of libating.[259]

To be sure, other reconstructions of these remains have been proposed. Cooley, for example, viewed these devices, not as evidence of a death cult at Ugarit, but as indicative of funerary rites on behalf of the dead. The libations were administered during the period lasting from burial to the complete decay of the body at which time the deceased was believed to have arrived in the netherworld. Libating ceased once the dead entered the netherworld for they could no longer influence the living. According to Cooley, this approach adequately accounts for the possibility of ritual libations as well as multiple burials in which the skeletal remains of earlier deceased were callously handled in order to make room for new burials. In other words, the death cult hypothesis does not sufficiently explain the

---

[256] Cf. Schaeffer 1939:46–56, followed by Sukenik 1940:59–65; Angi 1971:1–93, for a summary of his conclusions.

[257] Cf. Schumacher and Steuernagel 1908:19–22.

[258] Ribar 1973:45–50,75–76, followed by Heider 1985:383–400. Ribar's primary examples were Grabkammer II from Megiddo, following Schumacher and Steuernagel 1908:19–21 and Pl.6, and Tomb L and other installations from Ugarit, following Schaeffer 1939:46–56. Sukenik 1940:59–65 used Schaeffer's arguments to posit a death cult at Samaria. Lewis 1989:179–80 attempted to update Ribar by reference to Tomb I at Dothan, following Cooley 1983:47–58, esp. 50–51, but see below.

[259] Schaeffer 1939:46–56.

mistreatment of bones after decay.[260] Margueron offered another interpretation of the evidence based on his examination of the *Grand Bâtiment* at Ugarit. The only evidence for a libation installation was the funerary pit found inside the *Grand Bâtiment*. This Margueron saw as being used on the occasion of each new inhumation. This proposal is supported by the fact that several other tombs, with which such devices are related, preserve multiple burials.[261] Margueron understood these libations to have "served to conciliate the forces of the infernal world" and the pit at the center of the tomb to establish a close relation between the vault and the underworld. In other words, libations were not offered as a means to quench the thirst of the recently deceased. Rather, they were offered in an attempt to appease the netherworld gods.[262] Although not cited by Margueron, this practice is well documented in the Mesopotamian literary tradition.[263]

In other words, it appears then that the so-called libation devices can accommodate several interpretations. However, serious shortcomings surface upon closer examination of the first two proposals. The problematic nature of Schaeffer's first two assumptions has been exposed by Binford in his critique of the "rationalist-idealist" tradition beginning with the late nineteenth and early twentieth century anthropologists E. B. Tylor and J. G. Frazer. In this tradition, mortuary practices were studied within the context of primitive religion, and ideas and beliefs were invoked as reasons for particular practices, but as Binford pointed out, "by a referral of observed differences within one class of phenomena (behavior) to postulated differences within another (ideas), we are forced to seek the explanations for differences in ideas and in the conditions favoring their change."[264] The circularity in reasoning is self-evident.[265] Schaeffer's remaining two premises are debatable as well. The presence of Mycenaean artifacts may simply reflect the importation of foreign goods and not the presence of Mycenaean inhabitants or their beliefs.[266] The use of such foreign luxury goods as funerary gifts is known from Late Bronze

260 Cooley 1968:77,177,189–203, esp.198–201; 1983:47–58. Lewis 1989:180 quoted Cooley 1983:50–51 in an attempt to substantiate a death cult at Dothan by reference to the tomb window which was used for libations. But Cooley viewed this datum as evidence for funerary rites. Moreover, Cooley 1968:177 noted that it may have been believed that the dead could retrieve their own water supply from the jugs placed outside the tomb *via* the access provided by the window.

261 Margueron 1983a:8–9 also noted that two alabaster vases were found in the pit of the tomb. Their diameter was larger than the holes in the walls of the tomb by 1.4 cm. Thus, they comprised votive offerings made before the completion of the room.

262 Margueron 1983a:19.

263 The Third Dynasty of Ur, the Old Babylonian period, and the Late Assyrian period are represented in the texts found in Kramer 1944:6–12; 1967:114,118; Tsukimoto 1980:131; 1985:37–38,184–200; McGinnis 1987:4,9–10.

264 Binford 1972:208–43, esp. pp.209–10.

265 Cf. Morris 1992:1–30 for a survey of the recent intellectual history of the anthropology of death.

266 So Spronk 1986:144.

Byblos.[267] Moreover, the vaulted tombs at Ugarit which Schaeffer considered of Aegean influence have parallels in Syria and Mesopotamia,[268] but are only occasionally attested in the Aegean of that period.[269] In any case, Cooley's reconstruction is also unconvincing. This writer is unaware of any examples from the ancient Near East where it is claimed that the ghosts of the dead, once having arrived in the netherworld, could never return to haunt or, for that matter, serve the living. In fact, the frequent mention of ghosts of the dead causing distress for the living in Mesopotamian texts and the various ritualistic attempts to appease them reveal that they did indeed leave the netherworld.[270] To be sure, there are descriptions of the netherworld as a place of no return (Akkadian *erṣet la tāri*), but in view of the fact that the dead visited the living, this probably reflects their inability to return to their former state of life. It does not exclude the possibility that the dead might make contact with the living in the land of the living.

Margueron's assessment of the various devices found in the *Grand Bâtiment* presents some interesting possibilities vis-à-vis their application to the funerary data at Ugarit, but as the author recognized, much remains to be resolved. In the final analysis, we are left with the unavoidable conclusion that such devices can say nothing about Ugaritic or, for that matter, Canaanite beliefs beyond, perhaps, the mere fact that there was an afterlife. Besides, what would the so-called libation devices tell us about a supposed ancestor cult, if anything, had they a purely functional purpose? Ribar admitted that the ceiling holes, clay pipes, storage jars, etc., might testify to various techniques of ventilation or fumigation, alternate means of access, or even evidence of quarrying operations.[271] If such apertures were made to minimize offensive odors resulting from bodily decay, what could we surmise about the existence of an Ugaritic cult of the dead? The ceiling holes might have provided escape for the smoke of burning incense placed in the tomb for fumigation, or perhaps they served to ventilate the chamber,[272] or along with the other related libation apparatuses like the gutters and jars, they functioned to supply additional aromatic oils after burial.[273]

---

[267] Cf. Salles 1980:65–66.

[268] Cf. Strommenger 1957:588–89 and Tomb I at Megiddo.

[269] Cf. Courtois 1979:1200–01.

[270] Cf. e.g., Bottèro 1982:43 and the ghost expulsion texts in Scurlock 1988:29–102.

[271] Ribar 1973:45.

[272] Tufnell 1953(III):64 interpreted the ceiling holes in tombs at Lachish as air shafts.

[273] We know that the use of spices for the preparation of the corpse for burial was a common practice. Examples of such a practice can be found in 2 Chr. 16:14, a fragmentary funerary inscription from Byblos which refers to the body (of a dead king?) prepared "in myrrh and bdellium," *bmr wbbdl[ḥ . .]*, cf. Röllig 1974:1–15, and in a cuneiform text where the corpse of Nabonidus's mother, Adad-guppi, is said to have been covered in scented oil, cf. Gadd 1958:35–92; Longman 1991:267–79,282, esp. p.276 (H_2 A:III:15′ = H_1 A:III:31′ in *ANET* 1969:312).

A textual datum often cited in support of the death cult interpretation actually favors the first of the functional explanations offered above. Death cult adherents have identified the Ugaritic term *'urbt*, "aperture," with the holes used for regular food offerings found in the ceilings of tomb chambers at Ugarit.[274] The recent publication of a text from Ras Ibn Hani indicates that such an aperture could function as a passageway for incense (*RIH* 78/20:3): *kqṭr 'urbtm*, "like incense from an airhole."[275] If mortuary concerns are present in the list of duties of the faithful son in *KTU* 1.17:I:27, and this is by no means certain (cf. 3.3.4.), then the reference to "incense," or *qṭr*, there, might allude to its use in funerary rites. In honor of his father, the faithful son was expected to provide incense at his father's tomb until the decay of the body was complete.[276]

Another datum cited as evidence for a cult of the dead at Ugarit is the burial beneath houses.[277] But as Barrelet has demonstrated this understanding of the burial beneath houses is by no means certain. The burials in abandoned sections of villages in pre-Achaemenid Turkmenia should caution against too hasty conclusions, for without additional information we cannot know whether the dead were buried beneath the dwellings of surviving family members or in abandoned houses.[278] Even if it was granted that on occasion they were buried beneath a family dwelling, there is no way of knowing whether the family remained in the house or that they felt compelled to leave it. Perhaps, such burials were an attempt to conceal a grave should a conquering army seek to desecrate or rob it. We know that Ashurbanipal desecrated the bones of his enemies' ancestors.[279] As it stands, the data do not substantiate a domestic death or ancestor cult at Ugarit let alone the belief in the dead's supernatural benevolence.[280] Likewise, the practice of burying royalty beneath the palace can not establish a royal ancestor cult at

---

274 *KTU* 1.4:V:23; 1.109:19; cf. 3.3.3. Adherents include Gray 1966:173 n.2; 1978:102; Ribar 1973:64 n.8; Spronk 1986:145.

275 Cf. the *editio princeps* in Bordreuil and Caquot 1980:346–50. The simile likens the expulsion of an evil spirit to incense rising from an airhole, cf. Saracino 1982:338–43. Mayer 1976:362–74 has catalogued similar Mesopotamian formulae accompanying exorcisms.

276 Incense was used in the first millennium in the royal Assyrian funerary cult as a means of purification, cf. Parpola 1983:8 [Letter #4:5′] and, perhaps, fumigation (?), p.195 [Letter #197:8–9: NIG.NA *ša qutāri*, "incense burners"]; in the royal Babylonian funerary cult as a fumigant, cf. the Adad-guppi text, H_1 A:III:12′: *qutrinnu*, "censor" or "incense," and *ANET* 1969:312; Bayliss 1973:123–24; Tsukimoto 1985:120–23.

277 Most recently Spronk 1986:142–45 viewed this practice as evidence for "the care of the dead."

278 Barrelet 1980:20 and n.31. Thus the findings of Callot 1983:44–45,65–66, that at Ugarit a house was found with a grave beneath the floor and that the grave was accessible from the house, are mute with regard to a domestic cult.

279 E.g., the bones of the Elamite kings, cf. Luckenbill 1927(II):210; Brinkman 1984:102 and n.510.

280 Barrelet 1980:2–27, esp. pp.13–14.

Ugarit.[281] When seen in conjunction with the lack of references in the Ugaritic texts regarding royal burials or an attendant cult, such a choice of location for royal tombs might be explained as an attempt to hide the graves to avoid their desecration. This in turn might likewise explain the Babylonian king Nabonidus's concern to bury his mother in "a hidden location," or *ina niṣirti*.[282]

In concluding our evaluation of the material remains, we summarize the now well known findings of Ucko. Ucko has demonstrated that the presence of grave goods does not necessarily indicate a correlative set of afterlife beliefs. He noted that some items found in graves might have been deemed so personal that for that reason alone they were regarded as best buried with the dead. Others, like weapons, were likely deposited in simple recognition of the military prowess of the deceased. He astutely identified the problem inherent in the recovery of afterlife beliefs from material remains *via* the following question: "what will future archaeologists deduce about twentieth century beliefs in the afterlife from the discovery of a teddy bear, coats and blankets, collars, favorite toys and foods in the shape of rubber bones and actual chocolate which have been deposited with the dearly departed at Woodlands Private Animal Cemetery at Burwash in Sussex?"[283]

Returning to the interpretation of *lᵊmēṯ*, the remaining option "on account of the dead" offers a more likely rendering of the phrase. First, like Deut. 26:14, other biblical passages refer to the use of food or more specifically *leḥem*, "bread," within the context of mourning (Hos. 9:4; Jer. 16:7–8; and Ezek. 24:17,22).[284] In such instances, the mourners eat the bread. It is our contention that Deut. 26:14 points to the similar use of food in a mourning context. Commentators agree that

---

281 Cf. the royal tomb in Courtois 1979:1236.

282 Cf. H_2 A:III:16′ in *ANET* 1969:561 and cf. p.312; *CAD* 11^2(1981):276. McGinnis 1987:1–12 has recently published a Neo-Assyrian text mentioning a king's *bīt niṣirti*, "secret tomb." The relation of *niṣirtu* and Hebrew *nāṣûr* in Isa. 65:4 is discussed in 4.6.4. The burial of Mesopotamian kings in swamps may evince the same concern to hide their location, *contra* Beaulieu 1988:36–37. Moorey 1984:14 suggested that the paucity of literary references to the death and burial places of Mesopotamian kings was perhaps due to their taboo status.

283 Ucko 1969:262–80. In a paper presented at the SBL/AAR annual meeting, Pitard 1990, reviewed the mortuary data from Ugarit, Minet el-Beida, and Ras ibn-Hani. What has been commonly understood as reflective of a death or ancestor cult at Ugarit: libation pits, windows, ceiling holes, large jars, and libation tables, Pitard interprets as more likely associated with typical domestic activities unrelated to mortuary concerns. He suggests that the objects are respectively: disposal sumps, niches, holes resulting from the removal of capstones by pillagers, storage jars, and oil presses.

284 The MT of Jer. 16:7 reads *lāhem* "to them" probably under the influence of the same form in vv.5,6, but the LXX assumes *leḥem*, "bread," and cf. *RSV* and *JPS*. The MT of Ezek. 24:17,22 reads "bread of men" *leḥem ʾᵃnāšîm*, but the targum and Latin Vulgate read "bread of mourning," Hebrew *leḥem ʾônîm* after Hos. 9:4. In any case, the context of Ezek. 24:15–24 makes mention of the consumption of bread during mourning. Cf. also 2 Sam. 3:35 where David's refusal to eat bread may be due to the premature timing of the gesture.

the theme of death, or *mēṯ*, is central to the verse. This supports the interpretation of *bᵊʼōnî* in v.14a as a cognate form of *ʼāwen*, "in mourning" rather than as "in my strength."[285] Furthermore, the LXX *en odynei mou* assumed that mourning was in view.

Second, the form *lᵊmēṯ* of 26:14 shows up in the mourning context of Deut. 14:1 as the form *lāmēṯ* and in this instance it clearly refers to acts observed "on account of the dead," and not practices directed "to the dead" (cf. 4.4.1.). This rendering of the *lamed* preposition when its object refers to a dead person finds a semantic equivalent in the form *l-* + *nep̱eš*, "on account of the dead," in Lev. 19:28 (*lānep̱eš*) and 21:1 (*lᵊnep̱eš*).[286] In other words, what stands behind Deut. 26:14c is the custom of giving food as an act of consolation and nourishment to those in bereavement over the loss of a loved one, "nor have I given any of it (to those bereaving) on account of the dead."

It is now possible to be more specific as to what aspect of death dominates the whole of v.14, namely the theme of mourning. Mourning stands behind *lᵊmēṯ* in v.14c, *bᵊʼōnî*, "in my mourning," in v.14a, and *bᵊṭāmēʼ*, "in a state of uncleanness," in v.14b. According to Deut. 21:22–23; Num. 19:11–20; and Lev. 21:1–4; 22:4, contact with a corpse, or even proximity to it in the same dwelling, constitutes uncleanness. Likewise, Deut. 26:14 assumes that the corpse defiles the mourner and, for that matter, any food with which it or the contaminated mourner might come into close proximity. Furthermore, Hos. 9:4 specifically states that *leḥem ʼônîm* (< *ʼāwen*), "the bread of mourning," defiles.

Nevertheless, it is not the ritually defiling power of the corpse that stands at the forefront of the narrator's concern in v.14. Rather, as proposed previously, the narrator addresses what might be popularly viewed as legitimate excuses for having depleted the required amount of food set aside for the needy. But for our narrator, none of the mentioned reasons in v.14, in spite of the fact that they are related to the solemn act of mourning, suffice as a justification for skimping on one's tithe.

Admittedly, our author assumed the efficacy of the corpse's contaminating power, but for those who sought to observe mourning protocol, they must remember to hold fast their commitment to the underprivileged and use none of the tithe while in grief over the loss of a family member or in the hope to console another who had recently lost a loved one. This text then in no way suggests that the Israelite dead were worshipped, venerated, or even cared for on a regular basis.

---

[285] For "in my strength," cf. Craigie 1976:323. For Hebrew *ʼāwen*, "sorrow," cf. Rabin 1961:386–87; Andersen and Freedman 1980:526; Gen. 35:18; Hos. 9:4; perhaps Ezek. 24:17,22.

[286] On this use of *nep̱eš*, cf. Lev. 21:1; 22:4; see Seligson 1951 on *nap̱šōṯ mēṯ* in Lev. 21:11. In Jer. 16:6 the form *lāhem* evinces the same force of the preposition "on account of" as it likewise refers to the dead (cf. 4.6.1.).

The form *lᵊmēṯ* in 26:14c, as in 14:1, refers to a rite not of the death or ancestor cult, but of mourning.[287]

4.4.4. Summary

We have scrutinized the relevant deuteronomic legal texts for evidence documenting the existence of Israelite death and ancestor cult rites and necromantic practices. Our findings suggested that the texts were mute concerning the existence of any Israelite version of the ancestor cult. Deut. 14:1 was found to be a later dtr prohibition aimed at selected mourning rites, not death or ancestor cult rites. The dtr writer outlawed what were originally legitimate rites of tonsure and gashing owing to their symbolic identity of the living with the dead *via* physical appearance and their association of the world of the living with the world of death in terms of the latter's ever-present threat and inevitability. Likewise, the dtr text Deut. 26:14 forbade certain abuses associated with rites of mourning, not death or ancestral cult rites. The pledge regarding the tithe stipulated that no portion of the tithe was to be used for purposes other than to feed the needy. Within the purview of this proscription fell the use of the tithe in solemn acts of mourning. Should the regular supply of food become unclean through contact with the dead, the tithe was not to be eaten in its stead (v.14a). Furthermore, it was not to be discarded owing to its having become unclean through direct or indirect contact with the dead (v.14b). Finally, one was not to give it (*wᵊlōʾ-nāṯattî mimmennû*) as an act of consolation to others who were mourning on behalf of the dead (*lᵊmēṯ*; v.14c). In sum, the deuteronomic legal traditions do not record or polemicize against the observance of death or ancestor cult rites in general let alone those expressive of the worship or veneration of the dead. However, the belief in the supernatural beneficent power of the dead is documented in the dtr or post-dtr redactional passage Deut. 18:10–11. But like the dtr redactional texts embedded in the book of Isaiah, this text attests to the late introduction of necromancy. As our treatment of 1 Sam. 28:3–25 will demonstrate, the biblical polemic against necromancy reflects a significant degree of familiarity on the part of the dtr tradi-

287 If one assumed for the sake of argument that *lᵊmēṯ* referred to offerings "to the dead," and that this in turn reflected an Israelite funerary or ancestor cult, Mesopotamian funerary practices and ancestor cult rites such as the *kispum* ritual would explain the promulgation of a sanction against selected mortuary rites like those found in Deut. 26:14. For examples of roughly contemporary, Mesopotamian, funerary rites, cf. Parpola 1983:6–8 [Letter #4],190–91 [Letter #195],194–97 [Letters ##197,198],270–75 [Letter #280]; McGinnis 1987:1–12; cf. Tsukimoto 1985:107–24 for the first millennium *kispum* ritual.

tion and, perhaps, also some aspect of ancient Israelite society with contemporary Mesopotamian versions of this mantic art. To 1 Sam. 28:3–25 we now turn.

4.5. The Deuteronomistic History

In this section, we will inspect those passages in the DtrH that document rites reflective of the Israelite belief in the supernatural beneficent power of the dead. The pertinent texts exclusively concern the divinatory art of necromancy. Had ancestor worship or veneration enjoyed such popularity as has been so often presumed by scholars, we would have expected them or their corresponding rituals to show up in the DtrH as the object of dtr polemic. The traditions mentioning necromancy include king Saul's encounter with the woman diviner from Endor (1 Sam. 28:3–25) and king Manasseh's 'apostasy to' and Josiah's 'reforming of' necromancy in late pre-exilic Judah (2 Kgs. 21:6 and 2 Kgs. 23:24).

4.5.1. 1 Samuel 28:3–25

Saul's postmortem encounter with the prophet Samuel as narrated in 1 Sam. 28:3–25 has engendered a wide range of responses from Jewish and Christian scholars alike. Among others, Josephus, Justin Martyr, Origen, Augustine, John Chrysostom, Tertullian, Jerome, and later, Kimḥi, Martin Luther, and John Calvin have tried their hand at interpreting the inauspicious scene at the Endorian "witch's" abode.[288] Over the centuries, theologians have been at odds over whether what appeared was truly the ghost of Samuel or a pythonic spirit which was permitted to assume Samuel's form. Even among those who have advocated the view that it was Samuel, there is disagreement over the source of power behind his conjuration. Some view Israel's god, Yahweh, as the source while others make allowance for the possibility that the woman possessed the demonic(!) powers to bring Samuel up from the grave. To be sure, these opposing opinions do not exhaust the range of responses documented in the secondary literature.[289] The argument has been made that the witch, while in a state of ecstasy, might have deceived herself into imagining she saw Samuel and heard him speak or, perhaps, she deliberately

---

288 For the prominent role of women as necromancers, cf. the bibliography in Spronk 1986:254 n.3.

289 Kirkpatrick 1888:244–45 offered a survey of late nineteenth century opinion while Smelik 1979:160–78 has detailed much of the rabbinic and Christian exegesis prior to 800 C.E.

deceived Saul by pretending to see Samuel.[290] But, as noted previously, 1 Sam. 28:3–25 and Isa. 29:4 (4.3.5.) together establish the belief in the efficacy of the art of necromancy in at least some sectors of Israelite society whether they be those of the writers themselves or those of the more ancient societies depicted in the texts.[291] This conforms with what we know about the status of this divinatory art in other ancient cultures such as Mesopotamia and Greece (see below).

But what was the contextual setting underlying the mention of this practice and its proscription in the narratives spanning chapter 16 through 2 Samuel chapter 5, the extensive section known otherwise as the story of David's rise to power? Are the narrative elements of this account the actual goings-on of an Israelite king of the early Iron Age, who having previously outlawed necromancy, turns tail to embrace it as a last resort, or is this story a later writer's ideological and social concerns read back into earlier history? In an effort to find answers to these questions, we will first examine the compositional history of 1 Sam. 28:3–25. This passage is widely recognized as forming a sequel to 1 Samuel 15. The remark in 15:35, "Samuel did not see Saul again until the day of his death," anticipates the episode in 1 Sam. 28:3–25 (cf. esp. v.3).[292] Particular attention has been given to 28:17–18 which clearly presupposes chapter 15 where Samuel announces Yahweh's rejection of Saul in response to his failure to destroy completely the Amalekites.[293] If this connection holds, then it is safe to conclude that whatever date one assigns to chapter 15, the same or later can be proffered for 28:3–25. Others, however, have viewed vv.17–18 as a secondary addition to 28:3–25.[294] If this is in fact the case, then the remainder of 28:3–25 need not be taken as dependent upon chapter 15. But the isolated redactional character of 28:17–18 is doubtful. Together with vv.16 and 19, vv.17–18 form a unified prophetic speech: an accusation (in the form of a question, v.16), a rehearsal of past obedience

290 The LXX rendering of *'ôḇ* as *engastrimythos*, "ventriloquist," might be relevant here.

291 Recall that Isa. 8:19–20 rhetorically rejects the efficacy of necromancy, cf. 4.3.2. Necromancy's efficacy also conforms with the perspective reflected in Ecclesiasticus 46:20 that Samuel prophesied after his death.

292 Cf. Wellhausen 1899:251–52; Stoebe 1973:292; Veijola 1982:71 and n.13; Van Seters 1983:261; esp. Foresti 1984:130–31. The statement in 15:35 creates a tension with 19:18–24 which the redactor never resolved. For 19:24, the LXX has Saul speak in ecstasy "before them," or *enopion auton*, i.e., before the other prophets, rather than "before Samuel" with the MT *lip̄nê šᵊmû'ēl*, in an attempt to harmonize 19:24 with 15:35; 25:1; and 28:3.

293 Cf. Wellhausen 1973:259–61; Schunck 1963:94–96. 1 Sam. 15:28b reads *qāra' yhwh 'eṯ-maml*ᵊ*ḵûṯ yiśrā'ēl mē'ālêḵā*, "Yahweh has torn the kingship over Israel away from you"; 1 Sam. 28:17b reads *wayyiqra' yhwh 'eṯ-hammamlāḵāh miyyāḏeḵā*, "Yahweh has torn the kingship out of your hands." For the dtr character of this language, cf. 1 Kgs. 11:11,13,31; 2 Kgs. 17:21; Weinfeld 1972a:23 n.2, 355.

294 Cf. Budde 1902:182; Dhorme 1910:244; Hertzberg 1964:220; Dietrich 1972:86 (DtrN); Stoebe 1973:487,495; Veijola 1975:57–59 (DtrP); Beuken 1978:5–6 (DtrP); McCarter 1980:423 (a prophetic redactor); Klein 1983:270 (DtrP); Donner 1983:235–36; Foresti 1984:87–89,135 (DtrN).

(vv.17–18a), and an announcement of judgment (*'al-kēn*, v.18b) followed by a judgment speech (v.19).[295] Furthermore, Saul's answer to Samuel's question in v.15 anticipates Samuel's further response in v.16. Therefore, v.16 cannot be relegated to the level of an isolated redactional element. The same can be said for at least the second half of v.19 which is presupposed by v.20. On the basis of the unity of vv.16–19 and the links which vv.16,19 have with the immediate context, it is unlikely that any part of the speech is secondary to the immediate context.[296]

Therefore, given the probability that the whole of 28:3–25 comprises a sequel to chapter 15, it remains for us to detail the compositional history of the latter. There are several incongruities in the account of the Amalekite engagement in chapter 15.[297] First of all, the story of David's rise (1 Sam. 16:14–2 Sam. 5:12) does not recognize control of Judah by Saul as the story would have the reader believe. Moreover, the annihilation of the Amalekites does not account for David's later campaign against this group in 1 Samuel 30. Finally, the early stories about Saul (1 Sam. 9:1–10:16; 11:1–15; 13:2–14:46) reveal that Samuel had no role in Saul's monarchy. Such a role was the creation of a later redactional hand.[298] A related issue is the question of literary genre. Some have suggested that chapter 15 comprises an example of the "judgment speech to the individual," a literary form which has been dated to the pre-classical prophetic period.[299] On this basis, Birch dated 1 Samuel 15 to the late eighth century B.C.E.[300] In spite of the fact that the judgment speech to the individual is a narrative form which refers to Israel's earlier history, it forms part of the DtrH or a dtr redaction of the prophetic books where the lateness of the genre is evident.[301] This mitigates against locating this literary form only in early periods. Besides, an alternate literary genre has been proposed for chapter 15. This passage more appropriately exemplifies the

---

295 Following Van Seters 1983:262 n.55. For a critique of the redactional approach to the DtrH advocated by Dietrich 1972 and Veijola 1975 [DtrG followed by a redactor DtrP (post-exilic), followed by still another DtrN] and employed by Foresti 1984 and Tropper 1989:205–27 in 1 Sam. 28:3–25 in favor of the DtrH as a unified work of the exilic period with independent supplements (following Noth), cf. Van Seters 1983; for Kings, cf. Hoffmann 1980; McKenzie 1991.

296 Veijola 1975:58, followed by Beuken 1978:5–6, concluded that vv.17–18 comprised a later gloss by DtrP which maintained the two-part prophetic oracle of vv.16,19—annunciation and motivation. Not only is this an imprecise genre analysis of vv.16–19, but this view eliminates the scant evidence for the redactional nature of vv.17–18 which Veijola assumes.

297 Cf. Van Seters 1983:258–62 for what follows.

298 With perhaps the exception of the first story of Saul's youth, 9:1–10:16, but even in this case Samuel has a lesser role in the original version. Van Seters 1983:254–58 viewed the original lines of 9:1–10:16 as 9:1–8,10–14,18–19, 22–27*aab*; 10:2–6,9–13 (9:9,15–17,20–21,27*ac*,b; 10:1,7–8,14–16 are later additions).

299 Westermann 1967:129–63, esp. pp.137–38.

300 Birch 1976:98–108.

301 Cf. 1 Kgs. 13:1–3 and v.2 where the mention of Josiah establishes the lateness of this exemplar, so Rofé 1974:158–60.

prophetic didactic *legenda*. In this literary form, religious teachings are conveyed through the speeches of stereotypical characters in which the exaltation of Israel's god comes to the fore. In chapter 15, the lesson to be taught is: obedience is better than sacrifice—a theme also found at home in classical prophecy.[302] Furthermore, in this genre the prophet is depicted as the medium of the divine word, a portrayal characteristic of the DtrH in Kings and of the post-classical period more generally. Other examples of this genre include the stories of Naaman the leper (2 Kings 5), Elijah and the widow of Zarephath (1 Kgs. 17:8–24), and the healing of Hezekiah (2 Kgs. 20:1–11).[303]

We mention a further point in favor of the dtr or post-dtr character of 1 Samuel 15. The language and style of this chapter have clear affinities with the dtr tradition. The phrase *šᵊma' lᵊqôl (dibrê) yhwh*, "hearken to the voice of Yahweh," is dtr (vv.1b,19,20,22)[304] as is *kōh 'āmar yhwh ṣᵊbā'ôt*, "thus says Yahweh of hosts . . . ," (v.2).[305] The same applies in the case of the following phraseology: *'āśāh ḥesed*, "show loving-kindness" (v.6),[306] *wayᵊhî dᵊbar yhwh 'el-*, "the word of Yahweh came to . . . " (v.10),[307] *wᵊ'et-dᵊbāray lō' hēqîm*, "he did not confirm my word"(v.11),[308] *'āśāh hāra' bᵊ'ênê yhwh*, "do that which is evil in the eyes of Yahweh" (v.19),[309] *ḥērem*, "devoted to God" (v.21a),[310] and *'ābar 'et-pî-yhwh*, "violate Yahweh's command" (v.24).[311] The reciprocal judgment statement in which the king/people reject Yahweh and Yahweh rejects him/them is characteristically dtr (vv.23,26).[312] The description of the Amalekite opposition (v.2) shares similar language with Deut. 25:18 and the tearing of the cloak as a symbol of

302 As distinct from other prophetic *legendae*, neither the miraculous nor the figure of the prophet are of major concern. In fact, the way in which miracles are presented might constitute the object for critique, so Rofé 1974:145–53.

303 Rofé 1974:145–53.

304 E.g., Deut. 1:34; 5:28; 9:23; 13:5; Jer. 3:13,25; 7:23; cf. Weinfeld 1972a:337; Foresti 1984:89 (DtrN). Van Seters 1983:260 n.47 concluded that Yahwistic texts which contain this expression have been influenced by dtr style, cf. e.g., Gen. 22:18.

305 Cf. 2 Sam. 7:8, the prose sections of Jeremiah, e.g., 6:6,9; 9:6(ET 7),16(ET 17); 11:22; 19:11, and late texts dependent upon dtr, e.g., Mal. 1:4; 1 Chr. 17:7.

306 Cf. 1 Sam. 20:8,14; 2 Sam. 2:6; 3:8; 9:1,3,7; 10:2; 22:51; 1 Kgs. 2:7; 3:6; Foresti 1984:89 (DtrN).

307 Cf. 2 Sam. 7:4; as Van Seters 1983:260 n.49 has pointed out, the phrase shows up frequently in Jeremiah (e.g.,; 1:4,11; 2:1; 13:8; 16:1), Ezekiel (e.g.,; 3:16; 6:1; 7:1; 11:14), and the dtr stories of prophets in Kings (e.g., 1 Kgs. 13:20; 16:1,7; 17:2,8; 21:17,28).

308 Cf. Deut. 27:26; Jer. 34:28; 35:14,16; Van Seters 1983:260 n.50.

309 Cf. Deut. 4:25; 9:18; 17:2; 31:29; Judg. 2:11; 3:7,12; 4:1; 6:1; 10:6; 13:1; 2 Sam. 12:9; 1 Kgs. 11:6,14,22; 15:26,34 (over 40x total); Jer. 7:30; 18:10; 32:30; Weinfeld 1972a:339 against Mayes 1983:75.

310 Cf. Deut. 7:26; 13:18; Josh. 6:17,18; 7:1(2x) 7:11,12,13,15; 22:20; 1 Kgs. 20:42; Foresti 1984:89 (DtrN). Josh. 22:20 is a later P text according to Van Seters 1983:336.

311 Foresti 1984:89 labeled this as DtrN.

312 Cf. 1 Kgs. 17:15–20; Van Seters 1983:260 and n.51.

Yahweh's tearing of the kingdom away from a disobedient king (vv.27–28) finds a parallel in 1 Kgs. 11:29–31.[313] These several points when considered together point to the late dtr or post-dtr character of 1 Samuel 15.[314]

If 1 Samuel 15 is dtr and its linkage with 1 Sam. 28:17–18 is secure, then we can safely conclude that 1 Samuel 28 is likewise dtr or even post-dtr. To be sure, there are independent arguments for the post-dtr character of 28:3–25. First, 28:3a *ûš(ᵊ)mû'ēl mēṯ*, "Now Samuel was dead," is dependent upon the dtr text 25:1 because it presupposes the death of Samuel as something already known; 25:1 records *wayyāmoṯ šᵊmû'ēl*, "Now Samuel died."[315] Moreover, the latter part of 28:3a, "and all Israel had mourned for him and buried him in his own town of Ramah," is a revision of 25:1a, "and all Israel assembled and mourned for him, and they buried him at his home in Ramah."[316] The fact that v.3 repeats 25:1 raises the unlikelihood that the same author would cite the same facts twice.[317]

Critics have repeatedly pointed out that the presence of 28:3–25 creates a distinct disturbance in the geographical and chronological progression of the battle against the Philistines.[318] 28:2 has its direct continuation in 29:1. In 28:4–5, the Philistines are at Shunem, north of the Jezreel, while the Israelites are stationed on Mt. Gilboa, whereas in 29:1 the Philistines are at Aphek some distance away and Israel is encamped in the plain.[319] The Philistines arrive at Jezreel only in 29:11.[320] Thus, 28:3–25 comprises a secondary addition to the earlier story at the DtrH stratum in 28:1–2 + 29:1–11.[321]

---

[313] Cf. Van Seters 1983:260. For the dtr character of the phrase, *qāra' mamlāḵāh/mamlᵊḵûṯ mē'āl-*, "tear the kingdom from . . . ," cf. 1 Kgs. 11:11,13,31; 14:8; 2 Kgs. 17:21; Weinfeld 1972a:355; Foresti 1984:89 (DtrN).

[314] Cf. Schunck 1963:82–85; Foresti 1984. The latter assigned chapter 15 to DtrP.

[315] McCarter 1980:388; Van Seters 1983:262 n.56; Dietrich 1987:26. For the dtr character of 25:1, cf. Schunck 1963:94; Foresti 1984:132. Foresti 1984:132 n.132 noted that the inversion of subject and verb in 28:3 pointed to a past event (25:1), but one relevant to the present context.

[316] Schunck 1963:94; Van Seters 1983:262; Dietrich 1987:26–27.

[317] So Van Seters 1983:262; Foresti 1984:132–33.

[318] Wellhausen 1899:251–52.

[319] Van Seters 1983:n.57 outlined three possible locations for Aphek; in the Sharon south of Jezreel, in the plain of Acco, and in the region east of the Sea of Galilee.

[320] Driver 1913:213 noticed its dislocation and preferred to place it after chapters 29 and 30. McCarter 1980:422–23; Klein 1983:269 proposed that the narrator merely switched to a non-sequential perspective from David (to 28:2) to Saul (28:3–25) and back to David (29:1 and following). Van Seters 1983:262 concluded that 28:3–25 should not be placed after chapter 29 or chapter 30 owing to the fact that 28:4 would follow 29:1 and so depict a retreat up the mountain before the battle had begun. Cf. also Dietrich 1987:25–36.

[321] Van Seters 1983:262 concluded that, although secondary, 28:3–25 was not an independent tradition. Rather, it was dependent upon the previous compilation of the *Aufstiegsgeschichte* or the story of David's rise (1 Sam. 16:14–2 Sam. 5:12). Schunck 1963:95; Foresti 1984:133–34 have listed the linkage 28:3–25 has with accounts in 1 Sam. 7–14 and the *Aufstiegsgeschichte* which could only presuppose the synthesis comprising the DtrH.

The post-dtr character of 28:3–25 is given added confirmation in v.3b where the reform by Saul is mentioned. If this pericope was dtr, it would be exceptional for Saul not to have been commended for his reform.[322] Finally, the association of the root *q-s-m* with the terms *'ôb̲* and *yiddᵊ'ōnî* in v.8 points to a late compositional history. While all three terms refer to necromancy in our passage, the dtr lists of prohibited practices where *q-s-m* and our two terms appear together (e.g, Deut. 18:10–11; 2 Kgs. 21:6; and cf. 2 Chr. 33:6) make a clear distinction between augury and necromancy.[323] Only in later narrative texts does the root *q-s-m* take on a more generalized sense where it can encompass a variety of practices (cf. 1 Sam. 6:2; 15:23; Josh. 13:22[P]; Num. 22:7; 23:23).[324]

The above arguments indicate that 1 Sam. 28:3–25 is a late composition, probably post-dtr. As we pointed out in 4.2., the language and style point to its dependency upon such dtr passages as Deut. 18:11; 2 Kgs. 21:6; and 23:24, and to those elements it shares with the post-dtr texts Isa. 8:19; 9:3; and 29:4.[325] Furthermore, the deafening silence from some two millennia of Syria-Palestine with regard to the practice of necromancy together with its well-attested observance in Mesopotamia from the mid first millennium onwards supports a late compositional setting for 1 Sam. 28:3–25.[326]

The Assyrian kings Esarhaddon and Ashurbanipal employed various forms of divination to ascertain the intentions or activities of political and military enemies. Ashurbanipal was particularly concerned with the outcome of his struggle with his rebellious brother, Shamash-shumu-ukin, king of Babylon. Several extispicies dated to Ashurbanipal's reign inquire about the success of his planned military strategies and the eventual outcome of the engagements.[327] This is the function attributed to necromancy in 1 Samuel 28 where Saul clandestinely visits the woman of Endor to ascertain the strategy (and implicitly, the outcome) of the next day's battle with the Philistines (vv.4–7,15b). Once conjured up, however, Samuel's ghost not only conveys an unfavorable decision concerning the outcome of the battle (v.19), it also determines the future of his inquirer's royal aspirations (v.17).

While royal legitimacy was not Saul's direct concern in his having Samuel's ghost called up, legitimate kingship is a (if not, the) major theme in this section

---

322 So Van Seters 1983:262.

323 In Jer. 27:9, *q-s-m* shows up with other prohibited practices: false prophets, dreamers, soothsayers, and sorcerers.

324 On the compositional histories of Num. 22:7 and 23:23, cf. Rouillard 1985; Van Seters 1986:245–47.

325 Cf. similarly Foresti 1984:133 n.142.

326 On the Mesopotamian evidence see below and cf. also 4.3.3. for our treatment of necromancy in ancient Egyptian literature.

327 On the queries placed before the sun god, Shamash, and extispicy reports from the reigns of these kings, cf. Starr 1990:XIII-LXVII, esp. pp.XXX-XXXV and see his pp.262–70 for the use of divination to determine military strategy and to ascertain the outcome of a war.

of 1 Samuel. Moreover, the oracle spoken by Samuel's ghost addresses this issue and answers in the negative. Thus, a degree of irony has been infused into the plot. The association of legitimate kingship with necromancy is likewise attested in a diviner's letter to king Esarhaddon dated to 672 B.C.E. The question for which a decision was sought was whether or not Ashurbanipal should have been awarded the position of crown prince. The question is answered in the affirmative by means of consulting the ghost, or *eṭemmu*, of Esarhaddon's recently deceased wife Esharra-ḫamât:

> [The crown prince] explained [it as follows]: "The gods Ashur (and) Shamash ordained me to be the crown prince of Assyria because of her (= the dead queen's) truthfulness." (And) her ghost blesses him in the same degree as he has revered the ghost: "May his descendants rule over Assyria!" (As it is said), fear of the gods creates kindness, fear of the infernal gods returns life. Let the [king, my] lord give order.[328]

The late composition of 1 Samuel 28 finds additional collaboration in the preponderance of similar necromantic tales characteristic of late antiquity. Trencsényi-Waldapfel collected numerous Greek and Latin texts dealing specifically with the art of necromancy. These offer impressive parallels to the major motifs found in 1 Samuel 28: the consultation of the dead in spite of its illicit status, the role of the necromancer fulfilled by a woman, the ghost's reproach of the inquirer, the prediction of the downfall of a dynasty or king, the need for disguise, and the act of fasting.[329] Others have similarly noted parallels with Hellenistic literature such as the sustained power of the prophet both in life and in death (his is not a feeble shade), the role of a female medium, the advanced warning, and the precarious nature of the rite.[330] However, their full significance has not been appreciated by interpreters predisposed to seek out second millennium antecedents to 1 Samuel 28. Some have sought to anchor the early origins of the woman of Endor account in supposed parallels from second millennium Hittite and Mesopotamian sources. However, not only do they inadequately address the issue of the compositional history of the passage, frequently they misunderstand

---

[328] *LAS* 132 in Parpola 1970:107 and 1983:120: (beginning lost) ^{1} [. . . ^{2} . . .] *ú-saḫ-kim* ^{3} [*m*]*a-a ina ke-nu-ti-šá Aš-šur* ^{d}*Šá-maš* ^{4}*a-na* DUMU.LUGAL-*ú-te* KUR *Aš-šur*^{ki} ^{5}*iq-ti-bu-ú-ni e-ṭém-ma-šá* ^{6}*i-kar-rak-šú ki-i ša šu-u* ^{7}*e-ṭem-mu ip-laḫ-u-ni ma-a* MU-*šú* ^{8}NUMUM-*šú* KUR *Aš-šur*^{ki} *li-bé-lu* ^{9}[*p*]*a-laḫ* DINGIR^{meš} *da-ma-qu ul-lad* ^{10}[*p*]*a-laḫ* ^{d}*A-nun-na-ki ba-al-ṭu ú-tar* ^{11}[LUGAL *be*]-*li ṭè-e-*[*mu*] *liš-ku*[*n*] (remainder lost). The translation is that of Parpola, cf. also *CAD* 4(1958):397; 8(1971):396; Bayliss 1973:124; Finkel 1983–84:1,3; Tsukimoto 1985:159; Tropper 1989:76–83.

[329] Trencsényi-Waldapfel 1961:201–22. However, the motif of the dead as gods does not apply in the case of 1 Sam. 28:13 (*'ᵉlōhîm*), cf. below.

[330] Cf. e.g., Vattioni 1963:468 and n.43, 477 and n.73; Ebach and Rüterswörden 1980:212–13; Brown 1981:395.

Hebrew *'ôḇ* as related to the term "pit" (cf. 4.3.2.). Moreover, many of the early comparative examples cited do not concern necromancy per se.[331]

In view of the foregoing analysis, the post-dtr provenance of 1 Sam. 28:3–25 appears more likely than a late second millennium setting. Moreover, the post-dtr author's characterization of this mantic art as an ancient practice observed by the local Canaanites contradicts the comparative documentation for the late and exclusively Mesopotamian interest in necromancy and its absence in Canaanite (= Ugaritic) traditions otherwise. To be sure, Josh. 17:1–12 lists the city of Endor (v.11) and its dependencies among those Canaanite enclaves Israel failed to dispossess. According to this tradition, Israel was only able to force the inhabitants of Endor to pay tribute (v.13).[332] Thus, the author of 1 Sam. 28:3–25 might have built upon an older tradition by attributing Israel's observance of necromancy to her contacts with these Canaanites of the settlement period. But is this how such a tradition developed? The whole of Joshua chapters 14 to 17 may very well comprise the work of the exilic Priestly Writer.[333] The entire block of material reflects P's characteristic penchant for delineating the inheritance of individual tribes and families by lot.[334] The ideological concern reflected in such a scheme comes from the exilic period and attempts to justify the unfulfilled promise of land inheritance; Israel's failure to dispossess fully the Canaanites led to her apostasy.

As mentioned in 4.2., for the later biblical writers, the term Canaanite, like the terms Amorite and Hittite, functioned primarily as an ideological or rhetorical term for the pre-Israelite inhabitants of Palestine. These designations eventually came to epitomize the foreign occupations, including those of later times, which persistently threatened Israel's claim to the land and its blessings.[335] So, the question remains, why would the post-dtr hand responsible for 1 Sam. 28:3–25 seek to project this concern back into the history of an earlier period? Like the Deuteronomist, the Yahwist, and the Priestly Writer, our author sought to give his

---

331 Humphreys 1980:80–85 cites only Greek parallels to 1 Samuel 28 and 31, but otherwise draws upon the texts in Vieyra 1961:47–55; Hoffner 1967:385–401. Only one of the texts cited in Vieyra and Hoffner dealt with necromancy and it was Greek (*Odyssey* XI:23–29,34–43). Besides, the Hittite version of the Greek *chthonioi* (= infernal deities and the dead, on which see Guthrie 1955:221–22), the *katteres šiuneš* never appear in any of the examples. Lastly, none of the second millennium texts in Ebach and Rütersworden 1980:205–20 concern necromancy. We have leveled the same criticism against the works of Tropper 1989 and Moore 1990.

332 Endor is mentioned again only in Ps. 83:11(ET 10) in an allusion to Deborah's deliverance of Israel from the hands of Jabin, king of Canaan/Hazor, and his military commander Sisera, but the city is not explicitly mentioned in the related narrative account given in Judges 4.

333 Van Seters 1983:335,339.

334 For this distinctly priestly approach to the allotment of land over against the tendency in dtr to portray the inheritance of the land from the perspective of the nation as a whole, cf. von Rad 1966:79–93.

335 See Van Seters 1972:64–81; 1975:46–51.

polemic an historical basis in the past. Moreover, like those writers, he sought to attach his historical argument to biblical Israel's idealized enemy, the Canaanites.

A comparison of 1 Sam. 28:3–25 with the list of Manasseh's sins in 2 Kgs. 21:6, the cultic reform of Josiah in 2 Kgs. 23:24, and the dtr addition to the Mosaic law, Deut. 18:10–11, indicates that our author drew upon the stock dtr language of 'necromancy as taboo'. He also exemplified a dtr rhetorical strategy that utilized hoary antiquity, a different world, and a venerable figure of the past to insure the demise of this competing form of divination. With the insertion of the episode of the woman of Endor in 1 Sam. 28:3–25, necromancy could no longer be construed as the mere preoccupation of relatively late comers like the dtr ideologists. It was now an age old problem. Whereas the dtr circle condemned outbreaks of this form of divination as reflected in the account of Manasseh's apostasy in 2 Kgs. 21:6 (cf. 4.5.2.), the post-dtr writer established a much earlier precedent. According to the redactional hand responsible for 1 Sam. 28:3–25, Israel's first king, Saul, had violated the dtr law set forth in Deut. 18:11 (as we saw, itself inserted in a context thereby identifying it as the authoritative law of Moses) and Saul's complicity left its lasting mark on Israel's religion down to the exile and beyond (cf. 2 Kgs. 23:24 in 4.5.2.). It should be recalled that underlying the dtr ideology was the general premise that both the land and its blessings were dependent upon complete separation from foreigners and their religious practices. Viewed in this light, the legend of Saul underscores the point that in tolerating the presence of foreigners—like Israel of old in relation to the Canaanite—and by embracing their religious beliefs—like Saul in his rendezvous with the woman of Endor—the nation after the exile once again places itself in jeopardy with regard to her rights to the land and its blessings.

Several interpretative details in Saul's consultation with the Endorian 'hexter' demand further consideration. As we argued in 4.3.2., the mention of *'ôḇôṯ* and the *yiddᵊʿōnîm* (vv.3,7–9) refers neither to a class of professional mantics nor to ancestral images, but to the ghosts, "the Ones-who-return" and "the Knowers." In v.7, the witch is entitled *'ēšeṯ baʿᵃlaṯ 'ôḇ*, "a woman, controller of One-who-returns."[336] In v.8, the woman is asked to divine for Saul "by means of(?) One-who-returns." The form *bā'ôḇ* could designate either the indirect or direct object of the verbal form of *q-s-m*.[337] In any case, there is nothing in the general context that would suggest the involvement of a second necromancer or an image.

---

336 Based on the LXX *gynaika engastrimython/os*, McCarter 1980:418 conjectured that a conflation of *'ēšeṯ 'ôḇ* and *baʿᵃlaṯ 'ôḇ* has taken place, but cf. Driver 1913:215 (*'ēšeṯ* may be in the construct state in *suspenso*, cf. *GKC* #130[e]) or Stoebe 1973:485 (*'ēšeṯ* may be in the absolute state, cf. *GKC* #96).

337 Commentators usually interpret the *bet* preposition as signifying an indirect object, "divine for me by One-who-returns," but the parallel line, "bring up for me the one I shall name to you," in v.8d and the phraseology of 1 Chr. 10:13 where it is stated that Saul "consulted an *'ôḇ*," *liš'ôl bā'ôḇ*,

As we noted previously, the crucial passage in this regard is Lev. 20:27 where it is reported that a man or woman might have in them, *bāhem*, the *'ôḇ* or the *yiddᵊʻōnî*.[338] Furthermore, Isa. 29:4 locates the *'ôḇ* in the earth or dust, that is, the netherworld. This surely eliminates the necromancer and the image as serious interpretive options. While it is true that the related verbs often take inanimate things as their grammatical objects (in the case at hand, recall that both *'ôḇ* and *yiddᵊʻōnî* have been viewed as images), they can equally accommodate abstract or animate objects (or, as in the present context, their postmortem remains, cf. 4.3.2.). The verb *hēsîr* in v.3 can be translated "put aside" (e.g., matters; Josh. 11:15) or "reject" (prayer; Ps. 66:20) in addition to "drive out."[339] Similarly, *hiḵrîṯ* in v.9 can be rendered "forbid" (kindness; 1 Sam. 20:15) or "abolish" (one's name; Josh. 7:9) in addition to the more general "cut off."[340]

We now turn to the *crux interpretum* of 1 Sam. 28:3–25: the term *'ᵉlōhîm* in v.13 which is generally taken to refer to the dead Samuel. This is so in spite of the syntactic difficulties present. The witch's response to Saul's query in v.13, namely, that she saw *'ᵉlōhîm . . . ʻōlîm* "gods ascending," comprises a plural noun coupled with a plural participle. But Saul's immediate response in v.14 employs a singular pronominal suffix, "What is his/its appearance?"[341] Assuming that the *'ᵉlōhîm* of v.13 identified Samuel, Driver outlined two alternatives for the above discrepancy: (1) while the witch saw more than one figure, Saul in his anxiety inquired only about the one in whom he was interested or (2) *'ᵉlōhîm* is an honorific plural and denotes "a god,"[342] the plural *ʻōlîm* being merely a grammatical plural like *ḥayyîm* in *'ᵉlōhîm ḥayyîm*, a designation for Yahweh in 1 Sam. 17:26.[343] In the final analysis, independent data must be brought to bear in order to decide the issue.

The notion that the dead in Israel might be attributed divine status and depicted as "gods" has been recently reiterated. Evidence from Mesopotamia, Anatolia, and Syria has been cited as indicative of such a concept.[344] Often mentioned are the Akkadian *Ersatznamen*, the association of the *ilānu* with the *eṭemmū* in Akkadian texts from Assyria and Nuzi, the recently published parallel couplets

lends support to the translation of 28:8 as "augur for me One-who-returns," with the *bet* preposition governing the direct object.

338 Following Driver 1913:214.

339 The *JPS* translation rendered 1 Sam. 28:3b, "And Saul had *forbidden* [*recourse to*] ghosts and familiar spirits in the land."

340 *Contra* Hertzberg 1964:218. The *JPS* translation rendered 1 Sam. 28:9b, "You know what Saul has done, how he has *banned* [*the use of*] ghosts and familiar spirits in the land."

341 The LXX does not evince this discrepancy, for Saul's query of v.14 is phrased differently, *ti egnōs*, "What did you perceive?", on which, see below.

342 Cf. *GKC* #124^{g-i} and #132^{h}.

343 Driver 1913:215.

344 Cf. Spronk 1986:163, who also mentions Egypt; Lewis 1989:49–51,115.

involving the *ilānu* and the *mētū* in the Emar texts, the Ugaritic king list *KTU* 1.113 wherein the form *'il* is repeatedly followed by a personal royal name (i.e., "Divine So-and-So"), the *'ilm*, "gods," which parallel the *mtm*, "dead," in the Shapash fragment in the Baal-Mot myth in *KTU* 1.6.VI:45–49, the deification of the king at death in the Hittite *Totenrituale*, and the Phoenician inscription from Pyrgi wherein a buried god (cf. *qbr 'lm*) has been identified as a ghost.

While it has been repeatedly affirmed that the dead in Mesopotamia are designated by the lexeme *ilu*/*ilānu*, the cited data are sparse and highly controvertible. First, the *ilu* element in the so-called *Ersatznamen* may refer to "good fortune," "luck," or a "personal god" or a member of the pantheon, rather than to a deified ghost. In his extensive work on the *Ersatznamen*, Stamm had assumed that (1) since a god would not have been referred to as a brother, or *aḫu*, and only rarely as father, or *abu*, and (2) since a form of *ilu*, "god," often occurs in the position where one would expect to find a family designation like *aḫu* or *abu* in the construction of a personal name, then clear evidence was at hand for the deified status of that deceased family member.[345] But as Vorländer has demonstrated, among the wide range of epithets used to designate the personal god, family designations were utilized to express metaphorically that relationship.[346]

On the one hand, a name like *Ilum-ḫabil*, "the god is wronged/taken away," might refer to the abandonment of the personal god (who might have been a major deity) owing to some violation committed by a human protégé. Personal gods were known to abandon their human protégés on occasion leaving them to the mercy of the demons.[347] The offense and resultant abandonment might have been perceived as instigating some life threatening calamity during birth that marked the new born with some physical reminder such as a scar or deformity and so the newborn was given this name by the parents as a memorial. As such, it also served as an omen. On the other hand, a name like *Itūr-ilum*, "the god has returned," might refer to a similar situation, but one in which amends were speedily made allowing the personal god to exercise its protective powers and intervene on behalf of a newborn, thereby pre-empting any disaster.[348]

While the ghosts are associated on occasion with the *ilānu*, "gods," their supposed equation is another matter altogether. Often cited is the bilingual incantation text from Assyria, *CT* 17,37 "Y," 1–10: "the captive gods come forth from the grave, the *zaqīqu* come forth from the grave, for the offering of the *kispū*, for

345 Cf. Stamm 1939; for an in depth critique of Stamm's methods and assumptions, see Pitard 1993:1–20.

346 Cf. the inventory of epithets in Vorländer 1975:8–25; note pp.27–29 and our treatment of the personal god in 2.1.1.

347 Cf. Vorländer 1975:165–67.

348 Following *CAD* 7(1960):102 *contra* Lewis 1989:49–50. For a list of the names, cf. Stamm 1939:278–306.

the water libation, they come forth from the grave."[349] But the fact that the captive gods are located in the netherworld only confirms what we already knew, namely, that the Mesopotamian underworld was inhabited by sundry forms of numina. Furthermore, the *kispum* frequently comprised a gift offered to the gods of the underworld (*Totenbeigabe*) or a form of enticement to the infernal deities—particularly the Anunnaki—for protection from tormenting ghosts.[350] Most telling are the mid first millennium necromancy texts where offerings are made to various gods such as the Anunnaki, Pabilsag, Shamash and the primordial deities of the netherworld, Enmesarra, Ninmesarra, Endasurimma, Nindasurimma, Enkum, and Ninkum, for their aid in raising a ghost. In one necromantic incantation, Shamash is described as judge who brings the recently deceased from above down below, those long dead from below up above. Another text underscores this same role of Shamash in bringing up the ghost from below (for both texts, see below).

That the captive gods come up from their graves in the netherworld might be expressive of the Mesopotamian belief reflected in Enuma Elish that these gods, having been defeated in their rebellion against the established pantheon and perhaps imprisoned in their sepulchers, could nevertheless be released from the netherworld by the appropriate means whether it be the requisite incantational procedure or Marduk's decree at creation as in Enuma Elish.[351] It appears that there were many groups of such gods who comprised the defeated and slain divine enemies, not all of whom had apparently rebelled, been captured, and released at the creation of man. For example, many Asakku demons and Tammuzes show up after the death of the Asakku demon in Lugale and the death of Tammuz.[352] These slain divine enemies are given various titles: the ^{d}EN.LIL^{meš} *kišitti*, "conquered Enlils," the ^{d}UG$_5$.GA^{meš}, "dead gods," or the *abtūtu/šulputūtu*, "battered."[353] In fact, in a Seleucid period bilingual incantation, Shamash is said to be in charge of the DINGIR.UG$_5$.GA.ÀM, "dead gods" as well as "ghosts."[354]

---

[349] The Akkadian reads *ilānu ka-mu-ti iš-tu qab-rì it-ta-ṣu-ni za-qí-qu lim-nu-ti iš-tu qab-rì it-ta-ṣu-ni a-na ka-sa-ap ki-is-pi ú na-aq mé-e iš-tu qab-rì* KIMIN, cf. *CAD* 21(1961):59; most recently Tsukimoto 1985:148. *zaqīqu* has several possible renderings, e.g., "phantom," "wind," cf. *CAD* 21(1961):58–59; *AHw* 3(1981):1530a. In any case, usage reveals that the term cannot be simply equated with *eṭemmu*, "ghost of the dead."

[350] Cf. Tsukimoto 1985:140–45,184–200; Scurlock 1988:214–22.

[351] Cf. Enuma Elish IV:93–120 (esp. line 120); VI:11–34; VII:26–32 (on VII:26–27, see below).

[352] Lambert 1980:65.

[353] Cf. Enuma Elish IV:119–20; VI:151–54; Lambert 1980:65.

[354] *UVB* 15.36:9–10 in Falkenstein 1959:36–40. The Akkadian phraseology employed is *ra-bi-iṣ* DINGIR.UG$_5$.GA.ÀM *i-na qí-rib a-ra-al-li-i re-eṣ e-ṭem-mu mur-tap-pi-du šá du-ú-tú la-a paq-du*, "(Shamash) who watches over the dead gods in the netherworld, who helps the roving ghost who has no virility." On the insufficiency of parallelism alone to secure the equation of the dead gods and the deceased, see below.

It goes without saying, one cannot appeal to Enuma Elish VII:26–27 to buttress a simplistic equation of the captive gods and the ghosts.[355] The relevant lines read as follows: "Lord of the holy incantation who raises the dead to life, who has compassion on the captive gods."[356] While the captive gods are described as dead, the significance is not that the captive gods are to be equated with deceased mortals or their ghosts, for man had yet to be created. Rather, the following lines 28–29 make clear that, not only are the dead of line 26 the captive gods of line 27, but that both refer to those gods who were defeated for their rebellion against the great gods. These lines also point out that it is by the creation of man whose lot it is to relieve the captive gods of their service, that these defeated gods can be restored to their former place in the pantheon.

We turn now to the other texts cited in support of the equation of the gods and the ghosts. In the Neo-Assyrian version of the Legend of Etana, the *ilānu*, "gods," and the *eṭemmū*, "ghosts," show up as parallel members of a poetic bicolon. Contrary to widely held opinion, the parallelism alone cannot insure the equation of the *ilānu* with "the ghosts." A complementary force of the poetic parallelism might equally apply. The text reads, "I honored the gods, served the ghosts."[357] As we noted previously, the term *ilu*/*ilānu*, "god(s)," most frequently designates the gods of the pantheon and quite often the personal protective gods.[358] Thus, in the Legend of Etana, one would expect that the term *ilānu* refers to the personal gods, that is, if familial obligations are in view, if not, then to the gods of the pantheon. In other words, the text simply seeks to convey the widely held notion that the gods as well as the ghosts, two distinct groups of supra-natural beings, demand their respective service. The burden of proof is surely on those who would argue otherwise.

That the *ilānu* delineate the same group as that signified by the dead may be actually contradicted, not confirmed, by the handful of instances where the *ilānu* are mentioned alongside the *eṭemmū* at Nuzi and the *mētū* at Emar. In view of the general usage of *ilānu* outlined above and the non-poetic contexts in which these "parallel" pairs occur at Nuzi and Emar, it is most likely that some distinction was intended. We are otherwise forced to make the unwarranted assumption

---

355 Cf. e.g., Tsukimoto 1985:148 and n.490. Heidel 1963:153 and n.49 wrongly assumed that the captive gods in the incantation texts were the deceased and not the gods defeated at creation for "these were released after the creation of man."

356 The phraseology employed is *be-el šip-tu* KÙ-*tì mu-bal-liṭ mi-i-ti šá an* DINGIR.DINGIR *ka-mu-ti ir-šu-ú ta-a-a-ru*; cf. Tsukimoto 1985:148 n.490. Cf. also Pitard 1993:12 who pointed out that *mu-bal-liṭ mi-i-ti* can refer to the "one who revives those about to die."

357 The phraseology employed is *ilī ú-kab-bit e-ṭém-me ap-làḫ*; cf. Greenfield 1973:52; now Kinnier Wilson 1985:100 (lines 134–36).

358 Cf. our discussion of the use of the dingir sign in the so-called Eblaite king list in 2.1.1. and recall that the personal gods are at times identified as the gods of the pantheon, cf. van der Toorn 1985:44 where he cites TCL 18.85:25–26.

that the ancient writers in these instances were guilty of blatant redundancy. Some distinction is recognized even by those who seek to identify "gods" with "ghosts."[359]

In 3.2.1., it was noted that at Nuzi, both the *ilānu*, "gods," and the *eṭemmū*, "ghosts," are depicted as deserving of service (*palāḫu*). As in the case of the Legend of Etana, the *ilānu*, "gods," might just as conceivably refer to the family personal gods, which is what we would expect in the context of inheritance. The same can be said for the references to the *ilānu*, "gods," alongside the *mētū*, "dead," in the Emar texts in 3.2.2. In the genre of testament at Emar, the gods and the dead are "honored" (*kunnû*) and "called upon" (*nabû* A).[360] Again, the explicit mention of the gods together with the dead in a non-poetic context lends credence to the view that the former designate a group of supra-natural beings distinct from the dead. Within the context of inheritance, we would expect the *ilānu* to represent the family or personal gods.

In 3.1.6., we argued that the phrase *'il* + RN in the Ugaritic king list *KTU* 1.113 (= dingir + RN of the Eblaite king list in 2.1.1.) refers to a deceased king's personal god to whom ritual is directed.[361] Moreover, we argued in 3.1.7. that the terms *'ilm*, "gods," over against *mtm*, "the dead" or, better yet, "men," in the closing section of the Baal-Mot myth, *KTU* 1.6:VI:45ff., serve as antithetical rather than as synonymous elements. The above survey undermines the view that the dead in general or the deceased royalty in early Syria-Palestine attained the status of "gods." Even the oft-cited couplet *ilānu*//*eṭemmū* or *mētū* has been found to contain complementary elements, not synonymous ones.[362]

So again, who is the referent(s) behind the term *'ᵉlōhîm* in 1 Sam. 28:13? In an attempt to maintain some distinction between the high gods, and other "gods" such as the dead, Lewis has suggested that the term when applied to the deceased simply points to some type of transcendent character obtained at death. This character had in some way a lesser significance than that of the high gods, for the dead were not worshipped in the same way as the high gods. Accordingly, the term *'ᵉlōhîm* in

---

359 Tsukimoto 1985:104–05; Rouillard and Tropper 1987a:354–56 recognized the redundancy of merely equating these terms at Nuzi. Nevertheless, their commitment to relating the two resulted in the delineation between the *eṭemmū* as the recent identifiable ancestors and the *ilānu* as the remote unidentifiable ancestors.

360 Or, perhaps, "lamented" (*nabû* B). Even so, this alternative alone can not secure the status of *ilānu* as ghosts.

361 Our conclusions regarding the non-deified status of dead kings at Ugarit nevertheless conforms with the sacral nature of the Ugaritic royal ideology more generally.

362 Pitard 1993:14 noted the exceptional construction ᵈGIDIM (three occurrences) and rightly deemed it an idiosyncratic anomaly or possibly a Hittite conception which made its way into Sumero-Akkadian texts. Van der Toorn 1993:1–27 points out that such a construction occurs only in Akkadian texts written in Anatolia.

v.13 refers to the dead Samuel and should be translated as "preternatural being."[363] Our previous analysis renders questionable the assumption that the dead in Syria-Palestine obtained the status of "god" in any sense of the term. This in turn makes ineffectual any attempt to interpret *'ᵉlōhîm* in 1 Sam. 28:13 as the ghost of the deceased Samuel. Besides, if the deified status of a ghost provided the underlying conceptual background for this passage, then why was the singular form of *'ôḇôṯ* or *yiddᵊ'ōnîm* or *mēṯîm* or *'iṭṭîm* not used? These are the only "technical" terms for ghosts who participate in necromancy mentioned otherwise in the account or in the dtr traditions more generally. In other words, assuming that the dead were to be equated with the gods, the woman's identification of the ghost by the use of the term *'ᵉlōhîm* would be for her and Saul superfluous.[364]

There is a more suitable interpretation of the phrase *'ᵉlōhîm . . . 'ōlîm*, one that has its reflex in the necromantic texts from first millennium Mesopotamia. But before those texts are taken up, the history of necromancy in Mesopotamia will be reviewed. Evidence for necromancy in earlier periods of Mesopotamia has been identified in lines 238–43 of Enkidu and the Netherworld, in lines 4–7 of an Old Assyrian letter from Kültepe (*TC*[= TCL 4] 1,5) and in the lexical entry *mušēlû eṭemmi* (= lú-balag-gá, "a *balangu* singer/player") attested in second millennium lú professions lists.[365] But as for *mušēlû eṭemmi*, the *š* causative of *elû* might signify "to remove" in which case the *mušēlû eṭemmi* would be an exorcist, not a necromancer.[366] The same applies in the case of the phrase *šūlû ša eṭemmi* = bur_2. The term bur_2 is most often listed with Akkadian *pašāru* "to loosen, to free." So the question arises, is the meaning "to loosen a ghost (from its victim)" or "to free a ghost (from the netherworld)"?[367] The references in Gilgamesh and Kültepe are likewise controvertible. The first is a mythical context perhaps depicting an exceptional phenomenon not a known mantic practice. In any case, Enkidu is not explicitly identified as a ghost, or *eṭemmu*, but as šubur-a-ni, "servant," or *utukku*, "demon," in the Akkadian. The nineteenth century B.C.E. Kültepe text might be the strongest evidence for contact with a ghost in earlier periods. It is a letter written to a wealthy trader, Imdi-ilum, living in the Assyrian colony at Kanesh in central Anatolia. It is written by his wife, Šīmat-Aššur, and his sister, Tarām-Kūbī, both living in the city of Ashur. The two women had inquired of (*sâlū*) the women who interpret oracles (*šā'ilātum*), the women who interpret omens from entrails (*bariātum*), and the ghosts (*eṭemmū*), and on that basis warned Imdi-ilum that his

363 Lewis 1989:50,106,115–16. For "preternatural" as a translation of *'ᵉlōhîm* in 28:13, cf. also *NAB*. The English derives from the Latin *praeter naturam*, "beyond nature."

364 Our conclusions regarding Hebrew *'ᵉlōhîm* nullify the proposal of Niehr 1991:301–06 that 2 Sam. 12:16a preserves a reference to necromancy.

365 Cf. Finkel 1983–84:1–2; Tropper 1989:47–76.

366 Cf. *CAD* 4 (1958):134 #11c.

367 On bur_2, cf. Sjöberg 1984:195.

love for money had put his life at risk and so he should return immediately to Ashur to rectify matters.[368] The context makes clear neither the means nor ends of that inquiry. Whether or not Imdi-ilum had suffered adversity of recent, the stimulus for inquiry might approximate that found in the Egyptian letters to the dead where the dead are depicted as causing calamity among the living. Thus, inquiring of the ghosts would have provided the means to ascertaining whether or not a ghost had been offended. This is not necromancy as defined in chapter 1 and illustrated in a text like 1 Sam. 28:3–25. Moreover, the benevolence of the dead is nowhere in view. In any case, necromancy, per se, is attested in Mesopotamia only by the mid first millennium.

In several Neo-Assyrian and later texts recently published by Finkel and von Weiher, and re-edited by Scurlock, various deities including Shamash and the primordial deities of the netherworld are called upon in order to insure the appearance of the ghost.[369] In one such incantation, Shamash is depicted as follows: "Shamash, O' Judge, you bring those from above down below, those from below up above."[370] In another text, Shamash's central role in bringing up the ghost from below is likewise underscored:[371]

> [1][. . . [2] . . .] dust of the netherworld [. . .]. [3]May he (Shamash) bring up a ghost from the darkness for me! May he (put life back) into the dead man's limbs. [4]I call (upon you), O skull of skulls: [5]May he who

---

368 Cf. Larsen 1982:214–45; Tropper 1989:68–76.

369 For references, cf. Finkel 1983–84:1–17; von Weiher 1983:100–03; Scurlock 1988:5–8,103–12,318–42. On the role of the gods in Mesopotamian necromancy, cf. esp. Scurlock 1988:106–10 and note pp.79–81 where she lists the numerous epithets of Shamash as judge of, lord over, and retriever of the dead.

370 Cf. Finkel 1983–84:11; Scurlock 1988:327–28 [K 2779:13b–14a]: [d]UTU DI.KU_5 *ša e-la-a-ti ana šap-la-a-ti ša šap-la-a-ti ana e-la-a-ti túb-bal*. The verb *abālu* with the ventive can signify "to bring," rather than "to carry," cf. *CAD* 1(1964):14. Finkel 1983–84:7 noted that while this text belongs to the namburbi genre, it clearly contradicts the *raison d'etre* of averting evil, for here a ghost is willfully induced. As part of a manual listing the proper steps of undertaking the safe conjuration of a ghost, the namburbi procedures perhaps functioned as (1) the essential preliminary rites for manipulating the disposition of the ghost as well as (2) the rites crucial for averting any danger that subsequently resulted from contact with the ghost.

371 Cf. Finkel 1983–84:5,9; Scurlock 1988:322–23 (BM 36703:obv.ii:1–6): [1][. . . [2] . . .] ga še SAḪAR *qá-qá-r*[. . .][3] GIDIM *e-ṭu-ti li-š*[*e-l*]*a-an-ni* UZU.SA UG_7 *l*[*i-bal-liṭ-an-ni*] [4]*gul-gul gul-gul-la-at a-ša-as*-[*si-ka/ki*] [5]*ša* ŠÀ *gul-gul-la-ta li-pula*-[*an-ni*] [6]UTU *pe-tu-ú ek-le-t*[*i* (ÉN)]. Scurlock 1988:323 preferred to see here dust and tendons performing the retrieval, but the reference to Shamash as "opener of the darkness" in line 6 (the very "darkness" from which the ghost is specifically retrieved in line 3), the similar description of the solar deity as retriever of ghosts in the necromantic context of the previously mentioned text, and the numerous references to the role of the solar deity as judge of, lord over, and retriever of the dead cited by Scurlock on pp.79–81 clearly favor Shamash here. Besides, the problems of placement that Scurlock identified may be only apparent in view of the damaged state of the first two lines in the pertinent portion of the text.

is within the skull answer [me!] [6]O Shamash, who opens the darkne[ss. Incantation:].

In ancient Greece, the gods likewise participated in necromantic ritual by retrieving the dead. In fact, in one Greek magical papyrus, the sun god, Helios, is requested to send a ghost up during his cyclical journey so that the ghost might reveal some hidden knowledge to the living.[372] In view of the likelihood that the Syro-Palestinian and Mesopotamian dead were not equated with the gods, that the gods were active participants in the Mesopotamian necromancy rituals, and that the text of 1 Sam. 28:13 manifests a complex textual history, then the *'elōhîm* of v.13 might represent not the deified dead, but those gods known to be summoned—some from the netherworld—to assist in the retrieval of the ghost.[373] In support of this interpretation are the following additional factors.

In spite of the fact that the MT plural noun *'elōhîm* of v.13 is followed by a plural participle *'ōlîm*, a search for the antecedent to the singular pronominal suffix on *mah-to'orô* in v.14, "what does he/it look like?" has led interpreters to view the *'elōhîm . . . 'ōlîm* as a designation for the dead Samuel, "a god ascending." The same term *'elōhîm* shows up in v.15, but there it is followed by a singular finite verbal form of *sār* and given a singular force *'elōhîm sār mē'ālāy*, "(the) god (= Yahweh) has turned away from me." In Exod. 32:1, *'elōhîm* occurs with a plural finite verb and denotes multiple gods in this instance: *'elōhîm 'ašer yēlᵊḵû lᵊp̄ānênû*, "the gods who will go before us." Thus, the two occurrences of *'elōhîm* in 1 Sam 28:13,15—the first complimented by a plural verbal form, the other by a singular verbal form—might preserve a semantic as well as a morpho-syntactic distinction in number. In the first instance, v.13, more than one god is in view, in the second case, v.15, a single god is designated.

This offers a clue to resolving the apparent discrepancy involving a singular suffix on *to'orô* in v.14 and its supposed plural antecedent, *'elōhîm*, in v.13. Simply put, the antecedent for *to'orô*'s singular suffix is not v.13's "gods," or *'elōhîm*, but Samuel's ghost first alluded to in vv.11,12. The narrative plot develops as follows. Owing to the woman's newly acquired ability to identify Saul in v.12, Saul senses the presence of Samuel's ghost. He, therefore, urgently requests verification of Samuel's identity, *mah-to'orô*, "what does he/it look like?" The

---

372 Cf. *PGM* IV.1928–2005 (lines 1967–70) in Betz 1992:72–73. For the participation of the gods more generally, cf. e.g., Morrison 1981:87–114, esp. pp.88–91. I am indebted to Tim LaVallee for these references.

373 Hutter 1983:32–36 similarly concluded that "gods coming out of the earth" did not refer to Samuel's supernatural character, but simply affirmed the success of the necromantic process. However, he wrongly arrived at this *via* the Hittite incantations in which the underworld gods were summoned up from the "pit" and through the conjecture that necromancy was associated with such alien gods at Endor, cf. Josh. 17:11–13, and that Endor had an originally Hurrian name *enna durenna*.

same concern for the immediate disclosure of the identity of the ghost is reflected in the Mesopotamian necromantic incantations, for the wrong ghost could mean the wrong outcome! As described, the scene presupposes that Saul, although present, did not have direct access to the woman's vision. This finds confirmation in the fact that in the first millennium Mesopotamian necromancy incantations, only the one who performed the procedures involving recitations and the smearing of preparations on the face could see the ghost.[374]

The LXX might preserve a somewhat similar resolution to this exegetical conundrum. For the question posed in v.14, the LXX reads *ti egnōs* "what have you perceived?" Its underlying Hebrew *Vorlage* possibly read *mh t'rt*, "what did you make out" from Hebrew *t-'-r*, "to regard intently" (Qal) or "to form (a shape)" (Piel).[375] In other words, in the Greek tradition, the need to identify an antecedent in v.13 for the question posed in v.14 simply does not arise.[376] The LXX at 1 Sam. 28:13–14 merely records the outcome of the necromancer's successful appeal to the netherworld gods who, it was assumed, had brought up with them Samuel's ghost. Because Saul would not have had direct or immediate access to the witch's vision, he requested that she detail her experience (vv.13–14a):

> (11) At that, the woman said, "Whom shall I bring up for you?" He answered, "Bring up Samuel for me." (12) When the woman saw Samuel, she shrieked loudly, and the woman said to Saul, "Why have you deceived me? You are Saul!" (13) The king said to her, "Do not be afraid, what do you see?" And the woman said to Saul, "I see (chthonic) gods coming up from the earth." (14) Then he said to her, "(Now) what have you perceived (cf. LXX)?" And she said to him, "An old/upright[377] man coming up from the earth and he is wrapped in a robe."

---

[374] Cf. Finkel 1983–84:5,10; Scurlock 1988:324–26,337–42. The Mesopotamian necromancy texts describe how magic ointments must be smeared on the necromancer's face in order to make the spirit of the dead visible. This procedure gave access solely to the necromancer. One text states that "one must rub (ointment) on one's face and then one is able to look at the ghost and he will speak," cf. Finkel 1983–84:10.

[375] Perhaps a scribe misread the form as a noun from *r-'-h* and replaced the final *-t* with *-w* as in MT, the difference being one, possibly two, strokes. McCarter 1980:419 preferred the LXX and proposed *mh yd't* as its Hebrew *Vorlage*. Lewis 1989:109 favored the MT and offered *mh tr'y* (< *r-'-h*). Both presumed the equation of god and ghost.

[376] Moreover, the criterion of *lectio difficilior* is not a priori to be preferred, cf. now Tov 1992:302–05.

[377] Whether Samuel appeared in v.14 as "an old man" (MT), "an erect man" (LXX), or, perhaps, "a startling man," following Lewis 1989:116, is difficult to decide. If the narrator intended to convey the idea that Samuel had died in *old* age in 25:1, then congruence would favor that characteristic as the means of verification for the arrival of Samuel's ghost that Saul sought in 28:14 "What is his/its appearance?" The woman answered "an old man coming up. . . . "

The immediate narrative context in both of the preceding scenarios leaves the gods unidentified. These we have argued are the chthonic gods, but can we distinguish any of those gods more specifically? The Late Mesopotamian necromancy texts might offer a clue to the identity of at least one of those gods. These texts preserve several mechanical procedures that might be involved in performing a necromantic rite such as (1) offerings of food for the gods on altars or scattered on the ground, (2) offerings of jars with drink and libations of beer and wine, and (3) the participation of only one individual.[378] The central rite involved the preparation of magic salves which might be smeared either on the necromancer's face, on the figurine of the ghost, or on the skull which housed the ghost. Incantations were recited three or seven times over the ointment before its use. The salves took time to prepare and were required to stand overnight. The practitioner waited until morning for a response from the ghost. Only then was the dead consulted by applying the salve to the face, or to a figurine of the dead, or to a skull.[379] In one instance, it is stated that the salve is applied to the face *ana* IGI ^{d}UTU, "before Shamash."[380] In the light of the overnight preparations repeatedly mentioned in these texts and in view of Shamash's central role in necromancy, the procedural setting underlying 1 Sam. 28:3–25 would have entailed Saul's nocturnal arrival, the woman's preparations through the course of night, and her conjuration of the ghost in the morning at the rising of the sun god.[381] 1 Sam. 28:20 records as a temporal reference to the events described in the preceding verses that Saul "had not eaten all day or all night." If the version of necromancy reflected in 1 Sam. 28:3–25 is late and Mesopotamian in origin as we have argued above, then not only is the solar deity's presence alluded to, but Shamash imagery might have significantly informed the narrative. This certainly conforms with the knowledge of the Mesopotamian sun cult reflected elsewhere in dtr traditions (cf. e.g., 2 Kgs. 23:11 below in 4.5.2.).[382]

In conclusion, the late compositional setting of 1 Sam. 28:3–25, the explicit associations with Mesopotamian divination and necromancy, and the absence of necromancy in contemporary Syro-Palestinian, Anatolian, and Egyptian religions otherwise, point to the late eastern provenance of not only this text, but also its

---

378 In K 2779, where necromancy is set in the context of a namburbi ritual, *kispu* offerings were made in order to insure against the possibility that the ghost has been offended.

379 Cf. Finkel 1983–84:9; Scurlock 1988:104 and n.483.

380 Cf. Finkel 1983–84:8; Scurlock 1988:318–19.

381 Our interpretation also dispels the view that Saul's night visitation (v.8) was the appropriate time for consulting the dead, cf. e.g., Spronk 1986:168; Lewis 1989:114 following Hoffner 1967:393 who had noted the nocturnal rituals for the Greek *chthonioi*.

382 Had Yahweh taken over several of the characteristics of the solar deity as scholars have argued (whether one has in mind a Mesopotamian or a local version), any mortuary roles that might have been related to the solar deity would have been polemicized against in the dtr ideology.

tradition and the corresponding Israelite belief in the supernatural beneficent power of the dead. As to the rationale underlying the prohibition against necromancy, we will defer our speculative reconstructions to the conclusion of our study.

4.5.2. 2 Kings 21:6 and 23:24

The Late Mesopotamian Context for Israel's Belief in the Beneficent Dead

With this section we come to the two lone references to necromancy at the dtr level of the DtrH, 2 Kgs. 21:6 and 23:24.[383] Not only is the consultation of the *'ôḇ(ôṯ)* and *yiddᵊʿōnî(m)* listed among the "detestable practices" that the writer attributes to king Manasseh (2 Kgs. 21:6), it is also enumerated among those obliterated in what has been stylized as the subsequent Josianic "reform" (2 Kgs. 23:24).[384] While the Manasseh reference in 2 Kgs. 21:6 also occurs in the Chronistic History (i.e., 1 and 2 Chronicles hereafter ChrH) at 2 Chr. 33:6, the reference to necromancy in Josiah's reform (2 Kgs. 23:24–27) has no parallel in the Chronicler's account. It is mentioned, however, in the LXX of 2 Kgs. 23:24 (IV Reigns) and in the LXX of 2 Chr. 35:19 (= II Paralipomena). It may also appear in summary fashion in the paraphrase of 1 Esdr. 1:21–22.[385] The latter three probably reflect the same tradition or Hebrew *Vorlage*.

These factors suggest that either the Chronicler omitted the tradition associating the proscription of necromancy with Josiah or that it is not original to his *Vorlage* (cf. MT 2 Chr. 35:19+20 = MT 2 Kgs. 23:23+28). In any case, necromancy's absence in the Chronicler's account of Josiah conforms with his rendition of Manasseh in 2 Chr. 33:1–20 more generally.[386] In vv.10–20, the Chronicler recounts a story unparalleled in the MT or LXX of 2 Kings or 2 Chronicles

[383] Recall that 1 Sam. 28:3–25 is a post-dtr insertion. Its parallel, 1 Chr. 10:13, might be a later addition to Chronicles, so Ackroyd 1977:8; Braun 1986:151; but cf. Williamson 1982:95; de Vries 1989:121,397.

[384] As Ahlström 1982:68–81; 1993:735 has argued, Manasseh's "syncretism" of Canaanite religion was probably the creation of the dtr ideology. He was likely the traditionalist and the so-called reformers, Hezekiah and Josiah, the innovators.

[385] That 1 Esdr. 1:21–22 does not preserve an earlier text of Chronicles is suggested by its lack of mention of Manasseh, cf. Williamson 1977:16–20.

[386] On the lack of parallel to 2 Kgs. 23:24 in MT 2 Chr. 35:19–20 (= 2 Kgs. 23:23+28) and the relevance of LXX 2 Chr. 35:19 (= 2 Kgs. 23:24–27), and 1 Esdr. 1:21–22, cf. Williamson 1977:16–20; McKenzie 1984:160 and n.4,190–91; Dillard 1987:285–86; de Vries 1989:407. Williamson 1987b:112–13 has argued that the Chronicler's treatment of Manasseh in 2 Chronicles 33 is his own composition replete with his own theology and style (e.g., exile and restoration, retribution theology). It conflicts with the Kings account and Jer. 15:4 and even 33:22a. Williamson 1982:242–48; 1987a:9–

depicting Manasseh's captivity, repentance, and restoration. In fact, v.15 records how he rid the land of the "foreign gods" which he had previously introduced. As the Mesopotamian texts treated in 4.5.1. and 1 Sam. 28:13 illustrate, necromantic rites entailed the invocation of the gods to assist in the conjuration of the ghosts.[387] Therefore, for the writer of the ChrH (MT), Manasseh's policy to purge the foreign gods might have included a ban on necromancy as well. These factors explain why the Chronicler omitted any reference to necromancy elsewhere in his version of the Josianic reform. Manasseh had eventually taken care of the problem himself. This also conforms with his reconstruction of the life of king Manasseh in which his longevity and success were interpreted as the outgrowth of his repentance and reform.

But what relation do the two necromancy references in the DtrH have to the other biblical texts treated thus far? If, as we have argued, Deut. 18:10–11 and 1 Sam. 28:3–25 are post-dtr additions, its lack of mention in the apostasy and reform accounts of Manasseh's predecessors creates the impression that, from the perspective of the historians of the DtrH and ChrH, Israel had not embraced (Mesopotamian) necromancy prior to Manasseh's reign. But as we noted earlier, such a scenario conflicts with the impression created by Isa. 8:19 and 29:4 (cf. 4.2. and 4.3.2.-4.). In Isa. 8:19, necromancy is condemned in a context set some forty years prior to the reign of Manasseh during Ahaz's reign (perhaps on the eve of the Syro-Ephraimite war in 735 B.C.E.). But in the narrative worlds depicted in the DtrH and ChrH, necromancy goes unmentioned in the apostasy accounts of Ahaz (2 Kgs. 16:1–4,10–18//2 Chr. 28:1–4,21–25) and, for that matter, in the apostasy account of his northern contemporary, king Hoshea (2 Kgs. 17:7–23). It is also missing from the list of religious practices introduced by the foreigners from more easterly regions who had been deported and resettled in Samaria/Samerina by the Assyrians (2 Kgs. 17:24–41).[388] A similar discrepancy arises when Isa. 29:4 and the DtrH are compared. The oracle beginning with 29:1 is situated on the eve of Assyria's siege of Hezekiah's Jerusalem (701 B.C.E.). We have argued that the writer employs an ironic polemic against Judah's adoption of Assyrian necromancy. Thus, Assyria stands as the stimulus for Israel's illicit flirtation with necromancy *as well as* the bearer of her judgment. In the DtrH

15 has also argued that the Chronicler's account of Josiah's death, 2 Chr. 35:20–27, was probably drawn from an alternative version of the DtrH.

387 It should be noted as well that the subsequent apostasy of Amon in the ChrH only contributed to the partial perpetuation of that of Manasseh. Amon worshipped and sacrificed to the idols (*happᵊsîlîm*; 2 Chr. 33:22) or image(s?) (*hassemel*; 33:15b) that Manasseh had made (which we take to be the wrong images of Yahweh). However, he did not reinstate the "foreign gods" (*ʾᵉlōhê hannēḵār*) which Manasseh had purged (33:15a).

388 On the Chronicler's omission of the fall of the northern kingdom in 2 Kings 17, cf. Williamson 1977:117; McKenzie 1984:87,113; on its reapplication in 1 Chr. 5:25–26, cf. Williamson 1982:67,343–44; Braun 1986:75,78.

and the ChrH, however, the contemporary reform of Hezekiah lacks any mention of necromancy in Judah (2 Kgs. 18:3–6//2 Chr. 29:3–31:21).[389] When both the first Isaiah passages and the DtrH are read from a strictly historical point of view, necromancy's omission in the DtrH and ChrH accounts of earlier Judean kings creates a blatant discrepancy. Whereas the DtrH locates necromancy's introduction in the reign of Manasseh, Isa. 8:19 and 29:4 depict necromancy as widespread in Judah during the earlier reigns of Ahaz and Hezekiah.

Given our analyses thus far, the issue of necromancy's arrival on late pre-exilic Judean soil raises a prior question, namely, whether or not we should expect that the cults of eighth and seventh century Israel and Judah would have been influenced by Mesopotamian ritual and belief. If other Israelite or Judahite practices had Mesopotamian origins, then the likelihood increases that Israelite (or Judahite) adherence to necromancy and to death and ancestor cults—assuming that these rites existed—in the last days of Judah was stimulated by contact with Mesopotamia. In what follows, indications of such a stimulus will be evaluated with a view to assessing the resultant impact on our proposal. Of particular relevance are the foreign religious influences that scholars have extracted from the biblical depictions of the cult of king Ahaz, Manasseh's grandfather. According to 2 Kgs. 16:10–18, Ahaz's altar was built in the Jerusalem temple and modeled after an altar he saw while in the city of Damascus at which time he had sought an audience with the Assyrian king. Earlier scholarship interpreted the altar as an adaptation of an Assyrian prototype and therefore evidence for the introduction of Assyrian religion into Judah.[390] Some critics went so far as to conclude that in accordance with the presumed routine Assyrian policy of imposing the official Assyrian cult upon vassals, Ahaz was forced to adopt not only this altar, but the official Assyrian cult as well.[391]

---

[389] On the accounts of Hezekiah's reform in the DtrH and the ChrH, cf. Williamson 1977:119–25; 1982:350–78; McKenzie 1984:161–62,171–73; Dillard 1987:227–51. On the chronological and ideological relations of the reform and the revolt which resulted in Sennacherib's invasion and the relevance of 2 Chr. 29:3, cf. Williamson 1982:352; Cogan and Tadmor 1988:219–20. The general consensus is that the reform preceded the revolt. Nevertheless, Hoffmann 1980:151–55 deemed 2 Kgs. 18:1–6 a literary fiction and Donner 1986:332 viewed it as unreliable. Würthwein 1984:411–12 saw the account as a late recasting, but reflective of Hezekiah's removal of an Assyrian serpent symbol from the temple.

[390] For a listing of the elements in the cult of Ahaz that have been identified as Assyrian, cf. the surveys of McKay 1973:1–19; Cogan 1974:1–7,65–115; Spieckermann 1982:318–22,362–69; Holloway 1992:447–56; Cogan 1993:403–14, esp. p.409 and n.27.

[391] The late nineteenth century works of George Rawlinson set the stage for subsequent elaborations of the view that Assyria imposed its religion upon its vassals. According to Östreicher 1923:38; Olmstead 1931:452, local cults were eradicated in instances of Assyrian imposition; cf. the surveys of McKay 1973:1–4; Cogan 1974:1–7. Nicholson 1967:9–17 has outlined the implications of this theory for the role of the law book in Josiah's reform.

However, the monographs by McKay and Cogan, both published in the mid 1970's, challenged the notion that Assyria made it a policy to impose its official cult upon its subject nations.[392] According to these writers, the Assyrians never made it a regular policy to do so, at least not in the case of a vassal state such as Ahaz's.[393] McKay and Cogan concluded that the religion of the Judahite kings corresponds more closely to the regional Syro-Palestinian religions. The altar of Ahaz and the religious practices introduced by Manasseh, but rejected by Josiah, were Aramean and Canaanite in character, not Assyrian.[394] Nevertheless, while McKay and Cogan were willing to recognize neither the routine policy of Assyrian imposition, nor its causal role in creating the anti-reform and reform measures of the Judean kings, nor the special status of Mesopotamian gods in the Judean cult, they did acknowledge the likelihood that Mesopotamian religious influence found its way into the Judean cultural milieu of the eighth to seventh centuries B.C.E.[395]

In a 1982 monograph, Spieckermann defended the Assyrian imposition theory.[396] In order to set the theory on a more firm foundation, Spieckermann first offered an extensive study of late Assyrian religion which formed the basis for his identification of Assyrian religious elements in foreign contexts. As to the character of late Assyrian religion, he argued that with the loss of political strength, the royalty became increasingly fascinated with divination. Various oracular techniques involving the exclusive consultation of Shamash, the use of a horse in one such oracular rite, astronomical observations, omina (extispicy), hemerologies, menologies, apotropaic prayers, *namburbi* rituals, the substitute king ritual, and ecstatic prophecy all grew in prominence in the court of the Sargonid kings.

Spieckermann then asserted that the Assyrian kings did, indeed, routinely impose the royal cult not only upon provincial states but also upon vassals and others whom they conquered. Included in this policy of imposition were several of the above mentioned religious elements. Spieckermann also outlined the con-

392 McKay 1973; Cogan 1974.

393 Cogan 1974:65, while allowing for the occasional imposition of the Assyrian cult on provincial states, labeled Judah a vassal state throughout the Assyrian domination of Syria-Palestine (740–640 B.C.E.), but see below.

394 McKay 1973:25–27 assumed the normative nature of dtr Yahwism and accepted the judgment of apostasy against Manasseh made by the dtr tradition.

395 Cf. McKay 1973:15,18–19,69; Cogan 1974:93–95. Cogan envisioned such influence as realized through the mediation of Aramaic acculturation, cf. now Cogan 1993:412–13.

396 Spieckermann 1982. Prior to the response by Holloway 1992, Spieckermann's work had been largely neglected in the English speaking world, cf. e.g., the recent commentaries on 2 Kings by Jones 1984; Hobbs 1985; Cogan and Tadmor 1988; on 2 Chronicles by Dillard 1987. All of these follow McKay and Cogan. The first, second, and fourth engage Spieckermann only superficially while the third shows no explicit knowledge of his work. Of the recent German commentaries, Würthwein 1984:380–82,391,456–59 endorsed Spieckermann's general thesis, while Hentschel 1985 made no mention of him. Donner 1986:329–38; Lohfink 1987:467–68 have embraced the major outlines of his work.

comitant Assyrian practices of establishing garrisons in conquered regions, mass deportation, installation of *qēpu*-officials or "advisers" loyal to the Assyrians in foreign courts, and various forms of economic sanctions such as annual tribute, or *ma(d)dattu/mandattu*, display gifts, or *nāmurtu/tāmartu*, lucrative trade control, military levy, and corvée. He concluded that little distinction was made between provinces and vassaldoms in the application of these military and administrative intrusive policies.[397]

Spieckermann next examined primary sources indicative of the Assyrian intervention in the local cults of both provinces and vassal states.[398] The annals of Tiglathpileser III describe how he campaigned in Palestine in 734 and conquered (among others) the Philistine city-state of Gaza. According to Spieckermann, Gaza was never incorporated into the provincial state, it remained a vassal-state, for the southernmost province established by Tiglathpileser was Du'ru/Dor (north of Ashdod). According to Spieckermann, the gods of king Hanun of Gaza were taken as booty and the images of Assyrian gods and the royal statue were placed in the palace at Gaza.[399]

Likewise, the region of the Sealands was a provincial state and Sargon exacted regular annual tribute from the Hindaru tribe for the support of the cults of the Babylonian Bēl and Nabû.[400] In a banquet depiction prepared by Sargon during his eighth campaign in honor of his Mannaean vassal Ullusunu, the images(?) of Ashur and the Mannaean gods are represented.[401] In Esarhaddon's vassal treaties, the vassal was required to fear Ashur, his god, and to guard the images of Ashur, the king, the crown prince as well as their seals accompanying the treaty tablets.[402] In his second Egyptian campaign, Esarhaddon appointed officials over his new territories and established regular offerings for Ashur.[403] For their rebellion,

---

397 Spieckermann 1982:307–22.

398 Spieckermann 1982:246–301. That Assyrian religion generally impacted first millennium Syria-Palestine is confirmed by the undecorated limestone altars from Beer Sheba, cf. Ahlström 1993:726–27, and the epigraphic discoveries at Hamath, cf. Spieckermann 1982:293–94; Holloway 1992:242–47. Hamath was a vassal state under Tiglathpileser and a province under Sargon II. The twenty or so cuneiform texts found in the temple, or *Bâtiment* III of Stratum E (= the period 900–720 B.C.E.), include medical rituals, a hymn, an omen from the series *Šumma izbu*, magical texts, an exorcism text against sorcery, epistolary texts, and a lone *namburbi* against the evil of a snake. Owing to a reference to the city Anah of Suhi in one of the letters and the similarity in script and grammar it shares with the *namburbi*, scholars have dated both to 840–38 B.C.E. While *Bâtiment* III was probably dedicated to some Semitic deity or pantheon, for the chief goddess of Hamath during the ninth century was *Pahalatis*, Semitic *ba'alat*, the cuneiform texts indicate that under Assyrian stimulus, Mesopotamian divination was practiced alongside the local religion.

399 Spieckermann 1982:325–28.

400 Spieckermann 1982:330–31.

401 Spieckermann 1982:331–32.

402 Spieckermann 1982:333–38.

403 Spieckermann 1982:338–39.

Ashurbanipal punished the Arameans of the Sealands by appointing officials over them, demanding of them regular offerings to Ashur, Mulishu (a non-Babylonian god), and the great gods of Assyria, and by exacting tax and tribute.[404] Spieckermann paid particular attention to two data crucial to his thesis, Esarhaddon's Nahr el-Kelb and Zinjirli inscriptions. The first documents the seizure of the deities of Taharqa (690–644 B.C.E.) as booty during the 671 campaign against Memphis while the second, which recounts the events of the same expedition, states that regular offerings for the god Ashur were imposed on the Egyptians.[405] In another instance, after having an inscription describing the might of Ashur and his own name etched on Arabian divine statues, captured some twelve years earlier by Sennacherib, Esarhaddon released them to the penitent Arabian king Hazael. The statues served thereafter to focus attention in the local cult on the Assyrian god. The author pointed out that the territory of the Arabs never obtained the status of province, rather it remained a vassal state.[406]

For Spieckermann, the evidence establishes the lack of distinction between provinces and vassals in the matter of Assyrian cultic interference. In addition to their political and economic obligations, reverence for the gods of Assyria was demanded of both.[407] The Assyrians not only deported local national gods, but also introduced the worship of Ashur. On the basis of these examples and on the silence of the Assyrian royal annals, the author proposed that such acts reflected a routine Assyrian policy.[408] As to the question of Assyrian policy in Judah, he noted that many of the above mentioned practices have points of contact with religious observances in Judah prior to the reign of Manasseh. Spieckermann concluded that Assyria began to impose its official religion on Judah prior to Manasseh's reign and that Judah held the status of vassal as early as Ahaz's day.[409]

While he has set forth a strong case for the view that the Assyrians did in fact impose their religion upon vassal states as well as the provinces, on two important

404 Spieckermann 1982:340–43.

405 Spieckermann 1982:351–52.

406 Spieckermann 1982:355–57. Cogan 1974:35–37 minimized the importance of the Assyrian inscriptions on these statues. However, it is clear that this practice stands as an example of Assyrian cultic intervention in the case of a vassal. Therefore, not only does it severely undermine Cogan's explanation that Assyrian kings returned statues simply as a gesture of good will and that from the vassal's perspective the statue retained only historical and sentimental value (pp.30–34), but it contradicts his general thesis as well.

407 Spieckermann 1982:369–71.

408 Spieckermann 1982:351–52. Nevertheless, Tiglathpileser only imposed his gods on Gaza, mention of his taking the local gods as booty is never made. In view of the archaeological record which suggests that Iron Age religion in Palestine, whether one has in view Israel, Judah, or some other national entity, comprised a cult of many gods until after the exile, cf. Weippert 1988:620–31, it is better to view these practices not as strict policy.

409 Cf. Spieckermann 1982:362–69 on 2 Kgs. 16:10–16, Ahaz's altar, and in general, pp.307–72 *contra* McKay 1973:4,60–66 and Cogan 1974:42–61.

points issue must be taken with Spieckermann's thesis. First, his reliance upon the redaction-critical methods of Veijola, Smend, and Dietrich enables him to dismiss too easily, elements in the biblical reform accounts that do not readily lend themselves to a Mesopotamian interpretation.[410] The Göttingen approach employed by Spieckermann identifies as many as five extensive dtr and related levels in the DtrH. However, it has recently undergone a thorough critique.[411] Second, his evidence for the imposition of Assyrian religion in Judah is, at best, conjectural. In a recent work that augments Spieckermann's survey of late Assyrian religion, Holloway adds on a qualifier to his thesis: while Assyria might have imposed its cult on provinces, vassals, and other subjugated peoples, this was not a consistent policy of the empire. It was dictated by specific extenuating circumstances.[412]

The fact that a tradition like Ahaz's altar in 2 Kgs. 16:10–16 has perennially posed an enigma for would-be interpreters is indicative of the problems that surface over the question of Assyrian imposition in Judah, so much so, that several commentators have outlined detailed arguments in support of the non-Assyrian nature of the altar (see below).[413] Even if one were to grant an Assyrian origin for the altar, the context makes equal allowance for Ahaz's voluntary acceptance of Assyrian religion over against the imposition of the official Assyrian cult. Ahaz might have been the ruler of a satellite state by willful submission whereby he was able to avoid any heavy-handed administrative policy involving the imposition of official Assyrian religion as was the case with subject nations who rebelled against her sovereignty.[414]

In the world of Assyrian administrative policy, conquered kings and their principalities could be placed on one of three rungs of the geo-political ladder as either a *satellite* (or puppet), *vassal*, or *provincial* state. Having voluntarily submitted to Assyrian rule, satellite states experienced little Assyrian intervention in the social, religious, and administrative life so long as political and economic obligations such as providing labor, tribute, and military personnel were fulfilled (e.g., the Phoenician cities?). Vassal states comprised lands conquered for refusing to submit or for showing disloyalty. They therefore entailed greater Assyrian control of

[410] E.g., by attributing Manasseh's association with child sacrifice to a later dtr layer, Spieckermann 1982:165 avoids having to decide whether the *molk*-sacrifice is Canaanite or Arameo-Assyrian in origin and whether or not Manasseh observed this rite as an act of loyalty to Assyria.

[411] Cf. e.g., Hoffmann 1980 and see the critical reviews of the Göttingen approach in Provan 1988; O'Brien 1989; McKenzie 1991.

[412] Holloway 1992 esp. pp.532–36.

[413] Cf. Spieckermann 1982:362–69. While, Hoffmann 1980:144 earlier suggested that 2 Kgs. 16:10–16 had a post-exilic background, Würthwein 1984:389–409 agreed with Spieckermann. Donner 1986:330–31, who otherwise endorsed Spieckermann's general thesis, concluded that 2 Kgs. 16:10–16 remains ambiguous.

[414] Cf. Miller and Hayes 1986:346.

political and economic life including appointed Assyrian officials alongside local dynasts and sworn allegiance as expressed in vassal treaties. Provinces consisted of rebellious states crushed by Assyria and placed under the rule of a military governor. Various elements of the population were deported and settled elsewhere and new settlers were brought into the province. As stated above, this system was neither rigidly followed nor consistently applied.[415]

Several factors point first to Ahaz's original independent status, secondly to his subsequent voluntary submission to Assyrian sovereignty, and thirdly, to his position as ruler over a satellite state, not a vassal state.[416] It should be noted that prior to the sequence of events depicted in 2 Kgs. 16:7–9, the narrator never portrays Ahaz as having previously submitted to Assyrian sovereignty. The fact that Ahaz was bordered by both members of the opposing coalition in the Syro-Ephraimite war makes it highly unlikely that he could have succeeded in sending messengers ladened with a gift to Tiglathpileser III while his enemies, with which Judah had been at war since the days of Ahaz's father Jotham (cf. 15:37), remained at large. In other words, Ahaz probably sent his gift to the Assyrian king after Tiglathpileser had conquered Damascus in 732 B.C.E. and not before, and his payment was in response to the Assyrian king's presence in the region, not its motivation. The Assyrian Eponym Chronicle reports that Tiglathpileser campaigned in Philistia in 734 B.C.E. and in Damascus in 733/2 B.C.E.[417] The dtr writer connects Ahaz's gift with the latter (16:9, cf. 2 Chr. 28:20–21), while the former either goes unmentioned in the Hebrew Bible or the two are collapsed into one account.[418] Obviously, Ahaz could not expect Assyrian protection from the

415 So Miller and Hayes 1986:320–22; cf. Donner 1977:418–21,427,432. As an example of how this system functioned, Israel (i.e., the northern kingdom) made the transition from satellite (738 B.C.E.) to vassal (734 or 732 B.C.E.) to province (722 B.C.E.) in just a few short years. Pečírková 1987:162–75 has offered a brief, but helpful outline of the generally accepted two-tiered system of vassal and province. Machinist 1992:69–81, esp. p.71 offers a similar reconstruction. Like Holloway 1992:532–36, Cogan 1993:406–07 recognizes the need to revise the two tiered system.

416 Following Miller and Hayes 1986:341–46. In what follows, we will adopt an approach that presupposes the historicity of major portions of the DtrH. We do so in order to test the theory of Spieckermann as well as those of his dissenters on their own grounds, namely on the basis of the biblical texts as well as the extra-biblical evidence. In the summary in 4.5.3. and in our conclusion, the tendentiousness of the DtrH and the complexities involved in using it for historical reconstruction are appropriately highlighted.

417 Cf. Luckenbill 1927(II):436; Hughes 1990:201–04.

418 McKay 1973:6 viewed Ahaz's vassalship as initiated by the request of Tiglathpileser as he preferred 2 Chr. 28:20–21 over 2 Kgs. 16:7, but the Chronicler's account is more tendentious than that of the DtrH (see below). *Contra* Hughes 1990:202–03, Ahaz's tribute payment need not precede his becoming a vassal in 732. Soon after Tiglathpileser's campaign in Philistia in 734 against Hanun of Gaza (Eponym Chronicle), Aram, Tyre, and Israel formed an anti-Assyrian alliance (for the involvement of Tyre and Aram, cf. Tiglathpileser III table ND 4302 + rev.5f.). In response, Tiglathpileser returned in 733 and began a two year campaign against Damascus (Eponym Chronicle). Upon his arrival in the area, both Mitinti of Ashkelon and Jehoahaz of Judah paid tribute to the Assyrian king

Israelite-Syrian coalition of Pekah and Rezin prior to his becoming an Assyrian satellite. But this hardly justifies the dtr attempt to make the Assyrian king out as an opportunistic mercenary roaming the region in search of a *šōḥad*, "bribe," cf. 16:8.[419] Moreover, both 2 Chr. 28:21 and the relevant Assyrian royal inscription of Tiglathpileser describe the gift of Ahaz as a tribute, not a bribe.[420] It appears that the dtr writer has telescoped the events and altered them in order to make Ahaz out as a villain.[421] A strictly historical reconstruction reads as follows: Ahaz ruled an independent kingdom prior to the Assyrian campaign against Damascus in 732 B.C.E. At that time, he voluntarily submitted to Assyrian sovereignty, offered his gift or tribute as representative of a satellite state, and called upon his new overlord to provide protection from the coalition.

As mentioned above, other scholars have offered non-Assyrian origins for Ahaz's altar, namely Syrian or, less likely, Phoenician.[422] The Syrian interpretation is in part based on the argument that Assyrians did not offer burnt offerings and on 2 Chr. 28:23 which states that Ahaz worshipped Syrian gods. However, the "brazier," or *kanūnu*, was used in Neo-Assyrian temple worship and ritual and served to immolate animal sacrifices by fire.[423] Sheep were burned on a brazier before the god, Ashur.[424] Other gods, probably, had their own braziers.[425] Adad-nirari III commands the people of Guzana (Tell Halaf) to make a burnt offering to the god Adad.[426] This coincides with an Assyrian king's typical attitude toward local religion. Not only would he make concession for local custom but he might actually endorse it on occasion. If we assume for the sake of argument that Ahaz had constructed an Assyrian (or Syrian) style altar symbolic of his deference to

(Tiglathpileser III table K 3751). Of course, we would not expect the rebels, Tyre, Aram, and Israel, to be mentioned in this list of tribute. Immediately thereafter, Mitinti rebelled in 732, only to find that Rezin had been defeated and so Mitinti died (by suicide? Tiglathpileser III Annals 235–36).

419 On the term *šōḥad*, "bribe," in 2 Kgs. 16:8, cf. Cogan and Tadmor 1988:188. The related phrase "your servant and son" in 16:7 is likewise viewed as the creation of the dtr writer by Cogan and Tadmor 1988:187, but others have pointed out the connections with international treaty language, cf. e.g., Long 1992:177.

420 Cf. Luckenbill 1927(II):801; *ANET*³ 282. This is a clay tablet inscription of Tiglathpileser where Ahaz is listed as having paid tribute to Assyria, an act expected, in one form or another, of satellites, vassals, and provinces alike, so Miller and Hayes 1986:320–22; cf. also the survey on the economic obligations of nations subject to Assyria in Lowery 1991:130–34.

421 Cf. Jones 1984:532,536.

422 Others saw the altar as a purely aesthetic innovation, e.g., Šanda 1912(II):201; Skinner 1893:369–70. For criticisms of the Phoenician and aesthetic views, cf. McKay 1973:5–12; Cogan 1974:73–77.

423 Cf. *kinūnu* in *CAD* 8(1971):393–95, Neo-Assyrian *kanūnu*.

424 So Menzel 1981:T 33 6′–10′; cf. T 35 VII 44′–48′ which attest to other uses of a *kanūnu* with cooked meat in the Ashur temple.

425 So Parpola 1983:326.

426 Cf. *CAD* 10/1(1977):252 *ma-aq-lu-a-te qu-lu-a*. Among the burnt offerings are young goats, sheep, oxen, and doves, cf. also *CAD* 13(1983):70–71 *qalû*.

the Assyrian king, Tiglathpileser might have condoned it (if not supported the performance of burnt offerings) as the Assyrian kings were known to do from time to time.

In 2 Chr. 28:23b, the Chronicler cites as the motivation for Ahaz's worship of Syrian gods "because they helped them (the Syrians), I will sacrifice to them (the Syrian gods) so they will help me." But this can hardly be a logical deduction from 2 Kgs. 16:9, for the Syrian gods had been defeated previously by those of the Assyrians and Ahaz first saw the altar in Damascus only after the Assyrians had conquered the capital of his Syrian enemies according to the author of Kings. Besides, 2 Kgs. 15:37 depicts Judah at war with the Syrians since at least the days of Ahaz's father, Jotham, and there is no indication that the Syrian gods gained the victory in their battle against the god(s) of Judah.[427] So, then, what could possibly have motivated Ahaz to worship the gods of his perpetual foes as assumed by the Chronicler? Simply put, a strictly historical reading of the DtrH suggests that there was no occasion for Ahaz to esteem the Syrian gods as worthy of his devotion. That the ChrH account diverges widely from the DtrH tradition is further underscored by the direct conflict which 2 Chr. 28:23 presents in view of 2 Kgs. 16:13,15 where it is assumed that Ahaz offers sacrifices wholly compatible with (the dtr tradition's version of) the Yahwistic cult. In other words, the Syrian gods are not in view.[428] The conclusion usually drawn is that the Chronicler has intensified Ahaz's apostasy in an attempt to align the apostasy of Judah with that of Israel at the time of the schism (cf. 2 Chr. 13:8–9). From a strictly historical point of view, the Chronicler records less reliable information on this score.[429] Besides, one could argue that, owing to the fact that the DtrH and the ChrH both view Ahaz as a rampant "syncretist," both accounts were based on an earlier tradition in which Ahaz was portrayed as a king who simply embraced a range of Yahwistic religious forms, but many of which were too broad to be tolerated by later dtr writers.

Now Spieckermann has outlined a proposal that circumvents the problem of the dtr non-condemnation in the report of the altar construction by Ahaz, but which, nevertheless, upholds its Assyrian associations. He suggests that the new altar was reserved for Yahweh, while the small bronze (Solomonic) altar (1 Kgs. 8:64) was

---

[427] 2 Chr. 27:1–9 omits the war with Rezin and Pekah entirely and adds the account of Jotham's victory over the Ammonites. The unavoidable inference is that according to the Chronicler, Jotham's god(s) brought him success.

[428] This latter point has been frequently inferred from the type of sacrifices described in 16:13,15.

[429] Cf. Dillard 1987:223–24. The Chronicler has the temple closed whereas in the Kings account Ahaz uses the new altar in the temple. Hoffmann 1980:145 concluded that the Chronicler has given an interpretative rendition of the Kings account, cf. also Williamson 1982:349; McKenzie 1984:112. This is due in part to his reversal of the claims of 2 Chronicles 13 which dominates his version of Ahaz, cf. Williamson 1977:114–18; 1982:343–50; Dillard 1987:219–25 for this and other differences in the accounts.

moved aside and reserved for the gods of Assyria. Ezek. 9:2 might offer historical confirmation of Ahaz's altar reform and the silence in 1 Kings 7 might reflect the writer's disdain for the use to which the Solomonic altar was put in the divided monarchy. In any event, Ahaz was able to appease both his Assyrian overlord as well as the faithful Yahweh worshippers like Uriah the priest (2 Kgs. 16:10; Isa. 8:2). His proposal also explains why the new altar itself went uncondemned in the report comprising 2 Kgs. 16:10–18, while Ahaz's other additions and alterations to the cult were, perhaps, censured in the wider dtr context (cf. 2 Kgs. 16:2b–4 and 23:12).[430] Finally, if the deities served at the marginalized Solomonic altar were Assyrian, then the term *lᵊḇaqqēr*, "to consult," in 16:15b, which refers to Ahaz's use of the bronze altar, might signify, among other rites, various forms of Assyrian divination.[431]

Holloway has set forth several criticisms of Spieckermann's interpretation of the Ahaz altar reform.[432] He argues that while Assyrian religion probably did make its way into late pre-exilic Judahite religion, the altar of Ahaz is an unlikely example of that process for (1) Assyrian ritual installations did not elevate and support the one who sacrificed as described in 2 Kgs. 16:12–13,[433] (2) there is no evidence that the Assyrians forced their subject nations to construct Assyrian type altars, and (3) the need for Ahaz to appease Yahwists offended by the introduction of a foreign altar constitutes a projection of dtr ideology back into pre-exilic Judahite religion. Holloway also criticizes Spieckermann for his inconsistency in interpreting *lᵊḇaqqēr* in 16:15 as Assyrian divination since there is no evidence that Assyrian kings forced divination upon their vassals. He also offers an alternative approach to interpreting the account. The Ahaz altar reform as we have it in 2 Kings 16 is a literary creation of dtr ideological rhetoric. What once comprised a tradition about Ahaz's positive changes in the Yahweh cult, the dtr redactor has transformed into a polemic against Ahaz's adoption of Assyrian religion. He opines that it is a piece "composed with such calculated ambiguity, within an implied context of Ahaz's utter subservience to Tiglathpileser, that the audience/reader is expected to 'fill in the gaps' and conclude that these altar changes were made in order to introduce foreign cults into the Jerusalem temple."[434] If we understand Holloway

---

430 Might the reference to Josiah's pulling down of the roof top altars in Ahaz's upper chamber rhetorically encompass such introductions by Ahaz as the relocation of the bronze altar and the other cultic elements like the Sea and the cast metal seat and their new non-Yahwistic use (cf. similarly, Lowery 1991:127)?

431 Cf. Spieckermann 1982:362–69 followed by Ahlström 1993:687.

432 Holloway 1992:527–30; cf. Cogan 1993:409 and n.27.

433 Cf. Holloway 1992:169–74,268–69 for altars designed for use in the Neo-Assyrian cult.

434 Holloway 1992:447–56,527–30. The quote comes from pp.528–29.

correctly, he sees here a tacit polemic in the dtr account of Ahaz's reform, although the typical dtr formulaic language of condemnation is lacking.[435]

In view of his recognition of the inventive nature of 2 Kings, Holloway's first criticism actually comes as somewhat of a surprise. In order for him to disprove the identity of the altar as Assyrian, he must apply the criterion of historical accuracy to the dtr description of the altar's design and function. For him, the straightforward contrast of an Assyrian datum with a biblical one serves to prove that the Ahaz altar was not Assyrian. As his alternative interpretation of Ahaz's altar illustrates, this is an historical accuracy Holloway is not willing, otherwise, to grant to the dtr redaction. For Holloway, the non-Assyrian form of the altar is also consonant with its pre-Deuteronomic status as a local altar introduced by Ahaz to improve the Solomonic cult. But how does Holloway decide what is an historically accurate datum in the account and what is not? We will return to this question shortly.

His approach also cuts against the grain of his own evaluation of the account as one absorbed in ambiguity. Even if the ambiguity is purposeful as Holloway suggests, a strong case can be made for the originality of the imaging of the altar's form in Assyrian style and the secondary nature of its vaguely West Asiatic form as depicted in 16:12b. First, the earlier outlined arguments against Ahaz's adoption of a Syrian altar or Syrian religion favor an Assyrian type altar. Second, the broader narrative context underscores the explicitly Assyrian religio-political role of Ahaz's altar for our author. Ahaz's prior submission to the Assyrian king does not allow the reader to view Ahaz's altar as anything but Assyrian in terms of its religio-political function. Moreover, it would certainly be consistent with the narrative context to suggest that Ahaz visited an Assyrian designed temple in order to obtain plans for constructing his altar (2 Kgs. 16:6–11).[436] The subsequent comment in 16:18 on Ahaz's manipulation of the temple paraphernalia "in deference to the king of Assyria" likewise supports the Assyrian character of the altar. Hezekiah's rebellion against Assyria provides the still wider context in which to interpret the altar's function and character (cf. esp. 2 Kgs. 8:7) for Hezekiah serves (in the dtr rhetoric) as Ahaz's foil on the matter of the proper (dtr) response to Assyria's presence in the region. The fact that 16:10–18 is not couched in the familiar dtr language and style actually supports the proposal that

---

435 While Holloway 1992:451 and n.3 acknowledges that the dtr condemnation of non-Yahwistic imports is characteristically stylized (reforming kings subtract such elements from the Yahwistic cult while apostate kings add them), he cites Jotham as one exception to that style. Jotham is evaluated positively by the dtr tradition, although he had built a *bāmāh*. However, it should be noted that Ahaz is not positively evaluated and dtr language like *bāmāh* is missing from the altar account in 16:10–18.

436 As Holloway 1992:452 points out, the destruction of the associated temples was rather consistent with the capture of national capitals.

these verses are non-dtr and, perhaps, reflective of an earlier account (assuming that there was one). Following this logic, it would be more consistent to argue that, if the altar's Assyrian function was secondary, dtr redaction would be evident in 16:10–18. Finally, the originality of the altar's Assyrian elements is consistent with the dtr rhetorical strategy of revising a Mesopotamian practice so as to make it non-dtr Yahwistic and "Canaanite" as in the case of the traditions about necromancy. In other words, the altar's West Asiatic character is the invention of dtr redaction. Alternatively, the West Asiatic form of the altar might be the inadvertent creation of a dtr redactor removed by two centuries and two imperial cultures. Thus, it should come as no surprise that, redactionally, Ahaz's Assyrian altar—whether intentionally or unintentionally—ends up looking partially like a West Asiatic one in the final narrative development.

As for his second argument that there is no evidence that the Assyrians made their subject nations adopt Assyrian type altars, Holloway acknowledges that we presently lack the evidence to prove that Assyria did not.[437] In other words, on the basis of Assyrian evidence we cannot decide whether or not they made their subjects construct Assyrian style altars as a policy. However, the enforced worship of the Assyrian gods occasionally documented in the extra-biblical sources would slightly favor the idea that in at least isolated instances, corresponding paraphernalia such as an altar might also be needed, if not demanded.

Ironically, Holloway's third criticism is predicated on a narrow view of what it meant to be religious in pre-exilic Judah and on a reading of the reform narrative isolated from its broader context. Contrary to Holloway, the notion that sectors of Judahite society would have resisted Ahaz's acceptance of Assyrian sovereignty as symbolized in the introduction of the altar is a perfectly reasonable inference in spite of his suggestion that the pre-exilic Jerusalem cult might have represented a symbiosis of standard West Asiatic religions. In other words, to be a thoroughgoing local polytheist is one thing, but the fear of being one tyrannized by a foreign power might cause one to be mistaken for a rigid henotheist or monotheist. Holloway sets up a straw man in his suggesting that it is a projection of the exilic dtr ideological redaction into an earlier time period to adopt the notion that some Yahwists would have been offended by the presence of Assyrian religious forms. It is entirely credible to propose as Spieckermann does that the resistance of pre-exilic Judahite Yahwists to Ahaz's altar reform would have given rise to his brilliant solution of two altars. In fact, that there were those among the leaders of the contemporary Yahweh cult who opposed Ahaz's construction of an Assyrian altar and service to Assyrian gods finds support in the following Hezekiah narrative.

---

[437] Holloway 1992:527 n.4.

Although now highly idealized, the dtr account of Hezekiah's reform of Ahaz's cult and the related political resistance to Assyria might preserve some echoes of a reliable pre-exilic tradition.[438]

In any case, to find Yahwists, polytheistic or otherwise, who were not willing to accept the Assyrian sovereignty as epitomized in Ahaz's new altar is highly plausible and does not necessitate an equation of that pre-exilic ideology of Assyrian resistance with later dtr ideology. One could reasonably argue that adopting the religion and culture of one's foreign overlord was not the same for some Israelites or Judahites as adopting the local religions. The former would undoubtedly have presented wider ranging ideological and nationalistic implications. Of course, the contrast implied here is partially a false one as it is based on a 'syncretistic' model in which Israelite religion is distinguished from Canaanite as well as Mesopotamian religion. In other words, how could those Israelites who had willingly adopted Canaanite religion resist another foreign religion like that of the Assyrians? In response, it should be recalled that the Israelites never adopted Canaanite religion; they were essentially Canaanite.[439] In any case, in order to assess accurately the character of and relationships among the various religious traditions portrayed in the DtrH, one must keep in mind the rhetorical dimensions of the text.

Holloway's critique of Spieckermann's interpretation of *lᵊḇaqqēr*, likewise, lacks cogency. His statement that evidence is presently lacking for the Assyrian imposition of divination upon its subject peoples is an argument from silence. If we momentarily recognize Spieckermann's general thesis of forced imposition as a given and take into consideration the particular interest of late Assyrian kings in divination, one could reasonably conjecture that Assyria would have also imposed upon its subjects those forms of divination sanctioned by its royal court.[440] In any case, *lᵊḇaqqēr* might reflect a local version of divination willingly introduced by Ahaz, but one he nevertheless employed in the service of the king of Assyria. As such, while it could no longer be cited in support of Spieckermann's general thesis, neither would it undermine it. Holloway has not demonstrated that the Assyrian elements in the account are secondary and the product of dtr redaction while the reform otherwise is a faithful recounting of "positive" changes made by Ahaz in the

---

[438] Cf. similarly, Ahlström 1993:690–16, esp. p.701.

[439] Cf. similarly the syncretistic model implicit in Cogan 1993:403-14. On pp. 410-11, Cogan wrongly contrasts Solomon's 'syncretism' with that of Ahaz and Manasseh. A vassal's response to a foreign oppressor's religion and ideology is not in view in the case of Solomon's religious proclivities. Besides, the historicity of the Solomonic traditions cannot be simply assumed and then comparison made with the 2 Kings materials.

[440] Moreover, his implicit distinction between "religion" and "divination" is an artificial construct following the contours of dtr ideology.

pre-exilic Yahwistic cult. So while we, like many others, might postulate a pre-dtr tradition behind the account in 2 Kings 16, we do not envision a pre-Deuteronomic "pro-Ahaz source" (or any source for that matter) that has been reworked by the addition of Ahaz's construction of an Assyrian altar. Holloway's bifurcation of historiography and history at the seams of Assyrian and non-Assyrian or West Asiatic cultic elements in the reform account is unconvincing.[441]

How is it that critics are able to identify an originally pre-Deuteronomic tradition about a positive reform of the Yahwistic cult in the first place?[442] By what rationale does one remove the Assyrian elements of the narrative and arrive at an original source when one also acknowledges, like Holloway does, that Assyrian religion did in fact make its way into pre-exilic Judah and that the dtr redactor carefully calculated the ambiguity he has infused into the story—in other words, typical clues to dtr redaction are missing from 16:10–18?[443] The mere absence of dtr formulaic language and style in vv.10–18, on its own, cannot justify such a deduction. Is it because of the a priori assumption that the account comes from royal archival or temple records or is it because it constitutes the clearest biblical report of Assyrian religious influence on pre-exilic Judah? One could, in fact, reasonably argue that it was an ancient tradition about Ahaz's submission to Assyria involving his introduction of an Assyrian altar into the Solomonic cult that led the dtr redactor to adopt and embellish such an account (16:12b) in order to advance his polemic against Ahaz and to downplay Assyrian religious influence, replacing it instead with fictitious Canaanite or West Asiatic cultic influences.

Nevertheless, Holloway has appropriately nuanced Spieckermann's analysis of the Assyrian evidence: cult imposition was not a hard and fast Assyrian policy. Thus, Ahaz's altar can no longer be viewed as necessarily indicative of the *forced imposition* of Assyrian religion in pre-exilic Judah. At the level of story or historiography, we would also agree with Holloway that the account clearly warns its exilic audience living under the tyranny of their foreign overlords about the need to eschew both Mesopotamian and local non-dtr Yahwistic religions. However, at the level of historical and philological analysis, Holloway's critique of Spieckermann's interpretation of the Ahaz's altar reform is not persuasive.

We return now to our own assessment of Spieckermann's forced imposition theory. There is no compelling reason to conclude that Ahaz was forced into vassalship. As a ruler of a satellite state, he would not have been required to

---

441 Cf. e.g., Holloway 1992:454.

442 Cf. e.g., Cogan and Tadmor 1988:192–93 followed by Holloway 1992:528. Hoffmann 1980:142–43 sees here a unified post-DtrH tradition the priestly interest of which is distinctly non-dtr, but the DtrH shows an interest in priestly concerns, cf. 1 Kings 12 on Jeroboam's illicit cult.

443 As Holloway 1992:528–29 and others would have it (cf. also his p.449). Could this be a case of "the disappearing redactor" described by Barton 1984:45–60, esp. pp.56–58?

establish a local version of the official Assyrian cult to the eradication of his own existing cult. At most, he willingly incorporated into his cult certain aspects of Assyrian religion. That the writer points to, at least, some Assyrian religious forms as having found their way into the temple at this time finds confirmation in the phrase *mippᵊnê meleḵ 'aššûr*, "before the king of Assyria" or "in deference to the king of Assyria," in 2 Kgs. 16:18b. The phrase does not necessarily infer that the bronze oxen and other paraphernalia were removed in order to collect tribute money as so often proposed for it comes at the wrong point in the narrative. Rather, as it stands, it conveys Ahaz's willful submission to the Assyrian king on matters of religious concern as expressed in the temple renovations in vv.10–18a. Therefore, there is no need for the radical proposal of placing this clause immediately following v.17.[444]

2 Kgs. 16:17–18 outline several other alterations to the temple made by Ahaz. These too have been cited as evidence for his need to collect tribute payment for the Assyrian king. However, the emendation of *hēsēḇ*, "to turn about," in v.18 to *hēsîr*, "to remove," with reference to *mûsaḵ haššabbāṯ*, "the cast-metal seat(?),"[445] and *mᵊḇô' hammeleḵ haḥîṣônāh*, "the king's outer entrance," is unwarranted, motivated as it is by the desire to see in these verses a collection of precious metal for the payment of tribute to the Assyrian king.[446] The verb *hēsēḇ* makes good sense as it stands and depicts only Ahaz's repositioning of the cast-metal seat. This, in turn, points to his willingness to accommodate new elements from the Assyrian cult. In any case, there is no hint that the items were given to the Assyrian king as tribute and 2 Chr. 28:21 cannot be cited in support of the use of the items in 2 Kgs. 16:17–18 as tribute payment, for it more likely reinterprets Ahaz's gifts to the Assyrian king, in 2 Kgs. 16:7–10a, and a more fitting parallel to 2 Kgs. 16:17–18 can be found in 2 Chr. 28:24a.[447] The tribute interpretation has also given rise to the unwarranted speculation that "the Sea," or *hayyām*, (cf. *JPS* "tank") in 16:17 was moved so that Ahaz could use the material from the bronze oxen beneath it as tribute (cf. 1 Kgs. 7:25).[448] But the relocation of the Sea might have been motivated similarly by the need to reposition it in order to make room for Assyrian additions to the cult.

---

444 Cf. Hobbs 1985:218 against Jones 1984:541–42 following Šanda 1912:203–05. Olmstead 1931:452 went so far as to render the phrase as "from before the face of the king of Assyria" and took it to refer to a statue of the Assyrian king erected in the temple.

445 Cf. Mulder 1982:161–72.

446 Cf. e.g. Jones 1984:541–42.

447 Cf. the use of *qāṣaṣ* "cut off, take away" in both passages. 2 Chr. 28:24a comprises a summary of 2 Kgs. 16:17–18 for the phrase *kᵊlê ḇêṯ-hā'ᵉlōhîm*, "furnishings of the house of God," in 2 Chr. 28:24a refers to the same items listed in the 2 Kgs. 16:17–18 account.

448 Cf. e.g., Jones 1984:541; Cogan and Tadmor 1988:193.

Although the evidence remains ambiguous with regard to Assyrian cultic imposition on Ahaz, the above observations strongly favor the view that the DtrH preserves echoes or relics of Assyrian religious influence in Judah for the period immediately preceding the reign of Manasseh.[449] Therefore, the notion that Mesopotamian necromancy entered Judah not before the late pre-exilic period or sometime thereafter increases in probability. Whether one speaks of voluntary adoption or imperial imposition, either of these scenarios collaborates those traditions depicting necromancy's presence in Judah prior to Manasseh's reign. Isa. 8:19 and 29:4, when viewed within their respective Isaianic contexts, suggest that like other aspects of Assyrian religion, necromancy had taken hold in Judah during Ahaz's reign. Granting such a scenario, one could plausibly conclude that the DtrH account intended to depict Manasseh as the first Judahite *king* to embrace Mesopotamian necromancy. It had circulated in Judah only on the "popular" level in Ahaz's day. However, a narrowly construed historical reading of the biblical data tells against necromancy's introduction before Manasseh's reign.

Had necromancy become an adopted Judean practice prior to Manasseh's reign, that is to say, if the texts and underlying traditions of Isa. 8:19 and 29:4 reliably reflect pre-Manasseh, Judahite religion, surely the historian of the DtrH (and of the ChrH) would not have left necromancy unscathed. The needed precedents were in place for the dtr and related writers to claim that Ahaz also practiced necromancy for the dtr writers had firsthand knowledge of genuine Isaianic traditions.[450] They could have included it in the list of cult offenses of Ahaz and in Hezekiah's reform notwithstanding the programmatic nature of these accounts. Ahaz's reign brings full circle the chaotic days of the divided kingdom as Rehoboam and Ahaz open and close that history.[451] His reign ushers in the age of Assyrian sovereignty,

---

[449] Xella 1980:151–60 has pointed to further evidence for Judahite familiarity with Assyrian religion prior to Manasseh. In the dtr account of the encounter between Hezekiah's defenders of Jerusalem and the Assyrian official, the Rabshakeh, the Judahites are warned that they will be forced "to eat their own dung and drink their own urine" 2 Kgs. 18:27// Isa. 36:12. This comprises an allusion to the tragic destiny which awaited them in the netherworld where they would be forced to consume their own bodily wastes according to Mesopotamian belief. Others take this to refer to the Judahites as having to consume their own bodily wastes in the desperate hope of holding out against the Assyrian siege.

[450] Cf. e.g., Seitz 1991:116–18,133–35,140–41,185–88,195–96 for a detailed argument in favor of the priority of Isaiah 36–38 over "the prose narratives of Jeremiah, the DtrH, and the traditions of Second Isaiah" (p.141). Seitz suggests that Isaiah 36–38 were composed as an integral part of the proto-Isaianic traditions in the early years of Manasseh's reign (after 681 B.C.E., the death of Sennacherib). They formed a crucial contrast between Ahaz of chapters 6–8 and Hezekiah and served as the thematic basis for much of chapters 40–55. The same narratives were soon after integrated into Kings by the Dtr historian at 2 Kgs. 18:17–20:11 where their secondary character is observable and dtr redactional additions and modifications are identifiable (cf. esp. 2 Kgs. 18:14–16).

[451] Cf. Lowery 1991:140–41.

forever changing the course of Israelite religious history. For all that, the Dtr historian portrays him as the first southern king to incorporate into the Jerusalem cult, the loathsome practice of child sacrifice (16:3). Child sacrifice ranks high on the list of abominations which the dtr ideology invokes to epitomize the demise of the Davidic monarchy. This is further borne out by its placement at the penultimate position in the list of abominations embraced by the northern kings in 2 Kgs. 17:17.[452] Surely, necromancy's inclusion in Ahaz's cult would have likewise advanced such an ideological polemic.

Several additional lines of evidence favor the historical reliability of the tradition reflected in the DtrH and ChrH over against that suggested by the redaction of Isa. 8:19 and 29:4. That is to say, Manasseh's reign, rather than the administration of Ahaz, provided the probable context for Judah's adoption of Assyrian necromancy. As mentioned previously, it is our contention that in Ahaz's reign, Judah voluntarily submitted to Assyrian rule, became a satellite, and paid the expected tribute (2 Kgs. 16:7–10a; 2 Chr. 28:21). Judah thereby avoided the heavy-handed Assyrian policy which entailed forced imposition of the official Assyrian cult. Following Hezekiah's revolt however, Judah lost its status as a satellite and was reduced to the level of a vassal state (701 B.C.E.). Based on what details we know concerning Assyrian policy toward vassals, this might have entailed greater Assyrian control of Judah's political, economic, and religious life. In other words, more pervasive Assyrian religious influence is what we might expect on Judahite religion after Hezekiah's revolt in Manasseh's reign.

The Assyrian royal inscriptions verify Manasseh's status as a vassal (cf. also 2 Chr. 33:10–13).[453] In one instance, he and twenty-one other vassal kings of the West were required to transport timber and stone colossi from Lebanon to Nineveh for Esarhaddon's royal storehouse.[454] On another occasion, these same kings were enlisted to help build Port Esarhaddon on the site of the destroyed city of Sidon.[455] Ten years later, Manasseh and others was required to provide troops for Ashurbanipal's campaign against Egypt.[456] Whereas Ahaz had voluntarily submitted to Assyrian control and became a satellite, Manasseh came to the throne

---

452 Although it escaped explicit mention in Hezekiah's reform, on which see Heider 1985:288, the DtrH's lack of specific condemnation of child sacrifice is an unlikely indicator of dtr tolerance of this practice. Rather, it might indicate that the dtr writer knew of a tradition concerning Hezekiah's tolerance of child sacrifice and so he avoided any treatment of the topic as it pertained to that reformer. The possibility of purely rhetorical roles for both child sacrifice and necromancy in the DtrH is taken up in the summary, 4.5.3.

453 In the royal inscriptions, we find the mention of *Menasi/Minsi šar māt Iaudi*, "Manasseh, king of the land of Judah," cf. now Cogan and Tadmor 1988:265,339.

454 Cf. *ANET*^{3}, 291, Prism B of Esarhaddon and now Hughes 1990:224.

455 Cf. *ANET*^{3} 290b, Prism A of Esarhaddon and now Hughes 1990:224.

456 Cf. *ANET*^{3}, 294, the Rassam Prism and Prism C of Ashurbanipal, and now Hughes 1990:225.

following a major rebellion. In the days of Ahaz, Assyrian power was relatively unthreatened by developments in the region whereas just prior to Manasseh's reign, anti-Assyrian sentiment was widespread.

Moreover, Manasseh might have been hand-picked by the Assyrians. If the biblical texts preserve a reliable tradition regarding Manasseh's age at accession, then older siblings had been passed over. This suggests that the Assyrians were running the government initially. During this time, there appears to have been an extensive Assyrian presence in the region (cf. also Isa. 28:11–13; 33:19). We know that Assyrian troops were stationed in the region of Palestine after 701 B.C.E. (cf. e.g., the Assyrian palace ware found in the military settlements at Tell Jemme, Tell ed-Duweir, and Tell esh-Shārī'a). Lastly, Sennacherib's successor, Esarhaddon, occasionally required his subjects to swear an oath of allegiance to the Assyrian god Ashur in hopes of minimizing political infidelity.[457]

To be sure, critics have interpreted various other elements in Manasseh's official cult as Assyrian in origin. The deities, Baal and Asherah, of 21:3,7 have been viewed as West Asiatic versions of the Mesopotamian deities, Ashur and Ishtar, respectively. In view of 23:5,12, the host of heaven, or *ṣ*ᵊ*ḇā' haššāmayim*, mentioned in 21:3,5 has been taken to refer to the Mesopotamian astral cult: the Sun, or *haššemeš* = ᵈ*Šamaš*, the Moon, or *hayyārēah* = ᵈ*Sîn*, and the Constellation, or *mazzālôṯ* = *mazzalātu*/*manzalātu*.[458] The child sacrifice of 21:6 has been interpreted as an adaptation of a Mesopotamian cult (cf. also 16:3 and 17:31), and the killing of the innocent in 21:16 might allude to the substitute king ritual. Numerous practices attributed to Manasseh but mentioned only in Josiah's subsequent reform have been identified as Assyrian in origin as well. In 23:5, "the idolatrous priests," or *hakk*ᵊ*mārîm*, have been equated with the *kumrū* priests of cuneiform documents.[459] "The (male?) prostitutes," or *haqq*ᵊ*ḏēšîm*, of 23:7 have been cited as evidence for the introduction of an Assyrian version of hierodule perhaps related to the Ishtar cult (cf. e.g., Akkadian *ḫarīmtu*).[460]

In 23:8b, "the high places by the gates," or *bāmôṯ hašš*ᵊ*'ārîm*, have been emended to "the high places of the goat demons," or *bāmôṯ haśś*ᵊ*'irîm*, and seen as evidence for the presence of Assyrian rituals intended to propitiate malevolent ghosts (cf. also Lev. 17:7; 2 Chr. 11:15; Isa. 13:21; 34:14).[461] The *hassûsîm* . . . *mark*ᵊ*ḇôṯ haššemeš*, "horses . . . and chariots dedicated to the sun," in 23:11 have been interpreted as reflective of Assyrian oracular practices dedicated to

---

457 For the vassal treaties of Esarhaddon, cf. *ANET*³ 534–41, esp. p.538; for other indications of Assyrian presence, cf. Machinist 1992:75.

458 Cf. e.g., Spieckermann 1982:86–88,271–73.

459 Cf. e.g., Spieckermann 1982:84–86.

460 Cf. e.g., Spieckermann 1982:219 n.129; Donner 1986:335–37.

461 Cf. e.g., Spieckermann 1982:99–100 and n.140.

Shamash.[462] Lastly, the "rooftop altars," or *hammizbᵊḥôṯ ʾᵃšer ʿal-haggāg̱*, of 23:12 (cf. also Zech. 1:5) have their parallels in contemporary Assyrian religion.[463]

Admittedly, it is difficult to establish with any degree of certainty the *interpretationes canaanaicae* of the Assyrian deities proposed for the apostasy and reform accounts, but the mention of the goddess Asherah illustrates the feasibility of such an approach.[464] The argument that the *ʾᵃšērāh* in the book of Judges does not represent the Canaanite goddess Asherah of the first millennium but instead refers to her symbol and, by secondary association, to other goddesses such as Ashtarte has recently been defended.[465] While we would agree in principle that the dtr tradition had a marked tendency for rhetorical polemic in its use of the term *ʾᵃšērāh*, we do not accept the suggestion that the term is not a goddess in 2 Kgs. 21:7 and 23:4,6,7. A deity is most likely referred to as supported by the mention of the *pesel* or "image, idol" of Asherah in 21:7 and the clustering of "the Baals, the Asherah, and the host of heaven" in 23:4. The first and third are clearly deities (with, perhaps, implied Assyrian analogies?) and so we would expect the second to signify the same. That Asherah received *bāttîm*, "clothes(?)," (23:7) and was removed (23:6) confirms the likelihood that the image of a goddess is involved. Her image was erected in the temple in 21:7 and removed in 23:6.

Nevertheless, some dtr references to the term *ʾᵃšērāh* in which a deity is in view cannot be understood as historically reliable references to the goddess known by that name, but as a Canaanite interpretation of a foreign deity. In 1 Kgs. 18:19

---

462 As recognized by Cogan 1993:413. Taylor 1987:16–18; 1988b:561–64 has recently identified the four-legged animal immediately below the solar-disk on the top register of the cult stand from Taanach as a horse and connected it with the horses of the sun in 23:11. Others have identified the animal as a bull, cf., e.g. M. Smith 1989:116. The date of the cult stand and the identity of its makers and the inhabitants of Taanach remain problematic, cf. M. Smith 1989:19–20. In any case, M. Smith 1989:115–21, while acknowledging the absence of an indigenous sun cult, errs in his dismissal of possible Assyrian influence in the solar cult reflected in 2 Kgs. 23:11 solely on the grounds that "the notion that Neo-Assyrian rulers imposed their religious practices on their Levantine subjects has been discredited" (p.117 and n.17 citing McKay 1973; Cogan 1974). Holloway 1992:503–07 too easily dismisses the potential significance of the royal reliefs dating to the reign of Sennacherib that depict the horse as the mount of the anthropomorphic Shamash, for which cf. Schroer 1987:288–90. A "unique connection" between horses and the sun god in first millennium Mesopotamia is irrelevant to the possible influence of Mesopotamian solar imagery on the Judahite cult or on the dtr hand responsible for 2 Kgs. 23:11. It should be noted that horses of Shamash are referred to in a bilingual text from Boghazköi, cf. Cooper 1973:71,76.

463 Cf. Weinfeld 1972b:152–54; Spieckermann 1982:110–11,294–95. For surveys of proposed Assyrian entries in the cult of Manasseh, see now Donner 1986:329–38.

464 In this regard, the reconstruction of Delcor 1981:91–123 might be a more realistic reconstruction. Although one might challenge specific points of his proposal such as his tendency to view Assyrian influence as mediated through Aramean religion, he argued for more than one foreign provenance for the elements listed in Josiah's reform: Mesopotamian, Moabite, Ammonite, and Phoenician elements. Where Assyrian religion was imposed, it existed alongside the local religions (pp.95–104).

465 Cf. M. Smith 1989:15–21, 80–94. His view that the inscriptional evidence does not refer to the goddess Asherah is forced, cf. e.g., Freedman 1987:241–49.

where the term occurs, an historically reliable reference to the goddess Asherah is unlikely. She is never attested in any Tyrian text or anywhere in coastal Phoenicia during the Iron Age. In addition to its identity as a cultic symbol, the *'ᵃšērāh* was on occasion employed as a theologically programmatic term for (the cults of) foreign goddesses. An attractive possibility underlying this function is the Phoenician Ashtarte who perhaps posed a threat to northern Israel in the ninth century or to Yahwistic religion of the late monarchy or exile.[466] But Phoenician Ashtarte can be eliminated from consideration in 2 Kgs. 21:7 and 23:4,6,7, for she is mentioned independently in 23:13. That a "canaanization" of a Mesopotamian religious practice or belief has been employed in the case of some biblical references to Asherah (= Ishtar) finds support in the analogous rhetorical polemic employed by the dtr and related traditions concerning necromancy where a Mesopotamian practice has been ascribed older Canaanite origins.

The funerary custom of "making a fire," or *śārap̱ śᵊrēp̱āh*, provides a compelling example of either a literary or historical adaptation of another Assyrian mortuary custom by Manasseh's royal court. The cognate Akkadian phrase is *šuruptu šarpat*. It is first attested in the royal correspondence of Esarhaddon and his son Ashurbanipal, the Assyrian kings contemporary with king Manasseh.[467] This rite was performed in honor of a select few Judahite kings as confirmed by its occurrence in Jer. 34:5 (Zedekiah), 2 Chr. 16:14 (Asa), and 21:19 (Jehoram). Its absence in the DtrH is readily explicable. The writer of the DtrH either knew nothing of it or, being familiar with the royal Assyrian attachments of this rite, he avoided any mention of it. Any nonpolemical reference in the DtrH to a mortuary practice of Assyrian origin which had achieved customary status or was perceived as having attained such a status among earlier Judahite royalty would undermine the dtr polemic against the adoption of competing religious traditions. Therefore, the Dtr historian, unlike the Chronicler, purposely circumvented any mention of the royal funerary fire in his assessment of past kings.

On the other hand, the writers of Jeremiah 34 and Chronicles do make mention of the royal funerary fire and they portray it as one lacking any trace of such foreign attachments.[468] The author of Jeremiah 34 viewed the funerary fire as a laudatory royal Judahite tradition rather than as an adopted foreign practice. The writer creates the impression that such a rite was an ancient Judahite tradition as is made clear from the reference in the Zedekiah account to making the fire for "your (= Zedekiah's) fathers, the former kings who preceded you." The Chronicler likewise projected it back into selected accounts of Judah's earlier kings as a

---

[466] Cf. M. Smith 1990:88–90.

[467] Cf. Zwickel 1989:266–77.

[468] It is less likely the case that the author intended a comparison with Assyrian royalty for by attributing the practice to the period of Asa's reign, it lost any distinctly late Assyrian attachments.

positive criterion for evaluating their reigns. Although 2 Chr. 21:19 assumes that it was observed in honor of Jehoram's predecessors, that is "his fathers," the Chronicler makes no explicit mention of this practice prior to the reign of Asa (cf. 2 Chr. 16:14).

Thus, a strictly historical reading of the relevant biblical texts points to Israel's adoption of the Mesopotamian mortuary rite of necromancy in the period contemporary with Manasseh's reign. Admittedly, while not all of the preceding examples manifest equally compelling evidence for Assyrian influence, the cumulative effect is one which establishes a substantive Assyrian religious presence in late pre-exilic Judah. If Israelite necromancy owes its historical origins to mid first millennium Mesopotamia, then the dtr tradition might preserve—whether by accident or intent—a recollection of an historical development in which necromancy took hold in Judah during Manasseh's reign or thereafter. This, rather than its supposed compatibility, would explain why, from the dtr perspective, it apparently posed no threat to Yahwism in earlier times and why it was condemned only of late.[469]

4.5.3. Summary

The preceding arguments provide sufficient contextual support for advocating Judah's adoption of Assyrian necromancy during the period of Manasseh's reign: (1) the late compositional histories of the relevant biblical texts as well as their traditions, (2) the rise in popularity of various forms of divination among late Assyrian kings, (3) the preponderance of references to Mesopotamian necromancy from the Neo-Assyrian period onwards, (4) the political domination of Judah by the Mesopotamian imperial states of Assyria and Babylonia in the mid first millennium, and (5) the evidence for Mesopotamian influence on the religious life of late pre-exilic Judah—whether by means of willful adoption or imperial imposition. These considerations support the thesis that necromancy and the belief in the supernatural power of the beneficent dead entered Judahite religion and tradition from Mesopotamia in the mid first millennium. This thesis gains further support from the argument that (6) with the exception of the few late biblical references, necromancy remains otherwise unattested in Canaanite-Israelite or, for

[469] If ones assumes that necromancy was practiced but not mentioned in the list of abominations enacted by Ahaz in 2 Kgs. 16:1–4, that is to say, that the dtr writer failed to mention each and every one of Ahaz's actual illicit practices, then the silence regarding judgment against Ahaz in the report of his temple renovations in vv.10–18 cannot be used as a criterion for dating the temple narrative to the pre-exilic period, *contra* Spieckermann 1982:365–66 followed by Lowery 1991:123–24.

that matter, Mesopotamian, Egyptian, and Anatolian religions before the mid first millennium.

Having said all this, it must be conceded that while Manasseh's reign stands as the most likely historical context for the introduction of Assyrian necromancy, there remains the equally viable alternative that necromancy's arrival on pre-exilic Judahite soil is the idealization of concerns contemporary with the exilic and post-exilic dtr writers. That is to say, on the matter of the belief in the beneficent dead, these traditions might represent artificial literary constructs in which current ideological issues have been projected into the reconstructed past rather than reliable historical recollections of a pre-exilic past. In fact, an artificial literary nature for the whole of the DtrH has been recently reiterated by Hoffmann.[470] Hoffmann argues that the theme of cultic reform is basic to the entire DtrH from pre-monarchical to monarchical times. The dtr religious concerns stand out and are presented most fully in Josiah's reform which in Hoffmann's assessment has very little basis in historical reality. All the elements of the reform theme are brought together here and read back into the earlier reform accounts. The accounts throughout the DtrH are characteristic dtr compositions and the vocabulary is typical, rather than specific and singular, with the details giving only historic verisimilitude to the accounts. In each instance, there is little reflection of an actual cult reform. In the case of the monarchical period, the centrality of the reform theme is expressed in the alternating scheme of seven negative reforms and seven positive reforms. Those that introduce cultic elements alien to dtr Yahwism include 1 Kgs. 16:29–33: Ahab, 22:52–54: Ahaziah, 2 Kgs. 3:1–3: Joram, 9:4–10:31: Jehu, 13:1–9: Jehoahaz, 16:1–4,10–18: Ahaz, 21:1–16: Manasseh. Those that relate to the dtr purification of the cult are 1 Kgs. 15:9–15: Asa, 22:41–47: Jehoshaphat, 2 Kgs. 11:1–20: Jehoiada, 12:1–17(ET 11:21–12:16): Joash, 15:32–38: Jotham, 18:1–6: Hezekiah, 22:1–23:25: Josiah.

Moreover, Hoffmann has outlined an impressive argument in defense of Noth's theory concerning the single authorship of the DtrH and thereby its essential literary unity and character. One point is clear, the DtrH can no longer be considered the product of multiple extensive redactions. But there is one qualification that we would like to add to Hoffmann's theses. In his composition of the DtrH, the writer was not working purely on the basis of his ideological and literary theme of cultic reform.[471] Even the dtr polemic that resulted in the distortion of the traditional Yahwistic religion of Ahaz and Manasseh and the radical innovative tendencies of

[470] Hoffmann 1980; cf. Van Seters 1983:317–21,343–44; Long 1984:11–32. Donner 1986 maintains a healthy skepticism about what can be identified in the DtrH as reliable historical reconstruction although in the final analysis, he adopts the thesis of Spieckermann in its broad outlines.

[471] This is ultimately acknowledged by Hoffmann. While the reforms of Hezekiah and Josiah are considered literary fiction by Hoffmann 1980:155,268–69, the "anti-reform" accounts of Ahaz and Manasseh contain genuine pre-exilic backgrounds and were motivated by Assyrian influence

Hezekiah and Josiah presupposes at least some knowledge of the late pre-exilic period. The dtr writer exercised some degree of acquaintance with this period, however limited and biased, in order for his polemic to reflect the semblance of actuality which it does.[472]

Lowery has more recently reiterated the claim that the elements in the list of cultic crimes in a passage like 2 Kgs. 21:1–18 evince such a stylized character that it is impossible to substantiate the assertion that syncretism was on the rise in Manasseh's Judah as scholars like McKay and Cogan propose. According to Lowery, all of the crimes in the Manasseh account have been seen before in the Jerusalem temple and are derivative of Deut. 18:9–14.[473] But child sacrifice, while listed in Deut. 18:10, only appears in the summary account of the northern monarchy's fall (2 Kgs. 17:17) and in the account of Ahaz's reign (2 Kgs. 16:3). More to the point, necromancy is nowhere to be found in the DtrH's many crime lists preceding the account of Manasseh although it too is listed in Deut. 18:11. While one might agree in principle that the "syncretism" portrayed in the DtrH is the creation of the historian, the traditions indicate that the crime lists in Kings do not simply mimic the Deut. 18:10–11 list.[474] A detailed analysis of that passage (cf. 4.4.2.) reveals that the literary processes more likely moved in the opposite direction. Deut. 18:10–11 with its post-dtr list of seven or eight abominations comprises an expansion on 2 Kgs. 17:17 and 21:6 and other late traditions with, perhaps, Mesopotamian associations (e.g., the "sorcerer," or *mᵉḵaššēp̱*, and the "charmer," or *ḥōḇēr*). Besides, if the ban on necromancy in the law of Moses at Deut. 18:10–11 indeed preserved an older tradition as is often presumed, would it not have provided the needed literary-ideological precedent for the integration of necromancy into the apostasy and reform accounts of at least Manasseh's two immediate predecessors?

Furthermore, the mention of necromancy in 2 Kgs. 21:6 and 23:24 does not presuppose 1 Sam. 28:3–25. In fact, our study in 4.5.1 revealed that the literary development once again proceeded in the opposite direction. This post-dtr addition not only bolstered the dtr polemic by giving it the appearance of greater antiquity, but more specifically, together with 2 Kgs. 21:6, it established necromancy as the litmus test for the nation's two legitimate royal houses. In the

---

despite the presence of their theologically programmatic catalogues of tendentious sins (pp.144,164–66). Donner 1986:330–34 agrees as to the fictionality of Hezekiah's reform, is more skeptical about the Ahaz and Manasseh accounts, but he tends toward attributing greater reliability to the Josianic reform. Würthwein 1984:389–90,445–46,459–60 views the Ahaz, Manasseh, and Josiah accounts as reliable attestations of cultic impact by Assyria, but views Hezekiah's reform as a late recasting of anti-Assyrian measures.

472 Cf. similarly, Mayes 1983:12. The issue here is one of degree.

473 Lowery 1991:170,189.

474 *Contra* Lowery 1991:171,184–85.

case of 1 Sam. 28:3–25, participation in necromancy resulted in the 'death' of the nation's first legitimate royal house, the Saulide dynasty. Indications are that the *modus operandi* underlying the redactional insertions of Deut. 18:10–11 and 1 Sam. 28:3–25 reflects a more comprehensive ideological agenda set on placing sole blame for the Babylonian exile on Manasseh's shoulders.[475] As part of that same redaction, the pericopes in 2 Kgs. 21:16; 23:26–27 and 24:3–4, all of which explicitly blame Manasseh for the exile, were added to complete that picture. Prior to this redaction, the exile was attributed to the collective guilt of Judah's kings (cf. 2 Kgs. 21:11–15).[476] As was the case with the destruction of the north, the *raison d'etre* was the cumulative sin of the kings (cf. 2 Kings 17). Nevertheless, the DtrH represented Ahaz together with Manasseh, as advancing the extent of that collective Judean guilt, for both outdid their predecessors. Ahaz was the first child sacrificer and Manasseh was the first child sacrificer *and* necromancer. While Ahaz's misdeeds placed the Judahite monarchy on a level equal to the northern kings in terms of their villainy (17:17), Manasseh's iniquities thrust Judah well beyond the apostasy of Israel. No previous king (or commoner) of either the north or the south had engaged in necromancy (with the exception of Saul, but recall that this is a later redactional element in the DtrH)!

Manasseh's unique association with necromancy provided the starting point for the post-dtr redactor's ideological strategy. First, he directly linked Manasseh's crimes in 21:6, and in particular, necromancy, with the law of Moses by his insertion of Deut. 18:10–11. Thus, a *legal* precedent was established. Second, by inserting 1 Sam. 28:3–25, he provided the *historical* precedent for ascertaining the just punishment for an otherwise legitimate (i.e., Davidic) monarchy's embrace of necromancy, namely, its total destruction. As the straw that broke the camel's back, necromancy facilitated the downfall of the Saulide monarchy. By making necromancy an age old problem, the redactor could feature the utter perverseness of another legitimate king and his downfall, Manasseh the Judahite. The impression conveyed by the combined accounts of Saul and Manasseh in the final form of the DtrH is that necromancy, more than any other non-dtr Yahwistic practice, epitomized the apostasy of a legitimate king, be he a Saulide or Davidide. But given the undeniable ideological role of necromancy, why were the kings of the north also not accused of indulging in this prototype of royal abominations?

At the dtr level of the DtrH, the historian had underscored the gravity of the northern kings' perverseness by citing child sacrifice as justification for their

---

475 The dislocation of the short report in 2 Kgs. 23:24 likewise suggests the post-dtr redactional character of necromancy in that context (the list proper comprises 23:4–20), cf. now Long 1992:279–81.

476 Cf. Lowery 1991:175–82 who argues that the prophecy in 21:12–15 makes clear that v.11 is not suggesting Manasseh's sole responsibility.

destruction (17:17). He then accented the southern kingdom's iniquities by singularly attributing to Ahaz the same abomination (16:3). No other Judahite king had participated in child sacrifice. Thus, it was Ahaz's apostasy that initially signaled Judah's similar fate. However, for the post-dtr redactor, the gravity of Judah's apostasy could not be sufficiently highlighted by means of comparing its transgressions with those of an illegitimate kingdom like that of the north. Such a strategy could hardly explain why Judah's legitimate dynasty could suffer the same ignominious fate as a fraudulent ruling class like that of Israel. The redactor sought an ideologically more compelling analogy. With a heretofore unattested abomination like necromancy having been included in the list of iniquities committed by king Manasseh, our redactor created the needed legal and historical precedents by inserting Deut. 18:10–11 and 1 Sam. 28:3–25. In so doing, he was able to directly link the merited destruction of Judah with another legitimate kingdom of the nation from the past—that of the Saulides. The magnitude of Judah's sins were more convincingly paraded, its punishment more easily justified, and any facile comparison with the north supplanted.

Our extended study of a non-dtr Yahwistic religious practice like necromancy demonstrates that the literary and redactional processes involved in the composition of the DtrH are far too complex to accommodate easy generalizations. Nevertheless, the preceding analysis has identified one particular literary or ideological strategy that an Israelite writer might employ. A dtr writer might introduce into an account about a pre-exilic king (such as Saul), a foreign religious practice known only from periods subsequent to that represented in the narratives of that king. Whether one views Judahite necromancy as originally an historical intrusion, a literary adaptation, or both, it clearly stands as an exception to the stereotypical language of cult crime in the DtrH. Furthermore, contrary to what the dtr ideology would have the reader to believe, the sources underlying the DtrH apostasy accounts comprise a wide range of religious and literary traditions, not solely Canaanite or Mesopotamian, but foreign as well as indigenous, not real or rhetorical, but both fictitious and historical.

4.6. Exilic and Post-exilic Prophetic Texts

With the exilic and post-exilic prophetic texts, significant new possibilities arise vis-à-vis the existence of Israelite ancestor cults. Not only are the potential references significant, but the variation in the associated ritual is as well. Interpreters have recovered from these texts the supposed ancestor cult-related *bêṯ marzēaḥ* (Jer. 16:5), the burial of kings with attendant rites (Ezek. 43:7,9), and libations and offerings for the dead (Isa. 57:6). Necromancy is also documented in these texts.

While it is attested only once, its observance takes on a previously unattested form, a rite approximating what in later antiquity was identified as an incubation rite (Isa. 65:4).

4.6.1. Jeremiah 16:5

With the *bêṯ marzēaḥ* of Jer. 16:5, we return to the topic of the Israelite version of the *marzēaḥ* (cf. Amos 6:7 in 4.3.1.). This passage has been cited alongside the pertinent Ugaritic data in support of the theory that for a span of at least two millennia the West Asiatic *marzēaḥ* retained its death cult associations which involved, among other observances, licentious behavior and intoxication. Related to the character of the *bêṯ marzēaḥ* is the question of whether one or two social gatherings are prohibited in 16:5–9: a "sodality devoted to feasts for the dead," as the *bêṯ marzēaḥ* of v.5 has been described,[477] *and* a "drinking feast," or *bêṯ mišteh*, in v.8, or solely a ancestor cult feast, in which case the *bêṯ marzēaḥ* would be co-terminus with the *bêṯ mišteh*.[478] If the two are synonymous, then the festive nature of the gatherings of the *bêṯ marzēaḥ*—as supposedly attested in the pre-Hellenistic comparative data—finds added confirmation in the evidence of Jeremiah 16.

In order to come to some reasoned resolution of this *crux*, it will be necessary to survey what can be confidently said with regard to the structure of the larger pericope, Jer. 16:1–13. Although this passage has been considered a unit, 16:1–9 share no vocabulary with 16:10–13.[479] In any case, most commentators view 16:1–9 as comprising two sections, 16:1–4 and 16:5–9, which do share a common vocabulary and purpose. The former contains permanent prohibitions as the negative particle *lō'* occurs throughout, while the latter contains immediate prohibitions with *'al* negating the major verse lines in 16:5 and 8 (and see below).[480] A number of interpreters who assume the essential unity of 16:1–9, view 16:5–9 as a depiction of Jeremiah's proclamation of the divine word given in 16:1–4 in the form of a symbolic action.[481] This gains some support from the change in negative particles, from the *lō'* of 16:1–4 to the *'al* in 16:5–9, the presence of

[477] Cf. Pope 1977a:166 followed by King 1988a:138.

[478] Cf. Porten 1968:180–81; Pope 1977b:216; Bright 1965:110–11 who viewed these two elements as parallel. Lewis 1989:138–39 equated the *bêṯ marzēaḥ* of v.5 with the *bêṯ mišteh* of v.8 by way of an inclusio but completely omitted the crucial v.9 from his treatment.

[479] Holladay 1986:467 cited, as a second criterion, the notion that 16:1–9 comprises *Kunstprosa* or rhythmic prose whereas 16:10–13 does not, but cf. Thompson 1980:401–03; McKane 1986:363.

[480] Cf. Thompson 1980:400 n.4. Holladay 1986:467 emended *lō'* in v.8 to *'al*.

[481] Cf. e.g., Weiser 1962:135–39.

second person plural suffixes in 16:9, *lᵊʿênêḵem ûḇîmêḵem*, "before your eyes and in your days," and the assumed public announcement of 16:1–9 in 16:10.

Nevertheless, others who advocate extensive dtr redaction in 16:5–9 conclude that the Jeremianic nucleus preserves the historical Jeremiah's adherence to a vow of celibacy. His decision to remain in an unmarried state has been explained as owing to the demands of the prophetic office and/or to the hopelessness of the times.[482] Finally, more recent commentators view 16:5–9 neither as symbolic action nor as Jeremiah's personal practice. Rather, as this exilic passage contains an account of Jeremiah's loneliness, it comprises an artful comparison of the prophet's life-style with the fate of the community from which Yahweh has withdrawn his *šālôm*.[483]

The structure of 16:1–9 is also informative as to the character of the sixth century Judahite version of the *bêṯ marzēaḥ*. 16:1–4 comprises Yahweh's exhortation to his prophet Jeremiah to abstain from marriage owing to its procreative potential (16:1–2). The reason outlined is that in the face of impending national disaster, children and parents alike will die an ignominious death. In fact, the destruction will be so devastating that no one will survive to offer the proper burial and mourning rites on their behalf (16:3–4). An examination of the rhetorical structure of 16:1–9 reveals that two distinct occasions are in view in 16:5–9. As a unit, 16:1–9 contains a repeated twofold structure, three parallel main clauses accompanied by their respective motivational clauses each introduced with the particle *kî*. Two of these main clauses make up 16:5–9: 16:5a + 16:5b–7; and 16:8 + 16:9.[484] A comparison of 16:5–7 and 16:8–9 demonstrates that in vv.5–7, the *bêṯ marzēaḥ* forms part of a complex of solemn funerary rites, including lamentation (*s-p-d*) and consolation (*n-w-d*), whereas in vv.8–9, the *bêṯ mišteh* is mentioned within the context of a wedding as indicated by the reference to the *ḥāṯān*, "bridegroom," and the *kallāh*, "bride." It is further characterized by the sounds of joy, or *śāśôn*, and gladness, or *śimḥāh*.

In fact, v.9, with its mention of the bridegroom and bride, forms an inclusio with the prohibition against marrying in v.2, and not with the funerary rites of v.5.[485] That the *bêṯ mišteh* is intrinsically associated with marriage and not death can be established by the use of the term *mišteh* in Judg. 10:14,19. Moreover, in Eccl. 7:2, it is contrasted, not equated, with a "house of mourning," or *bêṯ ʾēḇel*. Lest it be wrongly presumed as typical of the *marzēaḥ* assemblies, it should be pointed out that mortuary rites do not appear as regular entries in the handful

[482] Cf. e.g., Rudolph 1958:98–99; Nicholson 1973:142–43; Thiel 1973:195–201.

[483] Thompson 1980:403; McKane 1986:367; cf. also Carroll 1986:340–42 for a similar mediating position.

[484] For the first instance of this repeated twofold structure, cf. 16:1–2 + 16:3–4.

[485] Thompson 1980:406; Holladay 1986:468; cf. McKane 1986:367 against Lewis 1989:138–39.

of references we have of the *(bt) mrzḥ* from pre-Hellenistic times. In fact, the mortuary connections are late and only occasional at that (cf. 4.3.1.). Furthermore, in the isolated instances where such a connection is made, funerary rites are in view, not death cult practices. This is surely the case with Jer. 16:1–9, where we have a veritable catalogue of funerary rites: lamentation (vv.4,5,6), burial (vv.4,6), grief (v.5), gashing (v.6), tonsure (v.6), and the giving of food and drink as consolation (v.7).[486]

Even the funerary character of the *marzēaḥ* for the time period reflected in the canonical context of Jer. 16:1–9 is controvertible. Following Thiel's general reconstruction of the compositional history of Jer. 16:1–9, Fabry has argued that the *bêṯ marzēaḥ* in this passage was not originally associated with mourning, but that this perspective was introduced into the text by later redactors. According to Fabry, 16:1,5,8 comprise the earliest compositional layer. 16:2,6,7 are secondary additions, and 16:3,4,9 as well as vv.10–13 are still later dtr additions.[487] This would make *bêṯ marzēaḥ* in v.5a and *bêṯ mišteh* in v.8 parallel members, in the pre-redacted form of the pericope and therefore lacking any mortuary associations. Moreover, in view of the non-ancestor cult attachments of the pre-Hellenistic form of the *marzēaḥ*, the *bêṯ marzēaḥ* and *bêṯ mišteh* should be understood as synonymous members in a chiastic structure in which v.5bc, "do not go to lament or to condole with them . . . ," forms the *antithetical* element interposed between *bêṯ marzēaḥ* and *bêṯ mišteh*:[488]

v.1	The word of the Lord came to me:	
v.5a	Do not go in the *marzēaḥ house*	[= Do not celebrate]
v.5bc	Do not lament or condole	[= Do not mourn]
v.8	Do not go in the drinking house	[= Do not celebrate]

In the final analysis, the time period one assigns to the funerary character of the *bêṯ marzēaḥ* reflected in Jer. 16:5 depends upon the level of probability one attaches to an extensive dtr redaction of the book of Jeremiah and 16:1–9 in particular. The difference here is a late pre-exilic setting or an exilic, possibly early post-exilic, setting. Admittedly, the theory of a systematic dtr redaction of

---

486 Likewise, contrary to commonly held opinion, inebriation cannot be considered a constituent element of the *marzēaḥ* as it is attested only on one occasion (*KTU* 1.114) in pre-Hellenistic times (cf. 3.1.5.).

487 Nicholson 1970:29,60–63,87; 1973:142–43 noted the dtr character of 16:4 (cf. Deut. 28:25) and 16:10–13 (cf. Deut. 29:21–27(ET 22–28)). Thiel 1973:195–201 offered a more extensive catalogue of dtr correspondences: 16:3b,4b,9* ("your eyes and in your days") as well as 16:10–13.

488 Fabry 1984:15 against Loretz 1982:87–93, esp. pp.88–90. Fabry labeled this structure a doubled antithetic parallelism.

Jeremiah as proposed by Thiel has fallen on hard times.[489] Nevertheless, a general consensus remains vis-à-vis the linguistic features shared by the book of Jeremiah and the dtr corpus. The debate centers on the significance of these shared elements. In view of such elements and the generally acknowledged redactional nature of the book, it is difficult to reject totally the theory of a dtr redaction of Jeremiah regardless of its extent. The remaining question is how much dtr influence can be identified in the production of the book of Jeremiah and in 16:1–9 in particular, an issue to which there is no easy answer.[490]

Our treatment of the extra-biblical materials demonstrated that the pre-Hellenistic *marzēaḥ* was an association foremost concerned with economic interests, in particular, real estate transactions. Its membership consisted of the upper echelons of society which held meetings in a "house," or *bt.* No direct evidence presented itself in support of the mortuary connections of the pre-Hellenistic *marzēaḥ*. This enhances the likelihood of the redactional nature of Jer. 16:1–9. That said, one cannot categorically eliminate the possibility that in an isolated instance in earlier periods, the *marzēaḥ* might have been involved with funerary matters, for such fraternities might have sought to acknowledge the death of one of their illustrious members by a solemn occasion.[491] It is nevertheless unwarranted to attach the technical term "house of mourning," or *Trauerhaus*, to the *bê<u>t</u> marzēaḥ* in Jer. 16:5.[492] In conclusion, an intermittent and late funerary association cannot be the basis for positing a hypothetical ancestor cult association inherent to the *marzēaḥ* of much earlier periods.

---

489 Like that of Thiel 1973, the opposing position of Weippert 1973 is too extreme, cf. the critiques of McKane 1981:220–37; 1986:xlii–lxxxix; Carroll 1986:38–50.

490 Although McKane 1986; Carroll 1986 reject Thiel's overall thesis, both recognize redactional processes that shaped the book. McKane's theory is one in which small pieces of pre-existing text trigger exegesis or commentary (1981:237; 1986:lxxxiii). This results in a text with its own character and orientation. But this does not eliminate dtr influence, rather, as the author acknowledged, dtr language will only be differently nuanced in Jeremiah (1986:xlvii). Carroll's theory of the book's composition in which a lengthy process of transmission and editorial activity often motivated by the needs of various groups (1986:34), likewise does not eliminate dtr influence. He in fact acknowledges such influence in the prose of Jeremiah in his defense of the extensive editorial nature of the book (cf. 1986:35–36, against the position of Holladay 1986:1–2). He rejects however the notion of a monolithic dtr redaction (1986:69). Even Holladay, in his rejection of the dtr editorial shaping of the prose of Jeremiah, maintains that such material is often modeled after the book of Deuteronomy (1986:1–2, and cf. p.351 on 11:1–14).

491 An earlier occasional incorporation of funerary rites into the social life of the *bt mrzḥ* like those reflected in Jer. 16:5 might have provided the stimulus for its more frequent connection with mortuary matters later *via* Greek rituals.

492 *Contra* e.g., Schreiner 1981:104.

4.6.2. Ezekiel 43:7, 9

Ezek. 43:7,9 are commonly cited in support of an Israelite ancestor cult.[493] Albright understood the phrase *pigrê malkêhem*, "the funerary stelae of their kings," in Ezek. 43:7 as a reference to an Israelite royal ancestor cult.[494] More recently, Heider has suggested that the phrase referred to "the *pagrū*-offerings to/for your (*sic* their) *malikū*," that is to say, animal sacrifices for the royal ancestors.[495] Based on the data from Mari and Ugarit, Ebach argued that the term in Ezekiel 43 denotes a (*Toten-*)*opfer* and cited the use of *peger* in Gen. 15:11 and Jer. 31:40 in support of this meaning.[496]

As demonstrated previously, neither the use of *pagrum* and *pagrā'um* at Mari (2.2.3.-2.2.4.) nor *pgr* at Ugarit (2.3.1.) support the meaning "stele," let alone "funerary stele."[497] In the remaining twenty instances of Hebrew *peger*, the contexts overwhelmingly favor the straightforward meaning "corpse."[498] Moreover, with one exception, the corpse is that of a human, the context is negative, and no indication of an offering is evident.[499] While the lone exception is Gen. 15:11, general usage suggests that Hebrew *peger* in this instance denotes an animal carcass, not an offering, as no altar, blood, or consumption by fire are mentioned.[500] Furthermore, in Jer. 31:40, the term probably refers to human corpses related to child sacrifice owing to the identification of the mentioned "valley of *happᵊgārîm* and ashes" with the valley of Hinnom, the notorious cult site for this parade abomination (cf. Jer. 17:31; 19:5; 32:35).[501] In any case, nowhere in the Priestly

---

493 Cf. e.g. Spronk 1986:250; Lewis 1989:139–142 following a long line of interpreters.

494 Cf. Albright 1957:242–48; 1968:203–06; 1969:103–04, following Neiman 1948:55–60 who understood *peger* as "stele," but as an implement of idolatry not of the death cult. Neiman cited Lev. 26:30 "the *pigrê* of their idols" against the corpse interpretation. But Lev. 26:30 is simply a poetic extension of the meaning of the term. Dr. John Day has pointed out in private communication the similar phrase in Jer. 16:18 *niblat šiqqûṣêhem*, "the carcasses of their detestable idols." Galling 1959:11, followed by Zimmerli 1983:417; Lust 1986:217 modified Neiman's proposal and suggested that the stelae were erected in memory of the dead. This is not an argument for veneration or worship of the dead, but for their commemoration. Nevertheless, "stele" is unlikely.

495 So Heider 1985:393–94 following Talon 1978:57 n.13,69–71, who viewed the cognate Akkadian *pagrā'um* as an animal sacrifice.

496 Ebach 1971:365–68 followed by Dietrich, Loretz, and Sanmartín 1973:289–91.

497 Cf. other occurrences of *peger* found in construct with a personal (pro)noun, cf. "your corpses," or *pigrêkem*, (Lev. 26:30) and "the corpses of the sons of Israel," or *pigrê bᵊnê yiśrā'ēl*, (Ezek. 6:5). These clearly do not refer to stelae.

498 Gen. 15:11; Lev. 26:30(2x); Num. 14:29,32,33; 1 Sam.14:29,32,33; 1 Sam. 17:46; 2 Kgs. 19:35 = Isa. 37:36; 2 Chr. 20:24,25; Amos 8:3; Isa. 14:19; 34:3; 66:24; Jer. 31:40; 33:5; 41:9; Ezek. 6:5; Nahum 3:3.

499 Furthermore, the corpse may be in a progressive state of decay as suggested by Isa. 34:3.

500 Following e.g., Sarna 1966:126.

501 For Jer. 31:40 as a reference to child sacrifice, cf. now Wright 1987:287 n.21. Heider 1985:360 also viewed this passage as a possible reference to child sacrifice, but interpreted *peger* as stele. Less

legislation on sacrifice is the term *peḡer* used to denote an offering. The fact that *peḡer* is qualified by the term *mēṯ*, "dead," in 2 Kgs. 19:35 (= Isa. 37:36) intimates that like English "body," *peḡer* can refer to man or animal as a material organism regardless of whether it is alive or dead. This would explain why in some instances, *peḡer* necessitated further qualification (e.g., 2 Kgs. 19:35) while in others it could stand alone when its mortuary character was otherwise explicit.

Having surveyed the range of opinions concerning *peḡer*, something must be said about the tendency of commentators to emend the vocalization of *bamôṯām*, "their high places," to read *bᵊmôṯām*, "at their death," in v.7. This emendation is frequently cited in support of an ancestor cult interpretation of Ezekiel 43. Arguments in favor of the change include the assumption that it would be rather odd for a high place to be located within the temple complex[502] or that high places would not have been built there after Josiah's reform.[503] However, both Jeremiah and Ezekiel attest to the limited success of Josiah's reform as it did not permanently eliminate all of the "apostate" practices. For example, the cult of child sacrifice at the Tophet soon reappeared after the reform, if it disappeared at all.[504] Therefore, that the *bāmāh* of Ezek. 43:7 might make its appearance in Israelite religion as a re-instituted abomination—regardless of its cultic associations—should come as no surprise. Moreover, by the time of the exile, the *bāmāh* might have evolved into a small elevation for cultic use.[505] Such an installation could easily fit in the temple complex envisioned by the writer of Ezekiel.

The phrase *pigrê malḵêhem* might, nevertheless, contain a reference to child sacrifice. The genitive noun "kings" in the phrase "corpses of the kings" might be a subjective genitive, i.e., "by the corpses which the (living) kings offered at their high places (reading *bāmôṯ*)." This interpretation finds some support from the immediate context. As noted previously, the high place, or *bāmāh*, is intimately connected with this abomination in Jer. 7:31; 19:5; and 32:35. But would one expect the location of a high place within the temple precinct irrespective of the issue surrounding its size? If the author intended by the mention of Yahweh's footstool and throne in 43:7 to symbolize Yahweh's presence, then, as 48:35 suggests, his presence might encompass all of the Jerusalem environs and not simply the confines of the temple. In other words, the narrator might not have

---

likely is the possibility of cremation, but cf. 1 Sam. 31:12–13; Amos 6:10; Ackroyd 1981:224 against Driver 1954:314–15; cf. Bieńkowski 1982:80–89. On the meaning of *haššᵊrēmôṯ* in the same verse, cf. Wright 1987:282–83 n.9 "gardens, fields" (< *śᵊḏēmôṯ*) and his critique of Lehmann 1953:361–71 who suggested "field (of the god) Mot."

502 Lewis 1989:141.

503 Zimmerli 1983:417.

504 Cf. Heider 1985:336–83.

505 Schunck 1977:141.

intended to restrict the *bāmāh* of 43:7 to the temple complex proper.[506] Assuming that *bāmāh* was a sizable "high place" and that *peger* can be connected with child sacrifice as in Jer. 31:40, *bāmāh* in our text might designate the cultic area near the Tophet or Hinnom valley and still be considered as located within the Jerusalem environs.

Admittedly, if the *bāmôṯ* designated locations where rites took place on a *regular* basis and if such rites observed at the *bāmôṯ* in Ezek. 43:7,9 were directed toward the dead kings (i.e., that they were not rites which the living kings supervised), then this passage might point to the late arrival of ancestor cult practices in the Judahite royal cult. Again, Assyria or Babylonia would serve as the most likely sources for the introduction of such a cult for the period in question. The royal *kispum* ritual is well documented for first millennium Mesopotamia and no comparable royal practice is attested for contemporary Syria-Palestine.[507] But this is all too speculative and it assumes that such a cult would be what one would expect in the social setting portrayed in these late biblical texts (against which, see our conclusion).

In sum, we are on safest ground in recognizing *peger* in Ezek. 43:7,9 as the corpse of a king which had been placed near the temple complex in total disregard for the priestly legislation aimed at the defiling power of human corpses.[508] Although the actual location of the tombs of Judah's kings remains shrouded in mystery, the writer of 1 and 2 Kings locates most of their tombs down to the time of Hezekiah in the capital city of Jerusalem and, more specifically, in the precinct known as the city of David.[509]

However, as for Hezekiah's death, the dtr writer recorded only that "he slept with his fathers," *wᵊyiškaḇ . . . ʿim-ʾᵃḇōṯāyw* (20:21). Unlike his predecessors beginning with Rehoboam and concluding with the apostate Ahaz, Hezekiah was not "buried with his fathers in the city of David." Furthermore, while his immediate successors, Manasseh and Amon, were given a burial site, it was an alternative one. 2 Kgs. 21:18 and 26 indicate that they were buried in the king's garden, or *gan bêṯ*, also named the garden of Uzza and not in the city of David. Likewise, its exact whereabouts is unknown. In view of the likelihood that the pre-exilic temple was a dynastic shrine, the royal garden was probably located in the palace complex and it might have been located in close proximity to the

506 Following Zimmerli 1983:415–16.

507 For Mesopotamia, cf. Tsukimoto 1985:107–24.

508 Owing to the concern with what they viewed as the late priestly tradition regarding the defilement of corpses, Wright 1987:115–28; Eichrodt 1970:551–55; and Wevers 1982:215–16 viewed Ezek. 43:7–9 as heavily redactional in nature. In any case, Ezek. 43:7,9 is probably related to Lev. 26:30 by way of the addition in Ezek. 6:5.

509 As to the exact coordinates of these areas, the archaeological data are inconclusive. For recent summaries, cf. Rahmani 1981:231–33; Wright 1987:115–28.

temple. The location of the corpses of the kings near the temple in Ezek. 43:7,9 would reflect the same orientation. The threshold, or *sap̱*, and doorposts, or *m*ᵊ*zûzôṯ*, associated with the corpses in 43:8 would then refer to a mausoleum-type structure that housed them. This in turn would allow for the regular observance of commemorative rites on behalf of the kings.[510]

Several indicators point to the prospect that the dtr tradition not only locates the corpses of Manasseh and Amon in a nontraditional burial plot, the royal garden, rather than in the city of David, but that the bones of the preceding kings of Judah from the city of David were also relocated there. The phrase *w*ᵊ*yiškaḇ . . . 'im-'*ᵃ*ḇōṯāyw*, "he slept with his fathers," is not simply a formula referring to a king's natural death, for in 2 Kgs. 14:22, it refers to the death of Amaziah who is slain as a result of a conspiracy. While it shows up repeatedly in the larger phrase "and he slept with his fathers and he was buried with his fathers in the city of David" or in versions thereof, it is more than a death formula. In 1 Kgs. 15:8, it describes the burial of Abijam, "he slept with his fathers. Now they buried him in the city of David." The element "with his fathers" immediately following "buried" in the latter phrase is missing. This suggests that "slept with his fathers" alone could refer to a king's burial with his ancestors and not simply his death.[511] The phrase, "Now they buried him in the city of David" in 15:8 would then serve only to identify the *exact* location of the burial.

While the phrase "slept with his fathers" suggests that both Hezekiah and Manasseh were thought to be buried with their ancestors, the corpses of neither Manasseh nor his ancestors were located "in the city of David." More to the point, Hezekiah's death introduces a curious ambiguity in the dtr formulaic style. Perhaps underlying that ambiguity is a tradition that claimed that Hezekiah relocated the bones of his ancestors in the palace complex in anticipation of the Assyrian siege.[512] Assyrian kings were known to desecrate the graves of the enemy royalty. Ashurbanipal carried away the bones of Elamite kings whose descendants he described as "the disturbers of the kings my ancestors."[513] But in keeping with the

---

510 The dtr tradition's account of Absalom's memorial (*maṣṣeḇeṯ*) in 2 Sam. 18:18 points to the same concern to commemorate the royal dead. It should be recalled that only the invocation of the name is mentioned: *hazkîr š*ᵊ*mî*, "commemorate my name." In other words, geneonymy is in view, not ancestor worship or veneration. Similar stelae established in memory of late Assyrian kings are well attested.

511 The related nominal formation, *miškāḇ*, denotes a grave in 2 Chr. 16:14 and Ezek. 32:25.

512 Merodach-Baladan II gathered the bones of his ancestors from their tombs and took them into exile with him. Alternatively, in view of the tradition that 185,000 Assyrian soldiers were smitten in an attempted siege of Jerusalem by Sennacherib (cf. 19:35), the dtr writer might have in view the idea that the extensive Assyrian casualties had polluted the city of David. This rendered the burial plots unfit for the Judahite royalty and so the tradition had them relocated.

513 Cf. Luckenbill 1927(II):310; Tsukimoto 1985:114–15; but note *CAD* 11^2(1981):349. This might explain the paucity of references in the cuneiform sources to the burial places of kings. As sug-

negative dtr assessment of Manasseh, the writer altered the tradition somewhat by omitting any reference as to where Hezekiah was exactly buried and by portraying Manasseh in Hezekiah's stead as the designer of the mausolea in the palace gardens where his ancestors were reburied.[514] Not only that, the writer might have modeled Manasseh's royal garden and the reburial of the royal ancestors in that garden after Mesopotamian practice. Royal gardens are well attested in first millennium Mesopotamian sources (cf. the Akkadian terms *kirû*, *kirmāḫu*, and *ambassu*) as is the burial of kings within the palace complex (or gardens?).[515]

4.6.3. Isaiah 57:6

Isa. 57:3–11 most likely comprises a post-exilic poem enumerating the nation's many violations against the standard of righteousness and justice.[516] While it is generally agreed that beginning with 57:5b, the writer initiates an invective against child sacrifice, a few commentators have proposed that beginning in v.6, the writer polemicizes against two death cult rites: offerings made as apotropaic rites to the deceased in v.6 and the art of necromancy in vv.9a and 13:

---

gested previously, this might also explain the burial of Mesopotamian kings in swamps, cf. Beaulieu 1988:36–37. Did the disturbers seek merely to defile the tombs and leave the ghosts uncared for or did they, by means of incantations, attempt to drive away the ghosts of the dead, defeated kings who haunted them owing to their desecration and neglect? Perhaps the disturbers employed necromantic incantations in order to gain information from these "captured" ghosts as military strategy (cf. 1 Sam. 28:15 and the use of *r-g-z*, "to disturb," there).

514 The Chronicler allows Ahaz to be buried in Jerusalem, but not in the royal tombs (2 Chr. 28:27). This is in keeping with relegating bad kings and kings who die untimely deaths to grave sites other than the royal tombs (cf. e.g., 2 Chr. 21:20; 22:9; 24:25; 26:23). He also locates Hezekiah in the city of David or more specifically, its ascent (2 Chr. 32:33). Like the dtr writer, he locates Manasseh's tomb in his palace (2 Chr. 33:20), but for Amon he offers no burial site (2 Chr. 33:24). Josiah might be buried back in the city of David "in the tombs of his fathers" (2 Chr. 35:24). Recall that Manasseh is a cultic innovator for the Chronicler.

515 On Mesopotamian royal gardens, cf. Wiseman 1983:137–44; on the exceptional mention of the burial of first millennium Assyrian and Babylonian kings in their palaces or swamps, cf. Moorey 1984.:14–15; Beaulieu 1988:36–37 respectively.

516 Ackerman 1992:111–14 argues that the poem must date from a time when the temple had not been rebuilt, for the performance of the condemned cult activities in 57:3–13 on Zion—fertility cults, death cults, and child sacrifice—demands such a date. As will be demonstrated, only one cult is evident in 57:3–13, namely child sacrifice, and as she acknowledges, it was performed not on Zion, but at the Tophet in the Hinnom valley. The post-exilic canonical context, the dtr language, and the lack of decisive evidence for a pre-exilic date are the strongest arguments in favor of a post-exilic date that can be mustered, cf. also Kennedy 1989:47; Ackerman 1992:111–14. These are more compelling than those offered for a pre-exilic date. In any case, no appeal to an historical Josianic reform can decide the matter as child sacrifice continued well into the sixth century and beyond (cf. Jer. 7:30–32; 19:5; 32:35; Ezek. 16:21; 20:31; 23:39).

(5)

You who burn with lust among the oaks,
under every verdant tree (*'ēlîm*);
who slay your children in the valleys,
under the clefts of the rocks.

(6)

Among the perished of the wadi (*bᵊḥallᵊqê-naḥal*)[517]
is your portion,
they, they, are your lot;
For them, you have poured out a libation,
you have offered up a cereal offering.
Should I be appeased for these things?

(9b)

You sent your envoys far off,
and sent (them) down even to Sheol.

(13)

When you cry out, let your gathered
(= rebellious deeds, *qibbûṣayik̠*)
deliver you!

In addition to such obvious death related language as the mention of child sacrifice in v.5b and in v.9a (cf. *mlk* = Molek or *molk*-sacrifices) and the journey to Sheol described in v.9b, death cult advocates have identified several other mortuary components in the passage in support of their thesis that 57:3–13 is replete with allusions and references to the Canaanite-Israelite cult of the dead. The listing below illustrates the terms so identified:

	The translations:		The new proposals:	
nᵊḥālîm	"wadis"	>	"burial sites"	(v.5)[518]
'ēlîm	"terebinths"	>	"deified dead"	(v.5)[519]
ḥallᵊqîm	"smooth (stones)"	>	"the perished"	(v.6)[520]

517 Commentators generally view the first occurrence of the root *ḥlq* as derived from "be smooth," *ḥlq* I, and the second from *ḥlq* II "to divide," cf. e.g., Westermann 1969:322 and see the treatments by Schunck 1980:444–47; Tsevat 1980:447–51. Westermann did entertain the notion that v.6 may refer to the place where the sacrificed children of v.5 were ritually buried "under the stones in the brook of the valley."

518 Irwin 1967:31–40; Lewis 1989:148; Kennedy 1989:47–52; Ackerman 1992:141–43,149; cf. 2 Kgs. 23:6; Jer. 31:40; Job 21:33.

519 Weise 1960:25–31; Lewis 1989:49–51,153–54.

520 Cf. Dahood 1964:408; Irwin 1967:32–33; Lewis 1989:148; Ackerman 1992:146–48. According to Irwin 1967:31–40, Ugaritic *ḥlq* III is occasionally found in contexts related to "death" or

miškāḇ	"bed"	>	"grave"	(vv.7,8)[521]
zikkārôn, yāḏ	"sign" "phallus"	>	"memorial monument"	(vv.7,8)[522]
šāp̱al	"to descend"	>	"*necromantic* descent"	(v.9b)[523]
qibbûṣîm	"gathered (idols)"	>	"gathered spirits"	(v.13).[524]

Some of the above proposals are more probable than others and a handful are altogether doubtful. Lewis understood the Hebrew *'ēlîm* of v.5 as "gods," rather than the "oaks" or "terebinths" against most commentators. He admitted that the latter is normally rendered *'êlîm* as in Isa. 1:29.[525] He cited as support the versional witnesses. For example, the LXX interpreted v.6 as follows: "that is your portion, this is your lot" referring to the "gods" or *'ēlîm* of v.5 which the Greek author rendered as "idols" < *eidōlon*.[526] In view of his conclusion that the dead ancestors in Israel could be identified by the word for god, either *'ēl* or *'ᵉlōhîm*, he suggested "dead spirits" for *'ēlîm* in 57:5 and posited a death cult background for not only these verses, but for the entirety of 56:9–57:13.[527] However, the conclusions reached in 4.5.1. demonstrate that the notion that the dead in ancient Israel were considered gods should be abandoned. Moreover, the translation of *'ēlîm* as "gods" is doubtful in view of the obvious parallelism in v.5:[528]

(5a)

You who burn with lust among (*bᵊ*-) the *'ēlîm*,
under (*taḥat*) every verdant tree;

Ugaritic *mt* (cf. Akk. *ḫalāqu* in *CAD* 6(1956):37b; Dahood 1964:408) and so the phrase *bᵊḥallᵊqê-naḥal*, Irwin translated "with the dead of the wadi" (others rendered *ḥallᵊqê* as "smooth serpents" for serpents were supposedly venerated in such cults). The following libations and offerings were likewise intended for the dead. This conforms with the fact that the Kidron was a place of burial as recorded in 2 Kgs. 23:6 and Jer. 31:40 and that the Hinnom valley was the place of child sacrifice. In any case, Irwin 1967:31–40 was doubtful about the legitimacy of his proposal owing to the admittedly scant evidence for an Israelite cult of the dead!

521 Lewis 1989:149–50, followed by Ackerman 1992:106–07,153–54.

522 Lewis 1989:149–50.

523 Lewis 1989:151.

524 Lewis 1989:151–52.

525 Following Weise 1960:25–32; Watts 1987:252,254; and the versions.

526 Similarly, the *NIV* adds "The idols among the smooth stones of the ravines are your portion."

527 Lewis 1989:143–58 = 1987:267–84; cf. Ribar 1973:74–75. Kennedy 1989:47–52 also adopted Irwin's interpretation and added the conjecture that *naḥal* signifies a tomb or grave (cf. pp.48–49).

528 Cf. Greenfield 1961:226–28.

(5b)

Who slaughter children among (*bᵊ-*) the wadis,
under[529] (*taḥat*) the clefts of the rocks.

The objects of the prepositions *bᵊ-* and *taḥat* in v.5b consist of two terms, "wadis," or *nᵊhālîm*, and "clefts of the rocks," or *sᵊʿip̱ê hassᵊlāʿîm*. Both point to the same place of reference, namely, where forbidden practices took place. The syntactic parallelisms between v.5a and v.5b and within v.5a itself favor the view that the term *ʾēlîm* signifies the same illicit locale as "verdant trees," or *ʿēṣ raʿanān*. The *JPS* translation retained the translation of *ʾēlîm* as terebinths and understood v.5 to be connected with what followed, for v.6 points back to the idolatrous practices mentioned there, "with such are your share and portion."[530]

Similar difficulties arise with the proposal that the terms *zikkārôn* or *yāḏ* are mortuary monuments. Unless one is predisposed toward a death cult background for 57:3–13, nothing in the context would demand such an interpretation. Furthermore, the dtr tradition, from which vv.3–13 draw much of their terminology, does not list these items or their associated practices as ones to be outlawed or condemned. In any case, the occurrence of *yād* and the phrase *hazkîr šᵊmî* in 2 Sam. 18:18 reflects a commemoration ritual and not a royal ancestor cult as so often assumed. Its commemorative function probably explains why it did not qualify for dtr proscription. Likewise, while the verb *šāp̱al*, or its Ugaritic cognate *špl*, can be used to denote netherworld descent as in its use in *KTU* 1.161:22, necromancy is not in view in either instance. Besides if necromancy were in view in Isa. 57:9, one would have expected the associated terminology to be present such as *ʾôḇ*, *yiddᵊʿōnî*, and related verbs such as *dāraš* or *šāʾal* or *yāraḏ*. In the light of the writer's familiarity with dtr and first Isaiah traditions, the lack of standard biblical necromantic terminology cannot be too easily dismissed.

The last proposal is *qibbûṣîm* of v.13. The immediate context suggests that *qibbûṣîm* signifies "gathered" in the sense of a repertoire of illicit maneuvers. The obvious parallelism with v.12 confirms that deeds of no account are in view and not the "gathered 'spirits'."[531] In fact, a necromantic interpretation of *qbwṣ* is the weakest link in the chain for it presupposes the death cult and necromantic

---

529 For this translation of *taḥat* in v.5b, cf. Day 1989:16 n.2.

530 The note to the verse states "the cult-trees referred to above in v.5." Along the same lines, Watts 1987:255 noted that the change of person from v.5 (2mpl) to v.6 (2fs) merely reflects the change of perspective from Israelite "evil doers" in general to the apostates of Jerusalem. Cf. also the criticisms of Ackerman 1992:102 n.6. Note, however, in her criticism she fails to recognize what for Lewis is a crucial distinction regarding *ʾēlîm* or consonantal *ʾlym* in 57:5 and *ʾêlîm* or consonantal *ʾylym* in 1:29.

531 The *RSV* suggests "collection of idols." Ackerman 1992:110–11 and n.21 proposes double duty for *qbwṣ* and for the negative *lʾ*. This is certainly possible, but ghosts are not in view.

elements identified elsewhere in 57:3–13: *'ēlîm*, *zikkārôn*, and *yāḏ*. As these are unlikely, the remaining death related language is to be associated with another cult mentioned in the context (see below). In any case, the cognate Ugaritic phrase *qbṣ ddn* or its parallel couplet *rp'i 'arṣ* cannot be invoked in defense of Hebrew *qbwṣ* as "gathered 'spirits'," for these constructions denote the gathered from among the living *Ditānu* and *rp'um*/Rephaim rather than the dead, royal ancestors (cf. 3.1.7.–9.).

Most of the remaining mortuary elements identified in 57:3–11 continue the poem's focus on the abomination of child sacrifice introduced in v.5. The wadis indicate where the child sacrifice was performed, namely in the Hinnom valley which was also known as a burial ground (perhaps for the victims?). "The perished of the wadi," or *ḥallᵊqê-naḥal*, in v.6 refer to the victims and *mlk* of v.9 refers to the deity Molek (see below and 4.4.2.). "The envoys who go down to Sheol" figuratively indicate the victims who had appeased Molek as if to underscore their function as messengers or intercessors(?) (v.9).[532] Lastly, the terms *miškāḇ* or bed and *yāḏ* or phallus occur in the context of the nation's figurative harlotry (vv.7–8) and the "sign," or *zikkārôn*, of that harlotry is the ritual of child sacrifice in vv.5–6,9–11.

Commentators frequently assume that a genuine fertility cult is polemicized against in v.5a and vv.7–8.[533] But the language in these verses is stereotypical and much more generalized than the language of child sacrifice. In fact, it is more akin to the rhetorical language of harlotry found elsewhere in biblical traditions. The close connection which the metaphor of national harlotry shares with child sacrifice confirms the metaphorical interpretation of the harlotry language in 57:3,5a,7–8. In Lev. 20:5, the language of harlotry is also applied to the Molek cult "I . . . will cut them off . . . him and all who follow him in playing the harlot (< *z-n-h*) after Molek."[534] In Isaiah 57, the theme of "playing the harlot after Molek" is first introduced in the depiction of the nation as a harlot in v.3 (note the derivative of *z-n-h*).[535] That Molek and not *molk*-sacrifice is in view in Isa. 57:9 and related

---

532 Did the recently sacrificed deliver communications to, or intercede on behalf of the living before, the underworld deity as weakened shades?

533 Following earlier commentators, Ackerman 1992:101–63, esp. p.155, has argued that three post-exilic cults were envisioned in 57:3–13: the fertility cult (vv.5a,7–8), child sacrifice (vv.5b,9a), and the cult of the dead (vv.6,9b).

534 Following Day 1989:10–12,82–83. Against Ackerman 1992:117–43, esp. p.137, Day 1989: 10–14,46–52 argues that there was a genuine deity Molek and that the offering of the first born to Yahweh was a distinct cult. While the biblical writers depict the existence of such a god, the question of whether or not the term was misunderstood or a deity invented to conceal its earlier Yahwistic associations is difficult to decide, for the extra-biblical testimony of an underworld deity named Molek who received child sacrifices remains unattested, cf. 3.1.8. and 4.4.2.

535 Day 1989:16,50–52 (and cf. Heider 1985:379–82) has rendered MT *meleḵ* in v.9 as "Molek" rather than "(living) king." Molek or *molk*-sacrifices finds support in the immediate context from the

passages finds confirmation in the fact that "playing the harlot after" is used in some forty instances in connection with the worship of other deities or numinous beings and never to the offering up of a sacrifice.[536]

With the language of harlotry in vv.5a,7–8 reinterpreted and the supposed death cult imagery of vv.6,9a rejected, one can convincingly maintain that child sacrifice occupies the whole of 57:3–9, even through v.11. Verse 10 then would allude to the efficacy of the rite by continuing the journey to Sheol mentioned in v.9.[537] 57:11 would demonstrate that, in this instance, the patron deity was not Yahweh as indicated by the question Yahweh poses "whom did you dread and fear so that you lied and did not remember me?"[538] For the biblical writer, that patron deity was none other than Molek as revealed in v.9.[539] The resultant structure of 57:3–11 is one in which vv.3–5a portray the alluring power of child sacrifice through an extended "awhoring" metaphor, vv.5b–6 condemn child sacrifice outright, vv.7–8 return to the "awhoring" metaphor, and vv.9–11 comprise a second direct assault on child sacrifice.[540]

---

mention of Sheol in vv.9–10 and the use of oil and ointments in v.9 which are closely associated with Molek worship in Ezek. 16:18–21.

536 Day 1989:10,83: Exod. 34:15,16; Lev. 17:7; Deut. 31:16; Judg. 2:17; 8:33; 1 Chr. 5:25; 2 Chr. 21:11,13; Ps. 106:39; Isa. 57:3; Jer. 3:1,2,6,8–9; Ezek. 6:9; 16:15,16,17,26,28,30,31,33,34,35,41; 20:30; 23:3; 23:5,19,37,43,44; Hos. 1,2; 2:7 (ET 5); 4:12; 5:3; Micah 1:7. The arguments of Day 1989:10–12,82–83 concerning the application of the phrase "playing the harlot after" to the ghosts, the *'ōḇôṯ*, or "Ones-who-return," and the *yiddᵊ'ōnîm*, or "Knowers," in Lev. 20:6 need only be modified to the extent that like gods, ghosts of the dead in necromantic ritual were viewed as numinous beings (but the two were not equated). Day interprets the phrase "playing the harlot after" as applied to Gideon's ephod in Judg. 8:27 to refer to the associated divine oracles, and ultimately (p.11) to the participating gods.

537 Cf. Day 1989:50–52. This would favor retaining the verb *tāšūrî* from *šūr* "to journey" in v.9 (cf. Song 4:8 and Ezek. 27:25) *contra* Ackerman 1992:107 n.16.

538 This verse contradicts the identification of Yahweh as patron deity of child sacrifice, at least from the perspective of the writer, *contra* Ackerman 1992:137. The reference to fear and dread in v.11 might alternatively be understood to refer to a crisis which occasioned the sacrifice like the king of Moab's sacrifice of his son while under Israelite siege in 2 Kgs. 3:27. Ackerman 1992:139–41 creates a false dichotomy between rituals occasioned by the routine cultic calendar and those dictated by crisis situations. Surely a given ritual might be performed in both situations. This in turn renders the question in v.6, "should I be appeased for these things" as a rhetorical question anticipating an ironic negative answer: "Obviously not, the victim is intended for Molek. You are unfaithful!"

539 Lust 1991:193–208 argues that *lmlk* in the Hebrew Bible did not originally refer to Molek or *molk*-sacrifice but was a title of Yahweh. Owing to what he deemed as inappropriate contexts, the LXX translator downgraded the title which he vocalized as *meleḵ* changing it to prince or leader, Greek *archōn*, rather than *basileus*, thereby making it a title for a lesser deity or a "devil."

540 Accordingly, the libations and offerings mentioned in v.6b are intended for the patron deity of child sacrifice. The construction *lāhem* would then be rendered "for them" functioning like the dative of respect "with respect to the sacrifice of children, you have poured out a libation, you have brought an offering (to Molek)." Alternatively, the offerings could be viewed as sustenance for the weakened dead while on their journey below.

4.6.4. Isaiah 65:4

As generally interpreted, the post-exilic text, Isa. 65:4, preserves rites which in later antiquity were associated with incubation. Incubation and its forerunners comprise a distinct form of dream divination that is widely attested in the ancient Near East.[541] In an incubation rite, one sleeps in a sacred place in order to obtain a revelation through a dream:

(3)

A people who provoke me
continually to my face,
who sacrifice in gardens,
burning incense on bricks/incense altars;[542]

(4)

who sit in graves (*qᵊḇārîm*),
and lodge (the night) in secret places (*nᵊṣûrîm*);
who eat the flesh of swine,
and the broth of a "desecrated sacrifice"[543]
is in their vessels;

The LXX translator most likely interpreted *nᵊṣûrîm* in v.4 as an allusion to incubation. The addition in the LXX *di' enupnia* "for the sake of (oracles received in) dreams" bears this out. While neither sleeping nor dreaming are mentioned per se, the parallel line in the MT v.4b *ûḇannᵊṣûrîm yālînû*, "and lodge (the night) in secret places," confirms that the writer had in mind an all night vigil at a burial site. It should be recalled that *niṣirtu*, the Akkadian cognate of Hebrew *nᵊṣûr*, likewise signified a secret place where graves were located.[544] In spite of the

541 Cf. Obermann 1946; Gaster 1950:270–71; Oppenheim 1956:187–91,211–12,245–52; Otten 1980:105; Parker 1989:100–01; Moore 1990:50–51,78–86,99; Ackerman 1992:194–202. The attempt of Oppenheim 1956:223 to connect the Mesopotamian *ša'ilu* and *ša'iltu*, necromancy, and incubation has at present no direct support, cf. Finkel 1983–84:1 n.1.

542 Most commentators translate *hallᵊḇēnîm* as "bricks," but for "incense altars" (< Hebrew *l ᵊḇōnāh*) cf. the survey in Ackerman 1992:169–94.

543 Cf. Wenham 1979:124–25,169–71 and contrast Wright 1987:140–43 on *piggûl*. Wright 1987:142 rendered *piggûl* in v.4 as "desecrated, profaned sacrifice," cf. also Lev. 11:7 and Deut. 14:8.

544 On Hebrew *n-ṣ-r* and Akkadian *niṣirtu*, "hidden thing," < *naṣāru*, "to guard, preserve," cf. Berger 1980:82–83 and note *CAD* 11^2(1981):276 against Healey 1976:433–34 who proposed a Syriac cognate, "to wail," "they sit in graves and spend the night in wailing/among the wailers." But this term is not attested in the Hebrew Bible. Cf. the "hidden location," or *ina niṣirti*, of Nabonidus' mother's tomb and the *bīt niṣirti*, "secret tomb," of a king in a recently published Neo-Assyrian text in McGinnis 1987:1–12 discussed in 4.4.3. In the light of the Mesopotamian practice of hiding royal

fact that neither the *'ôḇôṯ* and *yiddᵊ'ōnîm* nor the practitioners who conjure them up are mentioned in this passage,[545] the reference in v.4a to those "who sit in graves," or *hayyōšᵊḇîm baqqᵊḇārîm*, strongly suggests that the art of necromancy has been combined with incubation as a technique for contacting the dead in a dream.[546] The underlying belief made no distinction between the abode of the dead and the grave.[547] While this form of incubation is rather exceptional for the ancient Near East, Oppenheim notes that in a dream of Nabonidus, the ghost of Nebuchadnezzar, his royal predecessor, appears instead of the expected deity.[548] Greek literature knows this form of incubation as well.[549] Incubation when not associated with necromancy appears to be a legitimate means of contact with the other world in biblical tradition that is, if Gen. 28:10–22; 46:1–4; 1 Sam. 3:1–18; 28:15(?); 1 Kgs. 3:4–15 (= 2 Chr. 1:1–13); 9:2; 2 Kgs. 16:15; 19:1; Pss. 3:6; 4:9; 17:15; and 91:14–16 allude to Yahwistic incubation rites.[550] In any case, it is never condemned outright except in Isa. 65:4.

However, necromancy's connection with incubation does not establish the constituent nocturnal performance of the biblical version of necromancy. It should be recalled that in the necromancy texts of Mesopotamia, the expected time of revelation could be the morning. Furthermore, in view of the fact that dreams played the central role in the rite of incubation, the nocturnal aspect of the rite in 65:4 might derive from its association with incubation.[551] With regard to the remaining elements in 65:4, the eating of swine flesh and the broth of a "desecrated sacrifice" has been viewed as a meal shared in the context of the cult

---

graves, the mention in v.3 of gardens (cf. 4.5.2. and note Pope 1977b:224–26) and incense (cf. 4.4.3.) might indicate an instance in which death cult rites or necromancy were observed at a royal tomb.

545 For descriptions of the practitioner of necromancy, cf. Deut. 18:11: *šō'ēl 'ôḇ wᵊyiddᵊ'ōnî wᵊḏōrēš 'el-hammēṯîm*, "the inquirer of the One-who-returns and the Knower, namely, the conjurer of the dead," and 1 Sam. 28:7: *baᵃlaṯ-'ôḇ*, "the one who controls the One-who-returns."

546 Cf. also Tropper 1989:18,320–26.

547 Cf. Pedersen 1926:460–66.

548 Oppenheim 1956:191,250. Lewis 1989:142–43,158–60 viewed Isa. 45:18–19 as another example of necromancy combined with incubation. The phrase *bassēṯer*, "in secret," in v.19a suggests incubation and *'ereṣ ḥōšeḵ*, "land of darkness," in v.19b might denote the netherworld. Thus, the language of the line might suggest a form of necromancy along the lines of 65:4. Others have viewed the context in a more general way, cf. e.g., Muilenburg 1956:532; Westermann 1969:172–73. The LXX interpreted *tôhû* in vv.18–19, not as the power of death, but as a reference to vanity (v.18 *eis kenon*, "in vain"; v.19 *zētēsate*, "seek vanity"), cf. also Watts 1987:159–60,162.

549 Cf. e.g., Dodds 1951:110–11.

550 Ehrlich 1953:13–57 argued that 1 Kings 3 is the only genuine instance of incubation in the Hebrew Bible, but cf. Porter 1981:202 and n.28.

551 Cf. Oppenheim 1956:187–91 on the usual nocturnal dream. Daytime dreams are attested but this appears to be the exception not the rule.

of the dead, that is a *marzēaḥ*-type meal.[552] Apart from the proposed funerary nature of the Israelite *marzēaḥ*, a position which was shown to be inadequate, there is no evidence that Israelites partook of meals in honor of the dead although acts of commemoration might very well have been performed. Verse 4b more likely comprises one of three semi-independent themes; foreign gods, the dead, and abnormal food sources, which are included here primarily because all three share the common element of cultic impurity.[553] Elsewhere, these three are the repeated objects of considerable priestly legislation. Like the rites dedicated to foreign gods in v.3b, incubation, owing to its association with the dead, and the consumption of certain meat or the drinking of juices made from that meat were regarded as abnormal. This explains their collective condemnation.[554]

In closing, the remarks made in 4.2. concerning the relation of 65:4 to the first Isaiah necromancy references are worth repeating. If Isa. 8:19; 19:3; and 29:4 were part of the original Isaianic corpus, then the lack of reference to the *'ôḇôṯ* and *yiddᵊʻōnîm* in 65:4 supports the late redactional and compositional histories of these first Isaiah references to necromancy. Had they been original to first Isaiah, then one would have expected some mention of the *'ôḇôṯ* and *yiddᵊʻōnîm* in 65:4 in continuity with that authoritative tradition. This is especially so, if, as argued in 4.2., 65:4 was part of the post-exilic redaction of the *whole* of the Isaianic traditions. It seems that with the relatively late introduction of necromancy into biblical tradition, writers could exercise a significant degree of literary license when taking up the topic. In other words, there was yet to develop a long standing authoritative prophetic tradition dictating the language and form of polemic that an individual writer would be expected to invoke when discrediting necromancy.

4.6.5. Summary

Our examination of the exilic and post-exilic prophetic traditions indicates that ancestor worship or veneration were of no apparent concern to those responsible for the composition of these traditions. The *marzēaḥ* of Jer. 16:5, like its pre-Hellenistic form more generally, most likely concerned itself with the economic interests of its membership. It was not an institution inherently connected to mat-

---

552 Cf. Heider 1985:389. He noted that a reference to the drinking of the juices made from the flesh of child sacrifices has been proposed, but cf. his criticisms on pp. 190–92,391.

553 Cf. Westermann 1969:401 and Watts 1987:343. Ackerman 1992:193 suggests that the rites of v.3 have to do with illicit rites to Yahweh (burning incense) and Asherah (sacrificing in gardens).

554 De Vaux 1958:250–65, esp. pp.261–65, attempted to explain the prohibition against eating pork as owing to its chthonic associations in pagan religions, but cf. the critique of Wenham 1979:165–71 following Douglas 1966.

ters mortuary. Nevertheless, on a given occasion its members may have sponsored a funeral for one of its recently deceased associates. The *peger* envisioned in Ezek. 43:7,9 represents the corpse of the king which had been buried near or in the temple complex perhaps for the purpose of concealing the king's corpse. Nevertheless, to do so was, according to the author of Ezekiel, in violation of priestly legislation. This practice was therefore denounced not because it was related to the worship or veneration of the royal ancestors, but because it symbolized the Judahite monarchy's violation of prescribed boundaries of purity. Finally, Isa. 57:3–11 comprises a post-exilic poem denouncing the practice of child sacrifice which had apparently revived following the Babylonian exile. The worship of the ancestors is nowhere in view.

Matters are very different in the case of Isa. 65:4. A form of necromancy was apparently combined with dream divination or what came to be known as incubation in later antiquity. The context underscores the polluting power of not only this ritual, but those associated with foreign gods and the consumption of impure or abnormal food as well. In fact, it is only when combined with necromancy that an incubation-like ritual is condemned in the Hebrew Bible. Like Ezek. 43:7,9, Isa. 65:4 further highlights the *modus operandi* underlying the prohibition contained in Deut. 14:1, namely, that in dtr and priestly traditions, death rituals and, metonymically, corpses were singled out for severe censorship owing to the threat they posed to newly defined boundaries of social solidarity.

This concludes our investigation of passages located in what modern critical studies has identified as the major collections of tradition. Two types of data that do not fall with those perimeters but are nevertheless frequently cited in support of the existence of Israelite ancestor worship or veneration and necromancy remain to be considered. Various passages in the loosely constructed anthology of hymns known as the Psalms and the netherly character of the biblical Rephaim have been repeatedly cited as evidence for the existence of these ritual complexes in ancient Israelite society. To these we now turn.

4.7. The Psalms

A few isolated Psalms passages have been cited in support of the existence of Israelite ancestor cults and necromancy. Zolli interpreted the *qᵊḏôšîm*, "holy ones," in Ps. 16:3 as the mighty dead. This rendition, so it is argued, finds support in the phrase *'ᵃšer-bā'āreṣ*,[555] "in the earth," for *'ereṣ* is occasionally used to

---

555 Zolli 1950:149–50, followed by Spronk 1986:334–37; Smith and Bloch-Smith 1988:283; Lewis 1989:166.

designate the netherworld.[556] With this as a starting point, others have interpreted v.4 accordingly. Thus, "their libations of blood," or *niskêhem middām*, have been identified as sacrifices to the dead and the refusal to mention "their names," or *šᵊmôṯām*, has been viewed as a polemic against the invocation of the dead.[557] However, several obstacles stand in the way of this interpretation. A death cult interpretation requires emending *'addîrê*, "majestic," in v.3 to *'ᵃrûrîm*, "cursed," so as to cast a negative light on the associated practices.[558] Furthermore, elsewhere in biblical traditions, the holy ones are exclusively the angels (cf. e.g., Ps. 89:7–9(ET 6–8); Zech. 14:5; Dan. 8:13) or the living saints (cf. Lev. 11:44; Ps. 34:10 (ET 9); 2 Chr. 35:3), but never the dead. Thus, *bā'āreṣ*, "in the earth," would more likely indicate that the earthly saints are in view. Its designation as livable earth is by far its most common use. The "blood libations" in v.4 might be a figure for wine offerings to a deity as blood did not play a central role in ancient Near Eastern sacrificial ritual.[559] Wine is considered the "blood of grapes" in the Hebrew Bible (Gen. 49:11; Deut. 32:14).[560] In sum, Yahweh delights in pious Israelites (v.3), whereas he rejects the unfaithful who go after another god (v.4):[561]

(16:3)

As for the saints [= holy ones] in the land,
they are noble in whom I delight

(16:4)

Those who choose another [god] multiply their sorrows;
their libations of blood I will not pour out,
their names I will not take upon my lips.

---

556 Cf. Eaton 1976:163 "deities who are in the dust"; cf. Spronk 1986:336 n.3.

557 Spronk 1986:334–37; Smith and Bloch-Smith 1988:283; with qualified acceptance, Lewis 1989:166.

558 Otherwise the psalmist might be viewed as endorsing such a cult. Several commentators have identified the *qᵊḏôšîm* as foreign gods in order to avoid attributing to the psalmist such syncretistic tendencies. Anderson 1972:(I):142 "as for the so-called holy ones who are in the land, cursed are all who delight in them." Mannati 1972:359–61 was an exception for he concluded that these verses celebrated syncretism and was perfectly in harmony with the remainder of the psalm.

559 Cf. McCarthy 1969:166–76; Rainey 1975:196.

560 This presupposes that from the psalmist's perspective, the blood libations would be acceptable to Yahweh. Other interpreters viewed these as illegitimate offerings in the Yahweh cult or, perhaps, those made to the foreign gods, cf. Anderson 1972(I):143 "libations of blood to them." W. R. Smith 1880:347 suggested that the blood referred to "libations accompanying human sacrifice" cf. Isa. 57:5–6.

561 Following Kraus 1988:234,36–37. For the phrase *'aḥēr māhārû* in v.4, "those who barter for another [god]," cf. Exod. 34:14 *'ēl 'aḥēr*. The root *m-h-r* can signify an acquisition by payment of a purchase price, cf. Exod. 22:15(ET 16). In the passage at hand, perhaps the acquisition of idols is viewed as an illicit financial transaction, cf. also Jer. 2:11 and Ps. 106:20.

Smith and Bloch-Smith identified the ritual feeding of the dead in Ps. 22:30(ET 29).[562] But it is doubtful that "all the anointed of the earth," or *kôl-dišnê-'ereṣ*, are the dead. The Ugaritic phrase cited in support *mrqdm dšn*, which they translate as "the anointed dancers," in *KTU* 1.108:5 does not refer to the dead (or to the *rp'i 'arṣ*, cf. verso line 24), but to "ivory castanets."[563] Against Spronk, the MT *'āk̲ᵊlû*, "they eat," need not be emended to *'ak̲ lô*, "surely," as MT finds support in LXX *ephagon*.[564] In any case, Anderson viewed 22:30(ET 29) as expressive of the great distress the living might experience. It is as if they were dead.[565]

M. Smith argues that the phrase *qārᵊ'û b̲išmôt̲ām*, (lit.) "they call(ed) their names," in 49:12(ET 11) refers to the summoning of the dead ancestors.[566] He cites as support the death imagery in Psalm 49, the primary usage of *qr' b-šm* + object in cultic contexts where deities are summoned, and the use of *qr'* to invoke the ancestors in *KTU* 1.161. This interpretation is unlikely for several reasons. In 1.161, the relevant phrase is *qr'* + accusative object which conveys the commissioning of the weakened dead to perform a task down below (cf. 3.1.9.1.). The cultic associations of *qr' b-šm* are not readily apparent for Psalm 49. The construction *qr' b-šm* shows up often in non-cultic contexts where the called are commissioned for a specific task and the calling is that by a superior of an inferior. However, those called do not cross over cosmological worlds to arrive in the immediate presence of the superior as is presupposed with the summoning interpretation of *qr' b-šm*. For such a "summoning" we would expect *qr'* + *lᵊ* as in 1 Sam. 28:15. In any case, English "summoning" is inadequate in these instances, for in what sense does Yahweh "summon" Bezalel in Exod. 31:2; 35:30 or Israel in Isa. 43:1 and 45:4? Surely, the author does not mean to suggest that Bezalel ascended to the very presence of Yahweh. In any case, the obscure *'ᵃlê 'ᵃd̲āmôt̲* would be even more rare a designation for the netherworld than the occasionally used *bā'āreṣ*. As M. Smith acknowledges, most commentators understand the verse to refer to the naming of the land (*RSV* and *NAB*) or fame (cf. Ruth 4:11). Lastly, Ps. 49:6–11(ET 5–10),13–21(ET 12–20) is replete with the evils of pride, fame, and fortune and the pit, death, the grave, and Sheol are invoked only in their capacity to terminate such evils.

Many scholars understand "the sacrifices to/for the dead," or *zib̲ḥê mēt̲îm*, of Ps. 106:28 to refer to a cult of the dead.[567] This is presumably supported by

---

562 Smith and Bloch-Smith 1988:283.

563 Following Pardee 1988:98–99.

564 Spronk 1986:282 n.2.

565 Anderson 1972(I):194.

566 M. Smith 1993:105–07.

567 Cf. e.g., Oesterley 1939:451–52; Weiser 1962:677; Dahood 1970:73–74; Sabourin 1974:316; Pope 1977b:217; 1981:178–79; Brichto 1973:28; Xella 1982:657–65; Spronk 1986:231–33; Lewis 1989:92–93,167; Bloch-Smith 1992:123–24.

the dependence of 106:28 upon Num. 25:2 *zibḥê ʾelōhêhen*, "the sacrifices to their gods."[568] This connection has also resulted in the equation of the gods and the dead.[569] We have set forth extensive arguments against the equation of the gods and the dead in Syro-Palestinian traditions (cf. 4.5.1.). Confirmation of the death cult associations of the Baal Peor incident has been sought in the rabbinic connections of Baal Peor and the *marzēaḥ*. Both targum Pseudo-Jonathan and Sifre Num. 131 describe the events at Baal Peor as involving the *mrzḥn* = *marzēaḥ*. Moreover, the sixth century C.E. Madeba map depicts the region in the trans-Jordan where tradition locates the Baal Peor incident as a *betomarseas he k(ai) maioumas* or "a *marzēaḥ*-house, which is also a *mayumas*." The possibility that the *mayumas* comprised an orgiastic festival lends further credence to the excesses of the Baal Peor *marzēaḥ*.[570] Bryan has pointed out, however, that the rabbinic writers never referred to the *zibḥe mētîm* of Ps. 106:28 or to any other death cult practices in their association of Baal Peor and the *marzēaḥ*. It is more likely the case, that the excesses attached to the *marzēaḥ* in later periods under Hellenistic influence provided the catalyst for the connection made by the rabbis.[571]

In the light of Num. 25:2, Ps. 106:28 probably preserves a polemical depiction of foreign gods as "lifeless" or dead.[572] Several biblical texts employ similar literary imagery wherein foreign gods are portrayed as lifeless or dead (cf. 82:6–7; 115:4–7; 135:15–17; Isa. 44:9–20; Jer. 10:11). In the Wisdom of Solomon, foreign gods are explicitly called the dead (13:10; 15:15–17).[573]

---

568 Following Fishbane 1985:425–26 who views Ps. 106:27–30 as an aggadic treatment of Num. 25:1–9. Cf. Norin 1977:121 n.37 for a list of dates offered for Psalm 106. The reference to Ps. 106:47–48 in 1 Chr. 16:35–36 eliminates a Maccabean date. Its links with Joel 2:13 (106:45); Ezek. 16:20 (106:37); 20:23 (106:27), its close affinity with Isa. 61:7–14, and the presumed post-exilic setting of v.47 favor a post-exilic date despite attempts to uphold an exilic date, cf. Kraus 1989:316–18. The psalm is heavily influenced by dtr and priestly language and ideology in its rendition of Israel's history of rebellion, so Coats 1968:225–30; Kraus 1989:316–20.

569 So Spronk 1986:231–33; Lewis 1989:92–93,167.

570 Cf. Pope 1977b:217–18. On the licentious behavior and possible death cult relations of the *mayumas* festival of Hellenistic times, cf. Good 1986:100–14. On the historiographic fiction in the Madeba map, cf. now Donceel-Voûte 1988:519–42.

571 Cf. Bryan 1973:88–89 against Pope 1977b:217–18. Cavalletti 1981:135–36 similarly speculated that in Ps. 78:15, Yahweh took part in a *marzēaḥ*-type banquet like that reflected in *KTU* 1.114 in which El at Ugarit drank to satity in order to undergo a mystical experience.

572 Both earlier and recent commentators have upheld this view, cf. e.g., Delitzsch 1898:156; Briggs 1906–07:351; Gerstenberger, Jutzler, and Boecker 1972:172; Rogerson and McKay 1977:47; Jacquet 1979:139,147–48; Allen 1983:46,49; Kraus 1989:320–21. Andersen and Freedman 1980:632 emended *zibḥê mētîm*, "sacrifices of the dead," in Ps. 106:28 to *zibḥê mᵊtîm*, "sacrifices of men," that is, human sacrifices following *zibḥê ʾādām* in Hos. 13:2. But this ignores the obvious connection of Ps. 106:28–31 and Num. 25:1–9.

573 Wisdom 13:10: "But miserable are they and in dead things (*nekros*) are their hope, who called them gods (*theous*), which are the works of men's hands, gold and silver, to depict art, and

4.8. Excursus: The Israelite Rephaim

Scholars have repeatedly identified the biblical Rephaim, or *rᵊpāʾîm*, as the (semi-)divine, dead ancestors and thereby exemplary of the early Israelite belief in the supernatural, benefic power of the dead.[574] This, in turn, has generated a virtual consensus that the biblical Rephaim reflect an underlying Canaanite-Israelite ancestor cult aimed at manipulating those powers of the dead. As a matter of fact, the biblical texts testify to two distinct traditions with regard to the Rephaim. On the one hand, the Rephaim as the autochthonous populations of Palestine are depicted in narrative texts of the Pentateuch and the DtrH.[575] On the other hand, the prophetic, psalmic, and wisdom texts portray those Rephaim who were shades of the dead inhabiting the netherworld.[576] Although various scholarly theories vis-à-vis their relationship have developed, the biblical traditions never make any explicit association of the "pre-historic ethnic" Rephaim of the narratives and the Rephaim who are shades. Nevertheless, the history of interpretation has assumed some organic connection between the two.[577] The consensus is that the traditions concerning the "ethnic" Rephaim informed those reflective of the netherly Rephaim. What were once living entities, died, and then inhabited the netherworld. The Ugaritic *rpʾum* are repeatedly invoked as confirmation for the existence of both a living and dead biblical Rephaim.

De Moor's theory comprises the most compelling and thoroughgoing proposal to date. According to this author, the Ugaritic *rpʾi ʾarṣ* were the Rephaim who were originally the ruling aristocracy. These Rephaim (Ugaritic *rapiʾūma*/Hebrew *rōpᵊʾîm*) functioned as savior-healers of the country and worshipped Baal, *rpʾu mlk ʿlm*, "Savior, king of eternity," their patron deity. At death, they became deified royal ancestors, but continued in their capacity as savior-healers. However, with the late emphasis on Yahweh as *rōpēʾ*, "healer," (in direct contrast to Baal) and the general ban on ancestor worship, the Rephaim in Israel were no longer venerated or worshipped as heroes. Rather, in the polemical rhetoric of the biblical (poetic) traditions, the *rᵊpāʾîm*, whom de Moor relates to the *rōpᵊʾîm*, "healers," became

resemblances of men's hands, or stone good for nothing, the work of an ancient hand," cf. also Jacquet 1979:139,147–48; Kraus 1988:320–21.

574 Cf. recently Tropper 1989:124–26,142–45; M. Smith 1990:26,130; for a general survey of opinion, see Brown 1985.

575 The *rᵊpāʾîm* appear in Gen. 14:5; 15:20; Deut. 2:11,20(2x); 3:11,13; Josh. 12:4; 13:12; 17:15 (in the singular and plural). On the valley of Rephaim, or *ʿemeq-rᵊpāʾîm*, cf. Josh. 15:8; 18:16; 2 Sam. 5:18,22; 23:13; Isa. 17:5; 1 Chr. 11:15; 14:9. For the *yᵊlîdê hārāpāh*, cf. 2 Sam. 21:15–22; 1 Chr. 20:4–8; note 1 Samuel 17.

576 Isa. 14:9; 26:14,19; Ps. 88:11(ET 10); Prov. 2:18; 9:18; 21:16; Job 26:5 (only in the plural).

577 Neither the *yᵊlîdê hārāpāh*, "sons of the Weak One," (2 Sam. 21:15–22; 1 Chr. 20:4–8, see below) nor the *miyyeṯer hārᵊpāʾîm*, "remnant of the Rephaim," (Deut. 3:11; Josh. 12:4; 13:12) help to clarify our understanding of the related philological issues.

weakened and were relegated to the lower parts of the netherworld. Hence, the *rᵊpā'îm* came to be identified etymologically with Hebrew *rāpāh*, "to be weak," by means of such constructions as *yᵊlîdê hārāpāh* (which we take to mean "sons of the Weak One"). De Moor explains the "ethnic" Rephaim of the Hebrew Bible as reflecting a faint memory of the heroic savior-healers-turned-deified-ancestors known from Ugarit, while the weakened netherworld Rephaim reflect the later biblical polemic. He also explains the MT vocalization *rᵊpā'îm* as a secondary development of an original Hebrew *rōpᵊ'îm*, "physicians," as confirmed by the LXX translator's rendering of *iatroi*, "healers," (Ps. 87:11) for consonantal *rp'ym* in Ps. 88:11(ET 10) and in Isa. 26:14.[578] Lastly, his reconstruction draws upon elements found in the Greek hero traditions. He perceives an analogous Greek development in which "living" heroes, or *hērōs*, died and became *hērōs theos* with a divine status worthy of worship in the cult. These heroic ancestors could be portrayed as giants and identified as *iatroi*, "healers."[579]

Assuming for the sake of argument that the *opinio communis* is correct in concluding that some type of organic relationship originally obtained between the biblical "ethnic" Rephaim and the Rephaim who are shades, we would view that relationship quite differently. First, nowhere in the Ugaritic or, for that matter, the biblical texts are the *rp'um/rᵊpā'îm* explicitly portrayed or polemicized against in their specific capacity as savior-healers. Furthermore, no examples of the verbal form of the root *r-p-'* with the meaning "to heal" were found to exist at Ugarit in the survey offered in 3.1.9. As noted earlier, the location in the Ugaritic netherworld of a subgroup within the *rp'um*, the *rp'im qdmym*, is attested only on one occasion in *KTU* 1.161, so this occurrence is exceptional in nature. In any case, the text presupposes the weakened status of the netherworld *rp'im qdmym* (cf. 3.1.9.1.). They were merely called by name to gather at the netherworld entrance to transport the throne and the recently deceased king to their newly appointed place below. No supernatural powers with which to benefit the living are attributed to the *rp'im qdmym*. Moreover, the more inclusive group of Ugaritic *rp'um* were not royal deified ancestors. Rather, they reflected early mythic warrior traditions for which evidence of associated cultic practices, let alone for specific acts of worship or veneration, is entirely lacking. Instead, the *rp'um* name of the mythic traditions was adopted by bands of local living mercenaries, the *rp'i 'arṣ* and the *rp'u*. That a related patron deity existed is difficult to document for the equation of Baal with *rp'u mlk 'lm* is extremely problematic (cf. 3.1.8.) and the references to the

---

578 "We know for certain that even in the days of the translators of the Septuaginta the original vocalization of the word *rp'ym* was still not forgotten," de Moor 1976:340–41, i.e. *iatroi* = living aristocratic healer-saviors or *rōpᵊ'îm/rapi'ūma*.

579 De Moor 1976:323–45; cf. the more recent version articulated by his student Spronk 1986:161–96,227–29.

Ugaritic deity *Rp'u* never make any overt mention of his function as healer. Lastly, de Moor's citation of the Greek hero traditions is somewhat misleading. It was clearly the exception not the rule that a hero became *hērōs theos* after death. The same can be said of those given the epithet *iatroi*. Moreover, not all those who obtained this healer status were attributed gigantic size (and not all those with gigantic size were healers). In other words, the Greek traditions develop in a far more complex fashion.[580]

What is clear is that in the biblical poetic passages where the Rephaim are depicted as shades, like their Ugaritic counterparts, the *rp'im qdmym*, they are powerless. The term in these traditions only functioned to designate humanity's postmortem, weakened existence. Nowhere in the non-narrative contexts are living human beings identified as Rephaim or superhuman warrior heroes before their death. Isa. 14:9, perhaps the earliest biblical reference to the Rephaim as shades, states that the fallen tyrant (*meleḵ bāḇel*, cf. v.4) simply becomes weakened like the Rephaim. Contrary to general opinion, it is nowhere stated, assumed, or implied that the netherworld Rephaim, as the dead, ever possessed supernatural, beneficent powers. Furthermore, while the writer's polemic is aimed at the loss at death of a living king's power, this does not presuppose a long-standing Syro-Palestinian royal tradition in which such a loss of power at death was inconceivable. The focus of the Isaiah 14 passage is instead on death as the great equalizer.

If the Ugaritic and biblical traditions are to be associated, then what once comprised only a specific element within the *rp'um* traditions, the netherworld Rephaim or *rp'im qdmym*, was altered in the non-narrative traditions of the Hebrew Bible in two ways. Some biblical writers applied the unqualified term Rephaim (without the modifier "Old" or "Ancient," *qdmym*, Hebrew *qᵊḏāmîm*) to the deceased. For writers of poetic biblical texts, the *rᵊpā'îm* (= *rp'um*) replaced the *rp'im qdmym* in this capacity. The term used to denote living elites at Ugarit, *rp'um* (or *rp'i 'arṣ*), was now applied to those inhabiting the underworld. Whether this is to be explained as conscious compression or unwitting confusion of the earlier mythic, living, and deceased Rephaim traditions found at Ugarit is impossible to ascertain. In addition to this transformation, writers of other biblical poetic traditions incorporated the deceased from the common folk within the formerly elitist membership of the Syro-Palestinian Rephaim. In these biblical traditions, the dead Rephaim no longer denoted only the weakened elite.[581] They represented the feeble dead as an all inclusive class (cf. Ps. 88:11(ET 10); Isa. 26:14,19).

---

580 Cf. e.g., Coldstream 1976:8–17 and especially Snodgrass 1988:19–26. See also Antonaccio 1987; 1992:85–105; Whitley 1988:173–82; Morris 1988:750–61; 1991:147–69; 1992; Alcock 1991:447–67.

581 Isa. 14:9 is often cited as evidence for the elite status of the biblical Rephaim as shades. Usage and context suggest otherwise. The *rᵊpā'îm* of Isa. 14:9a form a synonymous parallelism with Sheol which is here personified as the dead who have been disturbed or quickened. The root *r-g-z*

De Moor's notion that the LXX translator knew the 'original vocalization' of consonantal *rp'ym* as *rōp̱ᵊ'îm* (= *iatroi*) some five hundred years after the writer of first Isaiah gets it wrong with *rᵊp̱ā'îm* in 14:9 is difficult to accept in the absence of convincing support. The two instances in which the LXX renders the Rephaim as *iatroi* or "healers" more likely reflect a confusion with a polemic against the "physicians" or Hebrew *rōp̱ᵊ'îm* (Ps. 88:11(ET 10) and Isa. 26:14). Some streams of tradition in ancient Judaism considered this profession one of seven that had no part in the blessed afterlife and was destined for hell.[582] In sum, evidence for the (semi-)divine benefic status of the Rephaim as shades, for a Syro-Palestinian cult in honor of their supernatural beneficence, and for a polemic against these traditions is lacking.

As for the "ethnic" Rephaim, Talmon has recently outlined what he understands to be the progressive stages of the tradition history behind this term. Originally the "ethnic" Rephaim represented a stratum of the pre-Israelite population of Canaan (Gen. 14:5; 15:20; Deut. 3:11; Josh. 13:12). Their abnormal height is an "epic aggrandizement of basic actual facts" (Deut. 2:11; 3:11) and the same applies to their association with the mythical Nephilim (Num. 13:33 and cf. Gen. 6:1–4). The connection of the *yᵊlîḏê hārāp̱āh* with the Philistines of David's day may be a secondary development resulting from the Philistine conquest of these autochthones.[583] He summarizes by stating that "the majority of these mentions of *rāp̱āh-rᵊp̱ā'îm* contain no unequivocal mythical allusions."[584] Regardless of Talmon's vague and questionable demarcation between historical and "mythopoeic" elements in these narratives, the tradition history can be viewed quite differently. The tradition about the superhuman size of a mythical Rephaim might very well be the earliest stage reflected in the Hebrew Bible.

In the biblical narratives about primeval peoples, two types of traditions were pressed into service. The first employs archaic names such as Hittites and Amorites

---

is similarly used in 1 Sam. 28:15 with reference to Samuel's ghost. For Sheol personified, cf. also Isa. 5:14; 38:18. Like the dead Rephaim in the biblical traditions generally, Sheol here represents the common dead. Only with v.14b does the focus change from the dead in general of v.14a to the deceased elite with the mention of "all the leaders of the earth," or *kōl-'attûḏê 'āreṣ*, and "the kings of the nations," or *malḵê gôyim*. The verb *hēqîm* (or *hāqîm*) serves double duty in v.14b. In the final analysis, Isa. 14:9 does not demonstrate that Rephaim was a technical term denoting dead kings and nobles in biblical tradition.

582 Cf. Abot de Rabbi Nathan 36:5 "the best physician was one of the seven who had no part in the world to come"; Qid. 4:14 (R. Yehudah = Qid. 82b) "the best physician is destined for hell"; for additional references, see Brown 1985:14–15,134–35.

583 Talmon 1983:237–40. The term *rᵊp̱ā'îm* does not serve as a gentilic name and shows up frequently alongside similar names probably denoting the character of the people, although in many instances the exact significance is irrecoverable (e.g., Anakim, Emim, Zamzumim, Zumim, Nephilim, and Perizzim).

584 Talmon 1983:240.

and is to be dated to sometime after the eighth century, probably the exile.[585] The other construes the inhabitants as giants: the Anakim or Rephaim who are associated elsewhere with the Nephilim (Num. 13:33; also thought to be giants). This portrayal of the "ethnic" Rephaim is preserved in the dtr redaction of Deuteronomy (2:11; 3:11) and in the DtrH (2 Sam. 21:15–22; 1 Chr. 20:4–8) where they or, more properly, the *yᵊlîḏê hārāp̄āh* are also connected with the Philistines. As at Ugarit, a mercenary association probably stands behind the Rephaim who are depicted as giant warriors employed by the Philistines in 2 Sam. 21:15–22.[586] The ideological significance of the pre-Israelite inhabitants' association with giants is made explicit in the account of David's encounter with Goliath in 1 Samuel 17. Goliath stands a head above the others as the embodiment of foreign defiance against Yahweh and his people.[587]

If one begins with the defensible position that the DtrH has chronological priority over the Yahwistic History (hereafter YH) vis-à-vis their respective compositional histories, then further developments can be detected in the subsequent YH. Whereas in Deut. 2:11 and 3:11, the Rephaim were depicted as only vaguely situated in the local geography, they are assigned smaller yet more specific regions of habitation by the Yahwist and the Priestly Writer. A comparison of Gen. 15:20 (YH) followed by 14:5 and the priestly texts Josh. 12:4; 13:12; 17:15 illustrates this tradition history. At the same time, their mythic characterization as giants gradually disappears (is it assumed or suppressed?) in the latter stages of the tradition. These transformations reflect a gradual process involving the historicization of myth.

In addition to the mercenary connections which the "ethnic" Rephaim share with their Ugaritic counterparts, they preserve certain associations with the related mythic warriors of the Ugaritic texts, "the Mighty Ones," or *rp'um*.[588] Nevertheless, the 'greatness' of the mythic Ugaritic *rp'um* was transformed in biblical narratives from one singularly focused on heroic military prowess to one which took on superhuman physical dimensions and pseudo-ethnic identity. This development approximates the kind of antiquarian concern to bring order to the numerous independent traditions about heroes and giants as found in the Greek

585 So Van Seters 1972:64–81.

586 In an effort to strengthen the polemic, they were secondarily identified as Philistines as in 1 Sam. 17:8. On the late compositional history of this story and David's rise to power, cf. Van Seters 1983:264–71. Talmon 1983:239–40 likewise noted that the descendants of Raphah are not Philistines but are depicted as having fought in the Philistine army as mercenaries (2 Sam. 21:15–22; 1 Chr. 20:4–8).

587 Cf. Van Seters 1972:75; 1975:117.

588 This aligns with the proposal offered previously: East Semitic *r-b-'* has a West Semitic correspondent in *r-p-'* II, "to be great, many."

traditions.[589] The Rephaim as pre-historic warrior heroes of Palestine also became the objects of biblical polemic. By employing the pseudo-ethnic marker *yᵊlîḏê hārāp̱āh* "the sons of the Weak One," the biblical writers could offer their occasional retrospective assessment of the power of Yahweh's enemy (or the lack thereof). The inhabitants of the land who opposed Yahweh and his people were found to be *yᵊlîḏê hārāp̱āh*, "the sons of the Weak One." The irony is enhanced through the description of these groups as giants who, although having initially struck fear into the hearts of the Israelite invaders of the promised land, were eventually conquered by them.

In sum, the *rep̱ā'îm* of the Hebrew Bible are neither identified as supernatural beneficent ghosts of the dead nor is such a status of the Rephaim unequivocally polemicized against anywhere in the biblical traditions. As underscored earlier, if the *rep̱ā'îm* who are shades are to be connected with the Ugaritic *rpi'm qdmym*, "the Mighty Ones from Old," this does not presuppose their original superhuman benefic power as ghosts. Like their Ugaritic forerunners, they are depicted as ghosts of inconsequential power and in need of care. Within the Rephaim as shades tradition, a change in the identity of the intended referents took place. That the earlier significance of the name was not fully comprehended in later biblical traditions is evidenced by the representation of the former "Mighty Ones (of Old)" as the ordinary and weak dead. The fact that a nominal form derived from *r-p-'* stands in non-narrative contexts where the weakness of the Rephaim is emphasized suggests not a polemic, but a loss of the intended referents' former heroic stature. Only fossilized elements of the name remained.[590] A similar process can be detected, perhaps, in the attachment of the epithet *hērōs* to the ordinary dead of no consequence by some Greek populations.[591] If an anti-Rephaim polemic exists, it appears in the narrative contexts where the *r-p-h* base ("to be weak") is associated with the "pre-historic ethnic" Rephaim through the construction *yᵊlîḏê hārāp̱āh*. Alternatively, it could be found perhaps in the purposeful omission in Isaiah 14 of the royal aspiration to be memorialized at death as one having attained the stature of the *rp'um* warrior heroes, but this would presuppose an acquaintace with those analogous Ugaritic traditions for which, in the case of the non-narrative biblical texts, we have no indication.

In the final analysis, their independence best explains the absence of any explicit connection between the two Rephaim traditions preserved in the Hebrew Bible. Perhaps, these two aspects of the ancient *rp'um* traditions had already obtained

---

[589] Cf. Van Seters 1988:1–22.

[590] The "Mighty-ness" of "the Mighty Ones of Old" derived from their original status as mythic heroes at Ugarit and not their secondary location in the netherworld where they were transformed into weakened shades.

[591] Garland 1985:10.

independent status by the time the Rephaim traditions reflected in the biblical texts were formulated. This might explain how the distinct developments evident in the growth of these traditions arose. Only in some of those biblical traditions did the Rephaim concept retain a remnant of its connection with the netherworld traditions. As with other biblical terms for the dead, the dead's weakened state was presupposed in those contexts where the term *rᵊp̄āʾîm* or Rephaim appears. In conclusion, the Rephaim concept nowhere presupposes an ancestor cult or the associated belief in the dead's supernatural beneficent power. At most, a former commemorative cult might underlie the Rephaim concept as now portrayed in the biblical traditions. The "ethnic" Rephaim of the narratives might reflect a polemical strategy bent on suppressing the memory of an earlier commemorative cult devoted to these Rephaim. They were formerly commemorated for their heroic acts in battle, but in the narrative traditions of the Hebrew Bible, they are depicted as the *yᵊlîḏê hārāp̄āh*, "the sons of the Weak One"; for these the Israelites ultimately defeated.

Conclusion

Two a priori assumptions frequently informing past studies on the Israelite ancestor cult govern our initial concluding remarks.[1] First, the existence of mortuary data indicative of funerary rites in a given culture does not guarantee the observance of the ancestor cult or, more specifically, ancestor veneration or worship. While various funerary rites—particularly those observed during mourning—are well attested in the ethnographic record, it would be a clear case of making too much of too little to infer from this that regular cultic rites indicative of the dead's supernatural benevolence necessarily ensued. As the comparative evidence reveals, not all peoples who solemnized the burying of their dead subsequently devoted significant rituals to remain on good terms with them. Even in societies that do develop post-funerary rituals for the dead, the beliefs underlying those rituals do not inherently presuppose the dead's supernatural beneficent powers.[2]

Second, mere geographic proximity and cultural contact cannot guarantee the adoption of one culture's mortuary beliefs by another. The argument does not hold that had populations of Syria-Palestine achieved geographical proximity to and cultural contact with other second millennium peoples who observed ancestor cult rites (e.g., the Hittites or Egyptians), then they would have necessarily observed like ceremony and belief. The same applies intra-regionally. Proximity and contact between the cultures of ancient Palestine and neighboring Syria do not provide guarantees on the matter. Again we cite as an argument by analogy, the fact that the Navajo culture never adopted the ancestor cults of the Pueblo. Considering the many loans that the Navajo made from Pueblo culture in the area of ceremonialism, this contrast is particularly striking. It was apparently the Navajo's morbid fear of the dead which impeded their acceptance of such cults (a topic to which we shall return shortly).[3]

---

[1] For a very recent endorsement of the Israelite ancestor cult theory, cf. now Levine 1993:468–79.

[2] Cf. also Morris 1991:147–69 on the distinctions between funerary rites (which he labels mortuary rites) and the ancestor cults and mortuary cults (which he identifies more generally as the ancestor cult).

[3] So Hultkrantz 1978:101; cf. also Opler 1983:368–92, esp. pp.376–80; Witherspoon 1983:570–78, esp. p.571 where the important distinction between a fear of death and the Navajo fear of the dead is underscored; Lamphere 1983:743–63, esp. p.754 where the Navajo belief in malevolent ghosts is contrasted with the Pueblo belief in the dead who became supernaturally empowered ancestors.

Having said all that, mortuary rites continuing beyond the burial of the dead are well attested in early Syro-Palestinian sources, but such rites reflect only the concern to care for or memorialize the dead. This brings to the fore one of the more critical issues addressed in our study: the absence of the ancestor cult or rites expressive of ancestor worship and veneration. The lack of these rites, however, is not indicative of the compatibility of such practices with earlier forms of Yahwism. Rather, our findings favor the view that the corresponding belief in the dead's supernatural beneficence was nonexistent throughout most, if not all, of the pre-exilic religious histories of Israel and Judah. Be that as it may, the conclusion that the ancestor cult was nonexistent in early Israelite or, for that matter, West Asiatic societies is not intended as a challenge to the obvious, namely, that ancient Israelite society was characterized by a strong bond between, kinship, family, and religion. Whether one has in mind the Israelite societies in which the authors themselves lived, the ideal society depicted in their texts, or a more ancient society constituting a historical past which we are able to reconstruct only in part, all indications are that kinship, family, and religion were closely intertwined. The care, feeding, and commemoration of the dead attested in the sources verifies the centrality of kinship and family in religious and social life. These rites, however, neither presupposed nor necessitated the belief in the supernatural beneficent power of the dead as expressed in ancestor veneration or worship or in the deification of the dead. That belief was a late foreign introduction motivated in part by the combination of prolonged social crises, the failure of traditional religion, and intensive contact with other cultures. The point to be underscored is that the belief in the supernatural beneficent power of the dead was not attached to the ancient kinship structures of Israelite society in the form of ancestor veneration or worship. It came to be ritually expressed in a belatedly adopted Mesopotamian form of divination, namely, necromancy.

Besides, if the dtr and priestly writers had been familiar with an indigenous, pre-exilic form of ancestor worship or veneration, then consistent with their polemical strategy against competing ideologies, one would have expected them to condemn explicitly these beliefs or their corresponding rites. But as our investigation has shown, general prohibitions against mortuary rites in the Hebrew Bible are late and limited only to two: mourning rites of self-mutilation and necromancy and, it should be recalled, the pre-exilic extra-biblical sources from the Levant only attest to the observance of selected mortuary rites such as mourning rites, care and feeding of the dead, and commemorative rites.[4] Ancestor worship and veneration are nowhere prohibited or, for that matter, mentioned, not because they were

[4] For our interpretation of what others have identified as prohibitions against such mortuary rites as feeding the dead, cf. 4.4.3. on Deut. 26:14.

deemed legitimate beliefs and practices, but because they were not observed. We arrived at the same conclusion regarding the deification of the deceased.[5]

The argument that ancestor cults did exist in early Israel but later biblical writers consciously suppressed them for they were incompatible with late Yahwistic religion is simply unconvincing.[6] If necromancy was depicted as having thrived from the late pre-exilic period onwards but was then prohibited in the traditions rather than simply expunged, would we not expect the same with ancestor veneration or worship for they express the same belief in the supernatural beneficent dead? Would they not have similarly posed a similar ideological threat to dtr Yahwism? Furthermore, the non-mention of necromancy and ancestor cults in traditions about earlier times such as we find in pre-exilic prophetic traditions like those of Hosea, Amos, and the oracles of Isaiah (chapters one to thirty-five) supports the pre-exilic *nonexistence* of these rites in early Israelite and Judahite cultures.

The royal mortuary and ancestor cults of first millennium Mesopotamia offer a fitting comparison. To decide whether these cults involved only the feeding, care, and commemoration of the royal dead or whether they belong to the ritual complex indicative of royal ancestor worship or veneration is beyond the scope of the present investigation.[7] We will assume for the moment that both kinds of cults were instituted and that they closely approximated each other in terms of their administrative and institutional demands. What is clear is that such cults were primarily, if not exclusively, designed for political legitimation. Assuming that analogous ritual and political worlds existed in ancient Israel and Judah, we would expect to find the royal mortuary or ancestor cult there, but we do not.[8] The Mesopotamian version of the royal mortuary and ancestor cults presupposed an institutional infrastructure sufficient to initiate and maintain them. Because these cults were (1) established by dynastic succession, (2) underwritten by enormous palatial economies, (3) managed by a vast professional priesthood, (4) performed at ideologically expedient ritual sites such as palaces and temples, and (5) incor-

---

[5] It cannot be assumed that the *exceptional* posthumous deification of kings associated with the likes of Sargon and Naram-Sin during the mid second millennium in Mesopotamia led to the "democratized deification" of the ordinary dead throughout Mesopotamia, let alone Syria-Palestine, in subsequent periods *contra* Hallo 1988:54–66; 1992:381–401.

[6] Loretz 1978:149–204, following a long line of predecessors, argued that traces of the cult of the dead had been eliminated by orthodox Yahwism after the exile. Prior to this such a cult was considered legitimate Yahwistic religion. See also M. Smith 1990:127–29.

[7] Cf. Tsukimoto 1985; note that Cooper 1992:19–33 interprets the Mesopotamian *kispu* offering merely as a *memorial* offering.

[8] It should be pointed out that the monument set up by Absalom in 2 Sam. 18:18 for his own personal commemoration does not necessarily presuppose a regular royal cult designed for political legitimation and dynastic succession. In fact, the account highlights the lack of a genealogically related successor.

porated into the festival calendars, it is doubtful that the requisite infrastructures to sustain them were present in the tyrannized Canaanite-Israelite-Judahite worlds of the mid first millennium. It would appear that these cults were historically the exclusive prerogative of "imperial" monarchies.

While Assyria's political domination undoubtedly resulted in her religious influence on subject nations, several factors would have impeded the incorporation of her mortuary or ancestor cults into the local Israelite and Judahite cults. For example, had Israel or Judah instituted local versions of the royal mortuary or ancestor cult inclusive of local dynastic genealogies, that cult would have presented a direct challenge to Assyrian claims of sovereignty over that region. Furthermore, the financial underwriting of such a cult would have severely hampered the local ruler's ability to make the expected payments of heavy tribute or taxes to the Assyrians. In the final analysis, we would not expect the attachment of either of these cults to a petty vassal or provincial state like that of late pre-exilic Israel or Judah.[9] The lack of associated monumental mortuary structures and paraphernalia in the archaeological record of Iron age Palestine might constitute further confirmation of our hypothesis.

Mari provides an exceptional example of a royal Syro-Palestinian mortuary cult that might have served to fulfill the functions of political legitimation and hereditary succession. As we pointed out previously, the Mari cult shares numerous elements with the mortuary cult at Pre-Sargonic Lagash. The comparison of the Mari and Lagash cults offers merely an illustration of what was possible in the broader Syro-Mesopotamian cultural context. At Lagash, the extensive mortuary cult was not expressive of the veneration or worship of the royal ancestors. That the Mari cult likewise functioned to simply care for or to commemorate the dead finds added support in the collective grouping of the *šarrānu* which, on the analogy of other cults such as those in East Asian ethnography, might point to their impersonal remoteness and powerlessness. The *kispū* offered to the statues of Sargon and Naram-Sin at Mari are indicative of the same concern to commemorate ancient royal figures and to legitimate the current dynasty by linking itself with the past.

In any event, it is not at all clear that the anonymous *šarrānu*, or kings, of the offering lists were actually former rulers of Mari and related genealogically to Zimri-Lim during whose reign, the relevant *kispu* offerings were made and recorded. Besides, the food offerings might have been made to appease the ghosts of displaced kings of former dynasties who, should they be neglected, might become angered. As Westenholz has noted, victors and defeated alike

[9] Of course, one might hypothesize that an unadulterated version of the Assyrian royal ancestor cult was imposed, but then this would not stand as evidence for an Israelite or Judahite adaptation of an Assyrian religious form.

during the Old Babylonian period had reason to fear the wrathful and restless ghosts of the royal and military dead. What Westenholz has proposed in the case of the unburied dead might equally apply in the case of neglected ghosts.[10] New dynasties might have feared the ghosts of former dynasties whom they succeeded; a fear which was only exasperated by the neglect of those unrelated ghosts. Thus, cults were established to placate those ghosts as well as the surviving sympathizers of the former administrations. In sum, extenuating circumstances might have given rise to the observance of a mortuary cult in early Syria like that at Mari. Be that as it may, a Mariote belief in the supernatural beneficence of the dead remains unattested.

But given what scholarship traditionally has described as ancient Israel's kinship structure, is this what we would expect in that context?[11] In a society that features corporate patrilineal descent groups whose members are tied to a certain territory by inherited land and ancestral graves, one might reasonably expect the observance of ancestor cults accompanied by sacrifice. As Wellhausen observed long ago, such a patrilineal society is presupposed in the narrative world of the Priestly writer. In that society, a specific male descent group held sole privilege of sacrifice and it performed that service on genealogically tenured territory. But is the Priestly writer's narrative world an accurate reflection of a pre-exilic Israelite society wherein patrilineal descent was exclusive? More to the point, would such a society have necessarily embraced ancestor cults and the associated beliefs in benevolent ghostly powers?

While it is often assumed that the biblical texts preserve a patrilineal descent system underlying the social structure of pre-exilic Israel, Jay has isolated several clues to an alternative form of lineage descent in the Yahwistic source (as traditionally defined).[12] According to her, the Yahwist has constructed a narrative world that is at least partially informed by a matrilineal descent system. Jay examines several passages where a number of interpretive problems and difficulties subside when a matrilineal system is taken into account. Sarah's blessing is problematic only on patrilineal grounds (Gen. 17:16a) and only Isaac, not Ishmael, could be a true heir because he could trace his descent through his mother. His descent from Abraham was not sufficient to guarantee his inheritance.[13] Likewise, the authority which Laban possesses to decide matters regarding the marriage of his

---

[10] Westenholz 1970:27–31; cf. Cooper 1992:27–29; Bottéro 1992:282–85.

[11] For an extensive treatment of ancient Israelite social structures, cf. Lemche 1985:231–74.

[12] Jay 1992:94–113; 1988:52–70.

[13] What has been generally recognized as the work of the Elohist resolves the conflict between matriliny and patriliny by the near sacrifice of Isaac (22:1–19). Thus, for the Elohist, Isaac ultimately receives his life not by birth from his mother but by the stayed hand of his father as directed by God, so Jay 1992:102. The work of the Elohist is viewed by Jay as an attempt to resolve the two competing systems of descent through the performance of sacrifice in favor of the patrilineal descent system.

sister Rebekah in Genesis 24 is due to his position as a mother's son (24:50–51). The fact that only Laban, Rebekah, and their mother receive gifts (and not Bethuel his father) suggests their positions of authority as well (24:53).[14] In such a system, the women are the preservers of the legitimate genealogical line.

The author has also proposed that the wife-sister stories in Genesis offer testimony to the existence of a matrilineal descent system underlying the non-priestly patriarchal traditions. As generally recognized, the practice of agnatic endogamous marriage (marriage within the patrilineal line) underlies these stories (Abraham and Sarah twice: Gen. 12:10–20; 20:1–18; and Isaac and Rebekah: 26:6–11).[15] Now Jay notes that if Abraham and Sarah had the same father but different mothers as Gen. 20:12 suggests, it is only as their mothers' offspring that their marriage was not incestuous. For Jay, this is "almost matrilineal."[16] The fact that the biblical writer(s) use agnatic endogamy to resolve the tension created by the coexistence of patrilineal and matrilineal descent systems exposes a latent bilateral structure in direct antithesis to patriliny.

If Jay's analysis is on the mark, the Yahwist's matrilineal descent system renders groundless the assumption that the ancestor cult necessarily constituted an essential institution of pre-exilic Israel.[17] Where lineage does not receive a strict definition either patrilineally or territorially there may be no ancestor cult. In non-patrilineal or non-territorial lineage systems, sacrifice is offered to divinities instead of ancestors, for the group is less corporate and so sacrifice is non-genealogically defined.[18] This more closely approximates what we find in the rival descent systems underlying the Yahwistic traditions. Finally, if one assumes for the sake of argument the early monarchical date of the Yahwistic work, then the matrilineal society portrayed therein would have precedent over the Priestly writer's later strictly patrilineal society.[19]

For the view that Gen. 22:1–19 is late (exilic or post-exilic) and perhaps Yahwistic, cf. the survey of opinion in Van Seters 1992:261–64.

[14] Jay 1992:104 notes that both the need to obtain Rebekah's consent (24:38) and the concluding blessing lavished on her and her descendants (24:60) are likewise inconsistent with patrilineal virilocal marriage.

[15] Lemche 1985:272–74.

[16] Jay 1992:99.

[17] Cf. Jay 1988:53–55,66–68; 1992:45–60,94–113,139–50.

[18] Cf. Jay 1988:52–70. In view of the argument of Van Seters 1992:227–45 that the land promise in biblical tradition was initially conditioned on loyalty to Yahweh and that only with the exilic Yahwist did it become unconditional and genealogically determined beginning with the patriarchs, it is difficult to offer a final verdict on the basis of the biblical traditions as to just how hereditarily bound to territory pre-exilic Israelite society viewed itself.

[19] If the Pentateuch and DtrH are to be identified as productions of the exile, the conflict between matrilineal and patrilineal descent systems is not one which entails the former's ancient priority as preserved in J and the latter's late and gradual ascendancy as articulated in P (cf. also the intriguing interpretation but questionable early dating of Gen. 49:26 by Jay 1992:109–10). Rather, the sources

These considerations confirm the superimposed nature of the priestly descent system as one perhaps derivative of some sector of post-exilic Israelite society with which the Priestly writer was familiar. By projecting this system into the past and by suppressing the matrilineal traditions in his genealogical reconstructions, he thereby enhanced his ideology of priesthood. More telling is the fact that if an ancestor cult was originally attached to the patrilineal system which informed that presented by the Priestly writer, no trace of that cult ever made it into the priestly tradition either by allusion or polemic. In other words, even the existence of an ancestor cult in the Priestly writer's Israelite patrilineal society is nowhere evident.

In any case, commemoration rites would have adequately served to perpetuate the genealogical lines for the Priestly writer's patrilineal system. The preservation and conveyance of genealogical descent could have served to legitimate and transfer power and hereditary ownership in both royal and non-royal contexts. The genealogical posterity would in turn sustain the immortality of the dead through the preservation and regular conveyance of their names and former deeds. In fact, because it does not presuppose the dead's supernatural beneficence, geneonymy would have been compatible with a priestly ideology that excluded competing supernatural powers. Moreover, patriliny or matriliny, with attendant commemoration rites and with, perhaps, pre-exilic antecedents, would have been compatible with the dismal netherworld existence of the dead as portrayed in both biblical and extra-biblical sources. Such a dreary afterlife suggests the strong likelihood that mortuary rites performed for the benefit of the ghosts located there maintained the sufferableness of that existence and no more.[20] Lastly, while the regularly or customarily observed practices of caring for and feeding of the dead, perhaps, perpetuated such personality traits as the deceased's form, consciousness, and memory, they do not presuppose the supernatural beneficent power of the Syro-Palestinian or, more specifically, the Israelite dead.[21]

---

might record the attempted resolution of roughly contemporary systems of conflicting descent which are reflective of the writers' ideological concerns and their own social realities. Nevertheless, in so far as Jay's argument that the traditions reflect multiple societal settings and lineage systems is limited to the narrative worlds of the biblical writers, it remains cogent.

[20] Wright 1990:152–53 distinguishes between commemoration and worship but follows Brichto in his vague definition of veneration and his notion that the dead could look forward to an afterlife of felicity or happiness if properly cared for or fed by the living kin. Wright unfortunately downplays the importance of commemoration in inheritance rites in the Israelite context through the perpetuation of genealogical lines of descent. In other words, the preservation of the patrimonial estate was the primary goal of the mortuary cult and not the happiness of the ancestors. The typical gloomy descriptions of the netherworld and the feeding of the dead as mere relief for the dead support this emphasis.

[21] Brichto 1973:48–49 imagines that the dead, in addition to some memory and consciousness of the living, possessed knowledge of the living's existence. This he derived from his analysis of

We turn now to the topic of necromancy. Our findings suggested that the repeated polemic against necromancy is not indicative of an early Israelite belief in the supernatural beneficent power of the dead. Rather, necromancy was introduced late, and it was of foreign provenance. Its non-mention in early pre-exilic texts is not an indicator of its original legitimacy in early Yahwistic circles.[22] Moreover, its subsequent condemnation was not a reaction to the threat that necromancy posed for pre-seventh century prophecy. The appearance of what was in origin a Mesopotamian rite, namely necromancy, alongside various practices of West Asiatic origin in the Josianic reform (and in Deuteronomy 18 and Leviticus), only serves to demonstrate that the dtr and priestly polemics held within their purview a far wider range of late pre-exilic and exilic practices and beliefs than those commonly identified as restricted to non-dtr, but Yahwistic religion. In addition to the demonization of non-dtr forms of Yahwism, the dtr and priestly traditions suppressed the eastern origin of those elements that made their way into the local culture from Mesopotamia of the seventh century and following (e.g., necromancy and cf. Ahaz's altar). The refusal of the dtr and priestly ideologies to acknowledge religious influence from Mesopotamia is consistent with their strategy of denying the ancient Israelite origins of the other practices outlawed in the Josianic reform. To deny contemporary religious influence from the culture of one's foreign master constitutes a rhetorical strategy in congruence with the repudiation of one's ancient, but now obsolete, local religious origin, for the

---

the biblical passages concerned with necromancy which he wrongly incorporated into his treatment of the ancestor cult complex. Anthropological studies demonstrate that these are distinct ritual complexes. Necromancy has no intrinsic familial associations. Moreover, necromancy was a late developing form of divination in the Levant. Thus, the Israelite family dead possessed no such knowledge and accessing that knowledge was not the *modus operandi* underlying the performance of mortuary rites. For recent summaries of the negative conceptions of the afterlife as imaged in the Hebrew Bible, cf. Spronk 1986:66–71; Knibb 1989:395–415, esp. pp.402–11; Mendenhall 1992:67–81. For similar conceptions in Mesopotamia, cf. Bottéro 1992:268–86; Cooper 1992:19–33. In Mesopotamian tradition, the care, feeding, and commemoration of the dead were not necessarily thought to be avenues for accessing the dead's knowledge of, or concern for, the living (*contra* Brichto 1973:48–49 for Israel), and were certainly not sufficient to make the dead's existence "felicitous" (*contra* Wright 1990:151–59 for Israel). Bottéro overstates the case when he emphasizes the dead's ability to assist the living, for his discussion depends in large part on his understanding of *mušēlu eṭemmi* in the lexical lists as an early reference to "the recaller of the dead" or necromancer. As we proposed in 4.5.1., the causative of *elû* might refer to "the one who drives the dead away" that is, an exorcist. In any case, necromancy appears in the Mesopotamian literary traditions rather late and as Bottéro and Cooper point out, references to the evil inclination of ghosts clearly dominate the textual evidence.

[22] If one embraced an early date for 1 Sam. 28:3–25 as most death cult advocates do, then that tradition would likewise disprove necromancy's compatibility with earlier Yahwism of the premonarchical period and with it the compatibility of the belief in the dead's supernatural beneficent power.

Canaanization of both contributed to the construction of an alternative form of Yahwism that was not only distinctive in character, but also ancient in origin.

Our results directly challenge the *opinio communis* regarding Israelite necromancy as most recently exemplified in Holloway's dissertation.[23] His conclusion that in Israel and Judah, necromancy had been around longer than the Assyrians is based on four doubtful or irrelevant points: (1) the existence of an Israelite belief in the afterlife based in part on the assumption that a diversity of grave goods necessarily entails such an afterlife belief, (2) the numerous references to rituals to the dead in the Hebrew Bible including necromancy, and (3) Bloch-Smith's conclusion that a lack of change in the archaeological record of Iron age mortuary artifacts points to the lack of change in practices and attitudes regarding the dead (according to Bloch-Smith, the divine ancestors, *'ᵉlōhê ābîw*, had continued as vital entities in Judahite religion and society as long as the kingdom existed).[24]

The mere existence of an afterlife says nothing in and of itself about the nature or power of those who attain it and diverse grave goods in and of themselves can say little or nothing about the underlying ideational concepts (cf. 4.4.3.). Holloway offers no detailed analysis of the biblical necromancy texts while ours demonstrates that necromancy was late and foreign. The numerous biblical references to a wide range of mortuary rites, if dtr in orientation and therefore exilic or post-exilic, can tell us little or nothing about pre-Assyrian beliefs in Israel or Judah. Neither can their mere presence in the textual tradition enhance the likelihood of an ancient necromantic tradition in Israel. In view of our analysis of the biblical and extra-biblical textual data, the lack of change evident in the archaeology of mortuary ritual more likely indicates that no changes took place regarding the weak and marginal role of the dead (and perhaps the maliciousness of those left unburied or neglected).[25] In any case, owing to the variability in ritual location and the paraphernalia associated with the performance of necromancy as well as the difficulties underlying the functional interpretation of non-epigraphic mortuary remains, the recovery of such material data, in and of itself, can contribute little if anything to the identification of necromancy in the historical record.

Furthermore, Holloway's statement that necromancy occupied only a marginal place in the repertoire of the Mesopotamian exorcist and diviner is based solely on a quantitative analysis of a limited corpus of texts (in the *ABL* corpus only 2 out of 61+ divinatory rites are entirely necromantic). He does not adequately account

---

[23] Holloway 1992:524–26.

[24] Bloch-Smith 1992:151. Bloch-Smith uses the results of her textual analyses to interpret the material remains. While methodologically viable, our investigation casts serious doubt on her interpretation of the textual evidence. For our view of the *'ᵉlōhê ābîw* or "gods of the fathers" as the personal gods of families, clans, and dynasties, cf. esp. our treatment of Ugaritic *'il'ib* in 3.1.3.

[25] The archaeological record also leaves open to textual verification the matter of the dead's exact function in society as embodied in commemoration rites.

for the fact that necromancy played a central role in the late Assyrian royal court of Esarhaddon where its enactment determined the legitimate successor to the Assyrian throne (cf. *LAS* 132 in 4.5.1.)![26] Finally, Holloway's more comprehensive and rather leveling analysis of the various Judahite cult reform practices that other scholars have identified as Mesopotamian, dictates the direction of his cursory treatment of necromancy. He does not allow for a sufficient degree of complexity in the dtr tradition-building process as is demanded by a detailed analysis of the evidence. For example, the various socio-political factors at play in these transformations do not get a serious hearing. To these we now turn.

The kinds of social influences at play in Israelite developments vis-à-vis the world of malevolent and benevolent ghosts can be illustrated by the transformations which took place in the spirit world of the Greeks. Generally speaking, the Greek dead were deemed objects worthy of fear only in the case of the special dead such as the unburied and the murdered. The ordinary dead were otherwise considered deserving of pity. In neither instance were the dead attributed supernatural beneficent powers. The beginning of the Greek belief in the dead's supernatural beneficent power is to be associated with the ideological and social transformations that coincided with the rise of the Greek *polis*. In fact, such a belief is first attested beginning, perhaps, as early as the eighth century but coming to prominence by the late sixth century with the rise of the veneration of the Greek heroes. While numerous factors, no doubt, contributed to the rise of the Greek hero cults, there stands a high correlation between the rise of such cults and the evolution of the Greek *polis*. As a new expression of broad based group solidarity these cults superseded the mortuary cult which formerly functioned in this capacity for the powerful aristocratic kinship groups. Whereas the heroes were venerated, the ancestors of earlier cults were only cared for and commemorated for legitimating purposes, and if proper respect for those dead ancestors was shortcoming, reprisals would come not from the dead but from the gods.[27] While the ordinary, pitied dead were buried outside the city in line with the new ideology of pollution and reclassification, the heroes were attributed supernatural powers and new cults were established in their honor. In other words, alongside the new social transformations that took place, status quo ritual systems were eradicated and new ones were introduced.

---

26 With a shade of the sardonic, Holloway violates his own criterion when he appeals to the same "paucity of hard evidence" argument to *support the likelihood* of necromancy's observance in early Syria-Palestine.

27 Cf. Burkert 1985:203–08; Garland 1985:1–12,88–93,118–23; 1992:31–34; the survey and critique of the archaeological data by Antonaccio 1987:7–21,358–75. For recent assessments of the history of interpretation of the Greek hero cult, cf. Coldstream 1976:8–17; Snodgrass 1988:19–26. See also Whitley 1988:173–82; Morris 1988:750–61; 1991:147–69; Alcock 1991:447–67; Antonaccio 1992:85–105.

A similar set of transformations in the spirit world can be identified in various sectors of late pre-exilic to post-exilic Israelite society. Three distinct "spirit worlds" can be discerned in ancient Israelite religion and tradition: (1) the spirit world of traditional polytheistic Yahwism,[28] (2) that accompanying the cultic innovations of the traditionalists, Ahaz and Manasseh, and (3) that presumed in the dtr and priestly traditions. The cosmology of traditional polytheistic Yahwism provides the starting point for our reconstruction. If the extra-biblical Syro-Palestinian mortuary rites of care, feeding, and commemoration as well as the cosmology of the netherworld preserved in biblical tradition are any indication of more broadly embraced pre-exilic beliefs, then at least the properly buried and regularly attended Israelite dead were pitied and their memory immortalized.[29] These considerations render doubtful the existence of the ancestor cult or necromancy as ritual complexes in pre-exilic Israelite or Judahite society. However, the gradual demise of the existing Israelite and Judahite social structures of the late eighth and seventh centuries gave rise to an increased skepticism in certain sectors of Israelite society about the viability of traditional Yahwistic polytheism. The social crises fomented by the domination of Assyria and that of Babylonia led to various constructions of new public and private reaffirmations of social solidarity which were given expression in the Israelite and Judahite cosmologies of the spirit world. The biblical traditions preserve two trends expressive of those cosmological transformations. As already mentioned, one is found in the cult innovations of kings Ahaz and Manasseh. The other is preserved in the dtr and priestly legislations concerning self-mutilation and necromancy.

The DtrH accounts of Ahaz and Manasseh preserve one strategy for identifying alternative sources of empowerment following the Assyrian conquest of Palestine and traditional Yahwism's loss of potency. For the dtr narrator, the initiation of ritual forms previously unattested in the accounts of their "apostatizing" predecessors epitomizes the superstitious spirit of the times and underscores Ahaz's and Manasseh's unprecedented sense of desperation. While one might be tempted to attribute this aura entirely to the rhetorical designs of the dtr traditions, it is, at least in part, predicated on the likelihood of Assyrian religious influence on pre-exilic Judah as our foregoing analysis demonstrates.[30]

---

[28] On the essentially polytheistic character of pre-exilic Yahwism, cf. now Lemche 1988 esp. pp.197–257; 1991b:97–115; Thompson 1992 esp. pp.12–16,415–23.

[29] As the following discussion will demonstrate, the fate of the Israelite dead who were neglected or who died prematurely is presently irrecoverable.

[30] Regardless of our present inability to reconstruct certain aspects of the world of ghosts in pre-exilic Israel i.e., whether they were malevolent and therefore feared or exclusively weak and therefore pitied, their benevolence is discernible only in late traditions. That the malevolence of ghosts might precede the development of their benevolent inclination has a precedent in the transformations that took place in the cosmology of first millennium Mesopotamia. Green 1984:80-105 has suggested that

We get our first glimpse at the desperation of the times in what the author conveys as the observance of human sacrifice by Ahaz and Manasseh (2 Kgs. 16:3; 21:6). According to the DtrH, no previous Judahite king had enacted this rite. The DtrH does depict Mesha, king of Moab, as offering up his eldest son as an act of efficacious apotropaic power (3:27). Human sacrifice is also listed in the dtr negative assessment of the entire northern dynasty which engaged in augury and sorcery as well (17:17). It is also attributed to the Mesopotamian populations deported by Assyria and resettled in Samerina/Samaria (17:31). There is a discernible pattern underlying the treatment of human sacrifice in the DtrH. First the foreign local populations are depicted as offering human sacrifice, followed by the illegitimate Israelite dynasty, and then the recently arrived Mesopotamian populations. Its embrace by Ahaz and Manasseh ought to be interpreted within these concentric circles of context. Human sacrifice serves to both distinguish Ahaz and Manasseh from their Judahite predecessors and to equate them with foreigners and with the rejected Israelite dynasty soon to be destroyed. In fact, 2 Kgs. 16:3 makes the claim that its avenue of entry into Judah was the local population not the northern cult.

Now the DtrH's portrayal of Manasseh's apostasy exceeds even that of Ahaz. None of Manasseh's predecessors of the divided monarchy, whether Israelite or Judahite, were recognized in the DtrH as having instituted the cults of human sacrifice *and* necromancy. Manasseh's unparalleled adoption of Mesopotamian necromancy underscores his unrivaled superstitious inclination. Desperate times demanded desperate measures. In fact, with his unrivaled observance of necromancy, Manasseh ends up looking very much like one of his superstitious Assyrian overlords that we have come to know through our treatment of the pertinent Neo-Assyrian texts. In the late Assyrian empire, the relevance of traditional religion was similarly weakening along with royal authority and the stability of the empire. An outgrowth of that crisis was the search for innovative ways to access numinous powers and the new role attributed to the divining arts in the Assyrian royal court gave unique expression to that quest.[31]

A pattern like that outlined for the DtrH treatment of human sacrifice is also discernible in the final form of the DtrH in its treatment of necromancy. Necromancy is similarly viewed as a practice observed by the local populations (1 Sam. 28:7–8) and by the rejected Israelite dynasty (of Saul; 1 Sam. 28:8,10–14). However, unlike human sacrifice, necromancy is not explicitly attributed Mesopotamian associations in the DtrH traditions. Rather, it is portrayed as a resurrected Canaanite

---

benevolent apparitions, or the benevolent inclination of existing demons, developed secondarily from an existing malevolent aspect in first millennium Mesopotamian cosmology as a means to counter negative powers.

[31] Cf. 4.2. and 4.5.1.

practice of hoary antiquity. Nevertheless, the ambiguity created by the DtrH's depiction of a centuries-long cessation of the rite following the days of Saul privileges the reader to speculate on the origin of its much later manifestation in late pre-exilic times. The note that the relocated Mesopotamian populations continued to worship their foreign gods, or *'ᵉlōhîm*, in 2 Kgs. 17:29,33,35,37 might tip the balance in favor of viewing *their* religious fervor as the stimulus behind the "reintroduction" of necromancy in Judah. For the dtr writer, those foreign gods might have included the chthonic deities responsible for the retrieval of the dead in necromancy. Perhaps then, the origin of necromancy was, at least rhetorically, taken to be Mesopotamian and only later thought to have become part of the local religious tradition of Manasseh's reign. Against this scenario stands its non-mention in the cults and reforms of Manasseh's predecessors, Ahaz and Hezekiah. Moreover, the fact that 2 Kgs. 17:24–41 does not explicitly describe the Mesopotamian populations relocated in Samaria as practicing necromancy (although they do observe human sacrifice) more likely serves to underscore the dtr writer's attempt to use the model of the superstitious late Assyrian king as the framework for his portrayal of Manasseh.[32] In the light of our foregoing arguments, its initial introduction in the reign of Manasseh remains more plausible.

Needless to say, not all sectors of late Judahite society searching for new avenues of empowerment tolerated the innovation attributed to Manasseh or the obsolete traditional Yahwistic polytheism. This brings us to the topic of the third "spirit world." More radical innovators like those represented by the dtr and priestly traditions combined elements of traditional polytheistic Yahwism like the cult of Asherah, and Mesopotamian innovations like necromancy, and depicted them as "the abominations of the Canaanite." The dtr traditions rhetorically identified Asherah as Baal's consort and necromancy as the pride of the ancient Canaanite city of Endor (and cf. Josh. 17:11–12). Thus, the spirit world of the dtr and priestly traditions was emptied of any and all superhuman beings that might possess benevolent powers except, of course, Yahweh.

The preceding considerations suggest the following traditio-historical reconstruction. The reign of Manasseh stands as the *terminus a quo* for the ghosts of Judah's dead having acquired beneficent supernatural powers (2 Kgs. 21:6; 23:24). Unlike other religious beliefs that were native to early Israelite or Judahite religion but polemized against in the dtr and related traditions and artificially ascribed foreign or Canaanite origins, this belief was of Mesopotamian origin. In the initial stage of expansion, the post-dtr redactor inserted Mesopotamian necromancy into traditions about the founding of the nation, attributed its observance to the Canaanites, and had it condemned in the law of the nation's founding father, Moses (Deut.

32 The formation *lᵊḇaqqēr* "to consult" in 16:15 might have necromancy in view, but rites performed at an altar more immediately suggest the regularly observed cult.

18:10–11). This redaction functioned as the 'legal precedent' against what was then read as necromancy's introduction several hundred years later by Manasseh (2 Kgs. 21:6; 23:24). The post-dtr redactor also extended necromancy into the stories about the formation of the nation's first monarchy. The story of Saul's encounter with the Endorian necromancer (1 Sam. 28:3–25) not only served to justify the rejection of the first Israelite dynasty, but it also provided the 'historical' precedent for necromancy's 'reintroduction' in the reign of Manasseh and, therefore by implication, the downfall of the second monarchy. This stage also saw the insertion of post-dtr anti-necromancy rhetoric in the oracles of Isaiah (Isa. 8:19; 19:3; 29:4) where the apostasy of necromancy was extended into the immediate past and attributed to the apostate Judahite king Ahaz and to the entire nation of Judah.

As to the rationale for necromancy's late proscription, the traditio-historical analysis of self-mutilation rites in biblical tradition outlined in 4.4.1. might offer some clarification by way of analogy. Although the legitimacy of self-mutilation was maintained in biblical traditions at least as late as the sixth century (Jer. 7:29; 41:5), these practices were eventually outlawed in dtr and priestly traditions. Clearly, their late proscription renders any appeal to a long-standing "Canaanite" origin unconvincing (cf. dtr Deut. 14:1 and the priestly texts Lev. 19:27–28; 21:5). Having eliminated any Canaanite associations, self-mutilation might be more appropriately viewed as an attempt to assuage the envy which the dead possess for the living by inflicting suffering on oneself or as a desperate attempt to disguise oneself from ghosts on the haunt by making oneself unrecognizable. Such a pronounced fear of the dead in pre-exilic Israelite or Judahite religion would also explain the scarcity of ancestor cults and necromancy. As the ethnographic data pertaining to the Navajos inform us, if one intensely fears the ghosts, one does not tend to invoke them.[33] But is there evidence for a pre-exilic Israelite fear of the dead?

To be sure, various malevolent demons are documented in West Asiatic religions, but as yet, none can be confidently identified as maligning ghosts.[34] Biblical traditions do not explicitly document a fear of the dead, although jewelry,

---

33 Cf. Spronk 1986:34–35,244–45,251–52 for the fear of the dead as a component of mourning in early Israel. His statement that "the positive side in the belief in powerful and wise spirits is better attested in the Old Testament" (p.252) is contradicted by our findings. It is late, foreign, and only occasionally attested in the form of necromancy.

34 For malevolent demons in Canaan, cf. now de Moor 1981–82:106–19; de Moor and Spronk 1984:237–49. Their view that some demons can be identified as malevolent and benevolent ghosts is highly conjectural. The early existence of benevolent ghosts in second millennium Canaan unfortunately rests on the equation of the *rp'um* and the *'ilm* with the dead at Ugarit. Against their reading *'ap zl* as an evil ghost in an incantation against evil demons from Ras Ibn Hani (*RIH* 78/20:15), cf. 3.1.9.2.

amulets, and figurines found in Iron age Judean burials have been cited as evidence of magical strategies designed to ward off malevolent apparitions including ghosts.[35] The epigraphic remains from first millennium Palestine might point in the same direction, at least as interpreted recently by Puech. The Uriyahu graffito dating to the early eighth century B.C.E. and incised in Tomb 2 at Khirbet el-Qôm (inscription 3) might refer to the deity's protection of the dead.[36] The concern for the deity's protection in warding off maligning demons is confirmed by its having been etched above an engraved right hand hanging in the position of an amulet "Uriyahu conjured his inscription. Blessed be Uriyahu before Yahweh, and from his adversaries by his Asherah save him. By Oniyahu and by his Asherah."[37] But this does not establish an underlying fear of the dead, for such fear, even in a mortuary context such as a tomb, might be caused by malicious demons other than the dead.

Puech also interprets some graffiti incised in tomb 1 at Khirbet el-Qôm as possessing magical and apotropaic powers. The inscribed letters *'alep* (or *'ayin*), *'alep*, *bet*, and *mem* might represent the initials of the four signs of the zodiac: "lion(-scorpion)," "lion," "virgo," and "libra." The protection invoked would be that sought during the liminal stage marking the deceased's journey to the netherworld. It is during this transition that malicious apparitions would most likely attack the deceased, for the newly dead were perhaps thought to be most vulnerable during this period. In any case, if supernatural powers are invoked for protection they are those of deities and not those of the dead.[38] Although malevolent apparitions are nowhere mentioned, they were undoubtedly the implied antagonists. Nevertheless, we cannot simply presume that these included malicious ghosts, for they are nowhere explicitly identified as such. In view of the lack of supporting biblical and extra-biblical evidence, the fear of the dead stands as an inadequate explanation for the observance of self-mutilation rites and the absence of ancestor cults and necromancy in the mid first millennium Levant. Nevertheless, the fear of the dead can perhaps explain the later transformations

[35] Cf. Bloch-Smith 1992:81–103. For possible biblical traces of exorcistic praxis and the mention of malevolent demons some of whom might conceal what were once believed to be evil ghosts, cf. Jirku 1912; Tromp 1969:160–67; Moore 1990:60–64.

[36] *Contra* Spronk 1986:307–10, following Mittmann 1981:143–44, this text does not preserve a belief in a beatific afterlife. Spronk's proposal depends upon unlikely textual readings, radical emendation justified on the basis of three supposed scribal errors, and his curious omission of lines 5–6. For a different rendering of the text, cf. Hadley 1987:51. Puech 1992:127–28 sees the inscription as possessing apotropaic powers.

[37] *'ryhw. hqšr. ktbh* (2) *brk. 'ryhw. lyhwh* (3) *wmṣryh. l'šrth. hwš'lh* (4) *l'nyhw* (5)*wl'šrth* (6) [. . . .]*h.*

[38] Puech 1992:127–29 also views the late seventh century Ketef Hinnom amulets that contain portions of a benediction similar to that of Num. 6:24–26 as having been placed in the tomb for the dead in order to continue the protective and apotropaic roles which they had fulfilled for the living.

that took place resulting in the dtr and priestly prohibitions against self-mutilation and necromancy, for both ritual complexes presuppose contact with the dead regardless of whether it is the dead's haunt or the living's summoning up that is in view.

On this point the Greek world offers another fitting analogy. An appeal to fear has been invoked to explain changes in the ancient Greek outlook regarding death. Coincident with the demise of Archaic Greece, the (re-)location of burial plots outside the city walls has been attributed to the ascendancy of a new fear of death (not to be confused with the fear of the dead). This fear led to an unease about tombs and so death was rationalized as pollution and given expression in the change from intramural to extramural burials.[39] Morris has demonstrated however that a new fear of death cannot adequately account for the concurrent non-mortuary transformations that took place in the classification systems of post-Archaic Greece. He also points out that evidence for a new fear of death is lacking in the textual and archaeological sources. While acknowledging that new ideas about pollution may have been behind such changes, Morris questioned the impetus behind the new ideas. He proposed that the sweeping ideological changes that took place with the rise of the Greek *polis* led to the development of a more rigid classification system vis-à-vis space and, in particular, man's central place in the cosmos as a citizen in the new social order. Boundaries between the living and the gods as well as between the living and the dead hardened. The resultant reclassification was given expression by the explicit spatial separation of their corresponding ritual sites. Religious activity was hitherto located in a discrete area over against the spatial indeterminacy characteristic of the previous so-called Dark age. In other words, the gods were more rigidly separated from humanity. Likewise, the movement of cemeteries expressed a similar concern to separate more strictly the living from the ordinary dead.[40] In support of his explanation for the introduction of extramural burials as well as the new temple locations, Morris invoked Douglas' notion that pollution beliefs provide a central means of defining norms and the intensity of those beliefs indicates the strength of concern with the definition of behavior. Such beliefs are designed to protect the "most vulnerable domains, where ambiguity would most weaken the fragile structure" of a given society, whether real or imagined.[41]

The restrictions placed on rites of mourning in biblical traditions are more appropriately viewed in this light, for mourning rites are liminal rites of the life cycle marking the transitional phase from life to death. In dtr and priestly circles, similar transformations were given expression through the reclassification of self-

39 Cf. Sourvinou-Inwood 1983:33–49.

40 Morris 1989:298–320.

41 Douglas 1975:47–59, esp. p.58.

laceration and tonsure as ritually polluting. They represented an anomaly that blurred the boundaries between life and death. They symbolized a convergence of the living's identity with that of the dead. One would expect, therefore, to find in the Hebrew Bible a comprehensive list of forbidden mourning rites. But of the many mourning rites mentioned in biblical traditions, only self-laceration and tonsure are singled out for censure. There must be more then to their being reclassified in the derisive manner in which they are.

As we proposed in 4.4.1., no other rite of mourning attested in the Hebrew Bible—including the (ritual) descent to the netherworld—can approximate the power to identify the living with the dead as embodied in self-mutilation. Through such excessive physical expression, the living achieve an unparalleled imitation of the dead. More than any other mourning rite, self-mutilation evokes a genuine sense of death's intrusion upon the world of the living. The resultant bodily scarifications stand as permanent reminders of death's inevitability and its ever-present threat.[42] Thus, self-mutilation as mourning so blurred the worlds of life and death in the tightly constructed and distinct worlds mapped out in the priestly and dtr legislations that they were singled out for censorship. Their exclusion insulated the idealized dtr and priestly social systems from the threat which death's inevitability presented.

In the narrative world of the dtr and priestly traditions and in the spatial organization of the Greek city, the development of pollution beliefs served to maintain the desired boundaries between the worlds of the gods, the living, and the dead. But in biblical traditions, while intimate identification with the dead like that expressed by self-mutilation was rationalized as pollution, it was necromancy, more than any other mortuary rite, that embodied the convergence of the worlds of the dead and the living. Mutilation was imitation of the dead, but in necromancy the dead themselves were thought to appear among the living. Not only that, necromancy was all the more anomalous owing to the appearance of the chthonic gods who assisted in the retrieval of the dead. Thus, necromancy was most vigorously denounced for it embodied the convergence of those three worlds which the dtr and priestly traditions sought to keep distinct—the worlds of the dead, the living, and the gods. But what led to rise of the idealized social systems that banned self-mutilation and necromancy in the first place?

In the case of the concurrent demise of Archaic Greek culture and the rise of the Greek *polis*, the quest to create a new national identity generated new forms of reaffirmation. These developments in the Greek world led to (1) the rise of the hero cults as a new expression of broad based group solidarity in the place

---

42 The ritualized descent was not a permanent reminder of death's presence and it did not embody a physical actualization. Therefore, it did not express as intensely death's encroachment. On the living's attempted identification with the dead in mourning, cf. now Feldman 1977:79–108.

of the former aristocratic ancestor cults, (2) the restriction of mortuary rites on behalf of the ordinary and aristocratic dead and the reclassification of corpses as pollution resulting in the relocation of cemeteries outside the city, and (3) the eventual replacement of hero cults by cults specifically designed to honor the war dead.[43]

The classification of Israelite self-mutilation and necromancy as ritually polluting likewise coincided with the need to institute new public and private reaffirmations of social solidarity in the exilic and post-exilic periods. In the aftermath of the social collapse brought on by the Babylonian invasions of the early sixth century, as in the case with the demise of Archaic Greek culture and the rise of the Greek *polis*, the quest to create a new national identity generated new forms of reaffirmation and the eradication of the status quo ritual system. Within the narrative world of the exilic biblical writers, rites whose performance conspicuously obscured those boundaries separating the realm of the living from those of the dead and the gods were rationalized as pollution, leaving in their place a more "tame death" and the possibility for the introduction of such new expressions of social solidarity as dtr Yahwism.

In other words, the dtr and priestly polemics were not aimed at breaking down clan fidelities fostered by local ancestor cults which were designed to legitimate land holdings and to insure the ancestors' blessings of fertility.[44] As we have argued, indications are that the ancestor cult played no role in the formation of dtr and priestly ideology and polemic. Moreover, landownership and the accompanying rites of the mortuary cult, care and feeding of the related dead, and the commemoration of the virtuous dead were not prohibited, but in fact employed by some biblical writers as a standard for the maintenance of the nation's relationship with her god. The dedication with which a son performed his duties on behalf of the weakened family dead stood as an ideal for the Israelite's loyalty to Yahweh.[45] The dtr and priestly prohibitions served instead to foster a new self-definition of Israel in the aftermath of the destruction of the first Temple. This self-definition provided an alternative to that afforded by traditional polytheistic Yahwism and those definitions advanced by new competing ideologies as exemplified in such ritual complexes as Mesopotamian necromancy. The dtr and priestly ideologies offered an innovative expression of social solidarity under the aegis of a radically restrictive form of Yahwism. The belief in the benevolent dead was a late development in Israelite or Judahite religion as is evidenced by both its introduction in

---

[43] Morris 1989:306; 1992:143–44.

[44] Cf. e.g., Bloch-Smith 1992:131-32 who views these fidelities as the object of polemic owing to the obstacle they presented to the centralization of the cult under the sole sovereignty of Yahweh and the administration of that cult by his prophets and priests of the eighth-seventh centuries B.C.E.

[45] Following Brichto 1973:1-54 and cf. Wright 1990:151-59.

the ritual form of Mesopotamian necromancy not before the seventh century B.C.E. and its subsequent renunciation in the dtr and priestly traditions. The foregoing analysis along with the application of an anthropologically informed lexicon reveals that ancestor veneration or worship played no role in the late third to mid first millennia cultures of the Levant. Simply put, the worship or veneration of the ancestors typically envisioned as underlying the mortuary rituals of ancient Israel comprises a cherished relic of nineteenth century anthropology. More to the point, mortuary data formerly identified as indicative of a primitive or syncretistic Israelite ancestor cult are neither primitive nor syncretistic nor of the ancestor cult. They witness instead to a variety of indigenous funerary, mourning and commemorative rites. Besides, not only does the enactment of commemorative rites (rather than in the ancestor cult) more adequately account for the details of the pertinent ritual data, it avoids the pitfalls endemic to the notion that the beneficence of the dead found early expression in the cultures of the Levant. Yet, it sustains the central roles that kinship structures and genealogies played in those societies. Ever since its rise to dominance at the turn of the century, mortuary data recovered from the Levant have been wrongly subsumed under the aegis of the ancestor cult and the notion of an early Israelite ancestor cult has persisted in biblical studies well beyond its allotted lifespan.[46]

Thus, the character of the seventh century Judahite religious spirit must be significantly revised. The syncretism commonly imagined by scholars is one that portrays various illicit Israelite or Judahite rituals as Canaanite in origin. As such, this image essentially follows the contours of the portrait sketched by the dtr writers. Assuming for the sake of argument that we can at least partially reconstruct the seventh century Judahite cult on the basis of the extra-biblical and biblical traditions, it is more likely the case that Ahaz and Manasseh were traditionalists who, for the most part, perpetuated the polytheistic Yahwism of their predecessors. Moreover, Josiah was an innovative monolatrist whom the later dtr writers held up as the ancient framer of their own ideological charter. If the term be employed at all, the syncretism that more accurately reflects the seventh century religious realia of Judah is one in which traditional polytheistic yahwists such as Manasseh adopted Mesopotamian practices like necromancy.[47] In a world in which traditional polytheistic Yahwism had lost its potency, a foreign practice like necromancy offered an alternative means of access to the power of the transcendent and a more adequate basis for broad based group solidarity. The

---

[46] Furthermore, while the available evidence points to the antiquity of the belief in the ghost's weakened state, it is silent on the matter of the dead's malevolence.

[47] We would therefore modify Ahlström's view that Ahaz and Manasseh were traditionalists and Hezekiah and Josiah were innovators. While Ahaz and Manasseh were for the most part traditionalists, Manasseh did introduce a radically new and foreign element into the Jerusalem cult.

dead now possessed the power to reveal the nation's future. As one among many responses to the social crisis that reached its zenith following Judah's vassalship to Assyria and that lasted well beyond the Babylonian invasions, necromancy posed a threat to the dtr brand of Yahwism that developed out the ashes of the exile. Therefore, like a number of non-dtr, but indigenous, Yahwistic rituals such as the mourning rites of self-mutilation, child sacrifice, and the cult of Asherah, the dtr writers reconfigured Mesopotamian necromancy as an ancient "Canaanite" ritual and had it condemned by such culture heroes as Moses, Isaiah, and Josiah.

In closing, a final qualification needs to be appended to the preceding argument. It must be conceded that the pervasiveness of the dtr rhetoric underscores the complexity involved in interpreting a biblical tradition that appears at once historical, at other times ideological, but more often than not, a combination thereof. It is this interplay between the ideological and the historical dimensions that significantly limits the scope of those reconstructions based solely on the biblical traditions that can be offered by the historian of religion. In fact, one could make the case that the dtr tradition's portrayal of seventh century Judahite religion was much more its own inventive creation. The form and style of the DtrH certainly could accomodate such an interpretation.[48] Therefore, one might be inclined to the view that the dtr writers held within their purview, a form of Mesopotamian necromancy with which they were directly familiar. Given such a scenario, the dtr writers would have themselves introduced necromancy into the narratives of the DtrH as the object of their polemic. This the dtr writers of the DtrH did in reaction to the threat which this Mesopotamian form of divination posed for the dtr Yahwism of their own day.

It has been the aim of this investigation to illustrate how the interface of text, artifact, and theory can significantly inform the modern interpretation of ancient cultures, how the comparative method can serve as a corrective to long revered paradigms based on antiquated versions of that same method and how the application of current anthropological data and theory can facilitate a revised reconstruction of the history of religions and, in particular, how it can inform the analysis of the mortuary data that have played so central a role in the re-imaging of that history.

---

[48] Cf. e.g., Hoffmann 1980.

Bibliography

Abbot 1966

W. M. Abbot (ed.), *The Documents of Vatican II.* New York, 1966.

Ackerman 1992

S. Ackerman, *Under Every Green Tree: Popular Religion in Sixth-century Judaism.* Atlanta, 1992.

Ackroyd 1977

P. R. Ackroyd, "The Chronicler as Exegete," *JSOT* 2(1977) 2–32.

Ackroyd 1981

P. R. Ackroyd, "The Death of Hezekiah—A Pointer to the Future," in *De la Tôrah au Messie: Études d'exégèse et d'herméneutique bibliques offertes à Henri Cazelles pour ses 25 années d'enseignement à l'Institut Catholique de Paris, octobre, 1979.* Éd. M. Carrez, J. Doré, et P. Grelot. Paris, 1981, 219–26.

Ahern 1973

E. M. Ahern, *The Cult of the Dead in a Chinese Village.* Stanford, 1973.

Ahlström 1982

G. W. Ahlström, *Royal Administration and National Religion in Ancient Palestine.* Leiden, 1982.

Ahlström 1993

G. W. Ahlström, *The History of Ancient Palestine from the Palaeolithic to Alexander's Conquest.* Ed. Diana V. Edelman. Sheffield, 1993.

Aistleitner 1967

J. Aistleitner, *Wörterbuch der ugaritischen Sprache.* Hrsg. O. Eissfeldt. Berlin, 1967^3.

Alberti 1985

A. Alberti, "A Reconstruction of the Abū Ṣalābīkh God List," *SEL* 2(1985) 3–23.

Albertz 1978

R. Albertz, *Persönliche Frömmigkeit und offizielle Religion: Religionsinterner Pluralismus in Israel und Babylon.* Stuttgart, 1978.

Albright 1944

W. F. Albright, "The 'Natural Force' of Moses in Light of Ugaritic," *BASOR* 94(1944) 32–35.

Albright 1953

W. F. Albright, "The Traditional Home of the Syrian Daniel," *BASOR* 130(1953) 26–27.

Albright 1957

W. F. Albright, "The High Place in Ancient Palestine," *SVT* 4(1957) 242–58.

Albright 1968

W. F. Albright, *Yahweh and the Gods of Canaan: A Historical Analysis of Two Contrasting Faiths*. London, 1968.

Albright 1969

W. F. Albright, *Archaeology and the Religion of Israel*. Garden City, 1969^5.

Alcock 1991

S. Alcock, "Tomb Cult and the Post-Classical Polis," *AJA* 95(1991) 447–67.

Al-Khalesi 1977

Y. M. Al-Khalesi, "The *Bīt Kispim* in Mesopotamian Architecture: Studies of Form and Function," *Mesopotamia* 12(1977) 53–81.

Al-Khalesi 1978

Y. M. Al-Khalesi, *The Court of the Palms: A Functional Interpretation of the Mari Palace*. Malibu, 1978.

Allen 1974

T. G. Allen, *The Book of the Dead or Going Forth by Day*. Chicago, 1974.

Allen 1983

L. C. Allen, *Psalms 101–150*. Waco, 1983.

Alster 1983

B. Alster, "The Mythology of Mourning," *Acta Sumerologica* 5(1983) 1–16.

Andersen and Freedman 1980

F. I. Andersen and D. N. Freedman, *Hosea*. Garden City, 1980.

Andersen and Freedman 1990

F. I. Andersen and D. N. Freedman, *Amos*. Garden City, 1990.

Anderson 1972

A. A. Anderson, *The Book of Psalms*. Grand Rapids, 1972.

Andrae 1952

W. Andrae, "Der kultische Garten," *WO* 1(1952) 485–94.

Angi 1971

B. J. Angi, "The Ugaritic Cult of the Dead: A Study of Some Beliefs and Practices that Pertain to the Ugaritians' Treatment of the Dead." M.A. thesis, McMaster University, 1971.

Antonaccio 1987

C. M. Antonaccio, "The Archaeology of Early Greek 'Hero Cult'." Ph.D. diss., Princeton University, 1987.

Antonaccio 1992

C. M. Antonaccio, "Terraces, Tombs, and the Early Argive Heraion," *Hesperia* 61(1992) 85-105.

Archi 1979–80

A. Archi, "Les dieux d'Ebla au IIIe millenaire avant J.C. et les dieux d'Ugarit," *AAAS* 29/30(1979–80) 167–71.

Archi 1985

A. Archi, *Testi amministrativi: Assegnazioni di tessuti.* Roma, 1985.

Archi 1986

A. Archi, "Die ersten zehn Könige von Ebla," *ZA* 76(1986) 213–17.

Archi 1988

A. Archi, "Cult of the Ancestors and Tutelary God at Ebla," in *Fucus: A Semitic/Afrasian Gathering in Remembrance of Albert Ehrmann.* Ed. Y. L. Arbeitman. Amsterdam and Philadelphia, 1988, 103–12.

Arnaud 1975a

D. Arnaud, "Catalogue des textes cunéiformes trouvés au cours des trois premières campagnes à Meskéné qadimé Ouest," *AAAS* 25(1975) 87–93.

Arnaud 1975b

D. Arnaud, "Les textes d'Emar et la chronologie de la fin du bronze récent," *Syria* 52(1975) 87–92.

Arnaud 1980a

D. Arnaud, "Les textes suméro-accadiens de Meskéné (Syrie) et l'Ancien Testament," *RHR* 197(1980) 116–18.

Arnaud 1980b

D. Arnaud, "Traditions urbaines et influences semi-nomades à Emar, à l'âge du Bronze Récent," in *Le Moyen Euphrates: Zone de contacts et d'échanges.* Éd. J. Margueron. Strasbourg, 1980, 245–64.

Arnaud 1981

D. Arnaud, "La religion à Emar," *Le Monde de la Bible* 20(1981) 34.

Arnaud 1982

D. Arnaud, "Les textes cunéiformes suméro-accadiens des campagnes 1979–1980 à Ras Shamra-Ougarit," *Syria* 59(1982) 199–222.

Arnaud 1985

D. Arnaud, "Religion assyro-babylonienne," *AEPHER* 92(1985) 231–36.

Arnaud 1986

D. Arnaud, *Recherches au pays d'Aštata. Emar VI.3: Textes sumériens et accadiens.* Paris, 1986.

Arnaud 1987

D. Arnaud, "La Syrie du moyen-Euphrate sous le protectorat hittite: contrats de droit privé," *AuOr* 5(1987) 211–41.

Arnaud and Kennedy 1979

D. Arnaud and D. Kennedy, "Les textes en cunéiformes syllabiques découverts en 1977 à Ibn Hani," *Syria* 56(1979) 317–24.

Aro 1961

J. Aro, Review of *Textes administratifs de la salle 5 du Palais*, by M. Birot, *OLZ* 56(1961) 603–05.

Artzi 1980

P. Artzi, "Mourning in International Relations," in *Death in Mesopotamia* [= RAI 26]. Ed. B. Alster. Copenhagen, 1980, 161–70.

Astour 1966

M. Astour, "Some New Divine Names from Ugarit," *JAOS* 86(1966) 277–84.

Astour 1968

M. Astour, "Two Ugaritic Snake Charms," *JNES* 27(1968) 13–36.

Astour 1975

M. Astour, "Place Names," in *Ras Shamra Parallels: The Texts from Ugarit and the Hebrew Bible*. Vol. 2. Ed. L. R. Fisher. Rome, 1975, 249–369.

Astour 1980

M. Astour, "The Netherworld and Its Denizens at Ugarit," in *Death in Mesopotamia* [= RAI 26]. Ed. B. Alster. Copenhagen, 1980, 227–38.

Attridge and Oden 1981

H. W. Attridge and R. A. Oden, Jr., *Philo of Byblos: The Phoenician History*. Washington D.C., 1981.

Avigad and Greenfield 1982

N. Avigad and J. C. Greenfield, "A Bronze *phialē* with a Phoenician Dedicatory Inscription," *IEJ* 32(1982) 118–28.

Avishur 1981

Y. Avishur, "The Ghost-Expelling Incantation from Ugarit (Ras Ibn Hani 78/20)," *UF* 13(1981) 13–25.

Avishur 1985

Y. Avishur, "The 'Duties of the Son' in the 'Story of Aqhat' and Ezekiel's Prophecy on Idolatry (Ch 8)," *UF* 17(1985) 49–60.

Baines 1991

J. Baines, "Society, Morality, and Religious Practice," in *Religion in Ancient Egypt: Gods, Myths, and Personal Practice*. Ed. B. E. Schafer. Ithaca, 1991, 123–200.

Barnett 1985

R. D. Barnett, "Assurbanipal's Feast," *EI* 18(1985) 1*–6* [Plate I].

Barnett 1986

R. D. Barnett, "Sirens and Rephaim," in *Ancient Anatolia: Aspects of Change and Cultural Development: Essays in Honor of Machteld J. Mellink*. Ed. J. V. Canby, E. Parada, B. S. Ridgway, and T. Stech. Madison, 1986, 112–20.

Barrelet 1980

M.-T. Barrelet, "Les pratiques funéraires de l'Iraq ancien et l'archéologie: Etat de la question et essai de prospective," *Akkadica* 16(1980) 2–27.

Barstad 1984

H. M. Barstad, *The Religious Polemics of Amos.* [= SVT 34] Leiden, 1984.

Barth 1977

H. Barth, *Die Jesaja-Worte in der Josiazeit.* Neukirchen-Vluyn, 1977.

Barton 1941

G. A. Barton, "Danel, A Pre-Israelite Hero of Galilee," *JBL* 60(1941) 213–25.

Barton 1984

J. Barton, *Reading the Old Testament: Method in Biblical Study.* Philadelphia, 1984.

Batto 1974

B. F. Batto, *Studies on Women at Mari.* Baltimore, 1974.

Bauer 1969

J. Bauer, "Zum Totenkult im altsumerischen Lagash," *Zeitschrift der Deutschen Morgenländischen Gesellschaft Supplementa* 1(1969) 107–14.

Baumann 1978

A. Baumann, "*dāmāh* II," in *Theological Dictionary of the Old Testament.* Vol. 3. Ed. G. J. Botterweck and H. Ringgren. Grand Rapids, 1978, 260–65 [= "*dāmāh* II," in *Theologisches Wörterbuch zum Alten Testament.* Hrsg. G. J. Botterweck, H. Ringgren, und H.-J. Fabry. Band 2. Stuttgart, 1977, 277–83].

Bayliss 1973

M. Bayliss, "The Cult of Dead Kin in Assyria and Babylonia," *Iraq* 35(1973) 115–25.

Beaulieu 1988

P.-A. Beaulieu, "Swamps as Burial Places for Babylonian Kings," *NABU* 2(1988) 36–37.

Beeston 1962

A. F. L. Beeston, *A Descriptive Grammar of Epigraphic South Arabian.* London, 1962.

Ben-Barak 1980

Z. Ben-Barak, "The Coronation Ceremony in Ancient Mesopotamia," *OLP* 11(1980) 55–67.

Ben-Barak 1988

Z. Ben-Barak, "The Legal Status of the Daughter as Heir in Nuzi and Emar," in *Society and Economy in the Eastern Mediterranean (1500–1000 B.C.).* Ed. M. Heltzer and E. Lipiński. Leuven, 1988, 87–97.

Berger 1980

P.-R. Berger, "Die Stadt auf dem Berge; zum kultur-historischen Hintergrund von Mt 5,14," in *Wort in der Zeit: Neutestamentliche Studien: Festgabe für Karl Heinrich Rengstorf zum 75. Geburtstag.* Hrsg. W. Haubeck und M. Bachmann. Leiden, 1980, 82–83.

Berndt 1970

R. M. Berndt, *Australian Aboriginal Anthropology: Modern Studies in the Social Anthropology of Australian Aborigines.* Nedlands, 1970.

Bertholet 1899

A. Bertholet, *Deuteronomium.* Tübingen, 1899.

Betz 1992

H. D. Betz, *The Greek Magical Papyri in Translation Including the Demotic Spells*. Chicago, 1992^2.

Beuken 1978

W. A. M. Beuken, "I Samuel 28: The Prophet as 'Hammer of Witches' ," *JSOT* 6(1978) 3–17.

Beyer 1985

B. E. Beyer, "Aspects of Religious Life at Ancient Mari as Seen through a Study of 'Archives royales de Mari 21'." Ph.D. diss., Hebrew Union College-Jewish Institute of Religion, 1985.

Biella 1982

J. C. Biella, *Dictionary of Old South Arabic: Sabaean Dialect*. Chico, 1982.

Bieńkowski 1982

P. A. Bieńkowski, "Some Remarks on the Practice of Cremation in the Levant," *Levant* 14(1982) 80–89.

Bietak 1979

M. Bietak, "Avaris and Piramesse. Archaeological Exploration in the Eastern Nile Delta," *Proceedings of the British Academy* 65(1979) 225–89.

Biga and Pomponio 1987

M. G. Biga and F. Pomponio, "Iš'ar-Damu, roi d'Ebla," *NABU* 4(1987) 60–61.

Biggs 1982

R. D. Biggs, "The Ebla Tablets: A 1981 Perspective," *BSMS* 2(1982) 9–24.

Biggs 1983

R. D. Biggs, "Lebermodelle," *RlA* 6(1983) 519–21.

Biggs 1992

R. D. Biggs, "Ebla Texts," in *The Anchor Bible Dictionary*. Vol. 2. Ed. D. N. Freedman. New York, 1992, 263–70.

Binford 1972

L. Binford, *An Archaeological Perspective*. New York, 1972.

Birch 1976

B. C. Birch, *The Rise of the Israelite Monarchy: The Growth and Development of 1 Samuel 7–15*. Missoula, 1976.

Birot 1980

M. Birot, "Fragment de rituel de Mari relatif au *kispum*," in *Death in Mesopotamia* [= RAI 26]. Ed. B. Alster. Copenhagen, 1980, 139–50.

Blau and Greenfield 1970

J. Blau and J. C. Greenfield, "Ugaritic Glosses," *BASOR* 200(1970) 11–17.

Bloch and Parry 1982

M. Bloch and J. Parry (eds.), *Death and the Regeneration of Life*. Cambridge, 1982.

Bloch-Smith 1992

E. M. Bloch-Smith, *Judahite Burial Practices and Beliefs about the Dead*. Sheffield, 1992.

Bonneterre 1983

D. Bonneterre, "À propos du *kispum* à Mari," *Recueil de travaux et communications de l'Association des Études du Proche-Orient Ancien* 1(1983) 26–31.

Bordreuil 1981

P. Bordreuil, "Les récentes découvertes épigraphiques à Ras Shamra et à Ras Ibn Hani," in *Ugarit in Retrospect: Fifty Years of Ugarit and Ugaritic*. Ed. G. D. Young. Winona Lake, 1981, 43–48.

Bordreuil and Caquot 1979

P. Bordreuil and A. Caquot, "Les textes en cunéiformes alphabétiques découverts en 1977 à Ibn Hani," *Syria* 56(1979) 295–315.

Bordreuil and Caquot 1980

P. Bordreuil and A. Caquot, "Les textes en cunéiformes alphabétiques découverts en 1978 à Ibn Hani," *Syria* 57(1980) 343–73.

Bordreuil and Pardee 1982

P. Bordreuil and D. Pardee, "Le rituel funéraire ougaritique *RS* 34.126," *Syria* 59(1982) 121–28.

Bordreuil and Pardee 1991

P. Bordreuil and D. Pardee, "Deuxième partie: les textes Ougaritiques: textes alphabétiques: 90-*RS* 34.126," in *Une bibliothèque au sud de la ville*. Ras Shamra-Ougarit VII. Paris, 1991, 151–63.

Borger 1988

R. Borger, "Amos 5,26, Apostelgeschichte 7,43 und Šurpu II,180," *ZAW* 100(1988) 70–81.

Borghouts 1976

J. F. Borghouts, *Ancient Egyptian Magical Texts*. Leiden, 1976.

Bottéro 1980

J. Bottéro, "La mythologie de la mort en Mésopotamie ancienne," in *Death in Mesopotamia* [= RAI 26]. Ed. B. Alster. Copenhagen, 1980, 25–52.

Bottéro 1982

J. Bottéro, "Les inscriptions cunéiformes funéraires," in *La mort, les morts dans les sociétés anciennes*. Éd. G. Gnoli et J.-P. Vernant. Cambridge, 1982, 373–406.

Bottéro 1983

J. Bottéro, "Les morts et l'au-delà dans les rituels en accadien contre l'action des revenants," *ZA* 73(1983) 153–203.

Bottéro 1992

J. Bottéro, *Mesopotamia: Writing, Reasoning, and the Gods*. Chicago, 1992.

Bourguignon 1987

E. Bourguignon, "Necromancy," in *Encyclopedia of Religion*. Vol. 10. Ed. M. Eliade. New York, 1987, 345–47.

Bowker 1991

J. Bowker, *The Meanings of Death*. Cambridge, 1991.

Braulik 1988

G. Braulik, "Zur Abfolge der Gesetze in Deuteronomium 16,18–21,23: Weitere Beobachtungen," *Biblica* 69(1988) 63–92.

Braun 1986

R. Braun, *1 Chronicles*. Waco, 1986.

Brekelmans 1989

C. Brekelmans, "Deuteronomistic Influence in Isaiah 1–12," in *The Book of Isaiah*. Éd. J. Vermeylen. Leuven, 1989, 167–76.

Brichto 1973

H. C. Brichto, "Kin, Cult, Land and Afterlife—A Biblical Complex," *HUCA* 44(1973) 1–55.

Briggs 1906–07

C. A. Briggs, *A Critical and Exegetical Commentary on the Book of Psalms*. 2 vols. Edinburgh, 1906–07.

Bright 1965

J. Bright, *Jeremiah*. Garden City, 1965.

Brinkman 1984

J. A. Brinkman, *Prelude to Empire: Babylonian Society and Politics, 747–626* B.C. Chicago, 1984.

Brown 1981

J. P. Brown, "The Mediterranean Seer and Shamanism," *ZAW* 93(1981) 374–400.

Brown 1985

M. L. Brown, " 'I am the Lord Your Healer.' A Philological Study of the Root 'RAPA' in the Hebrew Bible and the Ancient Near East." Ph.D. diss., New York University, 1985.

Bryan 1973

D. B. Bryan, "Texts Relating to the *Marzēaḥ*: A Study of an Ancient Semitic Institution." Ph.D. diss., The Johns Hopkins University, 1973.

Budd 1984

P. J. Budd, *Numbers*. Waco, 1984.

Budde 1902

K. Budde, *Die Bücher Samuel*. Tübingen, 1902.

Budde 1928

K. Budde, *Jesajas Erleben*. Gotha, 1928.

Burkert 1985

W. Burkert, *Greek Religion. Archaic and Classical.* Oxford, 1985. [= *Griechische Religion der archaischen und klassischen Epoche.* Stuttgart, 1977].

Burns 1970

J. B. Burns, "The Mythology of Death in the Old Testament." Ph.D. diss., The University of St. Andrews, 1970.

Burns 1973

J. B. Burns, "The Mythology of Death in the Old Testament," *SJT* 26(1973) 327–40.

Burns 1979

J. B. Burns, "Necromancy and the Spirits of the Dead in the Old Testament," *TGUOS* 26(1979) 1–14.

Burns 1989

J. B. Burns, "Some Personifications of Death in the Old Testament," *IBS* 11(1989) 23–34.

Callot 1983

O. Callot, *Une maison à Ougarit: Études d'architecture domestique.* Paris, 1983.

Caquot 1959

A. Caquot, "La divinité solaire ougaritique," *Syria* 36(1959) 90–101.

Caquot 1969

A. Caquot, "Nouveaux documents ougaritiens," *Syria* 46(1969) 241–65.

Caquot 1976a

A. Caquot, "Hébreu et araméen," *ACF* 75(1976) 423–32.

Caquot 1976b

A. Caquot, "La tablette RS 24.252 et la question des Rephaïm ougaritiques," *Syria* 53(1976) 296–304.

Caquot 1979

A. Caquot, "Ras Shamra: La littérature ugaritique," *Supplément au Dictionnaire de la Bible* 9(1979) 1361–1417.

Caquot 1981

A. Caquot, "Rephaïm," *Supplément au Dictionnaire de la Bible* 10(1981) 344–57.

Caquot 1984

A. Caquot, "Une nouvelle interprétation de la tablette ougaritique de Ras Ibn Hani 78/20," *Orientalia* n.s., 53(1984) 163–76.

Caquot and Sznycer 1980

A. Caquot and M. Sznycer, *Ugaritic Religion.* Leiden, 1980.

Caquot, Sznycer, and Herdner 1974

A. Caquot, M. Sznycer, and A. Herdner, *Textes Ougaritiques.* Tome I, *Mythes et légendes.* Paris, 1974.

Caquot, de Tarragon, and Cunchillos 1989

A. Caquot, J.-M. de Tarragon, and J.-L. Cunchillos, *Textes Ougaritiques.* Tome II, *Textes religieux et rituels*, par A. Caquot and J.-M. de Tarragon; *Correspondance*, par J.-L. Cunchillos. Paris, 1989.

Carmichael 1974
C. M. Carmichael, *The Laws of Deuteronomy.* Ithaca and London, 1974.

Carmichael 1976
C. M. Carmichael, "On Separating Life and Death: An Explanation of Some Biblical Laws," *HTR* 69(1976) 1–7.

Carroll 1986
R. P. Carroll, *Jeremiah: A Commentary.* Philadelphia, 1986.

Cassin 1958
E. Cassin, "Quelques remarques à propos des archives administratives de Nuzi," *RA* 52(1958) 16–28.

Cassin 1962
E. Cassin, "Tablettes inédites de Nuzi," *RA* 56(1962) 57–80.

Cassin 1981
E. Cassin, "Une querelle de famille," in *Studies on the Civilization and Culture of Nuzi and the Hurrians in Honor of Ernest R. Lacheman.* Ed. M. A. Morrison and D. I. Owen. Winona Lake, 1981, 37–46.

Cassin 1982
E. Cassin, "La mort: valeur et représentation en Mésopotamie ancienne," in *La mort, les morts dans les sociétés anciennes.* Éd. G. Gnoli et J.-P. Vernant. Cambridge, 1982, 355–72.

Cassuto 1975
U. Cassuto, *Biblical and Oriental Studies 2.* Jerusalem 1975.

Catastini 1985
A. Catastini, "Una nuova iscrizione fenicia e la 'Coppa di Yahweh' ," in *Studi in onore di Edda Bresciani.* A cura di S. F. Bondi et al. Pisa, 1985, 111–18.

Cathcart and Watson 1980
K. J. Cathcart and W. G. E. Watson, "Weathering a Wake: A Cure for Carousal. A Revised Translation of *Ugaritica V* Text 1," *PIBA* 4(1980) 35–58.

Cavalletti 1981
S. Cavalletti, "Il dio ebbro di vino," *Ricerche Bibliche e Religiose* 15(1981) 135–36.

Cazelles 1948
H. Cazelles, "Sur un rituel du Deutéronome (Deut. XXVI, 14)," *RB* 55(1948) 54–71.

Cazelles 1966
H. Cazelles, *La Deutéronome.* Paris, 1966.

Cecchini 1981
S. M. Cecchini, "*tḥt* in KAI 2,3 e in KTU 1.161, 22ss," *UF* 13(1981) 27–31.

Charpin 1984a
D. Charpin, "Inscriptions votives d'e'poque Assyrienne," *MARI* 3(1984) 41–81.

Charpin 1984b
D. Charpin, "Nouveaux documents du bureau de l'huile à l'époque assyrienne," *MARI* 3(1984) 83–126.

Charpin 1985a

D. Charpin, "Les archives d'époque 'assyrienne' dans le palais de Mari," *MARI* 4(1985) 243–68.

Charpin 1985b

D. Charpin, "Notes brèves," *RA* 79(1985) 91.

Charpin 1985c

D. Charpin, Review of *Mari and Karana*, by S. Dalley, *RA* 79(1985) 85–86.

Charpin 1986

D. Charpin, *Le clergé d'Ur au siècle d'Hammurabi.* Paris, 1986.

Charpin 1990

D. Charpin, "Les divinités familiales des Babyloniens d'après les légendes de leurs sceaux-cylindres," in *De la Babylonie à la Syrie en passant par Mari. Mélanges offerts à Monsieur J.-R. Kupper à l'occasion de son 70ᵉ anniversaire.* Ed. Ö. Tuncan. Liège, 1990, 59–78.

Charpin 1992

D. Charpin, "Mari entre l'est et l'ouest: politique, culture, religion," *Akkadica* 78(1992) 1–10.

Charpin and Durand 1985

D. Charpin and J.-M. Durand, "La prise du pouvoir par Zimri-Lim," *MARI* 4(1985) 293–343.

Charpin and Durand 1986

D. Charpin and J.-M. Durand, "«Fils de Sim'al»: Les origines tribales des rois de Mari," *RA* 80(1986) 141–83.

Charpin and Durand 1989

D. Charpin and J.-M. Durand, "Le tombeau de Yahdun-Lim," *NABU* 3(1989) 18–19.

Childs 1967

B. S. Childs, "Deuteronomic Formulae of the Exodus Traditions," *SVT* 16(1967) 30–39.

Cholewiński 1976

A. Cholewiński, *Heiligkeitsgesetz und Deuteronomium: Eine vergleichende Studie.* Rom, 1976.

Civil 1987

M. Civil, "KBo 26 53 and Funerary Personnel," *NABU* 1(1987) 4–5.

Clements 1981

R. E. Clements, *Isaiah 1–39.* Grand Rapids, 1981.

Clifford 1972

R. J. Clifford, *The Cosmic Mountain in Canaan and the Old Testament.* Cambridge, MA., 1972.

Coats 1968

G. W. Coats, *Rebellion in the Wilderness: The Murmuring Motif in the Wilderness Traditions of the Old Testament.* Nashville, 1968.

Cogan 1974
M. Cogan, *Imperialism and Religion: Assyria, Judah, and Israel in the Eighth and Seventh Centuries B.C.E.* Missoula, 1974.

Cogan 1993
M. Cogan, "Judah Under Assyrian Hegemony: A Re-examination of Imperialism and Religion," *JBL* 112(1993) 403–14.

Cogan and Tadmor 1988
M. Cogan and H. Tadmor, *II Kings*. Garden City, 1988.

Cohen 1978
H. R. Cohen, *Biblical Hapax Legomena in Light of Akkadian and Ugaritic*. Missoula, 1978.

Cohen 1993
M. E. Cohen, *The Cultic Calendars of the Ancient Near East*. Bethesda, 1993.

Coldstream 1976
J. N. Coldstream, "Hero-Cults in the Age of Homer," *Journal of Hellenic Studies* 96(1976) 8–17.

Conder 1896
C. R. Conder, "The Syrian Language," *PEF* 28(1896) 60–78.

Cooley 1968
R. E. Cooley, "The Contribution of Literary Sources to a Study of the Canaanite Burial Pattern." Ph.D. diss., New York University, 1968.

Cooley 1983
R. E. Cooley, "Gathered to His People: A Study of a Dothan Family Tomb," in *The Living and Active Word of God: Studies in Honor of Samuel J. Schultz*. Ed. M. Inch and R. Youngblood. Winona Lake, 1983, 47–58.

Cooper 1973
J. S. Cooper, "Bilinguals from Boghazköi," *ZA* 62(1973) 62–81.

Cooper 1981
A. Cooper, "Divine Names and Epithets in the Ugaritic Texts," in *Ras Shamra Parallels: The Texts from Ugarit and the Hebrew Bible*. Vol. 3. Ed. L. R. Fisher. Rome, 1981, 333–469.

Cooper 1987a
A. Cooper, "MLK ʻLM: 'Eternal King' or 'King of Eternity'?," in *Love & Death in the Ancient Near East: Essays in Honor of Marvin H. Pope*. Ed. J. H. Marks and R. M. Good. Guilford, 1987, 1–7.

Cooper 1987b
A. Cooper, "Phoenician Religion," in *Encyclopedia of Religion*. Vol. 11. Ed. M. Eliade. New York, 1987, 315–18.

Cooper 1992
J. S. Cooper, "The Fate of Mankind: Death and Afterlife in Ancient Mesopotamia," in

Death and Afterlife: Perspectives of World Religions. Ed. H. Obayashi. New York, 1992, 19–33.

Coote 1981
R. B. Coote, *Amos Among the Prophets: Composition and Theology.* Philadelphia, 1981.

Courtois 1969
J. C. Courtois, "La maison du prêtre aux modèles de poumon et de foies d'Ugarit' ," *Ugaritica VI* (1969) 91–119.

Courtois 1979
J. C. Courtois, "Ras Shamra, Archéologie," *Supplément au Dictionnaire de la Bible* 9(1979) 1126–1295.

Craigie 1976
P. C. Craigie, *The Book of Deuteronomy.* Grand Rapids, 1976.

Craigie 1981
P. C. Craigie, "Ugaritic and the Bible: Progress and Regress in 50 Years of Literary Study," in *Ugarit in Retrospect: Fifty Years of Ugarit and Ugaritic.* Ed. G. D. Young. Winona Lake, 1981, 99–111.

Craigie 1983
P. C. Craige, "Ugarit, Canaan, and Israel," *Tyndale Bulletin* 34(1983) 145–67.

Cross 1968
F. M. Cross, "The Canaanite Cuneiform Tablet from Taanach," *BASOR* 190(1968) 41–46.

Cross 1984
F. M. Cross, "An Old Canaanite Inscription Recently Found at Lachish," *TA* 11(1984) 71–76.

Dahood 1964
M. Dahood, "Hebrew-Ugaritic Lexicography II," *Biblica* 45(1964) 393–412.

Dahood 1965
M. Dahood, *Psalms I.* Garden City, 1965.

Dahood 1970
M. Dahood, *Psalms III.* Garden City, 1970.

Dahood 1977
M. Dahood, "The Ugaritic Parallel Pair *qra // qba* in Isaiah 62,2," *Biblica* 58(1977) 527–28.

Dahood 1987
M. Dahood, "Love and Death at Ebla and their Biblical Reflections," in *Love & Death in the Ancient Near East: Essays in Honor of Marvin H. Pope.* Ed. J. H. Marks and R. M. Good. Guilford, 1987, 93–99.

Dahood and Pettinato 1977
M. Dahood and G. Pettinato, "Ugaritic *ršp gn* and Eblaite *rasap gunu(m)*^{ki}," *Orientalia* n.s., 46(1977) 230–32.

Daiches 1921
S. Daiches, "Isaiah and Spiritualism," *The Jewish Chronicle Supplement* (July, 1921) 6.

Dalley 1979
S. Dalley, Review of *Archives royales de Mari* 10, by G. Dossin, *BO* 36(1979) 289–92.

Dalley 1984
S. Dalley, *Mari and Karana: Two Old Babylonian Cities*. London, 1984.

Dalley 1986
S. Dalley, "The God Ṣalmu and the Winged Disk," *Iraq* 48(1986) 85–101.

Dalley 1987
S. Dalley "Near Eastern Patron Deities of Mining and Smelting in the Late Bronze and Early Iron Ages," *Report of the Department of Antiquities, Cyprus* (1987) 61–66.

Dalman 1912
G. Dalman, *Neue Petra-Forschungen und der heilige Felsen von Jerusalem*. Leipzig, 1912.

Day 1985
J. Day, *God's Conflict with the Dragon and the Sea: Echoes of a Canaanite Myth in the Old Testament*. Cambridge, 1985.

Day 1989
J. Day, *Molech: A God of Human Sacrifice in the Old Testament*. Cambridge, 1989.

Deimel 1920
A. Deimel, "Die Listen über den Ahnenkult aus der Zeit Lugalandas und Urukaginas," *Orientalia* n.s., 2(1920) 32–51.

Delcor 1981
M. Delcor, "Les cultes étrangers en Israël au moment de la réforme de Josias d'après 2 R 23, Étude de religions sémitiques comparées," in *Mélanges bibliques et orientaux en l'honneur de M. Henri Cazelles*. Éd. A. Caquot et M. Delcor. Neukirchen-Vluyn, 1981, 91–123.

Delitzsch 1898
F. Delitzsch, *The Psalms*. Vol. 3. Edinburgh, 1898.

Deller 1981
K. Deller, "Die Hausgötter der Familie Šukrija S. Ḫuja," in *Studies on the Civilization and Culture of Nuzi and the Hurrians in Honor of Ernest R. Lacheman*. Ed. M. A. Morrison and D. I. Owen. Winona Lake, 1981, 47–76.

Demarée 1983
R. J. Demarée, *The 3ḫ ỉḳr n Rʿ-Stelae: On Ancestor Worship in Ancient Egypt*. Leiden, 1983.

Dhorme 1910
É. P. Dhorme, *Les livres de Samuel*. Paris, 1910.

Dhorme 1956
E. Dhorme, "Le dieu Baal et le dieu Moloch dans la tradition biblique," *AnSt* 6(1956) 57–61.

Dietrich and Loretz 1969
M. Dietrich and O. Loretz, "Beschriftete Lungen- und Lebermodelle aus Ugarit," *Ugaritica VI*(1969) 165–79.

Dietrich and Loretz 1980a
M. Dietrich and O. Loretz, "Gebrauch von Götterstatuen in der Mantik von Ugarit," *UF* 12(1980) 395–96.

Dietrich and Loretz 1980b
M. Dietrich and O. Loretz, "Totenverehrung in Māri (12803) und Ugarit (KTU 1.161)," *UF* 12(1980) 381–82.

Dietrich and Loretz 1981
M. Dietrich and O. Loretz, "*mḫrt* 'Brandopferaltar, Brand- Röststelle' (KTU 6.14, 3)," *UF* 13(1981) 297–98.

Dietrich and Loretz 1982
M. Dietrich and O. Loretz, "Der Vertrag eines *mrzḥ*-Klubs in Ugarit. Zum Verständnis von KTU 3.9," *UF* 14(1982) 71–76.

Dietrich and Loretz 1983
M. Dietrich and O. Loretz, "Neue Studien zu den Ritualtexten aus Ugarit (II) - Nr. 6- Epigraphische und inhaltliche Probleme in KTU 1.161," *UF* 15(1983) 17–24.

Dietrich and Loretz 1986
M. Dietrich and O. Loretz, "Die Trauer Els und Anats," *UF* 18(1986) 101–10.

Dietrich and Loretz 1988
M. Dietrich and O. Loretz, "Ugaritische Rituale und Beschwörungen," in *Texte aus der Umwelt des Alten Testaments.* Band 2/3 *Ritual und Beschwörungen.* Hrsg. W. Farber et. al. Gütersloh, 1988, 329–33.

Dietrich and Loretz 1990a
M. Dietrich and O. Loretz, *Mantik in Ugarit: Keilalphabetische Texte der Opferschau, Omensammlungen, Nekromantie.* Münster, 1990.

Dietrich and Loretz 1990b
M. Dietrich and O. Loretz, "*mt* 'Môt, Tod' und *mt* 'Krieger Held' im Ugaritischen," *UF* 22(1990) 57–65.

Dietrich and Loretz 1990c
M. Dietrich and O. Loretz, "Die ugaritischen Zeitangaben *ṣbu špš* ||*'rb špš* und *špšm*," *UF* 22(1990) 75–77.

Dietrich, Loretz, and Meyer 1989
M. Dietrich, O. Loretz, W. Meyer, "*sikkanum* Betyle," *UF* 20(1989) 133–39.

Dietrich, Loretz, and Sanmartín 1973
M. Dietrich, O. Loretz, and J. Sanmartín, "*Pgr* im Ugaritischen: Zur ugaritischen Lexikographie IX," *UF* 5(1973) 289–91.

Dietrich, Loretz, and Sanmartín 1974
M. Dietrich, O. Loretz, and J. Sanmartín, "Ugaritisch *ILIB* und hebräisch '*(W)B* 'Totengeist' ," *UF* 6(1974) 450–51.

Dietrich 1972

W. Dietrich, *Prophetie und Geschichte. Eine redaktionsgeschichtliche Untersuchung zum deuteronomistischen Geschichtswerk.* Göttingen, 1972.

Dietrich 1987

W. Dietrich, "Samuel, Saul und die Totenbeschwörerin (1 Sam 28)," in *David, Saul und die Propheten: Das Verhältnis von Religion und Politik nach den Prophetischen Überlieferungen vom frühesten Königtum in Israel.* Stuttgart, 1987, 25–36.

Dijkstra 1985

M. Dijkstra, "Once Again: The Closing Lines of the Ba'al Cycle (KTU 1.6.VI.42ff.)," *UF* 17(1985) 147–52.

Dijkstra, de Moor, and Spronk 1981

M. Dijkstra, J. C. de Moor, and K. Spronk, Review of *Die keilalphabetischen Texte aus Ugarit: Einschliesslich der keilalphabetischen Texte ausserhalb Ugarits*, by M. Dietrich, O. Loretz, and J. Sanmartín, *BO* 38(1981) 371–80.

Dillard 1987

R. B. Dillard, *2 Chronicles.* Waco, 1987.

Dillmann 1886

A. Dillmann, *Deuteronomium.* Leipzig, 1886^2.

Dion 1978

P. E. Dion, "Quelques aspects de l'interaction entre religion et politique dans le Deutéronome," *Science et Esprit* 30(1978) 39–55.

Dion 1985

P. E. Dion, "Deuteronomy and the Gentile World: A Study in Biblical Theology," *TJT* 1(1985) 200–21.

Diringer 1934

D. Diringer, *Le iscrizioni antico-ebraische Palestinesi.* Firenze, 1934.

Dodds 1951

E. R. Dodds, *The Greeks and the Irrational.* Berkeley, 1951.

Donceel-Voûte 1988

P. Donceel-Voûte, "La carte de Madaba: Cosmographie anachronisme et propagande," *RB* 95(1988) 519–42.

Donner 1977

H. Donner, "The Separate States of Israel and Judah," in *Israelite and Judaean History.* Ed. J. H. Hayes and J. M. Miller. Philadelphia, 1977, 381–434.

Donner 1983

H. Donner, *Die Verwerfung des Königs Saul.* Wiesbaden, 1983.

Donner 1986

H. Donner, *Geschichte des Volkes Israel und seiner Nachbarn in Grundzügen.* Teil 2, *Von der Königszeit bis zu Alexander dem Großen mit einem Ausblick auf die Geschichte des Judentums bis Bar Kochba.* Göttingen, 1986.

Donner and Röllig 1971–73

H. Donner and W. Röllig, *Kanaanäische und aramäische Inschriften.* 3 Bände. Wiesbaden, 1971–73.

Dossin 1938

G. Dossin, "Les archives épistolaires du palais de Mari," *Syria* 19(1938) 105–26.

Dossin 1939

G. Dossin, "Les archives économiques du palais de Mari," *Syria* 20(1939) 97–113.

Dossin 1948

G. Dossin, "Une révélation du dieu Dagan à Terqa," *RA* 42(1948) 125–34.

Dossin 1950

G. Dossin, "Le panthéon de Mari," in *Studia Mariana.* Éd. A. Parrot. Leiden, 1950, 41–50.

Douglas 1966

M. Douglas, *Purity and Danger: An Analysis of Concepts of Pollution and Taboo.* London, 1966.

Douglas 1975

M. Douglas, *Implicit Meanings: Essays in Anthropology.* London, 1975.

Dressler 1976

H. H. P. Dressler, "The Aqhat-Text: A New Transcription, Translation, Commentary and Introduction." Ph.D. diss., The University of Cambridge, 1976.

Driver 1902

S. R. Driver, *Deuteronomy.* Edinburgh, 1902^3.

Driver 1913

S. R. Driver, *Notes on the Hebrew Text and the Topography of the Books of Samuel with an Introduction on Hebrew Palaeography and the Ancient Versions and Facsimiles of Inscriptions and Maps.* Oxford, 1913^2.

Driver 1954

G. R. Driver, "A Hebrew Burial Custom," *ZAW* 25(1954) 314–15.

Driver 1956

G. R. Driver, *Canaanite Myths and Legends.* Edinburgh, 1956.

Driver 1968a

G. R. Driver, " 'Another Little Drink' — Isaiah 28:1–22," in *Words and Meanings: Essays Presented to David Winton Thomas on His Retirement from the Regius Professorship of Hebrew in the University of Cambridge, 1968.* Ed. P. R. Ackroyd and B. Lindars. Cambridge, 1968, 47–67.

Driver 1968b

G. R. Driver, "Isaiah I–XXXIX: Textual and Linguistic Problems," *JSS* 13(1968) 36–57.

Durand 1985a

J.-M. Durand, "Le culte des bétyles en Syrie," in *Miscellanea Babylonica: Mélanges offerts à Maurice Birot.* Réunis J.-M. Durand et J.-R. Kupper. Paris, 1985, 79–84.

Durand 1985b

J.-M. Durand, "Les dames du palais de Mari à l'époque du royaume de Haute-Mésopotamie," *MARI* 4(1985) 385–436.

Durand 1985c

J.-M. Durand, "La situation historique des Šakkanakku: Nouvelle approche," *MARI* 4(1985) 147–72.

Durand 1987a

J.-M. Durand, "Différentes questions à propos de la religion," *MARI* 5(1987) 611–15.

Durand 1987b

J.-M. Durand, "L'organisation de l'espace dans le palais de Mari: Le témoignage des textes," in *Le système palatial en Orient, en Grèce et à Rome.* Éd. E. Lévy. Leiden, 1987, 39–110.

Durand 1988a

J.-M. Durand, *Archives épistolaires de Mari I/1* [= ARM 26]. Paris, 1988.

Durand 1988b

J.-M. Durand, "Le nom des Bétyles à Ebla et en Anatolie," *NABU* 2(1988) 5–6.

Durand 1989

J.-M. Durand, "Tombes familiales et culte des ancêtres à Emar," *NABU* 3(1989) 85–88.

Durkheim 1915

E. Durkheim, *The Elementary Forms of the Religious Life.* New York, 1915.

Dussaud 1935

R. Dussaud, "Deux stèles de Ras Shamra portant une dédicace au dieu Dagon," *Syria* 16(1935) 177–80.

Eaton 1976

J. H. Eaton, *Kingship and the Psalms.* London, 1976.

Ebach 1971

J. H. Ebach, "*PGR* = (Toten-)opfer?: Ein Vorschlag zum Verständnis von Ez 43,7.9," *UF* 3(1971) 365–68.

Ebach and Rüterswörden 1977

J. H. Ebach and U. Rüterswörden, "Unterweltbeschwörung im Alten Testament: Untersuchungen zur Begriffs- und Religionsgeschichte des 'ōb: Teil I," *UF* 9(1977) 57–70.

Ebach and Rüterswörden 1980

J. H. Ebach and U. Rüterswörden, "Unterweltbeschwörung im Alten Testament: Untersuchungen zur Begriffs- und Religionsgeschichte des 'ōb: Teil II," *UF* 12(1980) 205–20.

Ebeling 1931

E. Ebeling, *Tod und Leben nach den Vorstellungen der Babylonier.* Berlin, 1931.

Ebeling 1959

E. Ebeling, "Garten," *RlA* 3(1959) 147–50.

Ehrlich 1953

E. L. Ehrlich, *Der Traum im Alten Testament.* Berlin, 1953.

Eichrodt 1970

W. Eichrodt, *Ezekiel: A Commentary*. Philadelphia, 1970 [= *Der Prophet Hesekiel*. Göttingen, 1959].

Eissfeldt 1966

O. Eissfeldt, "Etymologische und archäologische Erklärung alttestamentlicher Wörter," *OrAn* 5(1966) 165–76.

Eissfeldt 1969

O. Eissfeldt,"Kultvereine in Ugarit," *Ugaritica VI*(1969) 187–95.

Ellermeier 1968

F. Ellermeier, *Prophetie in Mari und Israel*. Herzberg, 1968.

Emerton 1962

J. A. Emerton, "Priests and Levites in Deuteronomy," *VT* 12(1962) 129–38.

Emerton 1972

J. A. Emerton, "A Difficult Part of Mot's Message to Baal in the Ugaritic Texts," *AJBA* 1(1972) 50–71.

Fabry 1984

H.-J. Fabry, "*marzēaḥ*," in *Theologisches Wörterbuch zum Alten Testament*. Hrsg. G. J. Botterweck, H. Ringgren, und H.-J. Fabry. Band 5. Stuttgart, 1984, 11–16.

Falkenstein 1956–57

A. Falkenstein, *Die neusumerischen Gerichtsurkunden*. München, 1956–57.

Falkenstein 1959

A. Falkenstein, "Zwei Rituale aus seleukidischer Zeit," *UVB* 15(1959) 36–40.

Farnell 1921

L. R. Farnell, *Greek Hero Cults and Ideas of Immortality*. Oxford, 1921.

Feldman 1977

E. Feldman, *Biblical and Post-Biblical Defilement and Mourning: Law as Theology*. New York, 1977.

Fensham 1971

F. C. Fensham, "Father and Son as Terminology for Treaty and Covenant," in *Near Eastern Studies in Honor of William Foxwell Albright*. Ed. H. Goedicke. Baltimore, 1971, 121–35.

Fenton 1969

T. L. Fenton, "Ugaritica-Biblica," *UF* 1(1969) 65–70.

Fenton 1977

T. L. Fenton, "The Claremont 'mrzḥ' Tablet, Its Text and Meaning," *UF* 9(1977) 71–75.

Figulla and Martin 1953

H. H. Figulla and W. J. Martin, *Letters and Documents of the Old-Babylonian Period* [= UET V]. London, 1953.

Finet 1985

A. Finet, "Une requête d'Išme-Dagan à Zimri-Lim," in *Miscellanea Babylonica:*

Mélanges offerts à Maurice Birot. Réunis J.-M. Durand et J.-R. Kupper. Paris, 1985, 87–90.

Finet 1987

A. Finet, "Usages et rites funeraires en Babylonie," in *Thanatos: Les coutumes funeraires en Egee à l'âge du bronze.* Éd. R. Laffineur. Liège, 1987, 235–44.

Finkel 1983–84

I. L. Finkel, "Necromancy in Ancient Mesopotamia," *AfO* 29–30(1983–84) 1–17.

Finkelstein 1966

J. J. Finkelstein, "The Genealogy of the Hammurabi Dynasty," *JCS* 20(1966) 95–118.

Finley 1977

M. I. Finley, "The Ancient City: From Coulanges to Max Weber and Beyond," *Comparative Studies in Society and History* 19(1977) 305–27.

Fishbane 1985

M. Fishbane, *Biblical Interpretation in Ancient Israel.* Oxford, 1985.

Fleming 1992

D. E. Fleming, *The Installation of Baal's High Priestess at Emar: A Window on Ancient Syrian Religion.* Atlanta, 1992.

Fleming 1993

D. E. Fleming, "Nābū and Munabbiātu: Two New Syrian Religious Personnel," *JAOS* 113(1993) 175–83

Ford 1992

J. N. Ford "The 'Living Rephaim' of Ugarit: Quick or Defunct?" *UF* 24(1992) 73–101.

Foresti 1984

F. Foresti, *The Rejection of Saul in the Perspective of the Deuteronomistic School: A Study of 1 Sm 15 and Related Texts.* Rome, 1984.

Fortes 1965

M. Fortes, "Some Reflections on Ancestor Worship in Africa," in *African Systems of Thought: Studies Presented and Discussed at the Third International African Seminar in Salisbury, December 1960.* Ed. M. Fortes and G. Dieterlen. London, 1965, 122–42.

Fortes 1976

M. Fortes, "An Introductary Commentary," in *Ancestors.* Ed. W. H. Newell. Paris, 1976, 1–16.

Fossey 1911

C. Fossey, "Textes Babyloniens inédits," *Babylonica* 4(1911) 248–49.

Foxvog 1980

D. A. Foxvog, "Funerary Furnishings in an Early Sumerian Text from Adab," in *Death in Mesopotamia* [= RAI 26]. Ed. B. Alster. Copenhagen, 1980, 67–75.

Frayne 1990

D. Frayne, *Old Babylonian Period (2003–1595 BC).* Toronto, 1990.

Freedman 1985

D. N. Freedman, "But Did King David Invent Musical Instruments?," *Bible Review* (Summer, 1985) 48–51.

Freedman 1987

D. N. Freedman, "Yahweh of Samaria and his Asherah," *BA* 50(1987) 241–49.

Freilich and Pardee 1984

D. Freilich and D. Pardee, "{ẓ} and {ṭ} in Ugaritic: A Re-examination of the Sign-Forms," *Syria* 61(1984) 25–36.

Friedman 1979–80

R. E. Friedman, "The Mrzḥ Tablet from Ugarit," *MAARAV* 2(1979–80) 187–206.

Fronzaroli 1988

P. Fronzaroli, "Il culto dei re defunti in *ARET* 3.178," in *Miscellanea Eblaitica 1*. A cura di P. Fronzaroli. Firenze, 1988, 1–33.

Fronzaroli 1989

P. Fronzaroli, "A proposito del culto dei re defunti a Ebla," *NABU* 3(1989) 1–2.

Fronzaroli 1993

P. Fronzaroli, "The Ritual Texts from Ebla," in *Literature and Literary Language at Ebla*. Ed. P. Fronzaroli. Florence, 1993, 163–85.

Frymer-Kensky 1987

T. Frymer-Kensky, "UTU," in *Encyclopedia of Religion*. Vol. 15. Ed. M. Eliade. New York, 1987, 162–63.

Fulco 1987

W. Fulco, "Resheph," in *Encyclopedia of Religion*. Vol. 12. Ed. M. Eliade. New York, 1987, 324–43.

Fustel de Coulanges 1864

N. D. Fustel de Coulanges, *La cité antique*. Paris, 1864 [= *The Ancient City*, 1873, rpt. Baltimore, 1980].

Gadd 1948

C. J. Gadd, *Ideas of Divine Rule in the Ancient Near East*. London, 1948.

Gadd 1958

C. J. Gadd, "The Harran Inscriptions of Nabonidus," *AnSt* 8(1958) 35–92.

Galling 1959

K. Galling, "Erwägungen zum Stelenheiligtum von Hazor," *ZDPV* 75(1959) 1–13.

Garbini 1986

G. Garbini, *Venti anni di epigrafia punica nel Magreb*. Roma, 1986.

García López 1984

F. García López, "Un profeta como Moisés. Estudio crítico de Dt 18,9–22," in *Simposio biblico español*. Ed. N. Fernandez Marcos, J. Trebolle Barrera, and J. Fernandez Vallina. Madrid, 1984, 289–308.

Gardiner 1930

A. H. Gardiner, "A New Letter to the Dead," *Journal of Egyptian Archaeology* 16(1930) 19–22.

Garland 1985

R. Garland, *The Greek Way of Death.* Ithaca, 1985.

Garland 1992

R. Garland, *Introducing New Gods: The Politics of Athenian Religion.* London, 1992.

Gaster 1950

T. H. Gaster, *Thespis: Ritual, Myth and Drama in the Ancient Near East.* New York, 1950.

Gaster 1976

T. H. Gaster, "An Ugaritic Feast of All Souls," in *Concepts Critiques and Comments: A Festschrift in Honor of David Rose.* Ed. B. Dibner and M. Rubien. [private publication] 1976, 97–106.

Gaster 1981

T. H. Gaster, *Myth, Legend and Custom in the Old Testament: A Comparative Study with Chapters from Sir James G. Frazer's Folklore in the Old Testament.* Reprint. New York, 1981.

Gelb 1957

I. J. Gelb, *Glossary of Old Akkadian.* Chicago, 1957.

Gelb 1980

I. J. Gelb, *Computer-aided Analysis of Amorite.* Chicago, 1980.

Gelb 1981

I. J. Gelb, "Ebla and Kish Civilization," in *La lingua di Ebla: Atti del convegno internazionale (Napoli, 21–23 aprile 1980).* A cura di L. Cagni. Napoli, 1981, 9–73.

Geller 1987

M. J. Geller, "The Lugal of Mari at Ebla and the Sumerian King List," in *Eblaitica: Essays on the Ebla Archives and Eblaite Language.* Vol. 1. Ed. C. H. Gordon, G. A. Rendsburg, and N. H. Winter. Winona Lake, 1987, 141–45.

van Gennep 1960

A. van Gennep, *The Rites of Passage.* London, 1960.

Gerstenberger, Jutzler, and Boecker 1972

E. Gerstenberger, K. Jutzler, and H. J. Boecker, *Psalmen in der Sprache unserer Zeit.* Neukirchen-Vluyn, 1972.

Gibson 1978

J. C. L. Gibson, *Canaanite Myths and Legends.* Edinburgh, 1978^2.

Gibson 1975

J. C. L. Gibson, *Textbook of Syrian Semitic Inscriptions: Aramaic Inscriptions.* Vol. 2. Oxford, 1975.

Gibson 1982

J. C. L. Gibson, *Textbook of Syrian Semitic Inscriptions: Phoenician Inscriptions including Inscriptions in the Mixed Dialect of Arslan Tash.* Vol. 3. Oxford, 1982.

Ginsberg 1936

H. L. Ginsberg, "The Rebellion and Death of Ba'lu," *Orientalia* n.s., 5(1936) 161–198.

Ginsberg 1946

H. L. Ginsberg, *The Legend of King Keret.* New Haven, 1946.

Ginsberg 1969

H. L. Ginsberg, "Ugaritic Myths, Epics, and Legends," "Aramaic Papyri from Elephantine," "Aramiac Proverbs and Precepts," and "Aramaic Letters," in *Ancient Near Eastern Texts: Relating to the Old Testament.* Ed. J. B. Pritchard. Princeton, 1969^3, 129–155, 427–30, 491–92, 633.

Glaeseman 1978

R. R. Glaeseman, "The Practice of the King's Meal at Mari: A System of Food Distribution in the 2nd Millennium B.C." Ph.D. diss., The University of California at Los Angeles, 1978.

Gluckman 1937

M. Gluckman, "Mortuary Customs and the Belief in Survival after Death among the South-Eastern Bantu," *Bantu Studies* 11(1937) 117–36.

Goetze 1938

A. Goetze, "The Tenses of Ugaritic," *JAOS* 58(1938) 266–309.

Good 1980

R. M. Good, "Supplementary Remarks on the Ugaritic Funerary Text RS 34.126," *BASOR* 239(1980) 41–42.

Good 1986

R. M. Good, "The Carthaginian *MAYUMAS*," *SEL* 3(1986) 99–114.

Goody 1962

J. Goody, *Death, Property, and the Ancestors: A Study of the Mortuary Customs of the Lo Dagaa of West Africa.* Stanford, 1962.

Gordon 1965

C. H. Gordon, *Ugaritic Textbook.* Rome, 1965.

Gosse 1992

B. Gosse, "Isaïe 1 dans la rédaction du livre d'Isaïe," *ZAW* 104(1992) 52–66.

Grabbe 1976

L. Grabbe, "The Seasonal Pattern and the Baal Cycle," *UF* 8(1976) 57–63.

Gray 1912

G. B. Gray, *The Book of Isaiah I-XXVII.* Edinburgh, 1912.

Gray 1949

J. Gray, "The Rephaim," *PEQ* 81(1949) 127–39.

Gray 1952

J. Gray, "*Dtn* and *Rp'um* in Ancient Ugarit," *PEQ* 84(1952) 39–41.

Gray 1965

J. Gray, *The Legacy of Canaan: The Ras Shamra Texts and Their Relevance to the Old Testament*. Leiden, 1965^2.

Gray 1966

J. Gray, "Social Aspects of Canaanite Religion," *SVT* 15(1966) 170–92.

Gray 1978

J. Gray, "Canaanite Religion and Old Testament Study in Light of New Alphabetic Texts from Ras Shamra," *Ugaritica VII*(1978) 79–108.

Grayson 1972

A. K. Grayson, *Assyrian Royal Inscriptions*. Vol. 1. Wiesbaden, 1972.

Grayson 1975

A. K. Grayson, *Babylonian Historical-literary Texts*. Toronto, 1975.

Grayson 1987

A. K. Grayson, *Assyrian Rulers of the Third and Second Millennia* BC *(to 1115* BC*)*. Toronto, 1987.

Green 1984

A. Green, "Beneficent Spirits and Malevolent Demons: The Iconography of Good and Evil in Ancient Assyria and Babylonia," *Visible Religion* 3(1984) 80–105.

Greenfield 1961

J. C. Greenfield, "The Prepositions B. . . . Taḥat. . . . in Jes 57₅," *ZAW* 73(1961) 226–28.

Greenfield 1973

J. C. Greenfield, "Un rite religieux araméen et ses parallèles," *RB* 80(1973) 46–52.

Greenfield 1974

J. C. Greenfield, "The *Marzēaḥ* as a Social Institution," *Acta Antiqua Academiae Scientiarum Hungaricae* 22(1974) 451–55.

Greenfield 1982

J. C. Greenfield, "Adi balṭu — Care for the Elderly and its Rewards," *AfO Beiheft* [= RAI 28] 19(1982) 309–16.

Greenfield 1987

J. C. Greenfield, "Aspects of Aramean Religion," in *Ancient Israelite Religion: Essays in Honor of Frank Moore Cross*. Ed. P. D. Miller, P. D. Hanson, and S. D. McBride. Philadelphia, 1987, 67–78.

Greenfield and Schaffer 1985

J. C. Greenfield and A. Schaffer, "Notes on the Curse Formulae of the Tell Fekherye Inscription," *RB* 92(1985) 47–59.

Gröndahl 1967

F. Gröndahl, *Die Personennamen der Texte aus Ugarit*. Rome, 1967.

Gruber 1980

M. I. Gruber, *Aspects of Nonverbal Communication in the Ancient Near East*. 2 vols. Rome, 1980.

Groneberg 1986

B. Groneberg, "Eine Einführungsszene in der altbabylonischen Literatur: Bemerkungen zum persönlichen Gott," in *Keilschriftliche Literaturen* [= RAI 32]. Hrsg. K. Hecker und W. Sommerfeld. Berlin, 1986, 93–108.

Gubel 1989

E. Gubel, "À propos du *marzeaḥ* d'Assurbanipal," in *Reflets des deux fleuves. Volume de mélanges offerts à André Finet*. Éd. M. Lebeau et Ph. Talon. Leuven, 1989, 47–53, 127–135.

Gurney 1981

O. R. Gurney, "The Babylonians and Hittites," in *Divination and Oracles*. Ed. M. Loewe and C. Blacker. London, 1981, 142–73.

Guthrie 1955

W. K. C. Guthrie, *The Greeks and Their Gods*. Boston, 1955.

Guzzo Amadasi 1987

M. G. Guzzo Amadasi, "Under Western Eyes," *SEL* 4(1987) 121–27.

Guzzo Amadasi and Karageorghis 1977

M. G. Guzzo Amadasi and V. Karageorghis, *Inscriptions Phéniciennes: Fouilles de Kition III*. Nicosia, 1977.

Hadley 1987

J. Hadley, "The Khirbet El-Qom Inscription," *VT* 37(1987) 50–62.

Halévy 1874

J. Halévy, *Mélanges d'épigraphie et d'archéologie semitiques*. Paris, 1874.

Halévy 1894

J. Halévy, "Les deux inscriptions hetéennes de Zindjîrlî," *Revue Sémitique* 2(1894) 25–60.

Hallo 1980

W. W. Hallo, "Royal Titles from the Mesopotamian Periphery," *AnSt* 30(1980) 189–95.

Hallo 1983

W. W. Hallo, "Dating the Mesopotamian Past," *BSMS* 6(1983) 7–18.

Hallo 1988

W. W. Hallo, "Texts, Statues and the Cult of the Divine King," *SVT* 40(1988) 54–66.

Hallo 1992

W. W. Hallo, "Royal Ancestor Worship in the Biblical World," in *Sha'arei Talmon: Studies in the Bible, Qumran, and the Ancient Near East Presented to Shemaryahu Talmon*. Ed. M. Fishbane and E. Tov. Winona Lake, 1992, 381–401.

Halpern 1979–80

B. Halpern, "A Landlord-Tenant Dispute at Ugarit?," *MAARAV* 2(1979–80) 121–40.

Halpern 1986

B. Halpern, " 'The Excremental Vision': The Doomed Priests of Doom in Isaiah 28," *HAR* 10(1986) 109–21.

Handy 1988
L. K. Handy, "A Solution for Many *mlkm*," *UF* 20(1988) 57–59.

Handy 1992
L. K. Handy, "Resheph," in *Anchor Bible Dictionary*. Vol. 5. Ed. D. N. Freedman. New York, 678–79.

Hardacre 1987
H. Hardacre, "Ancestors: Ancestor Worship," in *Encyclopedia of Religion*. Vol. 1. Ed. M. Eliade. New York, 1987, 263–68.

Harper 1905
W. R. Harper, *Amos and Hosea*. Edinburgh, 1905.

Hawkins 1980
D. Hawkins, "Late Hittite Funerary Monuments," in *Death in Mesopotamia* [= RAI 26]. Ed. B. Alster. Copenhagen, 1980, 213–25.

Hawley 1987
J. S. Hawley (ed.), *Saints and Virtues*. Berkeley, 1987.

Hayes and Irvine 1987
J. H. Hayes and S. A. Irvine, *Isaiah the Eighth Century Prophet: His Times and His Preaching*. Nashville, 1987.

Healey 1975
J. F. Healey, "Malkū: mlkm: Anunnaki," *UF* 7(1975) 235–38.

Healey 1976
J. F. Healey, "Syriac *nṣr*, Ugaritic *nṣr*, Hebrew *nṣr* II, Akkadian *nṣr* II," *VT* 26(1976) 429–37.

Healey 1977a
J. F. Healey, "Death, Underworld and Afterlife in the Ugaritic Texts." Ph.D. diss., The University of London, 1977.

Healey 1977b
J. F. Healey, "The Underworld Character of the God Dagan," *JNSL* 5(1977) 43–51.

Healey 1978a
J. F. Healey, "*MLKM/RP'UM* and the *kispum*," *UF* 10(1978) 89–91.

Healey 1978b
J. F. Healey, "Ritual Text KTU 1.161 — Translation and Notes," *UF* 10(1978) 83–88.

Healey 1979
J. F. Healey, "The *Pietas* of an Ideal Son at Ugarit," *UF* 11(1979) 353–56.

Healey 1980a
J. F. Healey, "The Sun Deity and the Underworld: Mesopotamia and Ugarit," in *Death in Mesopotamia* [= RAI 26]. Ed. B. Alster. Copenhagen, 1980, 239–42.

Healey 1980b
J. F. Healey, "Ugaritic *ḤTK*: A Note," *UF* 12(1980) 408–09.

Healey 1984
J. F. Healey, "The Immortality of the King: Ugarit and the Psalms," *Orientalia* n.s., 53(1984) 245–54.

Healey 1985
J. F. Healey, "The Akkadian 'Pantheon' List from Ugarit," *SEL* 2(1985) 115–25.

Healey 1986
J. F. Healey, "The Ugaritic Dead: Some Live Issues," *UF* 18(1986) 27–32.

Healey 1988
J. F. Healey, "The 'Pantheon' of Ugarit: Further Notes," *SEL* 5(1988) 103–11.

Healey 1989
J. F. Healey, "The Last of the Rephaim," in *Back to the Sources: Biblical and Near Eastern Studies in Honour of Dermot Ryan.* Ed. K. J. Cathcart and J. F. Healey. Dublin, 1989, 33–44.

Heidel 1963
A. Heidel, *The Babylonian Genesis: The Story of Creation.* Chicago, 1963^2.

Heider 1985
G. C. Heider, *The Cult of Molek: A Reassessment.* Sheffield, 1985.

Heimpel 1986
W. Heimpel, "The Sun at Night and the Doors of Heaven in Babylonian Texts," *JCS* 28(1986) 127–51.

Held 1982
M. Held, "Studies in Biblical Lexicography in Light of Akkadian," *EI* 16(1982) 76–85 [English summary 254.*].

Heltzer 1973
M. Heltzer, "Some Gleanings to the Ugaritic Texts Inscribed on Clay Lung and Liver Models," *AION* 23(1973) 93–97.

Heltzer 1978
M. Heltzer, "The *rabba'um* in Mari and the *rpi(m)* in Ugarit," *OLP* 9(1978) 5–20.

Heltzer 1981
M. Heltzer, *The Suteans.* Naples, 1981.

Hentschel 1985
G. Hentschel, *2. Könige.* Würzburg, 1985.

Herdner 1972
A. Herdner, "Une prière à Baal des Ugaritains en danger," *CRAIBL* (1972) 693–97.

Herdner 1978
A. Herdner, "Nouveaux textes alphabétiques de Ras Shamra — XXIVe campagne, 1961," *Ugaritica VII*(1978) 1–74.

Hertzberg 1964
H. W. Hertzberg, *I & II Samuel, a Commentary.* Philadelphia, 1964.

Hirsch 1963
H. Hirsch, "Die Inschriften der Könige von Agade," *AfO* 20(1963) 1–82.

Hobbs 1985

T. R. Hobbs, *2 Kings*. Waco, 1985.

Hoffmann 1980

H.-D. Hoffmann, *Reform und Reformen: Untersuchungen zu einem Grundthema der deuteronomistischen Geschichtsschreibung*. Zürich, 1980.

Hoffner 1967

H. A. Hoffner, "Second Millennium Antecedents to the Hebrew 'ôb," *JBL* 86(1967) 385–401.

Hoffner 1974

H. A. Hoffner, "*'ôb*," in *Theological Dictionary of the Old Testament*. Vol. 1. Ed. G. J. Botterweck and H. Ringgren. Grand Rapids, 1974, 130–34. [= "*'ôb*," in *Theologisches Wörterbuch zum Alten Testament*. Hrsg. G. J. Botterweck, H. Ringgren, und H.-J. Fabry. Band 1. Stuttgart, 1973, 141–45.

Holladay 1986

W. L. Holladay, *Jeremiah 1: A Commentary on the Book of the Prophet Jeremiah*. Chapters 1–25. Philadelphia, 1986.

Holloway 1992

S. Holloway, "The Case of Assyrian Religious Influence in Israel and Judah: Inference and Evidence." 2 vols. Ph.D. diss., The University of Chicago, 1992.

van Hoonacker 1897–98

A. van Hoonacker, "Divination by the 'Ôb amongst the Ancient Hebrews," *The Expository Times* 9(1897–98) 157–60.

Horst 1961

F. Horst, "Das Privilegrecht Jahwes," in *Gottes Recht. Studien zum Recht im Alten Testament*. Hrsg. H. W. Wolff. München, 1961, 17–154.

Horwitz 1979

W. J. Horwitz, "The Significance of the Rephaim," *JNSL* 7(1979) 37–43.

Huehnergard 1983

J. Huehnergard, "Five Tablets from the Vicinity of Emar," *RA* 77(1983) 11–43.

Huehnergard 1985

J. Huehnergard, "Biblical Notes on Some New Akkadian Texts from Emar (Syria)," *CBQ* 47(1985) 428–34.

Huehnergard 1987

J. Huehnergard, *Ugaritic Vocabulary in Syllabic Transcription*. Atlanta, 1987.

Huehnergard 1989

J. Huehnergard, *The Akkadian of Ugarit*. Atlanta, 1989.

Huffmon 1965

H. B. Huffmon, *Amorite Personal Names in the Mari Texts: A Structural and Lexical Study*. Baltimore, 1965.

Hughes 1990

J. Hughes, *Secrets of the Times: Myth and History in Biblical Chronology.* Sheffield, 1990.

Hultkrantz 1978

Å. Hultkrantz, "The Cult of the Dead among North American Indians," *Temenos* 14(1978) 97–126.

Humphreys 1987

S. C. Humphreys, "Fustel de Coulanges, N. D.," in *Encyclopedia of Religion.* Vol. 5. Ed. M. Eliade. New York, 1987, 459–60.

Humphreys and King 1981

S. C. Humphreys and H. King (eds.), *Mortality and Immortality: The Anthropology and Archaeology of Death.* London, 1981.

Humphreys 1980

W. L. Humphreys, "The Rise and Fall of King Saul: A Study of an Ancient Narrative Stratum in 1 Samuel," *JSOT* 18(1980) 74–90.

Hutter 1983

M. Hutter, "Religionsgeschichtliche Erwägungen zu *'lhm* in 1 Sam 28,13," *BN* 21(1983) 32–36.

Hvidberg 1962

F. F. Hvidberg, *Weeping and Laughter in the Old Testament: A Study of Canaanite-Israelite Religion.* Leiden, 1962 [= *Graad og Latter i det Gamle Testamente, en studie i kanaanæisk-israelitisk religion.* Copenhagen, 1938].

Ingholt 1967

H. Ingholt, "Palmyrene — Hatran — Nabataean," in *An Aramaic Handbook.* Part I/1. Ed. F. Rosenthal. Wiesbaden, 1967, 40–50 [cf. also Part I/2, pp.42–50].

Irwin 1967

W. H. Irwin, " 'The Smooth Stones of the Wady'? Isaiah 57,6," *CBQ* 29(1967) 31–40.

Irwin 1977

W. H. Irwin, *Isaiah 28–33, Translation with Philological Notes.* Rome, 1977.

Jacquet 1979

L. Jacquet, *Les Psaumes et le coeur de l'homme: Etude textuelle, litteraire et doctrinale.* Vol 3. Gembloux, 1979.

Jacob 1960

E. Jacob, *Ras Shamra-Ugarit et l'Ancien Testament.* Neuchâtel, 1960.

Jacobsen 1976

Th. Jacobsen, *The Treasures of Darkness: A History of Mesopotamian Religion.* New Haven, 1976.

Jacobs-Hornig 1978

B. Jacobs-Hornig, "*gan,*" in *Theological Dictionary of the Old Testament.* Vol. 3. Ed. G. J. Botterweck and H. Ringgren. Grand Rapids, 1978, 34–39 [= "*gan,*" in

Wörterbuch zum Alten Testament. Hrsg. G. J. Botterweck, H. Ringgren, und H.-J. Fabry. Band 2. Stuttgart, 1977, 35–41].

Jastrow 1903
M. Jastrow, *A Dictionary of the Targummim, the Talmud Babli and Yerushalmi, and the Midrashic Literature*. Brooklyn, 1903.

Jay 1988
N. Jay, "Sacrifice, Descent and the Patriarchs," *VT* 38(1988) 52–70.

Jay 1992
N. Jay, *Throughout Your Generations Forever: Sacrifice, Religon, and Paternity*. Chicago, 1992.

Jensen 1963
A. E. Jensen, *Myth and Cult among Primitive Peoples*. Chicago, 1963.

Jeremias 1971
J. Jeremias, "Die Bedeutung der Gerichtsworte Michas in der Exilszeit," *ZAW* 83(1971) 330–54.

Jirku 1912
A. Jirku, *Die Dämonen und ihre Abwehr im Alten Testament*. Leipzig, 1912.

Jirku 1965
A. Jirku, "Rapa'u der Fürst der Rap'auma-Rephaim," *ZAW* 77(1965) 82–83.

Jones 1984
G. H. Jones, *1 and 2 Kings*. 2 vols. Grand Rapids, 1984.

Joüon 1991
P. Joüon, *A Grammar of Biblical Hebrew*. 2 vols. Trans. and rev. by T. Muraoka. Rome, 1991.

Kaiser 1980
O. Kaiser, *Isaiah 13–39: A Commentary*. Philadelphia, 1980^2 [= *Der Prophet Jesaja. Kapitel 13–39*. Göttingen, 1973].

Kaiser 1983
O. Kaiser, *Isaiah 1–12: A Commentary*. Philadelphia, 1983^2 [= *Der Prophet Jesaja. Kapitel 1–12*. Göttingen, 1981^5].

Kaufman 1974
S. A. Kaufman, *The Akkadian Influences on Aramaic*. Chicago, 1974.

Kennedy 1987
C. A. Kennedy, "The Cult of the Dead at Corinth," in *Love & Death in the Ancient Near East: Essays in Honor of Marvin H. Pope*. Ed. J. H. Marks and R. M. Good. Guilford, 1987, 227–36.

Kennedy 1989
C. A. Kennedy, "Isaiah 57: 5–6: Tombs in the Rocks," *BASOR* 275(1989) 47–52.

Kerényi 1959
K. Kerényi, *The Heroes of the Greeks*. New York, 1959 [= *Die Heroen der Griechen*. Zürich, 1958].

Kilian 1986

R. Kilian, *Jesaja 1–12*. Würzburg, 1986.

King 1988a

P. J. King, *Amos, Hosea, Micah: An Archaeological Commentary*. Philadelphia, 1988.

King 1988b

P. King, "The *Marzeaḥ* Amos Denounces," *BAR* 14(1988) 34–44.

Kinnier Wilson 1985

J. V. Kinnier Wilson, *The Legend of Etana: A New Edition*. Chicago, 1985.

Kirkpatrick 1888

A. F. Kirkpatrick, *The First Book of Samuel*. Cambridge, 1888.

Kitchen 1977

K. A. Kitchen, "The King List of Ugarit," *UF* 9(1977) 131–42.

Klein 1981

J. Klein, *Three Shulgi Hymns: Sumerian Royal Hymns Glorifying King Shulgi of Ur*. Ramat-Gan, 1981.

Klein 1982

J. Klein, " 'Personal God' and Individual Prayer in Sumerian Religion," *AfO Beiheft* 19 [= RAI 28](1982) 295–306.

Klein 1983

R. W. Klein, *1 Samuel*. Waco, 1983.

Knibb 1989

M. A. Knibb, "Life and Death in the Old Testament," in *The World of Ancient Israel: Sociological, Anthropological, and Political Perspectives*. Ed. R. E. Clements. Cambridge, 1989, 395–415.

Knoppers 1992

G. N. Knoppers, " 'The God in His Temple': The Phoenician Text from Pyrge as a Funerary Inscription," *JNES* 51(1992) 105–20.

Knudtzon 1915

J. A. Knudtzon, *Die El-Amarna Tafeln*. 2 vols. Leipzig, 1915.

Kobayashi 1984

T. Kobayashi, "On the Meaning of the Offerings for the Statue of Entemena," *Orient* 20(1984) 43–65.

Kobayashi 1985

T. Kobayashi, "The Ki-a-nag of Enentarzi," *Orient* 21(1985) 10–30.

Kobayashi 1989

T. Kobayashi, "Was Mesandu the Personal Deity of Enentarzi?," *Orient* 25(1989) 22–42.

Koch 1967

K. Koch, "Die Sohnesverheißung an den ugaritischen Daniel," *ZA* 58(1967) 211–21.

König 1926

E. König, *Das Buch Jesaja*. Gütersloh, 1926.

Kramer 1944

S. N. Kramer, "The Death of Gilgamesh," *BASOR* 94(1944) 2–12.

Kramer 1967

S. N. Kramer, "The Death of Ur-Nammu and his Descent in the Netherworld," *JCS* 21(1967) 104–22.

Kraus 1965

F. Kraus, "Könige, die in Zelten wohnten. Betrachtungen über den Kern der assyrischen Königsliste," *Mededelingen der Koninklijke Nederlandse Akademie van Wetenschappen* 28(1965) 121–42.

Kraus 1987

F. Kraus, "Ein altbabylonisches Totenopfer," *ZA* 77(1987) 96–97.

Kraus 1966

H.-J. Kraus, *Psalmen*. Neukirchen-Vluyn, 1966[3].

Kraus 1988

H.-J. Kraus, *Psalms 1–59: A Commentary*. Minneapolis, 1988.

Kraus 1989

H.-J. Kraus, *Psalms 60–150: A Commentary*. Minneapolis, 1989.

Krebernik 1984

M. Krebernik, *Die Beschwörungen aus Fara und Ebla: Untersuchungen zur ältesten keilschriftlichen Beschwörungsliteratur*. Hildesheim, 1984.

Lacheman and Owen 1981

E. R. Lacheman and D. I. Owen, "Texts from Arrapha and from Nuzi in the Yale Babylonian Collection," in *Studies on the Civilization and Culture of Nuzi and the Hurrians in Honor of Ernest R. Lacheman*. Ed. M. A. Morrison and D. I. Owen. Winona Lake, 1981, 377–432.

Lafont 1984

"Chapitre 3. Textes no. 246 à 427," *Archives administrative de Mari 1*. ARM 23. Paris, 1984, 231–326.

Lambert 1956

M. Lambert, "Les «réformes» d'Urukagina," *RA* 50(1956) 169–84.

Lambert 1970

M. Lambert, "Textes de Mari — dix-huitième campagne — 1969," *Syria* 47(1970) 245–60.

Lambert 1960

W. G. Lambert, *Babylonian Wisdom Literature*. Oxford, 1960.

Lambert 1967

W. G. Lambert, "Enmeduranki and Related Matters," *JCS* 21(1967) 126–38.

Lambert 1968a

W. G. Lambert, "Another Look at Hammurabi's Ancestors," *JCS* 22(1968) 1–2.

Lambert 1968b

W. G. Lambert, "Myth and Ritual as Conceived by the Babylonians," *JSS* 13(1968) 104–12.

Lambert 1971

W. G. Lambert, "Götterlisten," *RlA* 3(1971) 473–79.

Lambert 1980

W. G. Lambert, "The Theology of Death," in *Death in Mesopotamia* [= RAI 26]. Ed. B. Alster. Copenhagen, 1980, 53–66.

Lambert 1981

W. G. Lambert, "Old Akkadian Ilaba = Ugaritic Ilib?," *UF* 13(1981) 299–301.

Lambert 1985a

W. G. Lambert, "The Pantheon of Mari," *MARI* 4(1985) 525–39.

Lambert 1985b

W. G. Lambert, "Trees, Snakes and Gods in Ancient Syria and Anatolia," *BSOAS* 48(1985) 435–51.

Lambert 1987

W. G. Lambert, Review of *Untersuchungen zur Totenpflege (kispum) im alten Mesopotamien*, by A. Tsukimoto, *Orientalia* n.s., 56(1987) 403–04.

Lamphere 1983

L. Lamphere, "Southwestern Ceremonialism," in *Handbook of North American Indians: Southwest.* Vol. 10. Ed. A. Ortiz. Washington, 1983:743–63.

Landsberger 1937

B. Landsberger, *Die Serie ana ittišu* [= MSL I]. Rome, 1937.

Landsberger 1974

B. Landsberger, *The Series ḪAR-ra = ḫubullu: Tablets XX–XXII* [= MSL XII]. Rome, 1959.

Lane 1863–93

E. W. Lane, *Arabic-English Lexicon.* 8 vols. London, 1863–93.

Lang 1988a

B. Lang, "Afterlife—Ancient Israel's Changing Vision of the World Beyond," *Bible Review* 4(1988) 12–23.

Lang 1988b

B. Lang, "Life after Death in the Prophetic Promise," *SVT* 40(1988) 144–56.

Laroche 1968

E. Laroche, "Documents en langue hourrite provenant de Ras Shamra," *Ugaritica V*(1969) 447–544.

Laroche 1976–77

E. Laroche, *Glossaire de la langue hourrite* [= RHA 34–35]. Paris, 1976–77.

Larsen 1982

M. T. Larsen, "Your Money or Your Life! A Portrait of an Assyrian Business Man," in

Societies and Languages of the Anciet Near East. Studies in Honor of I. M. Diakonoff. Warminster, 1982, 214–45.

Leach 1976

E. R. Leach, *Culture and Communication.* Cambridge 1976.

Lehmann 1953

M. R. Lehmann, "A New Interpretation of the Term *Śdmwt*," *VT* 3(1953) 361–71.

Lemche 1985

N. P. Lemche, *Early Israel: Anthropological and Historical Studies on the Israelite Society before the Monarchy.* Leiden, 1985.

Lemche 1988

N. P. Lemche, *Ancient Israel: A New History of Israelite Society.* Sheffield, 1988.

Lemche 1991a

N. P. Lemche, *The Canaanites and Their Land: The Tradition of the Canaanites.* Sheffield, 1991.

Lemche 1991b

N. P. Lemche, "The Development of the Israelite Religion in the Light of Recent Studies on the Early History of Israel,"in *Congress Volume. Leuven* [= SVT 43]. Ed. J. Emerton. Supplements to Vetus Testamentum 43. Leiden, 1991, 97–115.

Levenson 1985

J. D. Levenson, "A Technical Meaning for *n'm* in the Hebrew Bible," *VT* 35(1985) 61–67.

Levenson 1993

J. D. Levenson, *The Death and Resurrection of the Beloved Son: The Transformation of Child Sacrifice in Judaism and Christianity.* New Haven and London, 1993.

Levine 1993

Numbers 1–20. New York, 1993.

Levine and de Tarragon 1984

B. Levine and J.-M. de Tarragon, "Dead Kings and Rephaim: The Patrons of the Ugaritic Dynasty," *JAOS* 104(1984) 649–59.

Levine and de Tarragon 1988

B. Levine and J.-M. de Tarragon, " 'Shapshu Cries out in Heaven': Dealing with Snake-Bites at Ugarit (KTU 1.100, 1.107)," *RB* 95(1988) 481–518.

Lewis 1989

T. Lewis, *Cults of the Dead in Ancient Israel and Ugarit.* Atlanta, 1989.

L'Heureux 1974

C. E. L'Heureux, "The Ugaritic and Biblical Rephaim," *HTR* 67(1974) 265–74.

L'Heureux 1979

C. E. L'Heureux, *Rank Among the Canaanite Gods: El, Ba'al and the Repha'im.* Missoula, 1979.

Lichtheim 1980

M. Lichtheim, *Ancient Egyptian Literature: A Book of Readings.* Vol. 3, *The Late Period.* Los Angeles and London, 1980.

Lidzbarski 1915

M. Lidzbarski, *Ephemeris für semitische Epigraphik.* Band 3. New York, 1915.

Lie 1929

A. G. Lie, *The Inscriptions of Sargon II: King of Assyria.* Part I, *The Annals.* Paris, 1929.

Limet 1986

H. Limet, *Textes administratifs relatifs aux métaux.* Paris, 1986.

Lipiński 1978

E. Lipiński, "Ditānu," in *Studies in the Bible and the Ancient Near East Presented to Samuel E. Loewenstamm on His 70th Birthday.* Ed. Y. Avishur and J. Blau. Jerusalem, 1978, 91–110.

Lippert 1881

J. Lippert, *Der Seelencult in seinen Beziehungen zur althebräischen Religion: Eine ethnologische Studie.* Berlin, 1881.

Liverani 1974

M. Liverani, "La royauté syrienne de l'âge de bronze récent," in *Le palais et la royauté* [= RAI 19]. Éd. P. Garelli. Paris, 1974, 329–56.

Lods 1906

A. Lods, *La croyance à la vie future et le culte des morts dans l'antiquité israélite.* Paris, 1906.

Loewenstamm 1969

S. E. Loewenstamm, "Eine lehrhafte ugaritische Trinkburleske," *UF* 1(1969) 71–77.

Loewenstamm 1976

S. E. Loewenstamm, "r^{e}p̱ā'īm," *Entsiḳlopediyah Miḳra'it* 7(1976) 403–07.

Loewenstamm 1980

S. E. Loewenstamm, *Comparative Studies in Biblical and Ancient Oriental Literatures.* Neukirchen-Vluyn, 1980.

Lohfink 1971

N. Lohfink, "Die Sicherung der Wirksamkeit des Gotteswortes durch das Prinzip der Schriftlichkeit der Tora und durch das Prinzip der Gewaltenteilung nach den Ämtergesetz des Buches Deuteronomium (Dt 16,18–18,22)," in *Testimonium Veritati.* Hrsg. H. Wolter. Frankfurt am Main, 1971, 143–55.

Lohfink 1981

N. Lohfink, "Kerygmata des deuteronomistischen Geschichtswerks," in *Die Botschaft und die Boten: Festschrift für Hans Walter Wolff.* Hrsg. J. Jeremias und L. Perlitt. Neukirchen-Vluyn, 1981, 87–100.

Lohfink 1982

N. Lohfink, "*jāraš*," in *Theologisches Wörterbuch zum Alten Testament.* Hrsg. G. J.

Botterweck, H. Ringgren, und H. J. Fabry. Band 3, Lieferung 8/9. Stuttgart, 1982, col.953–85.

Lohfink 1987

N. Lohfink, "The Cult Reform of Josiah of Judah: 2 Kings 22–23 as a Source for the History of Israelite Religion," in *Ancient Israelite Religion: Essays in Honor of Frank Moore Cross.* Ed. P. D. Miller, P. D. Hanson, and S. D. McBride. Philadelphia, 1987:459–75.

Lohfink 1988

N. Lohfink, Review of *Von der politischen Gemeinschaft zur Gemeinde*, by U. Rüterswörden, *TLZ* 113(1988) 425–30.

Long 1984

B. O. Long, *1 Kings with an Introduction to Historical Literature.* Grand Rapids, 1984.

Long 1992

B. O. Long, *2 Kings.* Grand Rapids, 1992.

Long 1987

C. Long, "Mythic Ancestors," in *Encyclopedia of Religion.* Vol. 1. Ed. M. Eliade. New York, 1987, 268–70.

Longman 1991

T. Longman III, *Fictional Akkadian Royal Autobiography: A Generic and Comparative Study.* Winona Lake, 1991.

Lorenz 1990

B. Lorenz, "Bestattung und Totenkult im Alten Testament," *Zeitschrift für Religions- und Geistesgeschichte* 42(1990) 21–31.

Loretz 1978

O. Loretz, "Vom kanaanäischen Totenkult zur jüdischen Patriarchen- und Elternehrung. Historische und tiefenpsychologische Grundprobleme der Entstehung des biblischen Geschichtsbildes und der jüdischen Ethik," *Jahrbuch für Anthropologie und Religionsgeschichte* 3(1978) 149–204.

Loretz 1982

O. Loretz, "Ugaritisch-biblisch *mrzḥ* 'Kultmahl, Kultverein' Jer 16,5 und Am 6,7," in *Künder des Wortes: Beiträge zur Theologie der Propheten.* Hrsg. L. Ruppert. Würzburg, 1982, 87–93.

Lowery 1991

R. H. Lowery, *The Reforming Kings: Cults and Society in First Temple Judah.* Sheffield, 1991.

Luckenbill 1927

D. D. Luckenbill, *Ancient Records of Assyria and Babylonia.* 2 vols. Chicago, 1926–27.

von Luschan and Sachau 1893

F. von Luschan and E. Sachau, *Ausgrabungen in Sendscherli I.* Berlin, 1893.

Lust 1974

J. Lust, "On Wizards and Prophets," *SVT* 26(1974) 133–42.

Lust 1986

J. Lust, "Exegesis and Theology in the Septuagint of Ezekiel. The Longer 'Pluses' and Ezek 43: 1–9," in *VI Congress of the International Organization for Septuagint and Cognate Studies*. Ed. C. E. Cox. Atlanta, 1987, 201–32.

Lust 1991

J. Lust, "'Molek and APXŌN," in *Phoenicia and the Bible*. Ed. E. Lipiński. Leuven, 1991, 193-208.

Machinist 1992

P. Machinist, "Palestine, Administration of," in *Anchor Bible Dictionary*. Vol. 5. Ed. D. N. Freedman. New York, 66–81.

Magnanini 1973

P. Magnanini, *Le iscrizioni fenicie dell' Oriente*. Roma, 1973.

Malamat 1966

A. Malamat, "Prophetic Revelations in New Documents from Mari and the Bible," *SVT* 15(1966) 207–27.

Malamat 1968

A. Malamat, "King Lists of the Old Babylonian Period and Biblical Genealogies," *JAOS* 88(1968) 163–73.

Malamat 1989

A. Malamat, *Mari and the Early Israelite Experience*. Oxford, 1989.

Mannati 1972

M. Mannati, "Remarques sur Ps. XVI 1–3," *VT* 22(1972) 359–61.

Marcus 1987

D. Marcus, "A New Ugaritic Grammar," Review of *A Basic Grammar of the Ugaritic Language*, by S. Segert, *JAOS* 107(1987) 487–92.

Margalit 1976

B. Margalit, "Studia Ugaritica II: Studies in Krt and Aqht," *UF* 8(1976) 137–92.

Margalit 1979–80

B. Margalit, "The Ugaritic Feast of the Drunken Gods: Another Look at RS 24.258 (*KTU* 1.114)," *MAARAV* 2(1979–80) 65–120.

Margalit 1980a

B. Margalit, "Death and Dying in the Ugaritic Epics," in *Death in Mesopotamia* [= RAI 26]. Ed. B. Alster. Copenhagen, 1980, 243–54.

Margalit 1980b

B. Margalit, *A Matter of "Life" and "Death": A Study of the Baal-Mot Epic (CTA 4–5–6)*. Neukirchen-Vluyn, 1980.

Margalit 1981

B. Margalit, "The Geographical Setting of the *Aqht* Story and Its Ramifications," in *Ugarit in Retrospect: Fifty Years of Ugarit and Ugaritic*. Ed. G. D. Young. Winona Lake, 1981, 131–58.

Margalit 1989

B. Margalit, *The Ugaritic Poem of AQHT*. Berlin, 1989.

Margoliouth 1908

G. Margoliouth, "Ancestor-Worship and the Cult of the Dead [Hebrew]," *Encyclopedia of Religion and Ethics* 1(1908) 444–50.

Margueron 1982

J. Margueron, *Recherches sur les palais mésopotamiens de l'Âge du bronze*. 2 vols. Paris, 1982.

Margueron 1983a

J. Margueron, "Quelques reflexions sur certaines pratiques funeraires d'Ugarit," *Akkadica* 32(1983) 5–31.

Margueron 1983b

J. Margueron, Review of *The Court of the Palms: A Functional Interpretation of the Mari Palace*, by Y. M. Al-Khalesi, *RA* 77(1983) 185–86.

Margulis 1970

B. Margulis, "A Ugaritic Psalm (RŠ 24.252)," *JBL* 89(1970) 292–304 (= B. Margalit).

Materne 1983

J.-P. Materne, "L'Année de Kahat dans la chronologie de règne de Zimri-Lim," *MARI* 2(1983) 195–99.

Matthiae 1979

P. Matthiae, "Princely Cemetery and Ancestors Cult at Ebla during Middle Bronze II: A Proposal of Interpretation," *UF* 11(1979) 563–69.

Matthiae 1981

P. Matthiae, "A Hypothesis on the Princely Burial Area of Middle Bronze II at Ebla," *ArOr* 49(1981) 55–65.

Matthiae 1984

P. Matthiae, "New Discoveries at Ebla: The Excavation of the Western Palace and the Royal Necropolis of the Amorite Period," *BA* 47(1984) 18–32.

Matthiae 1990

P. Matthiae, "A Class of Old Syrian Bronze Statuettes and the Sanctuary B2 at Ebla," in *Resurrecting the Past: A Joint Tribute to Adnan Bounni*. Ed. P. Matthiae, M. van Loon, and H. Weiss. Istanbul, 1990, 349–54 [Plates 113–19].

Mayer 1976

W. R. Mayer, *Untersuchungen zur Formensprache der babylonischen "Gebetsbeschwörungen."* Rom, 1976.

Mayer 1978

W. R. Mayer, *Nuzi-Studien I*. Neukirchen-Vluyn, 1978.

Mayer-Opificius 1981

R. Mayer-Opificius, "Archäologischer Kommentar zur Statue des Idrimi von Alalaḫ," *UF* 13(1981) 279–90.

Mayes 1979

A. D. H. Mayes, *Deuteronomy.* Grand Rapids, 1979.

Mayes 1983

A. D. H. Mayes, *The Story of Israel between Settlement and Exile: A Redactional Study of the Deuteronomistic History.* London, 1983.

Mays 1969

J. L. Mays, *Hosea: A Commentary.* Philadelphia, 1969.

Mays 1976

J. L. Mays, *Micah: A Commentary.* Philadephia, 1976.

McCarter 1980

P. Kyle McCarter, *I Samuel.* Garden City, 1980.

McCarthy 1969

D. J. McCarthy, "The Symbolism of Blood and Sacrifice," *JBL* 88(1969) 166–76.

McGinnis 1987

J. McGinnis, "A Neo-Assyrian Text Describing A Royal Funeral," *State Archives of Assyria Bulletin* 1(1987) 1–12.

McKane 1981

W. McKane, "Relations between Poetry and Prose in the Book of Jeremiah with Special Reference to Jeremiah iii 6–11 and xii 14–17," *SVT* 32(1982) 220–37.

McKane 1986

W. McKane, *A Critical and Exegetical Commentary on Jeremiah.* Vol. 1, *Introduction and Commentary on Jeremiah I–XXV.* Edinburgh, 1986.

McKay 1973

J. W. McKay, *Religion in Judah under the Assyrians, 732–609 BC.* Naperville and London, 1973.

McKenzie 1984

S. L. McKenzie, *The Chronicler's Use of the Deuteronomistic History.* Atlanta, 1984.

McKenzie 1991

S. L. McKenzie, *The Trouble with Kings: The Composition of the Book of Kings in the Deuteronomistic History.* Leiden, 1991.

Meeks 1971

D. Meeks, "Génies, anges démons, en 'Egypte," in *Génies, anges et démons.* Paris, 1971, 25–26.

Mendenhall 1973

G. E. Mendenhall, *The Tenth Generation: The Origins of the Biblical Tradition.* Baltimore, 1973.

Mendenhall 1992

G. E. Mendenhall, "From Witchcraft to Justice: Death and Afterlife in the Old Testament," in *Death and Afterlife: Perspectives of World Religions.* Ed. H. Obayashi. New York, 1992, 67–81.

Menzel 1981

B. Menzel, *Assyrische Tempel*. Band 1, *Untersuchungen zu Kult, Administration und Personal*. Band 2, *Anmerkungen, Textbuch, Tabellen und Indices*. Rom, 1981.

Merendino 1969

R. P. Merendino, *Das deuteronomische Gesetz. Eine literarische, gattungs- und überlieferungsgeschichtliche Untersuchung zu Dt 12–26*. Bonn, 1969.

du Mesnil du Buisson 1962

R. du Mesnil du Buisson, *Les tessères et les monnaies de Palmyre*. Paris, 1962.

Metcalf and Huntington 1991

P. Metcalf and R. Huntington, *Celebrations of Death: The Anthropology of Mortuary Ritual*. Cambridge, 1991^2.

Meyer 1990

J.-W. Meyer "Zur Interpretation der Leber- und Lungenmodelle aus Ugarit," in *Mantik in Ugarit: Keilalphabetische Texte der Opferschau, Omensammlungen, Nekromantie*. By M. Dietrich and O. Loretz, Münster, 1990, 214-80.

Meyer 1979

R. Meyer, "Gegensinn und Mehrdeutigkeit in der althebräischen Wort- und Begriffsbildung," *UF* 11(1979) 601–12.

Michalowski 1983

P. Michalowski, "History as Charter: Some Observations on the Sumerian King List," *JAOS* 103(1983) 237–48.

Michalowski 1985

P. Michalowski, "Third Millennium Contacts: Observations on the Relationships Between Mari and Ebla," *JAOS* 105(1985) 293–302.

Michalowski 1988a

P. Michalowski, "Divine Heroes and Historical Self-Representation: From Gilgamish to Shulgi," *Canadian Society for Mesopotamian Studies Bulletin* 16(1988) 19–23.

Michalowski 1988b

P. Michalowski, "Thoughts about Ibrium," in *Wirtschaft und Gesellschaft von Ebla*. Hrsg. H. Waetzoldt und H. Hauptmann. Heidelberg, 1988, 267–77.

Michel 1984

W. L. Michel, "ṢLMWT, 'Deep Darkness' or 'Shadow of Death'?," *BR* 29(1984) 5–20.

Miller 1971

P. D. Miller, "The *Mrzḥ* Text," in *The Claremont Ras Shamra Tablets*. Ed. L. R. Fisher. Rome, 1971, 37–49.

Miller and Hayes 1986

J. M. Miller and J. H. Hayes, *A History of Ancient Israel and Judah*. Philadelphia, 1986.

Mittmann 1981

S. Mittmann, "Die Grabinschrift des Sängers Uriahu," *ZDPV* 97(1981) 139–52.

Momigliano 1977

A. Momigliano, "The Ancient City of Fustel de Coulanges," in *Essays in Ancient and Modern Historiography*. Middletown, 1977, 325–43.

Montalbano 1951

F. J. Montalbano, "Canaanite Dagon: Origin, Nature," *CBQ* 13(1951) 381–97.

Moon 1987

B. Moon, "Tears," in *Encyclopedia of Religion*. Vol. 14. Ed. M. Eliade. New York, 1987, 360–61.

de Moor 1969

J. C. de Moor, "Studies in the New Alphabetic Texts from Ras Shamra I," *UF* 1(1969) 167–88.

de Moor 1970

J. C. de Moor, "The Semitic Pantheon of Ugarit," *UF* 2(1970) 187–228.

de Moor 1971

J. C. de Moor, *The Seasonal Pattern in the Ugaritic Myth of Ba'lu according to the Version of Ilimilku*. Neukirchen-Vluyn, 1971.

de Moor 1972

J. C. de Moor, *New Year with Canaanites and Israelites*. 2 vols. Kampen, 1972.

de Moor 1976

J. C. de Moor, "Rāpi'ūma - Rephaim," *ZAW* 88(1976) 323–45.

de Moor 1980a

J. C. de Moor, "El, the Creator," in *The Bible World: Essays in Honor of Cyrus H. Gordon*. Ed. G. Rendsburg, R. Adler, M. Arfa, and N. H. Winter. New York, 1980, 171–87.

de Moor 1980b

J. C. de Moor, "An Incantation Against Evil Spirits (Ras Ibn Hani 78/20)," *UF* 12(1980) 429–32.

de Moor 1981–82

J. C. de Moor, "Demons in Canaan," *JEOL* 27(1981–82) 106–19.

de Moor 1985

J. C. de Moor, "The Ancestral Cult in KTU 1.17: I.26–28," *UF* 17(1985) 407–09.

de Moor 1990

J. C. de Moor, "Lovable Death in the Ancient Near East," *UF* 22(1990) 233–45.

de Moor and Sanders 1991

J. C. de Moor and P. Sanders "An Ugaritic Expiation Ritual and its Old Testament Parallels," *UF* 23(1991) 283–300.

de Moor and Spronk 1984

J. C. de Moor and K. Spronk "More on Demons in Ugarit (KTU 1.82)," *UF* 16(1984) 237–50.

Moore 1990

M. S. Moore, *The Balaam Traditions: Their Character and Development.* Atlanta, 1990.

Moorey 1977

P. R. S. Moorey, "What Do We Know about the People Buried in the Royal Cemetery?," *Expedition* 20(1977) 24–40.

Moorey 1984

P. R. S. Moorey, "Where Did They Bury the Kings of the IIIrd Dynasty of Ur?," *Iraq* 46(1984) 1–18.

Moorey and Fleming 1984

P. R. S. Moorey and S. Fleming, "Anthropomorphic Metal Statuary from Syro-Palestine before 330 B.C.," *Levant* 16(1984) 67–90.

Moran 1969

W. L. Moran, "New Evidence from Mari on the History of Prophecy," *Biblica* 50(1969) 15–56.

Moran 1984

W. L. Moran, "Additions to the Amarna Lexicon," *Orientalia* n.s., 53(1984) 297–302.

Moran 1987

W. L. Moran, *Les lettres d'El Amarna: Correspondance diplomatique du pharaon.* Paris, 1987.

Moran 1992

W. L. Moran, *The Amarna Letters.* Baltimore, 1992.

Morgenstern 1966

J. Morgenstern, *Rites of Birth, Marriage, Death, and Kindred Occasions among the Semites.* Cincinnati, 1966.

Morris 1987

I. Morris, *Burial and Ancient Society: The Rise of the Greek City-State.* Cambridge, 1987.

Morris 1988

I. Morris, "Tomb Cult and the 'Greek Renaissance': The Past in the Present in the 8th Century B.C.," *Antiquity* 62(1988) 750–61.

Morris 1989

I. Morris, "Attitudes Toward Death in Archaic Greece," *Classical Antiquity* 8(1989) 296–320.

Morris 1991

I. Morris, "The Archaeology of Ancestors: The Saxe/Goldstein Hypothesis Revisited," *Cambridge Archaeological Journal* 1(1991) 147–69.

Morris 1992

I. Morris, *Death-ritual and Social Structure in Classical Antiquity.* Cambridge, 1992.

Morrison 1981

J. S. Morrison, "The Classical World," in *Oracles and Divination.* Ed. M. Loewe and C. Blacker. London, 1981, 87–114.

Müller 1893

D. H. Müller, "Die altsemitischen Inschriften von Sendscherli," *Wiener Zeitschrift für die Kunde des Morgenlandes* 7(1893) 33–70.

Müller 1894

D. H. Müller, "The Excavations at Sendschirli," *The Contemporary Review* 65(1894) 563–75.

Müller 1937

K. F. Müller, *Das assyrische Ritual. Teil I: Texte zum assyrischen Königsritual* [= MVÄG 41/3]. Leipzig, 1937.

Müller 1975–76

H.-P. Müller, "Das Wort von den Totengeistern Jes. 8,19f.," *WO* 8(1975–76) 65–76.

Müller 1980

H.-P. Müller, "Religionsgeschichtliche Beobachtungen zu den Texten von Ebla," *ZDPV* 96(1980) 1–19.

Müller 1984

H.-P. Müller, "*mōlēk*" in *Theologisches Wörterbuch zum Alten Testament.* Hrsg. G. J. Botterweck, H. Ringgren, und H.-J. Fabry. Band 4, Lieferung 8/9. Stuttgart, 1984, 957–68.

Muilenburg 1956

J. Muilenburg, "The Book of Isaiah, Chapters 40–66: Introduction and Exegesis," in *Interpreter's Bible.* Vol. 5. Ed. G. A. Buttrick. Nashville, 1956, 532.

Mulder 1965

M. J. Mulder, *Kanaänitische Goden in het Oude Testament.* The Hague, 1965.

Mulder 1982

M. J. Mulder, "Was war die am Tempel gebaute 'Sabbathalle' in II Kön. 16,18?," in *Von Kanaan bis Kerala: Festschrift für Prof. Mag. Dr. Dr. J. P. M. van der Ploeg O. P. zur Vollendung des siebzigsten Lebenjahres am 4. Juli 1979.* Hrsg. W. C. Delsman., J. T. Nelis, J. R. T. M. Peters, W. H. Ph. Römer, und A. S. van der Woude. Neukirchen-Vluyn, 1982, 161–72.

Mullen 1980

E. T. Mullen, *The Divine Council in Canaanite and Early Hebrew Literature.* Chico, 1980.

Myerhoff, Camino, and Turner 1987

B. G. Myerhoff, L. A. Camino, and E. Turner, "Rites of Passage (An Overview)," in *Encyclopedia of Religion.* Vol. 12. Ed. M. Eliade. New York, 1987, 380–86.

Na'aman 1981

N. Na'aman, "The Recycling of a Silver Statue," *JNES* 40(1981) 47–48.

Nakata 1974

I. Nakata, "Deities in the Mari Texts: Complete Inventory of All the Information on the Deities Found in the Published Old Babylonian Cuneiform Texts from Mari and Analytical and Comparative Evaluation Thereof with regard to the Official and Popular Pantheons of Mari." Ph.D. diss., Columbia University, 1974.

Nakata 1975

I. Nakata, "A Mari Note: Ikrub-El and Related Matters," *Orient* 11(1975) 15–24.

Naveh 1967

J. Naveh, "Some Notes on Nabatean Inscriptions from 'Avdat," *IEJ* 17(1967) 187–89.

Negev 1961

A. Negev, "Nabatean Inscriptions from 'Avdat (Oboda)," *IEJ* 11 (1961) 127–38.

Negev 1963

A. Negev, "Nabatean Inscriptions from 'Avdat (Oboda)," *IEJ* 13 (1963) 113–24.

Negev 1987

A. Negev, "Nabatean Religion," in *Encyclopedia of Religion.* Vol. 10. Ed. M. Eliade. New York, 1987, 287–90.

Neiman 1948

D. Neiman, "*PGR*: A Canaanite Cult-Object in the Old Testament," *JBL* 67(1948) 55–60.

Newell 1976

W. H. Newell, "Good and Bad Ancestors," in *Ancestors.* Ed. W. H. Newell. Paris, 1976, 17–29.

Nicholson 1967

E. W. Nicholson, *Deuteronomy and Tradition.* Philadelphia, 1967.

Nicholson 1970

E. W. Nicholson, *Preaching to the Exiles: A Study of the Prose Tradition in the Book of Jeremiah.* Oxford, 1970.

Nicholson 1973

E. W. Nicholson, *The Book of the Prophet Jeremiah: Chapters 1–25.* Cambridge, 1973.

Nicholson 1975

E. W. Nicholson, "The Antiquity of the Tradition in Exodus XXIV 9–11," *VT* 25(1975) 69–79.

Nicholson 1986

E. W. Nicholson, *God and His People: Covenant and Theology in the Old Testament.* Oxford, 1986.

Niehr 1991

H. Niehr "Ein unerkannter Text zur Nekromantie in Israel," *UF* 23(1991) 301–306.

Nielsen 1954

E. Nielsen, "The Burial of Foreign Gods," *Studia Theologica* 8(1954) 103–22.

Nielsen 1977–78

E. Nielsen, "Historical Perspectives and Geographical Horizons: On the Question of

North-Israelite Elements in Deuteronomy," *Annual of the Swedish Theological Institute* 11(1977–78) 77–89.

Nielsen 1986
K. Nielsen, *Incense in Ancient Israel* [= SVT 38]. Leiden, 1986.

Nilsson 1950
M. P. Nilsson, *The Minoan-Mycenaean Religion and Its Survival in Greek Religion.* Lund, 1950^2.

Norin 1977
S. I. L. Norin, *Er spaltete das Meer: Die Auszugsüberlieferung in Psalmen und Kult des alten Israel.* Lund, 1977.

Noth 1965
M. Noth, *Leviticus: A Commentary.* Philadelphia, 1965.

Noth 1966
M. Noth, *The Laws in the Pentateuch and Other Studies.* Edinburgh, 1966 [= *Gesammelte Studien zum Alten Testament.* München, 1966^3].

Nougayrol 1955
J. Nougayrol, *Le palais royal d'Ugarit, publie sous la direction de Claude F.-A. Schaeffer.* Vol. 3, *Textes accadiens et hourrites des archives est, ouest et centrales.* Paris, 1955.

Nougayrol 1956
J. Nougayrol, *Le palais royal d'Ugarit, publie sous la direction de Claude F.-A. Schaeffer.* Vol. 4, *Textes accadiens archives sud.* Paris, 1956.

Nougayrol 1967
J. Nougayrol, "Rapports paléo-babyloniens d'haruspices," *JCS* 21 (1967) 219–35.

Nougayrol 1968
J. Nougayrol, "Textes suméro-accadiens des archives et bibliothèques privées d'Ugarit," *Ugaritica V*(1968) 1–446.

Obermann 1946
J. Obermann, *How Daniel Was Blessed with a Son: An Incubation Scene in Ugaritic.* New Haven, 1946.

O'Brian 1989
M. A. O'Brien, *The Deuteronomistic Hypothesis: A Reassessment.* Fribourg/Göttingen. 1989.

Oesterley 1939
W. O. E. Oesterley, *The Psalms.* 2 vols. London, 1939.

Oller 1977
G. Oller, "The Autobiography of Idrimi: A New Text Edition with Philological and Historical Commentary." Ph.D. diss., University of Pennsylvania, 1977.

del Olmo Lete 1981
G. del Olmo Lete, *Mitos y leyendas de Canaan segun la tradicion de Ugarit: Textos, version y estudio.* Madrid, 1981.

del Olmo Lete 1983
G. del Olmo Lete, "El mito de Ba'lu: Prosodia y hermenéutica," *AuOr* 1(1983) 167–78.

del Olmo Lete 1986a
G. del Olmo Lete, "The 'Divine' Names of the Ugaritic Kings," *UF* 18(1986) 83–95.

del Olmo Lete 1986b
G. del Olmo Lete, "Liturgia funeraria de los reyes de Ugarit (KTU 1.106)," *SEL* 3(1986) 55–71.

Olmstead 1931
A. T. E. Olmstead, *History of Palestine and Syria to the Macedonian Conquest.* New York, 1931.

Olyan 1988
S. M. Olyan, *Asherah and the Cult of Yahweh in Israel.* Atlanta, 1988.

Olyan and Smith 1987
S. M. Olyan and M. S. Smith, Review of *The Cult of Molek: A Reassessment*, by G. C. Heider, *RB* 94(1987) 273–75.

Oort 1881
H. Oort, "De doodenverering bij de Israëlieten," *Theologisch Tijdschrift* 14(1881) 350–63.

Östreicher 1923
T. Östreicher, *Das deuteronomische Grundgesetz.* Gütersloh, 1923.

Opler 1983
M. E. Opler, "The Apachean Culture Pattern and Its Origins," in *Handbook of North American Indians: Southwest.* Vol. 10. Ed. A. Ortiz. Washington, 1983, 368–92.

Oppenheim 1956
A. L. Oppenheim, "The Interpretation of Dreams in the Ancient Near East with a Translation of an Assyrian Dream Book," *TAPS* 46(1956) 179–373.

Oppenheim 1965
A. L. Oppenheim, "On Royal Gardens in Mesopotamia," *JNES* 24(1965) 328–33.

Oppenheim 1977
A. L. Oppenheim, *Ancient Mesopotamia. Portrait of a Dead Civilization.* Revised edition. Chicago, 1977.

Oswalt 1986
J. N. Oswalt, *The Book of Isaiah, Chapters 1–39.* Grand Rapids, 1986.

Otten 1951
H. Otten, "Die hethitischen 'Königslisten' und die altorientalische Chronologie," *Mitteilungen der Deutschen Orient-Gesellschaft zu Berlin* 83 (1951) 47–70.

Otten 1980
H. Otten, "Inkubation," *RlA* 5(1980) 105.

Palgi and Abramovitch 1984
P. Palgi and H. Abramovitch, "Death: A Cross-Cultural Perspective," *Annual Review of Anthropology* 13(1984) 385–417.

Paradise 1972
J. S. Paradise, "Nuzi Inheritance Practices." Ph.D. diss., University of Pennsylvania, 1972.

Paradise 1987
J. S. Paradise, "Daughters as 'Sons' at Nuzi," in *Studies on the Civilization and Culture of Nuzi and the Hurrians*. Vol. 2 *General Studies and Excavations at Nuzi 9/1*. Ed. M. A. Morrison and D. I. Owen. Winona Lake 1987, 203–13.

Parayne 1982
D. Parayne, "Les sépultures de Mari: typologie provisoire," *Akkadica* 29(1982) 1–29.

Pardee 1978
D. Pardee, "A Philological and Prosodic Analysis of the Ugaritic Serpent Incantation *UT* 607," *JANES* 10(1978) 73–108.

Pardee 1979
D. Pardee, "*m*^{e}*rôrăt-p*^{e}*tānîm* 'Venom' in Job 2014," *ZAW* 91(1979) 401–16.

Pardee 1980
D. Pardee, "The New Canaanite Myths and Legends," Review of *Canaanite Myths and Legends*, by J. C. L. Gibson, *BO* 37(1980) 269–91.

Pardee 1981–82
D. Pardee, "Ugaritic," *AfO* 28(1981–82) 259–72.

Pardee 1983
D. Pardee, "Visiting Ditanu—The Text of RS 24.272," *UF* 15(1983) 127–40.

Pardee 1987
D. Pardee, "Epigraphic and Philological Notes," *UF* 19(1987) 199–217.

Pardee 1988
D. Pardee, *Les textes para-mythologiques de la 24*^{e} *campagne (1961)*. Paris, 1988.

Pardee 1989
D. Pardee, Review of *I testi rituali di Ugarit*, by P. Xella, *JNES* 48(1989) 42–44.

Parker 1954
B. Parker, "The Nimrud Tablets, 1952 — Business Documents," *Iraq* 16(1954) 29–58.

Parker 1972
S. B. Parker, "The Ugaritic Deity Rāpi'u," *UF* 4(1972) 97–104.

Parker 1989
S. B. Parker, *The Pre-Biblical Narrative Tradition: Essays on the Ugaritic Poems Keret and Aqhat*. Atlanta, 1989.

Parpola 1970
S. Parpola, *Letters from Assyrian Scholars to the Kings Esarhaddon and Assurbanipal*. Neukirchen-Vluyn, 1970.

Parpola 1983
S. Parpola, *Letters from Assyrian Scholars to the Kings Esarhaddon and Assurbanipal*. Neukirchen-Vluyn, 1983.

Parrot 1975

A. Parrot, "La XXIe campagne des fouilles à Mari," *CRAIBL*(1975) 96–97.

Pečírková 1985

J. Pečírková, "Divination and Politics in the Late Assyrian Empire," *ArOr* 53(1985) 155–68.

Pečírková 1987

J. Pečírková, "The Administrative Methods of Assyrian Imperialism," *ArOr* 55(1987) 162–75.

Peckham 1987

B. Peckham, "Phoenicia and the Religion of Israel: The Epigraphic Evidence," in *Ancient Israelite Religion: Essays in Honor of Frank Moore Cross*. Ed. P. D. Miller, P. D. Hanson, and S. D. McBride. Philadelphia, 1987, 79–99.

Pedersen 1926

J. Pedersen, *Israel: Its Life and Culture I-II*. London, 1926.

Perles 1914

F. Perles, "*Eṭimmu* im Alten Testament und im Talmud," *OLZ* 17(1914) 108–10.

Pettinato 1966

G. Pettinato, *Die Ölwahrsagung bei den Babyloniern*. Rome, 1966.

Pettinato 1979a

G. Pettinato, *Catalogo dei testi cuneiformi di Tell Mardikh-Ebla*. Napoli, 1979.

Pettinato 1979b

G. Pettinato, *Culto ufficiale ad Ebla durante il regno di Ibbi-Sipiš. Con appendice di Pietro Mander* [= Orientis Antiqui Collectio 16]. Roma, 1979.

Pettinato 1979c

G. Pettinato, "Culto ufficiale ad Ebla durante il regno di Ibbi-Sipiš. Con appendice di Pietro Mander," *OrAn* 18(1979) 85–215.

Pettinato 1980

G. Pettinato, *Testi ammimistrative della biblioteca L.2769 – Parte I*. Napoli, 1980.

Pettinato 1981

G. Pettinato, *The Archives of Ebla: An Empire Inscribed in Clay*. Garden City, 1981.

Pettinato 1982

G. Pettinato, *Testi lessicali bilingui della biblioteca L.2769*. Napoli, 1982.

Pfeiffer and Speiser 1936

R. H. Pfeiffer and E. A. Speiser, *One Hundred New Selected Nuzi Texts* [= AASOR 16]. New Haven, 1936.

Pitard 1978

W. T. Pitard, "The Ugaritic Funerary Text RS 34.126," *BASOR* 232(1978) 65–75.

Pitard 1987

W. T. Pitard, "RS 34.126, Notes on the Text," *MAARAV* 4(1987) 75–86 [photographs and drawings, pp. 111–55].

Pitard 1990

W. T. Pitard, "The Tombs of Ugarit and the Care of the Dead," Paper delivered at the annual meeting of the Society of Biblical Literature, 1990, 1–18.

Pitard 1991

W. T. Pitard, "Post-Funeral Offerings to the Dead in Canaan and Israel," Paper delivered at the annual meeting of the Society of Biblical Literature, 1991, 1–13.

Pitard 1992a

W. T. Pitard, "A New Edition of the 'Rāpi'ūma' Texts: *KTU* 1.20–22," *BASOR* 285(1992) 33–77.

Pitard 1992b

W. T. Pitard, "The Practice and Function of Feeding the Dead in Canaan, Egypt, and Israel," Paper delivered at thc annual meeting of the Society of Biblical Literature, 1992, 1–21.

Pitard 1993

W. Pitard, "Gods and the Dead in Mesopotamia," Paper presented at the Annual Midwest AOS Meeting, 1993, 1–20.

Podella 1986

T. Podella, "Ein mediterraner Trauerritus," *UF* 18(1986) 263–69.

Podella 1989

T. Podella, *Ṣôm-Fasten: Kollektive Trauer um den verborgenen Gott im Alten Testament.* Neukirchen Vluyn, 1989.

Polley 1989

M. Polley, *Amos and the Davidic Empire: A Socio-historical Approach.* Oxford, 1989.

Pope 1972

M. H. Pope, "A Divine Banquet at Ugarit," in *The Use of the Old Testament in the New and Other Essays: Studies in Honor of William Franklin Stinespring*. Ed. J. M. Efird. Durham, 1972, 170–203.

Pope 1977a

M. H. Pope, "Notes on the Rephaim Texts from Ugarit," in *Essays on the Ancient Near East in Memory of Jacob Joel Finkelstein.* Ed. M. Ellis. Hamden, 1977, 163–82.

Pope 1977b

M. H. Pope, *Song of Songs.* Garden City, 1977.

Pope 1979–80

M. H. Pope, "Le MRZH à Ougarit et ailleurs," *AAAS* 29–30(1979–80) 141–43.

Pope 1981

M. H. Pope, "The Cult of the Dead at Ugarit," in *Ugarit in Retrospect: Fifty Years of Ugarit and Ugaritic.* Ed. G. D. Young. Winona Lake, 1981, 159–79.

Pope 1983

M. H. Pope, Review of *Rank among the Canaanite Gods, El, Ba'al, and the Rephaim,* by C. E. L'Heureux," *BASOR* 251(1983) 67–69.

Pope 1987

M. H. Pope, Review of *Beatific Afterlife in Ancient Israel and in the Ancient Near East*, by K. Spronk, *UF* 19(1987) 452–63.

Porten 1968

B. Porten, *Archives from Elephantine: The Life of an Ancient Jewish Military Colony*. Berkeley, 1968.

Porter 1981

J. R. Porter, "Ancient Israel," in *Divination and Oracles*. Ed. M. Loewe and C. Blacker. London, 1981, 191–214.

Porter 1989

J. R. Porter, "The Supposed Deuteronomic Redaction of the Prophets: Some Considerations," in *Schöpfung und Befreiung: Für Claus Westermann zum 80. Geburtstag*. Hrsg. R. Albertz, F. N. Gotka, und J. Kegler. Stuttgart, 1989, 69–78.

Preuss 1977

H. D. Preuss, "ʾ^{e}*lîl*," in *Theological Dictionary of the Old Testament*. Ed. G. J. Botterweck and H. Ringgren. Grand Rapids. 1(1977) 285–87 [= "ʾ^{e}*lîl*," in *Theologisches Wörterbuch zum Alten Testament*. Hrsg. G. J. Botterweck, H. Ringgren, und H.-J. Fabry. Band 1. Stuttgart, 1973, 305–08].

Preuss 1982

H. D. Preuss, *Deuteronomium*. Darmstadt, 1982.

Provan 1988

I. W. Provan, *Hezekiah and the Books of Kings*. Berlin, 1988.

Puech 1979

E. Puech, "Remarques sur quelques inscriptions phéniciennes de Chypre," *Semitica* 29(1979) 19–43.

Puech 1992

E. Puech, "Palestinian Funerary Inscriptions," in *The Anchor Bible Dictionary*. Vol. 5. Ed. D. N. Freedman. New York, 1992, 126–35.

Rabin 1961

C. Rabin, "Etymological Miscellanea," in *Scripta Heirosolymitana*. 8 (1961) 384–400.

von Rad 1966

G. von Rad, "The Promised Land and Yahweh's Land in the Hexateuch," in *The Problem of the Hexateuch and Other Essays*. London, 1966, 79–93.

Rahmani 1981

L. Y. Rahmani, "Ancient Jerusalem's Funerary Customs and Tombs," *BA* 44(1981) 171–77, 229–35.

Rainey 1965a

A. F. Rainey, "The Kingdom of Ugarit," *BA* 28(1965) 102–25.

Rainey 1965b

A. F. Rainey, "The Military Personnel of Ugarit," *JNES* 24(1965) 17–27.

Rainey 1970

A. F. Rainey, *El Amarna Tablets 359–379.* Neukirchen-Vluyn, 1970.

Rainey 1974

A. F. Rainey, "The Ugaritic Texts in Ugaritica 5," *JAOS* 94(1974) 184–94.

Rainey 1975

A. F. Rainey, "Sacrifice and Offerings," *Zondervan Pictorial Encyclopedia of the Bible* 5(1975) 194–211.

Rainey 1987

A. F. Rainey, "A New Grammar of Ugaritic," Review of *A Basic Grammar of the Ugaritic Language*, by S. Segert, *Orientalia* n.s., 56(1987) 391–402.

Raṭosh 1970–71

J. Raṭosh, "*'ēbr' bmqr' 'w 'rṣ h'brym'* [*'ebr* in Scripture or the Land of *h'brym*]," *Bet Mikra* 47(1970–71) 549–68.

Renaud 1977

B. Renaud, *La formation du livre de Michée: Tradition et actualisation.* Paris, 1977.

Reviv 1972

H. Reviv, "Some Comments on the Maryannu," *IEJ* 22(1972) 218–28.

Ribar 1973

J. W. Ribar, "Death Cult Practices in Ancient Palestine." Ph.D. diss., The University of Michigan, 1973.

Ribichini 1985

S. Ribichini, *Poenus Advena: Gli dei fenici e l'interpretazione classica.* Roma, 1985.

Ribichini and Xella 1979

S. Ribichini and P. Xella, "Milk'aštart, *mlk*(*m*) e la tradizione siropalestinese sui Refaim," *RSF* 7(1979) 145–58.

Ritner 1987

R. K. Ritner, "The Mechanics of Ancient Egyptian Magical Practice." 2 vols. Ph.D. diss., The University of Chicago, 1987.

Roberts 1970

J. J. M. Roberts, "A New Parallel to I Kings 18:28–29," *JBL* 89(1970) 76–77.

Roberts 1972

J. J. M. Roberts, *The Earliest Semitic Pantheon: A Study of the Semitic Deities Attested in Mesopotamia before Ur III.* Baltimore, 1972.

Röllig 1969

W. Röllig, "Zur Typologie und Entstehung der babylonischen und assyrischen Königslisten," in *lišān mitḫurti. Festschrift Wolfram Freiherr von Soden zum 19.4.1988 von Schülern und Mitarbeitern.* Hrsg. M. Dietrich und W. Röllig. Neukirchen-Vluyn, 1969, 265–77.

Röllig 1974

W. Röllig, "Eine Neue Phoenizische Inschrift aus Byblos," in *Neue Ephemeris für*

Semitische Epigraphik. Band 2. Hrsg. R. Degen, W. W. Müller, W. Röllig. Wiesbaden, 1974, 1–15.

Römer 1973

W. H. Römer, "Einige Bemerkungen zum dämonischen Gotte ^{d}*Kubu(m)*," in *Symbolae Biblicae et Mesopotamicae: Festschrift für F. M. Th. de Liagre Böhl.* Ed. M. A. Beek. Leiden, 1973, 310ff.

Rofé 1974

A. Rofé, "Classes in the Prophetic Stories: Didactic Legenda and Parable," *SVT* 26(1974) 143–64.

Rogerson and McKay 1977

J. Rogerson and J. McKay, *Psalms 101–50.* Vol. 3. Cambridge, 1977.

Roschinski 1988

H. P. Roschinski, "Die phönizische Weihinschrift aus Pyrgi," in *Texte aus der Umwelt des Alten Testaments.* Band 2/4 *Grab-, Sarg-, Votiv- und Bauinschriften.* Hrsg. O. Kaiser. Gütersloh, 1988, 602–05.

Rosengarten 1960

Y. Rosengarten, *Le concept sumérien de consommation dans la vie économique et religieuse.* Paris, 1960.

Rosenthal 1970

F. Rosenthal, *Knowledge Triumphant: The Concept of Knowledge in Medieval Islam.* Leiden, 1970.

Rost 1965

L. Rost, *Das kleine Credo und andere Studien zum Alten Testament.* Heidelberg, 1965.

Rouillard 1985

H. Rouillard, *La pericope de Balaam (Nombres 22–24): La prose et les "oracles".* Paris, 1985.

Rouillard and Tropper 1987a

H. Rouillard and J. Tropper, "*trpym*, rituels de guérison et culte des ancêtres d'après 1 Samuel XIX 11–17 et les textes parallèles d'Assur et de Nuzi," *VT* 37(1987) 340–61.

Rouillard and Tropper 1987b

H. Rouillard and J. Tropper, "Vom kanaanäischen Ahnenkult zur Zauberei. Eine Auslegungsgeschichte zu den hebräischen Begriffen *'wb* und *yd'ny*," *UF* 19(1987) 235–54.

Rowley 1963

H. H. Rowley, *Men of God: Studies in Old Testament History and Prophecy.* London, 1963.

Rudolph 1958

W. Rudolph, *Jeremia.* Tübingen, 1958^{2}.

Rüterswörden 1987

U. Rüterswörden, *Von der politischen Gemeinschaft zur Gemeinde: Studien zu Dt 16,18–18,22.* Frankfurt am Main, 1987.

Ryan 1954

D. J. Ryan, "Rpum and Rephaim. A Study in the Relationship between the Rpum of Ugarit and the Rephaim in the Old Testament." M.A. thesis, The National University of Ireland, 1954.

Sabourin 1974

L. Sabourin, *The Psalms: Their Origin and Meaning*. A New and Enlarged Edition. Staten Island, 1974^2.

Salles 1980

J.-F. Salles, *La nécropole "K" de Byblos*. Boulogne, 1980.

San Nicolò 1933

M. San Nicolò, "Parerga Babylonica X-XI: X. Bestattungs- und Totenkultverpflichtungen in den Keilschrifturkunden," *ArOr* 5(1933) 284–87.

Šanda 1912

A. Šanda, *Die Bücher der Könige*. Vol. 2. Münster, 1912.

Sapin 1983

J. Sapin, "Quelques systèmes socio-politiques en Syrie au 2° millénaire avant J.-C. et leur évolution historique d'après des documents réligieux (légendes, rituels, sanctuaires)," *UF* 15(1983) 157–90.

Saracino 1982

F. Saracino, "Ras Ibn Hani 78/20 and Some Old Testament Connections," *VT* 32(1982) 338–43.

Saracino 1984

F. Saracino, "Appunti in margine a RIH 78/20," *SEL* 1(1984) 69–83.

Sarna 1966

N. M. Sarna, *Understanding Genesis*. New York, 1966.

Sasson 1966

J. M. Sasson, "Canaanite Maritime Involvement in the Second Millennium B.C.," *JAOS* 86(1966) 126–38.

Sasson 1979

J. M. Sasson, "The Calendar and Festivals of Mari during the Reign of Zimri-Lim," in *Studies in Honor of J. B. Jones*. Ed. M. A. Powell and R. H. Sack. Neukirchen-Vluyn, 1979, 119–41.

Sasson 1981a

J. M. Sasson, "Literary Criticism, Folklore Scholarship, and Ugaritic Literature," in *Ugarit in Retrospect: Fifty Years of Ugarit and Ugaritic*. Ed. G. D. Young. Winona Lake, 1981, 81–98.

Sasson 1981b

J. M. Sasson, "On Idrimi and Šarruwa, the Scribe," in *Studies on the Civilization and Culture of Nuzi and the Hurrians in Honor of Ernest R. Lacheman*. Ed. M. A. Morrison and D. I. Owen. Winona Lake, 1981, 309–24.

Sasson 1982

J. M. Sasson, "Accounting Discrepancies in the Mari NÍ.GUB[NÍG.DU] Texts," in *Zikir šumim: Assyriological Studies Presented to F. R. Kraus on the Occasion of his Seventieth Birthday*. Ed. G. van Driel, T. J. H. Krispijn, M. Stol, and K. R. Veenhof. Leiden, 1982, 326–41.

Sasson 1983

J. M. Sasson, "Mari Dreams," *JAOS* 103(1983) 283–93.

Sasson 1984a

J. M. Sasson, "Thoughts of Zimri-Lim," *BA* 47(1984) 110–20.

Sasson 1984b

J. M. Sasson, "Zimri-Lim Takes the Grand Tour," *BA* 47(1984) 246–51.

Sasson 1985

J. M. Sasson, " 'Year: Zimri-Lim Offered a Great Throne to Shamash of Mahanum': An Overview of One Year in Mari Part I: The Presence of the King," *MARI* 4(1985) 437–52.

Sasson 1987

J. M. Sasson," 'Year: Zimri-Lim Dedicated His Statue to Addu of Halab': Locating One Year in Zimri-Lim's Reign," *MARI* 5(1987) 577–89.

Sauer 1966

G. Sauer, "Rephaim," *Biblisches Historisches Handwörterbuch* 3(1966) 1590–91.

Sayce 1909

A. H. Sayce, "An Aramaic Ostracon from Elephantine," *Proceedings of the Society of Biblical Archaeology* 31(1909) 154–55.

Schaeffer 1935

C. F.-A. Schaeffer, "Les fouilles de Minet-el-Beidha et de Ras Shamra: Sixième campagne (Printemps 1934)," *Syria* 16(1935) 141–76.

Schaeffer 1939

C. F.-A. Schaeffer, "Fertility Cult and Cult of the Dead at Ugarit," in *The Cuneiform Texts from Ras Shamra-Ugarit*. London, 1939, 46–56.

Schaeffer 1962

C. F.-A. Schaeffer, "Sacrifice à M-l-k, Moloch ou Melek," *Ugaritica IV*(1962) 77–83.

Schaeffer 1963

C. F.-A. Schaeffer, "Neue Entdeckungen in Ugarit. (23. und 24. Kampagne, 1960–1961)," *AfO* 20(1963) 206–15.

Schiffman and Schwartz 1992

L. Schiffman and M. Schwartz, *Hebrew and Aramaic Incantation Texts from the Cairo Genizah*. Sheffield, 1992.

Schmidt 1965

W. H. Schmidt, "Die deuteronomistische Redaktion des Amosbuches. Zu den theologischen Unterschieden zwischen dem Prophetenwort und seinem Sammler," *ZAW* 77(1965) 168–93.

Schreiner 1981

J. Schreiner, *Jeremia 1–25,14*. Würzburg, 1981.

Schroer 1987

S. Schroer, *In Israel gab es Bilder: Nachrichten von darstellender Kunst im Alten Testament*. Fribourg/Göttingen, 1987.

Schulman 1986

A. R. Schulman, "Some Observations on the 3ḫ ı'ḳr n R'-Stelae," *BO* 43(1986) 302–348.

Schumacher and Steuernagel 1908

G. Schumacher and C. Steuernagel, *Tell el Mutesellim* I. Leipzig, 1908.

Schunck 1963

K.-D. Schunck, *Benjamin: Untersuchungen zur Entstehung und Geschichte eines israelitischen Stammes*. Berlin, 1963.

Schunck 1977

K.-D. Schunck, "*bāmāh*," in *Theological Dictionary of the Old Testament*. Vol. 2. Ed. G. J. Botterweck and H. Ringgren. Grand Rapids, 1977, 139–45 [= "*bāmāh*," in *Theologisches Wörterbuch zum Alten Testament*. Hrsg. G. J. Botterweck, H. Ringgren, und H.-J. Fabry. Band 1. Stuttgart, 1973, 662–67].

Schunck 1980

K.-D. Schunck, "chālaq I," in *Theological Dictionary of the Old Testament*. Vol. 4. Ed. G. J. Botterweck and H. Ringgren. Grand Rapids, 1980, 444–47 [="ḥālaq I," in *Theologisches Wörterbuch zum Alten Testament*. Hrsg. G. J. Botterweck, H. Ringgren, und H.-J. Fabry. Band 2. Stuttgart, 1977, 1011–15].

Scurlock 1988

J. Scurlock, "Magical Means of Dealing with Ghosts in Ancient Mesopotamia." 2 vols. Ph.D. diss., The University of Chicago, 1988.

Scurlock 1993

J. Scurlock, "Once more *ku-bu-ru*," *NABU* 93/21(1993) 15–16.

Segert 1976

S. Segert, *A Grammar of Phoenician and Punic*. Munich, 1976.

Segert 1982

S. Segert, Review of *I testi rituali di Ugarit*, by P. Xella, *Wiener Zeitschrift für die Kunde des Morgenlandes* 74(1982) 239–41.

Segert 1984

S. Segert, *A Basic Grammar of the Ugaritic Language: With Selected Texts and Glossary*. Berkeley, 1984.

Seitz 1971

G. Seitz, *Redaktionsgeschichtliche Studien zum Deuteronomium*. Stuttgart, 1971.

Seitz 1991

G. Seitz, *Zion's Final Destiny*. Minneapolis, 1991.

Seligson 1951

M. Seligson, *The Meaning of npš mt in the Old Testament*. Helsinki, 1951.

van Selms 1954

A. van Selms, *Marriage and Family Life in Ugaritic Literature*. London, 1954.

Sigrist 1982

M. Sigrist, "Miscellanea," *JCS* 34(1982) 242–52.

Simpson, Faulkner, Wente 1973

W. K. Simpson, R. O. Faulkner, E. F. Wente, *Literature of Ancient Egypt: An Anthology of Stories, Instructions, and Poetry*. New Haven, 1973.

Singer 1948

A. D. Singer, "The Vocative in Ugaritic," *JCS* 2(1948) 1–10.

Singleton 1977

M. Singleton, "Ancestors, Adolescents, and the Absolute: An Exercise in Contextualization," *Pro Mundi Vita Bulletin* 68(1977) 2–35.

Sivan 1984

D. Sivan, *Grammatical Analysis and Glossary of the Northwest Semitic Vocables in Akkadian Texts of the 15th-13th Centuries* B.C. *from Canaan and Syria*. Neukirchen-Vluyn, 1984.

Sjöberg 1984

Å. W. Sjöberg, ed., *The Sumerian Dictionary*. Vol. 2, *B*. Philadelphia, 1984.

Skaist 1980

A. Skaist, "The Ancestor Cult and Succession in Mesopotamia," in *Death in Mesopotamia* [= RAI 26]. Ed. B Alster. Copenhagen, 1980, 123–28.

Skinner 1893

J. Skinner, *1 & 2 Kings*. Edinburgh, 1893.

Smelik 1979

K. A. D. Smelik "The Witch of Endor: I Samuel 28 in Rabbinic and Christian Exegesis Till 800 A. D.," *Vigiliae Christianae* 33(1979) 160–79.

Smith 1880

W. Robertson Smith, "The Sixteenth Psalm," *The Expositor* 4(1880) 341–72.

Smith 1889

W. Robertson Smith, *Lectures on the Religion of the Semites*. Edinburgh, 1889.

Smith 1899

H. P. Smith, *A Critical and Exegetical Commentary on the Books of Samuel*. Edinburgh, 1899.

Smith 1918

G. A. Smith, *The Book of Deuteronomy in the Revised Version: With Introduction and Notes*. Cambridge, 1918.

Smith 1987

J. Z. Smith, "Dying and Rising Gods," in *Encyclopedia of Religion*. Vol. 4. Ed. M. Eliade, 1987, 521–27.

Smith 1984

M. S. Smith, "The Magic of Kothar, The Ugaritic Craftsman God in KTU 1.6 VI 49–50," *RB* 91(1984) 377–80.

Smith 1985

M. S. Smith, "Baal in the Land of Death," *UF* 17(1985) 311–14.

Smith 1990

M. S. Smith, *The Early History of God: Yahweh and the Other Deities in Ancient Israel.* New York, 1989.

Smith 1993

M. S. Smith, "The Invocation of Deceased Ancestors in Psalm 49:12c," *JBL* 112(1993) 105-07.

Smith and Bloch-Smith 1988

M. S. Smith and E. M. Bloch-Smith, "Death and Afterlife in Ugarit and Israel," Review of *Beatific Afterlife in Ancient Israel and in the Ancient Near East,* by K. Spronk, *JAOS* 108(1988) 277–84.

Snell 1983–84

D. C. Snell, "The Cuneiform Tablet from El-Qiṭār," *Abr-Nahrain* 22(1983–84) 159–70.

Snodgrass 1982

A. Snodgrass, "Les origines du culte des héros dans la Grèce antique," in *La mort, les morts dans les sociétés anciennes.* Éd. G. Gnoli et J.-P. Vernant. Cambridge 1982, 107–19.

Snodgrass 1988

A. Snodgrass, "The Archaeology of the Hero," *Annali dipartimento di studi del mondo classico e del mediterraneo antico: Sezionee di archeologia e storia antica* 10(1988) 19-26.

von Soden 1985

W. F. von Soden, Review of *The Assyrian Dictionary of the Oriental Institute of the University of Chicago.* Vol. 13, *Q.* Ed. E. Reiner, *JSS* 30(1985) 274–78.

von Soden 1987

W. F. von Soden, Review of *Textes administratifs des salles 134 et 160 du Palais de Mari* [= ARMT 21], by J.-M. Durand; *Documents administratifs de la salle 135 du Palais de Mari* [=ARMT 22], by J.-R. Kupper; *Archives administratives de Mari, I* [= ARMT 23], by G. Bardet, F. Joannès, B. Lafont, D. Soubeyran, and P. Villard; and *Textes administratifs des salles Y et Z du Palais de Mari* [= ARMT 24], by P. Talon, *Orientalia* n.s., 56(1987) 97–105.

Soggin 1975

J. A. Soggin, " 'The Burial of the Godhead' in the Inscription of Pyrgi (Lines 8–9) and Parallel Motifs in the Old Testament," in *Old Testament and Oriental Studies.* Rome, 1975, 112–19.

Soggin 1987

J. A. Soggin, *The Prophet Amos: A Translation and Commentary.* London, 1987.

Sollberger 1986

E. Sollberger, *Administrative Texts Chiefly concerning Textiles: (L.2752)*. Rome, 1986.

Sourvinou-Inwood 1983

C. Sourvinou-Inwood, "A Trauma in Flux: Death in the Eighth Century and After," *The Greek Renaissance of the Eighth Century B.C.* Ed. R. Hägg. Stockholm, 1983, 33–49.

Spalinger 1977–78

A. Spalinger, "A Canaanite Ritual found in Egyptian Reliefs," *Journal of the Society for the Study of Egyptian Antiquities* 8(1977–78) 47–60.

Sperling 1971

D. S. Sperling, "Rephaim," in *Encyclopaedia Judaica*. Vol. 14. Ed. C. Roth. Jerusalem and New York, 1971, 79.

Spieckermann 1982

H. Spieckermann, *Juda unter Assur in der Sargonidenzeit*. Göttingen, 1982.

Spiess 1887

E. Spiess, *Entwicklungsgeschichte der Vorstellungen vom Zustande nach dem Tode auf Grund vergleichender Religionsforschung*. Jena, 1887.

Spronk 1986

K. Spronk, *Beatific Afterlife in Ancient Israel and in the Ancient Near East*. Neukirchen-Vluyn, 1986.

Spycket 1981

A. Spycket, *La statuaire du Proche-Orient Ancien*. Leiden, 1981.

Stamm 1939

J. J. Stamm, *Die akkadische Namengebung*. Leipzig, 1939.

Stamm 1979

J. J. Stamm, "Erwägungen zu RS 24.246," *UF* 11(1979) 753–58.

Starr 1990

I. Starr, *Queries to the Sungod: Divination and Politics in Sargonid Assyria*. Helsinki, 1990.

Steck 1972

O. Steck, "Bemerkungen zu Jesaja 6," *BZ* 16(1972) 188–206.

Stoebe 1973

H. J. Stoebe, *Das erste Buch Samuelis*. Gütersloh, 1973.

Stol 1976

M. Stol, *Studies in Old Babylonian History*. Istanbul, 1976.

Strommenger 1957

E. Strommenger, "Grab (I. Irak und Iran)," *RlA* 3(1957) 581–593.

Sukenik 1940

E. L. Sukenik, "Arrangements for the Cult of the Dead in Ugarit and Samaria," in *Mémorial Lagrange*. Paris, 1940, 59–65.

Sweeney 1988

M. A. Sweeney, *Isaiah 1-4 and the Post-Exilic Understanding of the Isaianic Tradition*. Berlin, 1988.

Talmon 1983

S. Talmon, "Biblical *repā'îm* and Ugaritic *rpu/i(m)*," in *Biblical and Other Studies in Honor of Robert Gordis* [=*HAR* 7]. Ed. R. Aharoni. Columbus, 1983, 235–49.

Talon 1974

Ph. Talon, "À propos d'une graphie présargonique de *ŠL* 577(Gídim)," *RA* 68(1974) 167–68.

Talon 1978

Ph. Talon, "Les offrandes funéraires à Mari," *Annuaire de l'Institut de Philologie et d'Histoire orientales et slaves* 22(1978) 53–75.

Talon 1979

Ph. Talon, Review of *The Court of the Palms: A Functional Interpretation of the Mari Palace*, by Y. M. Al-Khalesi, *BO* 36(1979) 331–33.

Talon 1980

Ph. Talon, "Un nouveau panthéon de Mari," *Akkadica* 20(1980) 12-17.

de Tarragon 1980

J.-M. de Tarragon, *Le culte à Ugarit: d'après les textes de la pratique en cunéiformes alphabétiques*. Paris, 1980.

Taylor 1984

J. G. Taylor, "Observations on the root QBA 'call', in Ugaritic," *Newsletter for Ugaritic Studies* 32(1984) 13.

Taylor 1985

J. G. Taylor, "A Long-Awaited Vocative Singular Noun with Final Aleph in Ugaritic (KTU 1.161.13)?," *UF* 17(1985) 315–18.

Taylor 1987

J. G. Taylor, "Yahweh and Asherah at Tenth Century Taanach," *Newsletter for Ugaritic Studies* 37/38(1987) 16–18.

Taylor 1988a

J. G. Taylor, "A First and Last Thing to do in Mourning *KTU* 1.161 and Some Parallels," in *Ascribe to the Lord: Biblical & Other Studies in Memory of Peter C. Craige*. Ed. L. Eslinger and G. Taylor. Sheffield, 1988, 151–77.

Taylor 1988b

J. G. Taylor, "The Two Earliest Representations of Yahweh," in *Ascribe to the Lord: Biblical & Other Studies in Memory of Peter C. Craige*. Ed. L. Eslinger and G. Taylor Sheffield, 1988, 557–66.

Teixidor 1987

J. Teixidor, "Aramean Religion," in *Encyclopedia of Religion*. Vol. 1. Ed. M. Eliade. New York, 1987, 367–72.

Thiel 1973
W. Thiel, *Die deuteronomistische Redaktion von Jeremia 1–25.* Neukirchen-Vluyn, 1973.

Thomas 1987
L.-V. Thomas, "Funeral Rites," in *Encyclopedia of Religion.* Vol. 5. Ed. M. Eliade. New York, 1987, 450–59.

Thompson 1980
J. A. Thompson, *The Book of Jeremiah.* Grand Rapids, 1980.

Thompson 1992
T. L. Thompson, *Early History of the Israelite People: From Written & Archaeological Sources.* Leiden, 1992.

Thureau-Dangin 1921
F. Thureau-Dangin, *Rituels accadiens.* Paris, 1921.

Tomback 1978
R. S. Tomback, *A Comparative Semitic Lexicon of the Phoenician and Punic Languages.* Missoula, 1978.

van der Toorn 1985
K. van der Toorn, *Sin and Sanction in Israel and Mesopotamia: A Comparative Study.* Assen, 1985.

van der Toorn 1988
K. van der Toorn, "Echoes of Judaean Necromancy in Isaiah 28,7–22," *ZAW* 100(1988) 199–217.

van der Toorn 1990
K. van der Toorn, "The Nature of the Biblical Teraphim in the Light of the Cuneiform Evidence," *CBQ* 52(1990) 203–22.

van der Toorn 1993
K. van der Toorn, "The Domestic Cult at Emar," unpublished paper, 1993.

Tov 1992
E. Tov, *Textual Criticism of the Hebrew Bible.* Minneapolis, 1992.

Trencsényi-Waldapfel 1961
I. Trencsényi-Waldapfel, "Die Hexe von Endor und die griechisch-römische Welt," *Acta Orientalia Academiae Scientiarum Hungaricae* 12 (1961) 201–22.

Tromp 1969
N. J. Tromp, *Primitive Conceptions of Death and the Netherworld in the Old Testament.* Rome, 1969.

Tropper 1989
J. Tropper, *Nekromantie: Totenbefragung im Alten Orient und im Alten Testament.* Neukirchen-Vluyn, 1989.

Tsevat 1980
M. Tsevat, "chālaq II," in *Theological Dictionary of the Old Testament.* Ed. G. J. Botterweck and H. Ringgren. Grand Rapids, 4(1980) 447–51 [= "chālaq II," in *Theologisches*

Wörterbuch zum Alten Testament. Hrsg. G. J. Botterweck, H. Ringgren, und H.-J. Fabry. Band 2. Stuttgart, 1977, 1032–36].

Tsukimoto 1980
A. Tsukimoto, "Aspekte von *kispu(m)* als 'Totenbeigabe' ," in *Death in Mesopotamia* [= RAI 26]. Ed. B. Alster. Copenhagen, 1980, 129–38.

Tsukimoto 1985
A. Tsukimoto, *Untersuchungen zur Totenpflege (kispum) im alten Mesopotamien.* Neukirchen-Vluyn, 1985.

Tsumura 1993
D. Tsumura, "The Interpretation of the Ugaritic Funerary Text *KTU* 1.161," in *Official Cult and Popular Religion in the Ancient Near East: Papers of the 1st Colloquim on the Ancient Near East – the City and its Life held at the Middle Eastern Cultural Center of Japan (Mitaka, Tokyo), March 20–22, 1992.* Ed. E. Matsuyama. Heidelberg, 1993, 40–55.

Tufnell 1953
O. Tufnell (et al.), *Lachish III (Tel ed Duweir) with Contributions by M. A. Murray and D. Diringer: The Iron Age.* London, 1953.

Tunča 1984
Ö. Tunča, *L'architecture religieuse protodynastique en Mesopotamie.* Leuven, 1984.

Tylor 1871
E. B. Tylor, *Primitive Culture: Researches into the Development of Mythology, Philosophy, Religion, Language Art and Custom.* London, 1871.

Ucko 1969
P. Ucko, "Ethnography and the Archaeological Interpretation of Funerary Remains," *World Archaeology* 1(1969) 262–80.

Ussishkin 1983
D. Ussishkin, "Excavations at Lachish 1978–1983, Second Preliminary Report," *TA* 10(1983) 97–175.

Van Seters 1972
J. Van Seters, "The Terms 'Amorite' and 'Hittite' in the Old Testament," *VT* 22(1972) 64–81.

Van Seters 1975
J. Van Seters, *Abraham in History and Tradition.* New Haven and London, 1975.

Van Seters 1983
J. Van Seters, *In Search of History: Historiography in the Ancient World and the Origins of Biblical History.* New Haven and London, 1983.

Van Seters 1986
J. Van Seters, Review of *La péricope de Balaam (Nombres 22–24)*, by H. Rouillard, *JSS* 31(1986) 245–47.

Van Seters 1988

J. Van Seters, "The Primeval Histories of Greece and Israel Compared," *ZAW* 100(1988) 1-22.

Van Seters 1992

J. Van Seters, *Prologue to History: The Yahwist as Historian in Genesis*. Louisville, 1992.

Vattioni 1963

F. Vattioni, "La necromanzia nell'Antico Testamento (1 Sam 28,3–25)," *Augustinianum* 3(1963) 461–81.

Vattioni 1980–81

F. Vattioni, "La bilingue latina e neopunica di El Amrouni," *Helikon* 20–21(1980–81) 293–99.

de Vaux 1958

R. de Vaux, "Les Sacrifices de porcs en Palestine et dans l'Ancien Orient," in *Von Ugarit nach Qumran: Beiträge zur alttestamentlichen und altorientalischen Forschung*. Hrsg. J. Hempel and L. Rost. Berlin, 1958, 250–65.

de Vaux 1961

R. de Vaux, *Ancient Israel: Its Life and Institutions*. Vol. 1. New York, 1961 [= Les Institutions de L'Ancien Testament. Paris, 1958].

Veijola 1975

T. Veijola, *Die ewige Dynastie: David und die Enstehung seiner Dynastie nach der deuteronomistischen Darstellung*. Helsinki, 1975.

Veijola 1982

T. Veijola, *Verheissung in der Krise. Studien zur Literatur und Theologie der Exilszeit anhand des 89. Psalms*. Helsinki, 1982.

Vermeylen 1977–78

J. Vermeylen, *Du Prophète Isaïe à l'apocalyptique: Isaïe, I–XXXV, miror d'un demi-millénaire d'experience religieuse en Israël*. 2 vols. Paris, 1977(I); 1978(II).

Verreet 1983

E. Verreet, "Das silbenschliessende Aleph im Ugaritischen," *UF* 15 (1983) 223–58.

Verreet 1984

E. Verreet, "Beobachtungen zum ugaritischen Verbalsystem," *UF* 16(1984) 307–21.

Verreet 1985

E. Verreet, "Beobachtungen zum ugaritischen Verbalsystem II," *UF* 17(1985) 319–44.

Vieyra 1961

M. Vieyra, "Les noms du 'mundus' en hittite et en assyrien et la pythonisse d'Endor," *RHA* 19(1961) 47–55.

Viganò and Pardee 1984

L. Viganò and D. Pardee, "Literary Sources for the History of Palestine and Syria: The Ebla Tablets," *BA* 47(1984) 6–16.

Virolleaud 1940

C. Virolleaud, "Les Rephaim," *RES-Babyloniaca* (1940) 77–83.

Virolleaud 1951

C. Virolleaud, "Six textes de Ras Shamra, provenant de la 14 campagne (1950)," *Syria* 28(1951) 163–79.

Virolleaud 1962

C. Virolleaud, "Les nouveaux textes alphabetiques de Ras Shamra," *CRAIBL* (1962) 92–97.

Virolleaud 1968

C. Virolleaud, *Ugaritica V.* Éd. C. F. A. Schaeffer et J.-C. Courtois. Paris, 1968.

Vorländer 1975

H. Vorländer, *Mein Gott. Die Vorstellungen vom persönlichen Gott im Alten Orient und im Alten Testament.* Kevelaer, 1975.

de Vries 1989

S. J. de Vries, *1 and 2 Chronicles.* Grand Rapids, 1989.

Wade 1911

G. W. Wade, *The Book of the Prophet Isaiah.* London, 1911.

Watson 1984

W. G. E. Watson, *Classical Hebrew Poetry: A Guide to Its Techniques.* Sheffield, 1984.

Watts 1985

J. D. W. Watts, *Isaiah 1–33.* Waco, 1985.

Watts 1987

J. D. W. Watts, *Isaiah 34–66.* Waco, 1987.

von Weiher 1983

E. von Weiher, *Spätbabylonische Texte aus Uruk II.* Berlin, 1983.

Weinfeld 1972a

M. Weinfeld, *Deuteronomy and the Deuteronomistic School.* Oxford, 1972.

Weinfeld 1972b

M. Weinfeld, "The Worship of Molech and the Queen of Heaven and its Background," *UF* 4(1972) 133–54.

Weippert 1973

H. Weippert, *Die Prosareden des Jeremiabuches.* Berlin, 1973.

Weippert 1988

H. Weippert, *Palästina in vorhellenistischer Zeit.* München, 1988.

Weise 1960

M. Weise, "Jesaja 57,5f.," *ZAW* 72(1960) 25–32.

Weiser 1962

A. Weiser, *The Psalms: A Commentary.* Philadelphia, 1962 [= Die Psalmen. Göttingen, 1959].

Wellhausen 1899

J. Wellhausen, *Die Composition des Hexateuchs und der historischen Bücher des alten Testaments*. Berlin, 1899^{3}.

Wellhausen 1973

J. Wellhausen, *Prolegomena to the History of Israel*. Gloucester, 1973.

Wenham 1979

G. J. Wenham. *The Book of Leviticus*. Grand Rapids, 1979.

Wensinck 1917

A. J. Wensinck, *Some Semitic Rites of Mourning and Religion: Studies on Their Origin and Mutual Relation*. Amsterdam, 1917.

Wente 1990

E. F. Wente, *Letters from Ancient Egypt*. Ed. E. S. Meltzer. Atlanta, 1990.

Westenholz 1970

A. Westenholz, "*berūtum, damtum*, and Old Akkadian KI.GAL: Burial of Dead Enemies in Ancient Mesopotamia," *AfO* 23(1970) 27–31.

Westermann 1967

C. Westermann, *Basic Forms of Prophetic Speech*. Philadelphia, 1967 [= *Grundformen prophetischer Rede*. München, 1960].

Westermann 1969

C. Westermann, *Isaiah 40–66, A Commentary*. Philadelphia 1969 [= *Das Buch Jesaja, 40–66*. Göttingen, 1966^{1}].

Wevers 1982

J. W. Wevers, *Ezekiel*. Grand Rapids, 1982.

White 1980

W. White, "rāpâ," in *Theological Wordbook of the Old Testament*. Vol. 2. Ed. R. L. Harris, G. L. Archer, Jr., and B. K. Waltke. Chicago, 1980, 858–59.

Whiting 1987

R. M. Whiting, Jr., *Old Babylonian Letters from Tell Asmar*. Chicago, 1987.

Whitley 1988

A. J. M. Whitley, "Early States and Hero Cults: A Reappraisal," *Journal of Hellenic Studies* 108(1988) 173-82.

Wiggerman 1992

F. A. M. Wiggerman, *Mesopotamian Protective Spirits: The Ritual Texts*. Groningen, 1992.

Wijngaards 1973

J. N. M. Wijngaards, "The Adoption of Pagan Rites in Early Israelite Liturgy," in *God's Word Among Men: Papers in Honor of Fr. Joseph Putz, Frs. J. Bayart, J. Volekaert, and P. De Letter*. Ed. G. Gispert-Sauch. Delhi, 1973, 247–56.

Wilcke 1983

C. Wilcke, "Nachlese zu A. Poebels Babylonian Legal and Business Documents from the Time of the First Dynasty of Babylon Chiefly from Nippur (BE 6/2). Teil 1," *ZA* 73(1983) 48–66.

Wilcke 1986

C. Wilcke, "Dagān-naḫmīs Traum," *WO* 17(1986) 11–16.

Wildberger 1972, 1978, 1982

H. Wildberger, *Jesaja: Das Buch, der Prophet, und seine Botschaft.* 1. Teilbd., *Jesaja 1–12*; 2. Teilbd., *Jesaja 13–27*; 3. Teilbd., *Jesaja 28–39.* Neukirchen-Vluyn, 1972; 1978; 1982.

Wilkinson 1986

R. H. Wilkinson, "Mesopotamian Coronation and Accession Rites in the Neo-Sumerian and Early Old Babylonian Periods c. 2100–1800 B.C." Ph.D. diss., The University of Minnesota, 1986.

Williamson 1977

H. G. M. Williamson, *Israel in the Books of Chronicles.* Cambridge, 1977.

Williamson 1982

H. G. M. Williamson, *1 and 2 Chronicles.* Grand Rapids, 1982.

Williamson 1987a

H. G. M. Williamson, "Reliving the Death of Josiah: A Reply to C. T. Begg," *VT* 37(1987) 9–15.

Williamson 1987b

H. G. M. Williamson, Review of *The Chronicler's Use of the Deuteronomistic History,* by S. McKenzie, *VT* 37(1987) 107–14.

Willi-Plein 1971

I. Willi-Plein, *Vorformen der Schriftexegese innerhalb des Alten Testaments. Untersuchungen zum literarischen Werden der auf Amos, Hosea und Micha zurückgehenden Bücher im hebräischen Zwölfprophetenbuch.* Berlin, 1971.

Wilson 1977

R. R. Wilson, *Genealogy and History in the Biblical World.* New Haven, 1977.

Wiseman 1965

D. J. Wiseman, Review of *Textes Administratifs de la Salle III du Palais* [=ARM XI], by M. L. Burke. *JSS* 10(1965) 124–26.

Wiseman 1983

D. J. Wiseman, "Mesopotamian Gardens," *AnSt* 33(1983) 137–44.

Witherspoon 1983

G. Witherspoon, "Language and Reality in the Navajo World View," in *Handbook of North American Indians: Southwest.* Vol 10. Ed. A. Ortiz. Washington, 1983, 570–78.

Wohlstein 1967

H. Wohlstein, "Zu einigen altisraelitischen Volksvorstellungen von Toten- und Ahnengeistern in biblischer Überlieferung," *ZRGG* 19 (1967) 348–55.

Wolff 1977

H. W. Wolff, *A Commentary on the Books of the Prophets Joel and Amos*. Philadelphia, 1977. [= *Dodekapropheton 2. Joel und Amos*. Neukirchen-Vluyn, 1975].

Wolff 1982

H. W. Wolff, *Dodekapropheton 4. Micha*. Neukirchen-Vluyn, 1982.

Wright 1990

C. J. H. Wright, *God's People in God's Land: Family, Land, and Property in the Old Testament*. Grand Rapids, 1990.

Wright, Shires, and Parker 1953

G. E. Wright, H. H. Shires, and P. Parker, "The Book of Deuteronomy," in *Interpreter's Bible*. Vol. 2. Ed. G. A. Buttrick et al. New York, 1953, 309–537.

Wright 1985

D. P. Wright, "Purification from Corpse-Contamination in Num XXXI 19–24," *VT* 35(1985) 213–23.

Wright 1987

D. P. Wright, *The Disposal of Impurity: Elimination Rites in the Bible and in Hittite and Mesopotamian Literature*. Atlanta, 1987.

Würthwein 1984

E. Würthwein, *Die Bücher der Könige: 1. Kön. 17–2. Kön. 25*. Teilbd. 2. Göttingen, 1984.

Wyatt 1980

N. Wyatt, "The Relationship of the Deities Dagan and Hadad," *UF* 12(1980) 375–79.

Xella 1978

P. Xella, "Un Testo Ugaritico recente (*RS* 24.266, *Verso* 9–19) e il 'Sacrifice dei primo nati' ," *RSF* 6(1978) 127–36.

Xella 1979

P. Xella, "KTU 1.19 (RS 19.15) e i sacrifici del re," *UF* 11(1979) 833–38.

Xella 1980

P. Xella, "Sur la nourriture des morts. Un aspect de l'eschatologie mésopotamienne," in *Death in Mesopotamia* [= RAI 26]. Ed. B. Alster. Copenhagen, 1980, 151–60.

Xella 1981a

P. Xella, *I testi rituali di Ugarit*. I testi. Roma, 1981.

Xella 1981b

P. Xella "Ilib, gli 'dei dei padre' e il dio ittita Zawalli," *Studi Storico-religiosi* 5/1(1981) 85–93.

Xella 1982

P. Xella, "Il culto dei morti nell' Antico Testamento: Tra telologia e storia delle religioni," *Religioni e Civiltà* 3(1982) 645–66.

Xella 1983

P. Xella, "Aspekte religiöser Vorstellungen in Syrien nach den Ebla- und Ugarit-Texten," *UF* 15(1983) 279–90.

Xella 1985
P. Xella, "La religione in siria durante l'età del Bronzo," in *Da Ebla a Damasco.* A cura di G. Garroni and E. Parcu. Milano, 1985, 72–79.
Xella 1988
P. Xella, "Culto dinastico tradizioni amorree nei rituali ugaritici," *SEL* 5(1988) 219–25.
Yon 1991
M. Yon, "Les stèles de pierre," in *Arts et industries de la pierre.* Éd. M. Yon. Paris, 1991, 273–344 [texts of the Dagan stelae are treated by P. Bordreuil and D. Pardee on pp.302–04; photographic plates on p.334].
Zayadine 1986
F. Zayadine, "A Symposiarch from Petra," in *The Archaeology of Jordan and Other Studies: Presented to Siegfried H. Horn.* Ed. L. T. Geraty and L. G. Herr. Berrien Springs, 1986, 465–74.
Zimmerli 1983
W. Zimmerli, *Ezekiel 2.* Philadelphia, 1983 [= Ezechiel. Neukirchen-Vluyn, 1969].
Zolli 1950
E. Zolli, "Die 'Heiligen' in Psalm 16,3," *Theologische Zeitschrift* 6(1950) 149–50.
Zwickel 1989
W. Zwickel, "Über das angebliche Verbrennen von Räucherwerk bei der Bestattung eines Königs," *ZAW* 101(1989) 266–77.

Indexes

Author

Subject

Extra-Biblical Texts

Akkadian

Aramaic

Eblaite

Greek

Hebrew

Hurrian

Nabatean

Phoenician/Punic

Sumerian

Ugaritic

Biblical Texts

106:27, 266
106:27–30, 266
106:28, 265, 266
106:28–31, 266
106:37, 266
106:39, 259
106:45, 266
106:47, 266
106:47–48, 266
115:4–7, 266
135:15–17, 266
136, 68

Proverbs
1:24–28, 148
2:18, 267
9:18, 267
17:10, 119
21:16, 267

Ecclesiastes
7:2, 247
7:12, 109

Song of Songs
4:8, 259

Isaiah
1, 140, 161
1:11, 140
1:19–20, 140, 148
1:29, 140, 256, 257
1:29–31, 140, 148
1:30, 140
1:31, 140
1–35, 148
2:4, 210
2:5–9, 184, 185
2:6, 184–186, 188
2:6c, 185
2:6–8, 186
2:6b–9a, 185
2:8, 140, 148, 157, 185
2:9b, 185
2:18, 157
2:20, 157
3:2, 184
3:2–3, 155
3:4, 155
3:10–11, 140, 148
3:24, 168
5:14, 270
6:1, 147, 148
6–8, 236
7:20, 166
8:2, 230
8:11, 149
8:15, 149
8:16, 150
8:16–18, 148, 149
8:18, 147
8:19, 139, 140, 142, 147–150, 153–155, 162–164, 179, 180, 188, 206, 221, 222, 236, 237, 262, 287
8:19a, 150
8:19b, 150
8:19–20, 148, 202
8:19–20a, 149
8:19–22, 147, 148, 154
8:19–23(ET 8:19–9:1), 147, 148, 153
8:20, 148–150
8:20a, 150
8:21, 149
8:21–22, 148
8:22, 149
8:23a(ET 9:1a), 148
9:3(ET 4), 206
9:6(ET 7), 147
9:13(ET 14), 155
10:10, 157
10:11, 157
13:1–14:23, 139
13:3, 115
13:17, 139
13:21, 238
13–23, 139, 155
14, 269
14:4, 269
14:9, 118, 267, 269, 270
14:9a, 269
14:14a, 270
14:14b, 270
14:19, 250
14:24–27, 155